# The Human Record

## SOURCES OF GLOBAL HISTORY

**VOLUME II: SINCE**

# 1500

## EIGHTH EDITION

**Alfred J. Andrea**
Emeritus Professor of History, University of Vermont

**James H. Overfield**
Emeritus Professor of History, University of Vermont

CENGAGE
Learning·

Australia • Brazil • Mexico • Singapore • United Kingdom • United States

8475252

D5
.A53
2016
C.2

**The Human Record: Sources of Global History, Vol. II: Since 1500, Eighth Edition**
Alfred J. Andrea and James H. Overfield

Product Team Manager: Cara St. Hilaire

Senior Content Developer: Tonya Lobato

Associate Content Developer: Cara Swan

Product Assistant: Andrew Newton

Media Developer: Kate MacLean

Marketing Development Manager:
   Kyle Zimmerman

Senior Content Project Manager:
   Carol Newman

Senior Art Director: Cate Rickard Barr

Manufacturing Planner: Sandee Milewski

Intellectual Property Analyst:
   Alexandra Ricciardi

Intellectual Property Manager: Amber Hosea

Production Service/Compositor: MPS Limited

Text Designer: Anthony L. Saizon,
   Saizon Design

Cover Designer: Dare Porter

Cover Image: Wooden sculpture of a drummer,
   of the variety kept in the Mbala chiefs'
   houses as symbols of authority. Mbala
   people, Zaire. 20th c./Werner Forman/
   Art Resource, NY

Library of Congress Control Number: 2014943058

ISBN-13: 978-1-285-87024-3

ISBN-10: 1-285-87024-7

**Cengage Learning**
20 Channel Center Street
Boston, MA 02210
USA

Cengage Learning is a leading provider of customized learning solutions with office locations around the globe, including Singapore, the United Kingdom, Australia, Mexico, Brazil and Japan. Locate your local office at **www.cengage.com/global**.

To learn more about Cengage Learning Solutions, visit **www.cengage.com**.

Purchase any of our products at your local college store or at our preferred online store **www.cengagebrain.com**.

Printed in the United States of America
Print Number: 02    Print Year: 2015

## DEDICATION

*As always, our love and thanks to*
*Juanita B. Andrea and Susan L. Overfield.*

# CONTENTS

# GEOGRAPHIC CONTENTS

## Western Hemisphere

# TOPICAL CONTENTS

## Western Expansion and Colonialism

# PREFACE

The eighth edition of *The Human Record: Sources of Global History* follows the principles that have guided the book since its inception in 1990. Foremost is our commitment to the proposition that all students of history must meet the challenge of analyzing primary sources, thereby becoming active inquirers into the past. Working with primary source evidence enables students to see that historical scholarship is an intellectual process of drawing inferences and discovering patterns from clues yielded by the past, not of memorizing someone else's judgments. Furthermore, such analysis motivates students to learn by stimulating their curiosity and imagination, and it helps them develop into critical thinkers who are equipped to deal with the complex intellectual challenges of life.

## Themes and Structure

We have compiled a source collection that traces the course of human history from the rise of the earliest civilizations to the present. Volume I follows the evolution of cultures that most significantly influenced the history of the world from around 3500 B.C.E. to 1500 C.E., with emphasis on the development of the major social, religious, intellectual, and political traditions of the societies that flourished in Eurasia and Africa. Although our focus in Volume I is on Afro-Eurasia, we do not neglect the Americas. Volume I concurrently develops the theme of the growing links and increasingly important exchanges among the world's cultures down to the dawn of full globalization that began with the trans-oceanic travels of the Portuguese and Spaniards. Fittingly, its last two sources focus on some of the reasons behind and immediate consequences of these voyages. Volume II, which begins in the 1400s, picks up this theme of growing human interconnectedness by tracing the gradual establishment of Western global hegemony; simultaneous historical developments in other civilizations and societies around the world; the anti-Western, anticolonial movements of the twentieth century; and the emergence of the twenty-first century's integrated but frequently divided world.

To address these themes in the depth and breadth that they deserve, we have chosen primary sources that combine to present an overview of global history in mosaic form. Each source serves two functions: It presents an intimate glimpse into some meaningful aspect of the human past and simultaneously contributes to the creation of a single large picture—an integrated history of the world.

In selecting and arranging the pieces of our mosaic, we have sought to create a balanced picture of human history that reflects many different perspectives and experiences. Believing that the study of history properly concerns every aspect of past human activity and thought, we have chosen sources that mirror the practices and concerns of as wide a variety of representative persons and groups as availability and space allow.

Our pursuit of historical balance has also led us into the arena of artifactual evidence. Although most historians center their research on documents, the discipline of history requires us to consider all of the clues surrendered by the past, and these include its artifacts. Moreover, we have discovered that students enjoy analyzing artifacts, remember vividly the insights they draw from them, and are eager to discuss this evidence in class and among themselves. For these reasons, we have included works of art and other artifacts that users of this book can and should analyze as historical sources.

## New to This Edition

We have been gratified with the positive response by colleagues and especially students to the first seven editions of *The Human Record*. Many have taken the trouble to write or otherwise contact us to express their satisfaction. No textbook is perfect, however, and these correspondents have been equally generous in sharing their ideas of how we might improve our book and meet more fully the needs of its readers. Such suggestions, when combined with continuing advances in historical scholarship, our deeper reflections on a variety of issues, and the march of time in this new century, have mandated periodic revisions. In the current revision, as was true in the previous seven editions, our intent has been to craft a book that not only reflects the most up-to-date scholarship but is as interesting and useful as possible to students and instructors alike.

In this continuing (and never-ending) pursuit of trying to find the best and most useful documents and artifacts, we have made several significant changes. First, we have introduced a large number of new sources. Inasmuch as many of the sources consist of two or more discrete elements, any number that we offer as an exact count is subject to debate, but the most conservative estimate is that, together, the two volumes contain well over one hundred new sources. Additionally, in a continuing effort to provide the most accurate and comprehensible versions of the sources that we have selected, the two volumes contain over twenty-seven new translations of sources from such languages as Chinese, Byzantine Greek, medieval Latin, Castilian, Portuguese, Spanish, German, French, and Tuscan.

Needless to say, in order to keep these volumes within manageable boundaries, we have had to excise many "old" sources, most of which undoubtedly have their advocates, who will be disappointed at their excision. Persons who disagree with our judgments as to what to cut and what to add should feel free to contact us (see "Feedback" below) and to argue their case. There will be a ninth edition.

Instructors who have used earlier editions of *The Human Record* will recognize immediately that we have, as in past editions, added a large number of new artifactual sources. As was the case with the seventh edition, they are in four-color reproduction, making it easy for student and instructor alike to identify details and allowing us greater latitude in selecting images. We do not need to reject an image because important elements would be lost in black and white.

Instructors who have read and used a variety of world history textbooks will also note that many of the artifactual sources that we selected for inclusion and analysis are unique to this work. In other words, many are the fruit of our own research and do not come from the usual cast of world history images. In fact, three of the artifacts come from the private collection of one of the editors. By their very inclusion, the artifacts that we have discovered in our travels and research will expand the store of important images, illustrations, and sources available to colleagues and students alike. Each, however, was not chosen because we thought it offbeat or uncommon or were overcome with whimsy. It was selected because we deemed it telling and important to the story of world history.

Multiple Voices, a feature that was new to the sixth edition, received near-universal acclaim from the instructors who used these exercises in the classroom. We retained and expanded this feature in the seventh edition and have further expanded it for the eighth edition, while also revising, in some cases radically so, several Multiple Voices exercises that appeared in the two previous editions. Whether new, revised, or recycled intact, a simple philosophy lies behind each Multiple Voices exercise. Two of the most important skills that every student of history must acquire and sharpen are an ability to identify, evaluate, and use evidence that reflects different perspectives and an ability to trace historical development over time.

Together, the two volumes contain sixteen Multiple Voices units, with each containing four to seven sources and clearly set apart from other elements in the chapter. We believe that this enables instructors to use each unit as a coherent whole in the classroom and as a focal point for out-of-class essays. Beyond that, we are confident that each Multiple Voices unit will help students acquire and deepen habits of the mind that are necessary for not only their successful mastery of history but also, more important, their functioning in the world as educated individuals and citizens. These include, but are not limited to, a high degree of comfort with nuance and ambiguity; a sensitivity to the ways in which personality, time, place, culture, and other circumstances influence perspectives; an understanding that change and continuity are equally important elements in the dynamics of human history; a willingness to offer provisional answers to complex phenomena in which some or much of the desired evidence is not available; and an intellectual humility that allows one to modify and even radically change previous judgments once new evidence or insights become available.

Beyond helping to stimulate these skills and habits of the mind, we also have an obligation to reflect in our work the most up-to-date scholarly discoveries and controversies. With that in mind, we have revised many of our introductions, commentaries, and notes. In several cases we have explicitly corrected statements made in previous editions that can no longer be held as valid in the light of new research.

As with past editions, more than one-third of the pages dedicated to editorial commentary and notes are either new or have been rewritten.

Each volume also has a few new topics, reflecting both new currents in scholarship and pedagogy and maybe even the perspectives of its author-editor (Andrea for Volume I and Overfield for Volume II).

The new topics in Volume I include expanded coverage of Mycenaean Greece, Mathuran Buddhist sculpture, and the Mound and Taino cultures of pre-Columbian North America and the Caribbean. Mathura often is overlooked in world history textbooks, which tend to give all the credit for the transition to humanistic representations of the Buddha to Gandhara, and the cultures of Mesoamerica and South America often eclipse those of the Caribbean and America north of the Rio Grande in those same textbooks.

The most significant change for Volume II is the addition of a new concluding chapter. Since the first edition of *The Human Record*, we have ended Volume II with a chapter titled "The Global Community since 1945." As years passed and the world changed, trying to cover this ever-expanding time-span became increasingly difficult and ultimately impossible. Chapter 13 now covers the period from the end of World War II to the late 1980s, and Chapter 14 covers the period from the end of the Cold War to the present. New topics covered in Chapter 14 include international relations since the end of the Cold War (speeches by George H. W. Bush and Vladimir Putin); neo-liberalism and its critics (an essay by a defender of free market capitalism and a critique of the same by the International Forum on Globalization); the Internet (exchanges between Secretary of State Clinton and the state-controlled Chinese press over Internet censorship); and terrorism (a declaration by Osama bin Laden and excerpts from the so-called "torture memos" produced by the Bush White House).

These are but some of many new sources and features that we hope will stimulate anew instructors who have used earlier editions and excite the imagination of their students. As for the many sources that are not new to this edition: Some treasures are too valuable to leave behind.

## Learning Aids

Source analysis can be a daunting challenge for any student. With this in mind, we have labored to make these sources as accessible as possible by providing the student-user with a variety of aids.

As in previous editions, each volume has a *Prologue,* in which we explain, initially in a theoretical manner and then concretely, how a historian interprets written and artifactual sources. Because we consider this Prologue to be one of *The Human Record*'s distinguishing and strongest features (and *The Human Record* pioneered the inclusion of such an essay in a history source book), we take pride in this essay and have continuously revised it over the course of the past quarter century. The eighth edition is no exception in this regard.

The book's Multiple Voices units are probably its most challenging elements, and because of that fact the Prologue offers a sample Multiple Voices exercise followed by our explanation of what insights we gleaned from these five sources and how we arrived at them (and users of the seventh edition will note that we have significantly expanded this Multiple Voices lesson). It is our firm hope and belief that after studying our step-by-step analysis of this Multiple Voices module, the student-reader will realize that source analysis is largely common sense and care to detail and is well within her or his ability.

Within the body of each volume, we offer *part, chapter, sub-chapter,* and *individual source introductions,* all to help the reader place each selection into a meaningful context and understand each source's significance. Because we consider *The Human Record* to be an interpretive overview of global history and therefore a survey of the major patterns of global history that stands on its own as a text, our introductions are significantly fuller than what one normally encounters in a book of sources.

Suggested *Questions for Analysis* precede each source; their purpose is to help the student make sense of each piece of evidence and wrest from it as much insight as possible. Ideally, and more often than not, the questions are presented in a three-tiered format designed to resemble the historian's approach to source analysis and to help students make historical comparisons on a global scale. The first several questions are usually quite specific and ask the reader to pick out important pieces of information. These initial questions require the student to address two issues: What does this document or artifact say, and what meaningful facts can I garner from it? Addressing concrete questions of this sort prepares the student researcher for the next, more significant, level of critical thinking and analysis: drawing inferences. Questions that demand inferential conclusions follow the fact-oriented questions. Finally, whenever possible, we offer a third tier of questions that challenge the student to compare the individual or society that produced a particular source with an individual, group, or culture encountered earlier in the volume. We believe such comparisons help students fix more firmly in their minds the distinguishing cultural characteristics of the various societies they encounter in their survey of world history. Beyond that, it underscores the fact that global history is, at least on one level, comparative history.

Another form of help we offer is to *gloss the sources,* explaining words and allusions that students cannot reasonably be expected to know. To facilitate reading and to encourage reference, the notes appear at the bottom of the page on which they are cited. A few documents also contain *interlinear notes* that serve as transitions or provide needed information.

Some instructors might use *The Human Record* as their sole textbook. Most, however, will use it as a supplement to a standard narrative textbook, and most of these will probably decide not to require their students to analyze every source. To assist instructors (and students) in selecting sources that best suit their interests and needs, we have prepared *two analytical tables of contents* for each volume. The first lists readings and artifacts by geographic and cultural area, the second by topic. The two tables suggest to professor and student alike the rich variety of material available within these pages, particularly for essays in comparative history.

In summary, our goal in crafting *The Human Record* has been to do our best to prepare the student-reader for success—*success* being defined as comfort with historical analysis, proficiency in critical thinking, learning to view history on a global scale, and a deepened awareness of the rich cultural varieties, as well as shared characteristics, of the human family.

## Using *The Human Record*: Suggestions from the Editors

We have also not forgotten our colleagues. Specific suggestions for assignments and classroom activities are provided in a PDF manual, accessible online. In it we explain why we have chosen the sources that appear in this book and what insights we believe students should be capable of drawing from them. We also describe classroom exercises for encouraging student thought and discussion on the various sources. The advice we present is the fruit of our own use of these sources in the classroom.

## Feedback

As already suggested, we want to receive comments and suggestions from instructors and students who use this book. Comments on the Prologue and Volume I should be addressed to A. J. Andrea, whose e-mail address is aandrea@uvm.edu; comments on Volume II should be addressed to J. H. Overfield at James.Overfield@uvm.edu.

## Acknowledgments

We are in debt to the many professionals who offered their expert advice and assistance during the various incarnations of *The Human Record*. Scholars and friends at The University of Vermont who generously shared their expertise with us over the years as we crafted these eight editions include Abbas Alnasrawi, Doris Bergen, Holly-Lynn Busier, Ernesto Capello, Robert V. Daniels, Carolyn Elliott, Bogac Ergene, Erik Esselstrom, Shirley Gedeon, Erik Gilbert, William Haviland, Walter Hawthorn, Dennis Herron, Richard Horowitz, Abigail McGowan, Wolfgang Mieder, William Mierse, George Moyser, Francis Nicosia, Sarah M. Paige, Kristin M. Peterson-Ishaq, Abubaker Saad, Wolfe W. Schmokel, Peter Seybolt, John W. Seyller, Sean Stilwell, Mark

Stoler, Marshall True, Diane Villemaire, Janet Whatley, and Denise Youngblood. Additionally, Ms. Tara Coram of the Arthur M. Sackler Gallery and Freer Gallery of Art of the Smithsonian Institution deserves special thanks for the assistance she rendered A. J. Andrea in his exploration of the Asian art holdings of the two museums. He also extends his appreciation to the Silkroad Foundation of Saratoga, California, and especially its executive director, Adela Lee. Participation in three summer seminars in China on the artifacts of the Silk Road enabled him to identify and study several of the sources that appear in Volume I. He also thanks Dr. Sun Yue, of Capital Normal University, Beijing, China, for translation assistance in our photo research efforts, and Mr. Liu Xu (Lancelot), also of Capital Normal University, for his graceful translations of five key sources. Finally, he must single out an act of great collegiality: John E. Hill shared his translation of the *Chronicle of the Western Regions*, inclusion of which has added immeasurably to the value of Chapter 5 of Volume I. Professor Overfield gratefully acknowledges the help of Professor Timon Screech of the University of London School of Oriental and African Studies for his insights into Shiba Kōkan's *A Meeting of Japan, China, and the West* in Chapter 7 of Volume II, and to James Cahill, Professor Emeritus of Art History at the University of California at Berkeley, for his help in locating Zhang Hong's landscape in Chapter 4 of that same volume.

We wish also to acknowledge the following instructors whose comments on the seventh edition helped guide our revision: Joseph Avitable, Quinnipiac University; David Bovee, Fort Hays State University; Richard Brabander, Bridgewater State University; Katherine Clark, SUNY College at Brockport; Andria Crosson, University of Texas at San Antonio; Paula De Vos, San Diego State University; Cheryl Golden, Newman University. Finally, our debt to our spouses is beyond payment, but the dedication to them of each edition reflects in some small way how deeply we appreciate their support and good-humored tolerance.

A. J. A. / J. H. O.

# PROLOGUE

## Primary Sources and How to Read Them

Imagine a course in chemistry in which you never set foot in a laboratory or a course on the history of jazz in which you never listen to a note of music. You undoubtedly would consider such courses deficient and might even complain to your academic advisor or college dean about flawed teaching methods and wasted tuition. And you would be right. No one can understand chemistry without doing experiments; no one can understand music without listening to performances.

In much the same way, no one can understand history without reading and analyzing *primary sources*. Simply defined, *in most instances, primary sources are historical records produced at the same time the event or period that is being studied took place or soon thereafter.* They are distinct from *secondary sources*—books, articles, television documentaries, and even historical films produced well after the events they describe and analyze. Secondary sources—"histories" in the conventional sense of the term—organize the jumble of past events into understandable narratives. They provide interpretations, sometimes make comparisons, and almost always discuss motive and causation. When done well, they provide insight and pleasure. But such works, no matter how well done, are still *secondary* in that they are written after the fact and derive their evidence and information from primary sources.

History is an ambitious discipline that deals with all aspects of past human activity and belief. This means that the primary sources historians use to recreate the past are equally wide-ranging and diverse. Most primary sources are written—government records, law codes, private correspondence, literary works, religious texts, merchants' account books, memoirs, and the list goes on. So important are written records to the study of history that some historians refer to societies and cultures with no system of writing as "prehistoric." This does not mean they lack a history; it means there is no way to construct a detailed narrative of their histories due to the lack of written records. Of course, even so-called prehistoric societies leave behind evidence of their experiences, creativity, and belief systems in their *oral traditions* and their *artifacts*.

Let us look first at oral traditions, which can include legends, religious beliefs and rituals, proverbs, genealogies, and a variety of other forms of wisdom and knowledge. Simply put, they constitute a society's remembered past as passed down by word of mouth. Reconstructing an accurate picture of the past from such sources presents significant difficulties for the historian. You are aware of how stories change as they are transmitted from person to person. Imagine how difficult it is to use such stories as historical evidence. Yet, despite the challenge they offer, these sources cannot be overlooked.

Many of the oral traditions of ancient societies were eventually set down in writing, but in most cases they were recorded long after they were first articulated. Regardless of this shortcoming, they are often the only documented evidence that we have of a far-distant society or event, and thus they are indispensable to the historian. One consequence of this fact is that the farther back in history we go, the more we see the inadequacy of the definition of primary sources that we offered above ("historical records produced at the same time the event or period that is being studied took place or soon thereafter"). The early chapters of Volume I contain quite a few primary sources based on oral traditions; in some cases, they were written down many centuries after the events and people they deal with. We will inform you when this is the case and offer information and suggestions as to what kinds of questions you can validly ask of them to enable you to use them effectively.

Artifacts—anything, other than a document, that was crafted by hand or machine—can help us place oral traditions into a clearer context by producing tangible evidence that supports or calls into question this form of testimony. Artifacts can also tell us something about prehistoric societies whose oral traditions are lost to us. They also serve as primary sources for historians who study literate cultures. Written records, no matter how extensive and diverse, never allow us to draw a complete picture of the past, and we can fill at least some of those gaps by studying what human hands have fashioned. Everyday objects—such as fabrics, tools, kitchen implements, weapons, farm equipment, jewelry, pieces of furniture, and family photographs—provide windows into the ways that people lived. Grander cultural products—paintings, sculpture, buildings, musical compositions, and, more recently, film—are equally important because they also reflect the values, attitudes, and styles of living of their creators and those for whom they were created.

To be a historian is to work with primary sources in all their diverse forms. But to do so effectively demands thoroughness and attention to detail. Each source provides only one glimpse of reality, and no single source by itself gives us the whole picture of past events and developments. Many sources are difficult to understand and can be interpreted only after the precise meaning of their words has been deciphered and the contexts of the documents have been thoroughly investigated. Many sources contain distortions and errors that can be discovered only by rigorous internal analysis and comparison with evidence from other sources. Only after all these source-related difficulties have been overcome can a historian hope to achieve a coherent and reasonably accurate understanding of the past.

To illustrate some of the challenges of working with primary sources, let us imagine a time in the future when a historian decides to write a history of your college class in connection with its fiftieth reunion. Since no one has written a book or article about your class, our historian has no secondary sources to consult and must rely entirely on primary sources. What primary sources might he or she use? Possible sources include the school catalogue or bulletin, class lists, academic transcripts, yearbooks, college rules and regulations, course syllabi, and similar official documents, most of which are now exclusively on-line and might or might not be recoverable fifty years from now. Some sources that might still exist in printed or handwritten form could include lecture notes (assuming not everyone takes notes on a personal device and then deletes them at semester's end), examinations, term papers, and textbooks (assuming that e-books do not totally replace printed books); diaries and private letters; articles from the campus newspaper; programs for sporting events, concerts, and plays; and posters and leaflets. Another potential source for the inquiring historian would be recollections written down or otherwise recorded by some of your classmates long after they graduated. With a bit of thought, you could add other items to the list, among them some artifacts, such as souvenirs sold in the campus store, recordings of music popular at the time, and photographs and videos of student life and activity.

Clearly, all the sources available to our future historian will be fortunate survivors. They will represent only a small percentage of the material generated by you and your classmates, professors, and administrators over a two- or four-year period. Wastebaskets and recycling bins will have claimed much written material; the "delete" function on computers and smart phones, inevitable changes in the technology of electronic communication, and old websites dumped as "obsolete" will make it impossible to retrieve some basic sources, such as your college's website, the electronic "blackboards" that you and your course instructors used for communication, e-mail, and a vast amount of other on-line materials, as we suggested above. It is also probable that certain groups within your class will present the historian with additional challenges when it comes to finding information about them. The past always has its so-called silent groups of people. Of course, they were never truly silent, but often their voices were muted by choice or circumstance. It is the historian's task to find whatever evidence exists that gives them a voice, but often that evidence is tantalizingly slim.

For these reasons, the evidence available to our future historian will be fragmentary at best. This is always the case when doing historical research. The records of the past cannot be retained in their totality, not even records that pertain to the recent past.

How will our future historian use the many individual pieces of surviving evidence about your class? As he or she reviews the list, it will quickly become apparent that no single primary source provides a complete or unbiased picture. Each source has its own perspective, value, and limitations. Imagine a situation in which the personal essays submitted by applicants for admission are a historian's only source of information about the student body. On reading them, our researcher might draw the false conclusion that the school attracted only the most gifted, talented, interesting, intellectually oriented, and socially committed students imaginable.

Despite their flaws, however, essays composed by applicants for admission are important pieces of historical evidence. They reflect the would-be students' perceptions of the school's cultural values and the types of people it hopes to attract, and usually the applicants are right on the mark because they have studied the college's or university's website and read the brochures prepared by its admissions office. Admissions materials and, to a degree, even the school's official catalogue or bulletin (assuming a fifty-year-old electronic publication can be recovered) are forms of creative advertising, and both present an idealized picture of campus life. But such publications have value for the researcher because they reflect the values of the faculty and administrators who composed them. The catalogue also provides useful information regarding rules and regulations, courses, instructors, school organizations, and similar items. Such factual information, however, is the raw material of history, not history itself, and certainly it does not reflect anything close to the full historical reality of your class's collective experience.

What is true of the catalogue is equally true of the student newspaper and every other piece of evidence pertinent to your class. Each primary source is part of a larger whole, but as we have already seen, we do not have all the pieces. Think of historical evidence in terms of a jigsaw puzzle. Many of the pieces are missing, but it is possible to put the remaining pieces together to form a fairly accurate and coherent picture. That picture will not be complete, but it is valid and useful, and from it, one can often make educated guesses as to what the missing pieces look like. The keys to putting together this historical puzzle are hard work and imagination. Each is necessary.

## Examining Primary Sources

Hard work speaks for itself, but students are often surprised to learn that historians also need imagination to reconstruct the past. After all, they ask, doesn't history consist of irrefutable dates, names, and facts? Where does imagination enter into the process of learning these facts? Again, let us consider your class's history and its documentary sources. Many of those documents provide factual data—dates, names, grades, statistics. While these data are important, individually and collectively they have no historical meaning until they have been *interpreted*. Your college class is more than a collection of statistics and facts. It is a group of individuals who, despite their differences, share and mold a collective experience. It is a community evolving within a particular time and place. Any valid or useful history of it written in the future must reach beyond dates, names, and facts and interpret the historical characteristics and role of your class. What were its values? How did it change and why? What impact did it have on its members, the school, and society? These are some of the important questions a historian asks of the evidence.

To arrive at answers, the historian must examine every piece of relevant evidence in its full context and wring from that evidence as many *inferences* as possible. *An inference is a logical conclusion drawn from evidence,* and it is the heart and soul of historical inquiry. Facts are the raw materials of history, but inferences are its finished products.

Every American schoolchild learns that "in fourteen hundred and ninety-two, Columbus sailed the ocean blue." In subsequent history classes, he or she might learn other facts about the famous explorer: that he was born in Genoa in 1451; that he made three other transatlantic voyages in 1493, 1497, and 1503; that he died in Spain in 1506. Knowing these facts is of little value, however, unless that knowledge contributes to our understanding of the motives, causes, and significance of Columbus's voyages. Why did Columbus sail west? Why did Spain support such enterprises? Why were Europeans willing and able to exploit, as they did, the so-called New World? What were the short- and long-term consequences of the European presence in the Americas? Finding answers to such questions are the historian's ultimate goal, and these answers can be reached only by studying primary sources.

One noted historian, Robin Winks, wrote a book entitled *The Historian as Detective,* and the image is appropriate although inexact. Like a detective, the historian examines evidence to reconstruct past events. Like a detective, the historian is interested in discovering "what happened, who did it, and why." Unlike the detective, however, the historian further asks "what did it all mean, and what were its immediate and long-term consequences?" Despite this difference, like a detective interrogating witnesses, *the historian must carefully examine the testimony of sources.*

First and foremost, the historian must evaluate the *validity* of the source. Is it what it purports to be? Artful forgeries have misled many historians. Even authentic sources still can be misleading if their authors lied or deliberately misrepresented reality. In addition, the historian can easily be led astray by not fully understanding the *perspective* reflected in a document. Any detective who has examined eyewitnesses to an event soon learns that even honest witnesses' accounts can differ widely. The detective has the opportunity to re-examine witnesses and offer them the opportunity to change their testimony in the light of new evidence and deeper reflection. The historian is not so fortunate. Even when the historian compares a piece of documentary evidence with other evidence in order to uncover its immediately apparent flaws, there is no way to probe more deeply by cross-examining its author. Given this fact, the historian must understand as fully as possible the source's perspective with an eye toward evaluating as fully as possible its level of credibility and worth. Thus, the historian must ask several key questions—all of which share the letter W:

- *What* kind of document is it?
- *Who* wrote it?
- For *whom* and *why?*
- *Where* was it composed and *when?*

*What* is important because understanding the nature of a source gives the historian an idea of what kind of information he or she can expect to find in it. Many sources simply do not address the questions a historian would like to ask of them, and knowing this can prevent a great deal of frustration. Your class's historian would be foolish to try to learn much about the academic quality of your school's courses from a study of the registrar's class lists and grade sheets; student and faculty class notes, copies of syllabi, examinations, student papers, and textbooks would be far more useful.

*Who, for whom,* and *why* are equally important questions. The official catalogue and publicity materials prepared by the admissions office undoubtedly address some issues pertaining to student academic and social life. But should documents such as these—designed to attract potential students and to place the school in the best possible light—be read and accepted uncritically? Obviously not. They must be tested against student testimony provided by such sources as private letters, memoirs, posters, the student newspaper, and the yearbook. Additional evidence that the historian should consult would be data, such as the school's graduation rate and the percentage of its students annually admitted to academic honor societies, that a reputable authority has gathered and recorded.

*Where* and *when* are also important questions to ask of any primary source. As a rule, distance from an event in space and time colors perceptions and can diminish the reliability of a source. Imagine that a classmate had celebrated the twenty-fifth class reunion by recording her or his memories and reflections. That document or video could be an insightful and valuable source of information for your class's historian. Conceivably this graduate would have had a perspective and information that he or she lacked a quarter of a century earlier. Just as conceivably, that person's memory of what college was like might have faded to the point where the recollections have little evidentiary value.

## You and the Sources

*This book will actively involve you in the work of historical inquiry by asking you to draw inferences based on your analysis of primary source evidence.* This might seem difficult at first, but it is well within your capability.

*You will analyze two types of evidence: documents and artifacts.* Each source in *The Human Record* is authentic, so you do not have to worry about validating it. Editorial material in this book also supplies you with the information necessary to place each piece of evidence into its proper context and will suggest questions you legitimately can and should ask of it.

It is important to keep in mind that historians approach each source with questions, even though they might be vaguely formulated. Like detectives, historians want to discover some particular truth or shed light on an issue. This requires asking specific questions of the witnesses or, in the historian's case, of the evidence. These questions should not be prejudgments. *One of the worst errors a historian can make is setting out to prove a point or to defend an ideological position.* Questions are essential, but they are starting points, nothing else. Therefore, as you approach a source, have your question or questions fixed in your mind, and constantly remind yourself as you work your way through a source what issue or issues you are investigating—but at the same time, keep an open mind. You are not an advocate or debater. Your mission is to discover the truth, insofar as you can, by following the evidence and asking the right questions of it. Each source in this anthology is preceded by a number of suggested *Questions for Analysis.* You or your professor might want to ask other questions. Whatever the case, keep focused on your questions and issues, and take notes as you read a source. Never rely on unaided memory; it will almost inevitably lead you astray.

*Above all else, you must be honest and thorough as you study a source.* Read each explanatory footnote carefully to avoid misunderstanding a word or an allusion.

Try to understand exactly what the source is saying and its author's perspective. Be careful not to wrench anything out of context, thereby distorting it. Be sure to read the entire source so that you understand as fully as possible what it says and does not say.

This is not as difficult as it sounds, but it does take concentration and work. And do not let the word "work" mislead you. True, primary source analysis demands attention to detail and some hard thought, but it is also rewarding. There is great satisfaction in developing a deeper and truer understanding of the past based on a careful exploration of the evidence. What is more, an ability to analyze and interpret evidence is a skill that will serve you well in whatever career you follow.

# Analyzing Sample Sources

To illustrate how you should go about this task and what is expected of you, we will now take you through an exercise. One of the features of this source book is what we call "Multiple Voices." Each Multiple Voices feature is a set of short source excerpts that illustrates one of three phenomena: (1) multiple, more-or-less contemporary perspectives on a common event or phenomenon; (2) multiple sources that illustrate how something changes over time; (3) multiple perspectives from different cultures regarding a common concern or issue. The sample exercise we have constructed for this Prologue is a Multiple Voices feature that illustrates the third phenomenon: multiple perspectives from different cultures regarding a common concern or issue. We have chosen four documents and an artifact that shed light on the importance and economic policies of the Indian port city of Calicut in the years preceding the entry on a large scale of Europeans into the Indian Ocean. We present this grouping of sources as it would appear in the book: first a bit of background; next a discussion of the individual sources; then suggested Questions for Analysis; and finally the sources themselves, with explanatory notes.

## Everyone Meets in Calicut

### BACKGROUND

On May 20, 1498, after almost eleven months of sailing, the Portuguese captain-major Vasco da Gama anchored his three ships a few miles from Kozhikode (known to the Arabs as Kalikut and later to the British as Calicut) on India's Malabar, or southwestern, Coast, thereby inaugurating Europe's entry into the markets of the Indian Ocean. At the time of da Gama's arrival, Calicut was the capital of the most important state in a region dotted with small powers. Despite lacking a good natural harbor, Calicut prospered as a center of trade for reasons suggested in the following sources. However, with the establishment of competitive Portuguese trading stations along the Malabar Coast and elsewhere in the Indian Ocean as a consequence of da Gama's initial contact with India and following da Gama's bombardment of the city in 1503, Calicut's fortunes rapidly declined, and its prominence ended.

## THE SOURCES

We begin with the most recent of our five sources, an account of Calicut contained in the anonymous *Logbook (Roteiro) of the First Voyage of Vasco da Gama*, often referred to simply as the *Roteiro*. The journal, which is incomplete, was kept by an anonymous crew member aboard the *San Rafael*. Although the author's identity is unknown, what is certain is that the *Roteiro* is authentic, and it clearly reflects why Western Europeans were so eager to reach this port-city. The next three sources, which span more than a century, suggest the continuity of policies that enabled Calicut to achieve and maintain its status as a rich marketplace for several hundred years before da Gama's arrival. Our fifth source completes the circle by revealing Western Europe's vision of India more than a century before da Gama sailed to Calicut.

The second source, Ibn Battuta's *Rihla*, or *A Gift to Those Who Contemplate the Wonders of Cities and the Marvels Encountered in Travel*, predates the *Roteiro* by almost a century and a half. Abu Abdallah Muhammad ibn Battuta (1304–1368?) left his home in Tangier on the coast of Morocco in 1325 at the age of 21 to begin a twenty-six-year journey throughout the Islamic world and beyond. When he returned to Morocco in 1349, he had logged about 73,000 miles of travel, including more than seven years spent as a *qadi*, or religious judge, in the Islamic sultanate of Delhi in northern India. In 1341, Sultan Muhammad Tughluq (r. 1325–1351) invited Ibn Battuta to travel to China as his ambassador. On his way to China, Ibn Battuta stopped at Calicut. In 1354, the traveler began to collaborate with a professional scribe, Ibn Juzayy, to fashion his many adventures into a *rihla*, or book of religious travels, one of the most popular forms of literature in the Islamic world. It took almost two years to complete his long and complex story. Some of that story was fabricated, as even contemporaries noticed, but most of the *rihla* has the ring of authenticity. The excerpt that appears here describes Calicut as seen in 1341 and remembered about fifteen years later, and there is no good reason to doubt that this is an eyewitness account.

The third source, *The Overall Survey of the Ocean's Shores*, is Chinese. Its author, Ma Huan (ca. 1380–after 1451), accompanied the fourth (1413–1415), sixth (1421–1423), and seventh (1431–1433) expeditions of the great Ming fleets that the Yongle Emperor (r. 1402–1424) and his successor sent into the Indian Ocean under the command of Admiral Zheng He (1371–1433). The main purpose of the seven expeditions, which began in 1405 and ended in 1433, was to reassert Chinese influence in coastal lands touched by the Indian Ocean. Ma Huan, who was a Chinese Muslim, served as an Arabic translator on his first voyage and upon his return home transcribed his notes into book form. After sailing on two additional expeditions, he amended his account accordingly and published a book around 1451 that encapsulated all three expeditions and described in detail the lands and peoples visited and actions taken by the fleets during those voyages. In this excerpt he describes Calicut, known to the Chinese as Guli, which he visited on each of his last two voyages.

Our fourth source is from the pen of a Persian scholar, Islamic jurist, and diplomat, Abd al-Razzaq (1413–1482), who served the Timurid ruler of western Central Asia, Shahrukh Bahadur, the son and successor of the would-be world conqueror

Amir Temur, known in the West as Tamerlane (Volume I, source 82). In 1442, Abd al-Razzaq traveled as an ambassador from the Timurid court at Herat (in present-day Afghanistan) to Vijayanagara, the most powerful Hindu state in southern India, where he remained until 1444. In 1463, al-Razzaq began writing *The Dawn of Two Auspicious Planets and the Meeting of Two Seas,* a history of the Turco-Mongol rulers of Persia from 1304 to 1470. He inserted into that history an account of his mission to Vijayanagara, which he had independently composed at an earlier date. In that account he described Calicut, to which he had sailed in early November 1442 and in which he resided until mid-April 1443. In a portion of his account not included below, he characterized the city as a "disagreeable place, where everything became a source of trouble and weariness," but despite his dislike for Calicut, his official position and four-and-a-half-month residence there provided him with an intimate insight into the workings and culture of the port-city.

The fifth source, an artifact, is a detail of the western portions of India and the adjoining Arabian Sea from the *Catalan World Atlas,* which was drawn in 1375 on the island of Majorca, probably by Abraham Cresques (1325–1387), a Jewish "master of maps of the world" who served the Catholic king of Aragon in northeastern Spain (Catalonia), which had seized Majorca from the Moors in 1229. Cresques's map was based on the best available literary and cartographic sources and reflected the facts and fictions regarding Afro-Eurasia (the vast connected landmass that constitutes Africa and Eurasia) that circulated in educated circles in late-fourteenth-century Western Europe. In the segment shown here, we see at the top the Three Magi on their way to visit the Christ Child. Below them is the sultan of Delhi, whose Muslim state dominated northern India; below him is the raja of Vijayanagara. Between them are an elephant and its handler. In the Arabian Sea, at the bottom of the map, are pearl divers, as described by Marco Polo in his widely circulated account of his late-thirteenth-century travels through Asia. Above the pearl divers is a vessel with two men in conical hats. You will need a magnifying glass to see the divers and details of the ship and sailors because of fading that has taken place over almost 650 years.

## QUESTIONS FOR ANALYSIS

1. According to the *Roteiro,* why was Calicut so important, and, by implication, why was it necessary for Portugal to gain direct access to it?

2. What does Ibn Battuta tell us about the roles of foreigners in Calicut, and specifically which foreigners?

3. Based on your analysis of the four documentary sources, what do you conclude were the factors that contributed to Calicut's prosperity?

4. What does the *Catalan World Atlas* allow us to infer about Western Europe's knowledge of the Malabar Coast and India in general by the late fourteenth century?

5. Overall, what can we say with certainty about Calicut prior to its rapid decline in the sixteenth century?

## 1 • Roteiro

From this country of Calicut . . . come the spices that are consumed in the East and the West, in Portugal, as in all other countries of the world, as also [are] precious stones of every description. The following spices are to be found in this city of Calicut, being its own produce: much ginger and pepper and cinnamon, although the last is not of so fine a quality as that brought from an island called Çillon [Ceylon],¹ which is eight days journey from Calicut. Calicut is the staple² for all this cinnamon. Cloves are brought to this city from an island called Melqua [Melaka].³ The Mecca vessels carry these spices from there to a city in Mecca⁴ called Judeâ [Jeddah],⁵ and from the said island to Judeâ is a voyage of 50 days sailing before the wind. . . . At Judeâ they discharge their cargoes, paying customs duties to the Grand Sultan.⁶ The merchandise is then transshipped to smaller vessels, which carry it through the Red Sea to a place close to Santa Catarina of Mount Sinai,⁷ called Tuuz [El Tûr]⁸ where customs dues are paid once more. From that place the merchants carry the spices on the backs of camels . . . to Quayro [Cairo], a journey occupying ten days. At Quayro duties are paid again. On this road to Cairo they are frequently robbed by thieves. . . .

At Cairo the spices are embarked on the river Nile . . . and descending⁹ that river for two days they reach a place called Roxette [Rosetta], where duties have to be paid once more. There they are placed on camels, and are conveyed in one day to a city called Alexandria, which is a sea-port.¹⁰ This city is visited by the galleys of Venice and Genoa, in search of these spices, which yield the Grand Sultan [an annual] revenue of 600,000 cruzados.¹¹

Source: From E. G. Ravenstein, ed. and trans., *A Journal of the First Voyage of Vasco da Gama*, 1497–1499 (Hakluyt Society, 1898), First Series, No. 99. Reproduced by Burt Franklin, 1963, pp. 11–18.

¹The present-day island nation of Sri Lanka. At this time, Ceylon alone produced true cinnamon. The other cinnamon-like spice is cassia, which is made from the bark of a related tree that originated in China.

²A staple is a place where merchants have been granted the exclusive right to purchase and export a particular commodity or group of commodities.

³The straits and city of Melaka (also known as Malacca) were not the source. Cloves came from the Southeast Asian islands known as the Moluccas (or Spice Islands), which today constitute the province of Maluku in the Republic of Indonesia.

⁴Actually Arabia, Mecca (or Makkah) being the inland holy city of Islam in the Arabian Peninsula. Today Mecca is located in Saudi Arabia.

⁵Jeddah (or Jidda) is the Arabian Peninsula's main port city on the Red Sea.

⁶The Mamluk dynasty of sultans that ruled Egypt from 1250 to 1517.

⁷Saint Catherine's Monastery—an ancient Christian monastery in Egypt that still exists.

⁸A port on Egypt's Sinai Peninsula.

⁹Sailing north.

¹⁰On the Mediterranean.

¹¹A Portuguese gold coin that received its name from the crusader cross emblazoned on it.

## 2 • Ibn Battuta, A Gift to Those Who Contemplate the Wonders of Cities and the Marvels Encountered in Travel

The sultan of Calicut is an infidel,¹ known as "the Samari."² . . . In this town too lives the famous ship-owner Mithqal,³ who possesses vast wealth and many ships for his trade with India, China, Yemen, and Fars.⁴ When we reached the city, the principal inhabitants and merchants and the sultan's representative came out to welcome us, with drums, trumpets, bugles and standards on their

Source: Travels in Asia and Africa, 1325–1354, H. A. R. Gibb, trans. (New York: Robert M. McBride & Co., 1929), pp. 234–237, passim. Modernized by A. J. Andrea.

¹A Hindu.

²In the local language, the title was *Samudri raja*, which means "Lord of the Sea." The Portuguese would corrupt this to "Zamorin."

³A strange name, very much like being called "Goldie" in English. A measure of weight throughout the Islamic world, a *mithqal* was 4.72 grams of gold. This might mean the man was a Muslim from across the Arabian Sea.

⁴Yemen is the southwestern tip of the Arabian Peninsula; Fars is the southern region of Iran along the Gulf of Oman.

ships. We entered the harbor in great pomp. . . . We stopped in the port of Calicut, in which there were at the time thirteen Chinese vessels, and disembarked. Every one of us was lodged in a house, and we stayed three months as the guests of the infidel, awaiting the season of the voyage to China.[5] On the Sea of China traveling is done in Chinese ships only. . . .

The Chinese vessels are of three kinds: large ships called *chunks* [junks],[6] middle-sized ones called *zaws* [dhows?],[7] and small ones called *kakams*.[8] The large ships have from twelve down to three sails, which are made of bamboo rods plaited like mats. They are never lowered, but turned according to the direction of the wind. . . . A ship carries a complement of a thousand men, six hundred of whom are sailors and four hundred men-at-arms, including archers . . . and arbalists, who throw naptha.[9] . . . The vessel has four decks and contains rooms, cabins, and salons for merchants; a cabin has chambers and a lavatory, and can be locked by its occupant, who takes along with him slave girls and wives. Often a man will live in his cabin unknown to any of the others on board until they meet on reaching some town. The sailors have their children on board ship, and they cultivate green stuffs, vegetables, and ginger in wooden tanks. The owner's factor [agent-in-charge] on board ship is like a great amir.[10] When he goes on shore he is preceded by archers and Abyssinians[11] with javelins, swords, drums, trumpets, and bugles. On reaching the house where he stays, they stand their lances on both sides of the door, and continue thus during his stay. Some of the Chinese own large numbers of ships on which their factors are sent to foreign countries. There is no people in the world wealthier than the Chinese. When the time came for the voyage to China, the sultan Samari made provision for us on one of the thirteen junks in the port of Calicut. The factor on the junk was called Sulayman of Safad,[12] in Syria. . . .

> Disaster strikes. Ibn Battuta's ship sinks in a storm in the harbor before he boards it, but it carries with it to the bottom all of his baggage, servants, and slaves.

Next morning we found the bodies of Sumbal and Zahir ad-Din,[13] and having prayed over them buried them. I saw the infidel, the sultan of Calicut . . . a fire lit before him on the beach; his police officers were beating the people to prevent them from plundering what the sea had cast up. In all the lands of Malabar, except in this one land alone, it is the custom that whenever a ship is wrecked all that is taken from it belongs to the treasury. At Calicut, however, it is retained by its owners, and for that reason Calicut has become a flourishing city and attracts large numbers of merchants.

---

[5]They awaited the lessening of the northeastern monsoon winds, which blow from late November to April. The period around April 11 was considered the best time to begin a voyage from the Malabar Coast to the Bay of Bengal, which lies east of India.

[6]The junk was the standard Chinese ocean-going ship since the second century C.E. and came in a variety of sizes.

[7]If he means dhows, he is incorrect. The dhow was (and is) a lateen-rigged vessel crafted by Indian, Arab, and East African shipwrights for sailing in the waters of the Indian Ocean and adjacent seas. It was not Chinese.

[8]This type of vessel is unknown. It cannot be the flat-bottomed sampan, which was used exclusively along China's coastal waters and in its rivers.

[9]Crossbowmen who shoot missiles containing a mixture of fiery materials.

[10]Lord or commander.

[11]Persons from the Horn of Africa—present-day Ethiopia, Eritrea, Djibouti, and Somalia—and maybe even farther south along the Swahili Coast.

[12]Zefat in present-day Israel.

[13]Envoys whom the sultan of Delhi had dispatched to accompany him.

## 3 • Ma Huan, The Overall Survey of the Ocean's Shores

### The Country of Guli

The inhabitants of Guli are divided into five classes: Muslims, Nankun, Zhedi, Geling and Mugua,[1] within which the king belongs to the second, and he venerates elephants and the ox due to his Buddhist belief.[2] All residents refrain from consuming beef; grand chiefs are Muslims who also refrain from partaking of pork. An earlier king made a compact with Muslim leaders that stated: "You people do not eat beef; we do not eat pork, and we will respect this taboo reciprocally from now on."[3] . . .

The king is assisted by two grand chiefs in administering governmental affairs. They are both Muslims; over half the people of Guli affirm the Islamic faith. They go to prayers every week, and there are twenty to thirty mosques round about.[4] . . . These two grand chiefs are recognized by the Chinese Court; hence, they are in full charge of the trade once the Chinese treasure boats arrive.[5] The king sends those chiefs alongside with a Zhedi termed the "Weinaji"[6] to keep the official books. A trade broker[7] accompanies them. The ship's commander decides the day for bargaining and trading. When that day arrives, the price of the pieces of [Chinese] silk clothing will be discussed, fixed, then registered in a contract for each party.[8] Guli chiefs, the Zhedi, and our great eunuch officer[9] shake hands; the broker then concludes that the price [on Chinese goods] has been determined with our hands' clasping. Whether it is over- or underpriced, there will be no regrets or further negotiations.

Afterwards, Zhedi people of wealth bring their precious stones, pearls, corals, and so on for price-evaluation and bargaining, which usually takes more than one day. It goes on for a month if done quickly; two to three months if not. When a price has been settled after bargaining, if one purchases pearls, the price payable is calculated by the chief agent and the "weinaji." The amount due is determined in raw textiles, such as hemp-silk, which is paid in exchange. Guli locals own no abacus,[10] but their calculations with both hands and feet are error-free and shockingly exceptional.

The Guli have a coin of sixty percent purity in gold . . . they also have smaller coins made of silver. . . .

The people of Guli know how to dye raw silk in varied colors and weave decorative stripes onto fine towels . . . ; every piece is sold for a hundred gold coins.

*Source:* Translated by Liu Xu from Ma Huan's *Ying Ya Sheng Lan* in Wan Ming edited & annotated version (Beijing, Haiyang Press, 2005), pp. 37–92, passim. Copyright © Liu Xu, 2014. All rights reserved.

[1]In his description of another port city, Cochin, Ma Huan makes it clear that these four "classes" of Hindus were *jatis*, or occupations, not *varnas*, or the four major castes of Indian society (Volume I, Chapter 3, source 15, and Chapter 5, source 32). The Nankun were rulers, the Zhedi were commercial accountants and business people (note 6), the Geling were commission agents (note 7), and the Muguas were fishermen and porters.
[2]Actually, he was a Hindu. His veneration of an ox (probably a bull) suggests that he was a devotee of Shiva.
[3]Hindus consider the cow and all other cattle sacred and do not eat beef; Muslims are prohibited from eating pork. In many areas of traditional India, where Muslims lived alongside Hindus, people refrained from eating the meat of both animals as an act of mutual respect.
[4]Compare this with the testimony of Abd al-Razzaq.

[5]The fleets commanded by Zheng He contained a significant number of treasure ships—large ships along the lines described by Ibn Battuta that carried Chinese trade goods and gifts, but which also were meant to carry back tribute, foreign trade goods, exotic items, and persons of importance invited (or compelled) to visit the imperial court. By extension, Ma Huan means any Chinese trading vessel.
[6]His attempt to transliterate the Malabar Coast term *Waligi Chitty,* or accountant.
[7]A Geling.
[8]India has produced silk since at least the third millennium (2000s) B.C.E., but Indians who could afford it favored Chinese silk as a superior luxury fabric.
[9]The reference is to Zheng He, a eunuch, who commanded the treasure ships that visited Calicut during these voyages, but more broadly it probably also refers to the commander of any Chinese ship.
[10]The traditional Chinese calculator.

Pepper is widely cultivated in countryside gardens; every October, ripe pepper corns are dried and sold to big pepper-collectors, then stored eventually at an official warehouse. Any purchase of pepper must be approved by the authorities, and taxed in accordance with the amount purchased. . . .

Foreign boats arrive for trade, the king sends out a chief and a clerk to oversee and to tax.

---

### 4 • Abd al-Razzaq, The Dawn of Two Auspicious Planets[1] and the Meeting of Two Seas[2]

Calicut is a perfectly secure harbor, which, like that of Hormuz,[3] brings together merchants from every city and from every country; in it are to be found an abundance of precious articles brought there from maritime countries, and especially from Abyssinia,[4] Zirbad,[5] and Zanzibar;[6] from time to time ships arrive there from the shores of the House of God[7] and other parts of the Hejaz,[8] and stay at will. . . . [T]he town is inhabited by infidels.[9] . . . It contains a considerable number of Muslims, who are constant residents and have built two mosques, in which they meet every Friday to offer up prayer. They have one qadi,[10] an imam,[11] and for the most part belong to the Shafi sect.[12] Security and justice are so firmly established in this city that the most wealthy merchants bring there from maritime countries considerable cargoes, which they unload, and unhesitatingly send into the markets and the bazaars, without thinking in the meantime of any necessity of checking the account or of keeping watch over the goods. The officers of the custom house take upon themselves the responsibility of looking after the merchandise, over which they keep watch day and night. When a sale is made, they levy a duty on the goods of one-fortieth; if the goods are not sold, they make no charge on them whatsoever.

In other ports a strange practice is adopted. When a vessel sets sail for a certain point and suddenly is driven by a decree of Divine Providence into another anchorage, the inhabitants, under the pretext that the wind has driven it there,[13] plunder the ship. But at Calicut every ship, whatever its place of origin or wherever it is bound for, is treated like other vessels when it puts into this port, and it has no trouble of any kind to put up with.

---

*Source:* Abd al-Razzaq: R. H. Major, ed. and trans., *India in the Fifteenth Century* (Hakluyt Society, 1857), First Series, No. 22., pp. 13–14. Modernized by A. J. Andrea.

[1] The Timurids bestowed the ancient royal title *Sahib-Qiran* (Lord of the Auspicious Conjunction) on their founder Amir Temur because it was believed that he had been born on April 8, 1336, when Mars and Jupiter were auspiciously conjoined.

[2] An ancient phrase that refers to any meeting of two discrete entities or cultures. This probably refers to the joining of Persian and Turco-Mongol cultures and peoples under the Mongol khans and their Timurid successors.

[3] An important trading port on an island at the mouth of the Persian Gulf.

[4] Ethiopia on the Horn of Africa.

[5] Southeast Asia.

[6] An island along the Swahili Coast of East Africa that was an important center of trade. (See Volume I, Chapter 10, source 67.)

[7] Mecca and its nearby port of Jeddah.

[8] The western region of the Arabian Peninsula that is bordered by the Red Sea.

[9] Hindus.

[10] A judge of Sharia, Islamic religious law.

[11] The leader of prayer in a mosque.

[12] One of four schools of jurisprudence within the Sunni branch of Islam. This school of legal interpretation emphasizes the rigorous application of legal principles based on the Quran and Hadith, or tradition. (See Volume I, Chapter 7, sources 45 and 46.)

[13] Thereby making it a derelict vessel. Anyone may rightfully take possession of such a ship and its cargo.

## 5 • The Catalan World Atlas

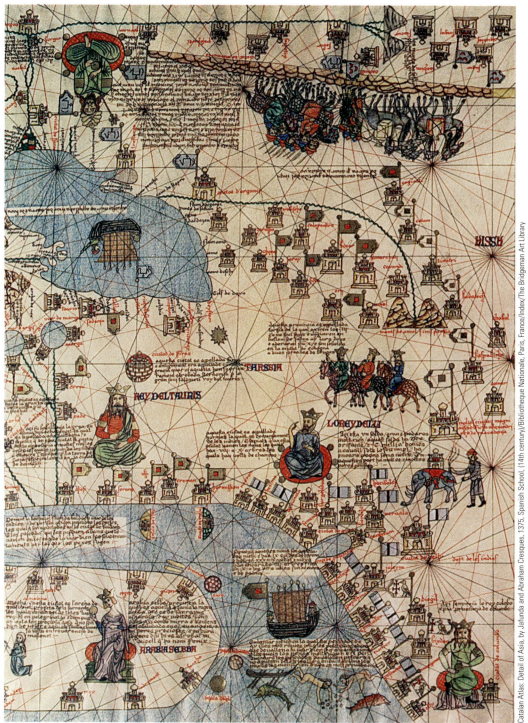

# Interpreting the Sources

These five pieces of evidence allow us to learn quite a bit about Calicut before Europeans established a strong presence in the Indian Ocean. Let us begin with the two Western sources.

The earlier of the two, the *Catalan World Atlas,* depicts what is unmistakably a Chinese junk off the west coast of India. Its plaited bamboo sails, which Ibn Battuta described, are difficult to discern with the unaided eye, but they are there to be seen if you look carefully. Moreover, the conical hats worn by the men at each end of the vessel were (and are) traditionally East Asian. Also, anyone who has ever seen a junk or a photo of one will recognize its distinctive high stern (the rear of the ship). Clearly, Westerners realized as early as the fourteenth century that the Chinese were major players in the commerce of the Indian subcontinent and descriptions of Chinese junks and clothing had made their way to Europe. The West's knowledge of the great wealth of India, as well as its high degree of urbanization and its political fragmentation, is equally obvious from the portraits of the sultan of Delhi and the raja of Vijayanagara, as well as the symbols for the many cities dotting the coastline and interior. The pearl divers, elephant, and Three Magi only add to the overall picture of India's riches and wonders. The fact is that between roughly 1250 and 1350, a significant number of Europeans, especially missionaries and merchants, had traveled, largely by land, to India and China, and some of them, such as Marco Polo, had written widely circulated accounts of their experiences. Even if you did not know that, you can infer from this map segment alone that the fourteenth-century West was not totally ignorant of India's geography and dynamics, including the importance of Chinese merchants in the commerce of the Malabar Coast.

The *Roteiro* illustrates why, with that knowledge, the Portuguese desired direct overseas access to the rich markets of India and beyond. Given the numerous duties and markups placed on spices that made their way to Egypt and from there to Europe, the Portuguese realized that access to the markets of the Malabar Coast and beyond would enable them cut out many of the middle agents who profited greatly from this lucrative trade. At this point, there is no good reason for you to know that the overland trade routes between Europe and the "Indies" (a vague term that referred to India, China, and other distant lands in Asia and East Africa) had largely broken down after about 1350 (see Volume I, Chapter 11) and that the closing down of those routes spurred Portugal and Spain to find alternate ways by sea. What you can easily infer from this source is that the Portuguese expected to make much more per year than the 600,000 *cruzados* that the sultan of Egypt enjoyed, once they had direct access to Calicut. As we learn from this anonymous author, not only was Calicut a major commercial emporium, it was also a center of spice and gemstone production.

The *Roteiro* also makes clear how important Calicut was to the commerce of Arabia and Egypt, Venice, Genoa, and the Spice Islands; likewise, Ibn Battuta, Ma Huan, and Abd al-Razzaq indicate how important Calicut was to the overseas trade of such widely separated regions as China, East Africa, Southeast Asia, Arabia, and Persia. It is no exaggeration to state that Calicut was a centrally located emporium that played a vital economic role for much of Afro-Eurasia.

Our Moroccan and Chinese eyewitnesses depict Calicut as a multicultural city, and Abd al-Razzaq notes that Calicut had a significant Muslim population, but in his description of this Muslim community, he serves as a corrective to several errors in Ma Huan's account. The Chinese visitor states that the population of the "country" (the city and surrounding lands) was largely Muslim and that it had twenty or thirty mosques. Both statements strain belief. Abd al-Razzaq, a pious Muslim jurist and scholar who spent more than four months in the city and therefore surely became well acquainted with its Muslim community, strongly (and correctly) implies that the city's population consisted largely of non-Muslims (infidels), and he further notes that the city had only two mosques, which were served by a single qadi and a single imam. It is unimaginable that there would have been any additional mosques in the surrounding countryside. It is not difficult to imagine that Ma Huan, who traveled to Calicut twice, was in the city for only short periods of time and did not have an opportunity to visit the twenty or more temples of worship that he assumed were mosques. All too often the eyes see what the brain prepares them to see. When Vasco da Gama first set foot in Calicut he worshiped at a temple dedicated to a Hindu goddess, believing it to be a church built by the legendary St. Thomas Christians and dedicated to the Virgin Mary. You do not need to know this fact about da Gama's error to reasonably conclude that Abd al-Razzaq is a far more trustworthy source than Ma Huan on the issue of Calicut's Muslim population and its religious life.

The three Muslim authors also shed light on policies adopted by the rulers of Calicut to encourage commerce and friendly relations with neighboring and far-distant powers.

Ibn Battuta tells us how his diplomatic party was received with great ceremony and how the *Samudri raja* arranged for his transportation aboard a Chinese vessel. Even more revealing are his descriptions of the sizes and types of the Chinese ships that did business at Calicut; the high status and honor accorded the factors, or agents-in-charge, of these Chinese ships; and the manner in which the ruler of Calicut protected the goods of shipwrecked merchants. The size of their ships alone suggests that the Chinese invested heavily in their trade with Calicut, but they did so because they knew that they would be welcomed and treated fairly at the port city. And why not? The rulers of Calicut understood that the prosperity of their city depended on the satisfaction of visiting merchants.

Ma Huan provides additional detail in this regard. The rajas of Calicut maintained a policy of religious toleration, which, given how much they depended on Muslim officials and merchants, was the only logical policy to follow. The rajas also provided for a well-run and honest marketplace by commissioning officials who were responsible for facilitating all commercial transactions and guaranteeing all contracts. Once a deal was struck, it was inviolate.

Finally, Ma Huan supports and supplements evidence from the *Roteiro* regarding Calicut's industries. Pepper production, which was carefully regulated by the state in regard to collection, storage, and sale (although the trees were apparently cultivated in small family garden plots), was a major staple of Calicut's economy. Likewise, Calicut's silk industry produced expensive bolts of silk, and the region was also a major source for coral and gemstones, especially pearls. Despite its native silk production, however, Calicut was a center for trade in Chinese embroidered silk. Apparently the high quality of this product allowed it to compete favorably with Indian silk.

Abd al-Razzaq supplements Ibn Battuta's testimony regarding the raja's protection of the cargoes of vessels that ran aground in the area by noting that every ship that happened to arrive in the area by accident was treated fairly and protected. He also adds a bit of detail to Ma Huan's account of the vital role played by the raja's officials in providing a secure and honest commercial environment. According to Abd al-Razzaq, local customs officials were responsible for inventorying and guarding all incoming cargoes and performed their duties so well that visiting merchants freely entrusted their goods to them. Finally, he informs us that a tariff of one-fortieth was levied on all sales of incoming merchandise. A tax of two and one-half percent on sales alone was not extortionate and ensured a heavy influx of merchandise, especially when merchants understood that all unsold items were tax-exempt.

In conclusion, inasmuch as this tax was paid into the ruler's treasury, it was in his best interest to grease the wheels of trade in every way possible and to provide two elements that merchants around the world and in all ages have deemed necessary for the success of their endeavors: certainty and security. The fact that, as Ma Huan informs us, the raja minted gold and silver coins suggests that these policies worked well—at least until the arrival in force of the Portuguese.

Well, as you can see, interpreting historical sources is not an arcane science or esoteric art. Yes, it is challenging, but it is a skill that you can master. Look at it this way: it is an exercise that mainly requires close attention and common sense. You must first read and study each source carefully and thoroughly. Then, using the evidence you have picked up from the documents and artifacts, answer the Questions for Analysis. It is that straightforward. If you work with us, trusting us to provide you with all of the necessary background information and clues that you need to make sense out of these sources, you will succeed.

One last word: Have fun doing it because you should find it enjoyable to meet the challenge of reconstructing the past through its human records.

# PART ONE

# An Era of Change and Increased Global Interaction: The Fifteenth Through Seventeenth Centuries

LTHOUGH CHANGES OCCURRED in each and every historical era, only a few of these eras can be considered true turning points in world history. The two centuries from the 1400s to the 1600s, when profound changes affected every part of the globe and every aspect of human existence, were just such an era.

In politics, the 1400s saw the consolidation of authority by the Ming dynasty in China and the establishment of new empires by the Ottoman Turks in Asia Minor and southeastern Europe, the Aztecs in Central Mexico, and the Incas in western South America. Political change continued in the 1500s and early 1600s, when the Songhai Empire in West Africa, the Safavid Empire in Iran, and the Mughal Empire in India emerged. Moreover, the Tokugawa clan ended decades of civil war in Japan, and the princes of Muscovy established a unified Russian state. Important changes also took place in politically divided Europe, which experienced decades of religious war.

Significant religious developments occurred in many parts of the world. These included the splintering of European Christendom as a result of the Protestant Reformation, and the emergence of the new monotheistic faith, Sikhism, in India. Islam continued to make converts in Africa and Southeast Asia, and Shiism, a branch of Islam dating from the seventh century, became the state religion in Iran.

In the realm of ideas and the arts, Europe experienced the climax of the Renaissance and the beginnings of the Scientific Revolution. In Asia, Confucian scholarship in China flourished, as did painting and poetry in India, Iran, and the Ottoman Empire. New technologies took root. Printed books (which had appeared in China and Korea centuries earlier) became an important cultural force in Europe after the art of printing by movable type was developed in the 1450s. Across Eurasia gunpowder weapons, invented in China several centuries earlier, proliferated. The world's population grew from approximately 350 million in 1400 to 550 million in 1600, despite catastrophic population losses in the Americas. Even the climate changed. Europe and parts of Asia experienced cold, harsh weather in the early 1300s, followed by a century and a half of warming and a return to colder temperatures in the late 1500s.

Although these events, individually and cumulatively, were hardly trivial, they were less important than two other interrelated developments that occurred between the 1450s and the 1600s: the increase in interaction and interconnectedness among the world's peoples and the emergence of Western Europe as a major force in world affairs. Although cross-cultural interchange had been a part of history from its beginnings, the world in 1400 still consisted of a number of culturally distinct regions whose peoples had limited contacts with and only vague knowledge of the rest of the world. The people of China, India, the Middle East, sub-Saharan Africa, Europe, and two regions that no one in Africa-Eurasia even knew existed, Oceania and the Americas, had distinctive religions, artistic styles, and technologies. They lived in a world in which transregional trade was negligible, long-distance travel was uncommon, and military threats and political interference from outside their region were rare or nonexistent. As a result, their histories followed trajectories that rarely intersected.

By the mid-seventeenth century, however, the world was far different. By then, the output of silver mines in Mexico and South America affected silk prices in China; the growing taste of Europeans for sweets led to the enslavement of Africans on sugar plantations in Brazil and the West Indies; statesmen in Lisbon, Madrid, and other European capitals controlled political affairs in North and South America; political disorders in seventeenth-century China stimulated the porcelain industry in the Netherlands and England; policies adopted by Japanese shoguns and Chinese emperors drew the attention of papal officials in Rome; wealthy Europeans kept warm by wearing coats and hats made from the furs of animals trapped in North America or Siberia; and Native Americans died from epidemics caused by pathogens imported from Europe and Africa.

All these developments can be traced back to the emerging global importance of Europe. In the early 1400s the Portuguese began to explore Africa's west coast, and by the 1450s, had set for themselves the more ambitious goal of reaching the Indian Ocean by sailing around the southern tip of Africa. The Portuguese captain Vasco da Gama accomplished this in 1498, six years after the Italian mariner in the service of Spain, Christopher Columbus, had discovered the Americas while seeking Asia. During the 1500s and 1600s Europe's expansion continued. The Portuguese pushed on from Africa and India to the East Indies, China, and Japan. Spain extended its power in the Americas. The French, Dutch, English, Danes, and Swedes struck claims to lands in the Americas and the Caribbean, and the Dutch challenged the Portuguese in Asia.

As important as it was, this first stage of Europe's global expansion must be kept in perspective. By the mid-1650s Europe was not the world's leading economic power and had not achieved military or technological superiority over the ancient centers of civilization in Asia. Europeans achieved political dominance only in the Americas, the Philippines, and the Atlantic islands off Africa's west coast, where political disunity, epidemics, and the native people's unsophisticated technology gave them an advantage. In Asia and most of Africa, they conquered and held a few coastal cities, but no more. Although Europe had become a new presence in world markets, its overall economic output was dwarfed by that of India and China. Europeans neither grew nor manufactured products that interested Asian buyers, meaning that they paid for their purchases in Asian markets with silver mined in the Americas. Without that silver, European's participation in world trade would have been negligible.

By the mid-seventeenth century, Europeans had changed the world in many ways. But it still was not Europe's world. This would be the case two hundred fifty years later, but only after the world had experienced a host of other far-reaching changes.

# Chapter 1

# Europe in an Age of Conflict and Expansion

F ROM THE 1400s THROUGH THE MID-1600s, Europe changed in many ways. Religious uniformity under the Roman Catholic Church gave way to religious diversity as new Protestant churches rejected papal authority and Catholic doctrine. A political order characterized by local aristocratic power and weak monarchies was undermined by the emergence of increasingly centralized and fiercely competitive states. Armies grew in size, and battles were fought with artillery, firearms, and landmines in addition to longbows, pikes, and lances. Intellectuals lost interest in the theological and philosophical speculations of their thirteenth-century predecessors, and inspired by rediscovered Greek and Roman texts, they broke new ground in science, philosophy, and political thought. Writers, artists, and architects developed new styles and themes, and explorers discovered new ocean routes to Africa, Asia, and the Americas.

Taken together, these changes mark the end of the Middle Ages, a long, formative period of European civilization that began with the fall of the Western Roman Empire in the fifth century C.E. These changes are generally viewed as indicators of progress and growth—an age of renaissance, or rebirth—after centuries of medieval stagnation. Such a view is problematic. Aside from belittling the impressive achievements of the Middle Ages, it ignores the many hardships, tensions, doubts, and conflicts that were part of the immediate post-medieval era.

The emergence of Protestantism, for example, ultimately led to an acceptance of religious diversity and toleration in most of Europe, but in the sixteenth and early seventeenth centuries, it was a source of religious persecution and war. Tens of thousands of Europeans were exiled, imprisoned, or executed because of their beliefs, and millions died in the religious wars that stretched from the 1520s to the 1640s. Similarly, the ideas of Copernicus, Kepler, and Galileo provided the foundation for Europe's Scientific Revolution, and the discoveries of Renaissance humanists

5

broadened Europe's intellectual perspectives by introducing scholars and the educated public to a wide range of previously unknown ancient philosophies. At the time, however, the proliferation of new and contending ideas led to the pessimistic view that humans could know little if anything with certainty. Nor did these scientists' and humanists' discoveries dispel irrational fears and superstitions. Witch hunts and witch trials claimed the lives of thousands of individuals, mostly women, who supposedly had pledged themselves to the Devil in return for supernatural powers.

The sixteenth century witnessed impressive economic growth. But inflation caused hardship for landlords and peasants, and beginning in the 1580s, plague, famine, and war slowed economic growth and caused a decline in Europe's overall standard of living. Political changes also increased tensions. Advocates of centralized monarchy contended with defenders of local autonomy, supporters of divine-right monarchy faced believers in regicide, and kings battled parliaments. Wars were fought to gain or protect territory, to advance the cause of Catholicism or Protestantism, to settle dynastic claims, or to fulfill personal ambitions. The Thirty Years' War (1618–1648) involved every major state and caused suffering unmatched in Europe until the wars of the twentieth century.

Expansionist Europe was not a stable, cohesive, and self-confident society. The Europeans, in their efforts to reach Asia by sailing west, luckily discovered the Americas, whose inhabitants were largely subdued after millions of them died from imported diseases. Elsewhere, the Europeans' aggressiveness, single-mindedness, and weaponry enabled them to expand their commercial activities and establish a measure of political power on the fringes of Africa and Asia. But these accomplishments, rightly deemed significant by historians, gave scant comfort to most Europeans, who faced a troubled present and anticipated the future with as much foreboding as hope.

# European Expansion: Goals and Motives

The Europeans' explorations, discoveries, and expansion from the fifteenth through the seventeenth centuries had ramifications for people across Eurasia, in much of Africa, and especially in the Americas. A story with elements of bravery, idealism, greed, and cruelty, and an event that brought wealth and power to some but suffering and death to others, Europe's expansion has been intensively studied and debated from the time it began to the present day. Nonetheless, its meaning and significance are frequently misunderstood.

One misconception is that during the early modern period "expansion and discovery" were unique European accomplishments. In truth, states in other regions were exploring and expanding, sometimes in what for them was "unknown territory." Between 1405 and 1433, China's emperors sponsored a series of maritime expeditions designed to establish a Chinese presence in the Indian Ocean basin. Commanded by Admiral Zheng He, Chinese fleets consisting of two hundred ships or more reached India, the Arabian Peninsula, and Africa's east coast. In addition, beginning in the 1500s, Russia began its eastward expansion, not halting until by the 1700s the Russians had conquered Siberia, reached the Pacific Ocean, and staked claims to Alaska and parts of the North American west coast.

Another misconception is that Europe's expansion was the result of the Europeans' superiority over the rest of the world's peoples. The Europeans, it is argued, took the lead in overseas exploration because they had better ships, a more sophisticated economy, better organized states, more freedom, and more effective weapons than anyone else in the world. Some go further to suggest it was the unique adventurous spirit of the Europeans that made the difference. None of these arguments holds up under careful scrutiny.

Instead, the causes of Europe's expansion are best understood if the issue is broken down into three questions. First, what developments in ship construction, navigational skills, and geographical knowledge enabled Europeans to sail across the world's oceans? Advances in ship design (ships outfitted with pintle and gudgeon rudders and a combination of triangular and square sails) and improved navigation techniques (better maps and instruments such as the compass, quadrant, astrolabe, and hourglass) are important parts of the story. Second, what advantages did Europeans have in their early encounters with the peoples of Asia, Africa, and the Western Hemisphere? European firearms and steel swords were important, but other factors, which varied from region to region, also played key roles. In the Americas, the susceptibility of the native populations to Old World diseases weakened resistance to the Europeans, as did political and religious divisions in Asia. A final question pertains to motive: What did explorers and the monarchs and investors who supported them hope to accomplish? Why did they pursue transoceanic discovery and expansion with such urgency? The sources in this section provide some answers to this third question.

# The Portuguese Imperial Venture

## 1 • AFONSO D'ALBUQUERQUE, SPEECH TO MEN OF THE PORTUGUESE FLEET BEFORE THE SECOND ATTACK ON MELAKA

Four men dominate the history of early Portuguese exploration and expansion: Prince Henry the Navigator (1394–1460), who sponsored the first Portuguese voyages down Africa's west coast; Bartholomeu Dias (1451–1500), who in 1488 first sailed around the tip of Africa; Vasco da Gama (1460–1524), who in 1498 reached India by sailing around Africa; and finally, Afonso d'Albuquerque (1453–1515), who in the wake of these discoveries created a Portuguese commercial empire stretching from Africa to Japan.

Known as the "Caesar of the East," Albuquerque was born to aristocratic parents and served as an officer in the Portuguese army before making his first voyage to India in 1503. On his return, he convinced King Manuel I of the feasibility of an ambitious plan to monopolize trade between Asia and Europe. The first step was to establish a string of fortified trading posts along Africa's coasts, the entrances to the Red Sea and Persian Gulf, and India's west coast. Farther east it meant establishing trading posts in the East Indies; taking control of Melaka, the prosperous trading city on the Malay Peninsula; and ultimately opening commercial contacts with China and Japan.

Following a failed Portuguese effort to take Melaka in 1509, Albuquerque returned in 1511 with a fleet of fourteen ships and approximately eleven hundred men. After the first Portuguese attack on the strongly defended city in late July failed, he delivered the following speech to his officers before a second attack on August 11. His words are recorded in a history of Albuquerque's exploits written by his son, Braz de Albuquerque, around 1515 and published in 1576 as *Commentarios do Grande Afonso de Albuquerque*. In the following speech, the elder Albuquerque reminds the Portuguese what is at stake, and in doing so, provides insights into the motives behind the Portuguese imperial enterprise.

## QUESTIONS FOR ANALYSIS

1. Why were Albuquerque's officers and men hesitant to support another attack on Melaka?
2. What does Albuquerque believe to be the overall religious significance of the Portuguese effort to take Melaka?
3. What does Albuquerque believe to be the overall economic significance of taking control of Melaka?
4. Why is Albuquerque confident that the Portuguese effort will succeed?

---

When the great Afonso de Albuquerque had completed all the necessary preparations for renewing the attack on the city, he heard that some of the captains were saying that it was not in the king's interest to keep Melaka or to build a fortress there. When he learnt this, he summoned them to his ship, together with all the noblemen and officers of his fleet, and addressed them thus:

"Gentlemen, you will recall that, when it was agreed that we should attack this city, it was also decided that we should build a fortress here, because we all considered it necessary.

Accordingly, once the city had been taken, I had no intention of abandoning it, and it was only

because you advised me to that I called off the attack and withdrew. Now that I am ready, as you see, to go back again and capture the city, I find that you have changed your opinion. . . . Since I have to give my own account of these matters and justify my actions to our lord, King Manuel, I do not wish to be the only one to take the blame for them. There are many reasons I could give you why we should take the city and build a fortress there to keep control of it. However, I will now only put to you two for not going back on what you have agreed.

The first of these is the great service we shall render to Our Lord by throwing the Muslims out of this country and preventing the fire of the

---

*Source:* T. F. Earle and John Villiers, trans. and eds., *Albuquerque: Caesar of the East* (Warminster, England: Aris & Phillips, 1990), pp. 79–82. Reprinted by permission of Oxbow Books.

Mohammedan sect from spreading any further. I hope in Our Lord[1] that, as a result of our doing this, the Muslims may be driven out of India[2] altogether, because most, if not all, of them live from the trade of this country and so have become powerful and rich and the owners of great treasures. I believe that the king of Melaka [Sultan Mahmud Shah] will not attempt to negotiate terms with us in order to safeguard his position. He has once already suffered defeat and experienced our strength and now, after sixteen days have passed, is no longer able to hope that any help will come to him from outside. I also believe that Our Lord will close his mind and harden his heart, because he wants this business of Melaka to be brought to a conclusion so as to open the route through the Straits [of Melaka] to us. The king of Portugal has often commanded me to go to the Straits, because it seemed to His Highness that this was the best place to intercept the trade which the Muslims of Cairo and of Mecca and Jiddah[3] carry on in these parts. So it was to do Our Lord's service that we were brought here; by taking Melaka, we would close the Straits so that never again would the Muslims be able to bring their spices by this route.

The other reason I put to you is the great service that we shall do to King Manuel by taking this city. It is the source of all the spices and drugs that the Muslims ship from here each year to the Straits, without our being able to stop them. If we cut them off from their traditional market, there will be no port or other place in the region as convenient as this that they can use. Since we gained control of the Malabar [southwest Indian] pepper trade, Cairo has not received any except what the Muslims have been able to take from this region. Forty or fifty [ships] sail every year from here bound for

Mecca, laden with all kinds of spices. They cannot be prevented without great expense and large fleets constantly patrolling the Gulf of Cape Comorin.[4] Malabar pepper, of which they might have some expectations, because the king of Calicut is their ally, is in our control under the eyes of the [Portuguese] governor of India, and the Muslims cannot take so much from there as they suppose. I am very sure that, if this Melaka trade is taken out of their hands, Cairo and Mecca will be completely lost and no spices will go to the Venetians except those that they go to Portugal to buy.

If it seems to you that Melaka, being a great city with a large population, will be difficult to hold, you need have no misgivings on that score. Once the city has been taken, all the rest of the kingdom is so small that the king would have no source of reinforcements. If you fear that the capture of the city will entail great expense and that then there will be nowhere where our men and ships can be re-equipped, I trust in God's mercy that, once we have gained mastery of Melaka with a fine fortress, and provided that the Portuguese crown appoints someone who knows well how to govern it and to make it grow rich, all its expenses will be met from local taxes. Once the merchants who frequent Melaka and are accustomed to live under the tyranny of the Malays have had a taste of our justice and honesty, our plain-dealing and clemency and see the decrees of King Manuel, our lord, in which he commands that all their vassals in these parts be well treated, I am convinced that they will come and settle here and build . . . their houses. All the things I am proposing to you are summed up in this one key point, which is that we build a fortress in this city of Melaka and hold it, that this country be governed by the Portuguese and that King Manuel

---

[1] "Our Lord" refers to Jesus Christ, not "our lord," the king of Portugal.
[2] A term used for the general region of South and Southeast Asia.
[3] Jiddah (also Jeddah or Jedda) is the major port city on the Arabian side of the Red Sea. Mecca, where Muhammad

received his revelations, was a caravan center and the destination of Muslim pilgrims from around the world. It is some 50 miles inland from Jiddah.
[4] The Gulf of Cape Comorin is off the southernmost tip of India.

be recognized as its rightful king. I therefore beg you as a favor to consider well the enterprise you have in hand and not to let it be lost."

When Afonso de Albuquerque had finished his discourse, as I have recorded it, the members of his council put forward varying opinions, some for and some against him. The result of their discussion was that the majority repeated their conviction that is was in the king's service to take the city of Melaka, to expel the Muslims, and to build a fortress there.

Afonso de Albuquerque . . . took the side of the majority and decided to attack Melaka and secure his position there. He decided to leave all the questions which had been raised on the other side in the hands of Our Lord Jesus Christ, because he would dispose everything according to his will. He ordered the secretary to draw up an agreement, which he and all the captains, noblemen and knights who were present signed.

## 1492: What Columbus and His Patrons Hoped to Gain

### 2 • FERDINAND OF ARAGON AND ISABELLA OF CASTILE, AGREEMENTS WITH COLUMBUS, APRIL 17 AND APRIL 30, 1492, AND COLUMBUS, PROLOGUE TO HIS DIARY OF HIS FIRST VOYAGE, APRIL 1493

Among the contributing factors to Europe's expansion in the early modern period, perhaps none was more important than simple human ambition. There is no better example of this truth than Christopher Columbus, the Genoese mariner credited with the discovery of the New World. Available evidence suggests that Columbus was born in 1451 into a weaver's family and went to sea as a teenager. As a young sailor, he gained experience on voyages as far north as Ireland, as far south as Mina on Africa's coast, and as far west as the Azores, an archipelago some 800 miles west of Portugal. Having taught himself to read, he studied geographical texts, travelers' accounts, maps, and even biblical passages that provided him with a set of assumptions about the earth's circumference, Europe's size, and the distance between Japan and the Asian mainland. Although inaccurate, these assumptions convinced him it would be possible to reach Asia by sailing west into the Atlantic. In 1484, Columbus sought support for an exploratory voyage from King João II of Portugal, but the king, convinced that sailing around Africa was a more promising route to Asia, denied his requests.

Undeterred, in 1486 Columbus gained an audience with the Spanish monarchs Ferdinand and Isabella, who on hearing his proposal gave him a small stipend and appointed a commission of "learned men and mariners" to examine his plan. For five years, he awaited a decision. Negotiations broke down in early 1492, when the monarchs balked at Columbus's demands. With Columbus preparing to take his ideas to the king of France, a last-minute appeal to Isabella resulted in an agreement. In two capitulations (sets of terms for an agreement, not "acts of surrender"), issued by Ferdinand and Isabella in April 1492, Columbus was promised a large share of any economic benefits that might accrue from his voyage and extensive authority over any lands he might discover. The monarchs also stood to benefit. Preparations could now begin for Columbus's historic voyage, which departed on August 3, 1492, and ended eleven weeks later, on October 12, when he and his crew landed on a small island in the Bahamas. On returning to Europe, he presented his royal patrons with a log of his voyage, to which he attached a prologue that sheds light on what he perceived to be the purpose and significance of his endeavor. It also gave him the opportunity to confirm the terms of the agreement he and the monarchs had made a year earlier.

Columbus never realized his dreams of wealth and power. After his discoveries failed to produce the gold and profits he had promised, he lost favor at court, and from 1495 onward, the agreements of 1492 were ignored by the monarchs and became the subject of protracted litigation. Columbus made his fourth and last voyage across the Atlantic in 1502, four years before he died in Spain, still pressing his claims with the crown and still convinced he had reached Asia.

## QUESTIONS FOR ANALYSIS

1. What assumptions underlie Columbus's and the monarchs' statements concerning the authority they expect to exercise in the lands Columbus discovers?
2. What kinds of authority will Columbus exercise over the lands he discovers? What role will be played by the monarchs?
3. What kind of material benefits do Columbus and the monarchs expect to gain from Columbus's discoveries? How will these gains be divided?
4. How do the stated and implied goals of Columbus's enterprise compare with the motives of Albuquerque in the conquest of Melaka?

---

## Agreement of April 17, 1492

The following favors, which at the request of Lord Cristóbal Colón [Columbus's Spanish name], your Highnesses give him as a reward for his discoveries in the Ocean Seas and the voyage which now, with the aid of God, he is about to make in the service of your Highnesses.

Firstly, that your Highnesses as Lords of the said Ocean Seas, make from this time and henceforth the said Lord Cristóbal Colón their Admiral[1] in all those islands and mainlands which by his hand and industry shall be discovered or acquired in the said oceans, for the rest of his life, and after his death, for his heirs and successors, from one to another in perpetuity, with all the rights and privileges belonging to the said office. . . .

Likewise, that your Highnesses make the said Lord Cristóbal their Viceroy and Governor-General[2] in all the said islands and mainlands which as has been stated, he may discover or acquire in the said seas; and that for the government of each of them, he may make selection of three persons for each

---

*Source:* J. B. Thatcher, *Christopher Columbus, His Life and Work* (New York and London: Putnam's Sons, 1903), Vol. 2, pp. 442–451.

[1]The office of admiral was originally applied to the Admiralty of Seville, a prestigious hereditary office dating back to the thirteenth century. The officeholder was responsible for the kingdom's navy and all seaborne commerce, which at the time was limited to Spain's immediate Atlantic and Mediterranean coasts.

[2]*Viceroy* is a title conferred on an official who officially represents the monarch; *governor* was an administrator of a province or region.

office, and that your Highnesses may choose and select the one who shall be most serviceable to you, and thus the lands which our Lord shall permit him to discover and acquire will be better governed, in the service of your Highnesses. . . .

All and whatever merchandise, whether it be pearls, precious stones, gold, silver, spices, and other goods of any kind, name, and manner it may be, which may be bought, bartered, discovered, acquired, or obtained within the limits of the said Admiralty, your Highnesses grant henceforth to the said Lord Cristóbal, and will that he may have and take for himself, the tenth part of all of them, after all expenses have been deducted; so that what remains free and clear, he may have and take the tenth part for himself, and do with it as he wills, the other nine parts remaining for your Highnesses. . . .

All the vessels which may be equipped for trade and negotiation, and as often as they may be equipped, the said Admiral Lord Cristóbal may, if he wishes, invest the eighth part of all that may be expended in the equipment. And also that he may have and take of the profit, the eighth part of all which may result from such equipment. . . .

## Agreement of April 30, 1492

Forasmuch as you, Cristóbal Colón, are going by our command, with some of our ships and with our subjects, to discover and acquire certain islands and mainlands in the ocean, and it is hoped that, by the help of God, some of the said islands and mainlands in the said ocean will be discovered and acquired by your pains and industry; and therefore it is a just and reasonable thing that since you incur the said danger for our service you should be rewarded for it . . . it is our will and pleasure that you, . . . after you have discovered and acquired the said islands and mainlands in the said ocean, or any of them whatsoever, shall be our Admiral of the said islands and mainland and Viceroy and Governor therein, and shall be empowered from that time forward to call and entitle yourself Lord Cristóbal Colón, and that your sons and successors in the said office and charge may likewise entitle and call themselves Lord and Admiral and Viceroy and Governor thereof; and that you may have power to use and exercise the said office of Admiral, together with the said office of Viceroy and Governor of the said islands and mainland . . . and to hear and determine all the suits and causes civil and criminal appertaining to the said office of Admiralty, Viceroy, and Governor according as you shall find by law, . . . and may have power to punish and chastise delinquents, and exercise the said offices . . . in all that concerns and appertains to the said offices . . . and that you shall have and levy the fees and salaries annexed, belonging and appertaining to the said offices and to each of them, according as our High Admiral in the Admiralty of our kingdoms levies and is accustomed to levy them.

## Columbus, Prologue to His Diary of His First Voyage (late 1492)

Because, O most Christian, and very high, most excellent, and most powerful Princes, . . . after your Highnesses had ended the war with the Muslims who reigned in Europe, and had finished it in the very great city of Granada, where in [1492] on January 2, by force of arms, I saw the royal banners of your Highnesses raised on the towers of Alhambra, the fortress of that city, and I saw the Muslim King come forth from the gates of the city and kiss the royal hands of your

*Source:* Julius E. Olson and Edward Gaylord Bourne, eds., *The Northmen, Columbus and Cabot, 985–1503, Original* *Narratives of Early American History.* New York: Charles Scribner's Sons, 1906.

Highnesses, . . . and presently in that same month, acting on the information that I had given to your Highnesses touching the land of India, and respecting a Prince who is called Grand Khan,[1] . . . how he and his ancestors had sent to Rome many times to ask for learned men of our holy faith to teach him, and how the Holy Father had never complied, insomuch that many people believing in idolatries were lost by receiving doctrine of perdition: Your Highnesses, as Catholic . . . Princes who love the holy Christian faith and the propagation of it, and who are enemies to the sect of Muhammad and to all idolatries and heresies, resolved to send me . . . to the said parts of India to see the said princes, and the cities and lands, and their disposition, with a view that they might be converted to our holy faith; and ordered that I should not go by land to the east, as had been customary, but that I should go by way of the west, whither up to this day, we do not know for certain that anyone has gone. . . . Thus, . . . your Highnesses gave orders to me that with a sufficient fleet I should go to the said parts of India, and for this they made great concessions to me, and ennobled me, so that henceforward I should be called "sir," and should be Chief Admiral of the Ocean Sea, perpetual Viceroy and Governor of all the islands and continents that I should discover and gain, and that I might hereafter discover and gain in the Ocean Sea, and that my eldest son should succeed, and so on from generation to generation forever . . .

---

[1] The "land of India" was a general term for Asia. There is some debate about what ruler Columbus had in mind in referring to the "Grand Khan." Most historians believe it referred to the emperor of China.

## Why England Should Sponsor Colonies

### 3 • RICHARD HAKLUYT, A DISCOURSE ON WESTERN PLANTING

Although King Henry VII and a group of Bristol merchants had dispatched the Italian mariner Giovanni Caboto (in English, John Cabot) to North America in 1497 to search for what came to be known as the Northwest Passage to Asia, no further exploration under English auspices took place until the reign of Elizabeth I (r. 1558–1603). Backed by investors in the Muscovy Company and the short-lived Company of Cathay (China), Martin Frobisher made three voyages to North America between 1576 and 1578 in search of gold and the Northwest Passage, but found neither. Five years later, an effort to colonize North America ended in tragedy when the expedition was lost at sea while sailing south from Newfoundland. These setbacks failed to discourage a small group of merchants, mariners, and courtiers who continued to devise plans for colonization and promote them at Elizabeth's court.

Included in this group was Richard Hakluyt (1552–1616), the son of a London merchant who was orphaned at age five and raised by a cousin, a lawyer. Through contacts with his cousin's friends and business associates, the young man developed an interest in trade and exploration. Although he studied Greek and Latin at Oxford, his passion was geography, which he learned from books, maps, and mariners' reports. Ordained a priest in the Church of England, Hakluyt still had time to write books on exploration and lobby Elizabeth and her officials on behalf of various proposals to colonize North America. Among them was a lengthy memorandum directed to the queen in 1584 in support of a proposal by Sir Walter Raleigh to colonize Norumbega, a name vaguely applied to northeastern North America. The excerpt below is the memorandum's concluding summary.

Elizabeth granted Raleigh a charter but declined to support the expedition financially, and thin funding was one of several reasons why Drake's project, the Roanoke Colony, failed. Hakluyt and others continued to promote their ideas, however, and during the reign of James I (1603–1625) the chartering of the Virginia Company and Plymouth Company marked the true beginnings of the English colonization of North America.

## QUESTIONS FOR ANALYSIS

1. According to Hakluyt, what economic advantages might England expect from colonizing Norumbega?
2. According to Hakluyt, how will colonization strengthen England and weaken its rivals?
3. According to Hakluyt, how will colonization help solve England's domestic problems?
4. How important is religion in Hakluyt's thinking about colonization?
5. How much concrete knowledge of the Americas does Hakluyt seem to have?

1. The soil yields and may be made to yield all the several commodities of Europe. . . .
2. The passage there and home is neither too long nor too short, but easy, and to be made twice in the year.
3. The passage cuts not near the trade of any prince, nor near any of their countries or territories, and is a safe passage, and not easy to be interfered with by prince or potentate.
4. The passage is to be performed at all times of the year, and in that respect surpasses our trades in the Levant Seas within the Straits of Gibraltar [the Mediterranean], and the trades in the seas within the King of Denmark's Strait [the Baltic Sea], and the trades to the ports of Norway and of Russia, etc. . . .
5. And whereas England now for more than a century, by the distinctive commodity of

wool, and of later years, by clothing of the same, has raised itself from meaner state to greater wealth and much higher honor, might, and power than before, . . . it comes now to pass that by the great increase of the trade of wool in Spain and in the West Indies,[1] now multiplying daily, that the wool of England, and the cloth made of the same, will become inferior, and every day more inferior than [the] other; which, prudently considered, behooves this realm, if it intends . . . to not negligently and sleepingly slide into beggary, to plan ahead and to plant [settle] at Norumbega or some like place, were it not for anything else but for the hope of the sale of our wool. . . .
6. This enterprise may prevent the Spanish king from flowing over all the face of that wild and uninhabited expanse of America, if we seed

*Source:* Richard Hakluyt, "A Discourse on Western Planting," in Charles Deane and Leonard Woods, *Documentary History of the State of Maine* (Collections of the Maine Historical Society, 2nd series, Vol. 2, 1877).

[1] Spain was famous for the fine wool produced by its herds of Merino sheep. Some of this wool was now being exported to Spain's possessions in the West Indies and the American mainland.

and plant there in time. . . . And England possessing the proposed place of planting, her Majesty may have plenty of excellent trees for masts, of goodly timber to build ships and to make great navies, of pitch, tar, hemp, and all things needed for a royal navy, and that for no cost. . . . How easy a matter may it be to this realm, swarming presently with valiant youths, degenerating and hurtful by lack of employment, and having good makers of cable and of all sorts of cordage [rope], and the best and most cunning shipwrights of the world, to be lords of all those seas, and to spoil Philip's Indian navy,[2] and to deprive him of yearly passage of his treasure to Europe, and consequently to abate the pride of Spain and of the supporter of the great Anti-christ of Rome [the papacy] and to . . . cut off the common mischiefs that come to all Europe by the abundance of his Indian treasure, and this without difficulty.

7. This voyage, although it may be accomplished by bark or smallest pinnace [small sailing ships] . . . yet for the distance, for burden [carrying capacity] and gain in trade, the merchant will not for profit's sake use it but by ships of great burden; so as this realm shall have by that means ships of great burden and of great strength for the defense of this realm. . . .

9. The great mass of wealth of the realm boarded in the merchants' ships . . . shall not . . . be driven by winds and tempests into ports of any foreign princes, as the Spanish ships of late years have been into our ports of the West countries, etc. . . .

10. No foreign commodity that comes into England comes without payment of custom once, twice, or thrice, before it comes into the realm, and so all foreign commodities become more expensive to the subjects of this realm; and by this route to Norumbega foreign princes' customs are avoided; and the foreign commodities cheaply purchased, they become cheap to the subjects of England, to the common benefit of the people, and to the saving of great treasure in the realm . . .

13. By making of ships and by preparing of things for the same, by making of cables and cordage, by planting of vines and olive trees, and by making of wine and oil, by husbandry, and by thousands of things there to be done, infinite numbers of the English nation may be set on work, to the unburdening of the realm with many that now live dependent on charity at home.

14. If the sea coast serve for making of salt, and the inland for wine, oils, oranges, lemons, figs, &c., and for making of iron, without sword drawn, we shall cut the comb[3] of the French, of the Spanish, of the Portuguese, and of enemies, and of doubtful friends, to the abating [reduction] of their wealth and force, and to the greater saving of the wealth of the realm.

15. We may out of those parts receive the mass of wrought [manufactured] wares that now we receive out of France, Flanders, Germany, &c.; and so we may daunt [subdue] the pride of some enemies of this realm, or at the least in part purchase those wares, that now we buy dearly of the French and Flemish, better cheap; and in the end, . . . drive them out of trade to idleness . . .

16. We shall by planting there enlarge the glory of the gospel, and from England plant sincere religion, and provide a safe and a sure place to receive people from all parts of the world that are forced to flee for the truth of God's word.

---

[2]Phillip II, king of Spain (r. 1556–1598); his "Indian navy" refers to Spanish ships carrying gold, silver, and other commodities between Europe and America.

[3]Comb refers to the red crest of a rooster. To "cut one's comb" is to humble or humiliate someone.

17. If frontier wars there chance to arise, and if thereupon we shall fortify, it will occasion the training up of our youth in the discipline of war, and make a number fit for the service of the wars and for the defense of our people there and at home.

18. The Spaniards govern in the Indies with all pride and tyranny; and like as when people of contrary nature at sea enter into galleys, where men are tied as slaves, all yell and cry with one voice, *Liberta, liberta*, as desirous of liberty and freedom, so no doubt whenever the Queen of England, a prince of such clemency, shall seat upon that broad expanse of America, and shall be reported throughout all that tract to use the natural people [Native Americans] there with all humanity, courtesy, and freedom, they will yield themselves to her government, and revolt clean from the Spaniard. . . .

20. Many men of excellent wits and of diverse singular gifts, overthrown by indebtedness or by some folly of youth, that are not able to live in England, may there be raised again, and do their country good service; and many needful uses there may (to great purpose) result in the saving of great numbers, that for trifles may otherwise be devoured by the gallows . . .

22. The fry[4] of the wandering beggars that grow up idly, and hurtful and burdensome to this realm, may there be unladen [unloaded], better bred up, and may populate waste countries to the home and foreign benefit, and to their own more happy state. . . .

---

[4]A "swarm" or crowd of insignificant persons.

# The Emergence of Protestantism

During the High Middle Ages, "the Age of Faith," devotion to the Catholic Church resulted in part from the clergy's moral example and leadership and in part from the Church's promise that its doctrines and practices, if followed, ensured eternal salvation. During the fourteenth and fifteenth centuries, however, the Church was rocked by schism, scandal, deficits, political challenges, and uninspired leadership. Anger over such abuses intensified, and many Europeans began to question the Church's ability to deliver the salvation they fervently sought. These doubts go far in explaining the success of the Protestant revolt, sparked in 1517 when a German friar, Martin Luther, challenged Catholic teachings, especially the doctrine that people could atone for their sins by purchasing indulgences. By 1650, Protestants dominated northern Germany, Scandinavia, England, Scotland, the Netherlands, and major Swiss cities and were a significant minority in France and parts of Central Europe.

No area of European life was unaffected by the Protestant Reformation. In the religious sphere, new Protestant churches (Lutheran, Reformed, Anglican, Presbyterian, and a host of smaller sects) proliferated, and Catholic reforms revitalized a church that had lost its spiritual focus and vitality. Education expanded because of the Protestants' emphasis on Bible reading by the laity and the needs of churches for educated leadership. Literacy among women increased as a result of Protestant educational efforts, and according to some historians, a more positive view of women resulted from the

Protestant affirmation of clerical marriage. Conversely, Protestant women made few appreciable legal or economic gains and were just as likely as their Catholic sisters to be victimized by witch hunts and witch trials. The religious struggles of the Reformation era also affected politics. With religious passions intensifying dynastic rivalries and internal conflicts, Europe endured a century of religious wars, including both civil wars and wars between states.

Most importantly, the Reformation era contributed to Europe's ongoing secularization. In the short run, the Protestant and Catholic reformations intensified religious feeling and thrust religion into the forefront of European life. In the long run, however, the proliferation of competing faiths divided and weakened Europe's churches, and years of religious intolerance and war discredited religion in the eyes of many. The gradual acceptance of religious diversity within individual states and Europe as a whole was a sign of the diminishing role of religion in European life and thought.

# A Protestant View of Christianity

## 4 • MARTIN LUTHER, TABLE TALK

The Protestant Reformation had many voices, but its first prophet was Martin Luther (1483–1546), whose Ninety-Five Theses of 1517 sparked the anti-Catholic rebellion. Born into the family of a German miner and educated at the University of Erfurt, Luther was preparing for a career as a lawyer when suddenly, in 1505, he changed course and became an Augustinian friar. Luther's decision followed a terrifying experience in a thunderstorm but at a deeper level resulted from his dissatisfaction over his relationship with God and doubts about his salvation. He hoped that life as a friar would shield him from the world's temptations and allow him to win God's favor by devoting himself to prayer, study, and the sacraments. His spiritual doubts remained, however. Intensely conscious of his inadequacies and failings, he was convinced he could never earn his salvation or live up to the high standards of selflessness, charity, and purity of Jesus' teachings as interpreted by the Catholic Church. He despaired of ever satisfying an angry, judging God and was terrorized by the prospect of eternal damnation.

During the 1510s, however, while teaching theology at the University of Wittenberg, Luther found spiritual peace through his reflections on the Scriptures. He concluded that weak, sinful human beings were incapable of earning their salvation by leading blameless lives and performing the pious acts enjoined by the Catholic Church. Rather, he came to view salvation as an unmerited divine gift, resulting from God-implanted faith in Jesus, especially in the redemptive power of his death and resurrection. This doctrine of "justification by faith alone" inspired the Ninety-Five Theses, in which Luther attacked Catholic teaching, especially the doctrine of indulgences, which taught that people could atone for their sins and ensure their own and their loved ones' salvation by contributing money to the Church. Within five years after posting the theses, Luther was the leader of a religious movement—Protestantism—that broke with the Catholic Church not only over the theology of salvation but also over a host of other issues concerning Christianity and the Christian life.

As Protestantism spread, Luther remained in Wittenberg as a pastor and professor and wrote hundreds of sermons, books, and treatises. He and his wife, Katharina, a former nun, made their home in the Augustinian convent where Luther had lived as a friar. Here they raised a family and entertained scores of visitors with whom Luther discussed the issues of the day. From 1522 to 1546, some of these guests recorded Luther's notable sayings as they remembered them, and from their journals we have what is known as Luther's *Table Talk*.

## QUESTIONS FOR ANALYSIS

1. According to Luther, what role should the Bible play in a Christian's life? In his view, how does the Roman Catholic Church obscure the Bible's meaning and message?
2. What does Luther mean by "good works"? Why does he believe that the Roman Catholic Church distorts the role of good works in a Christian's life?
3. What role does faith play in a Christian's life, according to Luther? Why is he convinced that faith is superior to external acts of devotion?
4. What are Luther's criticisms of the pope and other high officials of the Catholic Church?
5. Why does Luther single out monks and members of religious orders for special criticism? What are their shortcomings?

### Salvation and Damnation

Because as the everlasting, merciful God, through his Word and Sacraments,[1] talks and deals with us, all other creatures excluded, not of temporal things which pertain to this vanishing life . . . but as to where we shall go when we depart from here, and gives unto us his Son for a Savior, delivering us from sin and death, and purchasing for us everlasting righteousness, life, and salvation, therefore it is most certain, that we do not die away like the beasts that have no understanding; but so many of us . . . shall through him be raised again to life everlasting at the last day, and the ungodly to everlasting destruction.

### Faith versus Good Works

He that goes from the gospel to the law[2] thinking to be saved by good works,[3] falls as uneasily as he who falls from the true service of God to idolatry; for without Christ, all is idolatry and

*Source:* From *The Reformation Writings of Martin Luther*, Vol. 1, *The Basis of the Protestant Reformation*, translated and edited by Bertram Lee Woolf (London: Lutterworth Press, 1953). Reprinted with permission of Lutterworth Press.

[1] The *Word* is God's message as revealed through Jesus' life; *sacraments* are sacred rites that are outward, visible signs of an inward spiritual grace. Of the seven Catholic sacraments, Luther retained two, baptism and the Eucharist.

[2] By *law* Luther meant religious rules and regulations; he believed that futile human efforts to live strictly according to such laws undermined true faith.

[3] Ceremonies and pious activities such as pilgrimages, relic veneration, and attendance at Mass promoted by the Church as vehicles of God's grace.

fictitious imaginings of God, whether of the Turkish Quran, of the pope's decrees, or Moses' laws; if a man think thereby to be justified and saved before God, he is undone.

• • •

The gospel preaches nothing of the merit of works; he that says the gospel requires works for salvation, I say, flat and plain, is a liar.

Nothing that is properly good proceeds out of the works of the law, unless grace be present; for what we are forced to do, goes not from the heart. . . .

• • •

A Capuchin says: wear a grey coat and a hood, a rope round your body, and sandals on your feet. A Cordelier[4] says: put on a black hood; an ordinary papist says: do this or that work, hear Mass, pray, fast, give alms, etc. But a true Christian says: I am justified and saved only by faith in Christ, without any works or merits of my own; compare these together, and judge which is the true righteousness.

• • •

I have often been resolved to live uprightly, and to lead a true godly life, and to set everything aside that would hinder this, but it was far from being put in execution; even as it was with Peter,[5] when he swore he would lay down his life for Christ.

• • •

I will not lie or dissemble before my God, but will freely confess, I am not able to bring about that good which I intend, but await the happy hour when God shall be pleased to meet me with his grace.

• • •

A Christian's worshiping is not the external, hypocritical mask that our friars wear, when they chastise their bodies, torment and make themselves faint with ostentatious fasting, watching, singing, wearing hair shirts, scourging themselves, etc. Such worshiping God does not desire.

## The Bible

Great is the strength of the divine Word. . . . But we have neglected and scorned the pure and clear Word, and have drunk not of the fresh and cool spring; we are gone from the clear fountain to the foul puddle, and drunk its filthy water; that is, we have diligently read old writers and teachers, who went about with speculative reasonings, like the monks and friars.

• • •

The ungodly papists prefer the authority of the church far above God's Word; a blasphemy abominable and not to be endured; void of all shame and piety, they spit in God's face. Truly, God's patience is exceeding great, in that they are not destroyed; but so it always has been.

## The Papacy and the Monastic Orders

How does it happen that the popes pretend that they form the Church, when, all the while, they are bitter enemies of the Church, and have no knowledge, certainly no comprehension, of the holy gospel? Pope, cardinals, bishops, not a soul of them has read the Bible; it is a book unknown to them. They are a pack of guzzling, gluttonous wretches, rich, wallowing in wealth and laziness, resting secure in their power, and never, for a moment, thinking of accomplishing God's will.

• • •

---

[4]Capuchins and Cordeliers were branches of the Franciscan religious order noted for their austerity and strict poverty.
[5]One of Jesus' apostles. Following Jesus' arrest by Roman soldiers before his crucifixion, Peter three times denied any relationship with Jesus, despite having vowed shortly before to lay down his life for his teacher. It is thought that he was the first bishop of Rome and died there as a martyr.

Kings and princes coin money only out of metals, but the pope coins money out of everything—indulgences, ceremonies, dispensations, pardons; all fish come to his net. . . .

• • •

A gentleman being at the point of death, a monk from the next convent came to see what he could pick up, and said to the gentleman: Sir, will you give so and so to our monastery? The dying man, unable to speak, replied by a nod of the head, whereupon the monk, turning to the gentleman's son, said: You see, your father makes us this bequest. The son said to the father: Sir, is it your pleasure that I kick this monk down the stairs? The dying man nodded as before, and the son immediately drove the monk out of doors.

• • •

The papists took the invocation of saints from the pagans, who divided God into numberless images and idols, and ordained to each its particular office and work. . . . The invocation of saints is a most abominable blindness and heresy; yet the papists will not give it up, . . . for the calling on dead saints brings him infinite sums of money and riches, far more than he gets from the living.

• • •

In Italy, the monasteries are very wealthy. There are but three or four monks to each; the surplus of their revenues goes to the pope and his cardinals.

• • •

In Popedom they make priests, not to preach and teach God's Word, but only to celebrate Mass, and to roam about with the sacrament. For, when a bishop ordains a man, he says: Take the power to celebrate Mass, and to offer it for the living and the dead. But we ordain priests according to the command of Christ and St. Paul, namely, to preach the pure gospel and God's Word. The papists in their ordinations make no mention of preaching and teaching God's Word, therefore their consecrating and ordaining is false and wrong, for all worshiping which is not ordained of God, or erected by God's Word and command, is worthless, yea, mere idolatry.

## The Reform of the Church

The pope and his crew can in no way endure the idea of reformation; the mere word creates more alarm at Rome than thunderbolts from heaven or the Day of Judgment. A cardinal said the other day: Let them eat, and drink, and do what they will; but as to reforming us, we think that is a vain idea; we will not endure it. Neither will we Protestants be satisfied, though they administer the sacrament in both kinds, and permit priests to marry;[6] we will also have the doctrine of the faith pure and unfalsified, and the righteousness that justifies and saves before God, and which expels and drives away all idolatry and false-worshiping; with these gone and banished, the foundation on which Popedom is built also falls.

• • •

The chief cause that I fell out with the pope was this: the pope boasted that he was the head of the church, and condemned all that would not be under his power and authority. . . . Further, he took upon him power, rule, and authority over the Christian church, and over the Holy Scriptures, the Word of God; no man must presume to expound the Scriptures, but only he, and according to his ridiculous conceits; this was not to be endured. They who, against God's word, boast of the church's authority, are mere idiots.

---

[6]Two of the changes that Protestants demanded were allowing all Christians to receive the sacrament of the Eucharist in the forms of bread and wine (in medieval Catholic practice, only the priest drank the Eucharistic wine) and allowing priests to marry.

# Art as Protestant Propaganda

## 5 • LUCAS CRANACH THE YOUNGER, TWO KINDS OF PREACHING: EVANGELICAL AND PAPAL

Some seventy years before Luther posted his Ninety-Five Theses, another German, Johannes Gutenberg (ca. 1395–1468), perfected a method of printing books through movable metal type. Printing shops soon were established in Europe's major towns and cities, and by the mid-1500s, hundreds of thousands of books and pamphlets had been published.

Many of these publications played key roles in the era's religious struggles. The Ninety-Five Theses, intended by Luther to spark academic debate at the University of Wittenberg, instead brought him instant fame when they were translated into German and made available in inexpensive printed editions. Subsequently, Protestants, much more than Catholics, used the printed page to promote their ideas for learned audiences and, more tellingly, for the general population. Illustrations in the form of woodcuts were included in many of these works to make Protestant teachings accessible even to the illiterate.

One of the most famous of these illustrations is *Two Kinds of Preaching: Evangelical and Papal,* the work of a close friend of Luther's, Lucas Cranach the Younger (1515–1586). Produced in 1547, it was distributed as a broadsheet—a large printed sheet sold for a few small coins.

We have reproduced the woodcut on two pages, but in its original form it is undivided. The preacher facing left is Luther. Before him rests an open Bible, and on his side of the pulpit are words from the New Testament Book of Acts: "All prophets attest to this, that there is no other name in heaven than that of Christ." Above Luther is a dove, representing the Holy Spirit, the third person of the Holy Trinity, whose major functions are illumination, solace, and sanctification. Luther is pointing to three figures: the Paschal Lamb (a symbol of the risen Christ), the crucified Christ, and God the Father, who holds an orb. The crucified Christ directs these words to God the Father: "Holy Father, save them. I have sacrificed myself for them with my wounds." Directly below is written, "If we sin, we have an advocate before God, so let us turn in consolation to this means of grace." In the center and lower left corner, two Lutheran sacraments, baptism and the Eucharist, are depicted. Above the communion table and to the left of the crucified Christ are words uttered by Christ at the Last Supper according to Matthew 26:27, "Drink of it, all of you."

The right side of the woodcut is a Lutheran perspective on how Roman Catholicism has perverted Christianity. The preacher receives inspiration from an imp-like demon that pumps air into his ear with a bellows. The words above him state that the practices going on around him are theologically sound and offer an easy path to salvation. His audience consists mainly of clergy, with only a handful of laypeople. In the upper right corner, God rains down thunderbolts while Francis of Assisi, the founder of the Franciscan order and a revered medieval saint, vainly attempts to intercede on behalf of humanity. The rest of the scene ridicules various Catholic practices. They include, in

Lucas Cranach the Younger, *Two Kinds of Preaching: Evangelical*

Lucas Cranach the Younger, *Two Kinds of Preaching: Papal*

the lower right corner, the sale of indulgences by the pope, who holds a sign reading: "Because the coin rings, the soul to heaven springs." The sign on the money bag reads: "This is shame and vice, squeezed from your donations." Directly behind the pope is a priest celebrating a private Mass and an altar being consecrated by a bird-like demon. In the background is a dying man having his hair clipped in the style of a monk and having a monk's cowl, or hood, placed on his head, steps that supposedly would ensure his salvation. The attending nun sprinkles the man with holy water and holds a banner reading: "The cowl, the tonsure, and the water aid you." To the right of this scene, a bishop consecrates a bell. In the far background, two pilgrims approach a chapel, around which is a procession honoring the saint depicted on the banner. To Lutherans, such practices represent misguided rituals that replace faith with meaningless "works."

### QUESTIONS FOR ANALYSIS

1. What differences do you see in the makeup of the crowds surrounding the pulpits on the two sides of the picture? What point is Cranach trying to make?
2. What views of the Bible are presented in the woodcuts?
3. Examine the attire of the clergy crowded around the pulpit in the right half of the woodcut. What point is Cranach attempting to make?
4. The woodcuts depict the Catholic Church as full of abuses. What are these abuses, and how are they illustrated?
5. How many specific points made by Luther in his *Table Talk* can you find illustrated in the Cranach woodcut?

# Perspectives on Marriage, Families, and Gender

Since the 1960s, the family in all its dimensions—matrimony, child-rearing, conjugal attitudes, ideas of femininity and masculinity, generational relationships—has become a topic of extensive research among historians. This is especially true for the Renaissance and Reformation eras, whose historians have pored over legal codes, advice books, theological treatises, wills, private letters, municipal and church records, diaries, works of art and literature, and other relevant sources to understand how changes in family life affected and were affected by broader societal changes.

These historians agree that the one development that most affected marriage and family life in the early modern period was the Protestant Reformation. In the Middle Ages, even though marriage was a sacrament (and therefore a conduit of God's grace), in several respects married life was disparaged by the Catholic Church, which required celibacy of its priests, praised chastity and virginity, valued monks and nuns over married people, and taught that even for married couples the sole purpose of sex was to produce children. Such views had been challenged before the Reformation, but it was Luther who made the first decisive break with them when in 1522 he wrote a spirited defense of marriage and in 1525 married an ex-nun, Katharina von Bora, with whom he had six children. Wherever Protestantism took root, clerical celibacy was abandoned, convents and monasteries were closed, and laws and ordinances concerning marriage were taken over by secular governments. Men and women were encouraged to view marriage as a divine blessing, one that served God's purposes, contributed to human contentment, and was the foundation for a sound, God-fearing society.

Historians also agree on the dangers of making sweeping generalizations about "European marriage" or the "European family" in the early modern period. Not only did marriage and family life differ according to one's religion, social class, and economic standing, they also varied by region. Men and women in southern and eastern Europe were more likely to marry at a younger age, enter marriages planned and arranged by their parents, and live in multigenerational, extended families after marriage. In northern and western Europe people married later (on average around the age of 27 for men and 26 for women), had more control over their choice of mate, and after marriage established their own households.

Other issues pertaining to early modern marriage remain subjects of debate. Some historians see the period as one in which the ideal of "companionate marriage," based on conjugal affection and mutual sharing of rights and duties, made family life kinder and more equal. Others take a less positive view. Laws favoring husbands over wives, the frequent court cases involving abused or abandoned wives, and the near-universal acceptance of the idea of female inferiority all suggest that marriages based on love and conjugal parity were a model more praised than practiced. Even for those who accept the idea that companionate marriage increasingly became the norm, there is debate about what it meant for European women. Some historians see it as a positive step in that it lent dignity to the calling of wife and mother by according to married women the all-important responsibility of raising children, supervising servants, and exercising control of daily household affairs. Others argue that by consigning women to the separate sphere of home and family life, marriage patterns reinforced what for women was one of the most negative developments of the age—the erosion of career opportunities—as urban guilds excluded women from membership and municipal councils barred women from work as physicians, midwives, and apothecaries.

The written sources in this section, one representing Renaissance Italy and another seventeenth-century England, along with a fifteenth-century painting by the Flemish master Jan van Eyck, provide insight into the institution of marriage and in more general terms women's place in early modern European society.

# Upper-Class Marriage in Renaissance Florence

## 6 • LEON BATTISTA ALBERTI, ON THE FAMILY

Florence was the heart and soul of the Italian Renaissance. Its painters, sculptors, and architects produced works of great beauty, and its humanist scholars inspired a new appreciation and understanding of Greek and Roman antiquity.

None of this would have been possible without a relatively small number of elite Florentine families who made fortunes in business and, under the guidance and control of the Medici family, made up the city's political oligarchy. These families, along with patronage provided by the Catholic Church, funded humanist scholarship, the work of painters and sculptors, and the construction and remodeling of countless buildings.

Some members of the Florentine elite were artists and scholars in their own right. Such was the case with Leon Battista Alberti (1404–1472), viewed by many as a personification of the ideal "Renaissance man." The illegitimate son of one of Florence's wealthiest merchants, Alberti studied at the universities of Padua and Bologna before becoming a papal official in Rome. He wrote books on mathematics, ancient literature, painting, and architecture and designed churches and private residences in Florence and other Italian cities. He also wrote *On the Family* (1443), a dialogue among Alberti men that supposedly took place at the funeral of Alberti's father. Written in Italian and translated into the major European languages, Alberti's work expresses views of marriage and children common among wealthy and privileged Europeans of his era.

In the first section of the following excerpt Lionardo, a man in his late twenties or thirties, discusses marriage and the choice of wives; in the second section, an older gentleman, Gionnozzo, recalls the steps he took as a new husband to train his wife.

## QUESTIONS FOR ANALYSIS

1. According to the speaker Lionardo, what discourages young men from marrying?
2. What is the main purpose of marriage, according to the characters in the dialogue?
3. In arranging marriages, how much input did the future wife and husband have? Who else influenced the final choice of a mate?
4. According to Lionardo, what considerations should affect the choice of a future wife? What qualities of a future wife are most important?
5. What did Gionnozzo hope to accomplish when he showed his new bride around the house, especially his private apartment?
6. What views of women underlie Alberti's description of marriage?

## Arranging a Marriage

**LIONARDO:** Most times, the young do not appreciate the welfare of the family. Perhaps it seems to them that by bowing to matrimony they will lose much of their freedom in life. Perhaps they are overcome at times and caught in the clutches of a woman they love, as the comic poets are pleased to portray them. Perhaps the young find it most

*Source:* From *Della Famiglia*, Guido Guarino, trans. and ed., 1971, pp. 120–124, 216–219. Reprinted by permission of Bucknell University Press.

annoying having to maintain themselves, and therefore think that providing for a wife and children in addition to themselves is an overwhelming and hateful burden and are afraid they cannot properly take care of the needs which keep pace with the family's growth. Because of this, they consider the marriage bed too bothersome and avoid their duty honestly to enlarge the family. For these reasons, we must convince the young to marry by using reason, persuasion, rewards, and all other arguments so that the family may . . . grow in glory and the number of its young. . . .

• • •

Once the young men have been persuaded through the efforts and advice of all the elders of the family, the mothers and other old relatives and friends, who know the customs and behavior of almost all the girls of the city from the time they were born, must select all the well-born and properly-raised girls and propose their names to the youth who is to be married. The latter will choose the one he prefers, and the elders must not reject her as a daughter-in-law, unless she brings with her the breath of scandal or blame. . . . He should, however, follow the example of a good family-head who, when buying something, insists on examining the property many times before signing any contract. . . . One who wishes to marry must be even more diligent. My advice to him is to show forethought and, over a period of time and in various ways, learn what kind of woman his intended bride is, for he will be her husband and companion for the rest of his life. In his mind he must have two reasons for marrying: the first is to beget children, the other, to have a faithful and steadfast companion throughout his life. We must, therefore, seek a woman suited to childbearing and pleasant enough to be our constant companion. . . .

The first prerequisite of beauty in a woman is good habits. It is possible for a foolish, ignorant, slovenly, and drunken woman to have a beautiful body, but no one will deem her to be a beautiful wife. . . . As for physical beauty, we should not only take pleasure in comeliness, charm, and elegance, but should try to have in our house a wife well built for bearing children and strong of body to insure that they will be born strong and robust. . . . Physicians say that a wife should not be thin, but neither should she be burdened with fat, for the fat are very weak, have many obstructions, and are slow in conceiving. . . . They believe that a woman who is tall but full in all her limbs is very useful for begetting many children. They always prefer one of girlish age for many reasons, such as ease in conforming with her husband's wishes and others which we do not have to discuss here. Girls are pure because of their age, simple through inexperience, modest by nature and without malice. They are eager to learn their husbands' habits and desires and acquiesce without any reluctance. Thus we must follow all the precepts mentioned, for they are most useful for recognizing and choosing a prolific wife. To this we may add that it is a good sign for the girl to have many brothers, for you may then hope that she will be like her mother. . . .

Next comes the bride's family. . . . I believe first of all we must examine with care the life and ways of all those who will become our relatives. Many marriages have been the cause of great misfortunes to families because they became related with quarrelsome, contentious, proud, and hateful men. . . .

Therefore, . . . let one try to find new relatives who are not of vulgar blood, little wealth, or humble profession. In other things let them be modest and not too far above you so that their greatness will not cast a shadow on your honor and dignity and will not disturb your family's peace and tranquility. . . . Nor do I want these relatives to be inferior to you, for if it is an expense to aid the fallen relatives I mentioned above, these others will keep you in slavery. Let them, therefore, be your equals, modest, noble, and of honorable profession, as we have said.

Next comes the dowry,[1] which I believe should be modest, sure, and given at once rather than large, doubtful, and to be given in the future. . . . Let them not be too large, for the larger they are, the greater is the delay in receiving payment, the chance of litigation, and the reluctance to pay. In addition, in the case of a large dowry you will be much more inclined to undergo great expense in order to collect it. . . .

### Instructions for a New Wife

**LIONARDO** [Addressing Giannozzo]: You can be glad you had a most virtuous wife, perhaps more virtuous than others. I do not know where you could find another woman as industrious and prudent in managing the family as your wife was.

**GIANNOZZO:** She certainly was an excellent mother by nature and upbringing, but even more through my instruction. . . .

**LIONARDO:** How did you go about it?

**GIANNOZZO:** I shall tell you. When after a few days my wife began to feel at ease in my house and did not miss her mother and family so much, I took her by the hand and showed her the whole house. I showed her that upstairs was the place for storing grain and down in the cellar that for wine and firewood. I showed her where the tableware was and everything else in the house, so that she saw where everything was kept and knew its use. Then we returned to my room, and there, after closing the door, I showed her our valuables, silver, tapestries, clothes, and jewels, and pointed out their proper storage places.

I kept only the ledgers and business papers, my ancestors' as well as mine, locked so that my wife could not read them or even see them then or at any time. . . . I never allowed my wife to enter my study either alone or in my company, and I ordered her to turn over to me at once any papers of mine she should ever find. . . .

No matter how trifling a secret I had, I never shared it with my wife or with any other woman. I disapprove of those husbands who consult their wives and do not know how to keep any secret to themselves. They are mad to seek good advice and wisdom in women, and even more so if they think a wife can guard a secret. . . . O foolish husbands, is there ever a time when you chat with a woman without being reminded that women can do anything but keep silent?

**LIONARDO:** What an excellent warning! And you are no less prudent than fortunate if your wife was never able to draw out any of your secrets.

**GIANNOZZO:** She never did, my dear Lionardo, and I shall tell you why. First of all, she was very modest, and so never cared to know more than she should. Then, I never spoke to her about anything but household matters, habits, and our children. Of these subjects I spoke to her often and at length so that she might learn what to do. . . . As for the household goods, I deemed it proper . . . to entrust them to my wife's care, but not entirely, for I often wanted to know and see where the least thing was kept and how safe it was. After my wife had seen and understood where everything was to be kept, I said to her: ". . . You have seen our possessions, which, thank God, are such that we can well be satisfied. If we know how to take care of them, they will be useful to you, to me, and to our children. Therefore, my dear wife, it is your duty as well as mine to be diligent and take care of them."

**LIONARDO:** What did your wife answer?

---

[1]The dowry is the payment in money, goods, or land made by the bride's family to the groom. During the marriage the dowry was controlled by the husband, but if the husband died before the wife, it typically returned to the wife. Daughters whose families could not raise a suitable dowry typically joined a religious order and entered a convent.

GIANNOZZO: She answered that she had learned to obey her father and mother, and that they had instructed her to obey me always. She was ready, therefore, to do whatever I commanded. And I said to her: "Well then, my dear wife, one who knows how to obey her father and mother will soon learn to satisfy her husband." . . .

# A Fifteenth-Century Wedding (?)

## 7 • JAN VAN EYCK, ARNOLFINI PORTRAIT

Not all cultures value portraiture. Africa, for example, has a rich tradition of mask-making, but its masks do not portray actual chieftains or kings, but rather deities, ancestral spirits, mythological beings, animal spirits, and other beings believed to have power over humanity. In Jewish and Islamic cultures, portraiture smacks of idolatry and hence is rare. However, in other cultures such as Europe and China, where portraiture was valued, it can offer valuable insights into the past.

Like any other source, portraits need to be "read" with care. Each portrait results from decisions made by the artist, subject, and patron (who in many cases is also the subject). How will the subject be posed and in what setting? What will the subject's facial expression? What will he or she be wearing? What props and other human figures will be included? Answers to these questions are based on other considerations: What is the portrait's intended audience, and what message is it meant to convey about the subject's physical characteristics, values, social status, and personality? Such considerations should be kept in mind as this and other portraits in *The Human Record* are analyzed.

The Flemish artist Jan van Eyck's *Arnolfini Portrait* or *Arnolfini Marriage* is one of the most admired, enigmatic, and analyzed portraits in all of European art. Van Eyck, who was born in the town of Maaseik in present-day Belgium between 1370 and 1390, was living in the thriving Flemish city of Bruges as a court painter of Duke Philip the Good of Burgundy when he completed the painting sometime during or after 1434. Although there is little scholarly agreement about many of the painting's details, a few things can be said with certainty: For example, its setting is Bruges and it takes place during late spring, because a cherry tree can be seen blossoming through the window. It is agreed that despite her appearance, the woman is not pregnant; she is simply gathering the folds of her gown in front of her. It also is agreed that the man is a member of a wealthy Italian business family, the Arnolfini, which represented the interests of an even wealthier Italian business family, the Medici, in Bruges. For many years, it was thought that the subject of the painting is the betrothal or marriage ceremony of Giovanni di Arrigo Arnolfini and Giovanna Cenami, the daughter of another wealthy Italian merchant, in a Flemish bedchamber. Recent scholarship has revealed, however, that this marriage actually took place in 1447, six years after van Eyck's death. The male figure is now thought to be an older cousin, Giovanni di Nicolao Arnolfini, whose first wife, Constanza Trenta, died in 1433. This was a year before the event depicted in the painting took place. We know this because of the

Van Eyck, Arnolfini Portrait

message inscribed on the wall next to the bed, which states, "Johannes van Eyck was here, 1434." This new identification has given rise to theories that the painting depicts Giovanni's *second* wedding to an unknown but possibly Flemish woman, or that the painting is a memorial portrait to his first wife showing one dead and one living person. Most commentators believe the painting depicts a marriage ceremony, but some believe it is simply a portrait of a married couple; one art historian argues that what we see is a business agreement by which Giovanni di Nicolao agrees to give his wife control of his business interests while he is away from Bruges.

Barring the discovery of some new, revealing document, debates on the painting among scholars will undoubtedly continue. Why is there only one candle burning in the candelabra (on the side closer to the male figure)? What is the meaning of the convex mirror, which is surrounded by images of Christ's crucifixion and resurrection? Why can we see two figures reflected in the mirror, and who are they? Almost everyone believes one of them is van Eyck, but if so, why is he not shown painting the scene?

Meanwhile, non-experts can admire the painting for its beauty and gain insights from it about male–female relationships and fifteenth-century upper-class matrimony.

## QUESTIONS FOR ANALYSIS

1. Note the placement of the two figures, with the woman next to the bed and the man by the window. What might this signify?
2. Note how and where each of the two figures is looking, and how they are holding and gesturing with their hands. What message is the painter trying to communicate?
3. How does the painting illustrate the wealth of Arnolfini and his bride (or wife)?
4. The top of the far bedpost has an image of St. Margaret, the patron saint of pregnancy and childbirth. What other features of the painting emphasize the same theme?
5. On the sides of the mirror hang a brush or small broom and rosary beads (used in Catholic devotions to count certain prayers). What may these refer to?
6. What may be the significance of the small dog and the clogs, which the man has taken off?
7. Overall, how does the message of the painting compare with the views of marriage expressed by Alberti?

# A Puritan Guide to a Successful Marriage

## 8 • JOHN DOD AND ROBERT CLEAVER, A GODLY FORME OF HOUSEHOLD GOVERNMENT

The lifelong friendship of John Dod (1549–1645) and Robert Cleaver (c. 1561–1613) began while they were students at the University of Cambridge and continued during the twenty years they served as Protestant parsons in two neighboring rural parishes some seventy miles northwest of London. In addition to *A Godly Forme of Household Government*, an advice book on family life, the two men collaborated on several other books, including sermon collections and commentaries on the Ten Commandments, the Book of Proverbs, and Holy Communion. Both men were Puritans, a term applied to English Protestants who beginning in the late 1500s were drawn to the austere theology of the Geneva-based reformer John Calvin (1509–1564) and believed that the Church of England, although Protestant, remained too "Catholic" in matters of church governance, doctrine, and standards and expectations for personal behavior. Because of their views the two men were forced from their parishes by the conservative Anglican bishop of Oxford in 1607. With help from sympathetic Puritan patrons, Dod remained in the ministry until his death in 1645; Cleaver, it is thought, died in 1616.

*A Godly Forme of Household Government*, which went through more than a dozen editions after it was published in 1612, was one of several popular advice books for families written by Puritan clergymen in the 1600s. The authors' audience was neither the very rich nor the very poor, but moderately well-off families consisting of a husband and wife, their children, and perhaps a few servants. Dod and Cleaver discuss the Christian meaning of marriage, choosing a mate, courtship, the duties of wives and husbands, child-rearing, and dealings with servants. Dod, at least, brought to these subjects a wealth of personal experience: He was the youngest of seventeen children, the father of twelve, and the stepfather of several more children after he remarried following the death of his first wife. The authors' message was that achieving a "Godly forme of household government" was not easy. It involves careful planning, sensitivity, patience, compromise, respect, devotion (to one's spouse and to God), and ideally, love and affection.

## QUESTIONS FOR ANALYSIS:

1. According to Dod and Cleaver, what qualities should men and women look for when choosing a spouse? How do their recommendations differ from those of Alberti?
2. In the view of the two Puritan ministers, who should have the final word on the choice of a spouse? How do their views differ from those of Alberti?
3. According to Dod and Cleaver, what qualities should wives and husbands cultivate in an ideal marriage?
4. According to the authors, in what sense are husbands and wives equal in a marriage?
5. In the authors' view, what justifies the subservience of wives to husbands in marriage?
6. According to Dod and Cleaver, who has the main responsibility for maintaining harmony in marriage, the wife or husband?

## Courtship

There lies much weight in the wise election and the choice of a Wife. Just as he that will plant anything first considers the nature of the ground in which he has a mind to plant, even so much

---

Source: John Dod and Robert Cleaver, *A Godly Forme of Household Government* (London: Eliot's Court Press, 1630).

more ought a man have in respect to the condition of the woman out of whom he desires to plant children, the fruits of honesty and welfare. . . .

This is a thing worthy to be remembered, both on behalf of the suitor, and also on her as is wooed: namely that they deal plainly and faithfully with the other and not craftily deceive one another in body or goods. For they shall never use one another so lovingly and pleasantly as they hoped they might if one has fraudulently and deceitfully deceived the other either in body or substance. Therefore it would be much better that both parties disclose to one another the imperfections, infirmities, and wants [deficiencies] in their bodies, as also the mediocrity of their goods and substance [wealth], as the truth it is. . . .

There are certain signs of fitness and godliness both in the man and the woman, so that if the man desires to know a godly woman, or the woman would know a godly man, then let them observe and mark these six points: . . .

1. The report, name or fame [reputation] that he or she has, and what opinion honest folks have of them, because "As the market goes, so the market-men will take."[1] . . .

2. The next sign is The Look. Godliness is in the face of a man or a woman, and so likewise folly and wickedness may many times be seen and discerned by the face of a man or a woman. . . .

3. The third sign is her talk or speech, or rather her silence. Talking is the mirror and messenger of the mind, in which it may be commonly seen in the proverb: "Such as is the man or woman, such is their talk." . . .

4. The fourth sign is the apparel. . . . For doubtless by a man's or a woman's apparel, excessive laughter, and going about [behavior outside the home], it may be partly discerned of what

disposition they are. . . . Apparel often gives certain and sure testimony of pride, lightness, uncleanliness, and other vices or virtues, both for a man and a woman. . . .

5. The fifth sign is the Company. . . . For . . . good and honest folks are often stained and hurt by keeping the company of the wicked and ungodly. According to the common proverb, "Such like is everyone as the company is with whom they keep." . . .

6. The last sign is Education, which also gives great testimony, namely by whom and how everyone is brought up; whether the man or woman is acquainted with virtuous or vicious persons; whether the parties have continued in the nurture of the virtuous, and show themselves obedient to those who brought them up, or whether either of the parties have broken out of this discipline and followed his or her own willfulness. . . .

All these properties are not detected at three or four comings and meetings of the parties. He therefore who wants to know all his wife's qualities and she who wants to perceive her husband's dispositions and inclinations before being married need to see the other eating, walking, working, playing, talking, laughing and chiding too, or else it may be that one shall get with the other less or more than he or she looked for. . . .

## Betrothal and the Contract

[After agreeing to wed, the two parties swear a solemn oath that they are engaged to be married.]

We call this promise of marriage voluntary, because it must not come from the lips alone, but from the approval and consent of the heart. . . . For if either party be urged, constrained, or compelled by force of their parents or others by threatening the loss of health, of limb, of life, or by any other

---

[1]"Market" is to be understood as the public. In other words, what is being said publicly about a person will determine if that person is a good potential mate.

violent manner or dealing whatsoever, to make their promise, . . . this promise ought to be frustrated [unfulfilled] and broken, by the parents, or by such magistrates that may and ought to command and rule in such cases.

## The Benefits of Marriage

There is nothing that gives so much as does a good wife, no, not horses, oxen, servants, or farms. . . . She does more faithful and true service unto him than either a maid-servant or man-servant, who serve men for fear or else for wages. But your wife will be led only by love.

So a wife is called by God himself, a Helper, and not an impediment, or necessary evil, as some unadvisedly say, and as others say, "It is better to bury a wife than to marry one," or again, "If we could be without women, we should be without great troubles." Women are reasonable creatures, and have flexible wits both to good and evil, which with use, maturity, and good counsel, may be altered and changed. And although there may be some evil and lewd women, yet that does no more prove the malice of their nature, than of men.

## Duties of Husbands and Wives

There are few husbands or wives that know in truth how to love one another. If a man loves his wife only because she is rich, beautiful, noble, or because she contents and pleases him after the sensual appetite of the flesh, . . . that is no true love before God, for such love may be among harlots and whores, yea among brute beasts. But a Christian husband must love his wife, chiefly, because she is his sister in the profession of the Christian religion, and so an inheritor with him of the kingdom of heaven. The apostle Peter[2] teaches the husband his duty, that the more understanding and wisdom God has imbued him with, the more wisely and circumspectly he ought to behave

in bearing those unpleasantries which through his wife's weakness, oftentimes cause some dislike for one to another. Nevertheless, though she is by nature weaker than he is, it does not follow that she is therefore to be neglected. . . . On the contrary, she ought to be much more cared for. Like a weaker vessel, that the weaker it is ought to be favored and spared if we will have it continue, even so a wife because of her infirmities is so much the more to be favored. . . . And because the husband and wife are equal in that which is the most important matter, that is to say, in that gracious and free benefit, whereby they have everlasting life given them, the wife is not be despised although she be weak. . . .

The second point is that the husband should not be bitter, fierce and cruel unto his wife. . . . The husband must be careful to keep the bond of love, and beware that there never spring up the root of bitterness between him and his wife. If at any time there happens to arise any cause of unkindness between them then he must be careful to weed up the same with all lenience, gentleness, and patience. . . . And if he shall have occasion to speak sharply and sometimes reprove, he must be careful that he does not do so in the presence of others. . . . The husband is always to remember that he should not be fierce, rigorous, hasty, nor unpleasant with his wife, for then there never will be unity and concord between them. . . .

The best rule that a man may hold and practice with his wife to guard and govern her is to admonish her often, and to give her good instructions, to reprehend her seldom, never to lay violent hands on her, but if she be good and dutiful, to favor her, to the end she may continue so; and if she be shrewish and wayward, mildly to suffer her, to the end that she wax [become] no worse. But some husbands are so sour a nature and so unpleasant in their behavior, that they can hardly be loved, no not of their wives;

---

[2]According to tradition, the apostle Peter wrote two books of the New Testament, First and Second Peter.

their countenance is so glowering, their company so churlish, that they seem angry even when they are pleased.

This is also a duty . . . , namely that husbands be diligent and careful to make provision for their houses, to clothe their wives decently, to bring up their children virtuously, and to pay the servants duly. . . . The duty of the husband is to get the goods, and of the wife to save them. The duty of the husband is to travel abroad [go out of the house] to seek a living, and the wife's duty is to keep the house. The duty of the husband is to get money and provision; and of the wives, not vainly to spend it. . . . And order consists of this, that the husband follow his business, traffic, or calling without any interfering from his wife, who ought not to meddle . . . as also the husband is not to deal but soberly and in great discretion with affairs that are proper to the wife.

• • •

At any time it shall happen, that the wife shall anger or displease her husband by doing or speaking anything that shall grieve him, she ought never to rest until she has pacified him and gotten his favor again. And if he by chance blames her without a cause, and for that which she could not help or remedy you must bear it patiently and give him no uncomely or unkind words for it, but evermore look upon him with a loving and cheerful countenance, and so rather let her take fault upon her than seem to be displeased. Let her be always merry and cheerful in his company, but yet not with too much lightness. . . . True it is that some women are wiser and more discreet than their husbands. Yet still a great part of the discretion of such women shall rest in acknowledging their husbands to be their heads and loving the graces they have received from the lord that their husbands may be honored and not looked down upon. . . .

Another point . . . that [wives] do not wear gorgeous and sumptuous apparel, . . . but that they be sober in outward apparel and garnished and decked inwardly with virtues of their minds as with gentleness, meekness, quietness, and chastity, which are most precious things in the sight of God. . . .

# An Expanding Intellectual Universe

Between the fifteenth and seventeenth centuries European intellectuals and artists rejected much of their medieval heritage. That they did so does not diminish the achievements of the High Middle Ages (ca. 1000–1300 c.e.), an era for which the term "dark ages" could not be more inaccurate. These were centuries that saw the emergence of national literatures, technological innovation, the founding of Europe's first universities, profound discussions of law, religion, and philosophy, and wondrous artistic and architectural achievements.

Nonetheless, there were limitations to the medieval intellectual vision. Intellectuals were convinced that everything worth knowing already had been discovered by ancient authorities or revealed in the Bible. This meant, for example, that scientific inquiry in the Middle Ages involved poring over the works of the ancient Greek philosophers such as Aristotle and trying to understand the exact meaning of their words. Science, then called "natural philosophy," was carried on in one's study or a library, not a laboratory, and rarely generated new ideas. Innovation and originality also were discouraged by the strong religious atmosphere of the age. As brilliant as Aristotle and other ancient philosophers might have been, in the eyes of the Catholic Church and its theologians, nothing they wrote matched the authority of the Bible, the very word of God. Since any thinker who challenged Christian orthodoxy risked scorn, reprimand, and possible punishment, such thinkers were rare.

Between 1400 and the early 1600s, every one of these medieval assumptions faced serious challenges. We have already seen how Protestants rejected the Catholic Church's claims that it was the final arbiter of all intellectual disputes and provided Christians with the sole path to salvation. The secularism of the Italian Renaissance, geographical discoveries, and interactions with Africans, Asians, and Native Americans all changed Europe's intellectual landscape, but none of these developments matched the significance of a series of remarkable scientific discoveries that collectively have come to be known as the Scientific Revolution.

The first major break from ancient Greek science was made by the Polish astronomer Nicholas Copernicus, who, in *On the Revolution of the Heavenly Spheres* (1543), theorized that the sun, not the Earth, was the center of the universe. By the time of Galileo Galilei (1564–1642), most scientists accepted Copernican heliocentrism, even though it raised perplexing theoretical questions. Most of these questions were answered by Isaac Newton (1642–1727), whose *Mathematical Principles of Natural Philosophy* (1687) explained planetary and earthly motion through the law of universal gravitation. Newton's work was the crowning achievement of a 150-year period in which European thinkers transformed their understanding of astronomy and mechanics, made spectacular advances in mathematics, invented the microscope, telescope, and many other scientific instruments, and achieved new insights in the fields of anatomy and chemistry.

# Science and the Claims of Religion

## 9 • GALILEO GALILEI, LETTER TO THE GRAND DUCHESS CHRISTINA

Galileo, an Italian physicist, mathematician, and astronomer, was the greatest European scientist of the early 1600s. In the field of mechanics, he developed the theory of inertia and described the laws that dictate the movement of falling bodies. In astronomy, he pioneered the use of the telescope and defended the theory of a sun-centered universe. His public support of Copernicus disturbed Catholic theologians, who were convinced it undermined correct belief and Church authority. The Church officially condemned Copernican theory in 1616 and forced Galileo to renounce many of his ideas in 1632. Galileo's works continued to be read, however, and despite his condemnation, they contributed to the acceptance of Copernican theory and the new methodology of science.

In the following selection, Galileo, a devout Catholic, defends his approach to science in a published letter addressed to Christina, the grand duchess of Tuscany, in 1615.

## QUESTIONS FOR ANALYSIS

1. According to Galileo, what are his enemies' motives and why do they use religious arguments against him?
2. According to Galileo, why is it dangerous to apply passages of Scripture to science?
3. To Galileo, how does nature differ from the Bible as a source of truth?
4. In Galileo's view, what is the proper relationship between science and religion?

Some years ago, as Your Serene Highness well knows, I discovered in the heavens many things that had not been seen before our own age. The novelty of these things, as well as some consequences which followed from them in contradiction to the physical notions commonly held among academic philosophers, stirred up against me no small number of professors—as if I had placed these things in the sky with my own hands in order to upset nature and overturn the sciences. They seemed to forget that the increase of known truths stimulates the investigation, establishment, and growth of the arts; not their diminution or destruction.

Showing a greater fondness for their own opinions than for truth, they sought to deny and disprove the new things which, if they had cared to look for themselves, their own senses would have demonstrated to them. To this end they hurled various charges and published numerous writings filled with vain arguments, and they made the grave mistake of sprinkling these with passages taken from places in the Bible which they had failed to understand properly, and which were ill suited to their purposes.

Persisting in their original resolve to destroy me and everything mine by any means they can think of, these men are aware of my views in astronomy and philosophy. They know that as to the arrangement of the parts of the universe, I hold the sun to be situated motionless in the center of the revolution of the celestial orbs while the Earth rotates on its axis and revolves about the sun. They know also that I support this position not only by refuting the arguments of Ptolemy[1] and Aristotle, but by producing many counter-arguments; in particular, some which relate to physical effects whose causes can perhaps be assigned in no other way. In addition there are astronomical arguments derived from many things in my new celestial discoveries that plainly confute the Ptolemaic system while admirably agreeing with and confirming the contrary hypothesis. Possibly because they are disturbed by the known truth of other propositions of mine which differ from those commonly held . . . , these men have resolved to fabricate a shield for their fallacies out of the mantle of pretended religion and the authority of the Bible. These they apply, with little judgment, to the refutation of arguments that they do not understand and have not even listened to.

First they have endeavored to spread the opinion that such propositions in general are contrary to the Bible and are consequently damnable and heretical. . . . Next, becoming bolder, . . . they began scattering rumors among the people that before long this doctrine would be condemned by the supreme authority [the pope]. They know,

*Source:* From *Discoveries and Opinions of Galileo* by Galileo Galilei, translated by Stillman Drake. Copyright © 1957 by Stillman Drake. Used by permission of Doubleday, Doubleday, an imprint of the Knopf Doubleday Publishing Group, a division of Random House LLC. All rights reserved. Any third party use of this material, outside of this publication, is prohibited. Interested parties must apply directly to Random House LLC for permission.

[1]Ptolemy (ca. 100–170 C.E.), who spent most of his life in Alexandria, Egypt, was a Greek astronomer who propounded key aspects of the geocentric planetary system that prevailed in Europe until the time of Copernicus.

too, that official condemnation would not only suppress the two propositions which I have mentioned, but would render damnable all other astronomical and physical statements and observations that have any necessary relation or connection with these. . . .

To this end they make a shield of their hypocritical zeal for religion. They go about invoking the Bible, which they would have minister to their deceitful purposes. Contrary to the sense of the Bible and the intention of the holy Fathers, . . . they would have us altogether abandon reason and the evidence of our senses in favor of some biblical passage, though under the surface meaning of its words this passage may contain a different sense. . . .

The reason produced for condemning the opinion that the Earth moves and the sun stands still is that in many places in the Bible one may read that the sun moves and the Earth stands still. Since the Bible cannot err, it follows as a necessary consequence that anyone takes an erroneous and heretical position who maintains that the sun is inherently motionless and the earth movable.

With regard to this argument, I think in the first place that it is very pious to say and prudent to affirm that the holy Bible can never speak untruth—whenever its true meaning is understood. But I believe nobody will deny that it is often very abstruse, and may say things which are quite different from what its bare words signify. Hence in expounding the Bible if one were always to confine oneself to the unadorned grammatical meaning, one might fall into error. Not only contradictions and propositions far from true might thus be made to appear in the Bible, but even grave heresies and follies. Thus it would be necessary to assign to God feet, hands, and eyes, as well as corporeal and human affections, such as anger, repentance, hatred, and sometimes even the forgetting of things past and ignorance of those to come. . . .

This being granted, I think that in discussions of physical problems we ought to begin not from the authority of scriptural passages but from sense-experiences and necessary demonstrations. . . . It is necessary for the Bible, in order to be accommodated to the understanding of every man, to speak many things which appear to differ from the absolute truth so far as the bare meaning of the words is concerned. But Nature, on the other hand, is . . . immutable; she never transgresses the laws imposed upon her, or cares a whit whether her abstruse reasons and methods of operation are understandable to men. For that reason it appears that nothing physical which sense-experience sets before our eyes, or which necessary demonstrations prove to us, ought to be called in question (much less condemned) upon the testimony of biblical passages which may have some different meaning beneath their words. For the Bible is not chained in every expression to conditions as strict as those which govern all physical effects; nor is God any less excellently revealed in Nature's actions than in the sacred statements of the Bible.

# Chapter 2

# The Islamic Heartland and India

AFTER YEARS OF instability throughout much of South and Southwest Asia, three empires emerged between the mid-fifteenth and early sixteenth centuries. The first to take shape was that of the Ottoman Turks, a semi-nomadic people who, after migrating to Anatolia from Iran and Central Asia in the 1100s, embarked on successful conquests in Anatolia and southeastern Europe beginning in the 1290s. After recovering from a crushing defeat at the hands of the Turko-Mongol forces of Timur, leader of the Timurid Empire, in 1402, they conquered the last remnant of the Byzantine empire by capturing the imperial city, Constantinople, in 1453 and, as Istanbul, making it the seat of their government. After further conquests, by the mid-1500s the Ottomans ruled an empire that included Anatolia, Egypt, Syria, and Iraq, and lands in North Africa, the western coast of the Arabian Peninsula, and southeastern Europe.

The Ottoman Empire already was a major power by the time the Safavid and Mughal empires came into existence. On the Ottomans' eastern flank, following victories over Turkoman tribes, Armenia, and Azerbaijan, Ismail Safavi created the Safavid Empire in Iran, which was distinguished by its rulers' fervent devotion to Shia Islam. During the reign of Ismail's grandson, Abbas I (r. 1587–1629), the empire's military power reached its peak, as did its achievements in art, architecture, and philosophy. Finally, during the 1500s the Mughal Empire emerged in India as a result of the exploits of Babur (1483–1530), a military adventurer from Central Asia who conquered northwest India, and those of his grandson, Akbar (1542–1605), who extended and consolidated Mughal authority on the subcontinent.

The Ottoman, Mughal, and Safavid states are often referred to as "Islamic" empires, a designation that is not entirely accurate. Although the rulers were Muslims of varying degrees of devotion, their subjects were ethnically and religiously diverse. Ottoman subjects included Albanians, Armenians, Arabs, Bulgars, Croats, Circassians, Serbs, Greeks, and Turks; more than half of them were Christians or Jews. In Mughal India eighty percent of the population was Hindu, and even in Iran, where the rulers imposed Shia Islam on the country, significant Jewish and Christian communities existed.

Another popular term for these empires is "gunpowder empires," which focuses on the fact that all three empires were established by conquest and maintained by formidable armies that made effective use of gunpowder weapons, especially artillery. The basis of the empires' strength and durability, however, went beyond military prowess: It also involved strong leadership, effective central and provincial government, successful economic policies, and an ability to win the cooperation and support of diverse populations.

The Mughal and Safavid empires began to deteriorate in the late seventeenth century and effectively disappeared in the 1700s. The Ottomans' empire proved more resilient. Although it increasingly fell behind its European rivals in terms of wealth and power, its leadership proved capable of reforms in the face of changing circumstances. It lasted until 1922.

# Rulers and Their Challenges in the Ottoman and Mughal Empires

Although no historian any longer accepts the idea that the attributes and deeds of a few "great men" adequately explain historical events and developments, one cannot deny that in political entities such as the Mughal, Ottoman, and Safavid empires, where a supreme ruler made laws, set policy, appointed key officials, led armies into battle, and had the power of life and death over his subjects, individual rulers could and did make a difference. Each of the empires expanded and flourished under strong, dedicated rulers who suppressed dissent, maintained bureaucratic vigor, acted decisively, provided effective military leadership, and displayed a keen interest in the arts. After a time, however, the quality of leaders deteriorated, and this, along with numerous economic, political, and military factors, contributed to the decline and disappearance of the Mughal and Safavid empires and a host of problems for the Ottomans.

The sources in this section provide insights into the personalities and policies of two of the most renowned Islamic rulers of the sixteenth and seventeenth centuries—the Ottoman sultan Suleiman I and the Mughal emperor Jahangir. These sources provide an opportunity to analyze their styles of leadership and the strengths and weaknesses of their regimes.

## A European Diplomat's Impressions of Suleiman I

### 10 • OGIER GHISELIN DE BUSBECQ, TURKISH LETTERS

Suleiman I is remembered mainly for his military exploits, but his accomplishments go beyond the battlefield. He supported the work of historians, painters, and poets, oversaw the codification of Ottoman law, and through his patronage contributed to the architectural grandeur of Istanbul. He was one of the outstanding rulers of the age.

The following commentary on Suleiman and his empire is the work of Ogier Ghiselin de Busbecq (1522–1590), a Flemish nobleman who spent most of his life serving the Hapsburg dynasty, in particular Ferdinand I, who was archduke of Austria, king of Hungary and Bohemia, and Holy Roman Emperor from 1558 to 1564. In 1554 Ferdinand sent Busbecq to Istanbul to represent his interests in a dispute with Suleiman over the division of the kingdom of Hungary, which had broken apart after the Ottoman victory at the Battle of Mohács in 1526. After protracted discussions, the two sides agreed on a compromise by which the Hapsburgs controlled the western third of Hungary and portions of present-day Croatia, while the Ottomans held central and eastern Hungary. During his years in Turkey, Busbecq recorded his observations and impressions, which he sent in the form of four long letters to a friend Nicholas Michault, a Hapsburg official in a position to communicate Busbecq's views to Ferdinand and his advisors. The letters were first published in 1589 and in many subsequent editions and translations.

The following excerpt begins with a description of Busbecq's first meeting with Suleiman I in 1555 and goes on to discuss Ottoman military power. It concludes with a retelling of the events surrounding the assassination in 1553 of Suleiman's oldest son and likely successor, Mustafa. Mustafa's murder is an example of the conflicts and intrigue surrounding issues of succession in the Ottoman state, in which a son of the sultan would succeed his father but not necessarily the eldest. As Busbecq explains, Mustafa's interests clashed with the ambitions of Hurrem (also known as Roxelana), Suleiman's Ukrainian slave-concubine and later wife. To ensure that her son Selim would become sultan on Suleiman's death, she convinced her aging husband that Mustafa was plotting against him and had to be killed along with his children.

## QUESTIONS FOR ANALYSIS

1. What does Busbecq's first meeting with Suleiman reveal about the sultan's attitudes toward Europeans? What other insights into his attitudes are provided later in the excerpt?
2. What does Busbecq see as the main difference between Ottoman and European views of social privilege and inherited status? How, in his view, do these views affect Ottoman government?
3. What insights does Busbecq provide about the Ottoman military?
4. What does the episode of Mustafa's assassination reveal about the power and influence of Roxelana? About Ottoman attitudes toward the imperial succession? About Suleiman's character?
5. What advantages and disadvantages were there in the Ottoman practice of not making the eldest son the automatic heir of the reigning sultan?
6. Shortly after Suleiman's reign, some observers sensed that the Ottoman Empire was beginning to decline. What in Busbecq's account points to future problems?

## First Impressions

On our arrival at Amasya[1] we were taken to call on Achmet Pasha, the chief Vizier, and the other pashas[2]—for the Sultan himself was not then in the town—and commenced our negotiations with them touching the business entrusted to us by King Ferdinand. The pashas told us that the whole matter depended on the Sultan's pleasure. . . . On his arrival we were admitted to an audience; but the manner and spirit in which he listened to our address, our arguments, and our message was by no means favorable. . . . On entering we were separately conducted into the royal presence by the attendants, who grasped our arms. After having gone through a pretense of kissing his [Suleiman's] hand, we were conducted backwards to the wall opposite his seat, care being taken that we should never turn our backs on him. The Sultan then listened to what I had to say; but the language I used was not at all to his taste, for the demands of his Majesty [King Ferdinand] breathed a spirit of independence and dignity, which was by no means acceptable to one who deemed that his wish was law; and so he made no answer beyond saying in an impatient way, "Giusel, giusel," i.e., well, well. After this we were dismissed to our quarters.

The Sultan's hall was crowded with people, among whom were several officers of high rank. Besides these there were all the troopers of the Imperial guard and a large force of janissaries, but there was not in all that great assembly a single man who owed his position to anything save his valor and his merit.[3] No distinction is attached to birth among the Turks;

the respect to be paid to a man is measured by the position he holds in the public service. . . . It is by merit that men rise in the service, a system which ensures that posts should only be assigned to the competent. . . . Those who receive the highest offices from the Sultan are for the most part the sons of shepherds or herdsmen, and so far from being ashamed of their parentage, they actually glory in it, and consider it a matter of boasting that they owe nothing to the accident of birth; for they do not believe that high qualities are either natural or hereditary, nor do they think that they can be handed down from father to son, but that they are partly the gift of God, and partly the result of good training, great industry, and unwearied zeal. . . . Among the Turks, therefore, honors, high posts, and judgeships are the rewards of great ability and good service.

## Ottoman Military Strength

Against us stands Suleiman, that foe whom his own and his ancestors' exploits have made so terrible; he tramples the soil of Hungary with 200,000 horses, he is at the very gates of Austria, threatens the rest of Germany, and brings in his train all the nations that extend from our borders to those of Persia [Iran]. The army he leads is equipped with the wealth of many kingdoms. Of the three regions into which the world is divided [Asia, Africa, and Europe], there is not one that does not contribute its share towards our destruction. . . . The troops he leads are trained veterans, accustomed to his command; he fills the world with the terror of his name.

• • •

Source: Ogier Ghiselin de Busbecq, *The Life and Letters of Ogier Ghiselin de Busbecq* (London: Kegan Paul, 1881), pp. 113–120 (passim), 152–155, 218–220, 242–243, 255, 405.

[1]A provincial capital in north central Turkey where many royal sons were sent to be educated.

[2]*Pasha* was a title for a high-ranking military or government official; the *grand vizier* was the sultan's chief advisor and head of the Ottoman administration.

[3]Busbecq fails to mention that the janissaries and officials he observed were slaves recruited through the *devshirme*, or "child contribution" system, in which boys were taken from Christian families and converted to Islam. The brightest were educated in foreign languages, the law, and administrative procedures, after which they were employed in the sultan's "Inner Service" and could rise to the level of pasha. The less gifted joined the military and made up the core of the famous Ottoman janissary corps.

The Turkish monarch going to war takes with him over 40,000 camels and nearly as many baggage mules, of which a great part, when he is invading Persia, are loaded with rice and other kinds of grain. These mules and camels also carry tents and armor, and likewise tools and munitions for the campaign. The territories that bear the name of Persia are less fertile than our country, and even such crops as they bear are laid waste by the inhabitants in time of invasion in hopes of starving out the enemy, so that it is very dangerous for an army to invade Persia if it is not furnished with abundant supplies. . . .

• • •

After dinner I practice the Turkish bow, in the use of which weapon people here are marvelously expert. From the eighth, or even the seventh, year of their age they begin to shoot at a mark, and practice archery ten or twelve years. This constant exercise strengthens the muscles of their arms, and gives them such skill that they can hit the smallest marks with their arrows. . . . So sure is their aim that . . . they can hit a man in the eye or in any other exposed part they choose.

• • •

No nation in the world has shown greater readiness than the Turks to avail themselves of the useful inventions of foreigners, as is proved by their employment of cannons and mortars, and many other things invented by Christians. . . . The Turks [however] are much afraid of carbines and pistols, such as are used on horseback. The same, I hear, is the case with the Persians, on which account someone advised Rustem,[4] when he was setting out with the Sultan on a campaign against them, to raise from his household servants a troop of 200 horsemen and arm them with firearms, as they would cause much alarm . . . in the ranks of the enemy. Rustem,

in accordance with this advice, raised a troop of dragoons [mounted infantry], furnished them with firearms, and had them drilled. But they had not completed half the journey when their guns began to get out of order. Every day some essential part of their weapons was lost or broken, and it was not often that armorers could be found capable of repairing them. So, a large part of the firearms having been rendered unserviceable, the men took a dislike to the weapon; and this prejudice was increased by the dirt which its use entailed, the Turks being a very cleanly people; for the dragoons had their hands and clothes begrimed with gunpowder, and moreover presented such a sorry appearance, . . . that their comrades laughed at them. So . . . they gathered around Rustem and showing him their broken and useless firearms, asked what advantage he hoped to gain from them when they met the enemy, and demanded that he should relieve them of them, and give them their old arms again. Rustem, after considering their request carefully, thought there was no reason for refusing to comply with it, and so they got permission to resume their bows and arrows.

## Problems of Succession

Suleiman had a son by a concubine who came from the Crimea. . . . His name was Mustafa, and at the time of which I am speaking he was young, vigorous, and of high repute as a soldier. But Suleiman had also several other children, by a Russian woman [Roxelana]. . . . To the latter he was so much attached that he placed her in the position of wife. . . .

Mustafa's high qualities and matured years marked him out to the soldiers who loved him, and the people who supported him, as the successor of his father, who was now in the decline of life. On the other hand, his step-mother [Roxelana], by throwing the claim of a lawful wife onto the balance, was doing her utmost to counterbalance his

---

[4]Rustem, the grand vizier, was married to the daughter of Suleiman and Roxelana.

personal merits and his rights as eldest son, with a view to obtaining the throne for her own children. In this intrigue, she received the advice and assistance of Rustem, whose fortunes were inseparably linked with hers by his marriage with a daughter she had had by Suleiman.

Inasmuch as Rustem was chief Vizier, he had no difficulty in influencing his master's mind. The Turks, accordingly, are convinced that it was by the lies of Rustem and the spells of Roxelana . . . that the Sultan was so estranged from his son as to plan to get rid of him. A few believe that Mustafa, being aware of the plans, . . . was engaged in designs against his father's throne and person. The sons of Turkish Sultans are in the most wretched position in the world, for as soon as one of them succeeds his father the rest are doomed to certain death. The Turk can endure no rival to the throne, and, indeed, the conduct of the Janissaries renders it impossible for the new Sultan to spare his brothers; for if one of them survives, the Janissaries are forever asking generous favors. If these are refused, the cry is heard, "Long live the brother!" "God preserve the brother!"—a tolerably broad hint that they intend to place him on the throne. So that the Turkish Sultans are compelled to celebrate their succession by staining their hands with the blood of their nearest relatives. . . .

Being at war with Shah Tahmasp [of Iran] Suleiman had sent Rustem against him as a commander-in-chief of his armies. Just as he was about to enter Persian territory, Rustem suddenly halted, and hurried off dispatches to Suleiman, informing him that treason was rife; that . . . the soldiers cared for no one but Mustafa; and he must come at once if he wished to preserve his throne. Suleiman was seriously alarmed by these dispatches. He immediately hurried to the army, sent a letter to summon Mustafa, . . . inviting him to clear himself of those crimes of which he was suspected. . . .

There was great uneasiness among the soldiers, when Mustafa arrived. He was brought to his father's tent, and there everything betokened peace. . . . But there were in the tent certain mutes, strong and sturdy fellows, who had been appointed as his executioners. As soon as he entered the inner tent, they threw themselves upon him, and struggled to put the fatal noose around his neck. Mustafa, being a man of considerable strength, made a stout defense and fought—there being no doubt that if he escaped and threw himself among the Janissaries, the news of this outrage on their beloved prince would cause such indignation, that they would not only protect him, but also proclaim him Sultan. Suleiman, fearing this, and being only separated by the linen hangings of his tent from the stage on which this tragedy was being enacted, when he found there was an unexpected delay in the execution of his scheme, he thrust out his head from the chamber of his tent, and glared on the mutes with fierce and threatening eyes; at the same time, with gestures full of hideous meaning, he sternly rebuked their slackness. Hereupon the mutes, gaining fresh strength from the terror he inspired, threw Mustafa down, got the bowstring round his neck, and strangled him. Shortly afterwards they placed his body on a rug in front of the tent, so the Janissaries might see the man they had desired as their Sultan. . . .

Meanwhile, Roxelana, not content with removing Mustafa from her path, did not consider that she and her children were free from danger, so long as his offspring survived. . . . Information was brought to Suleiman that, whenever his grandson appeared in public, the boys . . . where he was being educated—shouted out, "God save the Prince, and may he long survive his father;" and that the meaning of these cries was to point him out as his grandsire's future successor, and his father's avenger. Moreover, he was bidden to remember that the Janissaries would be sure to support the son of Mustafa, so that the father's death had in no way secured the peace of the throne and realm. . . .

Suleiman was easily convinced by these arguments to sign the death-warrant of his grandson. He commissioned Ibrahim Pasha to go . . . with all speed, and put the innocent child to death.

# Ottoman History, Illustrated

## 11 • THREE PAINTINGS FROM THE BOOK OF SULEIMAN

Among the many literary and artistic masterpieces produced during the reign of Suleiman I, the *Suleymanname* (Book of Suleiman), a small book measuring only ten by fifteen inches, is among the most impressive. The last volume in a planned five-volume history of the world, it covers the reign of Suleiman I from his accession in 1520 until his death in 1556. The text was composed by Fethullah Arif Çelebi, an Iranian poet who had fled to Istanbul in 1547 after his patron was implicated in a plot to overthrow Shah Tahmasp. Winning the favor of Suleiman and his grand vizier, Rustem, he was given the job of providing the text and overseeing the production of this mammoth history project. Assisting Arif was a team of painters, calligraphers, bookbinders, papermakers, gilders, and leatherworkers who worked ten years on the project in a specially constructed studio in the sultan's palace. Of the five projected volumes, three were not completed or have been lost, but the *Book of Suleiman* by itself is sufficient proof of Arif's and his coworkers' skill and genius.

The *Book of Suleiman* contains sixty-nine watercolor paintings of battles, ceremonies, hunting scenes, diplomatic meetings, and other events described in the text. They are the work of five unidentified painters, whom art historians refer to as Painters A, B, C, D, and E. They all were undoubtedly attached to the Ottoman Academy of Painting, a studio and school founded in the 1470s. Here painters from across the empire learned and practiced the techniques of miniaturist painting, a genre developed in Iran in the thirteenth century.

We have chosen to include three paintings from the *Book of Suleiman*. The "Recruitment of Tribute Children" illustrates the first step in the Ottoman devshirme system, by which the government recruited and trained personnel to serve the state. Its setting is a town in southeastern Europe where a government official, with the help of a scribe, a guard, and two assistants, is enlisting six young boys who are about to embark on a trip to Istanbul, where they will be converted to Islam and trained in the palace school for careers as state officials or soldiers in the janissary corps. Except for the scribe, all the Ottoman officials can be identified as members of the janissary corps by their distinctive hats. In the background is a crowd of townspeople, made up mostly of women, and a priest.

The other two paintings depict the Battle of Mohács, which was fought on August 29, 1526, between an Ottoman army led by Suleiman I and the forces of King Louis II of Hungary. Having taken the Serbian city of Belgrade in 1521, in June 1526 Suleiman gathered an army of 100,000 men and marched to Hungary to ensure promised tribute payments from Louis II and to stave off a possible alliance between Hungary and Austria. In response, Louis cobbled together a smaller army consisting of Hungarian, Polish, and Croatian troops along with mercenaries and even a small contingent from the Papal States in central Italy. It was no match for the Ottoman army. In a battle lasting only a few hours, the Hungarian army was routed, with losses of between 15,000 and 20,000 troops compared to only 1,500 for the Ottomans.

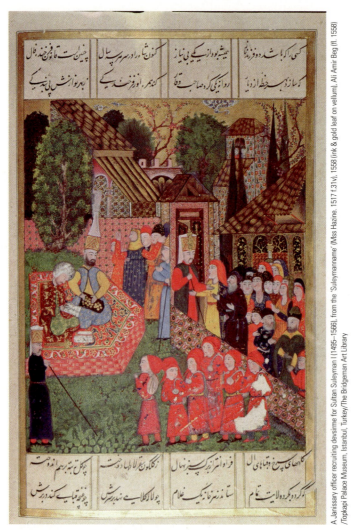

A Janissary officer recruiting devsirme for Sultan Suleyman I (1495–1566), from the 'Suleymanname' (Mss Hazine. 1517 f.31v), 1558 (ink & gold leaf on vellum), Ali Amir Beg (fl. 1558) /Topkapi Palace Museum, Istanbul, Turkey/The Bridgeman Art Library

The Recruitment of Tribute Children

For all intents and purposes the defeat at Mohács and the death of Louis II (who in retreat drowned by falling into a stream in full armor) meant the end of an independent Hungary and one more step in the expansion of Ottoman power.

The two paintings of the battle we have chosen can be considered two halves of one larger painting. Ottoman forces are on the right, with Suleiman and his handsome black horse at the center. They are surrounded by a barricade of cannons, two rows of janissaries, archers, cavalry troops, flag bearers, and a military band. Below them is a creek in which lie dead enemy troops and one of their horses. The painting on the left shows the beginning of an attack by the Ottomans on the enemy. From top to bottom, the painting shows three Ottoman officers attacking Hungarian leaders. Behind them are groups of Hungarian forces, some facing the enemy and some looking away.

The Battle of Mohacs, between the Turks and Hungarians, 1526, facsimile of a miniature conserved in the Topkapi Museum in Istanbul (colour litho), Turkish School, (16th century) (after)/Private Collection/Archives Charmet/The Bridgeman Art Library

Battle of Mohács

## QUESTIONS FOR ANALYSIS

1. In "The Recruitment of Tribute Children," examine the two groups of townspeople, the smaller one on the right side of the painting and the larger one in the middle. How are the townspeople reacting to the portrayed events?
2. In regard to the children, what age do they appear to be? What are their emotions?
3. In regard to the two paintings of the Battle of Mohács, what are the main differences between the two armies in terms of weaponry, organization, and dress?
4. How does the painter communicate the superiority of the Ottoman troops to the Hungarian troops?
5. In terms of style, what do the three paintings share in common? How do the artists indicate depth? What is their use of color? How do they depict trees, mountains, and other elements of the landscape?

# A Self-Portrait of Jahangir

## 12 • JAHANGIR, MEMOIRS

Jahangir, Mughal emperor from 1605 to 1627, modestly increased the empire's size through conquest, snuffed out several rebellions, and generally continued the policies of his illustrious father, Akbar. His lands provided him with enough wealth to indulge his tastes for formal gardens, entertaining, ceremony, sports, literature, and finely crafted books. In addition to subsidizing the work of hundreds of painters and writers, Jahangir himself contributed to the literature of his age by writing a memoir. In doing so he continued a tradition of writing or sponsoring royal histories that goes back to his great-grandfather, Babur, who wrote his memoirs in Turkish; it was continued by his father, Akbar, who commissioned his close friend and adviser Abul Fazl to chronicle his life. Jahangir wrote his memoirs with the assistance of several secretaries to whom he periodically handed over material for editing and organizing. The final version of the *Jahangirnama* (The Book of Jahangir) covers all but the last five years of his reign, but several other manuscripts exist that deal with shorter periods. The manuscript from which the following excerpt is drawn covers only the first thirteen years of Jahangir's reign. It contains much of the same material included in the final version of the work, but it also includes other matter as well, including a description of Jahangir's coronation celebration.

## QUESTIONS FOR ANALYSIS

1. Other than to glorify the person of the emperor, what political purposes might have been served by Jahangir's elaborate coronation ceremony?
2. What do the "twelve special regulations" issued at the beginning of Jahangir's reign reveal about his priorities as emperor?
3. How does Jahangir view his Hindu subjects? What are his reasons for allowing them to practice their religion?
4. What similarities and differences do you see in the authority and leadership style of Suleiman I and Jahangir?

## Jahangir's Coronation

On the eighth of the month of Jumada II, of the year of the Hegira one thousand and fourteen,[1] in the city of Agra, being then at the age of thirty-eight, I became Emperor, and under the most felicitous auspices, took my seat on the throne of my wishes. . . . Hence I assumed the titles of Jahangir Padashah, and Jahangir Shah: the world-subduing emperor; the world-subduing king. I ordained that the following legend should be stamped on the coinage of the empire: "Stricken at Agra by that safeguard of the world; the sovereign splendor of the faith; Jahangir son of the Emperor Akbar." On this occasion I made use of the throne prepared by my father, and enriched at an expense without parallel, for the celebration of the festival. . . . In the fabrication of the throne a sum not far short of ten krours of ashrafis[2] was expended in jewels alone. . . .

Having thus seated myself on the throne, I ordered the imperial crown, which my father had caused to be made after the manner of what was worn by the great kings of Persia, to be brought before me, and then, in the presence of the whole assembled Emirs [princes and royal governors], having placed it on my head, as an omen auspicious to the stability and happiness of my reign, kept it there for the space of a full hour. On each of the twelve points of this crown was a single diamond . . . all purchased by my father with the resources of his own government, not from anything he inherited from predecessors. At the point in the center of the top part of the crown was a single pearl . . . and on different parts of the same were set a total of two hundred rubies. . . .

For forty days and forty nights I caused the great imperial state drum to strike up without ceasing the sounds of joy and triumph; and . . . around my throne, the ground was spread with the most costly brocades and gold embroidered carpets. Censers of gold and silver were placed in different directions for the purpose of burning incense, and nearly three thousand wax lights . . . in branches of gold and silver illuminated the scene from night till morning. Numbers of beautiful young men . . . clad in dresses of the most costly materials, woven in silk and gold, with jewelry sparkling with the luster of the diamond, emerald, sapphire, and ruby, awaited my commands, rank after rank, and in attitude most respectful. And finally, the Emirs of the empire . . . stood round in brilliant array, also waiting for the commands of their sovereign. . . . For forty days and nights I kept up these scenes, furnishing an example of unparalleled imperial magnificence.

## The Emperor's Decrees

The very first ordinance that issued from me . . . related to the chain of justice,[3] one end of which I caused to be fastened to the battlements of the royal tower of the castle of Agra, and the other to a stone post near the bed of the Jumna River, so that whenever those charged with administering the courts were slack in dispensing justice to the downtrodden, he who had suffered injustice by applying his hand to the chain would find himself in the way of obtaining speedy redress. . . .

I issued twelve special regulations to be implemented and observed in all the realm.

*Source:* Major David Price, trans. *Memoirs of the Emperor Jahangueir Written by Himself* (London: Oriental Translation Committee, 1829), pp. 1–3, 5–10, 17–18, 34.
[1]October 10, 1605, according to the Muslim calendar.
[2]*Krour* is a measurement of weight, and *ashrafi* is a gold coin minted through much of the Islamic world. Although it is impossible to determine the exact value of ten "krours of ashrafis," it is an enormous sum.
[3]Pulling the chain would be the first step in bringing a perceived injustice to the emperor's attention. When in residence in Agra, Jahangir typically set aside two times a day when he would hear and respond to grievances of his subjects.

1. I canceled the *tamgha*, the *mirabari* [customs duties], and all other imposts the jagirdars[4] of every province and district had imposed for their own profit.

2. I ordered that when a district lay wasted by thieves and highway bandits or was destitute of people, that towns should be built, . . . and every effort made to protect the subjects from injury. I charged the jagirdars in such deserted places to erect mosques and . . . places for the accommodation of travelers, to make the district once more an inhabited country, and that men might again be able to travel back and forth safely. . . .

3. Merchants travelling through the country were not to have their bales or packs opened without their consent.

4. When a person dies and leaves children, no one was to interfere an iota with his property, and his property should be handed over to his heirs; but when he has no children or direct and unquestionable heirs his inheritance is to be spent on approved expenditures such as construction of mosques and caravansaries [roadside inns], repair of bridges, and the creation of watertanks and wells.

5. No person was permitted either to make or to sell wine or any other intoxicating liquor. I undertook to institute this regulation, although it is sufficiently well known that I myself have the strongest inclination for wine, in which from the age of sixteen I have liberally indulged.

6. No official was permitted to take up residency in the house of any subject of my realm. On the contrary, when troops enter any town, and can rent a place to live, it would be laudable; otherwise they were to pitch their tents outside the town and prepare dwellings for themselves. . . .

7. No person was to suffer, for any offence, the cutting off of a nose or ear. For theft, the offender was to be scourged with thorns, or deterred from further transgressions by an oath on the Quran.

8. I decreed that superintendents of royal lands and jagirdars were prohibited from seizing the lands of small landholders or cultivating the lands themselves for their own benefit . . .

9. The tax collectors of royal lands and jagirdars may not intermarry with the people of the districts in which they reside without my permission.[5]

10. Governors in all the large cities were directed to establish infirmaries or hospitals with competent medical aid for the treatment of the sick. Expenses are to be covered by income from royal lands until the patient is discharged with a sum of money sufficient for his needs.

11. During the month of my birth there could be no slaughter of animals in my realm both in town and country. . . . In every week also, on Thursday, that being the day of my accession, and Sunday, the day my father's birthday, the consumption of meat was forbidden. . . . For a period of more than eleven years a similar abstinence was observed by my father.[6] . . .

12. I issued a decree confirming the titles and jagirs of my father's servants in all that they had enjoyed while he was living; and where I found sufficient merit, I conferred an advance of rank. . . .

---

[4]A *jagirdar* was the holder of a grant of land (*jagir*) from the emperor. The jagirdar was *de facto* ruler of the land, and as such was entitled to collect taxes from his subjects. The income was used mainly to maintain troops who when needed would be made available to fight in the emperor's army.

[5]This was to prevent any tax collector or jagirdar from gaining a vested interest in the fortunes of a particular region or family.

[6]Akbar was famous for his moderate diet. He ate only one meal a day and gave up meat entirely toward the end of his life.

## Policy Toward Hindus

I am here led to relate that at the city of Benaras a temple had been erected [in which] . . . the principal idol . . . had on its head a tiara or cap, enriched with jewels. . . . [Also] placed in this temple, moreover, as the associates and ministering servants of the principal idol, [were] four other images of solid gold, each crowned with a tiara, similarly enriched with precious stones. It was the belief of these non-believers that a dead Hindu, provided when alive he had been a worshiper, when laid before this idol would be restored to life. As I could not possibly give credit to such a pretense, I employed a confidential person to ascertain the truth; and, as I justly supposed, the whole was detected to be an impudent fraud. . . .

On this subject I must however acknowledge, that having on one occasion asked my father [Akbar] the reason why he had forbidden anyone from preventing or interfering with the building of these haunts of idolatry, his reply was . . . : "My dear child," said he, "I find myself a powerful monarch, the shadow of God upon earth. I have seen that he bestows the blessing of his gracious providence upon all his creatures without distinction. . . . With all of the human race and with all of God's creatures, I am at peace: why then should I permit myself, under any consideration, to be the cause of molestation or aggression to anyone? Besides, are not five parts in six . . . either Hindus or aliens to the faith; and were I to be governed by motives of the kind suggested in your inquiry, what alternative can I have but to put them all to death! I have thought it therefore my wisest plan to let these men alone. Neither is it to be forgotten, that those of whom we are speaking . . . are usefully engaged, either in the pursuits of science or the arts, or of improvements for the benefit of mankind, and have in numerous instances arrived at the highest distinctions in the state, there being, indeed, to be found in this city men of every description, and of every religion on the face of the earth." . . .

• • •

In the practice of being burnt on the funeral pyre of their husbands[7] as sometimes exhibited among the widows of the Hindus, I had previously directed that no woman who was the mother of children should be thus made a sacrifice, however willing to die; and I now further ordained, that in no case was the practice to be permitted, when compulsion was in the slightest degree employed, whatever might be the opinions of the people. In other respects they were in no way to be molested in the duties of their religion, nor exposed to oppression or violence in any manner whatever. . . .

---

[7]A woman who burned herself in this way was known as *sati* (Sanskrit for "virtuous woman"). The word *sati* also is used to describe the burning itself.

# Religion and Society in South and Southwest Asia

At first glance one is struck by the differences between Islam and Hinduism, the two dominant faiths in South and Southwest Asia in the early modern period. Islam is distinguished by its uncompromising monotheism, the centrality of a single holy book, the Quran, and its origin in the prophecies communicated to a single human being, Muhammad. In contrast, Hinduism has a pantheon of thousands of gods, evolved over many centuries, and lacks a single creed or holy book.

Nonetheless, the two religions are similar in one important respect: Each rejects any separation between the religious and secular spheres. The two faiths not only guide each believer's spiritual development but also define the believer's role as a parent, spouse, subject, and worker. Secularism—the belief that religion should play no role in government, education, or other public aspects of society—is a foreign concept in both religions.

Islam is based on the prophecies and doctrines revealed by Allah (Arabic for God) to Muhammad (ca. 570–632 C.E.) and later recorded in the Quran. *Islam* in Arabic means "submission," and a Muslim is one who submits to God's will. Islam's creed is the statement that every follower must say daily: "There is no God but God, and Muhammad is the Prophet of God." All Muslims are expected to accept the Quran as the word of God, perform works of charity, fast during the month of Ramadan, say daily prayers, and, if possible, make a pilgrimage to Mecca, the city where Muhammad received Allah's revelation. Islam teaches that at death each person will be judged by Allah, with the faithful rewarded by Heaven and the unbelievers consigned to Hell.

Hinduism has no single creed, set of rituals, or holy book. It has thousands of deities, although all are believed to be manifestations of the Divine Essence or Absolute Reality, called Brahman. Some Hindus follow the "path of devotion," or *bhakti,* in which they focus their faith on devotion to a single god such as Vishnu or his incarnation, Krishna. Hindus believe that many paths lead to enlightenment, and as a result, Hinduism encompasses a wide range of beliefs and rituals.

All Hindus are part of the caste system, a religiously sanctioned order of social relationships that goes back to the beginnings of Indian civilization between 1500 and 1000 B.C.E. A person's caste, into which he or she is born, determines his or her social and legal status, restricts marriage partners to other caste members, limits the individual to certain professions, and, in effect, minimizes contacts with members of other castes. Hindus use two different words for caste: *varna* (color) and *jati* (birth). *Varna* refers only to the four most ancient and fundamental social-religious divisions: *Brahmins* (priests and teachers), *Kshatriyas* (warriors, nobles, and rulers), *Vaisyas* (landowners, merchants, and artisans), and *Sudras* (peasants and laborers). At the bottom of the Hindu hierarchy are the untouchables, who are relegated to despised tasks such as gathering manure, sweeping streets, and butchering animals. *Jati* refers to the many subdivisions of the four varna groups; by the 1600s, these local hereditary occupational groups numbered around three thousand.

The caste system is related to the doctrine of the transmigration of souls, or reincarnation. This is the belief that each individual soul, or *atman,* a fragment of the Universal Soul, or Brahman, strives through successive births to reunite with Brahman and win release from the cycle of death and rebirth. Reincarnation is based on one's *karma,* the fruit of one's actions, which is determined by how well or poorly a person has conformed to *dharma,* the duties required of members in each jati and varna. A person who fulfills his or her dharma will, in the next incarnation, move up the cosmic ladder, closer to ultimate reunion with the One.

# Sunni–Shia Conflict in the Early Sixteenth Century

## 13 • SULTAN SELIM I–SHAH ISMAIL I CORRESPONDENCE

The following letters, exchanged by the Ottoman sultan Selim I and the founder of the Safavid Empire, Ismail I, in early 1514 illustrate the bitterness of the centuries-old clash between Shia and Sunni Muslims. The origins of the Shia–Sunni schism go back to a series of disputes involving the major Arab clans over who should lead the Islamic community as caliph, or successor to the prophet, after the death of Muhammad in 632. One faction, the Shia, believed that descendants of Muhammad, and they alone, were qualified to serve as caliphs. Hence they became supporters of Ali, Muhammad's cousin and son-in-law, who served as the fourth caliph between 656 and 661. Their opponents, the Sunni, rejected the Shia position, believing that other factors should determine the choice of caliph. The Shia lost these early struggles. Ali was assassinated, and his son Husayn was killed in battle while leading a rebellion against Yazid I, the sixth caliph and a member of the powerful Umayyad clan. Under the Umayyad (661–750) and Abbasid (750–1258) caliphates (in which the office of caliph became hereditary), the Shia maintained a separate existence in Iraq, where they developed many beliefs and practices that made them anathema to Sunnis.

Selim, who in the Ottoman tradition was a Sunni, was deeply disturbed by the appearance of a Shia state in Iran under Ismail. Ismail, believed by his followers to have descended from Ali, had many supporters among the Turks of eastern Anatolia and had aided Selim's brother and rival, Ahmed, in the Ottoman succession conflict following Sultan Bayezid's death in 1512. When Ismail invaded eastern Ottoman territory in 1513, war seemed inevitable. Nonetheless, Selim wrote several letters to Ismail in early 1514 offering him an opportunity to avoid defeat by embracing Sunni Islam and abandoning his conquests. Ismail dismissed Selim's threats in his one letter to Selim. In August 1514, Selim's armies defeated Ismail's forces at the Battle of Chaldiran, forcing Ismail to retire to his palace until his death in 1520. Nonetheless, the Safavid Empire survived, and the rivalry with the Sunni Ottomans continued.

### QUESTIONS FOR ANALYSIS

1. Even though Selim's letter is designed to malign Ismail, not define Islam, it contains many references to essential Muslim beliefs. Which ones can you find?
2. According to Selim, what crimes has Ismail committed against the Islamic faith, and what are his flaws as a ruler?
3. How do the two rulers perceive themselves within the Islamic world?
4. Selim must have realized that the deeply religious Ismail was unlikely to abandon Shiism. Why might he have written the letter, despite the likelihood that its appeal would fall on deaf ears?

## Ottoman Sultan Selim I to Shah Ismail of Iran

This missive . . . has been graciously issued by our most glorious majesty – we who are the Caliph[1] of the God most high . . . ; haloed in victory, slayer of the wicked and the infidel, guardian of the noble and the pious, defender of the faith, champion, conqueror, lion . . . standard bearer of justice and righteousness, Sultan Selim—and is addressed to the ruler of the Persians, Ismail, the possessor of the land of tyranny and perversion, the captain of viciousness, the chief of maliciousness . . .

It has been heard repeatedly that you have subjected the upright community of Muhammad to your devious will, have undermined . . . the Faith, have unfurled the banner of oppression . . . , have incited your abominable Shi'i faction to unsanctimonious sexual union[2] and to the shedding of innocent blood[3] . . . that you have called the glorious Quran the myths of the Ancients . . . Thus when the Divine Decree . . . commended the eradication of the wicked infidels into our hands, we set out for their lands to enforce the order, "Leave not upon the Earth the Unbelievers, even one."[4] If God almighty wills . . . our avenging mace shall dash out the muddled brains of the enemies of the Faith as rations for the lion-hearted *ghazis* [warriors].

But . . . should you turn the countenance of submission . . . , should you lift the hand of oppression from the heads of your subjects, . . . should you take up a course of repentance, become like one blameless and return to the sublime straight path of the Sunna[5] and finally should you consider your lands and their people part of the well-protected Ottoman state, then shall you be granted our royal favor and our imperial patronage . . . On the other hand, if your evil, seditious habits have become part of your nature, that which has become essential can never be accidental. Then, with the support and assistance of God, I will crown the head of every gallows tree with the head of a crown-wearing Sufi.[6]

## Shah Ismail of Iran to Ottoman Sultan Selim I

May his Godly majesty, the refuge of Islam, the might of the kingdom . . . Sultan Selim Shah accept this affectionate greeting and this friendly letter, considering it a token of our good will. Your honored letters have arrived. Their contents, although indicative of hostility, are stated with boldness and vigor . . . The latter gives us much enjoyment and pleasure but we are ignorant of the reason for the former. The cause of your resentment and displeasure remains unknown. Dispute may fire words to such a heat that ancient houses be consumed in flames. We have always loved the *ghazi*- titled Ottoman house and we do not wish the outbreak of sedition and turmoil . . . There is no cause for improper words: indeed these vain, heretical imputations are the mere fabrications of opium-clouded minds . . . At this writing we are engaged upon a hunt near Isfahan, we now prepare our provisions and troops for the coming campaign. Bitter experience has taught . . . he who falls upon the house of Ali always fails. When war becomes inevitable, hesitation and delay must be set aside, and one must think on that which is to come. Farewell.

---

*Source:* Sultan Selim I–Ismail I Correspondence, 1514
[1] Successor of the Prophet Muhammad as head of the Islamic community.
[2] A reference to *muta*, a practice among the Shia in which a man and woman enter into a temporary marriage lasting anywhere from three days to a year.
[3] Following the Shia conquest of the city of Tabriz in 1501, numerous Sunnis were massacred.

[4] Quran LXXI: 26.
[5] The way of life prescribed for Muslims based on Muhammad's teachings and interpretations of the Quran.
[6] An approach to Islam that emphasizes a mystical approach to the faith. The Safavids trace their origins to a fourteenth-century Sufi order.

# Women and Islamic Law in the Ottoman Empire

## 14 • KHAYR AL-DIN RAMLI, LEGAL OPINIONS

Many of Muhammad's teachings were favorable to women. He taught that men and women were spiritual equals, and women were among his earliest and most important followers. As Islam evolved, however, women's status declined. Upper-class women were secluded in their homes and expected to wear clothes covering their bodies and faces in public. Their role in religious affairs virtually disappeared, and vocational and educational opportunities decreased. Some Muslims came to believe that Heaven itself was closed to females.

As the following legal opinions show, however, women in the Ottoman Empire were not without legal rights during the seventeenth century. The empire had a complex court system staffed by *qadi* (judges), who interpreted Islamic law (Sharia) and applied it to specific cases. In making decisions, they drew on their knowledge of the Quran and Hadith (traditions connected with Muhammad's life and teachings), legal precedent, and commentaries on Islamic law. They also considered *fatwas*, legal opinions of learned men known as *muftis*. Such opinions could be solicited by judges or by an individual involved in a court case. A fatwa was not a binding legal judgment but rather one scholar's opinion that would be included in the record of the trial and might affect the judge's decision.

The following fatwas were written by Khayr al-Din Ramli (1585–1671), who, after advanced studies in Cairo, returned to his native city of Ramla in Palestine, where he supported himself through farming, income from property, and teaching Islamic law. His fame, however, was based on his work as a mufti. By the 1650s, his reputation throughout Syria and Palestine was such that no judge would go against one of his opinions.

Many of the cases on which Khayr al-Din Ramli commented centered on relations between unmarried men and women, child custody, crimes against women, and sexual activity. The following examples provide many insights into male–female relations in seventeenth-century Syria-Palestine.

## QUESTIONS FOR ANALYSIS

1. In arranging marriages, how much legal authority is exercised by the following: the future husband and wife; fathers and grandfathers; male relatives of the future husband and wife?
2. What do the divorce cases reveal about the obligations of husbands to their wives?
3. What rights does a married woman have against an abusive husband?
4. How did Khayr al-Din Ramli view rapists and abductors of women? What penalties are prescribed for perpetrators of such crimes?
5. Taking all the cases together, what do they reveal about women's legal standing in seventeenth-century Syria-Palestine? What situations and legal opinions underscore women's legal inferiority to men? What situations and decisions accord women legal rights in their dealings with men?

## Arranging Marriages

QUESTION: A virgin in her legal majority [meaning she had reached puberty] and of sound mind was abducted by her brother and married off to an unsuitable man.[1] Does her father have the right to annul the marriage contract on the basis of the [husband's] unsuitability?

ANSWER: Yes, if the father asks for that, then the judge should separate the spouses whether or not the marriage was consummated, so long as she has not borne children, and is not pregnant, and did not receive the dower[2] before the marriage. . . . This is the case if her brother has married her off with her consent. But if she was given in marriage without her consent, she can reject [the marriage], and there is no need for the father [to ask for] separation [and raise] opposition, for he is not [in this case] a commissioned agent. [But] if she authorizes him to represent her, then he has the right to request from the judge an annulment of the marriage and a separation, and the judge should separate them. . . .

## Divorce and Annulment[3]

QUESTION: There is a poor woman whose husband is absent in a remote region and he left her without support or a legal provider, and she has suffered proven harm from that. She has made a claim against him for that [support], but the absent one is very poor. The resources [intended] for her support were left in his house and in his shop, but they are not sufficient for her to withstand her poverty. She therefore asked the . . . judge to annul the marriage, and he ordered her to bring proof. Two just men testified in conformity with what she had claimed, and so the judge annulled the marriage. . . . Then, following her waiting period, she married another man. Then the first husband returned and wanted to nullify the judgment. Can that be done for him, when it was all necessary and had ample justification?

ANSWER: When the harm is demonstrated and the evidence for that is witnessed, the annulment of the absent [one's marriage] is sound. . . .

• • •

QUESTION: There is a poor man who married a virgin in her legal majority, but he did not pay her stipulated dower expeditiously, nor did he provide support, nor did he clothe her. This caused her great harm. Must he follow one of God's two commands: "Either you maintain her well or you release her with kindness"? And if the judge annuls the marriage, is it on account of the severe harm being done to her?

ANSWER: Yes, the husband should do one of the two things, according to God's command: "maintain her well or release her with kindness." . . . You

---

Source: *In the House of the Law: Gender and Islamic Law in Ottoman Syria and Palestine*, by Judith E. Tucker, pp. 26, 47, 68, 69, 78, 83, and 165. © 1998 by the Regents of the University of California. Published by the University of California Press.
[1]Most marriages were arranged by legal guardians (usually fathers or grandfathers), often when the future wife and husband were children. On reaching a marriageable age, the young people had no choice but to acquiesce to their guardians' wishes and accept the planned marriage. For marriages arranged between adults, however, individuals had the right to reject a proposed match. Similarly, if a marriage was arranged by someone other than a father or grandfather for a minor, then on reaching adulthood the person could refuse.
[2]In contrast to practice in Europe, dowry payments were paid by the husband to the wife.

[3]Islamic law affirmed that no social good was served by continuing defective or unhappy marriages. Hence, divorce was permissible and fairly common. A husband could divorce his wife by saying before her and a witness, "I divorce you, I divorce you, I divorce you." This meant that the woman was irrevocably and finally divorced and could remarry if she wished. For a specified time or until the divorced wife remarried, the former husband was required to support her. A woman could also demand a divorce by demonstrating in court that her husband had failed to fulfill his financial or sexual obligations. She also could try to convince her husband to annul the marriage by offering him financial concessions—for example, by returning some or all of the dowry payment she had received.

cannot sustain [indefinitely] such needs through borrowing, and it appears that she does not have anyone to lend her money, and the husband has no actual wealth. . . .

• • •

QUESTION: A man consummated his marriage with his virgin legally major wife, and then claimed that he found her deflowered. He was asked, "How was that?" And he said, "I had intercourse with her several times and I found her deflowered." What is the legal judgment on that?

ANSWER: The judgment is that all of the dower is required, and it is fully and entirely incumbent on him. Her testimony on her own virginity [is sufficient] to remove the shame. And if he accuses her without [evidence], he is punished and his testimony is not accepted, as is her right. If he defamed her with a charge of adultery, he must now make a sworn allegation of adultery if she so requests, [and take the consequences].[4] Such is the case, and God knows best.

### Violence Against Women

QUESTION: A man approached a woman, a virgin in her legal majority who was married to someone else,[5] abducted her . . . , and took her to a village near her own village. He brought her to the shaykh[6] of the village, who welcomed him and gave him hospitality and protection. There the man

consummated the "marriage," saying "between us there are relations." Such is the way of the peasants. . . . What is the punishment for him and the man who helped him? . . . Should Muslim rulers halt these practices of the peasants . . .?

ANSWER: The punishment of the abductor and his accomplice for this grave crime is severe beating and long imprisonment, and even worse punishment until they show remorse. It is conceivable that the punishment could be execution because of the severity of this act of disobedience to God. . . . The one who commits this act, and those who remain silent about it, are like one who punches a hole in a ship, [an act] that will drown all the passengers. . . .

• • •

QUESTION: There is an evil man who harms his wife, hits her without right and rebukes her without cause. He swore many times to divorce her until she proved that a thrice divorce [a final and irrevocable divorce] had taken effect.

ANSWER: He is forbidden to do that, and he is rebuked and enjoined from her. If she has proved that a thrice divorce has taken place, it is permissible for her to kill him, according to many of the *'ulama'* [jurists] if he is not prevented [from approaching her] except by killing.

---

[4]To prove adultery an accuser had to present four witnesses to testify that it occurred. A failure to prove such an accusation carried severe legal penalties.

[5]The marriage had been legally contracted but not consummated.

[6]A village leader, often a man with some religious training and standing.

# Jews in Ottoman Lands

### 15 • NICHOLAS DE NICOLAY, VOYAGES AND TRAVELS TO TURKEY

The targets of persecution, mob violence, and expulsions that began in the eleventh century, many Jews in England, France, and Germany fled to join existing Jewish communities in Poland and Lithuania or to the Iberian Peninsula, where under tolerant

Muslim rulers, they built a prosperous and vibrant culture. Beginning in the mid-thirteenth century, however, as Islamic power waned in Iberia, Jews under their new Christian rulers were subjected to forced conversion campaigns, popular attacks, and exclusion from many professions. The anti-Jewish crusade reached a climax in March 1492, when Isabella I of Castile and Ferdinand II of Aragon, two months after their armies had conquered Grenada, the last Muslim bastion in Spain, ordered the expulsion of all Jews from Spain, to be completed no later than August. Some Jews converted, others made their way to Poland or Lithuania, but the majority—better than 300,000—sought new lives in the territory of the Ottoman Turks.

Here they found a situation far different from what they had faced in Europe. Jews entering Ottoman territory became part of the recently established millet system, in which the sultan's Christian and Jewish subjects paid a special tax but were allowed to live under their own leaders and maintain their own customs and laws. They could follow any profession they chose, engage in trade and commerce, manage their own schools and synagogues, and own property. Such policies were partly rooted in the perceived affinities between Islamic beliefs and those of Jews and Christians. Muslims drew inspiration from the teachings of Jewish prophets and Jesus, and like Jews and Christians worshiped a single god and relied on a single holy book (the Jewish Bible, the Christian New Testament, and the Quran). Tolerance also was rooted in self-interest. Ottoman rulers encouraged Jewish resettlement as a way of repopulating devastated areas and promoting trade and industry. Sultan Bayezid II (r. 1481–1512) dispatched the Ottoman navy to help evacuate fleeing Spanish Jews and issued proclamations that Jewish refugees were to be welcomed. By the mid-1500s the Ottoman Empire was the home of approximately 1.5 million Jews.

The following comments on Ottoman Jews are drawn from *Voyages and Travels to Turkey*, a book published in 1567 by the French aristocrat Nicholas de Nicolay. Nicolay, an inveterate traveler, spent his life in service to the French monarchy as a soldier, diplomat, cartographer, and geographer. His book on the Ottoman Empire grew out of a two-year visit to the court of Suleiman I in 1551–1552 as part of a mission to cement an alliance between France and the Ottoman Empire against their mutual enemy, the Hapsburgs. His comments reveal his admiration of the Ottomans' tolerant religious policies and his amazement at the achievements of the Jews, a people he personally despised.

## QUESTIONS FOR ANALYSIS

1. According to Nicolay, what contributions are the Jews making to Ottoman society?
2. How does Nicolay explain the success of the Jews in commerce and the practice of medicine?
3. How does the excerpt reveal certain misunderstandings on Nicolay's part of the Jews' status?
4. What is the basis of Nicolay's anti-Jewish prejudice?

## On the Physicians of Constantinople

In Turkey . . . are found numerous Turks who make a profession of the art of medicine and practice it, but a much greater number of Jews than Turks, who are very learned in theory and experienced in practice. The reason for this is that in this particular art they commonly exceed all other peoples in their knowledge of the Greek, Arabic, Chaldean,[1] and Hebrew languages and literature, in which languages the principal authors have written on medicine and the related fields of natural philosophy and astronomy. In addition to the physicians who serve the public, the sultan has his own, some Turks, and some Jews, whom he pays and rewards very generously. While I was there the most honored and authoritative physician was a Jew, Hamon,[2] who is more than sixty years old, esteemed for his wealth, knowledge, fame, and skill. . . . As for the physicians of Turkey, they dress no differently than the common people, except for the Jewish physicians, who instead of a yellow turban, which other Jews wear, wear a scarlet red pointed cap.

## Jewish Merchants Living in Constantinople and Other Places in Turkey and Greece

The number of Jews living in all the towns of Turkey and Greece, especially Constantinople [Istanbul], is so large that it is miraculous and almost unbelievable. The number of them making a business from barter and the trading of all kinds of merchandise, likewise money-lending, grows so much from one day to the next, that the value and abundance of the merchandise they handle from all parts of the world, some by land and some by sea, is so great that one can say . . . that they presently hold in their hands most of the trade in merchandise and money that is carried on in the whole region. Similarly, the most opulent shops and the best-furnished and best supplied warehouses . . . in Constantinople are those of the Jews. Furthermore, they have among them most excellent workers in all the crafts and manufactures, especially the Marranos,[3] recently banned and expelled from Spain and Portugal, who to the great damage and detriment of Christendom, have taught the Turks many inventions, crafts, and weapons, for example, artillery, harquebuses, gunpowder, shot, and other arms.[4] Similarly, they have set up a printing press, which previously had not been introduced in these regions; they have brought to light numerous books in various languages, including Greek, Italian, Spanish, Latin, and Hebrew. But they are not allowed to print anything in Turkish or Arabic.[5] Also, they have the convenience of being able to speak and understand all the other languages used in the Levant, which serves them very well in communication and commerce that they have with foreign nations,

---

*Source:* Nicholas de Nicolay, Nicholas de Nicolay, *Discourse et Histoire Veritable des Navigations et Voyages faict en Turquie* Anvers: A. Concinx, 1586), 114–115, 168–169. Digital copy on LOC website: http://hdl.loc.gov/loc.rbc/rosenwald.1207. Translated by J. Overfield.

[1]Chaldean refers to any one of several Semitic languages spoken by the people who lived originally in ancient Babylonia and later spread to other parts of present-day Iraq and Iran.

[2]The Hamon family, famous for its physicians, migrated to Constantinople at the end of the fifteenth century. Moise Hamon (1490–1554) was the physician for Selim I and Suleiman.

[3]*Marranos* was a Spanish term for "New Christians," Jewish converts to Christianity, most of whom returned to Judaism once in Ottoman territories.

[4]Although the Jews did bring a number of new technologies to Turkey, Ottoman armies had excellent artillery well before the influx of Iberian Jews in the late 1400s.

[5]Two brothers, David and Samuel ibn Nahmias, having fled from Spain to Istanbul, published in 1493 a fourteenth-century commentary on the Torah by Jacob ben Asher. Opposed by religious conservatives, the first printing press for the production of Turkish and Arabic books was introduced in Ottoman territories only in the eighteenth century.

for whom they often serve as a translator or interpreter. . . . In any event, the Jews as a people are full of trickery, fraud, cheating, and cunning deceptions, doing business without any conscience or regret, because having paid the tribute,[6] they can legally carry on their trade. They are remarkably stubborn in their infidelity, waiting for their Messiah every day, who will lead them to their Promised Land; the eyes of their understanding are so tightly covered by the veil of Moses that they cannot by any manner or means acknowledge the bright light of Jesus Christ, whom, through

unbelief, jealousy, and infinite wrath, they condemned and caused to die on the cross. . . .

The Turks will by no means dine with Jews, even less marry one of their women or girls, as they do with Christians, who are permitted to retain their laws, and with whom they are happy to dine and carry on a conversation. . . . The Jews, who reside in Constantinople, Adrianople, Bursa, Salonika, Gallipoli and other places in the dominions of the sultan, are all appareled in long robes, in the manner of the Greeks, but, for their mark to be recognized by others, they wear a yellow turban.[7]

---

[6]The poll tax levied on all non-Muslims.

[7]This was not necessarily a token of anti-Jewish prejudice (unlike the yellow badge or scarf Jews were forced to wear in Europe). *All* Ottoman subjects had to wear costumes of

certain fabrics and colors depending on their social standing and religious affiliation. Muslims, for example, were distinguished by their green clothing, white turbans, and yellow shoes.

## A Muslim's Description of Hindu Beliefs and Practices

### 16 • ABUL FAZL, AKBARNAMA

As Akbar, Mughal ruler from 1556 to 1605, expanded and strengthened his empire, at his side was Abul Fazl, his friend and advisor until 1602, when he was murdered by an assassin hired by Akbar's son and future emperor Jahangir. Abul Fazl is best known as the author of the *Akbarnama (Book of Akbar),* a laudatory history of Akbar's reign full of information about the emperor's personality and exploits. The third part of the work, often given its own title, *Ain-i-Akbari* (Constitution of Akbar), provides information on Akbar's administration and describes various features of Hindu society. Abul Fazl, who shared Akbar's tolerant religious views, was interested in presenting Hinduism favorably to his Islamic readers, many of whom were uncomfortable with Akbar's polices toward Hindus. Equally disturbing to his critics was Akbar's interest in Christianity, Jainism, and Zoroastrianism, all of which helped inspire his new religious cult, *Din-i Ilahi* (Divine Faith). In his book, Abul Fazl sought to lessen the concerns of orthodox Muslims that Hindus were guilty of what to Muslims were the two greatest sins—idolatry and polytheism. He also explained the Hindu caste system, whose rigid hierarchies were far removed from the Muslim belief in the spiritual equality of all believers. Our selection concludes with a description of marriage practices among the Brahmins, the highest of the four Indian varnas. There were seven other types of Hindu marriage, only one of which—Gandharva marriage—resulted from the mutual affection of the bride and groom.

## QUESTIONS FOR ANALYSIS

1. How does Abul Fazl counter the charge that Hindus are polytheists? Do you find his arguments convincing? Why or why not?
2. How does Abul Fazl address the charge that Hindus are idol worshipers?
3. In what ways do caste and karma provide Hindus with a moral understanding of the universe?
4. What do the dharmas of the castes reveal about Hindu social values?
5. Where do women fit into the structure of the ladder of reincarnation? What does this suggest about their status in Hindu society?
6. What are the notable features of marriage practices among the Brahmins? How do they compare with the practices described by Alberti (source 6) and Dod and Cleaver (source 8)?

As I was unfamiliar with the Sanskrit language and a competent interpreter was not available, the labor of repeated translations had to be undertaken. . . . It then became clear that . . . although with regard to some points there is room for controversy, the worship of one God and the profession of His Unity among this people appeared [to be] facts convincingly attested. It was indispensable for me, therefore, to bring into open evidence the system of philosophy . . . of this people in order that hostility towards them might abate, and the temporal sword be halted from the shedding of blood, that dissensions within and without be turned to peace, and the thorns of strife and enmity bloom into a garden of concord. They [Hindus] one and all believe in the unity of God, and as to the reverence they pay to images of stone and wood and the like, which simpletons regard as idolatry, it is not so. The writer of these words has exhaustively discussed the subject with many enlightened and upright men, and it became evident that these images . . . are fashioned as aids to fix the mind and keep the thoughts from

wandering, while the worship of God alone is required as indispensable. . . . Brahman is the Supreme Being; and is essential to existence and wisdom and also bliss. . . . Since according to their belief, the Supreme Deity can assume an elemental form . . . they first make various idols of gold and other substances to represent this ideal and gradually withdrawing the mind from this material worship, they become meditatively absorbed in the ocean of His mysterious Being. . . .

Brahma . . . they hold to be the Creator; Vishnu, the Nourisher and Preserver; and Rudra [Shiva], the Destroyer. Some maintain that God who is without equal [Brahman], manifested himself under these three divine forms, without thereby tarnishing the garment of His unblemished sanctity, as the Nazarenes [Christians] hold of the Messiah.[1]

## Caste

The Hindu philosophers reckon four states of fortune which they term *varna*. 1. *Brahmin*. 2. *Kshatriya*. 3. *Vaisya*. 4. *Sudra*. Other than these are termed *Mleccha*.[2] At the creation of the world

Source Abul Fazl, *The Ain-I-Akar* ed. and trans. by H. S. Jarrett (Calcutta, India: Baptist Mission Press, 1868–1894), Vol. 3, pp. 8, 114–119, 159–160, 225–232, 279, 284, 285–286, 291–292.
[1] Here Abul Fazl compares this Hindu trinity to the Christian Trinity (three divine and full separate persons in one God).
[2] Abul Fazl inaccurately uses this term to refer to all the various groups who were considered by Hindus to live outside the cultural community as defined by caste and thus were

known as "outcasts" or "untouchables." The term *Mleccha*, more narrowly defined, refers to a foreigner, and is used by caste Hindus in the same way ancient Greeks used the term "barbarian" for non-Greeks. In Abul Fazl's time the term might be applied to Christians, Muslims, or Buddhists. Mlecchas resembled other outcast groups in that caste Hindus avoided social contact with them because they were considered "unclean."

the first of these classes was produced from the mouth of Brahma . . . ; the second, from his arms; the third, from his thigh and the fourth from his feet; the fifth from the cow. . . .

The *Brahmins* have six recognized duties. 1. The study of the Vedas[3] and other sciences. 2. The instruction of others in the sacred texts. 3. The performance of the Jag, that is oblation [a religious offering] of money and goods to the Devatas [Hindu deities]. 4. Inciting others to the same. 5. Giving presents. 6. Receiving presents.

Of these six the *Kshatriya* must perform three. 1. Perusing the holy texts. 2. The performance of the Jag. 3. Giving presents. Further they must, 1. Minister to Brahmins. 2. Control the administration of worldly government. . . . 3. Protect religion. 4. Exact fines for illegal behavior. . . . 5. Punish in proportion to the offense. 6. Amass wealth and duly expend it. 7. Supervise the management of elephants, horses, and cattle and the functions of ministerial subordinates. 8. Declare war on due occasion. . . .

The *Vaisya* also must perform the same three duties of the Brahmin, and in addition must occupy himself in: 1. Service. 2. Agriculture. 3. Trade. 4. The care of cattle. 5. The carrying of loads. . . . The *Sudra* is incapable of any other privilege than to serve these three castes, wear their cast-off garments and eat their leavings. He may be a painter, goldsmith, blacksmith, carpenter, and trade in salt, honey, milk, butter-milk, clarified butter and grain. Those of the fifth class [*Mlecchas*] are reckoned as beyond the pale of religion, like infidels, Jews, and the like.[4]

By the intermarriages of these, sixteen other classes are formed. . . . In the same way still further ramifications are formed, each with different customs and modes of worship and each with infinite distinctions of habitation, profession, and rank of ancestry that defy computation. . . .

## Karma

. . . This is a system of knowledge of an amazing and extraordinary character. . . . It reveals the particular class of actions performed in a former birth which have occasioned the events that befall men in this present life, and prescribes the special expiation of each sin, one by one. It is of four kinds.

The first kind discloses the particular action which has brought a man into existence in one of the five classes into which mankind is divided, and the action which occasions the assumption of a male or female form. A *Kshatriya*, who lives purely, will in his next birth, be born a *Brahmin*. A *Vaisya* who risks his life to protect a Brahmin, will become a *Kshatriya*. A *Sudra* who lends money without interest and does not defile his tongue by demanding repayment, will be born a *Vaisya*. A *Mleccha* who serves a *Brahmin* and eats food from his house until his death, will become a *Sudra*. A *Brahmin* who undertakes the profession of a *Kshatriya* will become a *Kshatriya*, and thus a *Kshatriya* will become a *Vaisya*, and a *Vaisya* a *Sudra*, and a *Sudra* a *Mleccha*. Whosoever accepts in alms . . . the bed on which a man has died [an "unclean" object"] . . . will, in the next birth, from a man become a woman. Any woman or *Mleccha*, who in the temple . . . sees the form of *Narayana*,[5] and worships him with certain incantations, will in the next birth, if a woman, become a man, and if a *Mleccha*, a *Brahmin*. . . .

The second kind shows the strange effects of actions on the health. . . . Headache is caused by former violent language against one's father or mother. . . . Madness is the punishment of disobedience to father and mother. . . . Pain in the eyes arises from having looked upon another's wife. . . . Dumbness [lacking human speech] is the consequence of killing a sister. . . . Abdominal pain

[3]The four collections of ancient poetry that are sacred texts among Hindus.

[4]Abul Fazl is drawing an analogy for his Muslim readers. Just as Muslims consider all nonbelievers to be outside the community of God, so Hindus regard the Mleccha as outside their community.

[5]The personification of solar and cosmic energy underlying creation.

results from having eaten with an impious person or a liar. . . . Lameness is the result of having kicked a *Brahmin*. . . . Consumption is the punishment of killing a *Brahmin*. . . . Tumor is caused by killing a wife without fault on her part. . . .

The third kind indicates the class for actions which have caused sterility. . . . A WOMAN who does not menstruate, in a former existence . . . roughly drove away the children of her neighbors who had come as usual to play at her house. . . . A WOMAN who gives birth to only daughters is thus punished for having contemptuously regarded her husband. . . . A WOMAN who has given birth to a son that dies and to a daughter that lives, has, in her former existence, taken animal life. Some say that she had killed goats. . . .

The fourth kind treats of riches and poverty, and the like. Whoever distributes alms at auspicious times . . . will become rich and bountiful in his next existence. Whosoever when hungry and with food before him, hears the supplication of a poor man and bestows it all upon him, will be rich. Whoever when hungry and with food before him hears the supplications of a poor man and bestows it all upon him will be rich. . . .

## Marriage among the Brahmins

[The following ceremony takes place after the family of the marriageable daughter has approached the family of a man deemed suitable. After horoscopes are examined and lineages compared, the ceremony can go forward.]

The girl's father with other elders of the family visit the bridegroom and bring him to his house where the relations assemble. Then the grandfather, or brother, or any other male relation, or the mother, says before the company:—"I have bestowed such and such a maiden upon such and such a man." The bridegroom in the presence of the same company gives his consent. Certain incantations are then pronounced and a sacrifice is performed. It is then declared that the girl's mother has borne male children and was of smaller stature than her husband, and that the bridegroom is not impotent, and both parties declare that they are free of disease and deformity. . . .

The Brahmin next places the two hands of the bride in those of the bridegroom and repeats certain prayers; after which he binds them both with loose-spun cotton thread, and the girl's father taking her hand gives her to the bridegroom and says: 'May there be ever participation between you and this nursling of happiness in three things—in good works, in worldly goods, and tranquillity of life.' . . .

In the past, it was the rule for Brahmins to take wives from among all the castes, while the other three castes considered it unlawful to wed a Brahmin woman. The same practice applied to all superior and inferior castes reciprocally. In the present . . . no one chooses a wife outside his own caste, no, each of these four being subdivided into various branches, each subdivision asks in marriage only the daughters of their own equals. . . .

It is held expedient that the bride should not be under eight. . . . The man should be twenty-five, and marriage after fifty years of age, they regard as unbecoming. . . . It is not considered right for a man to have more than one wife, unless his first wife is sickly or proves barren, or her children die. In these cases, he may marry ten wives, but if the tenth proves defective, he may not marry again.

# Chapter 3

# Africa and the Americas

O F ALL THE WORLD'S REGIONS, Africa and the Americas were most affected by European expansion between the fifteenth and seventeenth centuries. On both sides of the Atlantic, the arrival of Europeans brought demographic changes, efforts to spread Christianity, political disruption, new patterns of trade, and the introduction of new weapons and new species of plants and animals. But the magnitude of Europe's impact on the two regions varied greatly, with the changes in the Americas many times more profound and disruptive than those in Africa.

Until the 1800s, the European presence in Africa primarily meant trade—trade in which Europeans exchanged iron, hardware, textiles, and other goods for pepper, gold, ivory, and, above all, human beings. European involvement in the slave trade began in 1441, when a Portuguese raiding party captured twelve Africans on a small coastal island and sold them into slavery in Portugal. After the plantation system of agriculture was established on São Tomé, Cape Verde, and other South Atlantic islands and later spread to the West Indies and the Americas, the sale of slaves grew from fewer than 1,000 a year in the fifteenth century, to 7,500 a year in the mid-seventeenth century, and to more than 50,000 a year in the eighteenth century. The slave trade, however, did not translate into European political dominance or permanent settlements in Africa. Europeans largely stayed on the coast, completed their business, and then departed. Missionary efforts were limited, and Portuguese dominance in Angola, in southwest Africa, is the only example of anything that approximated a European colony. As a result, Africans kept control of their political lives and experienced few cultural or religious changes until the late 1800s, when a new wave of European expansion occurred.

In the Americas, however, the Europeans' arrival had immediate and catastrophic consequences. By the mid-1600s, Portugal ruled Brazil; Spain controlled major Caribbean islands, Mexico, Central America, Florida, most of South America, and much of the present-day United States west of the Mississippi; Britain, France, and the Netherlands ruled territories in the West Indies, North America's Atlantic coastal regions, and the St. Lawrence River basin; Sweden and Denmark also had

small territorial claims. Throughout the Western Hemisphere, wealth was plundered, political structures were destroyed, millions of Native Americans were killed by Old World diseases, and traditional patterns of life and belief disappeared or managed only a tenuous survival.

Of the several factors that explain the differences in the African and the American experiences, two stand out. First, unlike the Americas, where more than half a dozen European states competed for trade and territory, in Africa only Portugal was involved. Portugal, having led the way in African exploration, by the end of the fifteenth century had established commercial contacts and trading posts in key areas on the African coasts. This discouraged European competitors until the seventeenth century, when merchants from other states showed an interest in the slave trade. Second, all Europeans were convinced that in comparison to other parts of the world, Africa offered relatively few economic rewards. Portugal's rulers and merchants concluded that their money and energy would better be spent on Asian trade and Brazilian development than on Africa. Neither they nor any other Europeans were willing to make the economic and military commitments necessary to support European settlement or establish political authority.

Europeans faced a far different situation in the Americas. Here was a region with easily exploitable sources of wealth such as gold, silver, and furs and a potential for growing profitable crops such as tobacco and sugar. These things were more or less theirs for the taking, not only in the thinly populated regions of North America and eastern and southern South America but also in the more populous regions of Mexico, Peru, and the Caribbean.

The Europeans' guns, steel swords, and horses certainly gave them an initial advantage over Native Americans. The relative ease of the European conquest, however, owed less to weapons than to the bacteria, viruses, and parasites Europeans and Africans carried in their bodies from across the Atlantic. Because of their long isolation, the Native Americans lacked immunity to diseases such as diphtheria, measles, chickenpox, whooping cough, yellow fever, influenza, dysentery, and smallpox. Thus the arrival of outsiders had devastating consequences. On the island of Hispaniola, where Columbus established the first Spanish settlement in the New World, the Tainos numbered between 300,000 and 400,000 in 1492 but had virtually disappeared 50 years later. In Mexico, within 50 years after the arrival of the Spaniards, the region's population had fallen by 90 percent, and in this case millions, not tens of thousands, were victimized.

Such devastation not only made it relatively easy for the Europeans to conquer or displace the Native Americans but also led to the enslavement of Africans in the New World. The massive die-offs created labor shortages that Europeans overcame by importing enslaved Africans. Before the transatlantic slave trade ended, as many as 11 million Africans had been sold into slavery in the Americas, and millions more died in slave raids and in the holds of slave ships crossing the Atlantic.

# Africa's Diversity Through Visitors' Eyes

## BACKGROUND

Writing Africa's early history is a daunting task. Because traditional non-Muslim and non-Christian societies in Africa left no written records, historians have had to rely on oral traditions, artifacts, rare travelers' accounts, and insights from the work of linguists, archeologists, and anthropologists. They have been able to reconstruct the broad outlines of Africa's early political and cultural development, but with many gaps and few details. The amount of available source material increases dramatically with the arrival of Europeans, who produced a trove of letters, diaries, memoirs, books, and business records pertaining to Africa. The utility of such records is limited by the cultural and religious biases of the Europeans and by the fact that they rarely traveled beyond Africa's coasts. Nonetheless, if used with care, the observations and commentaries of Europeans can provide much information about Africa's past.

Three of the four selections in this section were written by Europeans and one was written by a person who was born in Europe but moved to Africa at an early age. Describing societies in different parts of Africa, they provide insights into the rich diversity of African politics, religion, and society in the sixteenth and seventeenth centuries.

## THE SOURCES

The author of our first source, Leo Africanus, was born in 1494 as Al-Hassan ibn-Muhammad al Wazzan al-Fasi into a Muslim family in Granada, the last Muslim foothold in Spain. He was raised in Fez (in present-day Morocco), however, and entered the service of the sultan of Fez after studying Islamic law. His diplomatic and commercial missions for the sultan involved travel across North Africa and to places as far away as the Arabian Peninsula, Istanbul, and the eastern Mediterranean. After his capture by Spanish privateers, he was taken to Rome, became a Christian, and was given a new name, Giovanni Leo, by no less a figure than Pope Leo X. He remained in Italy for several years and came to be known as Leo Africanus after the book he completed in 1526, *The History and Description of Africa,* was published in a Latin version. Sometime after 1530, he moved to Tunis, in north Africa, returned to the fold of Islam, and died there in 1554.

In the following excerpts, Leo describes several places in the Western Sudan, a belt of dry grassland running from the Atlantic coast to the region of present-day eastern Nigeria. They include Gao, the capital of the Songhai Empire, the dominant state in the region, and Timbuktu, which was ruled by a governor in the name of the Songhai emperor. He also describes what was left of Mali, the dominant political power in the region before the rise of Songhai, and the kingdom of Bornu, which had recently displaced Kanem as the most powerful state in the region east of Songhai (see map on p. 68).

Our second excerpt is a description of the Kingdom of Benin, on Africa's Guinea Coast, taken from a Dutch work, *An Accurate Description of the Regions of Africa* (1668). Its author, Olfert Dapper (ca. 1635–1689), published a number of books describing regions where the Dutch carried on trade, all without his leaving the Netherlands. The section of his book on early seventeenth-century Benin includes information from interviews with Dutch merchants, who had begun trading in Africa in the early 1600s, and draws heavily on the records of the Dutch West India Company, a chartered company of Dutch merchants that established trading posts on the Gold Coast, the Slave Coast, and Angola. Historians have drawn extensively on Dapper's book. The Olfert Dapper Foundation, which seeks to foster interest in West African culture and maintains a museum of African art in Paris (the Musée Dapper), is named in his honor.

Our third source, which describes the newly created kingdom of Mutapa (to the Portuguese, Monomotapa) in southeastern Africa, is taken from the *Chronicle of King Manuel the Fortunate* by Damião de Góis (1502–1574). It recounts the principal events of Portuguese history during Manuel's reign (1495–1525), with an emphasis on the founding of Portugal's empire in Africa and Asia. De Góis never visited Africa, and instead found his information in the Portuguese royal archives, to which he had access after he was appointed Keeper of the Archives and Chronicler of the Kingdom in 1546. The archives contained a rich body of letters, documents, and reports on which de Góis based his description of Mutapa.

Our fourth source is written by Duarte Barbosa (ca. 1480–1521), a native of Lisbon, who between 1500 and 1516 played a major role in establishing Portugal's African/Asian empire. In addition to serving as an official in India and an agent for a number of Portuguese merchants, he mastered several Asian languages and served as a translator for Afonso d'Albuquerque in his dealings with the people of Melaka (see source 1). In the 1510s he returned to Portugal, where he completed his *Account of the Countries Bordering on the Indian Ocean and their Inhabitants*. The book describes dozens of political entities that Duarte had visited on his trips between Portugal and India.

## QUESTIONS FOR ANALYSIS

1. What insights do these documents provide into the biases and prejudices of their authors? In what terms do they describe the Africans and African societies they discuss?
2. What can be learned from these sources about the levels of technology in African societies?
3. What can be learned about the levels of literacy and scholarship in these particular societies?
4. In their descriptions of African governments, what information do these sources provide about the power of kings; military organization; legal institutions; and bureaucratic structure?
5. In terms of trade, what goods did Africans export and import? With whom did they trade? To what extent was Africa a part of the global economy?
6. Overall, are you more struck by the similarities or the diversity of the societies described in these four sources?

EUROPE

Azores

Madeira
Islands

Canary
Islands

Cape
Verde
Islands

Constantinople

Black Sea

Caspian Sea

PERSIA

Algiers

Tangier
Fez

Tunis

Mediterranean Sea

Tripoli

Alexandria

Cairo

Basra

Persian Gulf

Marrakech

MOROCCO

ARABIA

Medina

Tropic of Cancer

Muscat
OMAN

Taghaza

S A H A R A

Nile R.

Mecca

Aden

Gulf of Aden

Wadane

Saint-
Louis

Timbuktu

Gao

Agades

KANEM-
BORNO

Aksum

WOLOF

SENEGAMBIA

MALI

SONGHAI

Lake
Chad

ETHIOPIA

Koumbi
GHANA

Jenne

Niger R.

Sokoto

Katsina

Niani

SAHEL

HAUSALAND

Kano

N'gazargamu

Zaria

AFRICA

Sierra
Leone

YORUBA

OYO

DAHOMEY

BAULE ASHANTE

BENIN

AGNI

Gold Coast

Slave Coast

IGBO

Calabar

Bonny

Brass

To India

São Tomé

0° Equator

LOANGO

BUGANDA

GREAT
LAKES

SWAHILI COAST

INDIAN
OCEAN

Malindi

Mombasa
Pemba
Zanzibar

ATLANTIC
OCEAN

LUBA

KONGO

LUNDA

Luanda

Kilwa

NDONGO

Benguela

Zambezi R.

MOZAMBIQUE

MADAGASCAR

20°S

MUTAPA
(MONOMOTAPA)

Great Zimbabwe

Sofala

Tropic of Capricorn

NAMIB DESERT

KALAHARI
DESERT

KHOISAN

ZULU

SOUTH
AFRICA

Cape
Town
(founded
1650)

XHOSA

Cape of
Good Hope

Trans-Saharan trade route
Portuguese voyages before 1460
Portuguese voyages after 1460
Main coastal trading areas

0    400   800 Km.

0    400   800 Mi.

## 1 • Leo Africanus, History and Description of Africa

### The Kingdom of Mali

In this kingdom there is a large and ample village containing more than six thousand families, and named Mali, which is also the name of the whole kingdom. . . . The region itself yields great abundance of wheat, meat and cotton. Here are many craftsmen and merchants in all places: and yet the king honorably entertains all strangers. The inhabitants are rich and have plenty of merchandise. Here is a great number of temples, clergymen, and teachers, who read their lectures in the mosques because they have no colleges at all. . . .

### The City of Timbuktu

All its houses are . . . cottages, built of mud and covered with thatch. However, there is a most stately mosque to be seen, whose walls are made of stone and lime, and a princely palace also constructed by the highly skilled craftsmen of Granada.[1] Here there are many shops of artisans and merchants, especially of those who weave linen and cotton, and here Barbary [north African] merchants bring European cloth. The inhabitants, and especially resident foreigners, are exceedingly rich, since the present king [a vassal of the Songhai emperor] married both of his daughters to rich merchants. Here are many wells, containing sweet water. Whenever the Niger River overflows, they carry the water into town by means of sluices. This region yields great quantities of grain, cattle, milk, and butter, but salt is very scarce here, for it is brought here by land from Taghaza,[2] which is five hundred miles away. . . .

The rich king of Timbuktu . . . keeps a magnificent and well-furnished court. When he travels anywhere, he rides upon a camel, which is led by some of his noblemen. He does so likewise when going to war; and all his soldiers ride upon horses. Whoever wishes to speak to this king must first of all fall down before his feet and then taking up earth must sprinkle it on his own head and shoulders. . . . [The king] always has under arms 3,000 horsemen and a great number of foot soldiers who shoot poisoned arrows. They often skirmish with those who refuse to pay tribute and whomever they capture they sell as slaves to the merchants of Timbuktu. . . . Their best horses are brought out of North Africa. . . .

Here are great numbers of religious teachers, judges, scholars and other learned persons, who are bountifully maintained at the king's expense. Here too are brought various manuscripts or written books from Barbary, which are sold for more money than any other merchandise.

The coin of Timbuktu is gold, without any stamp or inscription, but in matters of small value they use certain shells from the kingdom of Persia.[3] . . .

The inhabitants are gentle and cheerful and spend a great part of the night in singing and dancing throughout the city streets. They keep large numbers of male and female slaves . . .

### The Town and Kingdom of Gao

Here are very rich merchants and to here journey large numbers of Negroes who purchase cloth from Barbary and Europe. . . . Here also is a certain place where slaves are sold, especially upon those days when merchants assemble. . . .

---

*Source:* Robert Brown, ed., *The History and Description of Africa* (London: The Hakluyt Society, 1896), Vol. 3, pp. 823–827, 832–834.

[1] Granada was the last Muslim emirate to fall to Spain in 1492.

[2] Founded in the tenth century, Taghaza was an important salt-mining center located in the northernmost region of present-day Mali.

[3] The reference is to cowrie shells, harvested in the Indian Ocean and widely used as currency in parts of Asia and Africa.

The king of this region has a certain private palace in which he keeps a large number of concubines and slaves, who are watched by eunuchs. To guard his person he maintains a sufficient troop of horsemen and foot soldiers. Between the first gate of the palace and the inner part, there is a walled enclosure wherein the king personally decides all of his subjects' controversies. Although the king is most diligent in this regard and conducts all business in these matters, he has in his company counselors and such other officers as his secretaries, treasurers, stewards and auditors.

It is a wonder to see the quality of merchandise that is daily brought here and how costly and sumptuous everything is. Horses purchased in Europe for ten ducats[4] are sold here for forty and sometimes fifty ducats apiece. There is no European cloth so coarse as to sell for less than four ducats an ell. If it is anywhere near fine quality, they will give fifteen ducats for an ell, and an ell of the scarlet of Venice or of Turkish cloth is here worth thirty ducats. A sword is here valued at three or four crowns[5] and likewise are spears, bridles and similar commodities, and spices are all sold at a high rate. . . .

The rest of this kingdom contains nothing but villages and hamlets inhabited by herdsmen and shepherds, who in winter cover their bodies with the skins of animals, but in summer go naked, save for their private parts. . . . They are an ignorant and rude people, and you will scarcely find one learned person in the square of a hundred miles. They are continually burdened by heavy taxes; to the point that they scarcely have anything left on which to live.

## The Kingdom of Borno

They have a most powerful prince. . . . He has in readiness as many as three thousand horsemen and a huge number of foot soldiers; for all his subjects are so obedient to him, that whenever he commands them, they will arm themselves and will follow him wherever he leads them. They pay him no tribute except tithes on their grain; neither does the king have any revenues to support his state except the spoils he gets from his enemies by frequent invasions and assaults. He is in a state of perpetual hostility with a certain people who live beyond the desert . . . who in times past marching with a huge army of footsoldiers over the said desert, devastated a great part of the Kingdom of Borno. Whereupon the king sent for the merchants of Barbary and ordered them to bring him a great store of horses: for in this country they exchange horses for slaves, and sometimes give fifteen or twenty slaves for a horse. And by this means there were a great many horses bought. . . .

---

[4]A *ducat* is an Italian coin; an *ell* is a measurement of length, approximately 45 inches.

[5]A gold coin worth substantially more than a ducat.

---

## 2 • Olfert Dapper, An Accurate Description of the Regions of Africa

Commercial dealings between foreigners and the inhabitants take place up the river Benin beside the village of Gotton,[1] which the Dutch reach in longboats and yachts. Such trade cannot take place without the King's permission. The King chooses certain *fiadors*[2] and merchants, and they alone are allowed to approach the Europeans, whom they call *"blanken"* [Whites]. Those enlisted as soldiers are wholly forbidden to trade with the white men;

---

Source: Olfert Dapper, *Description of Africa* (Madison, WI: African Studies Program, 1998).

[1]A village near Benin City where commercial transactions took place. Also known as Ughoton.

[2]This Dutch word is derived from the Portuguese word *feador*, or overseer. It refers to high appointed officials (sometimes translated as "major chiefs") who served as councilors to the king (oba) and in this case brokers between European and Beninese merchants.

govern the realm the King appoints . . . three
councilors called *fiadors*. . . . These are the
senior in the land next to the King; for above
nobody is closer to the King apart from the
-marshal [high military commander] and the
's mother. Each of them has authority over one
er, or ward, of the town, and they derive large
ts from this. In the same manner every town
verned by a certain number of nobles . . . who
esponsible for trying all cases not involving
oral punishment and for condemning the ac-
d man to certain punishments according to the
t of his misdeeds. But cases involving corpo-
unishment are referred to Great Benin where
igh court is and are tried there, the court sits
y day. Yet often the judges are bought over with
es of cowries without the King's knowledge.

The King comes out of his court only once
a year on an established feast-day and appears
before the populace on horseback, beautifully
adorned with all kinds of royal decorations and
in the company of three or four hundred noblemen, either on foot or on horseback, with many
players in front and behind making merry on all
kinds of instruments. He does not ride far, but
turns after a small distance and heads again for the
court. Then the King has certain tame leopards,
which he keeps for his amusement, paraded on
chains. . . . On this holiday ten, twelve, thirteen or
more slaves are killed by strangling or decapitation
in the King's honor. For they believe that these
slaves, after they have been dead a little while,
enter another land where they return to life and
live more pleasantly. . . .

## Damião de Góis, *Chronicle of King nuel the Fortunate*

king . . . is a great lord, because according to
rt his dominions are more than eight hundred
ues[1] in circumference, besides the lands of sev-
kings and lords who obey him and pay him a
ute of gold, the love of which had already been
arted to them many years before this time by
Moors [Muslims] who lived among them. . . .
ll this kingdom . . . is most abundant in provi-
s, fruits, and cattle; and there are such great
ls of wild elephants there that not a year passes
vhich the number killed by those who hunt
n does not amount to four or five thousand,
which means a large quantity of ivory is sent to
a. The land abounds in gold, which is found in
t quantity in mines, rivers, and marshy ground;
e of the mines are situated in the kingdom of
ua, the king of which is a vassal of the king. . . .

The inhabitants of the country are black with
woolly hair, and are commonly called Kaffirs.[2] They
do not make or worship idols, but believe in one
God, the creator of all things, whom they adore and
to whom they pray. . . . They have certain feast days
in their religion, among others the day on which
their king was born. No crime is punished among
them with such rigor as is witchcraft: all sorcerers
being executed by law, not one receiving pardon. . . .

This king . . . is served on bended knees with
reverence. When he drinks, coughs, or sighs, every
person in the house wishes him well in a loud
voice, and the same thing is done by those outside
the house, the word being passed . . . all round the
town, so that it is known that the king has drunk,
or coughed, or sighed. In this kingdom there are
no doors to the houses, with the exception of
those of the lords and principal persons, to whom
this privilege is granted by the king. They say that
houses are built with doors for fear of thieves and

---

ce: George McCall Theal, *Records of South-Eastern Africa*,
3 (Cape Town: C. Struik Ltd., for the government of
Cape Colony, 1899), pp. 128–131.
easure of length, anywhere from three to five miles.

[2]Based on the Arab word *kafir*, meaning black, *kaffir* was
used to refer to the Bantu-speaking peoples of southeast
Africa and more generally to non-Muslim black Africans.

indeed they dare not so much as enter the warehouse, let alone buy any European goods from
them. . . . Equally a merchant or *fiador* may not
take part in war, for each must remain within the
bounds of his occupation. . . .

Whenever a ship with its cargo has anchored on
this coast a *passadoor* [messenger] is sent to inform
the King, and he calls two or three *fiadors*, accompanied by twenty or thirty *veeljes* [merchants],
who are commanded to go down and trade with
the Whites. They go forthwith and travel posthaste
overland to Gotton, commandeering on their way
as many canoes and oarsmen as they require, taking them away everywhere, even when the owners
need them for themselves. If the owners complain
they remind them of the King and ask whether
they are not the King's slaves and whether all
their property does not belong to the King; they
command them to be silent in the future . . . and
threaten that they will be sent court. When they
[the merchants] arrive in Gotton . . . they choose
the best houses and dwellings and, without asking
the owners' leave, and use them to house all their
goods. . . . Also the owner is often obliged to cook
for them on the first day without receiving anything for his pains.

Whenever these *fiadors* come for the first visit
to the warehouses they are magnificently dressed,
wearing jasper necklaces; and kneeling, they bring
greetings from their king, from his mother, and
from the greatest *fiadors*, in whose names they
bring some gifts of food. With much ceremony
they then inquire about the state of the country
and the wars against their [the Whites'] enemies
and similar things. Afterwards there is drinking
and leave-taking, without there having been any
mention of trade. On the following days they return with a request to see the newly-arrived merchandise and a price is fixed.

The wares which the Ho[...]
ropeans acquire in exchang[...]
lands are cotton cloths, . . [...]
(none but women, because [...]
have men leave the country [...]
and . . . *akori*, a kind of blue [...]
by diving, because it grows, [...]
treelike upon stony groun[...]
people buy this *akori*, which [...]
how to polish into long blu[...]
Blacks of the Gold Coast.[3] [...]
them in their hair for the de[...]

In exchange for these thing[...]
the Blacks, among the wares [...]
lowing: gold and silver broca[...]
white cloth with a red stripe [...]
of fine cotton; linen; orang[...]
*paste* [beads]; red velvet; bras[...]
lavender and violet beads; co[...]
als; . . . fabrics with large flo[...]
and flowered; red glass earri[...]
mirrors; crystal beads; East I[...]
are used by them instead of n[...]

The larger cloths, particula[...]
our people re-sell on the Gol[...]
are greatly in demand; but th[...]
traded most in the region of C[...]

• • •

The weapons of these people [...]
bows, assegais,[5] and poisoned [...]
they maintain good order an[...]
nobody may yield a step even [...]
fore his eyes.

The king of Benin rules with [...]
power, and calls all his subjec[...]
what great nobles they may be [...]
stretches over many large an[...]
villages. . . . Also several kingd[...]

---

[3]A region of present-day Ghana, colonized by the Dutch
in 1598.

[4]Richly decorated fabrics often made [...]
gold and silver thread.
[5]An iron-tipped wooden spear.

malefactors, from whom it is the king's duty to protect his people and above all the poor. The houses are all built of wattles[3] plastered with clay.

The said king uses two insignia, one being a small hoe with an ivory point, which he always wears in his belt to show his subjects that they should cultivate and profit by the land . . . ; the other consists of two assegais [spears], showing that with one the king administers justice and with the other defends his people. He constantly keeps at his court all the sons of the kings and lords who are his vassals, the former that they may have filial affection for him, and the latter that their fathers may not rise against him with the lands which they hold from him. Whether in time of peace or war he always maintains a large standing army under

the command of Captain Zono to keep the land in a state of peace and to prevent the lords and kings who are subject to him from rising in rebellion.

Every year he sends a number of his chief courtiers through all his kingdoms and dominions to light new fires. . . . Each of these courtiers on reaching the houses of the kings and lords of the cities and towns commands all the fires in the place to be put out in the king's name, and after they are extinguished they all come as a sign of obedience and take fire from him, and anyone who does not do so is looked upon as a traitor and rebel, and the king commands him to be punished as such. If the offender is a powerful person, or represents a powerful town, the king sends the captain Zono against him, who is always present in the camp to attend to these matters.

[3]Poles interwoven with small branches or reeds.

## 4 • Duarte Barbosa, *Account of the Countries Bordering on the Indian Ocean and Their Inhabitants*

### Kilwa

Going along the coast, . . . there is an island hard by the mainland which is called Kilwa, on which is a Moorish [Muslim] town with many fair houses of stone and mortar, with many windows after our fashion, very well arranged in streets, with many flat roofs. The doors are of wood, well carved, with excellent joinery. . . . It has a Moorish king over it. From this place they trade with Sofala, from which they bring back gold, and from here they spread all over Arabia. . . . Of the Moors there are some fair and some black; they are finely clad in many rich garments of gold and silk and cotton, and the women as well; also with much gold and silver in chains and bracelets, which they wear on their legs and arms; and many jeweled earrings in their ears. . . .

### Mombasa

Further on, along the coast toward India, there is an island hard by the mainland, on which is a town called Mombasa. It is a very fair place, with lofty stone and mortar houses, well aligned in streets after the fashions of Kilwa. The wood is well-fitted with excellent joiner's work. It has its own king, himself a Moor. . . . This is a place of great trade, and has a good harbor, in which are always moored craft of many kinds and also great ships, both of those which come from Sofala[1] and those which go there, and others which come from the great kingdom of Cambay and from Malindi; others which sail to the islands of Zanzibar. . . .

### Mafia, Zanzibar, and Pemba

[These] are inhabited by Moors; they are very fertile islands, with plenty of provisions, rice, millet, and meat, and abundant oranges, lemons, and citrons. All the mountains are full of them; they produce

*Source:* Mansel Longworth Dames, ed., *The Book of Duarte Barbosa* (London: Hakluyt Society, 1918), pp. 6–8, 17, 18, 20–22, 26–28, 31, 39–42.

[1]Malindi and Sofala are east African port cities; Cambay is a major Indian port.

many sugar canes, but do not know how to make sugar. These islands have their kings. The inhabitants trade with the mainland with their provisions and fruits; they have small vessels, very loosely and badly made, without decks, and with a single mast; all their planks are sewn together with cords of reed or matting, and the sails are of palm mats. They are very feeble people, with very few and despicable weapons. In these islands they live in great luxury and abundance. . . . Their wives adorn themselves with many jewels of gold from Sofala, and silver, in chains, earrings, bracelets, and ankle rings, and are dressed in silk stuffs: and they have many mosques. . . .

## Mogodishu

Proceeding coastwise towards the Red Sea there is a very great Moorish town called Mogodishu; it has a king over it; the place has much trade in diverse kinds, by reason whereof many ships come hither from the great kingdom of Cambay, bringing great plenty of cloths of many sorts, and diverse other wares, also spices. And they carry away much gold, ivory, wax and many other things, whereby they make exceeding great profits in their dealings. . . .

They speak Arabic. The men are for the most part brown and black, but a few are fair. They have but few weapons, yet they use poisons on their arrows to defend themselves against their enemies.

## Kingdom of Prester John[2]

. . . This kingdom is very large and peopled with many cities, towns, and villages, with many inhabitants, and it has many kings subject to it and tributary kings. And in their country there are many who live in the fields and mountains, like Bedouins:[3] they are black men; very well made: they have many horses, and make use of them, and are good riders, and there are great sportsmen and hunters amongst them. These people are Christians of the doctrine of the blessed Saint Bartholomew.[4] . . . Many of them are deficient in our true faith, because the country is very large, and whilst in the principal city of Babel Melech,[5] where Prester John resides, they may be Christians, in many other distant parts they live in error and without being taught; so that they are only Christians in name. . . .

In this city [Babel Melech] a great feast takes place in August, for which so many kings and nobles come together, and so many people that they are innumerable: and they take an image out of a church, which is believed to be that of Our Lady, or that of St. Bartholomew, which image is of gold and of the size of a man; its eyes are of very large and beautiful rubies of great value, and the whole of it is adorned with many precious stones, and placing it in a great carriage of gold, they carry it in procession with very great veneration and ceremony, and Prester John goes in front of this carriage in another gold carriage very richly dressed in cloth of gold with much jewelry. And they begin to go out thus in the morning, and go in procession through all the city with much music of all sorts of instruments, until the evening, when they go home. And so many people throng to this procession, that in order to arrive at the carriage of the image many die of being squeezed and suffocated; and those who die in this way are held as saints and martyrs; and many old men and old women go with a good will to die in this manner.

---

[2]Prester John ("Priest John") is a name commonly used by the Portuguese for the king of Ethiopia in the sixteenth century. This usage was based on their assumption that they had finally made contact with the Christian king in the east long thought by Europeans to be a potential ally against Islam.
[3]Nomadic tribes of the Arabian, Syrian, or north African deserts.
[4]According to tradition, St. Bartholomew, one of Jesus' twelve disciples, introduced Christianity to Ethiopia in the first century C.E.

[5]Babel Melech is a Portuguese version of the Arabic term *Bab-el-Malik*, the "king's court." Duarte may be referring to Axum, the historic capital of the ancient kingdom of Axum. If so, he has misrepresented its importance. Although a significant religious center and the place where kings often held their coronation rituals, it was not a "capital city" in any sense. The royal court, consisting of thousands of nobles, soldiers, and retainers, moved from place to place every three or four months after exhausting food supplies in the surrounding region.

# Africans and the Portuguese

When the Portuguese began sending ships into the Atlantic to explore Africa's off-shore islands and west coast in the early 1400s, their goals were shaped by their limited and often inaccurate perceptions of Africa. They knew about Madeira and the Canary Islands, which French, Spanish, and Genoese mariners had visited in the late 1300s and perhaps even earlier. They knew that the North African coast was a Muslim stronghold, and that beyond the coast lay a vast desert. They also were convinced that south of the desert was a region rich in gold and pepper. Many also believed that in eastern Africa there existed a potential ally in the struggle against Islam—a Christian kingdom ruled by Prester John, whose existence had intrigued Europeans since the twelfth century. Based on this meager information and legend, the Portuguese gambled that their voyages down the African coast would enable them to bypass Muslim traders in North Africa and give them direct access to Africa's gold and pepper. They also dreamed of joining with Prester John in a new crusade against their common Muslim enemy.

In time, the Portuguese expanded their knowledge of Africa, and as they did, some of their original goals were abandoned and new ones emerged. They did find a Christian kingdom in eastern Africa, but it was not the realm of Prester John, but rather the kingdom of Ethiopia, a weak state vulnerable to attack by its neighbors. Elsewhere in Africa they discovered economic opportunities beyond trading for gold, pepper, and ivory. Beginning in the 1400s, purchasing slaves in Africa and transporting and reselling them throughout the Atlantic world became a major Portuguese enterprise.

In 1498, the Portuguese made an even more important discovery: that by sailing around Africa's southern tip, they could reach the rich markets of Asia by an all-ocean route. Having direct access to Asian luxury goods and spices generated opportunities for profits that trade in African goods could never match. From the 1500s onward the Portuguese came to view Africa mainly as a source of slaves for the New World and a place to sail around in order to reach Asia.

# Slavery and the Slave Trade in the Kingdom of Kongo

## 17 • CORRESPONDENCE BETWEEN NZINGA MBEMBA (AFONSO I), KING OF KONGO, AND JOÃO III, KING OF PORTUGAL

Interactions between Portugal and Kongo, a kingdom south of the Congo River on Africa's west coast, began in the 1480s when the Portuguese explorer Diogo Cão, in his efforts to circumnavigate Africa, twice dropped anchor at the mouth of the Congo River and made contact with Nzinga a Nkuwa, the king of Kongo. Their dealings were cordial at first. A number of Kongolese, including the king's son, accompanied Cão on his return trips to Portugal, where they learned European ways; the Portuguese soldiers who remained in Kongo fought for the king against rebellious nobles. The king and his nobility were intrigued by Christianity, and the Portuguese, of course, were eager to make converts. Both sides hoped to profit from trade. In 1491 King João II of Portugal dispatched to Kongo a contingent of priests, artisans, women (who were to teach "housekeeping"), soldiers, and officials, who brought with them gunpowder weapons and various European goods they hoped to exchange for ivory, copper, and slaves. In response the king agreed to an alliance with the Portuguese, and he, his son, and a number of prominent nobles took Portuguese names and were baptized as Catholics.

The king's son, Nzinga Mbemba, who took the name Afonso after his baptism, became king in 1506, and like his father promoted cooperation with the Portuguese. He proclaimed Christianity the state religion and imitated the trappings of Portuguese royalty. European firearms, horses, and cattle were introduced, regular trade began, and Afonso dreamed of achieving a powerful and prosperous kingdom with Portuguese help. By the mid-1520s, however, the slave trade threatened the Portuguese–Kongo alliance. Slaves, most of whom were captured in slave raids in surrounding regions, were widely owned in Kongo, and the king at first had no reservations about selling such slaves to the Portuguese in exchange for money and European goods. These goods, in turn, were distributed to nobles to ensure their loyalty to the king. This system broke down, however, in the 1510s and 1520s when Portuguese demand for slaves sharply increased. In Afonso's view, this had a number of harmful results, not the least of which was the loss of his monopoly on the sale of slaves. He expressed his concerns in two letters to King João III of Portugal in July and October 1526. Later, perhaps not until 1529, the king responded. At some point the two sides reached an agreement on how the slave markets should be organized and run, and in the 1530s, 4,000 to 5,000 slaves were deported from Kongo every year.

## QUESTIONS FOR ANALYSIS

1. According to Afonso, how has the Portuguese presence damaged his kingdom?
2. What do the letters reveal about the workings of the slave trade in the kingdom? Who participated in it?
3. What do the letters reveal about Afonso's attitude toward slavery?
4. What steps does Afonso propose to deal with the problems related to the slave trade?
5. How would you characterize Afonso's attitude toward the power and authority of the king of Portugal? Does he consider himself inferior to the Portuguese king or his equal?
6. What arguments does João III make to dissuade Afonso from ending the slave trade?
7. How would you characterize João III's attitude toward Afonso?

## King Afonso to King João III, July 6, 1526

Sir, Your Highness should know how our Kingdom is being lost in so many ways that it is convenient to provide for the necessary remedy, since this is caused by the excessive freedom given by your agents and officials to the men and merchants who are allowed to come to this Kingdom to set up shops with goods and many things which have been prohibited by us, and which they spread throughout our . . . Kingdoms and Domains in such an abundance that many of our vassals, whom we had in obedience, do not comply because they have the things in greater abundance than we ourselves; and it was with these things that we had them content and subjected under our vassalage and jurisdiction, so it is doing a great harm not only to the service of God, but the security and peace of our Kingdoms and State as well.

And we cannot reckon how great the damage is, since the mentioned merchants are taking every day our natives, sons of the land and the sons of our noblemen and vassals and our relatives, because the thieves and men of bad conscience grab them wishing to have the things and wares of this Kingdom which they are ambitious of; they grab them and get them to be sold; and so great, Sir, is the corruption and licentiousness that our country is being completely depopulated, and Your Highness should not agree with this nor accept. . . . And to avoid it we need from [your] Kingdom no more than some priests and a few people to teach in schools, and no other goods except wine and flour for the holy sacrament. That is why we beg of Your Highness to help and assist us in this matter, commanding your agents that they should not send here either merchants or wares, because it is *our will that in these Kingdoms there should not be any trade of slaves*

*nor outlet for them.* Concerning what is referred [to] above, again we beg of Your Highness to agree with it, since otherwise we cannot remedy such an obvious damage.

## King Afonso to King João III, October 26, 1526

Sir, . . . as the peace and the health of our Kingdom depend on us, . . . it happens that we have continuously many and different diseases which put us very often in such a weakness that we reach almost the last extreme; and the same happens to our children, relatives and people owing to the lack in this country of physicians and surgeons who might know how to cure properly such diseases. And as we have neither pharmacies nor drugs which might help us . . . , many of those who had been already confirmed and instructed in the holy faith of Our Lord Jesus Christ perish and die; and the rest of the people [largely] cure themselves with herbs and sticks and other ancient methods, so that they put all their faith in the mentioned herbs and ceremonies if they live, and believe that they are saved if they die; and this is not much in the service of God.

And to avoid such a great error and inconvenience, . . . we beg of you to be kind enough to send us two physicians and two apothecaries and one surgeon, so that they may come with their drug stores and all the necessary things to stay in our kingdoms, because we are in extreme need of them. . . .

Sir, . . . there is another great inconvenience, and this is that many of our people, keenly desirous as they are of the wares and things of your Kingdoms, which are brought here by your people, . . . seize many of our people, and very often . . . they kidnap even noblemen and the sons of noblemen, and our relatives, and take them to be sold to the

*Source:* From Bulliet, et al., *The Earth and Its Peoples,* 4E. © 2008 Cengage Learning.

white men who are in our Kingdoms . . . ; And as soon as they are taken by the white men they are immediately ironed and branded with fire, and when they are carried to be embarked [on ships], if they are caught by our guards, the whites allege that they have bought them but cannot say from whom, so that it is our duty to do justice and to restore to the freemen their freedom, but it cannot be done if your subjects feel offended, as they claim to be.

And to avoid such a great evil we passed a law so that any white man . . . wanting to purchase goods in any way should first inform three of our noblemen and officials of our court whom we rely upon in this matter, . . . who should investigate if the mentioned goods are captives or free men, and if cleared by them there will be no further doubt nor embargo for them to be taken and embarked. But if the white men do not comply with it they will lose the aforementioned goods.

## King João III to King Afonso (1529)

. . . You say in your letters that you do not want there to be any slave trade in your kingdom because it is depopulating your land. I can believe that you only say this as a result of the suffering that the Portuguese cause you, because I am told of the great size of Kongo and how it is so populated that it appears that not a single slave has left it. They also tell me that you send to buy them [slaves] outside [the country] and that you marry them and make them Christian, by which means the country is well populated. All this seems good to me and so now, with this order that the people carry and which you intend to send to the fairs [slave markets], it appears there will be many slaves.

As for those who are sold in this city, in order to know if they are natives or come from outside, there ought to be at the fair a designated place where they are sold and where there will be two of your servants who will know if the said slaves are sold in the houses in secret[1] and they shall not be sold without the said two men being present.

If I say now that I desire, as you request, that there shall not be any trade in slaves in your kingdom, I will still want to provide wheat and wine for use at Mass, and for this only one caravel[2] a year will be necessary. If this seems good to you, it shall be so. However, it does not seem to me to be to the honor of you or your kingdom because it would be more praiseworthy to draw each year from the Kongo 10,000 slaves and 10,000 *manilhas*[3] and as many tusks of ivory. If there is now to be no trade in the Kongo at all, and only one ship a year is to come there, this and more shall be as you desire.

You also sent to ask me for a ship, which astonishes me since all my ships are yours; and you ought to remember the ship which João de Melo lent you, who is still today owed 2,000 *reis*[4] for the costs he incurred, and in addition to this the suffering which you experienced in this. Nor do you take into account the [cost of the] boats, ships and [other] expenditures which my predecessors and I incurred on the sea, not to gain or acquire riches but only to secure the navigation and the route for sailors who make their living this way. It is these who profit by it, not the king, and this you have experienced yourself in your kingdom. . . .

If you do not want anyone to bring merchandise to Kongo, this would be against the custom of every country, because [merchandise] comes to Portugal from all parts of the world to be

---

*Source:* Malyn Newitt, ed. and trans. *The Portuguese in West Africa, 1415–1670* (Cambridge: Cambridge University Press, 2010), pp. 152, 153.
[1]By this is meant that the identity of slaves who are Kongolese is kept secret (i.e., "covered up").
[2]As opposed to the many dozens of ships currently involved.

[3]Copper or bronze rings, the size of bracelets or anklets, used as currency in Kongo and exported to Portugal.
[4]Afonso had requested a ship of his own to transport slaves. De Melo was the Portuguese agent in charge of administering the island of São Tomé. It is unclear why he was not paid for the ship he lent Afonso.

bought and sold. In this way the land is supplied with everything, and from Portugal, goods are sent to all parts; and if a *fidalgo* [a member of the nobility] of yours rebels against you and receives merchandise from Portugal, where will be your power and greatness because I well understand what constitutes your military strength and the fear that all have of you.

# Sixteenth-Century Benin Art and the Portuguese

## 18 • A BENIN-PORTUGUESE SALTCELLAR AND A BENIN WALL PLAQUE

Over many centuries, sub-Saharan Africans have produced some of the world's most impressive artworks, especially sculpture. Since at least 500 B.C.E., sculptors used clay, wood, ivory, and bronze to create masks, animal figures, images of rulers, and religious objects that had an important place in African society, politics, and religion. In some regions, bronze casting and ivory carving were royal monopolies carried on by highly trained professionals.

Such was the case in Benin, the kingdom described by Olfert Dapper in Multiple Voices I, source 2. The kingdom took shape in the 1200s and 1300s when a number of villages accepted the authority of an *oba*, or divine king, who ruled with a hierarchy of chiefs from the capital, Benin City. When the Portuguese arrived in 1485, Benin was a formidable military and commercial power and a center of state-sponsored artistic activity. Ivory carvers and bronze casters, organized into hereditary guilds, produced bronze heads, animal and human figures, pendants, plaques, musical instruments, drinking vessels, and armlets that were sold in trade or used in ceremonies.

The Portuguese affected Benin's art in two ways. First, their merchants, unable to establish Benin as a major source of slaves, turned to other commodities, including artworks, as objects of trade. Many ivory carvers received commissions from Portuguese merchants to produce condiment sets, utensils, and hunting horns for sale in Europe. Second, the Portuguese stimulated the production of artworks by purchasing African goods with copper, which was used to produce metallic plaques and sculptures.

The two sculptures in this section provide an opportunity to appreciate the skills of Benin artists while gaining insights into Beninese attitudes toward their rulers and Europeans. The ivory saltcellar was crafted in the sixteenth or early seventeenth century. It depicts two Portuguese officials (only one of which is visible in our photograph), flanked by two assistants. Above them is a Portuguese ship, with a man peering out of a crow's nest.

The second work is a sixteenth-century bronze plaque, approximately 18 inches high, to be displayed in the oba's palace. The central figure is the oba, who is holding a spear and shield. On each of his sides are three subordinate chiefs. The one on

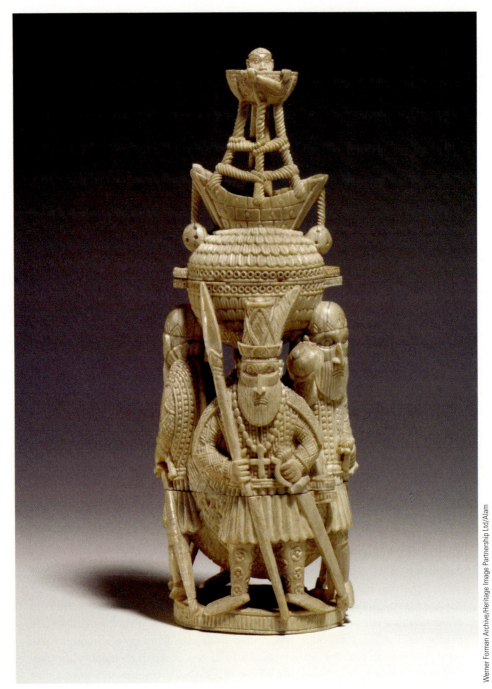

A Benin-Portuguese Saltcellar

A Benin Wall Plaque

the left is holding a C-shaped iron bar, used as currency in trade; the figure next to him is holding a ceremonial sword; the figure on the far right is playing a flute-like musical instrument. The two figures in the background, on each side of the oba's head, represent the Portuguese. In one hand, each figure holds a rectangular object, perhaps a glass mirror, and in the other hand what appears to be a goblet. These objects represent items the Portuguese traded for Beninese goods.

## QUESTIONS FOR ANALYSIS

1. In the saltcellar, notice what hangs around the standing figure's neck, what he holds in his hands, and his facial expression. What is the sculptor trying to communicate about this figure?
2. Why might this image of the Portuguese official have appealed to the European purchasers for which the carving was intended?
3. In the bronze plaque, what distinguishes the oba from the other figures? What details illustrate the oba's power and perhaps his divinity?
4. How does the representation of the oba compare to the description of his power in Dapper's *An Accurate Description of the Regions of Africa* (Multiple Voices I, source 2)?
5. What might you infer from these works about Portuguese–Benin relations and attitudes of the Beninese toward the Portuguese?

# Encounters in the Americas

The peoples who gradually populated the Americas began crossing the land bridge between northeast Siberia and present-day Alaska perhaps as early as 40,000 B.C.E. Then after 10,000 B.C.E., as the Ice Age ended and the oceans rose, this link between Asia and the Americas was submerged under the Bering Sea, and Native Americans were cut off from the rest of the world. Their isolation did not end until the arrival of Europeans in the wake of Columbus's discovery of the New World.

First on Caribbean islands, then in Mexico and Peru, and ultimately throughout the Americas, Native Americans faced the decision to resist, cooperate with, or retreat from the new European arrivals. Cooperation meant trade, and sometimes took the form of military alliances. In Mexico, for example, thousands of warriors fought on Cortés's side against their hated enemy, the Aztecs, and in North America the Hurons allied with the French and the Iroquois allied with the Dutch and the English in a long series of wars.

Many Native Americans chose to resist, however, and did so well into the nineteenth century. In Mexico and Peru, such resistance resulted in military defeat with Cortés's conquest of the Aztec Empire between 1519 and 1521 and Pizarro's overthrow of the Inca Empire between 1531 and 1533. In North America, Indian raids inflicted casualties and damage on early European settlements, but the colonists' reprisals were equally bloody and destructive, and in the Pequot War (1637) in Connecticut and the Algonquin-Dutch wars (1643–1645) in present-day New York and New Jersey, the Indians were routed and massacred. The long-term outcome of their resistance was never in doubt: The Europeans' single-mindedness and weaponry when combined with the toll of epidemics from Old World diseases made their victory inevitable.

# The Battle for Tenochtitlan

## 19 • BERNARDINO DE SAHAGÚN, GENERAL HISTORY OF THE THINGS OF NEW SPAIN

Bernardino de Sahagún (ca. 1499–1590), a Franciscan friar, was one of the earliest Spanish missionaries in Mexico, arriving in 1529. He soon developed a keen interest in the culture of the peoples of Mexico, for whom he had deep affection and respect. Having mastered Nahuatl, the language spoken by the Aztecs and other central Mexican peoples, in the 1540s he began to collect oral and pictorial information about Mexican culture. The result was his *General History of the Things of New Spain,* a major source of information about Mexico at the time of the conquest. Some Spaniards considered Sahagún's work dangerous because they feared his efforts to preserve the memory of native culture threatened their plans to exploit and Christianize the Indians. Thus in 1578, his writings were confiscated and sent to Spain, where they remained in an archive until discovered and published in the nineteenth century.

The following selection comes from Book Twelve of the *General History.* Based on interviews with Aztecs who had lived through the conquest some 25 years earlier, it recounts the conquest from the time Cortés arrived on the Mexican coast in April 1519 until the days following the Aztecs' capitulation in August 1521. Most scholars agree that it accurately portrays the events of the conquest from an Aztec perspective.

The excerpt begins in November 1519, by which time the Spaniards had allied with the Tlaxcalans, the Aztecs' bitter enemies, and were leaving Cholula, a city the Spaniards and their allies had sacked and looted because of its leaders' lack of cooperation. They were on their way to Tenochtitlan, the splendid Aztec capital on Lake Texcoco (spelled Tetzcoco in the reading), for an anticipated meeting with Emperor Moctezuma.

### QUESTIONS FOR ANALYSIS

1. What does the source reveal about the motives of the Spaniards and their Indian allies for their attack on the Aztecs?
2. What was Moctezuma's strategy for dealing with the Spaniards? Why did it fail?
3. Aside from their firearms, what other military advantages did the Spaniards have over their opponents?

4. On several occasions, the Aztecs routed the Spaniards. What explains these Aztec victories?
5. How did the Aztec view of war differ from that of the Spaniards?
6. What does the source reveal about Aztec religious beliefs and values?

---

After the dying in Cholula, the Spaniards set off on their way to Mexico,[1] coming gathered and bunched, raising dust. . . . Their iron lances and halberds[2] . . . seemed to sparkle and their iron swords were curved like a stream of water. . . . Some of them came wearing iron all over, turned into iron beings, gleaming, so that they . . . were generally seen with fear and dread. . . .

Thereupon Moteucçoma[3] named and sent noblemen and a great many other agents of his . . . to go meet [Cortés] . . . at Quauhtechcac. They gave [the Spaniards] golden banners, banners of precious feathers, and golden necklaces. And when they had given the things to them, they seemed to smile, to rejoice and to be very happy. Like monkeys they grabbed the gold. It was as though their hearts were put to rest, brightened, freshened. For gold was what they greatly thirsted for; they were gluttonous for it, starved for it, piggishly wanting it. They came lifting up the golden banners, waving them from side to side, showing them to each other. They seemed to babble; what they said to each other was in a babbling tongue. . . .

Another group of messengers—rainmakers, witches, and priests—had also gone out for an encounter, but nowhere were they able to do anything or to get sight of [the Spaniards]; they did not hit their target, they did not find the people they were looking for, they were not sufficient. . . .

---

> Cortés and his entourage continue their march.

---

And in a vain attempt Moteucçoma ordered that the roads and highways be closed off in various places. They planted magueys[4] in the road coming straight to Mexico here, directing them instead on the road going to Tetzcoco. . . . The Spaniards immediately recognized it, they saw that they had just blocked it, and they disregarded it. They took the magueys, kicked them far away, sent them flying. . . .

Then they set out in this direction, about to enter Mexico here. Then they all dressed and equipped themselves for war. They girded themselves, tying their battle gear tightly on themselves and then on their horses. Then they arranged themselves in rows, files, ranks.

Four horsemen came ahead going first, staying ahead, leading. . . .

Also the dogs, their dogs, came ahead, sniffing at things and constantly panting.

---

*Source:* The selections here from Book Twelve are translated from the Nahuatl by James Lockhart and appear in the book he edited, *We People Here: Nahuatl Accounts of the Conquest of Mexico*, University of California Press, 1993. Reprinted with permission of the author.

[1] Throughout this source, *Mexico* refers to the region around Tenochtitlan, the capital of the Aztec empire, and *Mexica* refers to the people who lived there.

[2] A pole weapon consisting of an axe, hook, and spike.

[3] One of several spellings of the Aztec emperor's name, including Moctezuma and Montezuma.

[4] *Agave americana* is a native Mexican plant with tough, spikey leaves.

By himself came marching ahead, all alone, the one who bore the standard on his shoulder. He came waving it about, making it spin, tossing it here and there. . . .

Following him came those with iron swords. Their iron swords came bare and gleaming. On their shoulders they bore their shields, of wood or leather.

The second contingent and file were horses carrying people, each with his . . . leather shield, his iron lance, and his iron sword hanging down from the horse's neck. They came with bells on, jingling or rattling. The horses . . . neighed, there was much neighing, and they would sweat a great deal; water seemed to fall from them. And their flecks of foam splatted on the ground, like soapsuds splatting. . . .

The third file were those with iron crossbows, the crossbowmen. . . . Their quivers went hanging at their sides, passed under their armpits, well filled, packed with arrows, with iron bolts. . . .

The fourth file were likewise horsemen; their outfits were the same as has been said.

The fifth group were those with harquebuses [heavy matchlock guns], the harquebusiers, shouldering their harquebuses; some held them [level]. And when they went into the great palace, the residence of the ruler, they repeatedly shot off their harquebuses. They exploded, sputtered, discharged, thundered, disgorged. Smoke spread, it grew dark with smoke, everyplace filled with smoke. The fetid smell made people dizzy and faint. . . .

Then all those from the various altepetl[5] on the other side of the mountains, the Tlaxcalans, the people of Tliliuhquitepec, of Huexotzinco, came following behind. They came outfitted for war with their cotton upper armor, shields, and bows, their quivers full and packed with feathered arrows, some barbed, some blunted, some with obsidian [volcanic glass] points. They went crouching, hitting their mouths with their hands yelling, singing . . . whistling, shaking their heads. . . . Some made bundles,

perhaps putting the bundles on their backs. Some dragged the large cannons, which went resting on wooden wheels, making a clamor as they came.

---

> Cortés and his army entered Tenochtitlan in November 1519 and were amicably received by Moctezuma, who was nonetheless taken captive by the Spaniards. Cortés's army was allowed to remain in a palace compound, but tensions grew the following spring. Pedro de Alvarado, in command while Cortés left to deal with a threat to his authority from the governor of Cuba, became concerned for the Spaniards' safety as the Aztecs prepared to celebrate the annual festival in honor of the god Huitzilopochtli.

---

And when it had dawned and was already the day of his [the god's] festivity, very early in the morning those who had made vows to him unveiled his face. Forming a single row before him they offered him incense; each in his place laid down before him offerings of food for fasting and rolled amaranth dough. And it was as though all the youthful warriors had gathered together and had hit on the idea of holding and observing the festivity in order to show the Spaniards something, to make them marvel and instruct them. . . .

When things were already going on, when the festivity was being observed and there was dancing and singing, with voices raised in song, the singing was like the noise of waves breaking against the rocks.

When it was time, when the moment had come for the Spaniards to do the killing, they came out equipped for battle. They came and closed off each of the places where people went in and out. . . . Then they surrounded those who were dancing, going among the cylindrical drums. They struck a drummer's arms; both of his hands were severed.

---

[5]The Nahuatl term for any sovereign state, especially the local states of central Mexico.

Then they struck his neck; his head landed far away. Then they stabbed everyone with iron lances and struck them with iron swords. They struck some in the belly, and then their entrails came spilling out. They split open the heads of some, they really cut their skulls to pieces, their skulls were cut up into little bits. And if someone still tried to run it was useless; he just dragged his intestines along. There was a stench as if of sulfur. Those who tried to escape could go nowhere. When anyone tried to go out, at the entryways they struck and stabbed him.

And when it became known what was happening, everyone cried out, "Mexica warriors, come running, get outfitted with devices, shields, and arrows, hurry, come running, the warriors are dying; they have died, perished, been annihilated, O Mexica warriors!" Thereupon there were war cries, shouting, and beating of hands against lips. The warriors quickly came outfitted, bunched together, carrying arrows and shields. Then the fighting began; they shot at them with barbed darts, spears, and tridents, and they hurled darts with broad obsidian points at them.

> The fighting drove the Spaniards back to the palace enclave, where they lacked a reliable supply of food and water. In July 1520 Cortés, who had returned with his power intact, led his followers on a desperate nocturnal escape from the city, but they were discovered and suffered heavy losses. They retreated to the other side of the lake, and the Aztecs believed the Spanish threat had passed.

Before the Spanish appeared to us, first an epidemic broke out, a sickness of pustules [smallpox]. . . . Large bumps spread on people; some were entirely covered. They spread everywhere, on the face,

the head, the chest, etc. The disease brought great desolation; a great many died of it. They could no longer walk about, but lay in their dwellings and sleeping places, no longer able to move or stir. . . . The pustules that covered people caused great desolation; very many people died of them, and many just starved to death; starvation reigned, and no one took care of others any longer.

On some people, the pustules appeared only far apart, and they did not suffer greatly, nor did many of them die of it. But many people's faces were spoiled by it, their faces and noses were made rough. Some lost an eye or were blinded. This disease of pustules lasted a full sixty days; after sixty days it abated and ended. When people were convalescing and reviving, the pustules disease began to move in the direction of the Chalco.[6] And many were disabled or paralyzed by it, but they were not disabled forever. . . . The Mexica warriors were greatly weakened by it.

And when things were in this state, the Spaniards came, moving toward us from Tetzcoco. . . .

> Having resupplied his army and having constructed a dozen cannon-carrying boats for use on the lake, Cortés resumed his offensive late in 1520. In April 1521 he reached Tenochtitlan and placed the city under a blockade.

The Tlatelolca fought in Coquipan, in war boats. And in Xoloco the Spaniards came to a place where there was a wall in the middle of the road, blocking it. They fired the big guns at it. At the first shot it did not give way, but the second time it began to crumble. The third time, at last parts of it fell to the ground, and the fourth time finally the wall went to the ground once and for all. . . .

Once they got two of their boats into the canal at Xocotitlan. When they had beached them, then

---

[6]A city on the southeast corner of Lake Texcoco.

they went looking into the house sites of the people of Xocotitlan. But Tzilacatzin and some other warriors who saw the Spaniards immediately came out to face them; they came running after them, throwing stones at them, and they scattered the Spaniards into the water. . . .

When they got to Tlilhuacan, the warriors crouched far down and hid themselves, hugging the ground, waiting for the war cry. . . . When the cry went up, "O Mexica, up and at them!" the Tlappanecatl Ecatzin, a warrior of Otomi[7] rank, faced the Spaniards and threw himself at them, saying, "Oh warriors, up and at them, who are these barbarians? Come running! " Then he went and threw a Spaniard down, knocking him to the ground; the one he threw down was the one who came first, who came leading them. And when he had thrown him down, he dragged the Spaniard off.

And at this point they let loose with all the warriors who had been crouching there; they came out and chased the Spaniards in the passageways, and when the Spaniards saw it the Mexica seemed to be intoxicated. The captives were taken. Many Tlaxcalans, and people of Acolhuacan, Chalco, Xochimilco, etc., were captured. A great abundance were captured and killed. . . .

Then they took the captives to Yacacolco, hurrying them along, going along herding their captives together. Some went weeping, some singing, some went shouting while hitting their hands against their mouths. When they got them to Yacacolco, they lined them all up. Each one went to the altar platform where the sacrifice was performed. The Spaniards went first, going in the lead; the people of the different altepetl just followed, coming last. And when the sacrifice was over, they strung the Spaniards' heads on poles on skull racks; they also strung up the horses' heads. They placed them below, and the Spaniards' heads were above them, strung up facing east. . . .

---

> Despite this victory the Aztecs could not overcome the problems of shortages of food, water, and warriors. In mid-July 1521 the Spaniards and their allies resumed their assault, and in early August the Aztecs decided to send into battle a quetzal-owl warrior, whose success or failure, it was believed, would reveal if the gods wished the Aztecs to continue fighting.

---

And all the common people suffered greatly. There was famine; many died of hunger. They no longer drank good, pure water, but the water they drank was salty. Many people died of it, and because of it many got dysentery and died. Everything was eaten: lizards, swallows, maize, straw, grass that grows on salt flats. And they chewed at wood, glue flowers, plaster, leather, and deerskin, which they roasted, baked, and toasted so that they could eat them, and they ground up medicinal herbs and adobe bricks. There had never been the like of such suffering. The siege was frightening, and great numbers died of hunger. . . .

And the ruler Quauhtemoctzin[8] and the warriors . . . took a great warrior named Tlapaltecatl Opochtzin . . . and outfitted him, dressing him in a quetzal-owl costume. . . . When they put it on him he looked very frightening and splendid. . . . They gave him the darts of the devil,[9] darts of wooden rods with flint tips. And the reason they did this was that it was as though the fate of the rulers of the Mexica were being determined.

When our enemies saw him, it was as though a mountain had fallen. Every one of the Spaniards

---

[7]Elite warriors bound by oath never to retreat.
[8]Quauhtemoctzin became Aztec emperor after the death of Moctezuma on June 19, 1520.

[9]Darts sacred to Huitzlopochtli.

was frightened; he intimidated them, they seemed to respect him a great deal. Then the quetzal-owl climbed up on the roof. But when some of our enemies had taken a good look at him they rose and turned him back, pursuing him. Then the quetzal-owl turned to them again and pursued them. Then he snatched up the precious feathers and gold and dropped down off the roof. He did not die, and our enemies did not carry him off. Also three of our enemies were captured. At that the war stopped for good. There was silence, nothing more happened. Then our enemies went away.

It was silent and nothing more happened until it got dark.

And the next day nothing more happened at all, no one made a sound. The common people just lay collapsed. The Spaniards did nothing more either, but lay still, looking at the people. Nothing was going on, they just lay still. . . .

---

> Two weeks passed before the Aztecs capitulated on August 13, 1521.

---

# Conflict in New Netherland

## 20 • DAVID PIETERZEN DEVRIES, VOYAGES FROM HOLLAND TO AMERICA

As a result of the efforts of Henry Hudson, who in 1609 explored present-day New York Harbor and the Hudson River, the Dutch claimed New Netherland, an area that included Long Island, eastern New York, and parts of New Jersey and Connecticut. To encourage colonization, the Dutch West India Company granted wealthy colonists large tracts of land, known as patroonships, with the understanding that each patroon would settle at least 50 tenants on the land within four years. At first, relations with the Native Americans (mainly members of the Lenape, or Delaware, tribe) in the area were generally cordial, but they deteriorated after Willem Kieft became director-general, or governor, of New Netherland in 1638. He sought to tax the Indians to pay for the construction of a fort and attempted to force them off their land to create new patroonships, even though few of them had attracted the minimum number of tenants. In 1643 Kieft ordered the massacre described by David DeVries in the following excerpt from his *Voyages from Holland to America*. Born in Rochelle, France, in 1592 or 1593, DeVries was a mariner before migrating to New Netherland and becoming a patroon in the late 1630s. In 1641 he was chosen to head the Council of Twelve, an elected body to advise the governor on Dutch–Indian relations. In the wake of the 1643 massacre, two years of fighting, known as Kieft's War, ensued. During the war a disillusioned DeVries returned to the Netherlands, where he died around 1662.

### QUESTIONS FOR ANALYSIS

1. Why does DeVries oppose the director-general's plan to attack the Indians?
2. What does this suggest about DeVries's attitude toward the Native Americans?
3. How did the Indians react immediately after the massacre?
4. What does the Indians' behavior suggest about their early relations with the Dutch?
5. What were the long-term results of the massacre?

The 24th of February, sitting at a table with the Governor, he [Kieft] began to state his intentions, that he had a mind to *wipe the mouths* of the savages; that he had been dining at the house of Jan Claesen Damen, where Maryn Adriaensen and Jan Claesen Damen, together with Jacob Planck, had presented a petition to him to begin this work. I answered him that they were not wise to request this; that such work could not be done without the approbation of the Twelve Men; that it could not take place without my assent, who was one of the Twelve Men; that moreover I was the first patroon, and no one else hitherto had risked there so many thousands, and also his person . . . ; and that he should consider what profit he could derive from this business, as he well knew that on account of trifling with the Indians we had lost our colony in the South River at Swanendael,[1] with thirty-two men, who were murdered in 1630; and that in 1640, the cause of my people being murdered on Staten Island was a difficulty which he had brought on with the Raritan Indians, where his soldiers had for some trifling thing killed some savages. . . . But it appeared that my speaking was of no avail. He had, with his co-murderers, determined to commit the murder, . . . deeming it a Roman deed,[2] and to do it without warning the inhabitants in the open lands [so] that each one might take care of himself against the retaliation of the savages. . . . When I had expressed all these things in full, sitting at the table, and the meal was over, he told me he wished me to go to the large hall, which he had been lately adding to his house. Coming to it, there stood all his soldiers ready to cross the river to Pavonia[3] to commit the murder. Then spoke I again to Governor Kieft: "Let this work alone; you wish to break the mouths of the Indians, but you will also murder our own nation, for there are none of the settlers in the open country who are aware of it. My own dwelling, my people, cattle, corn, and tobacco will be lost." He answered me, assuring me that there would be no danger; that some soldiers should go to my house to protect it. . . . So was this business begun. . . . I remained that night at the Governor's, sitting up. I went and sat by the kitchen fire, when about midnight I heard a great shrieking, and I ran to the ramparts of the fort, and looked over to Pavonia. Saw nothing but firing, and heard the shrieks of the savages murdered in their sleep. I returned again to the house by the fire. Having sat there awhile, there came an Indian with his squaw, whom I knew well, and who lived about an hour's walk from my house, and told me that they had fled in a small skiff, which they had taken from the shore at Pavonia; that the Indians from Fort Orange[4] had surprised them; and that they had come to conceal themselves in the fort. I told them that they must go away immediately; that this was no time for them to come to the fort to conceal themselves; that they who had killed their people at Pavonia were not Indians, but the Swannekens, as they call the Dutch, had done it. They then asked me how they should get out of the fort. I took them to the door, and there was no sentry there, and so they betook themselves to the woods. When it was day the soldiers returned to the fort, having massacred or murdered eighty Indians, and considering they had done a deed of Roman valor, in murdering so many in their sleep; where infants were torn from their mothers' breasts, and hacked to pieces in the presence of the parents, and the pieces thrown into the fire and in the water, and other sucklings, being bound to

---

*Source:* From David Pieterzen DeVries, *Voyages from Holland to America* (New York: Billin and Brothers, 1853), pp. 114–117.

[1] A Dutch colony in present-day Delaware.

[2] A glorious deed in the manner of the ancient Romans.

[3] The Dutch settlement on the west bank of the North River (Hudson River) that would become present-day Hudson County, New Jersey..

[4] A fortified trading post on the site of present-day Albany, New York.

small boards, were cut, stuck, and pierced, and miserably massacred in a manner to move a heart of stone. . . . Those who fled from this onslaught, and concealed themselves in the neighboring sedge [marsh grass], and when it was morning, came out to beg a piece of bread, and to be permitted to warm themselves, were murdered in cold blood and tossed into the fire or the water. . . . And these poor simple creatures, as also many of our own people, did not know any better than that they had been attacked by a party of other Indians. . . . After this exploit, the soldiers were rewarded for their services, and Director Kieft thanked them by taking them by the hand and congratulating them. At another place, on the same night, . . . forty Indians were in the same manner attacked in their sleep, and massacred there in the same manner. Did the Duke of Alva[5] in the Netherlands ever do anything more cruel? This is indeed a disgrace to our nation. . . . As soon as the savages understood that the Swannekens had so treated them, all the men whom they could surprise on the farmlands, they killed; but we have never heard that they have ever permitted women or children to be killed.

They burned all the houses, farms, barns, grain, haystacks, and destroyed everything they could get hold of. So a destructive war begun. They also burnt my farm, cattle, corn, barn, tobacco-house, and all the tobacco. . . . While my people were in alarm the savage whom I had aided to escape from the fort in the night came there, and told the other Indians that I was a good chief, that I had helped him out of the fort, and that the killing of the Indians took place contrary to my wish. Then they all cried out together to my people that they would not shoot them; that if they had not destroyed my cattle they would not do it, nor burn my house; that they would let my little brewery stand, though they wished to get the copper kettle, in order to make darts for their arrows; but hearing now that it had been done contrary to my wish, they all went away, and left my house unbesieged. When now the Indians had destroyed so many farms and men in revenge for their people, I went to Governor Willem Kieft, and asked him if it was not as I had said it would be. . . . Who would now compensate us for our losses? But he gave me no answer.

---

[5]Spanish general in the service of Philip II of Spain responsible for carrying out harsh anti-Protestant measures in the Netherlands in the 1560s.

# Land and Labor in Spanish America

Throughout its existence Spain's American empire was based on the exploitation of Native Americans. Such exploitation began in the 1490s when Columbus established a settlement on Hispaniola, an island he discovered in 1492. The settlers were determined to enrich themselves, and this spelled disaster for the island's Tainos, who were robbed of their food and forced to work as slaves for the Spaniards. In 1497 Columbus attempted to curb the rapaciousness of his countrymen by allocating groups of Tainos to individual Spaniards, who could demand tribute and labor from these Indians and these Indians alone. Abuses continued, however, and in 1512, the Crown issued the Laws of Burgos, which sought to regulate the treatment of Indians by requiring reasonable labor expectations, adequate food and housing, and restrictions on punishments. The laws were unenforceable, and by the mid-1500s were largely irrelevant: By then, African slaves were doing the Spaniards' work on Hispaniola. The Tainos, who numbered between 300,000 and 400,000 in 1492, had virtually disappeared as a result of agricultural disruption, excessive labor, and epidemics.

Elsewhere in Spanish America economic realities were no different from those in Hispaniola. Without cheap labor and tribute from the Indians, none of the Spaniards' objectives—income for the Crown, profit for individual Spaniards, and winning souls to Christ—could be attained. Although this rarely meant enslavement, Indians could be assigned to an individual Spaniard, or *encomendero,* who could demand tribute and labor from the Indians assigned to him in return for providing protection and religious instruction. Indians also could be required to pay tribute to the state or be subjected to state-controlled labor drafts. By the late 1500s some Indians accepted pittance wages for their work in the open market.

Reliance on native labor was hotly debated by settlers, clergy, and royal officials. Through what mechanisms should the Indians be compelled to work for the Spaniards? What kind of work could they reasonably be asked to do? What responsibilities did Spaniards have to protect Indians from mistreatment and abuse? Most fundamentally, how was it possible to reconcile the Spaniards' need to compel Indians to work for them with their responsibility to convert them to Christianity, civilize them, and treat them as human beings? The Spaniards never found satisfactory answers to these questions, even after three hundred years of colonial rule.

# Labor Problems in Mexico

## 21 • GONZALO GÓMEZ DE CERVANTES, OF THE AFFAIRS AND ADMINISTRATION OF MEXICO

Despite the objections of royal officials and the failure of the system on Hispaniola, Cortés, the conqueror of the Aztecs, established a version of the *encomienda* system in Mexico when he assigned the rights to Indian tribute and labor to his soldiers, who were to look after the material and spiritual well-being of their Indians. With little legislative guidance or judicial oversight, abuses were inevitable, and in response, Indian sympathizers, many drawn from Catholic religious orders, called for the suppression of the encomiendas. They got their wish in 1542, when the royal government issued the New Laws, a comprehensive legal code for Spanish America that along with much else ordered the end of all encomienda agreements after the deaths of current holders. In the face of protest from encomenderos, the Crown was forced to cancel some of the New Laws' provisions, but it continued to whittle away at the encomenderos' privileges. By the end of the century the encomienda system no longer was the prime source of Indian labor in New Spain. It had been replaced by a new system of draft labor—the *repartimiento*—in which native communities were required to provide a certain number of laborers for short periods of time to work in fields and mines and on road-building and other projects. Unlike Indians subject to the encomienda system, whose "pay" was religious instruction and protection, under the new system they received wages for their work. In addition, setting quotas for villages and allocating workers to specific projects became the responsibility of Spanish officials, who in theory would fairly balance the interests of the Indians and the needs of the Spaniards.

The repartimiento system was a double failure: Indian workers continued to be exploited and abused, and owners of agricultural estates and mines increasingly were forced to hire Indians on the open market when the system failed to meet their labor needs. The inadequacies of the repartimiento system are analyzed in the following excerpt, taken from a memorandum "Of the Affairs and Administration of Mexico and the Production of Silver and Grain," by Gonzalo Gómez de Cervantes. The son of one of Cortes's soldiers and a judge, landowner, and mine owner, Gómez began work on his memorandum late in his life. In 1599 he sent it to Eugenio de Salazar, a member of The Council of the Indies and former official in New Spain. It is a perceptive and knowledgeable commentary on the late sixteenth-century Mexican economy, but its effect on policy, if any, is unknown.

## QUESTIONS FOR ANALYSIS

1. What is the author's view of the overall importance of Indian labor in maintaining the Spanish empire?
2. What "injuries and hardships" are experienced by Indian farm and mine workers in the repartimiento system?
3. In what ways is the repartimiento system failing to meet the needs of landowners and mine owners? To what extent does the author ascribe these problems to policies adopted by the owners themselves?
4. What explanations have been offered by Spaniards for the dying off of the Indian population? Where does Gómez stand on this issue, and why?
5. Gómez proposes that having larger numbers of Indians working shorter shifts would improve the repartimiento system for all concerned. On the basis of information he himself provides, why is this an impractical suggestion?

## Concerning the Repartimiento of Indians for Wheat Farming

The injuries and offences against these Indians on the wheat farms are beyond the imagination. I have observed some of these as an eyewitness, which I discovered and punished as a judge, and about others I was informed of by a member of the clergy. To begin with, it is common to have a Negro[1] or servant accompany the Indians and speed them up in their work, forcing them to work harder than they are able due to their weak constitutions and lack of endurance. Even more disgusting, they beat and whip them, so they are very poorly treated. They even take away the food they brought with them and the serapes[2] they use to cover themselves. They keep the serapes to make

*Source:* Gonzalo Gómez de Cervantes, *La Vida Economica y Social de Nueva España al Finalizar el Siglo XVI*, Alberto Maria Carreño, ed. (Mexico City: Antigua Libreria Robredo, 1944), pp. 104, 107, 108, 109, 110, 137, 138. Trans. James H. Overfield.

[1]Large numbers of black slaves in New Spain were used as overseers of Indian workers.

[2]Indian laborers were expected to bring their own food during labor service; the serape is a blanket-like shawl that can be used as a pillow, a coat for keeping warm, or a bedcover.

sure the Indians will not flee. They lock the Indians up when they sleep, completely naked, something which causes great pity and sorrow. Others force them to work for fifteen or twenty days with all these discomforts. They Indians work, but always thinking about ways to escape . . .

Some employers pay their Indians with small dogs or little cats [for food]. Others, seeing that the food the workers have brought with them soon gives out because of the long time they have been at work, feed them, and at the end of their assignment deduct the cost of the food from what is owed for their labor. It should be noted that the Indians legally are required to work for only eight days. The landowners, however, seeing the value of their properties decline because it is impossible to farm them because of a shortage of labor, hold the Indians for fifteen or twenty days. Since the poor Indian only brought food for eight days and it soon gives out, he suffers hardship. Then when he returns home, he discovers that his wife or children have died, or his crops have been ruined by a lack of attention caused by his absence, or the cattle has eaten them, all because he has been required to work longer than they should be. . . .

The remedy is quite simple.[3] For indeed it is necessary that the repartimiento system remains in effect, because without them we would all starve and not be able to harvest a single grain of wheat. But no Indians would of their own free work a single day on the farms even if they were paid ten ducats, so great is their hatred and fear of the landowners.

## Regarding the Repartimiento of Indians Who Work in the Mines

Although it must be said that the Indians are treated poorly, their labor cannot be dispensed with, because then the mine owners would be done for, and the Royal *quintos*[4] would be lost and trade would shrink to the point of completely ending. The Indians are allotted the same way they are given to the landowners, and because the mine owners are so short of labor they keep the Indians not for eight days but for two to three weeks . . .

With the mines it is not possible to enforce the guidelines described in the previous chapter in regard to payment for the Indians, because mining is so hazardous and dangerous. . . . Furthermore, the mine owner or overseer would lose everything even if the Indians were absent for just an hour . . . Nonetheless, I have been witness to the abuse of the Indians in some mining operations. In particular, some of the mine owners require the Indians to carry the ore from inside the mine to the mine's mouth and from the mouth to the mill to the crushing mills, and from the crushing mills to the strainers and then to the fusers[5]—the poor Indian carrying it on his back in his own serape, which is worth five or six *reales*.[6] And since the ore is stone it tears the serape and ruins it, so if he is paid four reales for his work, as a result he works for nothing, and even loses money. Even worse, when he takes the ore from the mines, it is like mud, so that when the poor Indian goes to sleep, with his serape to cover himself, it is wet and full of mud. . . . It is necessary and unavoidable that certain procedures, such as carrying the ore to mouth of the mine, could not be done without Indian labor . . . But in justice those tasks that could be done with pack mules should not be forced on the wretched Indians. The Indians should be spared from harsh labor as much as possible . . .

---

[3]Gómez suggested that the number of workers allocated to work on farms and in mines should be increased, but the length of service should be no more than eight days.

[4]The *quinto* was a royal tax on all precious metals extracted from mines.

[5]The author is referring to the amalgamation process, in which silver is extracted from its ore by mixing it with mercury (quicksilver).

[6]A coin made of silver and copper, eight of which equaled a peso, the "Spanish dollar."

### Regarding the Repartimiento of Indians for the Property Owners of Mexico City and the Repair of their Houses

On the viceroy's orders, some Indians are allotted each week for the repair and service of the city dwellers' houses, and to do this an official is appointed . . . Some of those who receive an allotment of Indians make excessive requests, in order to use the Indians for other business. This goes against the intent of the repartimiento . . . The rate of pay is: for a carpenter and mason, two *reales* a day and meals; for a laborer, half a *real* per day. All the Indians are obliged to work when it is their turn. When a tailor, embroiderer, painter, silk worker, blacksmith, shoemaker or other tradesman is assigned to serve as a day laborer, in order not to go, since they earn six *reales* or more a day from their trade, they bargain with the other Indians who don't have a trade and only know how to work as laborers, to get them to substitute for them. They pay them a *real* or two a day in addition to what they would earn from the homeowner.

### Regarding the Decline in the Numbers of Indians in New Spain

An amazing thing has happened and is happening in New Spain, namely that Indians are dying off so quickly that from the time this kingdom was discovered, for every 1000 inhabitants, 900 are gone. I have been part of many discussions on this matter among clergy and laypeople, and almost all of them agree that this attrition is caused by the repartimientos and personal service demanded of the Indians on farms and in mines. I have concluded, however that this may not be the direct cause. For in the provinces of Tacupan and Tlaxcala there had been 300,000 Indians, and in these provinces there was no mandatory labor or repartimientos. Yet Tacupan today has only 20,000 Indians and Tlaxcala only 15,000. . . . The explanation that makes most sense to me is that the Indians while still pagans [before the arrival of the Spaniards] used to live to be 100 years and rarely suffered from any illnesses other than tiredness, headaches and other minor ailments . . . But since the Spaniards have arrived, there have been typhoid fever, measles, *dolor de castado*, erysipelas,[7] and other severe pestilences that ravage humans. The Indians are treated by Spaniards by bloodletting, cupping, mild purgatives and light diet,[8] or by other Indians according to their methods and customs. This cancels out the benefits received from the Spaniards, and the disease becomes established resulting in death. I cannot think of any general remedy for this.

---

[7]*Dolor de costado*, literally "flank pain," may be caused by kidney stones, various renal malfunctions, and infections of the abdominal cavity; erysipelas is a flu-like sickness accompanied by a painful, swollen rash on the body's extremities.

[8]These are all standard treatments in sixteenth-century European medicine, deigned to cure diseases by rectifying imbalances in the body's four humors—blood, yellow bile, black bile, and phlegm.

## The "Mountain of Silver" and the Mita System

### 22 • ANTONIO VAZQUEZ DE ESPINOSA, COMPENDIUM AND DESCRIPTION OF THE WEST INDIES

In 1545, an Indian herder lost his footing on a mountain in the eastern range of the Andes while chasing a llama. To keep from falling, he grabbed a bush, which he uprooted to reveal a rich vein of silver. This is one story of how the world learned of the silver mine at Potosí, in present-day Bolivia, but in the colonial era in the Viceroyalty of Peru. Located more than two miles above sea level in a cold, desolate region, Potosí became the site of the Western Hemisphere's first mining boomtown. By 1600, it had a population of 150,000, making it the largest city in the New World. With one-fifth of its silver going to the Spanish crown, Potosí had a major impact on the European Wars of Religion (it bankrolled Spanish military campaigns against the Protestants) and on world trade (its silver was used by Europeans to purchase goods throughout Asia).

The backbone of the Potosí operation was a system of government-controlled draft labor similar to the repartimiento system described in the previous source. It is known as the *mita*, a term used by the Incas for their preconquest system of required state labor. In the mita system, established in 1573, native communities were required to supply workers at fixed intervals for assignment to particular tasks, in this case work at the Potosí mine. In theory, required work was distributed evenly throughout each community, and an individual might go months or even years without being called for labor service.

The mita also was used to supply workers for another operation vital to Spanish silver production, the Santa Barbara mercury mine at Huancavelica, some 770 miles north of Potosí in present-day Peru. Mercury was necessary to extract silver from its ores using the amalgamation process, in which ore was mixed with salt and mercury and heated in shallow copper vessels.

The following description of the mita system is provided by Antonio Vazquez de Espinosa (d. 1630), a Spanish Carmelite friar who abandoned an academic career to perform priestly work in the Americas. During his retirement in the 1620s, he wrote several books on Spanish America, the best known of which is his *Compendium and Description of the West Indies*. It contains his observations of conditions in Mexico and Spanish South America. In this excerpt, he describes mercury mining at Huancavelica and the "mountain of silver" at Potosí.

## QUESTIONS FOR ANALYSIS

1. What was the range of annual wages for each laborer at Huancavelica? Compare the wages of the mita workers at Potosí with the wages paid those Native Americans who freely hired themselves out. What do you conclude from all these figures?
2. What were the major hazards connected with the extraction and production of mercury and silver?
3. What evidence does this source provide of Spanish concern for the welfare of the Indian workers? What evidence of indifference does it provide? Where does the weight of the evidence seem to lie?
4. What does the document tell us about the impact of the mita system on native society?
5. What similarities and differences do you see between the Mexican repartimiento described by Gómez de Cervantes (source 21) and the mita described by Vazquez?

## Huancavelica

. . . It contains 400 Spanish residents, as well as many temporary shops of dealers in merchandise and groceries, heads of trading houses, and transients, for the town has a lively commerce. It has a parish church . . . a Dominican convent, and a Royal Hospital under the Brethren of San Juan de Díos for the care of the sick, especially Indians on the range; it has a chaplain with a salary of 800 pesos[1] contributed by His Majesty; he is curate of the parish . . . for the Indians who have come to work in the mines and who have settled down there. . . .

Every 2 months His Majesty sends by the regular courier from Lima[2] 60,000 pesos to pay for the mita of the Indians, for the crews are changed every two months, so that merely for the Indian mita payment . . . 360,000 pesos are sent from Lima every year, not to speak of much besides, which all crosses at his risk that cold and desolate mountain country which has nothing on it but llama ranches.

Up on the range there are 3,000 or 4,000 Indians working in the mine; . . . The mine where the mercury is located is a large layer which they keep following downward. When I was in that town [in 1616] I went up on the range and down into the mine, which at that time was considerably more than 130 stades[3] deep. The ore was very rich black flint, and the excavation so extensive that it held more than 3,000 Indians working away hard with picks and hammers, breaking up that flint ore; and when they have filled their little sacks, the poor fellows, loaded down with ore, climb up those ladders or rigging, some like masts and others like cables, and so trying and distressing that a man empty-handed can hardly get up them. . . . Nor is that the greatest evil and difficulty; that is due to

thievish and undisciplined superintendents. As that great vein of ore keeps going down deeper and they follow its rich trail, in order to make sure that no section of that ore shall drop on top of them, they keep leaving supports or pillars of the ore itself, even if of the richest quality. . . . This being so, there are men so heartless that for the sake of stealing a little rich ore, they go down out of hours and deprive the innocent Indians of this protection by hollowing into these pillars to steal the rich ore in them, and then a great section is apt to fall in and kill all the Indians, and sometimes the unscrupulous and grasping superintendents themselves. . . .

On the other side of the town there are structures where they grind up the mercury ore and then put it in jars with . . . many little holes . . . and a channel for it to drip into and pass into the jar or place where it is to fall. Then they roast the ore with a straw fire. . . . Under the onset of this fire it melts and the mercury goes up in vapor until, passing through the holes in the first mold, it hits the body of the second, and there it coagulates, rests, and comes to stop where they have provided lodging for it. . . . Those who carry out the reduction of this ore have to be very careful and test cautiously; they must wait till the jars are cold before uncovering them for otherwise they may easily get mercury poisoning and if they do, they are of no further use; their teeth fall out, and some die.

## Potosí

According to His Majesty's warrant [authorization], the mine owners on this massive range have a right to the mita of 13,300 Indians. . . . It is the duty of the Corregidor[4] of Potosí to have them rounded up and to see that they come in from all the provinces. . . .

---

Source: Excerpt from Antonio Vazquez de Espinosa, *Description of the Indies* c. 1620, trans. by Charles Upson Clark, Smithsonian Institution Press, 1942.

[1] A silver coin equal to eight reales.

[2] The capital city of the Viceroyalty of Peru, one of the major administrative units of Spanish America.

[3] A measure of length, approximately 200 feet.

[4] A Spanish official with military and executive functions.

These Indians are sent out every year under a captain whom they choose in each village or tribe, for him to take them [to Potosí] and oversee them for the year each has to serve; every year they have a new election, for as some go out, others come in. This works out very badly, with great losses and gaps in the quotas of Indians, [since] the villages [are] being depopulated; and this gives rise to great extortions and abuses on the part of the inspectors toward the poor Indians, ruining them and thus depriving the caciques [chiefs] and chief Indians [the captains mentioned above] of their property and carrying them off in chains because they do not fill out the mita assignment, which they cannot do, for the reason given and for others which I do not bring forward.

These 13,300 are divided up every 4 months into 3 mitas, each consisting of 4,433 Indians, to work in the mines on the range and in the 120 smelters in the Potosí and Tarapaya areas; it is a good league [about three miles] between the two. These mita Indians earn each day for his labor, 4 reales. Besides these there are others not under obligation [mingados], who . . . hire themselves out voluntarily: these each get from 12 to 16 reales, and some up to 24, according to their reputation of wielding the pick and knowing how to get the ore out. These mingados will be over 4,000 in number. They and the mita Indians go up every Monday morning to the locality of Guayna Potosí which is at the foot of the range; the Corregidor arrives with all the provincial captains or chiefs who have charge of the Indians assigned them, and he there checks off and reports to each mine and smelter owner the number of Indians assigned him for his mine or smelter; that keeps him busy till 1 p.m., by which time the Indians are already turned over to these mine and smelter owners.

After each has eaten his ration, they climb up the hill, each to his mine, and go in, staying there from that hour until Saturday evening without coming out of the mine; their wives bring them food, but they stay constantly underground, excavating and carrying out the ore from which they get the silver. They all have tallow candles, lighted day and night; that is the light they work with, for as they are underground, they have need of it all the time. The mere cost of these candles used in the mines on this range will amount every year to more than 300,000 pesos, even though tallow is cheap in that country, being abundant; but this is a very great expense, and it is almost incredible, how much is spent for candles in the operation of breaking down and getting out the ore.

These Indians have different functions in the handling of the silver ore; some break it up with bar or pick, and dig down in, following the vein in the mine; others bring it up; others up above keep separating the good and the poor in piles; others are occupied in taking it down from the range to the mills on herds of llamas; every day they bring up more than 8,000 of these native beasts of burden for this task. These teamsters who carry the metal do not belong to the mita, but are mingados—hired.

So huge is the wealth which has been taken out of this range since the year 1545, when it was discovered, up to the present year of 1628, which makes 83 years that they have been working and reducing its ores, that merely from the registered mines . . . , 326,000,000 pesos have been taken out. At the beginning when the ore was richer and easier to get out, for then there were no mita Indians and no mercury process, . . . between 1545 and 1585, they took out 111,000,000 pesos of silver. From the year 1585 up to 1628, 43 years, although the mines are harder to work, for they are deeper down, with the assistance of 13,300 Indians whom His Majesty has granted to the mine owners on that range, and of other hired Indians, . . . and with the great advantage of the mercury process, in which none of the ore or the silver is wasted, and with the better knowledge of the technique which the miners now have, they have taken out 215,000,000 pesos. That, plus the 111,000,000 extracted in the 40 years previous to 1585, makes 326,000,000 pesos, not counting the great amount of silver secretly taken from these mines . . . and to other countries outside Spain. . . . Over and above that, such great treasure and riches have come from the Indies in gold and silver from all the other mines in New Spain and Peru, Honduras, the New Kingdom of Granada, Chile, New Galicia, New Vizcaya,[5] and other quarters since the discovery of the Indies, that they exceed 1,800 millions.

The parish church of this imperial town is very rich and well-served; it has three curates and one vicar, and two sacristan priests[6] . . . ; these are for the Spaniards. The church has many rich chapels, a large corps of musicians, and a very rich sacristy. [The city] contains two hospitals in which they care for indigent sick, both Spaniards and Indians. Both are excellent and wealthy but one is one of the best in the Indies; the richest and most important residents of the town have a Confraternity,[7] and so they serve the hospital and the invalids as brethren.

---

[5] New Galicia and New Vizcaya were regions and administrative jurisdictions located in north-central and northwestern Mexico.

[6] Priests in charge of the sacristy, a room where priestly vestments, sacred vessels, and church records were kept.

[7] An organization of laypeople for the purpose of supporting works of charity and devotion.

# Chapter 4

# Continuity and Change in East and Southeast Asia

|MPORTANT CHANGES TOOK PLACE in East and Southeast Asia in the early modern era: Islam continued to make converts in Southeast Asia and western China; a new dynasty, the Tokugawa, stabilized Japan after decades of civil war; the Chinese Ming Dynasty faced mounting problems in the late 1500s and was overthrown in 1644; contacts with European merchants and missionaries increased, and a few regions came under European political control. Nevertheless, in most respects continuity rather than change was the hallmark of the era.

One constant was the primacy of China. In terms of size, wealth, population, technology, trade, military might, and cultural influence, China, as it had for centuries, overshadowed the smaller states and nomadic societies that surrounded it. With some justification, the Chinese considered their country to be the "central kingdom" and viewed all other peoples as their inferiors. On China's periphery Japan, Korea, and Vietnam were politically independent, and in certain ways culturally distinct, but their religious practices, formal thought, writing systems, and political institutions all reflected centuries of Chinese influence. In Southeast Asia Chinese influence was less pervasive. Hinduism, Buddhism, and Islam had many adherents as a result of longstanding commercial and cultural contacts with India and Arabia. Nonetheless, China was the most important market for Southeast Asian merchants, and many Southeast Asian rulers paid tribute to the Chinese emperor as a token of their loyalty and subservience. The sparsely populated arid regions to the west and north of China lacked large cities and centralized states. They were populated by Uighurs, Khitans, Jurchens, Manchus, and Mongols, who supported themselves through pastoralism and limited agriculture. Their raids were a constant threat to China and sometimes developed into full-blown invasions. Four Chinese dynasties—the Liao, Jin, Yuan, and Qing—originated among these so-called barbarian peoples on China's northern and western flanks.

Another constant was East and Southeast Asia's importance in the world economy. Southeast Asia played an important role in regional trade and was a commercial crossroads linking Chinese and Japanese markets with those of India, Southwest Asia, Europe, and Africa. Southeast Asia also grew pepper, nutmeg, cloves, and mace—spices that were coveted throughout the Afro-Eurasian world. When Europeans began searching for ocean routes to Asia in the 1400s, their primary goal was direct access to the spice markets of Southeast Asia.

China, however, was the region's economic powerhouse. Its population in 1500 was between 100 and 125 million, well above Europe's estimated 80 million. Much Chinese economic activity was devoted to supplying this vast domestic market, but China also played a major role in international trade. Its main exports were silk textiles and ceramics, the high quality of which was recognized throughout Eurasia and Africa. Although the Chinese imported spices from Southeast Asia and cotton textiles from India, they were interested in few other foreign products. Thus, foreign merchants had no choice but to pay for Chinese goods with gold or silver, meaning that year after year, China had a favorable balance of trade.

Until the sixteenth century, contact between these Asian societies and Europe had been limited. Although trade between the two regions had existed for centuries, the goods exchanged had always been carried by Arab, Indian, or Central Asian intermediaries. The number of European travelers to China increased in the thirteenth century, but with the breakup of the Mongol Empire in the mid-fourteenth century and the antipathy toward foreigners of China's rulers, European contact with China was reduced to a trickle.

Then in the early 1500s, Portuguese merchants and missionaries arrived in the region, and the Spanish, Dutch, French, and English soon followed. The Portuguese captured the Malay port city of Melaka in 1511 and established trading posts in the Spice Islands, China, and Japan; beginning in the 1560s the Spaniards gradually subjugated the Philippines. Elsewhere, however, the Europeans' arrival was a relatively minor event. In Japan European missionaries introduced Christianity with some early (and short-lived) success, but the most significant development was the country's political recovery under the Tokugawa clan after decades of civil war. In China, emperors permitted the Portuguese to trade at a single port, Macao, and allowed a small number of Jesuit missionaries to reside at the imperial court in Beijing. Here they impressed the Chinese elite with their mechanical clocks and astronomical knowledge but had little effect on Chinese politics or culture.

# Confucianism in China and Japan

No philosopher has influenced the values and behavior of more human beings than the Chinese thinker Kong Fuzi (ca. 551–479 B.C.E.), known in the West by his Latinized name Confucius. Like other Chinese thinkers of his day, Confucius, a scholar intent on a career in public service, was distressed by the political fragmentation and turbulence plaguing China during the Eastern Zhou Era (771–256 B.C.E.). Only after failing to achieve a position as a ruler's advisor did he turn to teaching, a career in which he reputedly had more than 3,000 students.

Confucius taught that China's troubles were rooted in the failure of its people and leaders to understand and act according to the rules of proper conduct. Proper conduct meant actions conforming to the standards of an idealized past, when China was structured along lines paralleling those of a harmonious family. He taught that just as fathers, wives, sons, and daughters have specific familial roles and obligations, individuals, depending on age, gender, marital status, ancestry, and social standing, have specific roles and obligations in society. Subjects owed rulers obedience, just as children owed parents love and reverence. In turn, rulers were expected to be models of virtue and benevolence, just as parents, especially fathers, were expected to be kind and just. Children learned from parents, and subjects from rulers. Confucius also taught that whatever one's status, one must live according to the principles of *jen,* which means humaneness, benevolence, and love, and *li,* which encompasses the concepts of ceremony, propriety, and good manners. Because the wisdom and practices of ancient sages were central to his teaching, Confucius taught that one could achieve virtue by studying the literature, history, and rituals of the past. Education in traditional values and behavior was the path to sagehood, the quality of knowing what is proper and good and acting accordingly.

Although Confucius's philosophy competed with many other schools of thought in his own day, during the era of the Han Dynasty (206 B.C.E.–220 C.E.), it became the official program of studies for anyone seeking an office in the imperial administration. Mastery of the Confucian Classics became the path to success on the civil service examinations by which China chose its officials. Although the examination system was abolished by China's Mongol rulers during the Yuan Era (1264–1368), it was revived under the Ming (1368–1644) and continued in use until 1905. For almost 2,000 years, China was administered by a literary elite devoted to Confucianism.

Confucianism's influence was not limited to China. Although it had to compete with Buddhism and other indigenous religions, Confucianism deeply affected the thought, politics, and everyday life of Korea, Vietnam, and Japan.

# "Doing Good" in Seventeenth-Century China

## 23 • MERITORIOUS DEEDS AT NO COST

During the sixteenth and seventeenth centuries, interpreters of Confucianism mainly drew on the work of scholars from the Song Era (960–1279 C.E.). Known as Neo-Confucianists, these scholars had brought new energy and rigor to the study of Confucianism after years of stagnation and declining influence. The greatest Neo-Confucianist was Zhu Xi (1130–1200), who presided over a huge project of historical research and wrote detailed commentaries on most of the Confucian Classics.

His commentaries became the orthodox version of Confucianism and the official interpretation for evaluating performance on the civil service examinations.

Confucian scholarship in the 1500s and 1600s, however, involved more than re-hashing and refining of Neo-Confucian formulas. Ming-era scholars completed vast research projects on history, medicine, ethics, and literature. In reinterpreting Confucianism, they sought to apply the Sage's wisdom to their own society—one experiencing population growth, commercialization, urbanization, and ultimately dynastic decline and foreign conquest. Many endeavored to make Confucianism less elitist and more "popular."

Traditional Confucianism had taught that the erudition and virtue necessary for sagehood were theoretically attainable by anyone, but that in reality, they could be achieved only by small numbers of males who had the wealth and leisure for years of study and self-cultivation. Women, artisans, peasants, and even merchants were capable of understanding and internalizing some Confucian principles by observing the behavior of their superiors, but serious scholarship and true morality were beyond them. In the early 1500s, such ideas were challenged by the scholar-official Wang Yangming (1472–1529), who taught that everyone, regardless of station, was capable of achieving sagehood. He was convinced that a healthy Chinese polity depended on teaching sound moral principles to all classes of people.

Wang's ideas were well received in a China where urbanization, increased literacy, and growing wealth were increasing the demand for books, many of which brought Confucian ideas to the broad reading public. These included summaries and editions of the Confucian Classics, manuals to prepare candidates for the civil service examinations, and "morality books," which discussed proper behavior not only for the learned elite but also for common people. With titles such as *A Record of the Practice of Good Deeds* and *Establishing One's Own Destiny*, they taught that good deeds would be rewarded by worldly success, robust health, many sons, and a long life.

Among the most popular morality books was the anonymous *Meritorious Deeds at No Cost*, which appeared in the mid-seventeenth century. Unlike other such books, which recommended costly good deeds such as paying for family rituals connected with marriage, coming of age, funerals, and ancestral rites, it discussed laudable acts that required little or no money. It lists actions considered good for "people in general" but concentrates on good deeds appropriate to specific groups, ranging from local gentry and scholars to soldiers and household servants. Its prescriptions provide insights into both Confucian values and contemporary Chinese views of class, family, and gender.

*Meritorious Deeds at No Cost* begins with the "local gentry," individuals who have the rank and status of government officials but who reside at home and have social duties but no specific administrative responsibilities. The next group is "scholars," which refers to individuals at various stages of preparing for the civil service examinations. As educated individuals and potential officials, their status placed them below the gentry but above the common people. Many of them were teachers.

## QUESTIONS FOR ANALYSIS

1. In what ways do the responsibilities of the various groups differ from one another? In what ways do they reflect underlying assumptions about what makes a good society?
2. According to this document, what should be the attitude of the upper classes (gentry and scholars) to those below them? Conversely, how should peasants, merchants, and artisans view their superiors?
3. What views of women and sexuality are stated or implied in this treatise?
4. What views of money and moneymaking are stated or implied in this treatise?
5. According to this treatise, what specific kinds of behaviors and attitudes are components of filial piety?
6. Taking the document as a whole, what conclusions can be drawn about the ultimate purpose or highest good the author hopes to achieve through the various kinds of behaviors he describes?

### Local Gentry

Rectify your own conduct and transform the common people. . . .

If people have suffered a grave injustice, expose and correct it.

Settle disputes among your neighbors fairly.

When villagers commit misdeeds, admonish them boldly and persuade them to desist. . . .

Be tolerant of the mistakes of others.

Be willing to listen to that which is displeasing to your ears.

Do not make remarks about women's sexiness.

Do not harbor resentment when you are censured. . . .

Hold up for public admiration women who are faithful to their husbands and children who are obedient to their parents.

Restrain those who are stubborn and unfilial. . . .

Prevent the younger members of your family from oppressing others by taking advantage of your position. . . .

Do not be arrogant, because of your own power and wealth, toward relatives who are poor or of low status. . . .

Do not ignore your own relatives and treat others as if they were your kin.

Influence other families to cherish good deeds. . . .

Instruct your children, grandchildren, and nephews to be humane and compassionate toward all and to avoid anger and self-indulgence.

Do not deceive or oppress younger brothers or cousins.

Encourage others to read and study without minding the difficulties.

Urge others to esteem charity and disdain personal gain. . . .

Persuade others to settle lawsuits through conciliation . . .

Curb the strong and protect the weak.

Show respect to the aged and compassion for the poor.

Do not keep too many concubines.

### Scholars

Be loyal to the emperor and filial to your parents.

Honor your elder brothers and be faithful to your friends. . . .

Instruct the common people in the virtues of loyalty and filial piety. . . .

*Source:* From Tadao Saki, "Confucianism and Popular Educational Works," in *Self and Society & Ming Thought,* by Wm. Theodore de Bary, pp. 352–361. Copyright © 1970 Columbia University Press. Reprinted with permission of the author.

Be wholehearted in inspiring your students to study. . . .

Try to improve your speech and behavior.

Teach your students also to be mindful of their speech and behavior. . . .

Be patient in educating the younger members of poor families. . . .

Do not write or post notices which defame other people. . . .

Do not call other people names or compose songs making fun of them.

Do not attack or vilify commoners; do not oppress ignorant villagers. . . .

Do not ridicule other people's handwriting. . . .

Make others desist from unfiliality toward their parents or unkindness toward relatives and friends.

Educate the ignorant to show respect to their ancestors and live in harmony with their families. . . .

## Peasants

Do not miss the proper time for farm work. . . .

Do not obstruct or cut off paths. Fill up holes that might give trouble to a passersby . . .

Do not damage crops in your neighbors' fields by leaving animals to roam at large. . . .

Do not encroach [on others' property] beyond the boundaries of your own fields and watercourses. . . .

In plowing, do not infringe on graves or make them hard to find. . . .

Do not damage the crops in neighboring fields out of envy because they are so flourishing.

Do not instigate your landlord to take revenge on a neighbor on the pretext that the neighbor's animals have damaged your crops. . . .

Do not become lazy and cease being conscientious because you think your landlord does not provide enough food and wine or fails to pay you enough. . . .

Take good care of others' carts and tools. . . .

## Craftsmen

Whenever you make something, try to make it strong and durable.

Do not reveal and spread abroad the secrets of your master's house.

Do not make crude imitations.

Finish your work without delay.

In your trade with others, do not practice deceit through forgery.

Do not mix damaged articles with good.

Do not recklessly indulge in licentiousness. . . .

Do not steal the materials of others.

Do not use the materials of others carelessly. . . .

## Merchants

Do not deceive ignorant villagers when fixing the price of goods.

Do not raise the price of fuel and rice too high.

When the poor buy rice, do not give them short measure. . . .

When sick people have urgent need of something, do not raise the price unreasonably.

Do not deceitfully serve unclean dishes or leftover food to customers who are unaware of the fact.

Do not dispossess or deprive others of their business by devious means.

Do not envy the prosperity of others' business and speak ill of them. . . .

Treat the young and the aged on the same terms as the able-bodied.

When people come in the middle of the night with an urgent need to buy something, do not refuse them on the ground that it is too cold (for you to get up and serve them). . . .

Give fair value when you exchange silver for copper coins. Especially when changing money for the poor, be generous to them.

When a debtor owes you a small sum but is short of money, have mercy and forget about the difference. Do not bring him to bankruptcy and hatred by refusing to come to terms.

When the poor want to buy such things as mosquito nets, clothing, and quilts, have pity on them and reduce the price.

### People in General

Do not show anger or worry in your parents' sight.

Accept meekly the reproaches and anger of your parents.

Persuade your parents to correct their mistakes and return to the right path.

Do not divulge your parents' faults to others.

Do not let your parents do heavy work.

Do not be disgusted with your parents' behavior when they are old and sick.

Do not yell at your parents or give them angry looks.

Love your brothers. . . .

If you are poor, do not entertain thoughts of harming the rich.

If you are rich, do not deceive and cheat the poor. . . .

Do not speak of others' humble ancestry.

Do not talk about the private women's quarters of others. (Commentary: When others bring up such things, if they are of the younger generation, reprimand them with straight talk, and if they are older or of the same generation as you, change the subject.)

Respect women's chastity. . . .

Do not stir up your mind with lewd and wanton thoughts.

Do not intimidate others to satisfy your own ambition.

Do not assert your own superiority by bringing humiliation upon others. . . .

Do not dwell on others' faults while expounding at length on your own virtues.

Try to promote friendly relations among neighbors and relatives. . . .

When you hear someone speaking about the failings of others, make him stop.

When you hear a man praising the goodness of others, help him to do so. . . .

When you see a man about to go whoring or gambling, try to dissuade him. . . .

Do not make unreasonable demands for yourself, but be content to live modestly and within your means. . . .

Help those who are unmarried to be married. . . .

Make peace between husbands and wives who are about to separate. . . .

Help the blind and disabled to pass over dangerous bridges and roads. . . .

Cut down thorns by the roadside to keep them from tearing people's clothes. . . .

Put stones in muddy places [to make them passable].

At night, light a lamp for others. . . .

Do not listen to your wife or concubines if they should encourage you to neglect or abandon your parents. . . .

Do not stealthily peep at others' womenfolk when they are exposed by a fire in their home. . . .

Do not be impudent toward your superiors. . . .

Do not sell faithful dogs to dog butchers. . . .

Even if you see that the good sometimes suffer bad fortune and you yourself experience poverty, do not let it discourage you from doing good.

Even if you see bad men prosper, do not lose faith in ultimate recompense. . . .

In all undertakings, think of others.

# Teaching the Young in Tokugawa Japan

## 24 • KAIBARA AND TOKEN EKIKEN, COMMON SENSE TEACHINGS FOR JAPANESE CHILDREN AND GREATER LEARNING FOR WOMEN

Although Chinese Neo-Confucianism was brought to Japan by Zen Buddhist monks in the fourteenth and fifteenth centuries, it had little influence on Japan's aristocratic ruling class until the Tokugawa Era, when the new regime actively supported it.

Hayashi Razan (1583–1657), a leading Confucian scholar, was an advisor to Tokugawa Ieyasu, and the school founded by the Hayashi family at Edo in 1630 became a center of Confucian scholarship. Many provincial lords founded similar academies in their domains, and the education samurai received in these schools and from private tutors helped transform Japan's warrior aristocracy into a literate bureaucratic ruling class committed to Confucian values.

Among the Confucian scholars of the early Tokugawa Era, few matched the literary output and popularity of Kaibara Ekiken (1630–1714). After studying in Kyoto and Edo, he served the Kuroda lords of the Fukuoka domain in southwestern Japan as a physician, tutor, and scholar-in-residence. He wrote more than 100 books.

This selection draws on material from two of Ekiken's works. The first part is excerpted from his *Common Sense Teachings for Japanese Children*, a manual for tutors in aristocratic households. The second part is taken from *Greater Learning for Women*, a discussion of moral precepts for girls. This treatise was written in collaboration with Token, Ekiken's wife.

## QUESTIONS FOR ANALYSIS

1. According to *Common Sense Teachings for Japanese Children*, what moral qualities should be inculcated in students?
2. What attitudes toward the lower classes are expressed in these two treatises?
3. How do the goals and purposes of education differ for Japanese boys and girls? How are they similar?
4. What do these treatises say about Japanese marriage customs and family life?
5. What is there in these treatises that would have furthered the Tokugawa shoguns' ambition to provide Japan with stable and peaceful government (see Multiple Voices II)?

## Common Sense Teachings for Japanese Children

In January when children reach the age of six, teach them numbers one through ten, and the names given to designate 100, 1,000, 10,000 and 100,000,000. Let them know the four directions, East, West, North and South. Assess their native intelligence and differentiate between quick and slow learners. Teach them Japanese pronunciation from the age of six or seven, and let them learn how to write. . . . From this time on, teach them to respect their elders, and let them know the distinctions between the upper and lower classes and between the young and old. Let them learn to use the correct expressions.

When the children reach the age of seven, do not let the boys and girls sit together, nor must you allow them to dine together. . . .

For the eighth year. This is the age when the ancients began studying the book *Little Learning*.[1] Beginning at this time, teach the youngsters etiquette befitting their age, and caution them not

---

*Source:* From *Japan: A Documentary History* ed. and trans. by David J. Lu (Armonk, NY: M. E. Sharpe, 1997), pp. 258–261. Translation copyright © 1997 by David J. Lu. Reprinted with permission of M. E. Sharpe, Inc. All rights reserved. Not for reproduction.

[1]The *Little Learning* was written in 1187 by Liu Zucheng. A book for children, it contains rules of behavior and excerpts from the Classics and other works.

to commit an act of impoliteness. Among those which must be taught are: daily deportment, the manners set for appearing before one's senior and withdrawing from his presence, how to speak or respond to one's senior or guest, how to place a serving tray or replace it for one's senior, how to present a wine cup and pour rice wine and to serve side dishes to accompany it, and how to serve tea. Children must also learn how to behave while taking their meals.

Children must be taught by those who are close to them the virtues of filial piety and obedience. To serve the parents well is called filial piety, and to serve one's seniors well is called obedience. The one who lives close to the children and who is able to teach must instruct the children in the early years of their life that the first obligation of a human being is to revere the parents and serve them well. Then comes the next lesson which includes respect for one's seniors, listening to their commands and not holding them in contempt. One's seniors include elder brothers, elder sisters, uncles, aunts, and cousins who are older and worthy of respect. . . . As the children grow older, teach them to love their younger brothers and to be compassionate to the employees and servants. Teach them also the respect due the teachers and the behavior codes governing friends. The etiquette governing each movement toward important guests—such as standing, sitting, advancing forward, and retiring from their presence—and the language to be employed must be taught. Teach them how to pay respect to others according to the social positions held by them. Gradually the ways of filial piety and obedience, loyalty and trustworthiness, right deportment and decorum, and sense of shame must be inculcated in the children's minds and they must know

how to implement them. Caution them not to desire the possessions of others, or to stoop below one's dignity in consuming excessive amounts of food and drink. . . .

Once reaching the age of eight, children must follow and never lead their elders when entering a gate, sitting, or eating and drinking. From this time on they must be taught how to become humble and yield to others. Do not permit the children to behave as they please. It is important to caution them against "doing their own things."

At the age of ten, let the children be placed under the guidance of a teacher, and tell them about the general meaning of the five constant virtues and let them understand the way of the five human relationships.[2] Let them read books by the Sage [Confucius] and the wise men of old and cultivate the desire for learning. . . . When not engaged in reading, teach them the literary and military arts. . . .

Fifteen is the age when the ancients began the study of the *Great Learning*.[3] From this time on, concentrate on the learning of a sense of justice and duty. The students must also learn to cultivate their personalities and investigate the way of governing people. . . .

Those who are born in the high-ranking families have the heavy obligations of becoming leaders of the people, of having people entrusted to their care, and of governing them. Therefore, without fail, a teacher must be selected for them when they are still young. They must be taught how to read and be informed of the ways of old, of cultivating their personalities, and of the way of governing people. If they do not learn the way of governing people, they may injure the many people who are entrusted to their care by the Way of Heaven. That will be a serious disaster. . . .

---

[2] The *five virtues* are human-heartedness, righteousness, propriety, wisdom, and good faith. The *five relationships* are ruler–subject, father–son, husband–wife, older brother–younger brother, and friend–friend.

[3] The *Great Learning* consists of a short main text thought to have been written by Confucius and nine chapters of commentary written by Confucius's disciple, Zengzi.

## Greater Learning for Women

Seeing that it is a girl's destiny, on reaching womanhood, to go to a new home, and live in submission to her father-in-law, it is even more incumbent upon her than it is on a boy to receive with all reverence her parents' instructions. Should her parents, through their tenderness, allow her to grow up self-willed, she will infallibly show herself capricious in her husband's house, and thus alienate his affection; while, if her father-in-law be a man of correct principles, the girl will find the yoke of these principles intolerable. She will hate and decry her father-in-law, and the end of those domestic dissensions will be her dismissal from her husband's house and the covering of herself with ignominy. Her parents, forgetting the faulty education they gave her, may indeed lay all the blame on the father-in-law. But they will be in error; for the whole disaster should rightly be attributed to the faulty education the girl received from her parents.

• • •

From her earliest youth a girl should observe the line of demarcation separating women from men. The customs of antiquity did not allow men and women to sit in the same apartment, to keep their wearing apparel in the same place, to bathe in the same place, or to transmit to each other anything directly from hand to hand. A woman . . . must observe a certain distance in her relations even with her husband and with her brothers. In our days the women of lower classes, ignoring all rules of this nature, behave disorderly; they contaminate their reputations, bring down reproach upon the head of their parents and brothers, and spend their whole lives in an unprofitable manner. Is not this truly lamentable?

• • •

It is the chief duty of a girl living in the parental house to practice filial piety towards her father and mother. But after marriage her duty is to honor her father-in-law and mother-in-law, to honor them beyond her father and mother, to love and reverence them with all ardor, and to tend them with practice of every filial piety. . . . Even if your father-in-law and mother-in-law are inclined to hate and vilify you, do not be angry with them, and murmur not. If you carry piety towards them to its utmost limits, and minister to them in all sincerity, it cannot be but that they will end by becoming friendly to you.

• • •

The great lifelong duty of a woman is obedience. . . . When the husband issues his instructions, the wife must never disobey them. In a doubtful case, she should inquire of her husband and obediently follow his commands. . . .

Should her husband be roused at any time to anger, she must obey him with fear and trembling, and not set herself up against him in anger and forwardness. A woman should look upon her husband as if he were Heaven itself, and never weary of thinking how she may yield to her husband and thus escape celestial castigation.

• • •

Her treatment of her servant girls will require circumspection. Those low-born girls have had no proper education; they are stupid, obstinate, and vulgar in their speech. . . . Again, in her dealings with those lowly people, a woman will find many things to disapprove of. But if she be always reproving and scolding, . . . her household will be in a continual state of disturbance. When there is real wrongdoing, she should occasionally notice it, and point out the path of amendment, while lesser faults should be quietly endured. . . .

*Source:* From *Japan: A Documentary History,* ed. and trans. by David J. Lu (Armonk, NY: M.E. Sharpe, 1997), p. 191. Translation copyright © 1997 by David J. Lu. Reprinted with permission of M.E. Sharpe, Inc. All rights reserved. Not for reproduction.

# Humanity and Nature in Chinese Painting

## 25 • ZHANG HONG, *LANDSCAPE OF SHIXIE HILL* AND SHENG MAOYE, *SCHOLARS GAZING AT A WATERFALL*

Chinese painters over the centuries have produced portraits, religious works, pictures of animals and plants, and palace scenes, but their greatest contribution to the world's art has been their landscapes. Landscapes began to attract the interest of Chinese painters and patrons during the Tang Dynasty (618–907 C.E.), and by the eleventh and twelfth centuries artists had developed a distinctly Chinese approach to the genre. From then on, the painting of landscapes on silk or paper with ink and muted watercolor shading inspired China's greatest painters and attracted countless collectors and patrons.

The Chinese devotion to landscape painting was closely tied to views of nature in Daoism and Confucianism, both of which saw the natural world as a metaphor for the moral and metaphysical order underlying the universe. Thus, despite many different schools and styles, all Chinese landscape painters sought to capture the inner quality, or vital spirit (*qi*), of nature rather than simply reproducing what the eyes see. By communicating this inner quality, artists enabled viewers to see how the ever-changing phenomena of the visible landscape—wind, rain, mountains, rivers, lakes, trees, storms, mist, and snow—reveal higher realities and capture certain moods. Landscape painting had a strong appeal for many Confucian scholar-officials, who were the main patrons of landscape painters and in many instances were accomplished painters themselves. For them, being close to nature or being able to contemplate a painting of nature provided spiritual freedom from the pressures of their administrative duties.

In the Ming Era landscape painting was characterized by many different schools and individual styles. Some drew inspiration from the masters of the Song Era, while others sought to recapture the stylistic qualities of Yuan Era (1279–1368) painters. Different artists depicted nature's vital spirit as tranquil, powerful, charming, wild, forbidding, lonely, or cold. Each artist had a distinctive style of brushwork and color.

Because of this diversity, the two paintings included here cannot be considered "typical" Ming landscapes, but they do capture some of the general characteristics of the genre. Both paintings are large wall scrolls, and both were produced by painters from Suzhou, an important commercial hub and cultural center in the Yangzi Delta region. The first is Zhang Hong's *Landscape of Shixie Hill,* a painting in ink and light colors approximately five feet high and two feet wide. Although Zhang was an outstanding painter, little is known about him other than that he was born in 1557, lived most of his life in Suzhou, and died around 1652. The inscription on the upper-right corner of the painting reads, "In the summer of 1613, I traveled to Shixie with my revered older brother Chunyu and painted this for him." One must look closely to see the human beings in the painting. A group of travelers is gathering at the bridge as the bottom of the painting, perhaps planning a walk up the mountain. Mountains, which were close

Zhang Hong, Landscape of Shixie Hill

Sheng Maoye, Scholars Gazing at a Waterfall

to heaven and were believed to be the home of the "eight immortals" of Chinese folklore, were a common subject for Chinese landscape painters. Farther upstream, one finds four gentlemen-scholars gazing at a waterfall, while a Buddhist monk and his servant approach them with tea. Their two servants stand by, looking away.

The second painting is *Scholars Gazing at a Waterfall* by Sheng Maoye. Painted on silk in 1630, it is slightly longer and approximately a foot wider than Zhang's painting. Sheng's works are dated from 1594 to 1634, but the dates of his birth and death are unknown. Shang also lived in Suzhou and, like many Ming painters, included in his works lines of poetry. In this painting, the poetic inscription reads, "Pines and rocks lean fittingly for their age/Wisteria vines do not count the years." It is taken from a poem by an early Tang Era poet, Wang Bo (ca. 750–ca. 776). As in Zhang's painting, the learned scholars contemplate the rushing torrent, while their servants look away.

## QUESTIONS FOR ANALYSIS

1. How would you characterize the "inner spirit" of nature each artist seeks to communicate? How are the two artists' visions similar and different?
2. How are the human beings in each picture interacting with nature?
3. What message does each painting communicate about humanity's relationship to the natural world? Consider both the actions of the human beings in each painting as well as the manmade structures in Zhang's painting.
4. Both paintings show scholars contemplating a waterfall, a scene depicted in literally hundreds of Chinese landscape paintings. Why would the contemplation of a waterfall be particularly meaningful?
5. In each painting, the scholars' servants are not paying attention to the waterfall. What message does this communicate?

# Political Decline in China and Political Recovery in Japan

Eighteenth-century China and Japan were models of well-governed, prosperous states. This had seemed highly unlikely a century and a half earlier, when political problems plagued both societies: Japan, in the midst of a decades-long civil war, was on the brink of disintegration; China, meanwhile, was suffering from a host of problems, including the erratic rule of its Ming emperors.

The incessant civil strife of sixteenth-century Japan was rooted in longstanding tensions inherent in Japan's feudal society. In the 1300s, power began to shift away from the shogun, a military commander who ruled in the name of the emperor, to local military families who controlled districts and provinces. With a weak central government, feuding and fighting became endemic among the *daimyo,* the provincial lords, who enlisted *samurai,* lesser members of the nobility, and commoners to fight in their armies. Warfare intensified between the 1460s and the 1570s, an era known as the Warring States Period.

This ruinous feudal anarchy ended as a result of the efforts of three leaders bent on unifying Japan. Oda Nobunaga (1534–1582) brought approximately half of Japan under his rule before a traitorous vassal assassinated him. His successor, Toyotomi Hideyoshi (1536–1598), a commoner who rose through the ranks to become Nobunaga's ablest general, continued the work of consolidation. It was completed by Tokugawa Ieyasu (1542–1616), who conquered his rivals after Hideyoshi's death and declared himself shogun in 1603. Ieyasu and his successors stabilized Japan by imposing a sociopolitical order that lasted until 1867.

China's political problems had multiple causes, ranging from foreign military threats and fluctuations in the value of silver to a series of poor harvests after the weather turned cold and wet around 1600. Just as these problems were mounting, the quality and effectiveness of Ming rulers plummeted, especially during the long reign of the Wanli Emperor (r. 1572–1620). Disgusted with his bickering and quarrelsome advisors, Wanli withdrew from politics, ceased meeting with high officials, and failed to fill vacancies in the administration. Paralyzed by feuding between court eunuchs and Confucian officials, the central government drifted as China's problems worsened. Factional strife, oppressive taxation, corruption, unchecked banditry, and famine led to rebellion, the dynasty's collapse, and foreign conquest. In 1644, a rebel leader, Li Zicheng (1605–1645), captured Beijing, and in despair the last Ming emperor hanged himself. Within months, however, Li was driven from the city by the Manchus, northern invaders from the Amur River region. In the following decades, the Manchus extended their authority over all of China, established China's last dynasty, the Qing, and breathed new life into the imperial system.

# Symptoms of Ming Decline

### 26 • SHEN ZAN, FRAGMENTED PIECES ON RECENT EVENTS AND SONG YINGXING, UNOFFICIAL OPINONS

In the late sixteenth century, the formidable task of governing China became even harder. Manchu-Jurchen military pressure grew in the north, pirate raids increased on coastal cities, and in the 1590s Japan invaded China's client state, Korea. Peasant discontent boiled over into rebellion as rural misery deepened in the face of poor harvests, epidemics, worsening banditry, rising taxes, and currency fluctuations. From the 1580s onward, however, emperors ignored or were distracted from dealing with these challenges. They paid a price for their ineffectiveness: rebellion overwhelmed the government and brought about the fall of the Ming in 1644.

The following selections focus on several related issues confronting China in rhe final decades of Ming rule: lawlessness, budget shortfalls, taxes, and the role of eunuchs at court and in local administration. The first selection, written by the scholar/chronicler Shen Zan (1558-1612), describes a riot that took place in the silk-producing city of Suzhou in 1601. The main characters are Ge Xian, a silk weaver from Suzhou who led the riot, and the local tax commissioner, the powerful eunuch Sun Long, who had been appointed overseer of the imperial silk works in Suzhou. The second selection is drawn from the work of Song Yingxing (1587-1646?), a minor Ming official best known for his encyclopedic survey of Ming Era science and technology, *The Exploitation of the Works of Nature*. This particular excerpt, taken from one of his minor works, *Unofficial Opinions* (1636), describes the financial problems of Chinese salt merchants in the 1630s.

In both selections the villains are eunuchs, castrated males who traditionally had been relegated to the relatively minor role of managing the day-to-day business of the imperial palace but who in the 1580s assumed a much greater role in decision-making, appointments, and local administration. This occurred during the reign of the Wanli emperor (r. 1572-1620), who as a result of his feuds with Confucian officials and his disinterest in state affairs, gladly turned over the task of governing to eunuch favorites. Many were appointed as revenue officials charged with the task of raising taxes to help pay for the emperor's lavish ceremonies and construction projects. Eunuch power peaked between 1624 and 1627, when during the reign of the Tianqi emperor the eunuch Wei Zhongxian purged his enemies, levied new taxes, rewarded his cronies, and flouted rules and procedures. According to our author Song Yingxing, policies introduced by Wei were mainly responsible for the plight of the merchants in his account.

## QUESTIONS FOR ANALYSIS:

1. On the basis of Shen's account, what can one conclude about the motives of the individuals who supported the tax increase on silk?
2. What were Ge Xian's motives in leading the resistance to the new tax measures? What groups in Suzhou provided his main support?
3. Shen Zan admits that the ending of the affair was a "strange matter." What is "strange" in the summary of events in the last paragraph of Shen's account, and what may explain the events?
4. According to Song Yingxing, what was the situation of the Huai region salt merchants at the time he wrote his account?
5. What combination of factors contributed to their predicament?

---

## Shen Zan, Fragmented Pieces on Recent Events

Ge Xian was from Kunshan. He was hired to work as a silk weaver in the prefectural seat [Suzhou]. In the sixth moon of 1601, some treacherous people presented a plan to Tax Commissioner Sun which said: "We would like to propose a new tax law. A tax of three silver cents for every bolt of silk should be paid before it is marketed. We are willing to make efforts to take charge of this matter." They gathered substantial funds from several wealthy households to bribe the tax commissioner [to allow the tax]. The plan succeeded and the Commissioner made the announcement [of the tax] and let it be practiced.

All the artisans and silk dealers suffered from this and could find no method to stop it. Ge Xian then came forward and said: "I will be the leader and will eliminate this disorder for the people of Suzhou." He led dozens of people to the Xuan-miao Temple[1]. He made an arrangement with his followers, saying: "Let the palm-leaf fan in my hand be the signal for your actions." The crowd said: "We agree!" Thereupon, they first went to the homes of a certain Tang and a certain Xu who had first proposed the tax plan and beat them to death. Then they went to the house of an officer named Ding Yuanfu and the home of a certain rich family named Gui and burned their residences. Both Ding and Gui had helped in arranging loans to

---

*Source:* "1.1 Shen Zan's Account", "1.4 On the Management of the Salt Gabelle", translated by Pei Kai Cheng and Michael Lestz from *The Search for Modern China, A Documentary Collection* edited by Pei Kai Cheng, Michael Lestz, and Jonathan Spence. Copyright © 1999 by W.W. Norton & Company, Inc. Used by permission of W.W. Norton & Company, Inc. This selection may not be reproduced, stored in a retrieval system, or transmitted in any form or by any means without the prior written permission of the publisher.
[1]A Daoist temple dating from the third century C.E.

the local bullies for bribing the tax commissioner. The rioters forbade looting and nothing was taken. They split into two groups and went to the tax collection stations outside of the Lu and Xu Gates. They stopped at each station and beat all of the collectors to death. They then went in person to see the prefect[2] and said: "We want Tax Commissioner Sun or we won't be satisfied." The prefect tried to mollify them but dared not investigate. On the second day, the crowd still would not disperse. They said: "We won't stop until we get the Tax Commissioner!" Thereupon, Sun summoned garrison troops and local militia to make a display of force before his headquarters. Ge Xian and others also gathered a mob and approached the gate of the Tax Commission office.

Fortunately, Ge Xian's followers and the troops did not confront each other. At sunset, the mob dispersed. The Tax Commissioner took this opportunity to flee away with his escort and went to Hangzhou. Ge Xian then volunteered to go to prison. The prefect asked what he wanted. He replied: "There are many mosquitoes at night. I just need a mosquito net." People in the jail and outsiders who were not afraid of the consequences often praised him and brought wine and dried meat for him every day. Ge Xian expected that he must die but a memorial was presented and an order pardoning him was sent down. He is still in prison and is well. This is a strange matter!

## Song Yingxing, Unofficial Opinions

Everyone needs to eat salt and there is great profit for the state in its administration.[3] Management fails when corruption appears and merchants are impoverished when management is disorderly. It is human nature to seek profit and even risk death rushing after it. Since there is profit in trading in salt, who will not exhaust himself in pursuit of it? Why is it that the same merchants who once amassed jade and gold, have today emptied their purses and piled up debts? This is because the merchants are poor and the management of salt [production, transport, and sale] is not functioning,

Half of the state's salt levy comes from the Huai region.[4] The other half comes from Changlu, Xiechi, Liangzhe, the Sichuan wells, the Guangdong salt ponds, and the Fujian coast. Although the tax levy for Changlu and other places has been increased, the merchants there can still manage to pay. But for the Huai region, an increase is unbearable. The Huai tax quota was originally 930,000 taels. Now it has been increased to one million five hundred. If salt management was as effective as it was in the times of the Chenghua [r.1465–1487] and Hongzhi [r.1488–1505] emperors and if the merchants were still as rich as they were during the reigns of Longqing [r.1567–1572] and Wanli [r.1572–1620] then such an increase could be comfortably met. . .

The decline of the merchants started at the beginning of the Tianqi era [1621–1627]. For the state, the conflagration set by the eunuchs blazed out of control; for merchants, misfortunes were brought by spendthrift sons; in various localities, profit-seeking bullies assembled; officials became increasingly corrupt; and clerks . . . devised new, wicked techniques [to extort funds]. All of these problems grew worse each day. Just as the merchants were about to maneuver their way out of their straits, the new tax levy order

---

[2]A local administrator with limited authority in the area of law enforcement.

[3]The production and sale of salt was carried on by privileged merchants under strict state regulation. By the seventeenth century the salt tax was the second most important source of government revenue after the land tax.

[4]Although salt was produced throughout China, the major source of salt were the salt fields along the coast especially the Huai River region in present-day northern Jiangsu province.

fell down upon them and they were afflicted by the bandit invasions. When they could not pay the tax, the merchant's family members were arrested to force them to pay. Presently, half of them are poor and in debt. Their entire assembled capital is no more than five million taels; how could such a sum produce enough interest to pay the state's quota? . . .

# The Reunification of Japan Under Hideyoshi and the Tokugawa Clan

## BACKGROUND

In 1570 Japan had no effective central government, and warfare among its powerful aristocratic families, which had begun in the mid-1400s, showed no signs of ending. Portuguese traders and missionaries had arrived in 1543, and by 1570 large numbers of Japanese had accepted Christianity. Rural rebellion, brought on by new taxes, was widespread. And yet in a remarkably short time—by the early 1600s—the constant warfare had ended and order had been restored: Japan had been reunified, the foreigners had been expelled, Christianity had been outlawed, and rural violence had abated. Japan had entered what proved to be a 250-year period of peace and stability under the rule of the Tokugawa dynasty.

Japan's reunification resulted from the military prowess of Oda Nobunaga, Toyotomi Hideyoshi, and Tokugawa Ieyasu, but the country's long-term pacification resulted from more than battlefield victories. Stability was achieved by the rigorous enforcement of new policies that provided a foundation for a disciplined and stable Japan. The sources that follow—edicts issued by Hideyoshi and the early Tokugawa shoguns—provide insight into the range and substance of these new policies.

## THE SOURCES

The Edicts on Christianity were issued in 1587 by Toyotomi Hideyoshi, who by then was well on his way to bringing all of Japan under his control. To understand his motives for making these pronouncements, it is necessary to review the religious dynamics of Japan in the late 1580s. By 1587, Christianity had made impressive gains. On their arrival in 1549 Portuguese Jesuits converted a number of daimyo from Kyushu, the southernmost and westernmost of Japan's four major islands, and these daimyo in turn had used various forms of coercion to

convince their subjects to become Christians. The movement spread to other parts of Japan and by the late 1500s had garnered 200,000 to 300,000 converts. The Jesuits had the support of Oda Nobunaga, who had unified much of Japan before his death in 1582; for a time, they also were supported by his successor, Hideyoshi. Both rulers viewed Christianity as a counterweight to certain Buddhist sects that had established independent political bases or were connected with popular rebellion. These included the Honganji branch of the True Pure Land sect, which had many followers in central Japan and maintained fortified temples in key cities. Its doctrines, which emphasized the spiritual equality of all believers, inspired violent uprisings of *Ikkō-ikki*, loosely structured mobs made up mostly of peasant farmers who fought against taxes and samurai rule. It gained control of Kaga province in 1488 and was connected with insurrection and anti-tax movements in the 1500s.

By 1587 Hideyoshi had concluded that Christianity, like these Buddhist sects, also was a threat. His change of mind was prompted in part by events in the Philippines, where large-scale conversions to Christianity went hand in hand with the Spanish conquest. It also was no accident that the anti-Christian edicts were issued shortly after Hideyoshi invaded Kyushu, the center of Japanese Christianity.

The Sword Collection Edict (1588) and the Edict on Change of Status (1591), both issued by Hideyoshi, were designed to end the blurring of social distinctions that had occurred during decades of fighting. Specific concerns were the large number of commoners who had left farming to become soldiers and the smaller number of samurai and lesser nobles who had illegally changed masters or had abandoned their military obligations.

The Laws Governing Military Households (1615), proclaimed by Tokugawa Ieyasu (who continued to rule Japan until 1616, despite having named his son Hidetada shogun in 1605 to avoid a succession dispute), spelled out rules for members of Japan's aristocratic (daimyo) families. Their feuds had been largely responsible for Japan's civil wars.

The final edict, known as the Closed Country Edict, was issued by Tokugawa Iemitsu in 1635 to the two commissioners of Nagasaki, the city on the island of Kyushu that was the major port of entry for European traders. It addressed issues relating to trade and foreign relations and also clarified the status of Japanese Christians, who had been subjected to sporadic but brutal persecution since Hideyoshi had issued his anti-Christian edicts in 1587.

## QUESTIONS FOR ANALYSIS

1. What reasons does Hideyoshi provide to justify his move against Christianity in 1587? How are his views of Christianity shaped by his experience with Japan's Buddhist sects?
2. How are the Sword Collection Edict and the Edict on Change of Status related? What are their implications for the structuring of Japanese society?

3. In what ways does the edict on military households ensure the shogun's control of the daimyo?

4. Even though Tokugawa policies limited the independence of the daimyo, the daimyo retained certain political powers. How many such powers can be identified in the Laws Governing Military Households?

5. According to the Closed Country Edict, what is the greater threat to Japan: Christianity or trade with foreigners?

6. Did the Closed Country Edict really close Japan?

7. Based on the documents, what conclusions can be drawn about the political and social philosophies behind the efforts of Hideyoshi and the Tokugawa to bring order to Japan? What signs of Confucian teachings are discernable?

---

## 1 • Edicts on Christianity

### Notice

1. The matter of [becoming] a sectarian of the Bateren[1] shall be the free choice of the individual concerned.

2. That enfeoffed recipients[2] of provinces, districts, and estates should force peasants registered in [Buddhist] temples . . . against their will into the ranks of the Bateren sectarians is unreasonable beyond words and is outrageous. . . .

4. Persons holding above 200 *cho* of land or [who] can expect 2 or 3 thousand *kan* of rice harvest each year,[3] may become [followers of the] Bateren upon obtaining official permission, acceding to the pleasure of the lord of the *Tenka*.[4] . . .

6. The Bateren sectarians . . . are even more given to deceits . . . than the Ikkō Sect. The Ikkō Sect established temple precincts[5] in the provinces and districts and did not pay the yearly dues to their enfeoffed recipients [local lords]. Moreover, they made the entire Province of Kaga into [Ikkō] sectarians, chased out . . . the lord of the province, delivered the stipends over to [monks] of the Ikkō Sect. . . . That this was harmful to the *Tenka* is the undisguisable truth. . . .

7. That daimyo . . . should force their retainers into the ranks of the Bateren sectarians is even more undesirable by far than the Honganji[6] sectarians' establishment of temple precincts, and is bound to be of great harm to the *Tenka*. These individuals . . . shall be subject to punishment.

8. Bateren sectarians by their free choice, [insofar as they] are of the lower classes, shall be unmolested. . . .

---

*Source:* Excerpted from George Ellison, *Deus Destroyed: The Image of Christianity in Early Modern Japan* (Cambridge: Harvard University Council on East Studies, 1988), pp. 115–118.

[1]Japanese approximation of the word "padre," or father, a word used to designate a Catholic priest in Portugal, Spain, and Italy.

[2]Those invested by a higher authority with territory and, with it, various rights and duties connected with that territory; sometimes translated as "vassals."

[3]One *cho* equals approximately 2.9 acres; one *kan* equals approximately 8.25 pounds. Clearly, this provision refers to wealthy landowners—members of the aristocracy.

[4]A reference to Hideyoshi; *tenka* means the "whole realm."

[5]Villages or regions under the control of Buddhist monks connected with a temple or monastery.

[6]Honganji refers to a militant faction within the True Pure Land sect of Buddhism. The term also refers to the temples controlled by the faction. The Ishiyama Honganji in Osaka was controlled by the movement's most fanatical disciples, the Ikkō-ikki, and was burned to the ground by Nobunaga after a siege.

10. The sale of Japanese to China, South Barbary,[7] and Korea is outrageous[8] . . . .

11. Trade and slaughter of cattle and horses for use as food shall also be considered criminal.[9]

The above items shall rest under strict prohibition. Any transgressor shall immediately be put to severe punishment.

## Ordained

Japan is the Land of the Gods. Diffusion here from Christian Country of a pernicious doctrine is most undesirable.

To approach the people of our provinces and districts and, making them into [Christian] sectarians, cause them to destroy the shrines of the gods and the temples of the Buddhas is a thing unheard of in previous ages. . . . But to corrupt and stir up the lower classes is outrageous.

It is the judgment [of the lord of the *Tenka*] that since the Bateren by means of their clever doctrine amass parishioners as they please, the aforementioned violation of the Buddhist Law in these Precincts . . . has resulted. That being outrageous, the Bateren can hardly be allowed to remain on Japanese soil. Within twenty days they must make their preparations and return to their country. . . .

The purpose of the Black Ships [Spanish and Portuguese trading vessels] is trade, and that is a different matter. As years and months pass, trade may be carried on in all sorts of articles. . . .

---

[7]Europeans were called "Southern Barbarians," so South Barbary may refer to Europe itself, but it more likely refers to the parts of South Asia where the Portuguese had established a presence.

[8]There is evidence that European merchants for a time did purchase small numbers of Japanese and sell them as slaves to Asian trading partners. When confronted by Hideyoshi on this matter, the Jesuits denied any involvement and claimed they had no influence on the practices of European merchants.

[9]The Japanese, who considered the slaughter of animals as work suitable for the lowest groups in their social hierarchy, viewed the eating of useful animals such as horses and cattle as a sign of barbarism.

---

## 2 • Edict on the Collection of Swords (1588)

1. The farmers of all provinces are strictly forbidden to have in their possession any swords, bows, spears, firearms or other types of weapons. If unnecessary implements of war are kept, the collection of annual rent may become more difficult, and without provocation uprisings can be fomented. Therefore those who perpetrate improper acts against samurai . . . must be brought to trial and punished. . . .

2. The swords and short swords collected . . . will not be wasted. They will be used as nails and bolts in the construction of the Great Image of Buddha. In this way, the farmers will benefit not only in this life but also in lives to come.

3. If farmers possess only agricultural implements and devote themselves exclusively to cultivating the fields, they and their descendants will prosper. This compassionate concern for the well-being of the farmers is the reason for issuance of this edict, and such a concern is the foundation for the peace and security of the country and the joy and happiness of all the people. . . .

---

*Source:* From *Japan: A Documentary History*, ed. and trans., David J. Lu (Armonk, NY: M. E. Sharpe, 1997), p. 191. Translation copyright © 1997 by David J. Lu. Reprinted with permission of M. E. Sharpe, Inc. All rights reserved. Not for reproduction.

## 3 • Edict on Change of Status (1591)

1. If there should be living among you men who were in military service including those who served Hideyoshi, higher-ranking warriors [samurai] of the *daimyo*, those who took their orders from samurai, lowest-ranking warriors, and those who performed miscellaneous chores for samurai—who have assumed the identity of a townsman or farmer . . . they must be expelled. . . . If anyone as described is kept concealed, the entire town or village shall be held responsible and punished accordingly.

2. If any farmer abandons his fields and engages in trade or offers himself for hire for wages, not only is he to be punished, but also his fellow villagers. If there is anyone who neither serves in the military nor cultivates land, it is the responsibility of the deputies and other local officials to investigate and expel him. If they do not take action, those local officials shall be stripped of their posts on account of negligence. If a townsman is disguised as a farmer, and that fact is concealed, that county or town shall be regarded as committing a culpable offense.

3. No employment shall be given to a military retainer—be he a samurai, or . . . the lowest rank of warrior—who has left his former master without permission. In employing a retainer, you must investigate thoroughly his background, and insist on having a guarantor. If the above already has a master and that fact is discovered, he shall be arrested . . . and shall be returned to his former master. If this regulation is violated, and the offender is willfully set free, then three persons shall be beheaded in place of the one, and their heads sent to the offender's original master. . . .

Source: From *Japan: A Documentary History,* ed. and trans., David J. Lu (Armonk, NY: M. E. Sharpe, 1997), p. 194. Translation copyright © 1997 by David J. Lu. Reprinted with permission of M. E. Sharpe, Inc. All rights reserved. Not for reproduction.

## 4 • Laws Governing Military Households (1615)

1. The study of literature and the practice of the military arts, including archery and horsemanship, must be cultivated diligently. . . .

From of old the rule has been to practice "the arts of peace on the left hand, and the arts of war on the right"; both must be mastered. . . .

2. Avoid group drinking and wild parties. . .

3. Anyone who violates the law must not be harbored in any domain.

Law is the basis of social order. . . . Anyone who breaks the law must be severely punished.

4. Great lords [daimyo], the lesser lords, and [officials] should at once expel from their domains any among their retainers or soldiers who have been charged with treason or murder.

[Traitors] can become instruments for overturning the state and a deadly sword for destroying the people. How can this be tolerated?

5. Hereafter, do not allow people from other domains to . . . reside in your own domain. . . .

6. The castles in various domains may be repaired, provided the matter is reported [to the shogunate] without fail. New construction of any kind is prohibited.

Source: From *Japan: A Documentary History,* ed. and trans. David J. Lu (Armonk, NY: M. E. Sharpe, 1997), pp. 206–208. Translation copyright © 1997 by David J. Lu. Reprinted with permission of M. E. Sharpe, Inc. All rights reserved. Not for reproduction.

7. If innovations are being made or factions being formed in neighboring domains, they must be reported . . .

8. Marriage must not be contracted in private [without notifying the shogunate]. . . . To form a factional alliance by marriage is the root of treason.

9. The daimyo's visits to Edo must follow the following regulations.[1]

. . . For daimyo whose revenues range from 1,000,000 koku[2] down to 200,000 koku of rice, not more than twenty horsemen may accompany them. For those with an income of one hundred thousand koku or less, the number is to be proportionate to their income. . . .

10. Regulations in regard to dress materials must not be breached.

Lord and vassal, superior and inferior, must observe what is proper to their stations in life. . . .

11. Persons without rank are not to ride in palanquins.[3]

Traditionally there have been certain families entitled to ride in palanquins without special permission and others who have received such permission. Lately, however, even the ordinary retainers and soldiers of some families have taken to riding in palanquins, which is truly a wanton act. Hereafter, the daimyo of various domains, close relatives, and their distinguished officials may ride in palanquins . . . along with doctors and astrologers, persons over sixty years of age, the sick, and invalids.

12. The samurai of all domains must practice frugality.

When the rich proudly display their wealth, the poor are ashamed [and envious]. There is nothing which will corrupt public morality more than this.

13. The lords of the domains should select as their officials men of administrative ability.

The lord must recognize the merits and faults of his retainers so he can administer rewards and punishments. If a domain has good men, it flourishes . . . If it has no good men it is doomed . . .

---

[1]This refers to the policy of requiring daimyo to reside every other year in Edo, the seat of government.
[2]One *koku* equals five bushels.

[3]Enclosed carriages borne on the shoulders of carriers by means of poles.

---

## 5 • Closed Country Edict (1635)

1. Japanese ships are strictly forbidden to leave for foreign countries.

2. No Japanese is permitted to go abroad. If there is anyone who attempts to do so secretly, he must be executed. The ship so involved must be impounded and its owner arrested, and the matter must be reported to the higher authority.

2. If any Japanese returns from overseas after residing there, he must be put to death.

3. If there is any place where the teaching of the [Catholic] priests is practiced, the two of you[1] must order a thorough investigation.

4. Any informer revealing the whereabouts of the followers of the priests must be rewarded accordingly. If anyone reveals the whereabouts of a high-ranking priest, he must be given one hundred pieces of silver. For those of lower ranks, . . . the reward must be set accordingly. . . .

5. If there are any Southern Barbarians [Europeans] who propagate the teachings of the priests, or

*Source:* From *Japan: A Documentary History,* ed. and trans. David J. Lu (Armonk, NY: M. E. Sharpe, 1997), pp. 221–222. Translation copyright © 1997 by David J. Lu. Reprinted with permission of M. E. Sharpe, Inc. All rights reserved. Not for reproduction.

[1]The two commissioners of Nagasaki, to whom the edict is addressed.

otherwise commit crimes, they may be incarcerated in the prison. . . .

6. All incoming ships must be carefully searched for the followers of the priests.

7. No single trading city shall be permitted to purchase all the merchandise brought by foreign ships. . . .

12. After settling the price, all white yarns [raw silk] brought by foreign ships shall be allocated to the five trading cities[2] and other quarters as stipulated.

13. After settling the price of white yarns, other merchandise [brought by foreign ships] may be traded freely between the [licensed] dealers. . . .

14. The date of departure homeward of foreign ships shall not be later than the twentieth day of the ninth month. Any ships arriving in Japan later than usual shall depart within fifty days of their arrival. . . .

---

[2]The cities of Kyoto, Edo, Osaka, Sakai, and Nagasaki.

# Doing Business in Southeast Asia

Beginning in the 1400s and 1500s, Southeast Asian commerce entered a golden age as the world economy recovered from the ravages of the Black Death, the newly installed Ming Dynasty in China reopened trade with the outside world, and new supplies of gold and silver came into circulation. During this period of expansion, no single state controlled the region's trade, and cargo ships were unarmed. Port cities pursued an open-door policy, welcoming traders from all lands and faiths. In the early 1500s a visitor to Melaka, the Malay port, claimed to have heard no fewer than 84 languages on its streets.

Much of this changed in the 1500s with the arrival of Europeans, who came to the region with a mix of objectives and strategies. First came the Portuguese, with dreams of taking control of the sea routes between Europe and Asia while simultaneously spreading Christianity and wreaking havoc on Muslims, whom they fanatically hated. Their Southeast Asian venture got off to a promising start in 1511, when they conquered Melaka, giving them control of the key choke point between the Indian Ocean and the South China Sea (see source 1). They soon established a series of fortified trading stations in the spice-producing Moluccas, thereby increasing their control of the spice trade to Europe. Until the Dutch expelled the Portuguese from the region in the early 1600s, the spice trade enriched many individual Portuguese and provided much of the income for the Portuguese monarchy. The Portuguese, however, never achieved a monopoly over the region's trade. Indian, Arab, and local merchants avoided having to deal with them by shifting their commerce away from Melaka to other ports and by finding sources of spices in places other than the Moluccas. The Portuguese also failed to achieve their religious goals. Conversions to Christianity were miniscule, and paradoxically their presence in the region strengthened Islam, which became a symbol of resistance to the Portuguese, whose greed and cruelty were deeply resented.

The early forays of other European states into Southeast Asia had similar mixed results or were near-total failures. The Spaniards, who took the Philippines as a consolation prize after the Portuguese beat them to the Spice Islands, managed to convert most Filipinos to Catholicism but at first reaped few economic benefits. The efforts of France and England in the region barely got off the ground. After arriving at Aceh, in northern Sumatra, in 1602, the British East India Company established several trading posts, but in the face of Dutch opposition withdrew in the 1620s, choosing instead to focus on India. France organized the Company of the Moluccas in 1615 and one year later sent a well-armed fleet to the region, but in the face of stiff Dutch resistance it withdrew, leaving behind a small number of missionaries in Vietnam and Thailand.

By the early 1600s, only two European powers remained in Southeast Asia. One was Spain, which held the Philippines until its defeat in the Spanish-American War in 1898. The other was the Netherlands, which in the early 1600s under the auspices of the Dutch East India Company launched an aggressive campaign to replace Portugal as the dominant European power in the region and to block intrusions from the French and British. With enormous financial resources and a mandate from the Dutch government to raise an army, make alliances with native princes, and exercise all rights of sovereignty, the Company brought economic and political changes to the East Indies, but mainly in the eighteenth century. The role played by the Philippines in the world economy is spelled out in the selection that follows.

# Manila and the Galleon Trade: A World Economy Emerges

## 27 • ANTONIO DE MORGA, EVENTS OF THE PHILIPPINE ISLANDS

With the Portuguese firmly established in the Moluccas and other parts of the East Indies, the Spanish turned their attention to the Philippine Islands, a few of which had been claimed for Spain by Ferdinand Magellan before he was killed in a battle with native warriors in 1521. After Spanish expeditions to the Philippines in 1525, 1527, and 1542 all failed, the islands came under Spanish control following the arrival of the conquistador Miguel López de Legazpi in 1565. Within a decade Spanish settlements were established on the Cebu and Panay islands and in Manila, laying the foundations for extending and consolidating Spanish sovereignty in most of the archipelago.

The Spaniards found no spice-growing regions or gold mines in the Philippines, but in Manila they found a city whose location and deep-water harbor would soon make it one of the world's most important ports. It became the eastern terminus of the galleon trade, in which merchants from China, Japan, and other parts of Asia brought goods to exchange for American silver that had been shipped to Manila in Spanish galleons from Acapulco in New Spain. The galleons returned to Acapulco laden with Asian goods that were sold in Latin America or, after having been transported across Mexico and shipped across the Atlantic, in Europe. From 1571 to the early nineteenth century, when Mexico became independent from Spain, the galleon trade made Manila a wealthy city, sustained Spain's colonial enterprise in the Philippines, and was a prime symbol of the emerging global economy.

The following description of the galleon trade is provided by Antonio de Morga (1559–1636), a Spanish-born lawyer, who served as a judge and administrator in Spain, the Philippines, Mexico, and Peru. He is best known for his *Events of the Philippine Islands*, a two-volume history of the Philippines from the time of Magellan's visit in 1521 to 1603, when de Morga was transferred from the Philippines to Mexico. Based on documentary research and personal observation, the book is an invaluable source for the early history of Spanish colonization in the Philippines.

## QUESTIONS FOR ANALYSIS

1. How does the Spanish Crown benefit from the Manila trade?
2. To what extent is the Manila trade overseen by government officials? To what extent does it operate according to free-market principles?
3. To what extent are the goods brought to Manila for trade "luxury items"? What are some of the other general categories of goods?
4. What forms of payment are made for the goods purchased by the Spaniards?
5. What signs are there that Filipino natives participate in or benefit from the trade that goes on in Manila?
6. On the basis of the information provided in this source, what generalizations can be made about worldwide commercial relations around 1600?

Merchants and businessmen form the bulk of the residents of the islands, because of the great amount of merchandise brought there—in addition to native products—from China, Japan, the Moluccas, Melaka, Siam, Cambodia, Borneo, and other districts. They invest in this merchandise and export it annually in the vessels that sail to New Spain, and at times to Japan, where great profits are made from raw silk. Then on the return to Manila are brought the proceeds, which until now have resulted in large and splendid profits.

A considerable number of . . . junks[1] generally come from China to Manila, laden with merchandise. Every year thirty or even forty ships usually come, and although they do not come together, in the form of a convoy or war fleet, they still come in groups with the settled weather, which is generally in March. . . . These vessels come laden with merchandise, and bring wealthy merchants who own the ships, and their servants and agents of other merchants who remain in China. The merchandise that they bring and sell to the Spaniards consists

---

Source: Antonio de Morga, *History of the Philippine Islands*, Emma Helen Blair and James A. Robinson, ed. and trans. (Cleveland, OH: A. H. Clark Company, 1907), pp. 401–414, *passim*.

[1]Chinese cargo ships characterized by the so-called junk rig, a type of sail rig in which rigid strips of wood, called battens, span the full width of the sail and extend the sail forward of the mast.

of raw silk in bundles, and other silk of poorer quality; fine untwisted silk, white and of all colors, wound in small skeins; quantities of velvets, . . . some embroidered in all sorts of figures, colors, and fashions—others embroidered with gold; woven fabrics and brocades of gold and silver upon silk of various colors and patterns; quantities of gold and silver thread in skeins . . . ; damasks, satins, taffetas, and other cloths of all colors, some finer and better than others; a quantity of linen . . . and white cotton cloth of different kinds and qualities. They also bring musk [a scent derived from certain animals and some plants], benzoin resin [a scent derived from tree bark], and ivory; many bed ornaments, hangings, coverlets, and tapestries of embroidered velvet; tablecloths, cushions, and carpets; also some pearls and rubies, sapphires and crystal-stones; metal basins, copper kettles, and pots; . . . all sorts of nails, sheet-iron, tin and lead; saltpeter and gunpowder. They supply the Spaniards with wheat flour; preserves made of orange, peach, pear, nutmeg, and ginger, and other fruits of China; salt pork and other salted meats; live fowls and capons; oranges of all kinds; excellent chestnuts, walnuts, pears; . . . beds, tables, chairs, and gilded benches. They bring tame bison; geese; horses, some mules and donkeys; even caged birds, some of which talk, while others sing and play innumerable tricks. The Chinese furnish numerous other trinkets of little value, which are esteemed among the Spaniards; and curiosities of all kinds which, if I were to refer to them all, I would never finish, nor have sufficient paper for it.

As soon as the ship reaches the mouth of the bay of Manila, the watchman stationed at the island of Miraveles goes out to it in a light vessel. Having examined the ship, he puts a guard of two or three soldiers on it, so that it may anchor near the city, and to see that no one shall disembark from the vessel, or anyone enter it, until the vessel has been inspected. When the vessel has arrived [in Manila itself] and anchored, royal officials go to inspect it and the register of the merchandise. At the same time the valuation of the cargo is made . . . of what it is worth in Manila; for the vessel immediately pays three per cent on everything to his Majesty. Then the merchandise is immediately unloaded by another official into champans [small cargo boats], and taken to the Parian [the city's commercial district], or to other warehouses outside the city. There the goods are freely sold. . . .

The ordinary price of the silks and cloth—which form the bulk of the cargo—is settled leisurely, and by persons who understand it, both on the part of the Spaniards and that of the Sangleys.[2] The purchase price is paid in silver and *reals*,[3] for the Sangleys do not want gold, or any other articles, and will not take other things to China. All the trading must be completed by the end of May, or thereabout, in order that the Sangleys may return and the Spaniards have the goods ready to load upon the vessels that go to New Spain by the end of June. However, the larger dealers and those who have most money usually do their trading after that time, at lower rates, and keep the merchandise until the following year. Certain Sangleys remain in Manila for the same purpose, when they have not had a good sale, in order to go on selling it more leisurely. The Sangleys are very skillful and intelligent traders. . . . On the other hand, as they are a people without religion or conscience, and so greedy, they commit innumerable frauds and deceits. The purchaser must watch them very closely, in order not to be cheated by them. The purchasers, however, acquit themselves by their poor payments and the debts that they incur; and both sides keep the judges and the royal court quite busy.

---

[2]Sangley, or sanglay, was the word used for Chinese living in the Philippines or trading there.

[3]A silver coin, eight of which equaled one peso.

Some Japanese and Portuguese merchantmen [freighters] also come every year from the port of Nagasaki in Japan[4] . . . . The bulk of their cargo is excellent wheat-flour for the provisioning of Manila, and highly prized cured meats. They also bring some fine woven silk goods of mixed colors; beautiful and finely-decorated screens done in lacquer and gilt; all kinds of cutlery; many suits of armor, spears, and other weapons, all finely wrought; writing-cases, boxes and small cases of wood; excellent pears; barrels and casks of good salt tuna; cages of sweet-voiced larks, and other trifles. . . . The bulk of the merchandise is used in the Philippines, but some goods are exported to New Spain. The price is generally paid in *reals*, although they are not as greedy for them as the Chinese, for there is silver in Japan.

Some Portuguese vessels sail to Manila annually during the monsoon season from the Moluccas, Melaka, and India. They bring merchandise consisting of spices—cloves, cinnamon, and pepper; slaves, both blacks and mulattoes; cotton cloth of all sorts, fine muslins, linens, gauzes, . . . and other delicate and precious cloths; amber and ivory; bedcovers and rich coverlets from Bengal, Kochi,[5] and other countries; many gilt articles and curiosities; diamonds, rubies, sapphires, topazes, and other precious stones; many trinkets and ornaments; wine, raisins, and almonds; delicious preserves, and other fruits brought from Portugal and prepared in Goa; carpets and tapestries from Persia and Turkey; beds, writing-cases, parlor-chairs, and other finely-gilded furniture, made in Macao [a Portuguese colony in China]; needle-work of great beauty and perfection. Purchases of the above are paid in *reals* and gold. They carry to the Moluccas provisions of rice and wine, crockery, and other wares; while to Melaka they take only the gold or money, besides a few special trinkets and curiosities from Spain, and emeralds.

A few smaller vessels also sail from Borneo.[6] They sell their cargoes in their vessels. These consist of fine and well-made palm-mats, a few slaves for the natives, sago—a certain food of theirs prepared from the pith of palms—and large and small jars, glazed black and very fine; and excellent camphor, which is produced on that island. . . . These articles are bought mainly by natives rather than by the Spaniards. The articles taken back by the Borneans are provisions of wine and rice, cotton cloth, and other wares that are lacking in Borneo.

Very seldom a few vessels sail to Manila from Siam [Thailand] and Cambodia. They carry some benzoin, pepper, ivory, and cotton cloth; rubies and sapphires, badly cut and set; a few slaves; rhinoceros horns, and the hides, hoofs, and teeth of this animal; and other goods. In return they take the wares found in Manila.

In these classes of merchandise, the Spaniards make their purchases, investments, and exports for New Spain. They make these as best suits them, and load them on the vessels that are to make the voyage. They value and register these goods, for they pay into the royal treasury of Manila, before the voyage, the two per cent royal duties on exports, besides the freight charges of the vessel. . . . This latter is paid at the port of Acapulco into the royal treasury, in addition to the ten per cent duties for entrance and first sale in New Spain.

Since the ships which are dispatched with the said merchandise are his Majesty's enterprise, and other ships cannot be sent, there is generally not enough space for all the purchases. For that reason the governor divides the cargo-room among all

---

[4]The Portuguese sent one carrack, a large cargo ship, to trade in Nagasaki every year; they also were involved in the carrying trade, bringing Chinese goods from their base in Macao to Japan.

[5]Kachi is a port city in India's west coast; Bengal is a region in northeast India.

[6]The largest island in the Malay Archipelago, some eight hundred miles southwest of Manila. A Spanish effort to conquer the sultanate of Brunei on Borneo in 1578 had failed.

the shippers, according to their wealth and merits, after they have been examined by well-informed intelligent men appointed for that purpose. Consequently every man knows how much he can export, and only that amount is received in the vessel; and exact account is taken of it. Trustworthy persons are appointed who are present at the loading; and space is left for the provisions and passengers that are to go in the vessels. When the ships are and ready to sail, they are delivered to the general and the officials who have them in charge. Then they start on their voyage at the end of the month of June. . . .

This trade and commerce is so great and profitable, and easy to control—for it only lasts three months in the year . . . —that the Spaniards do not apply themselves to, or engage in, any other industry. Consequently, there is no husbandry or field-labor worthy of note. Neither do the Spaniards work the gold mines or placers,[7] which are numerous. They do not engage in many other industries that they could turn to with profit if the Chinese trade should fail them. That trade has been very hurtful and prejudicial in this respect, as well as for the occupations and farm industries in which the natives used to engage. Now the latter are abandoning and forgetting those labors. Besides, there is the great harm and loss resulting from the immense amount of silver that passes annually by this trade, into the possession of infidels, which can never, by any way, return into the possession of the Spaniards.

---

[7]Placer mining is mining for precious minerals, usually gold, in stream beds.

# PART TWO

# A Era of Transition and Transformation: The World from the Mid-Seventeenth to the Early Nineteenth Century

EVER-GREATER INTERACTION among the world's peoples and ongoing tensions between innovation and tradition are the major themes in world history from the mid-seventeenth to the early nineteenth century. Neither theme was new. Indeed, the degree of global interaction had considerably increased in the previous two hundred years as a result of the European discovery of the Americas and the growth of world trade. Similarly, the need to resolve conflicting claims of tradition and innovation had challenged many societies in the past. From the mid-1600s to the early 1800s, however, the pace of globalization quickened and the forces of change became more profound and intense, more threatening to old ways, and less avoidable.

Tensions between tradition and change were most pronounced in Europe and its offshoots in the Western Hemisphere. In the realm of ideas, intellectuals continued to abandon much of the heritage of the Middle Ages and Renaissance and formulated views of society, morality, and human nature that were secular and scientific. In politics revolutions on both sides of the Atlantic challenged royal authority, aristocratic privilege, and state-controlled churches and sought a new political order based on popular sovereignty, legal equality, and freedom. In economics the Atlantic assumed an ever-greater importance in world trade, while in Europe population growth, urbanization, and greater productivity in agriculture and manufacturing further undermined the traditional feudal-agrarian order. Such changes also set the stage for one of the great turning points in history, the Industrial Revolution, which began in England in the late 1700s.

The conflict between innovation and tradition was not limited to Europe and the Americas. In Russia a deep division opened between those who supported the Westernizing measures of Peter the Great (r. 1682–1725) and those who sought to preserve the essentials of Russian culture and religion. In the Ottoman Empire advocates of military and political reform clashed with religious leaders and upholders of the status quo. In Japan new intellectual currents, economic growth, and urbanization caused cracks in the foundations of Tokugawa rule, while in China the imposition of Manchu rule brought inevitable changes and adjustments.

The subjugation of China by the Manchus, subsequent Chinese expansion into Central Asia, and further Russian expansion into Siberia all are examples of how military conquest led to growing interaction among the world's peoples. But the main impetus to globalization was Europe's continuing commercial, demographic, and political expansion. Through migration and internal growth the number of Europeans in the Americas swelled, and in their churches, schools, political institutions, social mores, racial attitudes, and much else, they introduced European practices and perspectives to the Western Hemisphere. The growing importance of the Americas as a market for European goods and as a source of agricultural products and raw materials led to increased transatlantic trade, which in the eighteenth century included more than six million Africans who were sold into slavery in the Americas.

Europeans also intensified their involvement in Asia. In the 1600s the Dutch drove the Portuguese from Southeast Asia and took control of the island of Java. By the late 1700s the British ruled Bengal and a number of smaller Indian states, were flooding the Chinese market with opium, and were pressuring China to open more ports to foreign trade. Europeans in the late 1700s also began to explore, exploit, and settle New Zealand, Australia, and other South Pacific islands, bringing the world's last isolated region into global patterns of political influence, cultural interchange, and commerce. More so than at any other time in history, isolation among the world's peoples was melting away.

# Chapter 5

# Europe and the Americas in an Age of Science, Economic Growth, and Revolution

N OCTOBER 1648, the work of hundreds of diplomats and dozens of heads of state ended when signatures were affixed to the Treaty of Münster, which ended the longstanding Dutch Revolt against Spain, and the Treaty of Osnabrück, which ended the Thirty Years' War, Europe's deadliest and most demoralizing war until the twentieth century. With these treaties, the era of Europe's religious wars came to an end. After more than a century of attempting to exterminate each other with armies, the executioner's axe, and instruments of the torture chamber, Protestants and Catholics accepted the permanence of Europe's religious divisions.

Religion was not the only area in which tensions eased in the late seventeenth century. Conflicts between centralizing monarchs and independent-minded nobles and provinces ended in most European states with the triumph of absolutism—a form of government in which divinely sanctioned monarchs claimed the exclusive right to make and enforce laws. In a handful of states, notably the Netherlands and England, wealthy landowners and merchants were able to strengthen representative assemblies and limit royal authority, but in these states too, many conflicts over fundamental constitutional issues were resolved.

A resolution of uncertainties also took place in the realm of ideas. The work of Isaac Newton (1642–1727) settled perplexing scientific issues that had emerged in the 1500s when Nicholas Copernicus and others revealed the flaws of ancient Greek science but sought in vain for a coherent, all-encompassing model to replace it. Newton's theory of universal gravitation provided such a model. It enabled scientists to understand a host of natural phenomena, including the Earth's tides, the acceleration of falling bodies, and lunar and planetary movement. In the 1700s, the acceptance of Newton's theories along with advances in mathematics and other branches of science inspired secularism and confidence in human reason during Europe's Age of Enlightenment.

Europe in the eighteenth century was more civil, orderly, and tranquil than it had been in hundreds of years. Wars were fought, but none matched the devastation of the wars of religion. Steady economic growth—fueled by trade with the Americas, modest inflation, and greater agricultural productivity—increased per capita wealth within Europe's expanding population. Peasant revolts and urban violence declined, and old class antagonisms seemed to have abated.

The tranquility of the Atlantic world, however, was deceptive. A host of issues increasingly divided the governments of Spain, Portugal, and Great Britain from colonists across the Atlantic, many of whom now considered themselves more American than European. The result was a series of revolts between the 1770s and 1810s that resulted in the founding of more than a dozen new independent states in the Americas. Discontent also was growing in Europe itself. Peasants faced land shortages and higher rents as a result of rural population growth. Artisans were pinched by decades of gradual inflation. Many merchants, manufacturers, lawyers, and other members of the middle class prospered, but they resented the nobles' privileges and their rulers' ineffectiveness. The intellectual atmosphere of the Age of Enlightenment, with its belief in reason and progress, heightened political expectations, as did events in North America, where the Thirteen Colonies threw off British rule and established the United States of America, a state based on constitutionalism and popular sovereignty. The meeting of France's representative assembly, the Estates General, in May 1789 was the first step in the French Revolution, a revolution that reverberated throughout the world.

In England another revolution, an economic revolution, also was under way by century's end. The adoption of new spinning and weaving devices driven by water power and steam was transforming the textile industry, while new methods of smelting and casting were bringing fundamental changes to iron production. By the early 1800s, as domestic industry gave way to factory production, output soared, urban populations swelled, and work was redefined. Collectively known as the Industrial Revolution, these changes reshaped the human condition to a degree even greater than did the political revolutions in France and the Americas.

# An Age of Science and Enlightenment

Although secularism had been a growing force in European intellectual life since the time of the Renaissance, only in the eighteenth century during the Age of Enlightenment did it eclipse religion as the dominant influence on thought and culture. Catholic and Protestant churches still had millions of followers, and new religious movements such as English Methodism were evidence of religious vitality. Nonetheless, eighteenth-century intellectuals were largely hostile or indifferent to religion, artists painted fewer religious scenes, and rulers gave little thought to religion in making decisions.

The main inspiration for the secularism of the eighteenth century was the Scientific Revolution, especially the work of Isaac Newton. When Newton revealed the physical laws that determined the movement of bodies throughout the universe, and did so without relying on religious authority or ancient texts, he demonstrated to eighteenth-century intellectuals the full power of human reason. These intellectuals, known as *philosophes* (French for philosophers), disagreed on many issues, but all were convinced that reason could be applied to social, political, and economic problems with results as spectacular as those achieved by Newton and other scientists. Specifically, reason could expose the weaknesses, flaws, and injustices carried over from Europe's "unenlightened" past. With this new faith, the philosophes became social and political critics who scrutinized and frequently condemned their era's laws, schools, churches, governments, wars, sexual mores, class privileges, and much else.

The Enlightenment was not, however, purely negative. The philosophes rejected passive acceptance of the status quo and proclaimed that human beings through reason could plan and achieve a better future. They disagreed about what that future would be, but none doubted that improvement of the human condition was not only possible but even inevitable, if reason were given freedom to inquire, question, plan, and inspire.

# Two Images of Seventeenth-Century Science

## 28 • SÉBASTIEN LE CLERC, THE ROYAL ACADEMY AND ITS PROTECTORS AND A DISSECTION AT THE JARDIN DES PLANTES

Many contributors to Europe's scientific revolution were solitary scholars who had few contacts with others who shared their interests. By the late 1600s, however, most leading scientists were members of one of several newly founded scientific societies that provided opportunities for exchanging ideas through meetings and publications. The four most prestigious academies were the Academy of Experiment, founded in 1657 in Florence by Prince Leopold de Medici; the Royal Society of London, licensed but not financially supported by Charles II in 1660; the French Royal Academy of Sciences, founded in 1661 and supported by Louis XIV; and the Berlin Academy of Sciences, created in 1700 under the auspices of Elector Frederick III of Brandenburg-Prussia. Although these academies varied in size, organization, and activities, each contributed to Europe's ongoing scientific development.

Many Europeans were introduced to the ideals and goals of the French Royal Academy of Sciences through the engravings of Sébastien Le Clerc (1637–1714), an artist with a lifelong interest in science. As the engraver for many of the Academy's books, he set a new standard for accurate scientific illustration. Among his works was a series of engravings depicting the activities of the academicians themselves. These engravings appeared in several of the Academy's publications, with individual copies made for the king, interested courtiers, and collectors. Two of them, both produced in 1671, are reproduced here.

The first, *The Royal Academy and Its Protectors*, centers on Louis XIV, with two aristocrats, the Prince of Condé and the Duke of Orléans, on his right and Jean-Baptiste Colbert, the French controller-general of finances, on his left. They are surrounded by members of the Academy and their scientific instruments. Seen through the window are a formal garden and the Royal Observatory, which is under construction.

At the center of the second engraving, *A Dissection at the Jardin des Plantes* (botanical gardens), two academicians are dissecting a fox, with their observations being recorded by the individual seated at their right. In the foreground, an academician points to a printed book, in which the results of the dissection will be published, and behind the table stands Le Clerc, pointing to a page of his scientific engravings. On the far left, two figures are making observations with a magnifying glass and a microscope, while on the right stand Colbert and another courtier.

Neither engraving is realistic: Louis XIV made his first visit to the Academy in 1681, ten years after *The Royal Academy and Its Protectors* was engraved. Furthermore, the room where dissections were carried out was notoriously rank, probably closer in appearance and smell to a butcher shop than the genteel scene portrayed by Le Clerc. The artist's goal, however, was not to depict the day-to-day reality of the Academy's activities but rather to communicate an idealized vision of the methods and purposes of science.

## QUESTIONS FOR ANALYSIS

1. How many different pieces of scientific equipment can you identify in the engravings? What does the equipment and other paraphernalia reveal about the scientific interests and methodology of the academicians?
2. What is the significance of the picture toward which Colbert is pointing? What might be the significance of the map on the floor?
3. What point is Le Clerc trying to make in the following details from the engraving of the dissection room: the two figures at the window, the figure pointing to the book, and the artist pointing to the page of engravings?
4. Note the formal gardens that can be seen through the windows in both engravings. What attitude toward nature is expressed in gardens such as these?
5. How does this view of nature differ from that expressed in the two Ming Era landscape paintings in Chapter 4 (source 25)?

Sébastien Le Clerc, The Royal Academy and Its Protectors

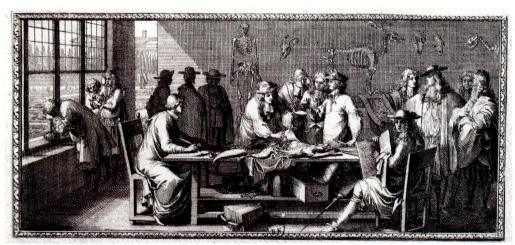

Sébastien Le Clerc, A Dissection at the Jardin des Plantes

# A Plea for Religious Understanding and Tolerance

### 29 • VOLTAIRE, TREATISE ON TOLERATION

Francis-Marie Arouet (1694–1778), better known as Voltaire, combined wit, literary elegance, and a passionate social conscience in a long literary career that epitomizes the values and spirit of the Age of Enlightenment. Born into a well-to-do Parisian family, Voltaire published his first work, the tragic drama *Oedipus,* in 1717. In the next 61 years, he wrote thousands of poems, histories, satires, novels, short stories, essays, and reviews. The European reading public avidly bought his works, making him one of the first authors to make a fortune through the sale of his writings.

Although Voltaire's output and popularity ensured his influence on the Enlightenment at many different levels, one contribution stands out: his devotion to the principles of religious toleration and freedom of thought. Voltaire was convinced that the intolerance of organized religions, not just Christianity, had caused much of the world's suffering and conflict. He was angered that even in the "enlightened" eighteenth century Protestant–Catholic enmity resulted in episodes such as the torture and execution in 1762 of Jean Calas, a French Protestant convicted of murdering his son, supposedly after learning of the son's intent to become a Catholic. Voltaire's devotion to religious toleration is revealed in the following selection, taken from his *Treatise on Toleration,* written in 1763 in response to the execution of Calas.

### QUESTIONS FOR ANALYSIS

1. Does Voltaire believe that intolerance is a unique trait of Christianity, or does it characterize other religions as well?
2. What point is Voltaire trying to make in his reference to the various dialects of the Italian language?

3. What does Voltaire believe to be the essence of a truly religious person?
4. What attitude toward humankind does Voltaire express in the "Prayer to God"?
5. What does the excerpt tell us about Voltaire's views of the nature of God?

## Of Universal Tolerance

One does not need great art and skilful eloquence to prove that Christians ought to tolerate each other—nay, even to regard all men as brothers. Why, you say, is the Turk, the Chinese, or the Jew my brother? Yes, of course, are we not all children of the same father, creatures of the same God?

But these people despise us and treat us as idolators. Very well; I will tell them that they are quite wrong. It seems to me that I might astonish, at least, the stubborn pride of a Muslim or a Buddhist priest if I spoke to them somewhat as follows:—

This little globe, which is but a tiny point, travels in space like many other globes; we are lost in this immensity. Man, about five feet tall, is certainly a small thing in the universe. One of these imperceptible beings says to some of his neighbors in Arabia or South Africa: "Listen to me, for the God of all these worlds has enlightened me. There are nine hundred million little ants like us on the earth, but my ant-hole alone is dear to God. All the others are eternally deemed unworthy by him. Mine alone will be happy."

They would then interrupt me, and ask who was the fool that talked all this nonsense. I should be obliged to tell them that it was they themselves. I would then try to calm them down them, which would be difficult.

I would next address myself to the Christians, and would venture to say to, for instance, a Dominican friar—an inquisitor of the faith:[1] "Brother, you are aware that each province in Italy

has its own dialect, and that people do not speak at Venice and Bergamo as they do at Florence. The Academy of La Crusca[2] has fixed the language. Its dictionary is a rule that has to be followed, and the grammar of Mattei[3] is an infallible guide. But do you think that the consul of the Academy, or Matei in his absence, could in conscience cut out the tongues of all the Venetians and the Bergamese who persisted in speaking their own dialect?"

The inquisitor replies: "The two cases are very different. In our case it is a question of your eternal salvation. It is for your good that the heads of the inquisition direct that you shall be seized on the information of any one person, however infamous or criminal; that you shall have no advocate [lawyer] to defend you; that the name of your accuser shall not be made known to you; that the inquisitor shall promise you pardon and then condemn you; and that you shall then be subjected to five kinds of torture, and afterwards either flogged or sent to the galleys or ceremoniously burned." . . .

I would take the liberty of replying: "Brother, possibly you are right. I am convinced that you wish to do me good. But could I not be saved without all that?"

It is true that these absurd horrors do not stain the face of the earth every day; but they have often done so, and the record of them would make up a volume much longer than the gospels which condemn them. Not only is it cruel to persecute, in this brief life, those who differ from us, but I am not sure if it is not [being] too bold to declare that they are damned eternally. It seems to me that it is

---

*Source:* Voltaire, *Treatise on Tolerance and Other Essays,* Joseph McCabe, ed. and trans. (New York: Putnam's and Sons, 1912), pp. 211–214.
[1]A Catholic official responsible for uncovering and punishing erroneous belief.

[2]The Florentine Academy of Letters, founded in 1582.
[3]Loretto Mattei, a seventeen-century grammarian.

not the place of the atoms of a moment, such as we are, thus to anticipate the decrees of the Creator. Far be it from me to question the principle," Out of the Church there is no salvation." I respect it, and all that it teaches; but do we really know all the ways of God, and the full range of his mercies? May we not hope in him as much as fear him? . . . Must each individual usurp the rights of the Deity, and decide, before he does, the eternal lot of all men?

Followers of a merciful God, if you were cruel of heart; if, in worshipping him whose whole law consisted in loving one's neighbor as oneself, you have burdened this pure and holy law with sophistry and unintelligible disputes; if you had lit the fires of discord for the sake of a new word or a single letter of the alphabet; if you had attached eternal torment to the omission of a few words or ceremonies that other peoples could not know, I should say to you:—

"Transport yourselves with me to the day on which all men will be judged, when God will deal with each according to his works. I see all the dead of former ages and of our own stand in his presence. Are you sure that our Creator and Father will say to the wise and virtuous Confucius, to the lawgiver Solon, to Pythagoras, to Zaleucus, to Socrates, to Plato, to the divine Antonines, to the good Trajan, to Titus, the delight of the human race, to Epictetus. and to so many other model men:[4] "Go, monsters, go and submit to a chastisement infinite in its intensity and duration; your torment shall be as eternal as I. And you, my beloved, Jean Chatel, Ravaillac, Damiens, Cartouche, etc. who have died with the prescribed formulae, come and share my empire and felicity forever."[5]

You shrink with horror from such sentiments; and, now that they have escaped me, I have no more to say to you.

[4]Moralists, enlightened rulers, and philosophers who were not Christians.
[5]Châtel, a devout Catholic, in 1594 attempted to assassinate King Henry IV, who had granted toleration to French

Protestants; Ravaillac, another Catholic, actually did assassinate Henry in 1610; Damiens attempted to assassinate Louis XV; Cartouche was a notorious bandit, captured and executed in 1711.

## Prayer to God

I no longer address myself to men, but to thee, God of all beings, all worlds, and all ages. If indeed it is allowable for feeble creatures, lost in immensity and imperceptible to the rest of the universe, to dare ask anything of Thee who hast given all things, whose decrees are as immutable as they are eternal, deign to look with compassion upon the failings inherent in our nature, and grant that these failings lead us not into calamity.

Thou didst not give us hearts that we should hate each other or hands that we should cut each other's throats. Grant that we may help each other bear the burden of our painful and brief lives; that the slight difference in the clothing with which we cover our puny bodies, in our inadequate tongues, in all our

ridiculous customs, in all our imperfect laws, in all our insensate opinions, in all our stations in life so disproportionate in our eyes but so equal in Thy sight, that all these little variations that differentiate the atoms called *man,* may not be the signals for hatred and persecution. . . .

May all men remember that they are brothers; may they hold in horror tyranny that is exercised over souls, just as they hold in execration the brigandage that snatches away by force the fruits of labor and peaceful industry. If the scourge of war is inevitable, let us not hate each other, let us not tear each other apart in the lap of peace; but let us use the brief moment of our existence in blessing in a thousand different tongues, from Siam to California, Thy goodness which has bestowed this moment upon us.

*Source:* From *Les Philosophes,* ed. and trans. by Norman L. Torrey (New York: Capricorn Books, 1961), 170–171.

# An Affirmation of Human Progress

## 30 • MARQUIS DE CONDORCET, SKETCH OF THE PROGRESS OF THE HUMAN MIND

Throughout history most human beings have valued tradition and resisted change. Reform of governments and religious institutions was deemed possible, but it often meant going back to recapture a lost "golden age" rather than moving forward to something new. Thinkers who studied the past and contemplated the future concluded that the human condition had always been more or less the same, or that history ran in cycles or was the story of gradual decline. Only in the West in the eighteenth and nineteenth centuries did intellectuals and much of the general populace come to believe that the past was a burden and that human beings were capable of effecting changes that were beneficial, not destructive. In a word, people began to believe in progress.

This belief in progress began in the eighteenth century, when many thinkers became convinced that well-intentioned human beings could employ reason to erase at least some of the cruelties, superstitions, and prejudices that had diminished the human condition in the past. By the end of the century, some went further and developed a theory of progress that saw humanity ascending from ignorance and darkness to a utopian future. The most famous prophet of progress was the Marquis de Condorcet (1743–1794), a mathematician, philosopher, and educational reformer. He supported the French Revolution but like many moderates fell afoul of the radical Jacobins and was forced into hiding in July 1793. It was then that he wrote his *Sketch of the Progress of the Human Mind*, which traces human progress in ten epochs from the dawn of history to the French Revolution and beyond. Having completed his work in March 1794, he emerged from hiding, was arrested immediately, and was found dead the next morning of unknown causes.

### QUESTIONS FOR ANALYSIS

1. What factors, according to Condorcet, have impeded progress in the past?
2. According to Condorcet, scientific achievement was the outstanding feature of humanity's "ninth stage." In what ways did science in this era change human thinking and affect human society?
3. Condorcet is not proud of the Europeans' record in dealing with the peoples of Asia, Africa, and the Americas. What groups does he blame for the Europeans' unenlightened behavior in these regions?
4. Why is Condorcet confident that Europeans will modify their behavior in Asia and Africa? What will be the result? Does Condorcet show any interest in preserving the customs and beliefs of Asians and Africans?
5. According to Condorcet, what caused the oppression of women in the past? Why does he reject such oppression, and what positive results in his view will result from ending it?

## Ninth Epoch

### From Descartes to the Formation of the French Republic

Humanity was finally permitted to boldly proclaim the long-ignored right to submit every opinion to reason, that is, to utilize the only instrument given to us for grasping and recognizing the truth. Each human learned with a sort of pride that nature had never destined him to believe the word of others. The superstitions of antiquity and the abasement of reason before the madness of supernatural religion disappeared from society just as they had disappeared from philosophy. . . .

If we were to limit ourselves to showing the benefits derived from the immediate applications of the sciences, or in their applications to man-made devices for the well-being of individuals and the prosperity of nations, we would be making known only a slim part of their benefits. The most important, perhaps, is having destroyed prejudices and re-established human intelligence, which until then had been forced to bend down to false instructions instilled in it by absurd beliefs passed on to the children of each generation by the terrors of superstition and the fear of tyranny. . . .

## Tenth Epoch

### The Future Progress of the Human Mind

Our hopes for the future of humanity may be reduced to three important points: the destruction of inequality among nations; the progress of equality within nations themselves; and finally, the real improvement of humanity. Should not all the nations of the world approach one day the state of civilization reached by the most enlightened peoples such as the French and the Anglo-Americans? Will not the slavery of nations subjected to kings,

the barbarity of African tribes, and the ignorance of savages gradually disappear? Are there on the globe countries whose very nature has condemned them never to enjoy liberty and never exercise their reason?

Can it be doubted that either wisdom or the senseless feuds of the European nations themselves, working with the slow but certain effects of progress in their colonies, will not soon produce the independence of the new world; and that then the European population, spreading rapidly across that immense land, must either civilize or make disappear the savage peoples that now inhabit these vast continents?

If one runs through the history of our undertakings . . . in Africa and Asia, you will see our commercial monopolies, our treacheries, our bloodthirsty contempt for people of a different color and belief; the insolence of our usurpations; the extravagant missionary activities and intrigues of our priests which destroy their feelings of respect and benevolence that the superiority of our enlightenment and the advantages of our commerce had first obtained. But the moment is approaching, without any doubt, when ceasing to present ourselves to these peoples as tyrants or corrupters, we will become instruments of their improvement and their noble liberators. . . .

> Slavery will be abolished, free trade established on the world's oceans, and European political authority in Asia and Africa ended.

Then the Europeans, limiting themselves to free trade, too knowledgeable of their own rights to show contempt for the rights of others, will respect this independence that until now they have violated. . . . Then their settlements, instead of being filled with government favorites . . . who

Source: Esquisse d'un tableau historique des progrès de l'esprit humain (Paris: Firmin Didot Frères, 1847), pp. 186–187, 223–225, 229–231, 237–244, 250–251, 255–256, 263–266, 272–276, trans. by James Overfield.

hasten by pillaging and dishonesty to amass fortunes so they can return to Europe to buy honors and titles, will be populated by hard-working men, seeking in these happy climates the affluence that eluded them in their homeland. . . . Settlements of robbers will become colonies of citizens who will plant in Africa and Asia the principles and the example of European liberty, enlightenment, and reason. In place of clergy who carry to these people nothing but the most shameful superstitions and who disgust them and menace them with a new form of domination, one will see men taking their place who are devoted to spreading among the nations useful truths about their happiness, and explaining to them both the concept of their own interest and of their rights. . . .

Thus the day will come when the sun will shine only on free men born knowing no other master but their reason; where tyrants and their slaves, priests and their ignorant, hypocritical writings will exist only in the history books and theaters; where we will only be occupied with mourning their victims and their dupes; . . . when we will learn to recognize and stifle by the force of reason the first seeds of superstition and tyranny, if ever they dare to appear!

> Condorcet explains how education and scientific knowledge will be made available to all.

If we consider the human creations based on scientific theories, we shall see that their progress can have no limits; that the procedures in constructing them can be improved and simplified just like those of scientific procedures; that new tools, machines, and looms will add every day to the capabilities and skill of humans; they will improve and perfect . . . their products while decreasing the amount of time and labor needed to produce them. Then the obstacles in the path of this progress will disappear, accidents will be foreseen and

prevented, the unhealthful conditions that are due either to the work itself or the climate will be eliminated.

A smaller piece of land will be able to produce commodities of greater usefulness and value than before; greater benefits will be obtained with less waste; the production of the same industrial product will result in less destruction of raw materials and greater durability. We will be able to choose for each type of soil the production of goods that will satisfy the greatest number of wants with the least amount of labor and expenditure. . . . Thus each individual will work less but more productively and will be able to better satisfy his needs. . . .

Among the advances of the human mind we should reckon as most important for the general welfare the complete destruction of those prejudices that have established an inequality of rights between the sexes, an inequality damaging even to the party it favors. One will look in vain for reasons to justify it on the basis of differences in physical make-up, the strength of intellect, and moral sensibility. This inequality has no other root cause than the abuse of force, and it is to no purpose to try to excuse it through sophistical arguments. We will show how the abolition of practices condoned by this prejudice will increase the well-being of families and encourage domestic virtues, the prime foundation of all others; how it will favor the progress of education, and especially make it truly universal, partly because it will be extended to both sexes more equitably, and partly because it cannot be truly universal even for males without the cooperation of mothers in families. . . .

The most enlightened people, having seized for themselves the right to control their life and treasure, will slowly come to perceive war as the deadliest plague and the most monstrous of crimes. . . . They will understand that they cannot become conquerors without losing their liberty; that perpetual alliances are the only way to preserve independence; and that they should seek their security, not power. . . .

We may conclude then that the perfectibility of humanity is indefinite. However, until now, we have imagined humanity with the same natural abilities and physical make-up as at the present. How great will our certitude be, and how limitless our hopes, if one were to believe that these natural abilities themselves, this physical make-up, are also capable of improvement? This is the last question we shall consider. . . .

No one can doubt that progress in preventive medicine, the use of healthier food and housing, a way of living that increases strength through exercise without destroying it through excess, and finally, the destruction of the two most persistent causes of deterioration, poverty and excessive wealth, will lengthen for human beings the average life span and assure more good health and a stronger constitution. Clearly, improvements in medical practices . . . will cause transmittable and contagious diseases to disappear as well as diseases caused by climate, nourishment, and certain vocations. . . . [We] will arrive at a time when death will be nothing more than the result of extraordinary accidents or of the gradual destruction of vital forces, and that as a result, the interval between birth and the time of that destruction will no longer have a fixed term. . . .

Finally, can we not also extend the same hopes to the intellectual and moral faculties? . . . Is it not also probable that education, while perfecting these qualities, will also influence, modify, and improve that bodily nature itself? Analogy, analysis of the development of human faculties, and even certain facts seem to prove the reality of such conjectures, which extend even further the limits of our hopes. . . .

How much does this picture of the human species, freed of all chains, released from the empire of blind fate and the enemies of progress, and marching with a firm and sure pace on the path of truth, virtue, and honor, present the philosopher with a scene that consoles him for the errors, crimes, and injustices that still defile the earth . . . ? In contemplation of this scene he receives the reward for his efforts on behalf of the advance of reason and the defense of liberty. . . . Such contemplation is a place of refuge where the memories of his persecutors cannot follow him, where living with the thought of humans established in their natural rights and dignity, he forgets the way greed, fear, and envy have tormented and corrupted them. It is there he truly exists with his fellow humans in an Elysium[1] which his reason has created and which his love of humanity adorns with the purest pleasures.

---

[1]In Greek mythology, Elysium, also known as the Elysian Fields on the Isles of the Blessed, was the dwelling place after death of virtuous mortals or those given immortality by divine favor.

# From Mercantilism to Laissez Faire

During the seventeenth and eighteenth centuries European governments pursued an economic policy known as *mercantilism*, a system of regulation designed to strengthen the state and increase its supply of gold and silver by encouraging industry, the growth of commerce, and self-sufficiency in agriculture and raw materials. Although Europe's national and local governments had regulated economic activity since the Middle Ages, mercantilism was a new approach to regulation that reflected the increased competiveness of the European state system and the overall expansion of government. Mercantilists viewed commerce as a form of warfare in which each nation competed for economic advantages that would augment tax revenue, increase the amount of gold and silver in circulation, maintain high employment, and sustain a favorable balance of trade, all at the expense of its rivals.

By the late eighteenth century mercantilism had many critics who argued that it inflated prices, stifled innovation, and smothered the entrepreneurial spirit. In addition, mercantilism was opposed by many Enlightenment thinkers who prized individual liberty, deplored government intrusiveness, and were convinced that a nation's economy worked best when its own "natural laws" operated without interference. French critics of mercantilism were known as Physiocrats, a term meaning "rule of nature."

The most famous critic of mercantilism was a Scot, Adam Smith, whose *Wealth of Nations* (1776) called for free trade, the reduction of government regulation, and economic competition at every level. His disciples, the economic liberals of the nineteenth century, sought to convince governments to abandon economic meddling, and by doing so, to give entrepreneurs and investors the chance to take advantage of the unparalleled opportunities provided by industrialization.

# The Advantages of Mercantilism

## 31 • JEAN-BAPTISTE COLBERT, MEMORANDUM ON ENGLISH ALLIANCES AND MEMORANDUM TO THE KING ON FINANCES

Born to a family of merchants in Reims in 1619, Jean-Baptiste Colbert became Louis XIV's most powerful minister. Between 1665 and 1683, when he died, Colbert held several positions in the royal administration, the most important of which was controller-general of finance. Colbert's goal was to strengthen the French economy to provide Louis the resources needed to fight his wars. No statesman better represents the policies of seventeenth-century mercantilism. Indeed, for the French, the words *mercantilisme* and *Colbertisme* are virtually synonymous.

The following selection consists of excerpts from two memoranda Colbert prepared for the king. The first was written in 1669, while the French and English were negotiating a possible alliance against their common commercial rival, the Dutch. The second, written in 1670, describes the goals and achievements of Colbert's economic policies.

### QUESTIONS FOR ANALYSIS

1. Why is Colbert convinced that French commercial expansion can come only at the expense of France's economic competitors?
2. To what degree are Colbert's policies motivated by a wish to improve economic conditions among the French people?
3. What social and economic groups in France would stand to benefit most from Colbert's policies? Who would be hurt?
4. What is the basis of Colbert's conviction that international commerce is a form of war?
5. What industries is Colbert especially interested in encouraging? What do his choices reveal about the general purposes of French mercantilism?

## Memorandum on English Alliances

Based on every piece of information and after a very exacting review, one is able to assert with certainty that the commerce of all of Europe is carried on by 20,000 ships of every size; and one can readily agree that this number cannot be increased, because the number of people in all states remains the same and the consumption of goods also remains the same. . . .

It must be added that commerce causes a perpetual combat both in peacetime and during war among the nations of Europe as to who will win the most of it. . . . Each nation works incessantly to have its legitimate share of it and to gain an advantage over other nations. The Dutch currently are fighting this war with 15,000 to 16,000 ships, a government of merchants, all of whose principles and power are directed solely toward preservation and increase of their commerce, and more dedication, hard work, and thrift than any other nation.

The English fight with 3,000 to 4,000 vessels, less industriousness and attention, and more expenses. The French fight with 500 to 600 ships. The last two cannot improve their commerce except by increasing their number of vessels, and cannot increase this number except from the 20,000 that carry all the commerce, and consequently by cutting into the 15,000 or 16,000 of the Dutch.

## Memorandum to The King on Finances

Without a doubt, the king's revenues are derived from a part of the goods and money his subjects accumulate through their labors, by the fruits they harvest from the earth, and by what their industry gains for them. Everything that the people accumulate is divided into three parts: first, what they can set aside for their subsistence and their small savings; second, for their lord who is the owner of the land they cultivate; third, for the king. This is the normal distribution. But when authority is at the level where Your Majesty has put it, it is certain . . . that the people, who fear and respect the royal authority, begin by paying their taxes [to the king] and have little left for their own sustenance, and pay little or nothing to their lords. And since the people need at least something before they think of meeting their tax obligations, and since these taxes must always be proportionate to the amount of money people have, the financial administration . . . must make every effort and [use] all Your Majesty's authority to attract money into the realm, and to distribute the money throughout the provinces so that the people have the ability to live and pay their taxes.

. . . The well-being and economic recovery of the people depend on apportioning what they pay into the public treasury with the amount of money that circulates in commerce. This ratio has always been 150 million livres [in circulation] to 45 million livres.[1] [in taxes and expenditures] . . . But at present it appears that there are no more than 120 million livres in public commerce . . . and that taxes and expenditures are at 70 million livres. As a result, it is in excess by a wide margin, and as would be expected, the people are falling into great misery.

It will be necessary to do one of two things to stop this evil: either lower tax obligations and expenditures, or increase the amount of money in public commerce. For the first, taxes have been lowered already. . . . For the second, it consists of three parts: increase money in public commerce by drawing it away from other countries; by keeping it inside the kingdom and keeping it from leaving; by giving the people the means to make a profit from it.

In these points reside the greatness and the power of the state and the magnificence of the king, . . . and this magnificence is all the greater in

*Source:* Pierre Clément, ed., *Lettres, Instructions, et Mémoires de Colbert,* Vol. 6 (Paris: Imprimerie Impériale, 1869), pp. 264–266, 269, and Vol. 7 (Paris: Imprimerie Impériale, 1869), pp. 237–240, 264, 268, 269. Trans: J. H. Overfield

[1]The livre was the basic unit of the French currency.

that it simultaneously weakens all the neighboring states, because there being only a fixed quantity of money circulating in all of Europe, and this quantity is increased from time to time by what comes in from the western Indies,[2] it is certain and clear if there is only 150,000,000 livres that circulate publicly in France, that one cannot succeed in increasing it . . . without at the same time taking the same quantity from neighboring states; this is the cause of the double success that one has seen so noticeably in the past few years, the one increasing the power and greatness of Your Majesty, the other reducing that of his enemies. . . .

Thus in these areas all the work and attention to finances since the beginning of Your Majesty's administration has been focused; and since it is commerce alone and what depends on it that can produce such a great result, it was a task to introduce it into the realm because neither the general population nor individuals have applied themselves to it, and in a way it is even contrary to the genius of the nation.[3] . . .

The Dutch, English, and other nations take from the kingdom wine, brandy, vinegars, linen, paper, certain articles of clothing, and wheat when they need it. . . . But they brought us woolen cloth and other goods made of wool and fur; sugar, tobacco, and indigo from the American islands; all the spices, drugs, silks, cotton cloths, leather goods, and an infinity of other goods from the East Indies; the same merchandise from the Levant [the eastern Mediterranean]. . . . All the goods necessary for ship construction, such as wood, masts, iron, copper, tar, iron . . . , cannons, hemp, rope, tin-coated sheet iron, brass, navigation instruments, musket balls, iron anchors, and generally everything necessary for the construction of vessels for the fleet for the king and for his subjects. Gunpowder, fuses,

muskets, cannon shot, lead, pewter, clothes, . . . silk and wool stockings from England, . . . fabrics from Flanders, lacework from Venice and Holland, embroidery from Flanders, camlet [a woven fabric] from Brussels, carpets of Flanders; beef and mutton from Germany, hides and horses from every land, silk fabrics from Milan, Genoa, and Holland. All the commerce from port to port, even inside the kingdom [France], used to be carried on by Dutchmen, so that no sea commerce was carried on by the king's subjects.

By these means . . . the Dutch, English, merchants of Hamburg, and others bring into the kingdom a quantity of merchandise much greater than they take away, withdraw the surplus in cash, which produced both their prosperity and [our] poverty, and as a result, unquestionably, added to their power and our weakness.

It is necessary next to examine the steps taken to change this fate. First, in 1662, Your Majesty maintained his right to [charge a duty of] 50 *sols*[4] for ton of freight carried on foreign vessels, which impressively had the result that the number of French ships has increased every year, and in seven or eight years the Dutch have been almost excluded from port-to-port commerce. . . . Finally, . . . Your Majesty ordered the tariff of 1664, in which the duties are regulated by a completely different principle, that is, all the merchandise and manufactured goods of the realm were notably favored, and the prices of foreign goods increased; . . . this change began to offer the opportunity to manufacture these same items in the kingdom; and to this end:

The fabric manufacture of Sedan was reestablished, and the number of looms increased from 12 to 62. New establishments have been built at Abbeville, Dieppe, Fécamp, and Rouen, at which there are presently more than 200 looms; the

---

[2]A term for the Americas.
[3]Under Colbert, the government encouraged manufacturing by building roads and canals, promulgated a commercial code to replace local customary laws pertaining to business,

and subsidized industries through tax exemptions and monopolies.
[4]A French coin (also *sous*), twenty of which equaled a livre.

factory for barracan[5] was established at Ferte-sous-Jouarre with 120 looms. . . .

---

> Colbert goes on to enumerate more than 100 towns and cities where new factories have been established to produce lace, metal products, and especially textiles. The lace industry, he claims, produced jobs for 20,000 workers.

---

The search for saltpeter,[6] [was encouraged] and at the same time the manufacture of gunpowder; . . . the establishment of the manufacture of muskets and weapons of all sorts . . . ; the distribution of stud horses, which has produced and certainly will continue to produce the re-establishment of stud farms and will considerably decrease the import of foreign horses. . . .

And since Your Majesty wished to work diligently for the restoration of his navy . . . it was absolutely necessary to strive to find within the kingdom, or to establish everything needed for the great design.

---

> Colbert lists the towns and regions where factories have been established to produce tar, iron cannons, anchors, sailcloth, cloth for flags, navigation instruments, and wood for ship construction and masts.

---

Iron, which was obtained from Sweden and Biscay [in Spain], is now made within the kingdom. High-quality hemp for rope, which came from Prussia and Piedmont, is now obtained from Burgundy, Mâconnais, Bresse, and Dauphiné. In a word, everything needed for the construction of vessels is now established in the kingdom, so that Your Majesty can do without foreigners for the navy, and even in a short time will be able to supply them with what they need and extract their money. . . .

In addition, to prevent the Dutch from profiting from the American islands, which they have gotten hold of and excluded the French . . . , Your Majesty has established the West India Company[7] and invested in it almost 4 million livres; he has also had the satisfaction of taking away from the Dutch that million livres per year that maintained more than 4,000 of their subjects who continually sailed among these islands on their 200 ships. . . . In addition, to prevent the same Dutch from taking more than 10 million livres out of the kingdom through all the goods they bring from the East Indies and the Levant, Your Majesty formed companies for the same areas, in which he has invested more than 5 million livres. . . .

All these great undertakings, however, and an infinity of others that are in a sense innovations . . . are still in their infancy and can be carried to perfection only with work and stubborn application and can exist only with the resources of the state, since considerable expenditures are always necessary to support all of this great system. . . .

---

[5]A thick, heavy fabric.
[6]Potassium nitrate, used for making gunpowder.

[7]The French West India Company was founded in 1664 and dissolved in 1674 because of its massive debt.

# Capitalism's Prophet

## 32 • ADAM SMITH, THE WEALTH OF NATIONS

Born in 1723 in a Scottish fishing village and educated at the universities of Glasgow and Oxford, Adam Smith taught logic and moral philosophy at the University of Glasgow between 1751 and 1763, served for a time as tutor for a Scottish aristocrat's son, and from 1778 until his death in 1790 served as commissioner of the customs of Scotland. He was an eccentric but likable individual who felt most comfortable in the company of his books and in conversations with other intellectuals. In 1764 he made his one trip to Europe, where he met Voltaire and other prominent Enlightenment figures. His conversations with the economic thinkers Anne-Robert-Jacques Turgot and François Quesnay influenced his views on the sources of national wealth and free trade, topics he examined fully in *The Wealth of Nations*, published in 1776.

## QUESTIONS FOR ANALYSIS

1. Smith denies that a nation's wealth consists of the amount of gold and silver within its borders. What arguments does he present to defend his position, and what are their implications for trade policy?
2. Smith proposes that each individual, by pursuing his or her self-interest, promotes the general welfare. What examples of this paradox does he provide?
3. What implications does this paradox have for government policy?
4. According to Smith, what determines prices and wages?
5. What groups in society would you expect to be most enthusiastic about Smith's ideas? Why? What groups might be expected to oppose them?

## Self-Interest and the Free Market

This division of labor,[1] from which so many advantages are derived, is not originally the effect of any human wisdom, which foresees and intends that general opulence to which it gives occasion. It is the necessary, though very slow and gradual consequence of a certain propensity in human nature which has in view no such extensive utility; the propensity to . . . barter and exchange one thing for another.

. . . It is common to all men, and to be found in no other race of animals, which seem to know neither this nor any other species of contracts. . . . Nobody ever saw one animal by its gestures and natural cries signify to another, this is mine, that yours; I am willing to give this for that. . . . In almost every other race of animals each individual, when it is grown up to maturity, is entirely independent, and in its natural state has occasion for the assistance of no other living creature. But man has almost constant occasion for the help of his brethren, and it is in vain for him to expect it from their benevolence only. He will be more likely to prevail if he can interest their self-love in his favor, and show them that it is for their own advantage to do for him what he requires of them. Whoever offers to another a bargain of any kind, proposes to do this. Give me that which I want, and you shall have this which you want, is the meaning of every such offer; and it is in this manner that we obtain from one another the far greater part of those good offices which we stand in need of. It is not from the benevolence of the butcher, the brewer, or the baker, that we expect our dinner,

*Source:* Adam Smith, *An Inquiry into the Nature and Causes of the Wealth of Nations* (Hartford, Connecticut: Cooke and Hale, 1818), Vol. 7, pp. 10–12, 40, 43, 299–304, 316, 317, 319, 330, 331.

[1]Economic specialization, in terms both of different professions and also in terms of the separate tasks carried out by different individuals in the process of manufacturing or preparing commodities for the market.

but from their regard to their own interest. We address ourselves, not to their humanity but to their self-love, and never talk to them of our own necessities but of their advantages. . . .

## Prices and the Free Market

It is the interest of all those who employ their land, labor, or stock [money] in bringing any commodity to market, that the quantity never should exceed the effectual demand; and it is the interest of all other people that it never should fall short of that demand.

If at any time it exceeds the effectual demand, some of the component parts of its price must be paid below their natural rate. If it is rent,[2] the interest of the landlords will immediately prompt them to withdraw a part of their land; and if it is wages or profit, the interest of the laborers in the one case, and of their employers in the other, will prompt them to withdraw a part of their labor or stock from this employment. The quantity brought to market will soon be no more than sufficient to supply the effectual demand. All the different parts of its price will rise to their natural rate, and the whole price to its natural price.

If, on the contrary, the quantity brought to market should at any time fall short of the effectual demand, some of the component parts of its price must rise above their natural rate. If it is rent, the interest of all other landlords will naturally prompt them to prepare more land for the raising of this commodity; if it is wages or profit, the interest of all other laborers and dealers will soon prompt them to employ more labor and stock in preparing and bringing it to market. The quantity brought thither will soon be sufficient to supply the effectual demand. All the different parts of its price will soon sink to their natural rate, and the whole price to its natural price. . . .

The monopolists, by keeping the market constantly under-stocked, by never fully supplying the effectual demand, sell their commodities much above the natural price, and raise their emoluments [benefits], whether they consist in wages or profit, greatly above their natural rate.

The price of monopoly is upon every occasion the highest which can be got. The natural price, or the price of free competition, on the contrary, is the lowest which can be taken, not upon every occasion, indeed, but for any considerable time together. The one is upon every occasion the highest which can be squeezed out of the buyers, or which, it is supposed, they will consent to give: The other is the lowest which the sellers can commonly afford to take, and at the same time continue their business.

The exclusive privileges of corporations, statutes of apprenticeship,[3] and all those laws which restrain . . . the competition to a smaller number than might otherwise go into them, have the same tendency, though in a less degree. They are a sort of enlarged monopolies, and may frequently, for ages together and in whole classes.

## Mercantilist Fallacies

. . . A rich country, in the same manner as a rich man, is supposed to be a country abounding in money; and to heap up gold and silver in any country is supposed to be the readiest way to enrich it. . . .

In consequence of these popular notions, all the different nations of Europe have studied, though to little purpose, every possible means of accumulating gold and silver in their respective countries. Spain and Portugal, the proprietors of the principal mines which supply Europe with those metals, have either prohibited their exportation under the severest penalties, or subjected it to a considerable duty. The like prohibition seems anciently to have [been]

---

[2]Payments made by tenants to their landlord.
[3]Laws that restricted the number of individuals who could receive training in trades through apprenticeship.

made a part of the policy of most other European nations. When those countries became commercial, the merchants found this prohibition, upon many occasions, extremely inconvenient. . . .

They represented [stated forcefully], first, that the exportation of gold and silver in order to purchase foreign goods, did not always diminish the quantity of those metals in the kingdom. . . . They represented, secondly, that this prohibition could not hinder the exportation of gold and silver, which, on account of the smallness of their bulk in proportion to their value, could easily be smuggled abroad. . . .

Those arguments . . . were solid. . . . But they were sophistical in supposing, that either to preserve or to augment the quantity of those metals required more the attention of government, than to preserve or to augment the quantity of any other useful commodities, which the freedom of trade, without any such attention, never fails to supply in the proper quantity. . . .

A country that has no mines of its own must undoubtedly draw its gold and silver from foreign countries, in the same manner as one that has no vineyards of its own must draw its wines. It does not seem necessary, however, that the attention of government should be more turned towards the one than towards the other object. A country that has wherewithal to buy wine, will always get the wine which it has occasion for; and a country that has wherewithal to buy gold and silver, will never be in want of those metals. They are to be bought for a certain price like all other commodities, and as they are the price of all other commodities, so all other commodities are the price of those metals. We trust with perfect security that the freedom of trade, without any attention of government, will always supply us with the wine which we have occasion for: and we may trust with equal security that it will always supply us with all the gold and silver which we can afford to purchase or to employ, either in circulating our commodities, or in other uses.

• • •

By restraining, either by high duties, or by absolute prohibitions, the importation of such goods from foreign countries as can be produced at home, the monopoly of the home market is more or less secured to the domestic industry. . . . But whether it tends either to increase the general industry of the society, or to give it the most advantageous direction, is not, perhaps, altogether so evident. . . .

Every individual is continually exerting himself to find out the most advantageous employment for whatever capital he can command. It is his own advantage, indeed, and not that of the society, which he has in view. But the study of his own advantage, naturally, or rather necessarily, leads him to prefer that employment which is most advantageous to the society.

First, every individual endeavors to employ his capital as near home as he can, and consequently as much as he can in the support of domestic industry, provided always that he can thereby obtain the ordinary, or not a great deal less than the ordinary, profits of stock. Secondly, every individual who employs his capital in the support of domestic industry, necessarily endeavors so to direct that industry, that its produce may be of the greatest possible value. . . .

As every individual, therefore, endeavors . . . both to employ his capital in the support of domestic industry, and so to direct that industry that its produce may be of the greatest value, every individual necessarily labors to render the annual revenue of the society as great as he can. He generally, indeed, neither intends to promote the public interest, nor knows how much he is promoting it. By preferring the support of domestic to that of foreign industry, he intends only his own security; and by directing that industry in such a manner as its produce may be of the greatest value, he intends only his own gain, and he is in this, as in many other cases, led by an invisible hand to promote an end which was no part of his intention. . . . By pursuing his own interest he frequently promotes that of the society more effectually than when he really intends to promote it. . . .

To give the monopoly of the home market to the produce of domestic industry, in any particular art or manufacture, is in some measure to direct private people in what manner they ought to employ their capital, and must, in almost all cases, be either a useless or a hurtful regulation. If the produce of domestic [industry] can be brought there as cheap as that of foreign industry, the regulation is evidently useless. If it cannot, it must generally be hurtful. It is the maxim of every prudent master of a family, never to attempt to make at home what it will cost him more to make than to buy. . . .

What is prudence in the conduct of every private family, can scarce be folly in that of a great kingdom. If a foreign country can supply us with a commodity cheaper than we ourselves can make it, better buy it of them with some part of the produce of our own industry, employed in a way in which we have some advantage. . . .

To expect, indeed, that the freedom of trade should ever be entirely restored in Great Britain, is as absurd as to expect that an Oceana or Utopia should ever be established in it. Not only the prejudices of the public, but what is much more unconquerable, the private interests of many individuals, irresistibly oppose it. . . .

The undertaker of a great manufacture, who, by the home markets being suddenly laid open to the competition of foreigners, should be obliged to abandon his trade, would no doubt suffer very considerably. That part of his capital which had usually been employed in purchasing materials and in paying his workmen might, without much difficulty perhaps, find another employment. But that part of it which was fixed in workhouses, and in the instruments of trade, could scarce be disposed of without considerable loss. The equitable regard, therefore, to his interest requires that changes of this kind should never be introduced suddenly, but slowly, gradually, and after a very long warning.

# Russia and the West

After two centuries of Mongol rule ended in the late 1400s, Russia embarked on a period of remarkable expansion in which the tsars consolidated their control of European Russia, then extended their authority eastward across the Urals and into Siberia. By the 1630s Russia stretched all the way to the Pacific and was the largest nation in the world.

Russia's western border, however, remained insecure. The Livonian War (1558–1583) against Poland and Sweden resulted in territorial losses, and during the period of political breakdown known as the Time of Troubles (1604–1613), Poland and Sweden sent armies deep into Russian territory. In 1612 the Russians drove them out, and for the next several decades European rulers were diverted from Russian adventures by the Thirty Years' War (1618–1648). The Turks remained a threat, however, and in the late 1600s the Poles and the Swedes resumed their pressure.

Russia's inability to translate its enormous size into military victories underscored the extent to which Russia lagged behind neighboring states in almost every activity that affects state power. Manufacturing was negligible, commerce was limited to small amounts of trade in amber, furs, and timber, and agricultural productivity was constrained by Russia's long winters and the inefficiencies of an agrarian order based on serfdom. With little economic development and an ineffective system of tax collection, Russia lacked the resources to match its rivals' armies.

How to respond to their nation's weakness deeply divided the Russian people in the eighteenth century. Some, most notably Tsar Peter I (the Great), were convinced that Russia could overcome its backwardness only by adopting the institutions, customs, and attitudes of the technologically superior, wealthier, and more powerful states of Western Europe. This would mean discarding much of Russia's distinctive past, but in Peter's view Russia had no choice. Many Russians disagreed. Devoted to Russia's unique Slavic and Orthodox Christian traditions, they argued that abandonment of Russia's past was too high a price to pay for Europeanization.

# Peter the Great's Blueprint for Russia

### 33 • PETER THE GREAT, EDICTS AND DECREES

The growth of centralized government in Russia, halted during two centuries of Mongol rule and impeded by decades of turmoil and foreign invasion following the death of Ivan IV in 1584, resumed during the reigns of Alexis (r. 1645–1676) and his son Peter the Great. Alexis streamlined the central bureaucracy, extended his control over church affairs, issued a new law code, and generally ignored advisory bodies such as the Council of State and Assembly of the Land. Alexis also initiated reforms of the Russian military and founded state-sponsored factories for manufacturing weapons, glass, brick, textiles, and agricultural equipment.

Despite Alexis's accomplishments, when Peter became tsar, Russia still lagged behind the nations of Western Europe. Peter learned this bitter truth in November 1700 at the Battle of Narva, the first major battle in the Great Northern War, when a Swedish army of just over eight thousand routed a poorly trained and equipped Russian army four times its size. Peter responded with characteristic energy. Already enamored of Western European technology, military drill, shipbuilding, fashion, and government as a result of boyhood contacts with European visitors to Moscow and his travels through Europe in 1697 and 1698, Peter threw himself into a campaign to transform Russia along Western European lines. Issuing no fewer than three thousand decrees in the next twenty-five years on everything from the structure of government to male shaving habits, Peter became the first ruler who sought to transform his country through a process of state-imposed Westernization.

## QUESTIONS FOR ANALYSIS

1. What do these decrees reveal about Peter the Great's motives for his reforms?
2. What can be learned from these decrees about Russian social relationships and the state of the Russian economy?
3. Why do you think Peter believed it was necessary for Russians to change their dress, shaving habits, and calendar?

4. What evidence do these edicts provide about opposition or indifference to Peter's reforms on the part of his subjects?

5. What do these edicts reveal about Peter's views of the state and its relationship to his subjects?

6. What groups within Russia might have been most likely to oppose Peter's reforms? Why?

## Learning from Europe

### Decree on the New Calendar (1699)

It is known to His Majesty that not only many European Christian lands, but also Slavic nations in total accord with our Eastern Orthodox Church . . . count their years from the eighth day after the birth of Christ, from the first day of January, and not from the creation of the world,[1] . . . It is now the year 1699 . . . and from the first of January will begin both the new year 1700 and a new century; and so His Majesty has ordered. . . . And to celebrate this good undertaking . . . in Moscow let the reputable citizens arrange decorations of pine, fir, and juniper trees and boughs along the busiest main streets and by the houses of eminent church and lay persons of rank. . . . Poorer persons should place at least one shrub or bough on their gates or on their house. . . . Also, . . . as a sign of rejoicing, wishes for the new year and century will be exchanged, and the following will be organized: when fireworks are lit and guns fired on the great Red Square, let the boyars,[2] the Lords of the Palace, of the Chamber, and the Council, and the eminent personages of Court, Army, and Merchant ranks, each in his own grounds, fire three times from small guns, if they have any, or from muskets and other small arms, and shoot some rockets into the air.

### Decree on the Invitation of Foreigners (1702)

Since our accession to the throne all our efforts and intentions have tended to govern this realm in such a way that all of our subjects should, through our care for the general good, become more and more prosperous. For this end we have always tried to maintain internal order, to defend the state . . . , and to improve and to extend trade. With this purpose we have been compelled to make some necessary and salutary changes in the administration, in order that our subjects might . . . become more skillful in their commercial relations. We have therefore given orders . . . and founded institutions indispensable for increasing our trade with foreigners, and shall do the same in the future. Nevertheless we fear that matters are not in such a good condition as we desire. . . .

To attain these worthy aims, we have endeavored to improve our military forces, which are the protection of our State, so that our troops may consist of well-drilled men, maintained in perfect order and discipline. In order to obtain greater improvement in this respect, and to encourage foreigners, who are able to assist us in this way, as well as artisans profitable to the State, to come in numbers to our country, we have issued this manifesto, and have ordered printed copies of it to be sent throughout Europe. . . . And as in our residence

Source: Marte Blinoff, Life and Thought in Old Russia (University Park: Pennsylvania State University Press, 1961), pp. 49–50; Eugene Schuyler, Peter the Great, Vol. 2, pp. 176–177; L. Jay Oliva, Peter the Great (Englewood Cliffs, NJ: Prentice-Hall, 1970), p. 50; George Vernadsky et al., A Source Book for Russian History from Early Times to 1917, Vol. 2 (New Haven and London: Yale University Press, 1972), pp. 347, 329, 357.

[1]Before January 1, 1700, the Russian calendar started from the date of the creation of the world, which was reckoned at 5508 B.C.E. The year began on September 1.

[2]Members of the hereditary nobility.

of Moscow, the free exercise of religion of all other sects, although not agreeing with our church, is already allowed, so shall this be hereby confirmed anew in such manner that we . . . shall exercise no compulsion over the consciences of men, and shall gladly allow every Christian to care for his own salvation at his own risk.

### An Instruction to Russian Students Abroad Studying Navigation (1714)

1. Learn how to draw plans and charts and how to use the compass and other naval indicators.

2. Learn how to navigate a vessel in battle as well as in a simple maneuver, and learn how to use all appropriate tools and instruments; namely, sails, ropes, and oars, and the like matters, on row boats and other vessels.

3. Discover . . . how to put ships to sea during a naval battle. . . . Obtain from foreign naval officers written statements, bearing their signatures and seals, of how adequately you are prepared for naval duties.

4. If, upon his return, anyone wishes to receive from the Tsar greater favors, he should learn, in addition to the above enumerated instructions, how to construct those vessels [aboard] which he would like to demonstrate his skills.

5. Upon his return to Moscow, every foreign-trained Russian should bring with him at his own expense, for which he will later be reimbursed, at least two experienced masters of naval science. They [the returnees] will be assigned soldiers, one soldier per returnee, to teach them what they have learned abroad. . . .

## Creating a New Russian

### Decree on Western Dress (1701)

Western dress shall be worn by all the boyars, members of our councils and of our court, . . . gentry of Moscow, secretaries, . . . provincial gentry, gosti [merchants], government officials, streltsy [members of the imperial guard], members of the guilds, . . . citizens of Moscow of all ranks, and residents of provincial cities . . . excepting the clergy and peasant tillers of the soil. The upper dress shall be of French or Saxon cut, and the lower dress . . . —waistcoat, trousers, boots, shoes, and hats—shall be of the German type. They shall also ride German saddles. Likewise the women-folk of all ranks, including the priests', deacons', and church attendants' wives, the wives of the dragoons, the soldiers, and the streltsy, and their children, shall wear Western dresses, hats, jackets, and underwear—undervests and petticoats—and shoes. From now on no one of the above-mentioned is to wear Russian dress . . . , sheepskin coats, or Russian peasant coats, trousers, boots, and shoes.

### Decree on Shaving (1705)

Henceforth all court attendants, . . . provincial service men, government officials of all ranks, military men, all the gosti, members of the wholesale merchants' guild, and members of the guilds purveying for our household must shave their beards and moustaches. But, if it happens that some of them do not wish to shave their beards and moustaches, let a yearly tax be collected from such persons. . . . As for the peasants, let a toll of two half-copecks[3] per beard be collected at the town gates each time they enter or leave a town; and do not let the peasants pass the town gates, into or out of town, without paying this toll.

## Military and Economic Reforms

### Decree on Promotion to Officer's Rank (1714)

Since there are many who promote to officer rank their relatives and friends—young men who do not know the fundamentals of soldiering, not having served in the lower ranks—and since even those who serve do so for a few weeks or months only,

---

[3]One twentieth of a ruble, the basic unit of Russian currency.

as a formality; therefore . . . henceforth there shall be no promotion of men of noble extraction or of any others who have not first served as privates in the Guards. This decree does not apply to soldiers of lowly origin who, after long service in the ranks, have received their commissions through honest service or to those who are promoted on the basis of merit, now or in the future. . . .

### Statute for the College of Manufactures[4] (1723)

His Imperial Majesty is diligently striving to establish and develop . . . such manufacturing plants and factories as are found in other states, for the general welfare and prosperity of his subjects. He [therefore] most graciously charges the College of Manufactures to exert itself in devising the means to introduce, with the least expense, and to spread in the Russian Empire these and other ingenious arts, and especially those for which materials can be found within the empire. . . .

His Imperial Majesty gives permission to everyone, without distinction of rank or condition, to open factories wherever he may find suitable. . . .

Factory owners must be closely supervised, in order that they have at their plants good and experienced [foreign] master craftsmen, who are able to train Russians in such a way that these, in turn, may themselves become masters, so that their produce may bring glory to the Russian manufactures. . . .

By the former decrees of His Majesty commercial people were forbidden to buy villages [i.e., to own serfs], the reason being that they were not engaged in any other activity beneficial for the state save commerce; but since it is now clear to all that many of them have started to found manufacturing establishments and build plants, . . . which tend to increase the welfare of the state . . . therefore permission is granted both to the gentry and to men of commerce to acquire villages for these factories without hindrance. . . .

In order to stimulate voluntary immigration of various craftsmen from other countries into the Russian Empire, and to encourage them to establish factories and manufacturing plants freely and at their own expense, the College of Manufactures must send appropriate announcements to the Russian envoys accredited at foreign courts. The envoys should then, in an appropriate way, bring these announcements to the attention of men of various professions, urge them to come to settle in Russia, and help them to move.

---

[4]One of several administrative boards created in 1717 by Peter and modeled on Swedish practice.

# Revolutions in England and France

Political revolutions involve more than changing leaders or replacing one ruling faction with another. Revolutions bring about fundamental changes in the political order itself, often resulting in the transfer of power from one social group to another. Moreover, they affect more than politics. Revolutions reshape legal systems, education, religious life, economic practices, and social relationships. Because revolutions occur in societies already undergoing intellectual, economic, and social transformations, it is not surprising that history's first revolutions took place in Western Europe and the Americas in the seventeenth through nineteenth centuries, when economic change undermined existing social hierarchies and the emergence of new secular values weakened the foundations of divine right monarchies and privileged churches.

In the 1600s England experienced two revolutions: the Puritan Revolution (also known as the English Revolution or English Civil War) in the 1640s and 1650s and the Glorious Revolution of 1688 and 1689. They limited royal authority, confirmed the fiscal and legislative powers of Parliament, and guaranteed basic rights for the English people, mainly those with property. They also affirmed the principle that governments must operate according to established laws that apply to subjects and rulers alike, and not according to the whims of individual rulers.

The French Revolution, which began in 1789, had a greater impact than that of the English revolutions. More social groups—peasants, urban workers, and women—participated, and it inspired more people around the globe. More importantly, the French Revolution went beyond the principles of constitutionalism and representative government. It championed the democratic principles that every person, irrespective of social standing, should have a voice in government and that all people should be treated equally before the law. It also gave rise to the first nationalist movements in Europe and inspired disaffected groups throughout the world to seek political and social change through revolution.

# Foundations of Parliamentary Supremacy in England

## 34 • ENGLISH BILL OF RIGHTS

The English Bill of Rights, accepted in 1689, kept England on a path that set it apart from the absolutist governments then taking hold in most of continental Europe. It also ended a clash between the Crown and Parliament that had convulsed English politics for almost a century. Ever since the reigns of James I (r. 1603–1625) and his son Charles I (r. 1625–1649), landowners, merchants, and lawyers in the House of Commons had fought the monarchy over religion, economic policies, foreign relations, and political issues that all centered on the question of Parliament's place in England's government. An impasse over new taxes led to civil war between parliamentarians and royalists in 1642. After a triumphant Parliament ordered the execution of Charles I in 1649, a faction of Puritans led by Oliver Cromwell seized power and imposed strict Protestant beliefs on the country for eleven years. The Puritans' grip on England loosened after the death of Cromwell in 1658 and was lost altogether when a newly elected parliament restored the Stuarts in 1660.

Charles II (r. 1660–1685) and his brother James II (r. 1685–1688), however, alienated their subjects through pro-French, pro-Catholic policies and a disregard for Parliament. James II was a professed Catholic, and when a male heir was born in 1688, this raised the possibility of a long line of English Catholic kings. Many of his predominantly Protestant subjects found this unacceptable, and the result was the Glorious Revolution of 1688–1689. In what was more of a *coup d'état* than a revolution, Parliament offered the crown to James's Protestant daughter Mary and her husband, William of Orange of Holland. After James mounted only token resistance and fled the country, his son-in-law and daughter became King William III and Queen Mary II after signing the Bill of Rights, presented to them by Parliament in 1689. By signing, they accepted limitations on royal authority that became a permanent part of England's constitution.

## QUESTIONS FOR ANALYSIS

1. What abuses of royal power seem to have most disturbed the authors of the English Bill of Rights?
2. Were the authors of the Bill of Rights most concerned with political, economic, or religious issues?
3. What political role does the Bill of Rights envision for the English Crown?
4. When the Bill of Rights speaks of "rights," whose rights is it referring to?
5. In what ways might the common people of England benefit from the Bill of Rights?

---

Whereas the late King James the Second, by the assistance of diverse evil counselors, judges and ministers employed by him, did endeavor to subvert and extirpate the Protestant religion and the laws and liberties of this kingdom . . .

[The] said Lords Spiritual and Temporal and Commons,[1] pursuant to their respective letters and elections, being now assembled in a full and free representation of the nation, taking into their most serious consideration the best means for attaining the ends aforesaid, do in the first place . . . for the vindicating and asserting their ancient rights and liberties declare:

That the pretended power of suspending of laws or the execution of laws by regal authority without consent of Parliament is illegal; . . .

That the commission for erecting the late Court of Commissioners for Ecclesiastical Causes,[2] and all other commissions and courts of like nature, are illegal and pernicious;

That levying money for or to the use of the Crown by pretense of prerogative, without grant of Parliament . . . , is illegal;

That it is the right of the Subjects to petition the king, and all commitments[3] and prosecutions for such petitioning are illegal;

That the raising or keeping a standing army within the kingdom in time of peace, unless it be with consent of Parliament, is against law;

That the subjects which are Protestants may have arms for their defense suitable to their conditions and as allowed by law;

That election of members of Parliament ought to be free;

That the freedom of speech and debates or proceedings in Parliament ought not to be impeached or questioned in any court or place out of Parliament;

That excessive bail ought not to be required, nor excessive fines imposed nor cruel and unusual punishments inflicted; . . .

That all grants and promises of fines and forfeitures of particular persons before conviction are illegal and void;

And that for redress of all grievances, and for the amending, strengthening and preserving of the laws, Parliaments ought to be held frequently. . . .

---

*Source: The Statutes: Revised Edition* (London: Eyre and Spottiswoode, 1871), Vol. I, pp. 10–12.

[1]The Lords Spiritual were the prelates of the Anglican Church who sat in the House of Lords; the Lords Temporal were titled peers who also sat in the House of Lords; Commons refers to the House of Commons, to which nontitled Englishmen were elected.

[2]A royal court in which religious cases were tried.

[3]A written court order to confine someone to prison.

Having therefore an entire confidence that his said Highness . . . will perfect the deliverance [a formal announcement] so far advanced by him, and will still preserve them from the violation of their rights, which they have asserted here, and from all other attempts upon their religion, rights, and liberties:

The said Lords Spiritual and Temporal, and Commons, do resolve,

That William and Mary, Prince and Princess of Orange, be, and be declared King and Queen of England, France,[4] and Ireland. . . .

---

[4]This title was first adopted in 1340 by Edward III, who claimed the French throne after the death of his uncle Charles IV of France. This claim, which precipitated the Hundred Years' War, was not abandoned until 1801.

## Principles of the French Revolution

### 35 • DECLARATION OF THE RIGHTS OF MAN AND OF THE CITIZEN

The French Revolution began because of a problem that has plagued rulers since the beginning of organized government—Louis XVI (r. 1774–1792) and his ministers could not balance the government's budget. Having exhausted every other solution, the king agreed to convene the Estates General, France's ancient representative assembly, which had last met in 1614. He hoped it would solve the government's fiscal plight by approving new taxes, while nobles sensed it would be an opportunity to strengthen their role in government. For both the king and nobility, the calling of the Estates General had unexpected results: the nobility lost its privileges, and the king lost power and, ultimately his life, when in 1793 a revolutionary assembly judged him a traitor and ordered his execution. Neither Louis nor the nobles had comprehended the depth of the French people's disgust with royal absolutism and aristocratic privilege. Nor had they sensed the degree to which the Enlightenment and the English and American revolutions had committed the people to fundamental change.

The Estates General convened at Versailles on May 5, 1789. After six weeks of debating voting procedures, in mid-June representatives of the Third Estate (commoners), and a handful of clergy and nobles, broke away to form a National Assembly and pledged to continue meeting until they wrote a constitution. On June 27, the king gave his grudging approval to the new assembly and ordered all representatives of the clergy and nobility to join its deliberations. The revolution was under way.

Among the National Assembly's most notable achievements was the approval of the Declaration of the Rights of Man and of the Citizen on August 26, 1789. Drawing on the principles of English constitutionalism, the American Revolution, and the Enlightenment, this document summarizes the political and social goals of the French Revolution in its early stages.

### QUESTIONS FOR ANALYSIS

1. In what ways does the Declaration limit the power of the Crown and the authority of government?

2. According to the Declaration, what rights and responsibilities does citizenship entail?

3. What does the Declaration state about the origin and purpose of law?

4. How does the concept of rights in the Declaration differ from the concept of rights in the English Bill of Rights (source 34)?

---

The representatives of the people of France, empowered to act as a national assembly, taking into consideration that ignorance, oblivion, or scorn of the rights of man are the only cause of public misery and the corruption of government, have resolved to state in a solemn declaration the natural, inalienable, and sacred rights of man, so that this declaration, continually offered to all the members of society, may forever recall them to their rights and duties; so that the actions of the legislative and executive power, able to be compared at every instant to the goal of any political institution, may be more respected; so that the demands of the citizens, from now on based on straightforward and incontestable principles, will revolve around the maintenance of the constitution and the happiness of everyone.

Consequently, the National Assembly recognizes and declares, in the presence and under the auspices of the Supreme Being, the following rights of man and citizen:

*Article 1.* Men are born and remain free and equal in rights; social distinctions can be established only for the common benefit.

2. The goal of every political association is the conservation of the natural and indefeasible rights of man; these rights are liberty, property, security, and resistance to oppression.

3. The source of all sovereignty is located essentially in the nation; no body, no individual can exercise authority which does not emanate from it expressly.

4. Liberty consists in being able to do anything that does not harm another. Thus the exercise of the natural rights of each man has no limits except those which assure to other members of society the enjoyment of these same rights; these limits can be determined only by law.

5. The law has the right to prohibit only those actions harmful to society. All that is not prohibited by the law cannot be hindered, and no one can be forced to do what it does not order.

6. The law is the expression of the general will; all citizens have the right to concur personally or through their representatives in its formation; it must be the same for everyone, whether it protects or punishes. All citizens, being equal in its eyes, are equally admissible to all honors, offices, and public employments, according to their abilities and without any distinction other than those of their virtues and talents.

7. No man can be accused, arrested, or detained except in instances determined by the law, and according to the practices which it has prescribed. Those who solicit, draw up, carry out, or have carried out arbitrary orders must be punished; but any citizen summoned or seized by virtue of the law must obey instantly; he renders himself guilty by resisting.

8. The law must establish only penalties that are strictly and plainly necessary, and no one can be punished except in virtue of a law established and published prior to the offense and legally applied.

9. Every man being presumed innocent until he has been declared guilty, if it is judged indispensable to arrest him, all harshness that is not necessary for making secure his person must be severely limited by the law.

---

*Source:* "Declaration of the Rights of Man and of the Citizen," in Buchez and Roux, *Histoire parlementaire de la Révolution française* (Paris: Librarie Paulin, 1834), Vol. 11, pp. 404–406.

10. No one may be disturbed because of his opinions, even religious, provided that their public manifestation does not disturb the public order established by law.

11. The free communication of thoughts and opinions is one of the most precious rights of man: every citizen can therefore freely speak, write, and print, except he is answerable for abuses of this liberty in instances determined by the law.

12. The guaranteeing of the rights of man and citizen requires a public force; this force is therefore instituted for the advantage of everyone, and not for the private use of those to whom it is entrusted.

13. For the maintenance of the public force, and for the expenses of administration, a tax supported in common is indispensable; it must be apportioned among all citizens on grounds of their capacities to pay.

14. All citizens have the right to determine for themselves or through their representatives the need for taxation of the public, to consent to it freely, to investigate its use, and to determine its rate, basis, collection, and duration.

15. Society has the right to demand an accountability from every public agent of his management.

16. Any society in which guarantees of rights are not assured nor the separation of powers determined has no constitution.

17. Property being an inviolable and sacred right, no one may be deprived of it except when public necessity, legally determined, requires it, and on condition of a just and predetermined compensation.

## Multiple Voices III

# Nationalism and Revolution in France

## BACKGROUND

Nationalism combines allegiance to the interests and purposes of one's nation-state, a sense of being a part of a national community with shared values and traditions, and a conviction that these values and traditions are equal or superior to those of other nations and national communities. This powerful ideology emerged only in the 1790s, during the first years of the French Revolution, when the French people transformed themselves from subjects to citizens by abolishing monarchy and establishing a regime based on equality and popular sovereignty. For millions of French, *la patrie*, or the fatherland, became more than their ancestral territory: It was their spiritual homeland and a beacon of liberty and equality for which citizens were willing to sacrifice and soldiers were prepared to die.

## THE SOURCES

When war broke out between France and antirevolutionary Austria and Prussia in April 1792, many thousands of Frenchmen volunteered to serve in the army, especially after the enemy pushed across the French frontier and threatened Paris in July and August. The French repulsed the Austro-Prussian threat and, in the fall of 1792, pushed into German territory to the east and the Austrian Netherlands to the north. At that point, the newly elected National Convention turned the war into an ideological crusade by pledging aid to all peoples "who wish to recover their liberty." In its Decree for Proclaiming the Liberty and Sovereignty of All Peoples of December 15, 1792, our first excerpt, the Convention ordered its generals to implement the full program of the revolution in conquered territories.

In 1793, however, disaster again threatened. With new enemies, including Britain, Holland, and Spain, and reversals on every front, the Committee of Public Safety, the government's twelve-man executive committee, took action. On August 23, it asked the Convention to approve an edict implementing a *levée en masse* (mass levy), a program to requisition the nation's human and material resources for the war effort. Attached to the proposed decree was our second source, "A Report Accompanying the Proposal for a Levée en Masse," which spells out the decree's underlying moral principles.

Despite some resistance, the *levée* within a year resulted in an army of over one million men, of whom approximately 800,000 were trained and equipped for battle. It was the largest army Europe had ever seen. More importantly, the fighting men were largely citizen-soldiers committed to their cause and country, not indifferent mercenaries or unwilling recruits; officers won their commissions on merit, not through purchase or privilege.

Our last two sources are examples of how throughout the fighting, the Committee of Public Safety made efforts to maintain the nation's revolutionary fervor by ordering schools to instill patriotism in their students and by sponsoring patriotic clubs, festivals, ceremonies, musical performances, theatrical productions, and monuments. The third excerpt, "Report of the Committee of Public Safety on Drafting Poets and Citizens for the Cause of Revolution," describes a plan to enlist France's writers on behalf of the revolution. The fourth, "A Report of the Committee of Public Safety on Revolutionary Education," describes a plan to found a School of Mars (the Roman god of war), to train elite highly qualified sixteen- and seventeen-year-old boys for service to the revolution.

## QUESTIONS FOR ANALYSIS

1. How do these decrees and proposals characterize France and its mission?
2. According to these documents, what principles does the French Revolution represent?
3. How do these documents represent France's prerevolutionary government and France's foreign enemies?
4. What does the French fatherland (*patrie*) provide for its citizens? What does it expect in return?
5. Do these edicts and proposals represent what you understand to be "propaganda"? Why or why not?

## Decree for Proclaiming the Liberty and Sovereignty of All Peoples (December 15, 1792)

In the countries which are or shall be occupied by the armies of the Republic, the generals shall proclaim at once, in the name of the French nation, the sovereignty of the people, the suppression of all the established authorities and of the existing imposts and taxes, the abolition of the tithe, of feudalism, of seigniorial rights, . . . of real and personal servitude, of the privileges of hunting and fishing, of *corvées,* of the nobility, and generally of all privileges.[1] . . . They shall announce to the people that they shall bring them peace, assistance, fraternity, liberty and equality, and that they will convoke them directly in primary and communal assemblies to create an administration. . . .

The French nation declares that it will treat as enemies the people who, refusing liberty and equality, or renouncing them, may wish to preserve, recall, or deal with the prince and the privileged estates [nobles and clergy]; it promises not to lay down its arms until after the establishment of the sovereignty and independence of the people whose territory the troops of the Republic have entered upon and who shall have adopted the principles of equality, and established a free and popular government.

[Addressing the liberated people]: "You are from this moment brothers and friends, all citizens, all equal in rights, and all equally called to govern, to serve and to defend your fatherland. . . . The agents of the French republic will cooperate with you in order to assure your welfare and the brotherhood which ought to exist between us."

*Source:* Frank Maloy Anderson, *Constitutions and Other Select Documents Illustrative of the History of France, 1789–1901* (Minneapolis: Wilson, 1904), pp. 129–132.
[1]In other words, generals should impose on conquered territories what already had been accomplished in France—the end of privileges for noble and ecclesiastical landowners. These included payments (seigniorial dues) and unpaid labor (*corvée service*) owed by peasants to their lords and certain other privileges, such as exclusive hunting and fishing rights on the estate for the landowners.

## Report Accompanying Proposal for a Levée en Masse (August 23, 1793)

Let us proclaim a lofty truth: liberty has become the creditor of all citizens. Some owe it their labor, others their wealth, some their wisdom, others the strength of their arms; all owe it the blood which flows in their veins. Thus all the French, men and women alike, people of all ages, are called by the fatherland to defend liberty. All physical and intellectual abilities, all political and economic resources belong to it by right. . . . Let everyone take up his post; let everyone behave as he should in this national and military outpouring that . . . the campaign requires, and all will soon be proud that they had worked together to save the fatherland. . . .

Here we are all united. The metal worker and the legislator; the physician and the surgeon; the intellectual and the manual worker; the gunmaker and the colonel; the arms manufacturer and the general; the patriot and the banker; the poor artisan and the rich landowner; the artistic person and the maker of cannons; fortification engineers and the manufacturer of pikes; country folk and townsmen: All are united; all are brothers; all are valuable; all will be honored. Men, women and

*Source:* Translated from original text: *Rapport et décrêt, du 23 août, l'an II de la République, sur la réquisition civique des jeunes citoyens pour la defense de la Patrie* (Paris: 1793).

children . . . the call of the fatherland summons all of you in the name of liberty and equality. . . .

Young men will fight . . . [and] are entrusted to conquer. Married men will forge arms, transport military baggage and guns and will prepare food supplies. Women, who finally are to take their rightful place in the revolution and follow their true destiny, will forget their everyday tasks: their delicate hands will work at making uniforms for soldiers; they will make tents and extend their tender care to shelters where the defenders of the fatherland will receive the help that their wounds require. Children will make lint of old cloth. It is for them that we fight; children . . . destined to gather all the fruits of the revolution, will raise their pure hands toward the skies. And old men, performing their missions again, as in the past, will be guided to the public squares of cities where they will inspire the courage of young warriors and preach the doctrines of hate for kings and the unity of the Republic.

## Report of the Committee of Public Safety on Drafting Poets and Citizens for the Cause of Revolution (May 16, 1794)

The Committee of Public Safety summons poets to celebrate the principal events of the French Revolution, to compose patriotic hymns and poems and republican dramas, to proclaim the heroic deeds of the soldiers of liberty, the qualities of courage and loyalty of republicans, and the victories won by French arms. It also summons citizens who cultivate literature to preserve for posterity the most noteworthy facts and great epochs in the rebirth of the French people, to give to history that pure and resolute character which befits the annals of a great people engaged in winning the liberty which all the tyrants of Europe are attacking. It bids them to . . . inject republican morality into works intended for public instruction, while the Committee will be preparing for the Convention a type of national award to be decreed for their labors. . . .

*Source:* Translated from original text in F. A. Aulard, *Recueil des actes du Comité de salut public, avec la correspondence officielle des représentants en mission et le registre du Conseil executif provisoire* (Paris: Imprimerie nationale, 1889–1951) XIII, 546.

## Report of the Committee of Public Safety on Revolutionary Education (June 1, 1794)

What is involved here is the procedure that must be followed quickly to nurture republican defenders of the fatherland *and* to revolutionize the youth just as we have revolutionized the armies. . . . The young man of sixteen, seventeen, or seventeen and a half, is best prepared to receive a republican education. Nature's work is accomplished. At that moment the fatherland *asks* each citizen: What will you do for me? What means will you employ to defend my unity and my laws, my territory and my independence?

The Convention gives its reply to the fatherland today: a School of Mars is going to open its doors. Three thousand youthful citizens, the strongest, the most intelligent and the most commendable in conduct, are going to attend this new establishment. Three thousand children of honorable parents are going to devote themselves to shared tasks and to themselves for military service. They will . . . dedicate their toil and their blood to their country. . . .

*Source:* Translated from *Rapport fait à la Convention nationale . . . dans la séance de du 13 prairial* (Paris: 1794). Trans. J. H. Overfield.

Love for the fatherland, this pure and generous sentiment which knows no sacrifice that it cannot make . . . ; love for the fatherland which was only a myth in the monarchies and which has filled the annals of the Republic with heroism and virtue, will become the ruling passion of the pupils of the School of Mars. . . .

In founding this outstanding revolutionary establishment, the National Convention ought thus to address the families of the youthful citizens it calls to the School of Mars: "Citizens, for too long ignorance has dwelt in the countryside and workshops; for too long fanaticism and tyranny have prevailed over the convictions of youthful citizens to impede their development. It is not for slaves or mercenaries to nurture free men; the fatherland itself today assumes this important function, which it will never relinquish to prejudice, deviousness, and aristocracy. Loyalty to your own families must end when the great family calls you. The Republic leaves to parents the guidance of your first years, but as soon as your intelligence develops, it loudly proclaims the right it has over you. You are born for the Republic, not to be the pride of family despotism or its victims. It takes you at that happy age when your ardent feelings are directed to virtue and respond naturally to enthusiasm for the good of and love of the fatherland."

# Images of the Emperor: Napoleon

## 36 • JACQUES-LOUIS DAVID, NAPOLEON CROSSING THE ALPS AND NAPOLEON IN HIS STUDY

Napoleon Bonaparte, who between 1799 and 1815 ruled France as first consul, first consul for life, and finally as emperor, is a prime example of how the French Revolution provided opportunities for men of talent and ambition. Born into the minor nobility of Corsica shortly after the island's annexation by France, his military schooling in France would have done him little good in France's pre-1789 army, where birth, wealth, and connections won commissions and determined promotions. But when many antirevolutionary officers left France in the early 1790s, Bonaparte became a general while still in his twenties and, after two brilliant campaigns in Italy against the Austrians and an invasion of Egypt, a national hero.

In the late 1790s, France needed heroes. Controlled by the five-man executive board known as the Directory, the government sought to maintain a moderate republican regime after Jacobin rule had collapsed in 1794. Unloved by democrats and monarchists alike, the Directory was plagued by inflation, corruption, and military setbacks. In 1799, Napoleon and a small group of politicians engineered a *coup d'état* that replaced the Directory with a regime known as the Consulate. Napoleon began as first consul, but in 1804, at age 35, he became emperor.

Napoleon promoted himself as a supporter and savior of the Revolution, but few historians agree with his self-assessment. Although supportive of legal equality and religious freedom, he subverted representative government and respected individual liberties only when it suited his purposes. His government eliminated basic freedoms, not just by censoring newspapers, plays, art, classroom instruction, and books, but also by using them as instruments of propaganda.

Napoleon's use of art as a means of self-promotion took several forms. He generously supported the art museum at the Louvre, a royal palace that in the 1790s had been turned into a public museum for the display of royal and confiscated émigré art. The money he donated was used to fill the museum with works taken from collections in the Vatican, Florence, and Egypt to remind viewers of his conquests. Renamed the Musée Napoléon in 1803, it became a venue for the display of paintings that centered on the emperor. The paintings included many portrayals of his battlefield victories, but since Napoleon wanted to be known as more than a great general, many of them depicted him in other roles—as the defender of the revolution, the sage statesman, the champion of science and progress, and the enlightened lawgiver.

The two paintings we have included are by Jacques-Louis David (1748–1825), the most prominent painter of his age and an ardent supporter of the Revolution. As a member of the Convention, he voted for the execution of King Louis XVI (causing his royalist wife to divorce him) and organized dozens of revolutionary ceremonies and festivals inspired by his friend, Robespierre. Imprisoned after the fall of Robespierre, he was released in 1797 (with the help of his ex-wife, whom he remarried) and gained the notice of Napoleon, whom David came to admire. After Napoleon became first consul, David accepted a commission from King Charles IV of Spain, who was interested in currying Napoleon's favor, to commemorate the crossing of the Alps by Napoleon's army into Italy in 1800 and his subsequent victory over Austria at Marengo. After consulting with Napoleon, David produced *Napoleon Crossing the Alps,* which so impressed Napoleon that he ordered four other versions. The painting commissioned by Charles IV is shown here.

Although leading an army of sixty thousand through the snow and mud of the Alps in May was an impressive achievement, David embellished it. As Napoleon's soldiers trudge by in the background, the first consul is shown on a rearing horse (not the mule he actually rode) and dressed in tights and a flowing cape (not the mud-spattered coat he wore). On stones below the horse's front legs are inscribed the names of Hannibal (247–183 B.C.E.), the Carthaginian general who led an army through the Saint Bernard Pass to attack Rome in the Second Punic War, and Charlemagne, who as king of the Franks also led an army through the pass in 773 C.E. when he attacked the Lombards.

The second painting, *The Emperor Napoleon in His Study at the Tuileries* (1812), shows Napoleon rising from his desk after a long night of work to leave his office and review his troops. Napoleon is dressed in a military uniform and stands next to his desk, where a number of maps have been placed. As can be seen by the words on the paper on top of the pile, he also has been working on the Civil Code, the mammoth codification of French law that was one of his regime's lasting achievements. David's painting is deceptive in that most of the work on the Civil Code was done by a panel of experts Napoleon appointed. Another notable detail is the copy on the floor of Plutarch's *Lives,* biographical sketches of ancient Greek statesmen written in the first century C.E. He is wearing the medallion of the Legion of Honor, an organization founded by Napoleon to honor outstanding military achievement and other service to the state. Although Napoleon did not pose for the painting, after he saw it, he told the painter, "You have understood me well, my dear David."

## QUESTIONS FOR ANALYSIS

1. In the painting of Napoleon crossing the Alps, why did David include soldiers in the background and the stones with the names of Hannibal and Charlemagne?
2. What is significant about the bearing of the horse, the posture of Napoleon, his gestures, his gaze, and his dress? What impressions of Napoleon is David trying to communicate through these details?
3. In the painting of Napoleon in his study, what clues does David provide to show that Napoleon has been working through the night?
4. Why did he include the book by Plutarch, the sword, the maps, and the papers scattered across the desk?
5. What significance do you find in the glimpse of the library shown on the far left?

Napoleon Crossing the Alps

Napoleon (1769–1821) Crossing the Alps at the St Bernard Pass, 20th May 1800, c.1800–01 (oil on canvas). David, Jacques Louis (1748–1825)/Musee National du Chateau de Malmaison, Rueil-Malmaison, France/Giraudon/The Bridgeman Art Library

Napoleon Bonaparte in his Study at the Tuileries, 1812 (oil on canvas) (see also PHD 320), David, Jacques Louis (1748–1825)/Private Collection/Giraudon/The Bridgeman Art Library

Napoleon in His Study

# Anticolonialism and Revolution in the Americas

Despite the many differences between the British colonies of North America, the French colony of Saint-Domingue, and the Portuguese/Spanish colonies of Latin America, all of them achieved their independence between the 1770s and the 1830s. In the Thirteen Colonies and Latin America, the independence movements were stoked by similar grievances and inspired by similar ideals. Grievances included mercantilist restrictions on trade, high taxes, and a lack of self-government; ideals were drawn from English constitutionalism, the Enlightenment, and, in the case of Latin America, the revolutions in North America and France. In Saint-Domingue, however, only a handful of wealthy white landowners worried about French-imposed restrictions on trade and the absence of local self-government. In this tiny colony on the western third of the island of Hispaniola, slavery and race were the key elements. The revolution was instigated by slaves who launched a massive revolt in August 1791 and was driven forward by slaves and free people of color (ex-slaves and mulattoes). In the chaotic years that followed they often were at odds, but they came together between 1802 and 1804 to defeat an invading French army and to found the independent republic of Haiti.

In the Thirteen Colonies, opponents of British rule coalesced into a unified movement under the Continental Congress and George Washington, and after independence, they preserved this unity to found a single state, the United States of America. Federal and state governments drew on the principles of English constitutionalism to guarantee basic freedoms and extend political rights to a majority of adult white males. Although the new government preserved slavery and continued to restrict women's legal and political rights, widespread property holding, a fluid class structure, and economic expansion meant that not just the political elite but also the common people would benefit from independence.

In Latin America, however, the end of colonialism resulted in more than a dozen independent states, all controlled by wealthy landowners of European descent who successfully excluded the peasant masses from politics. Continuation of the colonial class structure meant that the economic and social chasm between propertyless Indian peasants and the tiny elite of white property owners remained intact. In this respect, the independence movement in Latin America ended colonialism but lacked important features of a true revolution.

The people of Saint-Domingue/Haiti experienced great changes as a result of their revolution. The white ruling class was destroyed, and slavery, the condition of close to ninety percent of the population before 1791, was abolished. Political unity and prosperity proved elusive goals, however. Plagued by regionalism, foreign debt, the lack of natural and cultural resources, and widespread poverty, Haiti experienced a civil war between 1806 and 1820, followed by a series of coups, dictatorships, and foreign interventions that impeded the development of stable political institutions and a diversified economy.

# The Thirteen Colonies Declare Their Freedom

## 37 • THE DECLARATION OF INDEPENDENCE

After more than a decade of growing tension, in April 1775 the American Revolution began with a clash between British and American troops at the battles of Lexington and Concord. In the following months Americans vigorously debated whether the colonies should declare their independence from Great Britain. Many had misgivings, but gradually those favoring independence gained the upper hand. The debate ended in June and early July 1776. On June 7 Richard Henry Lee of Virginia proposed an independence resolution to the Second Continental Congress, meeting in Philadelphia. On July 2 twelve states voted for independence, with the delegates from New York abstaining because they needed approval from the New York Provincial Congress before voting. Two days later the Congress voted by the same margin to accept the Declaration of Independence, which was largely the work of the Virginia planter Thomas Jefferson. The Declaration powerfully stated humanity's right to revolution and eloquently justified the colonies' actions. New York ultimately made the vote for independence unanimous when on July 9 the New York Provincial Congress reconvened and directed the New York delegates to vote their approval.

## QUESTIONS FOR ANALYSIS

1. According to the Declaration, what are the purposes of government?
2. According to the Declaration, under what circumstances are people justified in overthrowing their government?
3. To what extent does the Declaration restate principles of the English Bill of Rights (source 34)?
4. How many religious references can you find in the document? How central are they to its arguments?
5. How do the principles of the Declaration of Independence resemble and differ from those of the Declaration of the Rights of Man and of the Citizen (source 35)?

When in the Course of human events, it becomes necessary for one people to dissolve the political bands which have connected them with another, and to assume among the powers of the earth, the separate and equal station to which the Laws of Nature and of Nature's God entitle them, a decent respect to the opinions of mankind requires that they should declare the causes which impel them to the separation.

We hold these truths to be self-evident, that all men are created equal, that they are endowed by their Creator with certain unalienable Rights, that among these are Life, Liberty and the pursuit of Happiness.—That to secure these rights, Governments are instituted among Men, deriving their just powers from the consent of the governed,— That whenever any Form of Government becomes destructive of these ends, it is the Right of the People to alter or to abolish it, and to institute new Government, laying its foundation on such principles and organizing its powers in such form, as to them shall seem most likely to effect their Safety and Happiness. Prudence, indeed, will dictate that Governments long established should not be changed for light and transient causes; and accordingly all experience hath shewn, that mankind are more disposed to suffer, while evils are sufferable, than to right themselves by abolishing the forms to which they are accustomed. But when a long train of abuses and usurpations, pursuing invariably the same Object evinces a design to reduce them under absolute Despotism, it is their right, it is their duty, to throw off such Government, and to provide new Guards for their future security.—Such has been the patient sufferance of these Colonies; and such is now the necessity which constrains them to alter their former Systems of Government. The history of the present King of Great Britain is a history of repeated injuries and usurpations, all having in direct object the establishment of an absolute Tyranny over these States. To prove this, let Facts be submitted to a candid world. . . .

---

> *A list of grievances follows.*

---

In every stage of these Oppressions We have Petitioned for Redress in the most humble terms: Our repeated Petitions have been answered only by repeated injury. A Prince whose character is thus marked by every act which may define a Tyrant, is unfit to be the ruler of a free people.

Nor have We been wanting in attentions to our British brethren. We have warned them from time to time of attempts by their legislature to extend an unwarrantable jurisdiction over us. We have reminded them of the circumstances of our emigration and settlement here. We have appealed to their native justice and magnanimity, and we have conjured them by the ties of our common kindred

to disavow these usurpations, which would inevitably interrupt our connections and correspondence. They too have been deaf to the voice of justice and of consanguinity. We must, therefore, acquiesce in the necessity, which denounces our Separation, and hold them, as we hold the rest of mankind, Enemies in War, in Peace Friends.

We, therefore, the Representatives of the united States of America, in General Congress, Assembled, appealing to the Supreme Judge of the world for the rectitude of our intentions, do, in the Name, and by Authority of the good People of these Colonies, solemnly publish and declare, That these United Colonies are, and of Right ought to be Free and Independent States; that they are Absolved from all Allegiance to the British Crown, and that all political connection between them and the State of Great Britain, is and ought to be totally dissolved; and that as Free and Independent States, they have full Power to levy War, conclude Peace, contract Alliances, establish Commerce, and to do all other Acts and Things which Independent States may of right do. And for the support of this Declaration, with a firm reliance on the protection of divine Providence, we mutually pledge to each other our Lives, our Fortunes and our sacred Honor.

## Toussaint Louverture and the Revolution in Saint-Domingue

### 38 • EXCERPTS FROM FORCED LABOR DECREE OF 1800, CONSTITUTION OF 1801, AND PROCLAMATION OF NOVEMBER 25, 1801

The Saint-Domingue Revolution, which culminated in the founding of the Republic of Haiti in 1804, can be divided into three periods. In the first, between 1789 and 1791, white colonists, who numbered 40,000 and owned most of the colony's nearly 500,000 slaves and 8,000 plantations, sought greater autonomy from France and the end of French economic restrictions. Simultaneously, free blacks and mulattoes— "free people of color"—achieved political equality with whites as a result of a decree adopted by the French National Assembly in May 1791. The revolution's middle phase, which lasted until 1801, began in August 1791, when a massive slave revolt erupted in the Northern Province and fighting broke out between whites and free people of color in the south and west. It was marked by the invasion of Saint-Domingue by Spain and Great Britain in 1793; the abolition of slavery in 1793 by a French colonial official; massive destruction of plantations and cities as fighting raged among troops fighting for France, foreign powers, white landowners, poor whites, mulattos, and ex-slaves; the withdrawal from Saint-Domingue of Spain in 1795 and Great Britain in 1798; and finally, in 1799–1800, at a point when French power in its colony had all but disappeared, a brutal civil war—"The War of the Knives"—between rival native leaders. Only in the third period, between 1802 and 1804, did the revolution become a war of independence after Napoleon sent to Saint-Domingue 20,000 troops under General Charles Leclerc to restore French authority and in all likelihood reinstitute slavery.

The leader who won the civil war of 1799–1800 and led the early resistance to the French invasion in 1802 was Toussaint Louverture, Haiti's best-known revolutionary figure. Born into slavery in 1743, he received a modest education and was freed around the age of thirty. Like many other ex-slaves and mulattoes, he acquired a small plantation and a few slaves. Nonetheless, in August 1793, two years after the slave rebellion had begun, he joined the forces of Georges Biassou, whose army of insurgent slaves was fighting for Spain against the French administration. A gifted commander who quickly rose through the ranks, in May 1794 Louverture defected to the French after a falling out with Biassou and in response to the French government's decision to abolish slavery throughout its empire. After leading his army of ex-slaves on successful campaigns against the Spanish and British, Louverture was promoted by the French to the offices of lieutenant governor of the colony in 1796 and commander-in-chief of all French forces in 1797. By early 1800, after defeating the forces of the mulatto general André Rigaud in the "War of the Knives" and with French authority at low ebb, Louverture was the most powerful man in Saint-Domingue.

This gave Louverture the opportunity to implement his vision for Saint-Domingue. In keeping with his conviction that blacks, whites, and people of mixed race could live side by side on the basis of equality, he named many mulattoes and whites to key administrative positions. He also issued decrees that praised marriage, banned divorce, took steps to limit illegitimacy, and required parents to teach their children the Catholic faith.

His greatest challenges, however, were economic and political. He was determined to revive the colony's plantation system, which before 1791 had produced almost half the world's supply of coffee and sugar. The problem was how to do this without slaves, who after their emancipation had migrated to towns or claimed small plots on abandoned plantations and took up subsistence farming. In politics his main concern was to secure his personal rule, which he was convinced was the key to Saint-Domingue's future.

Louverture's solutions to these challenges are spelled out in the three following excerpts. The first, which deals with plantation labor, is taken from his "Regulations Concerning Field Labor" of October 1800. An excerpt from the Constitution of

1801 follows. Written by Louverture and his advisors, it delineates Louverture's claims to political power. The third excerpt is from a decree of November 25, 1801, which had both economic and political implications.

For better or for worse, Louverture was unable to implement his plans. In June 1802, when it appeared that the Leclerc expedition had restored French authority and even Louverture had withdrawn from the fight, he was lured from his home by a French general, who took him prisoner. He was then taken to France and imprisoned in a fortress in the Jura Mountains, where he died on April 7, 1803. By then Saint-Domingue was once more slipping away from the French. Napoleon's decision to reinstitute slavery in the French colonies in May 1802 rekindled the insurgency at a time when yellow fever was taking a terrible toll on French soldiers. In November 1803 a rebel army commanded by Jean-Jacques Dessalines, a former lieutenant of Louverture, defeated the French and forced the French commander to sue for peace. It was Dessalines who proclaimed the founding of the Republic of Haiti on January 1, 1804. As supreme governor, one of his first acts was to order the murder of three thousand to five thousand whites, including women, children, and infants, who remained in the new country. In September he proclaimed himself Emperor Jacques I of Haiti, a title he held until he was assassinated in 1806.

## QUESTIONS FOR ANALYSIS

1. What information do these sources provide about the behavior of former slaves after the emancipation decree of 1793?
2. What information is provided about Louverture's strategy to bring ex-slaves back to their pre-1793 plantations?
3. What is the constitution's position on slavery and race relations?
4. What powers are accorded to Louverture according to the Constitution of 1801?
5. When he first read a copy of Louverture's 1801 constitution, Napoleon supposedly was livid. What may have caused his anger?
6. To what extent do these documents agree with the ideas expressed in the Declaration of the Rights of Man and of the Citizen (source 35)? In what ways do they go against these ideas?

### Regulations Respecting Field Labor

Whereas, since the revolution, laborers of both sexes . . . refuse to go to it [agricultural work] under pretext of freedom, spend their time wandering about, and give a bad example to the other cultivators; while, on the other hand, the generals, officers, and soldiers, are in a state of constant activity to maintain the sacred rights

*Source:* Regulations Respecting Field Labor, from *Supplement to the Royal Gazette,* Vol. VVII, no. 47, November 15–22, 1800, pp. 9–10.

of the people . . . I do most urgently order as follows:

All overseers, drivers,[1] and field Negroes are bound to observe, with exactness, submission, and obedience, their duty in the same manner as soldiers.

All overseers, drivers, and field-laborers, who will not perform . . . the duties required of them, shall be arrested and punished as severely as soldiers deviating from their duty. After which punishment, if the offender be an overseer, he shall be enlisted in one of the regiments of the army. . . . If a driver, he shall be dismissed from employment and placed among the field-Negroes. . . . And, if a common-laborer, he shall be punished with the same activity as a private soldier, according to his guilt.

All field-laborers, men and women, now in a state of idleness, living in towns, villages, and on other plantations than those to which they belong, with an intention to evade work, even those . . . who have not been employed in field labor since the revolution, are required to return immediately to their respective plantations if in the course of eight days from the promulgation of this present regulation, they shall not produce sufficient proof of their having some useful occupation or means of livelihood. . . .

Parents are earnestly entreated to attend to their duty towards their children; which is, to make them good citizens; for that purpose they must instruct them in good morals, in the Christian religion, and the fear of God. Above all . . . they must be brought up in some specific business or profession to enable them not only to earn their living, but also to contribute to the expenses of the Government.

All persons residing in towns and villages who shall harbor laborers of either sex, all proprietors . . . who shall allow on their plantations laborers belonging to other estates, without immediately making it known to the Commandant of the district . . . shall pay a fine of 200 or 800 *livres*, according to the abilities of the delinquent; in case of repetition of the offense, they shall pay three times as much. . . .

The overseers and drivers of every plantation shall . . . inform the commanding officer of the district in regard to the conduct of the laborers under their management; as well as of those who shall absent themselves from their plantations without a pass; and of those who, residing on the plantations shall refuse to work. They shall be forced to go to the labor of the field, and if they prove obstinate, they shall be arrested and carried before the military commandant, in order to suffer punishment. . . .

The commandants of the towns, or the officers in the villages, shall not suffer the laborers or field-Negroes to spend [weeks] in town; they shall also take care that they do not conceal themselves. . . .

All the municipal administrations of Saint-Domingue are requested to take the wisest measures . . . to inform themselves whether those who call themselves domestics [household servants] really are so, observing that plantation Negroes cannot be domestics. Any person keeping them in that quality will be liable to pay the above-mentioned fine. . . .

I command all the Generals of departments . . . , and other principal Officers in the districts to attend to the execution of this regulation, for which they shall be personally responsible. And I flatter myself that their zeal in assisting me to restore the public prosperity will not be momentary, convinced as they must be, that liberty cannot exist without industry.

---

[1] A supervisor was an overseer of field workers; a driver was an assistant to the overseer.

## Constitution of 1801

### On the territory

The entire extent of Saint-Domingue, . . . and other adjacent islands, form the territory of one colony that is part of the French Empire, but is subject to particular laws.

### On its inhabitants

There can be no slaves in this territory; servitude has been forever abolished. All men are born, live and die there free and French.

All men can work at all forms of employment, whatever their color.

No other distinctions exist than those of virtues and talents, nor any other superiority than that granted by the law in the exercise of a public charge. The law is the same for all, whether it punishes or protects.

### On religion

The Catholic religion, Apostolic and Roman, is the only one publicly professed.

### On cultivation and commerce

The colony, being essentially agricultural, cannot allow the least interruption in its labor and cultivation. Every plantation is a factory that demands a gathering together of cultivators and workers; it shall represent the tranquil haven of an active and constant family, of which the owner of the land or his representative is necessarily the father. Every cultivator and worker is a member of the family and a shareholder in its revenues. . . .

The introduction of the cultivators indispensable to the re-establishment and the growth of agriculture will take place in Saint-Domingue. The Constitution charges the governor [Louverture] to take the appropriate measures to encourage and favor this increase in manpower . . . , and to assure and guarantee the carrying out of the respective engagements resulting from this introduction.

*Source:* Constitution of 1801, from website Marxist Internet Archive http://www.marxists.org/history/haiti/1801/constitution.htm Translated by Mitch Abidor.

### On government

The administrative reins of the colony are confided to a Governor, who directly corresponds with the government of the metropole [France] in all matters relating to the colony. The Constitution names as governor Citizen Toussaint Louverture, General-in-Chief of the army of Saint-Domingue and, in consideration of the important services that the general has rendered to the colony in the most critical circumstances of the revolution, and per the wishes of the grateful inhabitants, the reins are confided to him for the rest of his glorious life. . . .

In order to strengthen the tranquility that the colony owes to the firmness, activity, indefatigable zeal, and rare virtues of General Louverture, and as a sign of the unlimited confidence of the inhabitants of Saint-Domingue, the Constitution attributes exclusively to this general the right to choose the citizen who, in the unhappy instance of his death, shall immediately replace him. . . .

The Governor seals and promulgates the laws; he names men to all civil and military posts. He commands the armed forces and is charged with its organization; the ships of State docked in the ports of the colony receive his orders. . . .

He influences the general policies of the inhabitants and manufactories, and ensures that owners, farmers and their representatives observe their obligations towards the cultivators and workers, and the obligations of cultivators and workers towards the owners, farmers and their representatives . . .

He directs the collection, the payment and the use of the finances of the colony and, to this effect, gives all orders.

He oversees and censors, via commissioners, every writing meant for publication on the island. He suppresses all those coming from foreign countries that will tend to corrupt the morals or again trouble the colony. He punishes the authors or sellers, according to the seriousness of the case.

If the Governor is informed that there is in the works some conspiracy against the tranquility of the colony, he has arrested the persons presumed to be its authors, executors or accomplices. After having had them submit to an extra-judiciary interrogation if it is called for he has them brought before a competent tribunal.

## Proclamation of November 25, 1801

In all the communes of the colony . . . all male and female citizens who live in them, whatever their quality or condition, must obtain a security card. Such card shall contain the name, family name, address, civil state, profession and quality, age and sex of those who bear them. It shall be signed by the mayor and the police superintendent of the quarter in which lives the individual to which it shall be delivered. . . .

It is expressly ordered that municipal administrators are only to deliver security cards to persons having a known profession or state, irreproachable conduct and well assured means of existence. All those who cannot fulfill the conditions rigorously necessary to obtain it will be sent to the fields if they are Creole [born in Saint-Domingue], or sent away from the colony if they are foreigners. Two weeks after the publication of the present act, any person found without a security card shall be sent to the fields if they are Creole and if they are foreigners deported from the colony without any form of trial if they don't prefer to serve in the troops of the line. . . .

Source: Proclamation of November 25, 1801, from Decree of Nov 25, 1801, from the Marxist Internet Archive, translated by Mitch Abidor: http://www.marxists.org/reference/archive/toussaint-louverture/1801/dictatorial.htm

# Bolívar's Dreams for Latin America

## 39 • SIMÓN BOLÍVAR, THE JAMAICA LETTER

Simón Bolívar, the most renowned leader of the Latin American independence movement, was born to a wealthy Venezuelan landowning family in 1783. Orphaned at an early age, he was educated by a private tutor who inspired in his pupil an enthusiasm for the principles of the Enlightenment and republicanism. After spending three years in Europe, Bolívar returned in 1803 to Venezuela, where the death of his new bride plunged him into grief and caused his return to Europe. In 1805, in Rome, he took a vow to dedicate his life to liberating his native land from Spain. On his return, he became a leading member of a republican-minded group in Caracas that in 1810 deposed the colonial governor and created the Republic of Venezuela. Until his death in 1830, Bolívar dedicated himself to the independence movement as a publicist, diplomat, and statesman. His greatest contribution was as the general who led the armies that defeated the Spaniards and liberated the northern regions of South America.

The so-called Jamaica Letter was written in 1815 during a temporary self-imposed exile in Jamaica. It was addressed to "an English gentleman," probably the island's governor. The Venezuelan Republic had collapsed in May as a result of a viciously fought Spanish counteroffensive, divisions among the revolutionaries, and opposition from many Indians, blacks, and mulattos, who viewed the Creole landowners, not the Spaniards, as their oppressors. The letter was in response to a request from the Englishman for Bolívar's thoughts about the background and prospects of the liberation movement.

## QUESTIONS FOR ANALYSIS

1. According to Bolívar, what will doom Spain's efforts to hold on to its colonies?
2. According to Bolívar, what Spanish policies made Spanish rule odious to him and other revolutionaries?
3. In Bolívar's view, what complicates the task of predicting Spanish America's political future?
4. Does Bolívar's letter reveal concern for the economic and social condition of South America's nonwhite population? What are some of the implications of Bolívar's attitudes?
5. Based on your reading of Bolívar, what guesses can you make about the reasons that the new nations of South America found it difficult to achieve stable republican governments?

Success will crown our efforts, because the destiny of America has been irrevocably decided; the tie that bound her to Spain has been severed. . . . That which formerly bound them now divides them. The hatred that the [Iberian] Peninsula inspired in us is greater than the ocean between us. It would be easier to have the two continents meet than to reconcile the spirits of the two countries. The habit of obedience; a community of interest, of understanding, of religion; mutual goodwill; a tender regard for the birthplace and good name of our forefathers; in short, all that gave rise to our hopes, came to us from Spain. As a result there was born a principle of affinity that seemed eternal. . . . At present the contrary attitude persists: we are threatened with the fear of death, dishonor, and every harm; there is nothing we have not suffered at the hands of that unnatural stepmother—Spain. . . . We have already seen the light, and it is not our desire to be thrust back into darkness. . . .

The role of the inhabitants of the American hemisphere has for centuries been purely passive. Politically they were non-existent. We are still in a position lower than slavery, and therefore it is more difficult for us to rise to the enjoyment of freedom. . . . States are slaves because of either the nature or the misuse of their constitutions; a people is therefore enslaved when the government, by its nature or its vices, infringes on and usurps the rights of the citizen or subject. Applying these principles, we find that America was denied not only its freedom but even an active and effective tyranny. Under absolutism there are no recognized limits to the exercise of governmental powers. The will of the great sultan, khan, bey, and other despotic rulers is the supreme law, carried out more or less arbitrarily by the lesser pashas, khans, and satraps of Turkey and Persia, who have an organized system of oppression in which inferiors participate according to the authority vested in them. To them is entrusted the administration of civil, military, political, religious, and tax matters. But, after all is said and done, the rulers of Isfahan are Persians; the viziers of the Grand Turk are Turks; and the sultans of Tartary [the steppe region of Central Asia] are Tartars. . . .

How different is our situation! We have been harassed by a conduct which has not only deprived us of our rights but has kept us in a sort of permanent infancy with regard to public affairs. If we could at least have managed our domestic affairs and our internal administration, we could have acquainted

*Source:* From Simón Bolívar, *Selected Writings*, ed. Harold A. Bierck, Jr., trans. by Lewis Bertrand (New York: Colonial Press, 1951), pp. 103–122.

ourselves with the processes and mechanics of public affairs. . . .

Americans today, and perhaps to a greater extent than ever before, who live within the Spanish system occupy a position in society no better than that of serfs destined for labor. . . . Yet even this status is surrounded with galling restrictions, such as being forbidden to grow European crops, or to store products which are royal monopolies, or to establish factories of a type the Peninsula itself does not possess. To this add the exclusive trading privileges, even in articles of prime necessity, and the barriers between American provinces designed to prevent all exchange of trade, traffic, and understanding. In short, do you wish to know what our future held?—simply the cultivation of the fields of indigo, grain, coffee, sugar cane, cacao, and cotton; cattle raising on the broad plains; hunting wild game in the jungles; digging in the earth to mine its gold—but even these limitations could never satisfy the greed of Spain. So negative was our existence that I can find nothing comparable in any other civilized society. . . .

As I have just explained, we were cut off and, as it were, removed from the world in relation to the science of government and administration of the state. We were never viceroys or governors, save in the rarest of instances; seldom archbishops and bishops; diplomats never; as military men, only subordinates; as nobles, without royal privileges. In brief, we were neither magistrates nor financiers and seldom merchants—all in flagrant contradiction to our institutions. . . .

It is harder . . . to release a nation from servitude than to enslave a free nation. This truth is proven by the annals of all times, which reveal that most free nations have been put under the yoke, but very few enslaved nations have recovered their liberty. Despite the convictions of history, South Americans have made efforts to obtain liberal, even perfect, institutions, doubtless out of that instinct to aspire to the greatest possible happiness, which, common to all men, is bound to follow in civil societies founded on the principles of justice, liberty, and equality. But are we capable of maintaining in proper balance the difficult charge of a republic? Is it conceivable that a newly emancipated people can soar to the heights of liberty, and, unlike Icarus, neither have its wings melt nor fall into an abyss? Such a marvel is inconceivable and without precedent. There is no reasonable probability to bolster our hopes.

More than anyone, I desire to see America fashioned into the greatest nation in the world, greatest not so much by virtue of her area and wealth as by her freedom and glory. Although I seek perfection for the government of my country, I cannot persuade myself that the New World can, at the moment, be organized as a great republic. Since it is impossible, I dare not desire it; yet much less do I desire to have all America a monarchy because this plan is not only impracticable but also impossible. Wrongs now existing could not be righted, and our emancipation would be fruitless. The American states need the care of paternal governments to heal the sores and wounds of despotism and war. . . .

From the foregoing, we can draw these conclusions: The American provinces are fighting for their freedom, and they will ultimately succeed. Some provinces as a matter of course will form federal and some central republics; the larger areas will inevitably establish monarchies, some of which will fare so badly that they will disintegrate in either present or future revolutions. To consolidate a great monarchy will be no easy task, but it will be utterly impossible to consolidate a great republic. . . .

When success is not assured, when the state is weak, and when results are distantly seen, all men hesitate; opinion is divided, passions rage, and the enemy fans these passions in order to win an easy victory because of them. As soon as we are strong and under the guidance of a liberal nation which will lend us her protection, we will achieve accord in cultivating the virtues and talents that lead to glory. Then will we march majestically toward that great prosperity for which South America is destined. . . .

# Chapter 6

# Africa, Southwest Asia, and India in the Seventeenth and Eighteenth Centuries

AROUND 1600, SOUTHWEST ASIA and India, two huge regions dominated by three large and powerful empires, would seem to have had little in common with Africa, a continent of hundreds of kingdoms, confederations, chiefdoms, city-states, and regions with no formal states. In comparison to Africa, India and Southwest Asia had more people, more cities, and more commercial and cultural contacts with Europe and East Asia. Moreover, India and Southwest Asia were dominated by just two major faiths, Islam and Hinduism, while Africa had many religions: Islam in the Mediterranean north, the Sudan, and on the east coast; Christianity in Egypt and Ethiopia; and many varieties of native religions throughout the continent.

Despite these differences, the regions' histories in the seventeenth and eighteenth centuries were similar in several respects. All three areas, for example, experienced political instability, which in some cases led to the demise of once-formidable states. In Southwest Asia, the Safavid Empire collapsed in the 1730s, and in India the Mughal Empire had been reduced to impotence and irrelevance by the mid-1700s. The Ottoman Empire remained a large, formidable state, but its failure to take Vienna in a two-month siege in 1683 was the beginning of a prolonged period of military setbacks and territorial losses. In west Africa, the Songhai Empire fell apart after a defeat by invading Moroccans in 1591, and in the southeast, the kingdom of Mutapa, following years of Portuguese penetration, was overrun by the Changamire kingdom in the 1680s. Other African states experienced civil war, invasion, or gradual decline.

Increased interaction with Europe is another common thread in the histories of these regions. In South and Southwest Asia, trade expanded, especially between Europe and India. In India, however, interaction with Europeans went beyond commerce. Beginning in the 1750s, officials of the British East India Company took advantage of the Mughal Empire's disintegration to establish the Company's authority over Bengal in the northeast and other regions of the subcontinent. In Africa, increased interaction with Europe included the first permanent European settlement with the arrival of Dutch farmers in southern Africa in 1652. It also meant a substantial expansion of the slave trade on Africa's west and east coasts, with just over six million African slaves transported to the Americas and the West Indies in the 1700s, and smaller numbers to the Middle East, India, and French-controlled islands in the Indian Ocean. This spectacular growth in the slave trade underlined Africa's vulnerability in an age of growing global interaction.

# The African Slave Trade and Its Critics

Slavery has been practiced throughout history in every corner of the globe. Since the 1500s, however, it has uniquely affected the people of Africa, who became a source of unpaid labor in many parts of the world, especially the Americas. The transatlantic slave trade began in the fifteenth century under the Portuguese, who first shipped Africans to Portugal to serve as domestics and then to the Canary Islands, the Madeiras, and São Tomé to work on sugar plantations. By 1500, Portuguese merchants were exporting approximately five hundred slaves each year. That number grew in the mid-1500s, when the plantation system was established in Brazil and subsequently spread to parts of Spanish America, the West Indies, and British North America. In the 1700s, when Great Britain was the leading purveyor of slaves, the transatlantic slave trade peaked, with more than six million slaves transported to the Americas and the Caribbean.

Almost every aspect of the Atlantic slave trade is the subject of debate among historians. Did the enslavement of Africans result from racism, or were Africans enslaved because they were available and convenient to the market across the Atlantic? Did the loss of millions of individuals to slavery have serious or minimal demographic consequences for Africa? Was political instability in Africa linked to the slave trade or to other factors? To what extent did reliance on selling slaves to Europeans impede Africa's economic development? What combination of humanitarianism, religious conviction, and hard-headed economic calculation led to the abolition of the slave trade?

One thing is certain: For the millions of Africans who were captured, shackled, wrenched from their families, branded, sold, packed into the holds of ships, sold once more, and put to work in the mines and fields of the Western Hemisphere, slavery meant pain, debasement, and fear. For them, it was an unmitigated disaster.

# The Path to Enslavement in America

## 40 • OLAUDAH EQUIANO, THE INTERESTING NARRATIVE OF OLAUDAH EQUIANO WRITTEN BY HIMSELF

In 1789, no fewer than 100 abolitionist books and pamphlets were published in England, but none had more readers than the autobiography of the former slave Olaudah Equiano. In his memoir, Equiano relates that he was born in 1745 in Igboland, in the southern part of modern-day Nigeria. He was captured and sold into slavery at the age of eleven, and after a harrowing Atlantic crossing, served three masters, including an officer in the British navy; an English sea captain who took him to the West Indian island of Montserrat; and finally, Robert King, a Quaker merchant from Philadelphia.

In many ways, Equiano's experiences as a slave were unique. He never served as a plantation worker, and he learned to read and write while owned by his first master. He made numerous trips back and forth across the Atlantic and, in the process, learned skills relating to navigation, bookkeeping, and commerce. After purchasing his freedom from his last owner in 1766, he took up residence in England, where he supported himself as a barber, servant, and sailor. In the 1780s, he joined the English abolitionist movement. As a result of contacts he made with the movement's leaders, in the late 1780s he was given a government post with the responsibility of arranging the transfer of provisions to Sierra Leone, a newly founded colony that abolitionists hoped would serve as a homeland for freed slaves. Dismissed after a year, Equiano turned to writing his autobiography, which was published with the financial support of leading abolitionists. Heavily promoted by Equiano on lecture tours, his book went through eight editions in the 1790s.

How factual is Equiano's narrative? Historians must raise this question about any historical source, especially autobiographies, whose authors cannot be expected to be totally objective when writing about themselves or totally accurate in recalling childhood events. Equiano's memoirs, furthermore, were written with a specific purpose: to discredit slavery and garner support for the abolitionist cause. One scholar, Vincent Carretta of the University of Maryland, has suggested that Equiano fabricated the account of his kidnapping and his voyage across the Atlantic on a slave ship. A baptismal certificate and a Royal Navy document, he argues, show that Equiano was actually born in South Carolina.

Scholars who consider Carretta's evidence inconclusive believe that the memoir is generally accurate. Certainly, a comparison of Equiano's description of his slave experience with what we know from other sources suggests that his work is free of exaggeration and distortion. This includes the following excerpt, which describes his harsh introduction to slavery.

### QUESTIONS FOR ANALYSIS

1. On the basis of Equiano's account, what is the role of Africans in the slave trade?
2. What does Equiano's account reveal about the effect of slavery and the slave trade on African society?

3. What were the characteristics of slavery that Equiano encountered in Africa?

4. Once the slaves were on board the slave ship, what experiences contributed to their despair and demoralization, according to Equiano?

5. What factors might have contributed to the brutal treatment of the slaves by the ship's crew?

---

## Taken Captive

One day, when all our people were gone out to their work as usual and only I and my dear sister were left to mind the house, two men and a woman got over our walls, and in a moment seized us both, and without giving us time to cry out or make resistance they stopped our mouths and ran off with us into the nearest wood. . . .

For a long time we had kept to the woods, but at last we came into a road which I believed I knew. I had now some hopes of being delivered, for we had advanced but a little way before I discovered some people at a distance, on which I began to cry out for their assistance: but my cries had no other effect than to make them tie me faster and stop my mouth, and then they put me into a large sack. They also stopped my sister's mouth and tied her hands, and in this manner we proceeded till we were out of the sight of these people. When we went to rest the following night they offered us some victuals, but we refused it, and the only comfort we had was in being in one another's arms all that night and bathing each other with our tears. But alas! we were soon deprived of even the small comfort of weeping together. The next day proved a day of greater sorrow than I had yet experienced, for my sister and I were then separated while we lay clasped in each other's arms. It was in vain that we besought them not to part us; she was torn from me and immediately carried away, while I was left in a state of distraction not to be described. At length, after many days' traveling . . . , I got into

the hands of a chieftain in a very pleasant country. This man had two wives and some children, and they all used me extremely well and did all they could to comfort me, particularly the first wife, who was something like my mother. . . . This first master of mine, as I may call him, was a smith, and my principal employment was working his bellows, which were the same kind as I had seen in my vicinity. . . . I was there about a month, and they at last used to trust me some little distance from the house. This liberty I used in embracing every opportunity to inquire the way to my own home: and I also sometimes, for the same purpose, went with the maidens in the cool of the evenings to bring pitchers of water from the springs for the use of the house.

---

> Equiano escapes, but terrified of being alone in the forest at night returns to his household.

---

Soon after this my master's only daughter and child by his first wife sickened and died, which affected him so much that for some time he was almost frantic, and really would have killed himself had he not been watched and prevented. However, in a small time afterwards he recovered and I was again sold. I was now carried to the left of the sun's rising, through many different countries and a number of large woods. The people I was sold to used to carry me very often when I was tired either

---

Source: *The Interesting Narrative of the Life of Olaudah Equiano, or Gustavus Vassa, the African. Written By Himself* (New York: William Durell, 1791), pp. 34–36, 41–43, 48–50, 52, 53, 55–59, 61–62.

on their shoulders or on their backs. I saw many convenient well-built sheds along the roads at proper distances, to accommodate the merchants and travelers who lay in those buildings along with their wives, who often accompany them; and they always go well armed.

---

> Equiano encounters his sister, but again they are quickly separated.

---

I did not long remain after my sister [departed]. I was again sold and carried through a number of places till, after traveling a considerable time, I came to a town called Tinmah. . . . I was sold here by a merchant who lived and brought me there. I had been about two or three days at his house when a wealthy widow came there one evening, and brought with her an only son, a young gentleman about my own age and size. Here they saw me; and, having taken a fancy to me, I was bought of the merchant, and went home with them. . . . The next day I was washed and perfumed, and when meal-time came I was led into the presence of my mistress, and ate and drank before her with her son. This filled me with astonishment; and I could scarce help expressing my surprise that the young gentleman should suffer me, who was bound, to eat with him who was free. . . . There were likewise slaves daily to attend us, while my young master and I with other boys sported with our darts and bows and arrows, as I had been used to do at home. I now began to think I was to be adopted into the family . . . when all at once the delusion vanished; for without the least previous knowledge, one morning early, while my dear master was still asleep, I was wakened out of my reverie to fresh sorrow, and hurried away. . . . Thus I continued to travel, sometimes by land, sometimes by water, through different countries and various nations, till at the end of six or seven months after I had been kidnapped I arrived at the sea coast.

## The Slave Ship

The first object which saluted my eyes when I arrived on the coast was the sea, and a slave ship which was then riding at anchor and waiting for its cargo. These filled me with astonishment, which was soon converted into terror when I was carried on board. I was immediately handled and tossed up to see if I were sound by some of the crew, and I was now persuaded that I had gotten into a world of bad spirits and that they were going to kill me. Their complexions differing so much from ours, their long hair and the language they spoke united to confirm me in this belief. . . . When I looked round the ship too and saw a large furnace boiling and a multitude of black people of every description chained together, every one of their countenances expressing dejection and sorrow, I no longer doubted of my fate; and quite overpowered with horror and anguish, I fell motionless on the deck and fainted. When I recovered a little I found some black people about me, who I believed were some of those who had brought me on board and had been receiving their pay; they talked to me in order to cheer me, but all in vain. . . .

I was soon put down under the decks, and there I received such a salutation in my nostrils as I had never experienced in my life: so that with the loathsomeness of the stench and crying together, I became so sick and low that I was not able to eat. . . . I now wished for the last friend, death, to relieve me; but soon, to my grief, two of the white men offered me eatables, and on my refusing to eat, one of them held me fast by the hands while the other flogged me severely. I had never experienced anything of this kind before, and although, not being used to the water, I naturally feared that element the first time I saw it, yet nevertheless could I have got over the nettings I would have jumped over the side, but I could not; and besides, the crew used to watch us very closely . . . lest we should leap into the water: and I have seen some of these poor African prisoners most severely cut for attempting to do so, and hourly whipped for not eating. . . . In a little time after, . . . I found some of my own nation, which in a small degree gave ease to my mind. I inquired of these what was to be done with us; they gave me to understand we were to be carried to these white people's country to work for them. I then was a little revived, and thought if it were no worse than working, my situation was not so desperate: but still I feared I should be put to death, the white people looked and acted, in so savage a manner; for I had never seen . . . such instances of brutal cruelty, and this not only shown towards us blacks but also to some of the whites themselves. One white man in particular I saw, when we were permitted to be on deck, flogged so unmercifully with a large rope near the foremast that he died in consequence of it; and they tossed him over the side as they would have done a brute. . . .

At last, when the ship we were in had got in all her cargo, they made ready with many fearful noises, and we were all put under deck so that we could not see how they managed the vessel. But this disappointment was the last of my sorrow. The stench of the hold while we were on the coast was so intolerably loathsome that it was dangerous to remain there for any time, and some of us had been permitted to stay on the deck for the fresh air; but now that the whole ship's cargo were confined together it became absolutely pestilential. The closeness of the place and the heat of the climate, added to the number in the ship, which was so crowded that each had scarcely room to turn himself, almost suffocated us. This produced copious perspirations, so that the air soon became unfit for respiration from a variety of loathsome smells, and brought on a sickness among the slaves, of which many died. . . . This wretched situation was again aggravated by the galling of the chains, now become insupportable,

and the filth of the necessary tubs [latrines], into which the children often fell and were almost suffocated. The shrieks of the women and the groans of the dying rendered the whole a scene of horror almost inconceivable. Happily perhaps for myself I was soon reduced so low here that it was thought necessary to keep me almost always on deck, and from my extreme youth I was not put in fetters. . . .

At last we came in sight of the island of Barbados, at which the whites on board gave a great shout and made many signs of joy to us. We did not know what to think of this, but as the vessel drew nearer we plainly saw the harbor and other ships of different kinds and sizes, and we soon anchored amongst them off Bridgetown. Many merchants and planters now came on board. . . . They put us in separate parcels and examined us attentively. They also made us jump, and pointed to the land, signifying we were to go there. . . .

We were not many days in the merchant's custody before we were sold after their usual manner, which is this: On a signal given, the buyers rush at once into the yard where the slaves are confined, and make choice of that parcel they like best. The noise and clamor with which this is attended and the eagerness visible in the countenances of the buyers serve not a little to increase the apprehensions of the terrified Africans. . . . In this manner, without scruple, are relations and friends separated, most of them never to see each other again. I remember in the vessel in which I was brought over, in the men's apartment there were several brothers who, in the sale, were sold in different lots; and it was very moving to see and hear their cries at parting.

O, ye nominal Christians! might not an African ask you, learned you this from your God who says unto you, Do unto all men as you would men should do unto you?

# Ending the Slave Trade: European and African Perspectives

## BACKGROUND

In 1453, in his *Chronicle of the Discovery and Conquest of Guinea,* the Portuguese author Gomes Eannes de Azurara became one of the first Europeans to record his thoughts and feelings about the slave trade. Eannes acknowledged that he was deeply saddened by the sight of African slaves disembarking from a ship in the Portuguese port city of Lagos. He deplored their "wretched state" and was reduced to tears by the sobs of families about to be broken apart and sold to different owners. His remorse was fleeting, however. He took comfort in the fact that in Portugal the slaves would be converted to Christianity, treated well, and given an opportunity to overcome their "bestial sloth."

For the next three centuries, many Europeans depended on such rationalizations to dull their unease about the slave trade. Others defended it as an economic necessity. Most ignored it. As a result, the slave trade grew, until in the eighteenth century, just over six million Africans were transported across the Atlantic as slaves. At century's end, however, the institution of slavery was on the defensive. Antislavery societies were founded in England, the United States, and France; in 1792 the government of Denmark issued a ban on Danish participation in the slave trade that would take effect in 1803; in 1794, the government of revolutionary France outlawed slavery throughout its empire; and in 1807 the United States and Great Britain outlawed the slave trade. Great Britain's decision turned the world's leading slave-trading nation into its leading opponent.

What explains the sudden rise in antislavery sentiment? Some Europeans turned against slavery out of religious conviction. Many early abolitionists were Quakers, members of the Religious Society of Friends, a small English religious organization with a tradition of egalitarianism and pacifism. They wrote many of the first antislavery treatises and were prime movers in the founding of the first antislavery societies. Others had ties with Methodism, an offshoot of the Church of England with a commitment to personal rebirth and social reform. Opposition to the slave trade also was encouraged by the intellectual atmosphere of the Enlightenment, with its emphasis on freedom, natural rights, and progress. Finally, the campaign against slavery was strengthened by the American and French revolutions, movements dedicated to furthering the rights of man—even though many of their leaders were slaveholders.

Abolitionists were opposed by slave traders, plantation owners, and some politicians, who marshaled religious, economic, and political arguments to support their cause. Ending the slave trade also was opposed by Africans who depended on the capture and sale of slaves as a source of wealth and power. Slavery's defenders failed, however. When Brazil outlawed slavery in 1888, slavery and the slave trade in the Atlantic world had come to an end. By then, however, untold damage had been done, and slavery's racist legacy remained.

## THE SOURCES

Our first excerpt is from the pamphlet "Thoughts Upon Slavery," written by the charismatic Methodist leader John Wesley in 1774. Wesley's widely read treatise demonstrates the moral earnestness and emotional fervor of evangelical Protestant abolitionists. The second excerpt is from a speech delivered in 1790 by an unknown speaker to the French National Assembly, which had legislative authority in the early stages of the French Revolution. The speaker draws on moral principles derived from the Enlightenment and the early stages of the French Revolution to oppose the slave trade.

The views of those who favored the continuation of the slave trade are represented by two sources. The first is a memorandum prepared in 1797 by Willem S. van Ryneveld, a prominent member of the Dutch settler community in the Cape Colony of southern Africa. After the British seized the colony from the Dutch in 1795 to prevent it from coming under French control, the British governor sought his views on a variety of issues, including the feasibility of ending the slave trade in a colony where more than fifty percent of the white population owned slaves and slaves outnumbered whites by a margin of just under fifteen thousand to just under fourteen thousand.

The final source contains the words of Osei Bonsu, the king of Asante, as recorded by Joseph Dupuis, a British envoy sent to Asante in 1820 to discuss Asante–British commerce. Asante, a powerful state on the Guinea Coast, derived much of its income from the sale of criminals, debtors, and prisoners of war to European slavers.

## QUESTIONS FOR ANALYSIS

1. Consider the arguments of Wesley and the author representing the Society of the Friends of Blacks. On what do they agree and disagree? What are their reasons for opposing the slave trade and slavery? What can be inferred about the intended audience for their writings? How do they try to appeal to that audience?
2. Obviously van Ryneveld and Osei Bonsu both oppose the arguments of Wesley and the French abolitionists. On what other matters do this African king and this wealthy European agree and disagree?
3. On the basis of these four excerpts, what conclusions can you draw about the reasons that the abolitionists, not the defenders of slavery, were successful in attaining their goals?

# Political Change in South and Southwest Asia

Halfway through the seventeenth century, the Ottoman, Safavid, and Mughal dynasties ruled three of the world's four largest and most powerful empires; only China had more territory, subjects, and wealth. Within a century, however, the Safavid Empire had collapsed, and an impoverished powerless Mughal emperor ruled only a tiny scrap of territory around Delhi. The Ottoman Empire survived, and indeed would do so until 1922, making it one of the longest-lasting empires in history, but by the mid-1700s, it had many problems—military defeats, territorial losses, weakened central authority, budget deficits, scandals, bribery, and a string of sultans who ranged from unremarkable to incompetent. However, it also showed a resiliency and strength that spared it the fate of the two other Islamic empires.

The Safavid Empire's decline began soon after the death of Shah Abbas II (r. 1642–1667). His successor Shah Soleyman (Safi II), drank excessively, built a sumptuous palace in Isfahan, and richly rewarded his favorites but thought little about governing. His son Husain (r. 1694–1722) was uninformed, superstitious, and easily influenced, qualities one might expect in a ruler who had been confined to the palace harem for all of his twenty-six years before becoming shah. He paid the price in 1722, when Isfahan fell to an army of Afghan warriors. In the wake of this defeat the Safavids fled to the hills, leaving Iran open to Ottoman and Russian invasions, decades of anarchy, and the establishment of the weak Qajar Dynasty in the 1790s.

In India, the empire's problems began in the reign of Aurangzeb (r. 1658–1707), who after years of military campaigning extended Mughal authority in the northwest and south, but who also alienated his Hindu and Sikh subjects by abandoning the tolerant religious policies of his predecessors. He and his successors faced rebellions from powerful Hindu princes, Sikhs, and the Marathas, who broke away from the empire and established a sizable kingdom in western India. Following a turbulent period from 1713 to 1719, which was marked by succession wars, the overthrow of two emperors, and the deaths of two others who ruled for a matter of days before dying, Muhammad Shah reigned from 1719 to 1748. By then, however, local officials, princely rulers, and provincial governors had stopped remitting taxes to the Mughal treasury and had become de facto independent territorial rulers. Such was the decrepit state of the Mughal Empire when the warlord Nadir Shah led his Afghan army into India in 1739, decisively defeated the Mughal army, and ordered the sack of Delhi at the cost of twenty thousand to thirty thousand lives.

Ottoman history followed a different course. Beginning in the 1600s Ottoman expansion gave way to Ottoman contraction, and by the middle decades of the eighteenth century the empire had lost large chunks of territory to European powers. It also had ceded virtual autonomy to a number of provincial rulers. Concurrently, many of the key institutions and practices of an earlier age had been abandoned.

Taxes were now collected by independent contractors (tax farmers) rather than by government agents; the devshirme system, in which Christian boys were recruited by force to serve as soldiers and officials had been abandoned; the vaunted Janissary corps had degenerated into a poorly trained organization of part-time soldiers mainly concerned with protecting their stipends and privileges; Ottoman princes, who once had gained valuable experience through service in the army or provincial administration, were now confined to the harem to prevent rebellion.

But these were signs of change, not necessarily decay. In the eighteenth century Ottoman agriculture, artisan production, and international and domestic commerce grew. Impressive building projects were undertaken and cultural innovations of all types flourished under imperial patronage. Translations from Arabic, Persian, and European languages into Turkish were encouraged, and in 1729 an Istanbul publisher began printing books in Turkish for the first time. Land surveys were undertaken to increase tax revenue, and sultans and their chief ministers called meetings of prominent officials to debate policy. By the end of the century, however, the Ottomans suffered one-sided defeats by Austria and Russia and faced a spate of provincial rebellions. In light of these setbacks, in 1789 a new sultan, Selim III, and his close advisors concluded that substantial military and administrative changes were necessary and began to institute a "new order" modeled on European practices.

# Selim III's New Order Army

## 41 • MUSTAFA RESHID CELEBI, A DEFENSE OF THE NEW ORDER ARMY

Before becoming sultan, Selim III, unlike his predecessors, had been educated outside the harem until age thirteen, and thus had some knowledge of the outside world and military affairs. During the disastrous wars fought against Austria and Russia between 1787 and 1792 he consulted with high-ranking Ottoman officials about the need for reform, surrounded himself with advisers who shared his commitment to change, and solicited reports from twenty-three experts, including two foreigners, about what steps should be taken. When the wars ended he announced a series of reforms, the most important of which was the creation of the New Order Army, a corps of full-time troops outfitted with up-to-date weapons and trained in European tactics. His reforms, though modest, provoked strong opposition, especially from the Janissary corps, which at the time of Suleiman the Great in the 1500s had been the core of the Ottoman army, but which by the eighteenth century was a bloated organization of part-time soldiers mainly committed to preserving their stipends and privileges. Selim persevered with his plans until 1806, when to placate his conservative opponents he revoked his reforms and named conservatives to key positions. His enemies were not satisfied, however. In 1807 they forced his deposition and a few months later arranged for his murder.

Although there is some debate about the authorship and exact dating of the following document, the weight of evidence suggests it appeared around 1804 and

was written by a key figure in Selim III's administration, Mustafa Reshid Celebi. A friend and confidant of Selim and an advocate of reform, Celebi served for a time as director of the New Order Army. In 1806, when conservatives became ascendant, he saved his life by escaping from Istanbul in disguise. He returned to government service under Selim's successor and died in 1819 in his nineties. It is thought Celebi wrote this treatise at the suggestion of the sultan, who hoped it would silence some of his critics. It offers insights into the views of both the supporters and opponents of Selim's reforms.

## QUESTIONS FOR ANALYSIS

1. According to this account, what developments inspired Selim to embark on his reforms?
2. What are the author's views of the military capabilities of the Janissaries?
3. In Celebi's view, in what ways are the troops of the New Order Army superior to the Janissaries?
4. According to the author, why did the Janissaries oppose Selim's reforms?
5. What religious objections were offered to Selim's new programs?
6. What new fiscal policies were part of Selim's reforms? Why were they necessary?

The Russian infidels have recently greatly improved the state of their dominions within the space of seventy or eighty years, and manifested their thirst of glory by their arrogant and insolent interference in the affairs of other States, and having annexed several foreign countries to their own dominions, especially the kingdom of Poland, . . . God forbid that so cunning an enemy should find us in an unguarded posture. . . .

That therefore, as it is an established maxim that in an emergency some remedy must be sought . . . there was no other method of removing the danger . . . , but by keeping a body of troops [the New Order Army] on foot ready for service . . . and provided with requisite supply of artillery, ammunition, and military stores; and such troops should not, like the rest of our forces, be composed of sellers of pastry, boatmen, fishermen, coffee-house keepers, vegetable sellers and others[1]

who are engaged in trades, but of well disciplined men, who would take care to have their cannon and muskets ready for service, and in an emergency. After these points had been taken into serious consideration, some men were dispatched to the corps of the Janissaries for the purpose of selecting from them some young and chosen soldiers, whom they were to discipline and train to the use of arms. Upon this, our heroes considering that if they were obliged to attend punctually to the exercise of cannon and small arms, they would be occupied with that instead of their private affairs, . . . began to ponder the matter, stroaking their beards and mustaches, and to vent their discontent by saying, "We are not made for this sort of work, and we will have nothing to do with it." Whatever pains were taken to enlighten their understandings, they obstinately persisted, addressing each other by these or similar terms,

---

*Source:* William Wilkinson, *An Account of the Principalities of Wallachia and Moldavia* (London: Longman, Hurst, Rees, Orme, and Brown, 1820), pp. 227, 232, 233–236, 253, 262, 263, 266–268, 273, 274, 287–291, 293, 294.

[1]Some of the trades commonly pursued by Janissaries.

"Ho . . . what say you to this business? the exercise of the New Order Army is now introduced; henceforth no pay is to be had without service, and what they call drill is a very troublesome service; it is true that drawing up in a line makes a better show; but if they send us to war, we can fire our muskets, and then charging sword in hand, we can put the Russians to flight and storm their camp. May Heaven preserve from decay our corps and our chiefs!" . . .

There are indeed certain considerations which may induce us to pardon those detractors of the New Order Army, who are . . . connected with the old corps; but do those persons who are by no means attached to them, and who know the difference between . . . good and evil, show any sense in daring to abuse so noble a science?

They suggest . . . that as the men who were inscribed in the corps of the New Order Army performed an exercise similar to that of the Christians, the Muslim faith is thereby injured. Although these blockheads had never before given themselves any concern about our faith or government, and indeed knew nothing of what belongs to Muslim purity; yet, they showed a mighty anxiety for religion, and by that means prevented many persons from inscribing their names, and encouraged many who were already engaged to desert. . . .

## The Old Corps and the New Corps Compared

The soldiers of our ancient corps, are not at all clothed alike; from this the following bad effect results: if . . . any of them should desert from the army, as there are no marks by which we can distinguish whether the deserters belong to the troops, or whether they are tradesmen, or servants, they have the opportunities of escaping without being known. Whereas the new troops have a particular uniform of their own, so that the stragglers would be soon discovered. . . .

Our old forces, when in presence of the enemy, do not remain drawn up in a line, but stand confusedly like a crowd in a place of entertainment. Some load their muskets, and fire once, some twice, or oftener, just as they think proper, while others being at their wits' end, and not knowing what they are about turn from side to side like fabulous storytellers.[2] If . . . the officers endeavor to make the troops fall back a little, some will obey them, others will not, everyone does just as he likes. . . .

But the new troops remain drawn up in line . . . , the rear ranks being exactly parallel with the front, and consisting of the same number of companies, neither more nor less, so that, when it is necessary, they turn with as much precision as a watch. . . .

The following is another of the advantages of the new troops. If it should happen that the enemies have obtained the victory by their superior numbers, and that the new forces were defeated, they will not lose courage and disperse themselves. . . . But if our old corps meet with a small check, they run, throw themselves into the water, and get drowned.

We trust, that by the favor of Heaven, that when . . . the New Order Army shall have become sufficiently numerous, it . . . will perpetuate the duration of the Sublime Government even to the end of the world. . . .

## Financing the New Order Army

When Suleiman the Great . . . thought proper to form the Janissaries, considered that these troops could not be assembled and kept together for the love of God only, but that it was also necessary to establish funds for the purpose of providing meat, drink, &c. for them, as well as to appoint them pay suitable to their expenses.

---

[2]Popular entertainers noted for their dramatic gestures and movements as they told their stories.

After consulting with the wise and experienced men of the time, he regulated the administration of the revenue in the following manner. A small part of the monies drawn from the provinces that had . . . become subject to his illustrious predecessors, was appropriated to the subsistence of military men who served on horseback and otherwise. . . .

Such a system worked well, but the price of commodities has greatly risen since the time his policy was implemented. . . .

The truth is, that the treasury does not possess a fixed revenue sufficient to defray contingent expenses, and as two hundred and forty-five years have elapsed since the publication of Suleiman's plan, the Emperor has labored to establish a revenue proportioned to the amount of expenditure of these times. But . . . the arrangement is this: that when the right to collect a tax, which

belongs by right to the treasury, falls vacant, it is no longer farmed out in consideration of a small sum, but is taken possession of by the Sublime Government, and the management of it is carried on for the benefit of the new treasury; the sum which continues to be paid to the crown is . . . appropriated to the pay, clothing, and allowances of the New Order troops, and to the special needs of the war department, such as the providing of cannon, ammunition, tents, camp equipage, military stores, and the expenses of the train of artillery. . . .

This business has been conducted in so masterly a manner that no just cause is left to any one to cry out against it; and the new revenue . . . causes no loss or damage to any man, but, on the contrary, tends manifestly to perpetuate the duration of the empire and of the people of Islam to understanding.

# European Designs on India

## 42 • JOSEPH FRANÇOIS DUPLEIX, MEMORANDUM TO THE DIRECTORS OF THE FRENCH EAST INDIA COMPANY; ROBERT CLIVE, LETTER TO WILLIAM PITT THE ELDER

As the Mughal Empire disintegrated in the 1700s, Indian–European relations underwent a dramatic change. Until then (with a few exceptions, such as the Portuguese colony at Goa), European merchants had stayed out of Indian politics and were content to trade from coastal cities, where with the approval of the emperor and local rulers they built wharves, warehouses, and offices. As Mughal authority deteriorated, however, agents of the British East India Company and the French East India Company saw an opportunity to improve their companies' financial situations by forging alliances with local princes who granted them trading privileges or the right to collect certain taxes in return for military support. By mid-century, they were laying plans for actual territorial conquest.

A Frenchman, Joseph François Dupleix (1697–1763), and an Englishman, Robert Clive (1725–1774), were the two principal advocates of greater European involvement in India. Dupleix, the son of a merchant, was sent by his father on a voyage to India in 1715 to divert him from a career in science to one in commerce. The father's strategy was successful. His son, after amassing a fortune in Indian trade, was appointed governor-general of the French East India Company's operations in India in 1742. He was convinced that the French could gain a decisive advantage over their British rivals by gaining political control of Indian territories and using local tax revenues to increase profits and pay the costs of fighting the British. In 1746 the French took the city of Madras (present-day Chennai), in 1749 defended the French-held city of Pondichéri (Pondicherry) from a British attack, and in the following four years launched a diplomatic and military campaign to extend their influence in southern India. Worried about expenses, the directors of the French East India Company opposed such ventures, and to overcome their doubts, Dupleix sent them the following memorandum in 1753. His efforts failed, however, and in 1754 he was recalled in disgrace when he defied the directors' orders to abandon his policies.

The dismissal of Dupleix provided an opening for his rival, Robert Clive. The son of a landowner and politician, Clive entered the service of the East India Company and sailed to India in 1744 at age eighteen. Having abandoned his clerk's job for a commission in the company army, in 1751 he distinguished himself in the defeat of the French and their Indian allies at the Battle of Arcot in 1751, and in 1757 led British forces to another important victory at the Battle of Plassey. In the wake of their victory, the British placed in power their own puppet, Mir Jafar as nawab of Bengal, who in return for British support in his quarrels with neighboring princes was happy to grant the British rights to collect taxes in a few districts around Calcutta and to mint their own coins.

Less than three years later, having realized that the costs of maintaining their increasingly unreliable ally Mir Jafar were higher than expected, Clive began to formulate a plan to bring Bengal under direct British control. He outlined his ambitions in a letter he wrote on January 7, 1759 to the secretary of state William Pitt the Elder, who since 1757 had directed the fight against France in the Seven Years' War (1756–1763).

## QUESTIONS FOR ANALYSIS

1. According to Dupleix, what are the anticipated benefits from the extension of French political authority in India?
2. To what extent is Dupleix's thinking influenced by the principles of mercantilism (see Colbert's memoranda, source 31)?
3. According to Clive, what benefits will accrue to Great Britain once it establishes its authority in India? How do his views resemble and differ from those of Dupleix?
4. Why are Dupleix and Clive convinced that the Europeans will encounter little difficulty in establishing their political authority in India?
5. What does Clive's letter reveal about the state of the Mughal Empire in the mid-1700s?
6. What does Clive's letter reveal about his attitudes toward the Indians and their rulers?

## Joseph Dupleix, Memorandum to the Directors of the French East India Company (1753)

All the Company's commerce in India is shared with the English, Dutch, Portuguese and Danes. This division of trade, or rather this rivalry, has served to raise considerably the price of merchandise here and has contributed quite a little toward cheapening the quality—two unfortunate circumstances which further reduce the price and profits in Europe. . . . Our Company can hope for no monopoly in the Indian trade. We shall always share whatever we deal in with other countries. We can, therefore, hope for no other profits than those being made at present. We should even anticipate that instead of increasing, they are likely to decline and that very soon. . . . The only possible way of making profits on inferior merchandise would be to have a large and regular revenue; then the losses could be offset by our income. Those of our rivals who did not have such a resource would be obliged to give up this branch of commerce, or else restrict themselves to their national market. . . .

I pass now to the second truth, which is that every commercial company should avoid the exportation of bullion [gold and silver] from the kingdom. It is a maxim long established that the more the specie [coined money] circulates in a state, the more flourishing is the state's condition, and the more the state can be helped and sustained by it. It is, then, good policy to seek every means of preventing its exportation. But it is very hard to trade in China and India without exporting specie. . . . Since it is obviously impossible to keep all our specie in France, we should neglect nothing to reduce to a minimum its exportation to India, whence it will never flow back to Europe. Our manufactures can diminish such exportation, but not to the extent we desire; we need something else, and this can only be found in a fixed, constant, and abundant local revenue. . . .

Let us suppose that the Company is obliged yearly to send twelve millions to India. Wool, cloth, and other exported manufactures amount to two millions, so there remains ten millions to be sent in specie, a large sum and one exported only too frequently. It could be reduced by at least half, and might even entirely cease, if the local revenue amounted to ten millions . . .

This work would have been already accomplished, if I had been better supported, not only here but in my native land, which has looked upon the benefits I have acquired for it with too great indifference. . . . I shall content myself by saying that, in spite of all the obstacles, I have succeeded in procuring for my nation a revenue of at least five millions. My intention was to raise it to ten millions . . . I can truly say that if what [military support] has arrived this year had been drawn from France's regular troops, all the fighting would now be over and the Company would be enjoying more than ten millions in revenue.

## Robert Clive, Letter to William Pitt the Elder

The great revolution that has been effected here by the success of the English arms, and the vast advantages gained to the Company . . . have, I observe, in some measure, engaged the public attention; but much more may yet in time be done, if the Company will exert themselves in the manner

*Source:* (1) Joseph Francois Dupleix, "Memorandum to the Directors of the French East India Company," from Virginia Thompson, *Dupleix and His Letters* (New York: Baillou, 1933), pp. 801–802. (2) Robert Clive in a letter to William Pitt, in John Malcolm, *The Life of Robert, Lord Clive* (London: John Murray, 1836), Vol. 2, pp. 119–125.

the importance of their present possessions and future prospects deserves. I have represented to them [the Company directors] in the strongest terms the expediency of sending out and keeping up constantly such a force as will enable them to embrace the first opportunity of further aggrandizing themselves; and I dare pronounce, from a thorough knowledge of this country's government, and of the genius of the people, acquired by two years' application and experience, that such an opportunity will soon offer. The reigning Subah,[1] whom the victory at Plassey invested with the sovereignty of these provinces, still, it is true, retains his attachment to us, and probably, while he has no other support, will continue to do so; but Muslims are so little influenced by gratitude, that should he ever think it his interest to break with us, the obligations he owes us would prove no restraint. . . . Moreover, he is advanced in years; and his son is so cruel, worthless a young fellow, and so apparently an enemy to the English, that it will be almost unsafe trusting him with the succession. So small a body as two thousand Europeans will secure us against any apprehensions from either the one or the other; and, in case of their daring to be troublesome, enable the Company to take the sovereignty upon themselves.

There will be the less difficulty in bringing about such an event, as the natives themselves have no attachment whatever to particular princes; and as, under the present Government, they have no security for their lives or properties, they would rejoice in so happy an exchange as that of a mild for a despotic Government: and there is little room to doubt our easily obtaining the Mughal's [Mughal emperor's] grant in confirmation thereof, provided we agreed to pay him the stipulated allotment out of the revenues, viz. fifty lacs[2] annually. . . .

But so large a sovereignty may possibly be an object too extensive for a mercantile Company; and it is to be feared they are not of themselves able, without the nation's assistance, to maintain so wide a dominion. I have therefore presumed, Sir, to represent this matter to you, and submit it to your consideration, whether the execution of a design, that may hereafter be still carried to greater lengths, be worthy of the Government's taking it into hand. . . . Now I leave you to judge, whether an income yearly of upwards of two millions sterling, with the possession of three provinces [Bengal, Bihar, and Orissa] abounding in the most valuable productions of nature and of art, be an object deserving the public attention; and whether it be worth the nation's while to take the proper measures to secure such an acquisition—an acquisition which, under the management of so able and disinterested a minister, would prove a source of immense wealth to the kingdom, and might in time be appropriated in part as a fund towards diminishing the heavy load of debt under which we at present labor. Add to these advantages the influence we shall thereby acquire over the several European nations engaged in the commerce here, which these could no longer carry on but through our indulgence, and under such limitations as we should think fit to prescribe. It is well worthy of consideration, that this project may be brought about without draining the mother country, as has been too much the case with our possessions in America. A small force from home will be sufficient, as we always make sure of any number we please of black [Indian] troops, who, being both much better paid and treated by us than by the country powers, will very readily enter into our service. . . .

---

[1]A synonym for nawab, governor of an Indian province. This specific reference is to Mir Jafar, the British puppet installed in power after the Battle of Plassey.

[2]Synonymous with lakh, meaning 100,000. Clive states that the British will pay five million rupees (in British currency approximately 260,000 pounds) per year to the emperor.

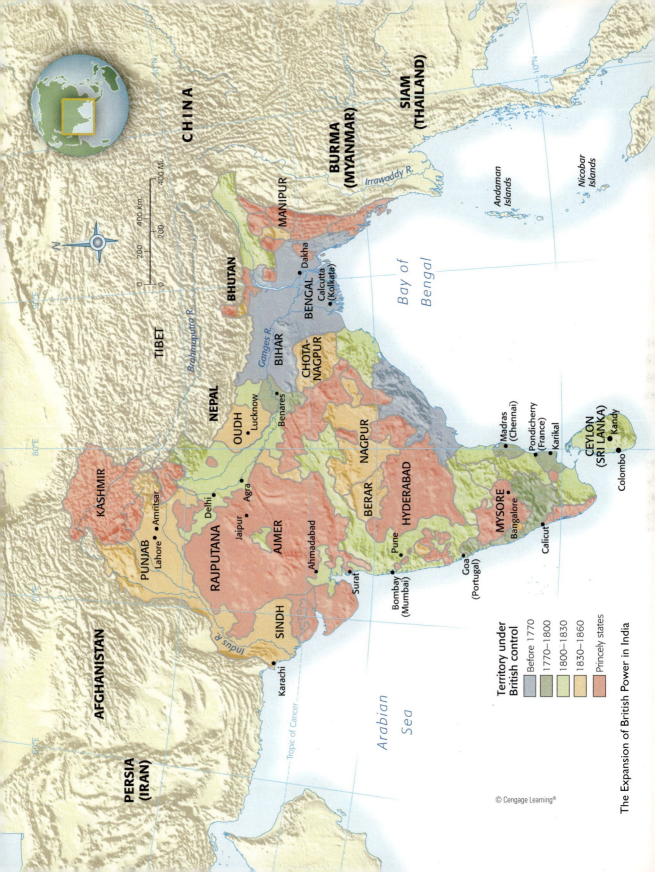

The Expansion of British Power in India

**CHINA**

**BURMA (MYANMAR)**

**SIAM (THAILAND)**

Irrawaddy R.

MANIPUR

**BHUTAN**

Andaman Islands

Nicobar Islands

Dakha

BENGAL

Calcutta (Kolkata)

*Bay of Bengal*

**TIBET**

Brahmaputra R.

Ganges R.

BIHAR

CHOTA-NAGPUR

**NEPAL**

OUDH

Lucknow

Benares

NAGPUR

Madras (Chennai)

Pondicherry (France)

Karikal

**CEYLON (SRI LANKA)**

Kandy

KASHMIR

Delhi

Agra

RAJPUTANA

Jaipur

AJMER

BERAR

HYDERABAD

MYSORE

Bangalore

Calicut

Colombo

PUNJAB

Lahore

Amritsar

Ahmadabad

Surat

Pune

Goa (Portugal)

SINDH

Indus R.

Karachi

Bombay (Mumbai)

*Arabian Sea*

Tropic of Cancer

**AFGHANISTAN**

**PERSIA (IRAN)**

N

0   200   400 Km.

0   200   400 Mi.

Territory under British control

Before 1770

1770–1800

1800–1830

1830–1860

Princely states

© Cengage Learning®

# The Continuing Vitality of Islam

Despite the demoralizing failures of the major Muslim empires, the eighteenth century was in many ways a period of reform and revitalization for Islam. The religion continued to make converts in Southeast Asia and Africa and spread into areas such as eastern Bengal through migration. In addition, movements of reform and renewal took root in many parts of the Islamic world, including the religion's historic center in Arabia and its outermost fringes in Southeast Asia and West Africa.

Although eighteenth-century Muslim reform movements varied greatly, most were led by scholars or devotees of Sufism, the mystical movement that emphasizes closeness to God through devotion. Many reformers traveled widely and drew inspiration from experiences in religious centers such as Baghdad, Cairo, and Mecca. Some called for a purification of Muslim practices and a return to Islam's fundamentals as revealed in the Quran and the teachings and deeds of Muhammad. Many were convinced that Islam had been tainted by accommodating itself to local religious practices and beliefs. Some urged Muslims to seek social justice, while others preached a message of puritanical rigor and personal regeneration. A few called on their followers to take up the sword against unbelievers and heretics.

## A Call to Recapture Islam's Purity

### 43 • ABDULLAH WAHHAB, THE HISTORY AND DOCTRINES OF THE WAHHABIS

Wahhabism, the dominant form of Islam in Saudi Arabia and Qatar and a growing influence in many parts of the Islamic world, traces its origins to Muhammad Ibn Abd al-Wahhab (1703–1792), whose teachings gave rise to a movement whose followers called themselves *Muwahhidun,* or "those who advocate oneness," because they rejected any belief or practice that even slightly detracted from the exclusive worship of one all-powerful god, Allah. Wahhab was a native of Nejd, a region in the east-central part of the Arabian Peninsula, who as a student and teacher visited Mecca, Medina, Basra, Damascus, and Baghdad. After he returned to Arabia, he began to denounce the Arabs' perceived religious failings. These included magical rituals, faith in holy men, worship of saints and their tombs, and veneration of supposedly sacred wells and trees. He also rejected Sufi mysticism, Shiism, and rationalist attempts to understand God's nature and purposes.

A key development in the history of the Wahhabi movement was the alliance forged in 1744 between Wahhab, the movement's founder, and Muhammad Ibn Saud, the leader of the Saudi clan. Saud, who sought to extend his authority in Arabia, provided protection for Wahhab, who in turn supported his claims to political authority. Although he therefore approved the Saudi's military campaigns, he never was willing to endorse them as jihads, or holy wars.

This changed after his death in 1792. In 1802, his followers captured Karbala in present-day Iraq and destroyed the tomb of the revered Shia Imam Husayn. One year later, they captured the holy city of Mecca, the immediate aftermath of which is described in the following selection. It is the work of the founder's grandson, Abdullah Wahhab, who participated in the conquest of Mecca and was executed when an army sent by the Ottoman sultan took the city in 1813. Abdullah Wahhab wrote this piece to answer critics and clarify the beliefs of the Muwahhidun.

## QUESTIONS FOR ANALYSIS

1. In the Wahhabi view, what are the most serious threats to the purity of Islam?
2. How did the Wahhabis attempt to change Mecca after they captured it? What do their acts reveal about their beliefs and purposes?
3. The Wahhabis have been characterized as puritanical and intolerant. Is such a view justified on the basis of this document?
4. The Wahhabis strongly opposed Shiism and the use of logic as a means of discovering religious truth. Why? (See the introduction to source 14 for a discussion of Shiism.)
5. How do the Wahhabis perceive their role in the history of Islam?

---

. . . Now I was engaged in the holy war, carried on by those who truly believe in the Unity of God, when God graciously permitted us to enter Mecca, the holy, the exalted, at midday, on the 6th day of the week on the 8th of the month Muharram, 1218, Hijri [April 1803]. Before this, Saud,[1] our leader in the holy war, had summoned the nobles, the divines, and the common people of Mecca; for indeed the leaders of the pilgrims and the rulers of Mecca had resolved on battle, and had risen up against us in the holy place, to exclude us from the house of God. But when the army of the true believers advanced, the Lord filled their hearts with terror, and they fled. . . . Then our commander gave protection to everyone within the holy place, while we entered with safety, crying "Labbayka,"[2]

without fear of any created being, and only of the Lord God. Now, though we were more numerous, better armed and disciplined than the people of Mecca, yet we did not cut down their trees, neither did we hunt[3] nor shed any blood. . . .

When our pilgrimage was over, we gathered the people together . . . , and our leader explained to the divines what we required of the people, . . . namely, a pure belief in the Unity of God Almighty. He pointed out to them that there was no dispute between us and them except on two points, and that one of these was a sincere belief in the unity of God, and a knowledge of the different kinds of prayer, of which *dua*[4] was one. He added that to show the significance of *shirk*,[5] the prophet [Muhammud] had put people to death on account

---

*Source:* J. O'Kinealy, "Translation of an Arabic Pamphlet on the History and Doctrines of the Wahhabis, Written by 'Abdullah, Grandson of 'Abdul Wahhab, the Founder of the Wahhabis," *Journal of the Asiatic Society of Bengal,* Vol. 43 (1874), pp. 68–82.
[1] Saud ibn Abdul Aziz ibn Muhammad al Saud, head of the house of Saud from 1803 to 1814.
[2] The loud cry uttered as Muslims begin their pilgrimage activities in Mecca.

[3] Not cutting down a defeated enemy's trees or hunting the enemy's animals was considered an act of mercy.
[4] A personal prayer uttered by a Muslim.
[5] *Shirk* is the opposite of surrender to God and the acceptance and recognition of His reality. It may mean atheism, paganism, or polytheism. According to Muslim doctrine, it is the root of all sin.

of it; that he had continued to call upon them to believe in the Unity of God for some time after he became inspired, and that he had abandoned shirk before the Lord had declared to him the remaining four pillars[6] of Islam. . . .

. . . They then acknowledged our belief, and there was not one among them who doubted or hesitated to believe that that for which we condemned men to death, was the truth pure and unsullied. And they swore a binding oath, although we had not asked them, that their hearts had been opened and their doubts removed, and that they were convinced whoever said, "Oh prophet of God!" or "Oh Ibn 'Abbas!" or "Oh 'Abdul Qadir!"[7] or called on any other created being, thus entreating him to turn away evil or grant what is good, such as recovery from sickness, or victory over enemies, or protection from temptation, etc. is guilty of the most heinous form of shirk, his blood shall be shed and property confiscated. Nor is it any excuse that he believes the effective first cause in the movements of the universe is God, and only supplicates those mortals to intercede for him or bring him nearer the presence of God. . . . Again, the tombs which had been erected over the remains of the pious, had become in these times as it were idols where the people went to pray for what they required; they humbled themselves before them, and called upon those lying in them, in their distress, just as did those who were in darkness before the coming of Muhammad.

When this was over, we razed all the large tombs in the city which the people generally worshipped

and believed in, and by which they hoped to obtain benefits or ward off evil, so that there did not remain an idol to be adored in that pure city. Then the taxes and customs we abolished, all the different kinds of instruments for using tobacco we destroyed, and tobacco itself we proclaimed forbidden.[8] Next we burned the dwellings of those selling *hashish,* and living in open wickedness, and issued a proclamation directing the people to constantly exercise themselves in prayer. They were not to pray in separate groups according to the different Imams;[9] but all were directed to arrange themselves at each time of prayer behind any Imam who is a follower of any of the four Imams. For in this way the Lord would be worshiped by one voice, the faithful of all sects would become friendly disposed towards each other, and all dissensions would cease. . . .

We believe that good and evil proceed from God, the exalted; that nothing happens in His kingdom, but what He commands. . . . We believe that the faithful will see Him in the end, but we do not know under what form, as it was beyond our comprehension. . . . [We] do not reject anyone who follows any of the four Imams, as do the Shias. Nor do we admit them in any way to act openly according to their vicious creeds; on the contrary, we compelled them to follow one of the four Imams. We do not claim to exercise our reason in all matters of religion, and of our faith, save that we follow our judgment where a point is clearly demonstrated to us in either the Quran or the Sunnah.[10] . . . We do not command the destruction of any writings except such as tend to cast people into infidelity

---

[6]The first pillar of Islam is the creed, which affirms "There is no god but God, and Muhammad is the messenger of God." The other four pillars are daily prayer, almsgiving, fasting during the month of Ramadan, and pilgrimage, at least once in every Muslim's life if possible, to Mecca, the city of Muhammad's birth and revelation.

[7]Calling out in prayer the name of Muhammad or these early caliphs in the Abbasid line detracted from the majesty of God.

[8]The Wahhabis saw no Quranic basis for the use of tobacco; its use is still rare in present-day Saudi Arabia.

[9]The author uses the term *imam* to refer to the founders of the four major schools of Sunni Muslim jurisprudence: Abu Hanifa (d. 767), founder of the Hanafite school; Malik ibn Anas (d. 795), founder of the Malikite school; al-Shafi (d. 820), founder of the Shafiite school; and Ahmad ibn Hanbal (d. 855), founder of the Hanbali school. The Wahhabis were Hanbalis but did not reject the authority of the other schools.

[10]The body of traditional social and legal thought and practice that represent the proper observance of Islam.

to injure their faith, such as those on Logic, which have been prohibited by all Divines. But we are not very exacting with regard to books or documents of this nature; if they appear to assist our opponents, we destroy them. . . . We do not consider it proper to make Arabs prisoners of war, nor have we done so, neither do we fight with other nations. Finally, we do not consider it lawful to kill women or children. . . .

We do not deny miraculous powers to the saints. . . . They are under the guidance of the Lord, so long as they continue to follow the way pointed out in the laws and obey the prescribed rules. But whether alive or dead, they must not be made the object of any form of worship. . . .

We prohibit those forms of Bidah[11] that affect religion or pious works. Thus drinking coffee, reciting poetry, praising kings, do not affect religion or pious works and are not prohibited. . . . All games are lawful. Our prophet allowed play in his mosque. So it is lawful to chide and punish persons in various ways; to train them in the use of different weapons; or to use anything which tends to encourage warriors in battle such as a war-drum. But it must not be accompanied with musical instruments. These are forbidden. . . .

Whoever is desirous of knowing our belief, let him come to us at al Diriyya,[12] and he will see what will gladden his heart. . . . He will see God praised in a pleasing manner; the assistance He gives in establishing the true faith; the kindness, which He exerts among the weak and feeble, between inhabitants and travelers. . . . He is our Agent, our Master, our Deliverer.

---

[11]Erroneous or improper customs that grew after the third generation of Muslims died out.

[12]The Wahhabi capital.

## Jihad in the Western Sudan

### 44 • USMAN DAN FODIO, SELECTIONS FROM HIS WRITINGS

Although merchants and teachers from North Africa and Arabia had introduced Islam to Africa's western and central Sudan (the region south of the Saharan and Libyan deserts) as early as the tenth century, in 1800 the region's conversion to Islam was still incomplete. Islam was largely a religion of the cities, where resident Muslim traders had established Islamic communities, built mosques, introduced Arabic, and made converts. Many converts, however, continued non-Muslim religious rites and festivals, and in rural areas, peasants and herders remained animists. Rulers became Muslims in name, but often less for religious reasons than to ingratiate themselves with the merchant community and attract Islamic scholars to their service as advisors, interpreters, and scribes. Most rulers tolerated their subjects' pagan practices, and many participated in such practices themselves.

This changed as a result of a series of holy wars that swept across the Sudan in the eighteenth and nineteenth centuries. Dedicated Muslims took up arms against nonbelievers and, after seizing power, imposed a strict form of Islam on their new subjects. In a matter of decades, these movements redrew the region's political and religious map.

The first major jihad of the era, known as the Sokoto Jihad, took place in Hausaland in the early nineteenth century under the leadership of Usman dan Fodio

(1754–1817). Hausaland, an area that straddles the Niger River and today makes up the northern part of Nigeria, had been settled by Hausa speakers in the tenth century but also had substantial numbers of Fulani-pastoralists who had migrated into the area beginning in the 1500s. In 1800 it consisted of a dozen principalities.

Usman dan Fodio, a member of a Fulani clan with a tradition of Islamic scholarship and teaching, was a member of the *Qadiriyya,* a Sufi brotherhood dating from the twelfth century. Beginning in the 1770s, he began to travel and preach in Hausaland, denouncing corrupt Islamic practices and the rulers who tolerated them. His calls for religious and political renewal won followers among the Fulani, who considered themselves oppressed by their rulers, and among some Hausa farmers, who were feeling the effects of drought and land shortages. In 1804, when the sultan of Gobir denounced Usman and prepared to attack his followers, Usman called on his supporters to take up arms against Hausaland's rulers. By the late 1810s, Usman controlled Hausaland and established the Kingdom of Sokoto. After his retirement from public life, Usman's son and brother extended the campaign to the south and east of the kingdom. The era of Sudanese jihads had begun in earnest.

Usman wrote nearly one hundred treatises on politics, religion, marriage customs, and education. Brief excerpts from four of them follow. Together they provide a sampling of his thoughts on religion, government, and society.

## QUESTIONS FOR ANALYSIS

1. What policies and values of the Hausa sultans does Usman criticize? Why?
2. How do the religious failings of the Hausa princes prevent them from being just and equitable rulers?
3. What groups in Hausa society would have been most likely to respond positively to Usman's criticisms of the sultans?
4. What is Usman's message concerning the treatment of Muslim women? Is it a message of equality with men?

## The Faults of the Hausa Rulers[1]

And one of the ways of their government is the building of their sovereignty upon three things: the people's persons, their honor, and their possessions; and whomsoever they wish to kill or exile or violate his honor or devour his wealth they do so in pursuit of their lusts, without any right in the *Sharia.*[2] . . . One of the ways of their government is their intentionally eating whatever food they wish, . . . and wearing whatever

*Source:* Usman dan Fodio, "The Book of Differences," from M. Hiskett, "Kitab al-farq: A Work on the Habe Kingdoms Attributed to Uth-mann dan Fodio," in *Bulletin of the School of Oriental and African Studies,* Vol. 23 (1960); "Concerning the Government of Our Country," from Tanbih al-ikhwan, translation in Thomas Hodgkin, *Nigerian Perspectives* (Oxford: Oxford University Press, 1975), pp. 244, 245; "Light of Intellectuals," from Nur al-albab, in Hodgkin, pp. 254–255; "Dispatch to the Folk of the Sudan," from A. D. H. Bivar, "The Whatiqat ah al-Sudan: A Manifesto of the Fulani Jihad," in *The Journal of African History,* Vol. 2 (1961).
[1]From "The Book of Differences between the Government of Muslims and Unbelievers," written around 1806.
[2]*Sharia* is the body of Islamic law.

clothes they wish, . . . and drinking what beverages they wish, and riding whatever riding beasts they wish, . . . and taking what women they wish without marriage contract, and living in decorated palaces, and spreading soft carpets as they wish, whether religiously permitted or forbidden.

. . . One of the ways of their government is to place many women in their houses, until the number of women of some of them amounts to one thousand or more. . . . One of the ways of their government is to delay in the paying of a debt, and this is injustice. One of the ways of their government is what the superintendent of the market [a royal official] takes from all the parties to a sale, and the meat which he takes on each market day from the butchers, . . . and one of the ways of their government is the cotton and other things which they take in the course of the markets. . . . One of the ways of their government is the taking of people's beasts of burden without their permission to carry the sultan's food to him.

. . . One of the ways of their government which is also well known is that whoever dies in their country, they take his property, and they call it "inheritance," and they know that it is without doubt injustice.[3] One of the ways of their government is to impose a tax on merchants, and other travelers. One of the ways of their government, which is also well known, is that one may not pass by their farms, nor cross them without suffering bad treatment from their slaves. One of the ways of their government, which is also well known, is that if the people's animals go among their animals, they do not come out again unless they give a proportion of them, and if the sultan's animals stray, and are found spoiling the cultivated land and other things, they are not driven off. . . .

One of the ways of their government, which is also well known, is that if you have an adversary in law and he precedes you to them [the government], and gives them some money, then your word will not be accepted by them, even though they know for a certainty of your truthfulness, unless you give them more than your adversary gave. One of the ways of their government is to shut the door in the face of the needy. . . . Therefore do not follow their way in their government, and do not imitate them. . . .

## Royal Religion[4]

It is well known that in our time Islam . . . is widespread among people other than the sultans. As for the sultans, they are undoubtedly unbelievers, even though they may profess the religion of Islam, because they practice polytheistic rituals and turn people away from the path of God and raise the flag of a worldly kingdom above the banner of Islam. . . .

The government of a country is the government of its king. If the king is a Muslim, his land is Muslim; if he is an Unbeliever, his land is a land of Unbelievers. . . . There is no dispute that the sultans of these countries venerate certain places, certain trees, and certain rocks and offer sacrifice to them. This constitutes unbelief according to the consensus of opinion [of the Muslim community]. I say this on the basis of the common practice known about them, but I do not deny the existence of some Muslims here and there among them. Those however are rare and there is no place for what is rare in legal decisions.

## The Treatment of Women and Slaves[5]

Most of our educated men leave their wives, their daughters, and the slaves morally abandoned, like beasts, without teaching them what God prescribes should be taught them, and without

---

[3]A grievance of foreign Muslim merchants who might die while residing in a Hausa city.
[4]From "Concerning the Government of Our Country . . . ," written around 1811.

[5]From "Light of the Intellects."

instructing them in the articles of the Law which concern them. Thus, they leave them ignorant of the rules regarding ablutions [ritual cleansing], prayer, fasting, business dealings, and other duties which they have to fulfil, and which God commands that they should be taught.

Men treat these beings like household implements which become broken after long use and which are then thrown out on the dung-heap. This is an abominable crime! Alas! How can they thus shut up their wives, their daughters, and their slaves in the darkness of ignorance? . . . Muslim women—Do not listen to the speech of those who are misguided and who sow the seed of error in the heart of another; they deceive you when they stress obedience to your husbands without telling you of obedience to God and to his Messenger [Muhammad], and when they say that the woman finds her happiness in obedience to her husband.

They seek only their own satisfaction, and that is why they impose upon you tasks which the Law of God and that of his Prophet have never especially assigned to you. Such are—the preparation of food-stuffs, the washing of clothes, and other duties which they like to impose upon you, while they neglect to teach you what God and the Prophet have prescribed for you.

---

[6]From "Dispatch to the Folk of the Sudan and to Whom so Allah Wills Among the Brethren," probably written in 1804 or 1805.

Yes, the woman owes submission to her husband, publicly as well as in intimacy, even if he is one of the humble people of the world, and to disobey him is a crime, at least so long as he does not command what God condemns; in that case she must refuse, since it is wrong of a human creature to disobey the Creator.

## The Call to Holy War[6]

That to make war upon the heathen king who does not say "There is no God but Allah" on account of the custom of his town, and who makes no profession of Islam, is obligatory . . . and that to take the government from him is obligatory. And that to make war upon the king who has abandoned Islam for the religion of heathendom is obligatory . . . and that to take the government from him is obligatory. And that to make war against the king who has not abandoned Islam as far as the profession of it is concerned, but who mingles the observances of Islam with the observances of heathendom, like the kings of Hausaland for the most part—is also obligatory, that to take the government from him is obligatory.

And to enslave the freeborn among the Muslims is unlawful by assent, whether they reside in the territory of Islam, or in enemy territory. . . .

# Chapter 7

# Change and Continuity in East Asia

FOR THE OTTOMAN, SAFAVID, AND MUGHAL empires, the seventeenth and eighteenth centuries were times of military decline and retrenchment after an era of strength and expansion. In East Asia, this pattern was reversed. For Japan, its "time of troubles" occurred in the sixteenth century, an era of civil war and social discord, made worse by the arrival of Europeans, who introduced firearms and converted large numbers of Japanese to Christianity. For China, problems mounted in the late sixteenth and early seventeenth centuries, when fiscal and diplomatic challenges increased, factionalism paralyzed the central administration, and peasant violence escalated in response to rising taxes, higher rents, and natural catastrophes. This paved the way for the invasion of China by the Manchus, who poured into China from their homeland to the northeast and established a new dynasty, the Qing, in 1644.

During the seventeenth century, however, conflicts and tensions abated in both China and Japan. In Japan, recovery began in 1603 when the Tokugawa clan took power and ended the decades-long civil war, while in China, it began soon after the Manchus established their authority. Although the two countries did not lack problems in the seventeenth and eighteenth centuries, compared to what had come before and what would follow, these were years of orderly government and social harmony.

These also were years in which European pressures on the region eased. China's rulers continued to limit European merchants' activities to Macao and Guangzhou, began to curtail European missionary activity in the early 1700s, and checked Russian expansion in the Amur Valley. In Japan, the Tokugawa shoguns soon after taking power expelled all foreigners, outlawed Christianity, and limited trade with Europeans to one Dutch ship a year. In the East Indies, the Dutch, after forcing out the Portuguese and establishing a political base in Java, were content after the mid-1600s to protect rather than extend their gains.

By the late 1700s, however, signs of change were evident. In Japan, economic expansion, urbanization, and years of political stability created new tensions by enriching

205

merchants and undermining the function and financial base of the military aristocracy. In China, population growth caused hardship among peasants by driving up the cost of land; moreover, around 1800, budgetary shortfalls, higher taxes, abuses of the civil service examination system, court favoritism, and neglect of roads, bridges, and dikes were early signs of dynastic decline.

In addition, European pressures in the region were building. In the late 1700s, the English began to settle Australia and New Zealand. French missionaries increased their activities in Vietnam. In 1800, the Dutch government stripped the bankrupt Dutch East India Company of its administrative responsibilities in the East Indies and tightened its control of the colony's economy. From their base in India, British merchants opened a new chapter in the history of trade with China after finding a product that millions of Chinese deeply craved. The product—grown and processed in India, packed into 133-pound chests, shipped to Guangzhou, and purchased for silver by Chinese traders who sold it to millions of addicts—was opium. A new era of upheaval was about to begin.

# China's Revival Under the Qing

On taking power, the Manchus made it clear that they were the rulers and the Chinese their subjects. They imposed the Manchu banner system on the organization of the Chinese army. They ordered courtiers and officials to abandon the loose-fitting robes of the Ming for the high-collared tight jackets worn by the Manchus. They also required males to shave their foreheads and braid their hair in back in a style favored by the Manchus. In other ways, however, the Manchus adapted to Chinese culture. They embraced the principle of centralized monarchy, learned Chinese, and supported Confucian scholarship. They reinstated the civil service examinations, which had been neglected during the last decades of Ming rule. Although Manchus were disproportionately represented in the bureaucracy, Chinese were allocated a major share of all important offices, and gradually Chinese scholar-officials began to support and serve the new dynasty.

From 1661 through 1799, China had but three emperors: Kangxi (r. 1661–1722), Yongzhen (r. 1722–1736), and Qianlong (r. 1736–1796), who abdicated in 1796 to avoid exceeding the long reign of his grandfather Kangxi but actually ruled until 1799. Their reigns were among the most impressive in all of Chinese history. China reached its greatest size as a result of military campaigns in central Asia. Agriculture flourished, trade expanded, and China's population grew. China's cultural vitality was no less remarkable. Painting and scholarship flourished, and the era's literary output included what many consider China's greatest novel, Cao Xueqin's *The Dream of the Red Chamber*.

Toward the end of Qianlong's reign, however, problems emerged. Rural poverty worsened, military effectiveness declined, and factionalism and favoritism at the imperial court resurfaced. Nonetheless, it was neither far-fetched nor fanciful when France's leading eighteenth-century writer, Voltaire, described China as a model of moral and ethical government and praised Qianlong as the ideal philosopher-king.

# Emperor Kangxi Views His World

## 45 • KANGXI, EDICTS AND OTHER WRITINGS

In 1661, a seven-year-old boy became the second Qing emperor. He took as his reign name Kangxi, and during his long reign, which lasted until 1722, he crushed the last vestiges of Ming resistance, fortified China's borders, revitalized the civil service examination system, won the support of Chinese scholar-officials, eased tensions between ethnic Chinese and their Manchu conquerors, promoted economic growth, and brought vigor and direction to the government. A generous supporter of writers, artists, poets, scholars, and craftsmen, Kangxi himself was a scholar and writer of distinction. He studied Confucianism, learned Latin, and was intrigued by Western music, mathematics, and science. He also left behind a rich store of writings, including official pronouncements, poems, essays, aphorisms, and letters.

The following excerpts fall into the period between 1693 (the year of Kangxi's edict on Russian trade) and 1718 (the year of his edict on trade with the "southern barbarians," or Europeans). They all shed light on Kangxi's personal ruling style and his perceptions of his role as emperor.

### QUESTIONS FOR ANALYSIS

1. According to Kangxi, what were the flaws of the Ming government in the years before its collapse? What steps did he take to avoid making the same mistakes?
2. What does the selection reveal about the challenge of establishing Manchu rule in China? How does the emperor approach this problem?
3. What does the excerpt reveal about the state of China's rural economy?
4. What evidence does the selection provide about Kangxi's views of foreigners?
5. What evidence does it provide about his attitudes and policies concerning foreign trade?

## Thoughts on Government

Good government cannot come about if eunuchs are employed as responsible officials. The validity of this statement has been proved in every dynasty of China's past. The harm is even greater if the eunuchs are allowed not only to enjoy power but also to build a larger following who do the eunuchs' bidding. . . . It is for this reason that T'ai-tsu [Taizu] and T'ai-tsung [Taizong],[1] knowing about the eunuchs' abuse of power . . . did not introduce in the imperial court the institution of eunuchs. It was also for this reason that my immediate predecessor [Sunzhi, r. 1638–1661] confined the duties of the eunuchs to those of a servile nature and that when they were entrusted with positions of authority he did not forget that they were evil and conspiratorial. In one of his last decrees he reminded us that the downfall of the Ming dynasty was caused primarily by the employment of eunuchs in positions of power. . . . I shall be most diligent insofar as the observation of eunuchs' behavior is concerned. . . .

• • •

Source: Dun J. Li, *The Civilization of China from the Formative Period to the Coming of the West* (New York: Scribner's Sons, 1975), pp. 311, 313, 314.

[1]Taizu (r. 927–976) was founder of the Song dynasty; he was succeeded by his younger brother Taizong (r. 976–997). Both were considered to be outstanding emperors.

[One] cannot but be impressed with the openness with which the king and his ministers discussed national issues during the reigns of Yao and Shun.[2] . . . The king and his ministers acted toward each other like members of one family: the king consequently was able to suppress evil and elevate goodness. . . . The situation was totally different toward the end of the Ming dynasty, when a wide gap existed between the king and his ministers, and the king had no way of knowing how much the people really suffered. Since the establishment of this dynasty all the officials of the empire have been cooperating fully in reporting the true condition of the people. They do whatever they can to improve their living conditions, sometimes under very difficult circumstances.

## The Rural Economy

I was surprised to learn that peasants who volunteer to cultivate abandoned fields can enjoy tax exemption for only a six-year period. . . . The peasants cultivating abandoned fields are among the poorest in the nation. . . . Having to pay taxes that increase their burden, they may decide to abandon the fields and thus become unemployed. About this I am deeply concerned. Let it be known that peasants who volunteer to cultivate abandoned fields will not be taxed for a ten-year period.

Last year the harvests . . . were less than abundant, and the authorities . . . reported the condition of famine and petitioned the imperial government for tax exemptions and emergency relief. Had these authorities lived up to their responsibility of promoting saving during the good years, the deplorable situation . . . would have been avoided. Lest the people become extravagant again, I am instructing all officials . . . to urge people to be thrifty so that enough grain can be stored away for relief when harvests may not be so abundant.

Having traveled extensively I think I know the people's economic conditions. The reason that people are less affluent . . . stems from the simple fact that as peace has prevailed for a long time, population increases enormously, while total cultivated acreage remains substantially the same. It is no wonder that people have become less well-to-do.

[2]Mythological emperors from China's past noted for their wisdom and benevolence.

## Manchu and Chinese Officials

I've tried to be impartial between Manchus and Chinese, and not separate one from the other in judgments. . . . There are certainly differences in their characters: the Manchus are direct and open, whereas the Chinese think it better not to let any anger or joy show on their faces. And the Manchus are often tougher and braver than the Chinese Bannermen,[1] and treat both slaves and horses better. But the Manchus' scholarship is often in no way inferior to that of the Chinese and, even if they commit some abuses—riding their horses into the civil officials' yamens [offices and residences] or disrupting proceedings in the courts—there is no need for a senior official like Shao-kan [Shaogan] to plead that people are bound to be fearful of him since he is a Manchu. And though Manchu vice-president Salai had to be demoted for drinking too heavily and playing the dice—and drinking and gambling were prevalent in the army, and even among the Manchu nobles—Han T'an [Handan] too drank heavily as Chancellor

*Source:* Jonathan D. Spence, *Emperor of China Self-Portrait of Kang-Hsi* (New York: Random House, 1974), pp. 43, 44.
[2]Mythological emperors from China's past noted for their wisdom and benevolence.

[1]Soldiers in the Qing army, which by now was organized into twenty-four banners, or units.

of the Hanlin Academy and continued to do so as president of the Board of Rites,[2] while many

of the Hanlin scholars drank also or wasted their time playing chess.

[2]The Hanlin Academy was an elite group of Confucian scholars who performed literary, archival, and secretarial work for the court. The equally prestigious Board of Rites administered court ceremonies and the imperial civil service examinations.

## Regulating Foreign Trade

In 1693 the Emperor approved the following:

"When the Russian merchants come to Peking [Beijing] for trade, they should number no more than two hundred and should come only once every three years. They should furnish their own horses and camels. Their commodities should not be taxed, but they are not allowed to trade in contraband [prohibited] goods. After they arrive in Peking they are to be located in the Russian House.[1] They are not to receive government provisions. They may remain only eighty days." . . .

In 1716 the Emperor decreed:

"Chang Po-hsing [Zhang Boxing, an advisor of the emperor] has memorialized that the rice of Kiangnan [Jiangnan] and Chekiang [Zhejiang][2] was being mostly exported. This statement is not necessarily true, but We cannot neglect to prevent any such procedure before it takes place. When our seafarers go abroad to trade . . . they should bring only sufficient rice for their journey and not more than that amount." . . .

"Beyond the ocean lie Luzon, Batavia,[3] and other places which serve as asylum for Chinese outlaws. From the time of the Ming dynasty these places have been the headquarters of the Chinese pirates. However, when our government sea-patrols discover that pirate ships outnumber them five to one,

they cannot attack. Moreover, the sailors will not be eager to use their oars, and so our officers may become helpless. The government ships can only lag behind the pirates. How can this method achieve their annihilation? Moreover, our commercial ships are allowed to trade in the Eastern ocean, but they are not allowed in the Southern ocean.[4] We allow only the ships of the red-haired barbarians [Europeans] to come from the Southern oceans. . . ."

"The people of Taiwan and the Chinese in Luzon often exchange visits; We must prevent this. Moreover, to gather more information on this matter all the natives of the maritime provinces . . . residing in the capital city [Beijing] should be questioned by you people [the emperor's advisors]. Then We wish to discuss this matter in person. After one hundred years we are afraid that the Middle Kingdom [China] will suffer injury from the overseas countries, for example, from the European countries. This is only a prediction." . . .

In 1718 the emperor approved the following:

". . . the barbarian merchants profit through trading with China and have long obeyed us. Scores of years they have lived peacefully, therefore we should allow them to trade as usual. . . . [That] we search their ships for firearms, remove them before their ships enter our harbor, that we establish another maritime customs officer to control

*Source:* Fu, Lo-shu, *A Documentary Chronicle of Sino-Western Relations*, Vol. I (Tucson: University of Arizona Press, 1966), pp. 106, 107, 122, 123, 126, 127.
[1]A structure where visiting Russian officials and merchants were expected to stay.
[2]Two regions of eastern China below the lower reaches of the Yangzi River, including the southern part of the Yangzi Delta.

[3]Luzon is the largest island in the Philippines and the site of Manila; Batavia, or Jakarta, is a city on the island of Java and was the center of Dutch trade in the East Indies.
[4]Both are vaguely used terms. Trade in the "Eastern ocean" generally refers to trade with Japan; trade in the "Southern ocean" refers to trade with the Philippines, the East Indies, and mainland Southeast Asia.

them, and that foreign merchants should come one at a time throughout the year—this need not be discussed further. However . . . whenever the barbarian ships arrive on our coast we should order the civil and military magistrates to guard our harbor day and night so that they will continue to be subject to our orders and dare not act in a disorderly manner."

# Painting and Imperial Power Under Qianlong

## 46 • THE QIANLONG EMPEROR IN CEREMONIAL ARMOR ON HORSEBACK; QIANLONG IN HIS STUDY; QIANLONG AS A CHINESE SCHOLAR AND ART LOVER PLAYING THE ZITHER IN FRONT OF A PAINTING OF HIS OWN; THE QIANLONG EMPEROR TAKES A STAG; TEN THOUSAND ENVOYS COME TO PAY TRIBUTE

Although many Chinese emperors were patrons and connoisseurs of painting, the fourth Qing emperor, Qianlong (r. 1736–1796), stands out for his devotion to this particular form of artistic expression. An accomplished calligrapher and a respectable painter himself, he expanded the imperial painting studios and purchased many paintings from private collectors to enrich his collection. The one hundred sixty artists employed at the imperial studios, including a number of European painters, produced thousands of works that were displayed within the palace grounds in Beijing and at other sites where the emperor resided. Most of these paintings featured Qianlong, and almost all of them sought to glorify the emperor.

Unlike Ming rulers, who had viewed China as a Confucian state in which all subjects were expected to adhere to the same universal principles, early Qing rulers, including Qianlong, viewed the empire as a confederation of several distinct ethnic groups whose cultures should be respected and whose allegiance needed to be won. These groups included not only Manchus and ethnic Chinese, but also Mongols, Tibetans, and Turkish-speaking peoples of Central Asia. As ruler of all of them, Qianlong promoted Confucian scholarship; took steps to preserve Manchu culture; learned to speak Mongolian, Uighur, Tibetan, and Tangut; took a Uighur woman as a concubine and allowed her to remain a Muslim; and built a replica of a famous Tibetan Buddhist temple at his summer palace, mainly to please his mother, a devotee of Buddhism.

Many of the paintings produced in the imperial studios were designed to promote this imperial ideal. For his Buddhist subjects in Tibet, for example, he was portrayed in several paintings as the incarnation of a Buddhist saint. For members of his own ethnic group, the Manchus, as well as his other nomadic Mongol, Tibetan, and Uighur subjects, he was depicted as a warrior, skilled horseman, and fearless hunter. For his Chinese subjects, he was depicted as a supporter of the Confucian values of scholarship, filial piety, and traditional court ceremony. As was the case with the portraits of Napoleon (see source 36, pp. 165–166) paintings featuring Qianlong all had political messages.

The first painting, *The Qianlong Emperor in Ceremonial Armor on Horseback (1758)*, is attributed to the Italian Giuseppe Castiglione, who served as a court painter between 1715 and 1766; the painting is thought to have been completed in 1758. Painted in the style of equestrian portraits of European monarchs, with which Castiglione was undoubtedly familiar, it shows the almost life-size emperor in full battle array, wearing armor decorated with imperial dragons and sitting on a splendid pinto horse. He wears a silver helmet, topped with a horsehair tassel. Although he carries a quiver of arrows and a bow (barely visible behind the horse's mane), his outfit was purely ceremonial, worn only while reviewing troops or welcoming victorious armies. Although Qianlong paid close attention to military affairs and took pride in his armies' victories (almost doubling the empire's size through conquests in Central Asia), he never led troops in battle.

The second painting, *Qianlong in his Study,* is a collaborative work of Castiglione and the Chinese artist, Jin Tingbaiao; it was completed around 1767. Qianlong is depicted in the garb of a Confucian scholar stroking his wispy beard (often considered a mark of sagehood) as he ponders his words while writing a poem. He sits at his desk with his window open to the outside world of nature. On his desk are the Chinese literary man's "four treasures"-- rice paper, writing brush, ink, and ink stone.

The next painting, *Qianlong as a Chinese Scholar and Art Lover Playing the Zither in front of a Painting of his Own,* was painted by an unknown artist sometime in the 1760s, when Qianlong was his sixties. The painting centers on the emperor, who is seated at an elaborate desk playing a *qin,* an ancient stringed instrument, often

IMAGE ASSET MANAGEMEN/World History Archive/AGE Fotostock

The Qianlong Emperor in Ceremonial Armor on Horseback

called a zither, the mastery of which was, in addition to the mastery of painting and calligraphy, an attribute of sagehood. On his left and right are young boys, probably three of his many grandchildren. Behind him is Qianlong's painting of a bleak and bare plum tree, a tree with special significance in Chinese thought: it is the first fruit-bearing tree to blossom, often during the cold and snowy weeks of late winter. For this reason the tree is connected with the qualities of endurance, strength, and regeneration. A blooming plum tree provides the backdrop for Qianlong's painting.

As a side note, it is likely that the zither in the painting is an ancient instrument, created in 1120, which Qianlong revered despite his modest skills as a musician. He had a special case made for it and had his name inscribed on the instrument's back. In 2010 this particular zither sold for over $20 million when put up for auction in Hong Kong.

The fourth painting, *Emperor Qianlong Taking a Stag*, created by Castiglione in the 1750s, shows the emperor displaying his skills as a hunter as hundreds of his subjects look on. The scene takes place at the Mulan Imperial Hunting Park, some two hundred thirty miles north of Beijing. This vast area of forests and grasslands was the summer destination of as many as thirty thousand courtiers, soldiers, and attendants who hunted a wide range of animals. Qianlong was a skilled rider, an expert archer, and an avid hunter, who

Giuseppe Castiglione and Jin Tingbaiao, Qianlong in His Study

Hu Weibiao/Panorama/The Image Works

Qianlong as a Chinese Scholar and Art Lover Playing the Zither in front of a
Painting of his Own

Giuseppe Castiglione, Emperor Qianlong Taking a Stag

over his lifetime killed thousands of deer, elk, and caribou and much smaller numbers of bear, tigers, and panthers, three animals that could be hunted only by the emperor.

The final painting, *Ten Thousand Envoys Come to Pay Tribute,* the work of an anonymous painter in the 1760s, does not feature Qianlong, who presumably is in the Hall of Supreme Harmony, in the upper left corner, awaiting the arrival of the "10,000" envoys from nearby states in Asia and Europe. The work of anonymous court painters, it is an idealized picture of a practice that goes far back in Asian history. Smaller states on China's periphery were expected annually or every two or three years to send gift-bearing emissaries to Beijing, where they would acknowledge China's cultural and political superiority and pay homage to the emperor. In return, the emperor gave them presents, promised their states continued protection, and granted their merchants permission to trade. This painting shows a crowd of emissaries from dozens of states gathering just inside the courtyard of the imperial grounds in Beijing, from which point they will proceed through the Gate of Supreme Harmony to the site of their audience with the emperor, the Hall of Supreme Harmony. Inside the courtyard, blue-robed Chinese officials gather to greet the visitors. If one were to count the number of envoys in the painting, he or she would come up with a number much smaller than 10,000. Indeed, during the 1700s fewer than twenty nations sent tribute missions to China, and only a few – Annam (Vietnam), Korea, Laos, and the Ryuko Islands-- did so regularly.

## QUESTIONS FOR ANALYSIS

1. In the four paintings that feature Qianlong, what message does the painter seek to convey in each of them, and what characteristics of Qianlong does each one communicate?
2. What does *Ten Thousand Envoys Come to Pay Tribute* reveal about China's views of foreigners and China's place in the world? How do the depicted actions of the foreigners and their placement in the painting show their subservience to the emperor?
3. What is your judgment about the effectiveness of each of the works in communicating its message?
4. What do these paintings reveal about the usefulness of paintings such as these as sources for the historian?

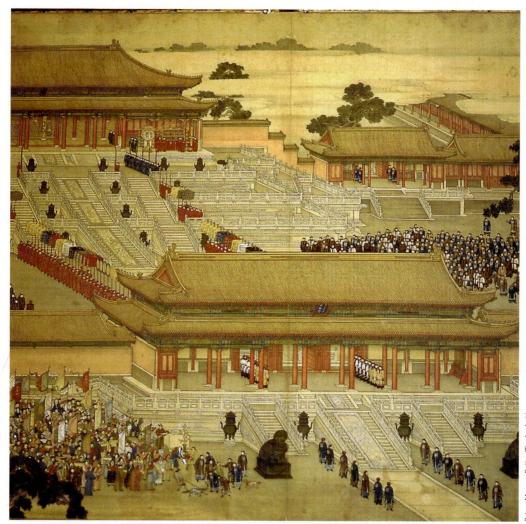

Ten Thousand Envoys Come to Pay Tribute

Palace Museum Beijing/The Art Archive

# Negotiating with the Qianlong Emperor

## 47 • EMPEROR QIANLONG, EDICT ON TRADE WITH GREAT BRITAIN

Chinese restrictions on commerce increasingly frustrated the British in the eighteenth century. They and other Europeans could do business in the environs of only one city, Guangzhou, and only during the trading season, which ran from October to March. Subject to Chinese laws, they were barred from entering Guangzhou, learning Chinese, and being accompanied by their wives. Furthermore, they were required to deal exclusively with a small number of merchant companies that formed a merchants' guild, the Cohong, which had a monopoly on trading with Westerners. Any grievance or dispute had to be referred to these merchants, who would pass it on to the *hoppo*, a government official who oversaw Guangzhou trade. The hoppo might make a decision himself, forward the grievance to Beijing, or simply ignore it. Efforts by the British East India Company to have the system modified got nowhere. When it sent an agent to China in 1759 to negotiate trade issues with the emperor, the envoy was imprisoned for three years on charges of learning Chinese, sailing to unapproved ports, and improperly addressing the emperor.

By the 1780s, with demand for Chinese tea soaring, the British government decided to send its own embassy to China to discuss trade. This time, it would be led by a representative of the king, not the company. The first such embassy, dispatched in 1787, never reached China; its leader died en route, and the British ships returned home. A second embassy, headed by the career diplomat George Macartney, arrived in Beijing in June 1793. After Macartney was granted permission to kneel and bow before the emperor rather than prostrate himself in the ritual known as the kowtow, he presented his requests. One day later Qianlong rejected each and every British proposal in an edict addressed to King George III. Macartney's mission had failed, and Sino-British relations continued to deteriorate until the Opium War (1839–1842) settled the two nations' disputes through force rather than diplomacy.

### QUESTIONS FOR ANALYSIS

1. What views of China's place in the world are revealed in Qianlong's edict?
2. What does the letter reveal about Qianlong's views of foreigners in general and the British in particular?
3. What are the emperor's stated reasons for rejecting any expansion of trade with Great Britain?
4. What unstated reasons might also have influenced his decision?

---

You, O King, from afar have yearned after the blessings of our civilization, and . . . have sent an Embassy across the sea bearing a memorial [memorandum]. I have already taken note of your respectful spirit of submission, have treated your mission with extreme favor and loaded it

*Source*: Emperor Qianlong, "Edict on Trade with Great Britain," in J. O. P. Brand, *Annals and Memoirs of the Court of Peking* (Boston: Houghton Mifflin, 1914), pp. 325–331.

with gifts, besides issuing a mandate to you, O King, and honoring you with the bestowal of valuable presents. Thus has my indulgence been manifested.

Yesterday your Ambassador petitioned my Ministers to memorialize me regarding your trade with China, but his proposal is not consistent with our dynastic practice and cannot be entertained. Hitherto, all European nations, including your own country's barbarian merchants, have carried on their trade with our Celestial Empire at Guangzhou. Such has been the procedure for many years, although our Celestial Empire possesses all things in prolific abundance and lacks no product within its own borders. There was therefore no need to import the manufactures of outside barbarians in exchange for our own products. But as the tea, silk, and porcelain which the Celestial Empire produces are absolute necessities to European nations . . . , we have permitted, as a signal mark of favor, that merchant guilds should be established at Guangzhou, so that your wants might be supplied and your country thus participate in our beneficence. But your Ambassador has now put forward new requests which completely fail to recognize the Throne's principle to "treat strangers from afar with indulgence," and to exercise a pacifying control over barbarian tribes the world over. Moreover, our dynasty, ruling over the myriad races of the globe, extends the same benevolence towards all. England is not the only nation trading at Guangzhou. If other nations, following your bad example, wrongfully importune my ear with impossible requests, how will it be possible for me to treat them with indulgence? Nevertheless, I do not forget the lonely remoteness of your island, cut off from the world by intervening wastes of sea, nor do I overlook your excusable ignorance of the usages of our Celestial Empire. I have consequently commanded

my Ministers to enlighten your Ambassador on the subject, and have ordered the departure of the mission. But I have doubts that after your Envoy's return he may fail to acquaint you with my view in detail or that he may be lacking in lucidity, so that I shall now proceed . . . to issue my mandate on each question separately. In this way you will, I trust, comprehend my meaning. . . .

Your request for a small island near Zhoushan, where your merchants may reside and goods be warehoused, arises from your desire to develop trade. As there are neither merchant guilds nor interpreters in or near Zhoushan, where none of your ships has ever called,[1] such an island would be utterly useless for your purposes. Every inch of our Empire is marked on the map and the strictest vigilance is exercised over it all: even tiny islets and far-lying sand-banks are clearly defined as part of the provinces to which they belong. Consider, moreover, that England is not the only barbarian land which wishes to establish trade with our Empire: supposing that other nations were all to imitate your evil example and beseech me to present them each and all with a site for trading purposes, how could I possibly comply? This . . . cannot possibly be entertained.

The next request, for a small site in the vicinity of Guangzhou, where your barbarian merchants may lodge or, alternatively, that there be no longer any restrictions over their movements at Macao[2] has arisen from the following causes. Hitherto, the barbarian merchants of Europe have had a definite locality assigned to them at Macao for residence and trade, and have been forbidden to encroach an inch beyond the limits assigned to that locality. . . . If these restrictions were withdrawn, friction would inevitably occur between the Chinese and your barbarian subjects, and the results would work against

---

[1]Zhoushon is a city on a group of islands at the entrance to Hangzhou Bay, south of Shanghai. Contrary to the emperor's statement, the East India Company had established a trading post there in the early 1700s but abandoned it after three years.

[2]A Portuguese island colony west of present-day Hong Kong.

the benevolent regard that I feel towards you. From every point of view, therefore, it is best that the regulations now in force should continue unchanged. . . .

Regarding your nation's worship of the Lord of Heaven, it is the same religion as that of other European nations. Ever since the beginning of history, sage Emperors and wise rulers have bestowed on China a moral system and inculcated a code [Confucianism], which from time immemorial has been religiously observed by my subjects. There has been no hankering after heterodox doctrines. Even the European officials [missionaries] in my capital are forbidden to have contacts with Chinese subjects; they are restricted within the limits of their appointed residences, and may not go about propagating their religion. The distinction between Chinese and barbarian is most strict, and your Ambassador's request that barbarians shall be given full liberty to disseminate their religion is utterly unreasonable.

It may be, O King, that the above proposals have been wantonly made by your Ambassador on his own responsibility, or perhaps you yourself are ignorant of our dynastic regulations and had no intention of transgressing them when you expressed these wild ideas and hopes. . . . If, after the receipt of this decree, you . . . allow your barbarian merchants to proceed to Zhejiang and Tianjin[3] with the object of landing and trading there, the ordinances of my Celestial Empire are strict in the extreme, and the local officials . . . are required to obey the law of the land. Should your vessels touch the shore, your merchants will assuredly never be permitted to land or to reside there, but will be subject to instant expulsion. In that event your barbarian merchants will have had a long journey for nothing. Do not say that you were not warned in due time! Tremblingly obey and show no negligence! A special mandate!

---

[3]Chinese port cities.

# Social Change and Intellectual Ferment in Tokugawa Japan

In the 1600s Tokugawa Ieyasu and his successors implemented a four-part plan to stabilize Japan. They tightened control of powerful daimyo families; severed almost all contacts between Japan and the outside world; officially sanctioned and supported Confucianism; and sought to freeze class divisions with military aristocrats (daimyo and samurai) at the top and farmers, artisans, and merchants below them. These policies were remarkably successful. Their subjects, who yearned for order as much as their rulers, experienced internal peace and stable government for many years.

Paradoxically, by the mid-eighteenth century the very success of Tokugawa policies was generating tensions and problems. Decades of peace fostered economic expansion, population growth, urbanization, and social mobility. Japan's population grew from approximately eighteen million in 1600 to thirty million by the 1750s, and Edo (present-day Tokyo) grew from a small village into a city of over a million. These changes increased demand for all types of goods, especially rice, and as a result, richer peasants and merchants prospered. Most peasants, however, could not take advantage of the commercialization of agriculture, and many experienced hardship from land shortages and rising rents. In addition, Japan's military aristocrats failed to benefit from the economic boom. Lavish spending and the daimyo's need to maintain dual residences in Edo and their own domains led to massive indebtedness.

While economic change was undermining the social basis of the Tokugawa regime, intellectual ferment was eroding its ideological underpinnings. As the memory of earlier civil wars faded, Confucian conservatism lost some of its appeal and foreign ideas seemed less dangerous. In the eighteenth century, two intellectual movements challenged state-sponsored Confucianism. Proponents of National Learning, or *Kokugaku,* rejected Chinese influence, especially Confucianism, and promoted the study and glorification of Japan's ancient literature and religion. Other Japanese developed an interest in European medicine, botany, cartography, and gunnery. Their endeavors were known as Dutch Studies because their sources of information about Europe were the Dutch, who continued to trade on a limited basis with Japan even after the seclusion policy had been adopted. By the late eighteenth century, those who were dissatisfied with the Tokugawa regime had models for a different future, something that solidly Confucian China lacked.

# The National Learning Movement

## 48 • KAMO NO MABUCHI, A STUDY OF THE IDEA OF THE NATION

The son of a Shinto priest, Kamo No Mabuchi (1697–1769) received training in both ancient Japanese literature and Confucianism. He contributed to the National Learning Movement in two ways. As a poet, he sought to imitate the style of ancient Japanese poetry, and as a scholar, he promoted the study of ancient Japanese verse. As the following selection illustrates, his intent was to reveal the original simplicity and spontaneity of the Japanese people before their corruption by Chinese influence.

### QUESTIONS FOR ANALYSIS

1. What arguments does Mabuchi make to show the worthlessness of Confucianism?
2. According to Mabuchi, how was the very nature of the Japanese people affected when Confucianism was introduced?
3. What is Mabuchi's vision for Japan's future?
4. According to Mabuchi, what are the drawbacks of Chinese as a written language? What language reforms does he propose for the Japanese?
5. On the basis of your knowledge of Confucianism and Chinese history, in your view, how valid are his criticisms of Chinese thought and the Chinese in general?

---

Someone remarked to me, "I pay no heed to such petty trifles as Japanese poetry; what interests me is the Chinese Way of governing a nation." I smiled at this and did not answer. Later, when I met the same man he asked, "You seem to have

---

*Source:* From *Sources of Japanese Tradition,* by William Theodore de Bary, pp. 515–518. Copyright © 1966 Columbia University Press. Reprinted with permission of the publisher.

an opinion on every subject—why did you merely keep smiling when I spoke to you?"

I answered, "You mean when you were talking about the Chinese Confucian teachings or whatever you call them? They are no more than a human invention which reduces the heart of Heaven and Earth to something trivial." At these words he became enraged, "How dare you call our Great Way trivial?" I answered, "I would be interested in hearing whether or not the Chinese Confucian learning has actually helped to govern a country successfully." He immediately cited the instances of Yao, Shun, Hsia, Yin, Chou, and so on.[1] I asked if there were no later examples, but he informed me that there were not.

I pursued the matter, asking this time about how far back Chinese traditions went. He answered that thousands of years had passed from Yao's day to the present. I then asked, "Why then did the Way of Yao continue only until the Chou [Era] and afterwards cease? I am sure that it is because you restrict yourself to citing events which took place thousands of years ago that the Way seems so good. But those are merely ancient legends. It takes more than such specious ideas to run a country!" . . .

Despite the fact that their country [China] has been torn for centuries by disturbances and has never really been well administered, they think that they can explain with their Way of Confucius the principles governing the whole world. Indeed, when one has heard them through, there is nothing to be said: anyone can quickly grasp their doctrines because they consist of mere quibbling. What they value most and insist on is the establishment and maintenance of good government. Everybody in China would seem to have been in agreement on this point, but belief in it did not in fact lie very deep. It is obvious that many gave superficial assent who did not assent in their hearts. Yet when these principles were introduced to this country it was stated that China

had obtained good government through the adoption of them. This was a complete fabrication. . . .

Japan in ancient days was governed in accordance with the natural laws of Heaven and earth. There was never any indulgence in such petty rationalizing as marked China, but when suddenly these teachings were transmitted here from abroad, they quickly spread, for the men of old in their simplicity took them for the truth. In Japan there had been generation after generation, extending back to the remote past, which had known prosperity, but no sooner were these Confucian teachings propagated here than in the time of Temmu[2] a great rebellion occurred. Later . . . the palace, dress, and ceremonies were [made to look Chinese] and everything took on a superficial elegance; under the surface, however, contentiousness and dishonesty became more prevalent. Confucianism made men crafty, and led them to worship the ruler to such an excessive degree that the whole country acquired a servant's mentality. . . .

Just as roads are naturally created when people live in uncultivated woodlands or fields, so the Way of the Age of the Gods spontaneously took hold in Japan. Because it was a Way indigenous to the country it caused our emperors to wax increasingly in prosperity. However, the Confucian teachings had not only repeatedly thrown China into disorder, but they now had the same effect in Japan. Yet there are those unwitting of these facts who reverence Confucianism and think that it is the Way to govern the country! This is a deplorable attitude. . . .

When ruling the country a knowledge of Chinese things is of no help in the face of an emergency . . . In the same way, doctors often study and master Chinese texts, but very seldom do they cure any sickness. On the other hand, medicines which have been transmitted naturally in this country with no reasons or theoretical knowledge behind them, infallibly cure all maladies. . . .

---

[1] Yao and Shun are mythical enlightened rulers from China's ancient past. Xia, Yin, and Zhou are the names of the first three Chinese dynasties described in historical records. The Yin Dynasty is also known as the Shang.

[2] Emperor Temmu (r. 631–686) assumed the throne after raising an army and defeating the forces of his nephew and reigning emperor, Kōbun.

People also tell me, "We had no writing in this country and therefore had to use Chinese characters. From this one fact you can know everything about the relative importance of our countries." I answer, "I need not recite again how troublesome, evil, turbulent a country China is. To mention just one instance—there is the matter of their picture-writing. There are about 38,000 characters in common use. . . . Every place name and plant name has a separate character for it which has no other use but to designate that particular place or plant. Can any man, even one who devotes himself to the task earnestly, learn all these many characters? Sometimes people miswrite characters, sometimes the characters themselves change from one generation to the next. What a nuisance, a waste of effort, and a bother! In India, on the other hand, fifty letters suffice for the writing of the more than 5,000 volumes of the Buddhist scriptures. . . . In Holland, I understand, they use twenty-five letters. In this country there should be fifty. The appearance of letters used in all countries is in general the same, except for China where they invented their bothersome system. . . .

As long as a few teachings were carefully observed and we worked in accordance with the Will of Heaven and earth, the country would be well off without any special instruction. Nevertheless, Chinese doctrines were introduced and corrupted men's hearts; . . . they were of the kind which heard in the morning are forgotten by evening. Our country in ancient times was not like that. It obeyed the laws of Heaven and earth. The emperor was the sun and moon and the subjects the stars. . . . Just as the sun, moon, and stars have always been in Heaven, so our imperial sun and moon, and the stars his vassals, have existed without change from ancient days, and have ruled the world fairly. . . .

## Curing Japan's Social Ills

### 49 • HONDA TOSHIAKI, A SECRET PLAN FOR GOVERNMENT

Honda Toshiaki (1744–1821), a perceptive critic of late Tokugawa society and a prophet of Japan's future, was born in northern Japan, where his samurai father had fled after killing a man. Educated in Confucianism, he increasingly was drawn to the study of Western mathematics, science, and geography. As a young man he opened a school in Edo for teaching mathematics but spent much of his life traveling about Japan to observe and analyze economic and social conditions, especially of the poor. He concluded that as an island nation, Japan needed to expand commerce and colonize rather than simply focus on agriculture, as a large continental country like China could do. He believed Japan should end its seclusion and strive to learn European skills in navigation and manufacturing.

Honda's *A Secret Plan for Government*, written in 1798, is his most important work. In it, he outlines a strategy for Japan based on what he calls the "four imperative needs": to learn the effective use of gunpowder, to develop metallurgy, to increase trade, and to colonize nearby islands and the Kamchatka Peninsula. The following excerpt, in which he analyzes the roots of Japan's problems, comes at the end of a long discussion of Japanese history.

#### QUESTIONS FOR ANALYSIS

1. What is Honda's view of the daimyo?
2. How do merchants contribute to Japan's problems, according to Honda?

3. How does Honda justify his assertion that fifteen-sixteenths of all Japanese rice production goes to the merchants? Are his arguments plausible?

4. According to Honda, why is Europe rather than China the better model for Japan's revival?

5. What Confucian influence is evident in Honda's *Plan*? In what ways does Honda reject Confucianism?

6. In your view, what would Kamo No Mabuchi (source 48) have thought of Honda's ideas?

---

Not until Tokugawa Ieyasu[1] used his power to control the strong and give succor to the weak did the warfare that had lasted for three hundred years without a halt suddenly abate. . . . It must have been because he realized how difficult it would be to preserve the empire for all ages to come if the people were not honest in their hearts that Ieyasu, in his testament, exhorted shoguns who would succeed him to abstain from any irregularities in government, and to rule on a basis of benevolence and honesty. It was his counsel that the shoguns should serve as models to the people, and by their honesty train the people in the ways of humanity and justice. He taught that the shogun should not compel obedience merely by the use of force, but by his acts of benevolence. . . .

He taught the daimyo that the duties of a governor consisted in the careful attempt to guide the people of their domains in such a way as both to bring about the prosperity of the land and to encourage the literary and military arts. However, in recent days there has been the spectacle of lords confiscating the allocated property of their retainers[2] on the pretext of paying back debts to the merchants. The debts do not then decrease, but usually seem rather to grow larger. One daimyo with an income of 60,000 *koku*[3] so increased his borrowings that he could not make good his debts, and there was a public suit. . . . Even if repayment had been attempted on the basis of his income of 60,000 koku, the debt would not have been completely settled for fifty or sixty years, so long a time that it is difficult to imagine the day would actually come.

All the daimyo are not in this position, but there is not one who has not borrowed from the merchants. Is this not a sad state of affairs? The merchant . . . must feel like a fisherman who sees a fish swim into his net. Officials of the daimyo harass the farmers for money, which they claim they need to repay the daimyo's debts, but the debts do not diminish. Instead, the daimyo go on contracting new ones year after year. The [daimyo's] officials are blamed for this situation, and are dismissed as incompetent. New officials then harass and afflict the farmers in much the same way as the old ones, and so it goes on. . . .

No matter how hard the daimyo and their officials rack their brains, they do not seem to be able to reduce the debts. The lords are "sunk in a pool of debts," as it is popularly said, a pool from which their children and grandchildren will be unable to escape. Everything will be as the merchants wish it. The daimyo turn over their domains to the merchants, receiving in return an allowance with which to pay their public and private expenses. . . .

---

*Source:* Excerpts from Donald Keene, *The Japanese Discovery of Europe, 1720–1830,* revised edition. Copyright © 1952 and 1969 by Donald Keene. All rights reserved. With the permission of Stanford University Press, www.sup.org.

[1]The founder of the Tokugawa Shogunate.
[2]A reference to the *samurai,* lesser members of the military aristocracy.
[3]One *koku* is approximately five bushels of rice.

Many fields have turned into wasteland since the famine of 1783, when thousands of farmers starved to death.[4] Wherever one goes . . . , one hears people say, "There used to be a village here. . . . The land over there was once part of such-and-such a county, but now there is no village and no revenue comes from the land." . . . When so many farmers starved, reducing still further their already insufficient numbers, the amount of uncultivated land greatly increased. If the wicked practice of infanticide, now so prevalent, is not stopped, the farming population will dwindle until it tends to die out altogether. . . .

The Confucian scholars of ancient and modern times have talked a great deal about benevolence and compassion, but they possess neither in their hearts. Officials and authorities talk about benevolent government, but they have no understanding of what that means. Whose fault is it that the farmers are dying of starvation and that good fields are turning into wasteland? The fault lies entirely with the ruler. . . .

> There follows an enthusiastic but often inaccurate account of Europe's accomplishments.

Because astronomy, calendar making, and mathematics are considered the ruler's business, the European kings are well versed in celestial and terrestrial principles, and instruct the common people in them. Thus even among the lower classes one finds men who show great ability in their particular fields. The Europeans as a result have been able to establish industries with which the rest of the world is unfamiliar. It is for this reason that all the treasures of the world are said to be attracted to Europe. There is nowhere the Europeans' ships do not go in order to obtain different products and treasures.

. . . They trade their own rare products, superior implements, and unusual inventions for the precious metals and valuable goods of others, which they bring back to enrich their own countries. Their prosperity makes them strong, and it is because of their strength that they are never invaded or pillaged, whereas for their part they have invaded countless non-European countries. . . .

It may be wondered in what way this supremacy was achieved. In the first place, the European nations have behind them a history of five to six thousand years. In this period they have delved deep into the beauties of the [mechanical] arts, have divined the foundations of government, and have established a system based on an examination of the factors that naturally make a nation prosperous. Because of their proficiency in mathematics, they have excelled also in astronomy, calendar making, and surveying. They have elaborated laws of navigation such that there is nothing simpler for them than to sail the oceans of the world. . . .

In spite of this example, however, the Japanese do not look elsewhere than to China for good or beautiful things, so tainted are the customs and temperament of Japan by Chinese teachings. . . . China is a mountainous country that extends as far as Europe and Africa. . . . Since it is impossible to feed the huge population of cities when transport can be effected only by human or animal strength, there are no big cities in China away from the coast. China is therefore a much less favored country than Japan, which is surrounded by water, and this factor shows in the deficiencies and faults of Chinese state policies. China does not merit being used as a model. Since Japan is a maritime nation, shipping and trade should be the chief concerns of the ruler. Ships should be sent to all countries to obtain products needed for national consumption and to bring precious metals to Japan. A maritime nation is equipped with the means to increase her national strength.

---

[4]A reference to the Tenmei famine (1783–1786), one of the three famines in eighteenth-century Japan. The famines had various causes, including flooding, drought, typhoons, insect damage, and volcanic eruptions.

By contrast, a nation that attempts to get along on its own resources will grow steadily weaker. . . . To put the matter bluntly, the policies followed by the various ruling families until now have determined that the lower classes must lead a hand-to-mouth existence. The best part of the harvests of the farmers . . . is wrenched away from them. The lords spend all they take within the same year, and if they then do not have enough, they oppress the farmers all the more cruelly in an effort to obtain additional funds. This goes on year after year. . . .

Soon all the gold and silver currency will pass into the hands of the merchants, and only merchants will be deserving of the epithets "rich" and "mighty." Their power will thus grow until they stand first among the four classes. When I investigated the incomes of present-day merchants, I discovered that fifteen-sixteenths of the total income of Japan goes to the merchants, with only one-sixteenth left for the samurai. As proof of this statement, I cite the following case. When there are good rice harvests at Yonezawa in Dewa or in Semboku-gun in Akita[5] the price is five or six *mon* for one *sho.*[6] The rice is sold to merchants who ship it to Edo, where the price is about 100 mon, regardless of the original cost. At this rate, if one bought 10,000 ryos[7] worth of rice in Dewa, sent it to Edo, and sold it there, one's capital would be increased to

160,000 ryo. If the 160,000 ryo in turn were used as capital, the return in Edo would be 2,560,000 ryo. With only two exchanges of trade it is possible to make enormous profits.

It may be claimed that of this sum, part must go for shipping expenses and pack-horse charges, but the fact remains that one gets back sixteen times what one has paid for the rice. It is thus apparent that fifteen-sixteenths of the nation's income goes to the merchants. In terms of the production of an individual farmer, out of thirty days a month he works twenty-eight for the merchants and two for the samurai . . . Clearly, then, unless the samurai store grain it is impossible for them to offer any relief to the farmers in years of famine. This may be why they can do no more than look on when the farmers are dying of starvation. And all this because the right system has not been established.

By means of the plans outlined in the account of the four imperative needs . . . the present society could be restored to its former prosperity and strength. The ancient glories of the warrior-nation of Japan would be revived. Colonization projects would gradually be commenced and would meet with great success. . . . Then, under enlightened government, Japan could certainly be made the richest and strongest country in the world.

---

[5]Dewa and Akita are provinces in northern Honshu.
[6]A *mon* was a copper coin; a *sho* was about 3.2 pints.

[7]Also known as a *koban,* a *ryo* was a Japanese gold coin.

# A Meeting of Cultures

## 50 • SHIBA KŌKAN, A MEETING OF JAPAN, CHINA, AND THE WEST

Born into the family of a wealthy Edo merchant, Shiba Kōkan (1747–1818) was trained in Chinese and Japanese painting, but in the 1780s he became intrigued by the European prints and paintings circulating in Edo. He experimented with oil-based paints, sought realism in his paintings through shading and perspective, and learned the techniques of copperplate engraving and etching. His visit to Nagasaki, the Dutch commercial center, introduced him to Western science and geography. Beginning in the 1780s, he illustrated and wrote a number of books on these subjects, notable for their laudatory but fanciful descriptions of Europe.

In the 1790s, Kōkan painted *A Meeting of Japan, China, and the West*, a hanging silk scroll. At the bottom are three figures: on the left a Chinese Confucian scholar, in the middle a Japanese samurai, and on the right a European. The European is holding an anatomical treatise opened to show a drawing of the human skeleton. Before the Chinese scholar is a scroll of his writings, a *ruyi* scepter (a symbol of power and a talisman thought to bring good luck), and what may be a medicinal herb in a Chinese-style vase. The samurai has one hand on a fan and has a small white snake, perhaps a talisman to ward off disease around his wrist.

At the top of the painting, Japanese, Chinese, and Westerners interact in a very different context. While flames engulf a pagoda, the Chinese firefighters on the left are throwing small buckets of water on the flames; the Europeans are using a modern pump and hose; and the Japanese, represented by sumo wrestlers, have large tubs of water available but are using the water to bathe, not to subdue the fire.

### QUESTIONS FOR ANALYSIS

1. Consider the postures, seating arrangements, and facial expressions of the three men seated at the table. What do they suggest about the message of the painting?
2. What might be the significance of the following details—the vase with the herb, the Chinese scroll, the printed book, the fan, and the white snake?
3. What is the meaning of the scene depicted at the top of the painting?
4. If Kamo No Mabuchi (source 48) and Honda Toshiaki (source 49) had seen this painting, what might they have thought of it?

Shiba Kōkan, A Meeting of Japan, China, and the West

# PART THREE

# The World in the Age of Western Dominance: 1800–1914

N O PART OF THE world better illustrates the seismic changes in world relationships in the nineteenth century than Africa. Before the 1800s Europeans had exploited the continent by their centuries-long involvement in the transatlantic slave trade, but aside from the tenuous Portuguese claim to Angola, they established no colonies; and apart from the small numbers of Dutch and French who migrated to the Cape Colony in southern Africa, there were no permanent European settlements. In 1800, with the slave trade under attack in Europe and the Americas, it would not have been unreasonable to think Europe's engagement in Africa would shrink even further in the coming century.

By 1914, however, except for Ethiopia and Liberia, all of Africa was under the political control of European powers. In 1884 and 1885, rules for carving up Africa were laid down at the Berlin West Africa Conference, attended by representatives of eleven European nations, the Ottoman Empire, and the United States. They agreed that each power had to give the others proper notice if it intended to annex African territory and could not do so by simply stamping its name on a map: it had to have real troops or administrators on the scene. The stage was set for the "scramble for Africa," one of the largest and most rapid conquests in history.

The European takeover of Africa was striking in its speed and magnitude, but it was not unique. Burma, India, Vietnam, Cambodia, Laos, small states on the Malay Peninsula and in the East Indies, and hundreds of South Pacific islands also came under direct European or U.S. control in the nineteenth century. Independent states such as Nicaragua, Haiti, the Dominican Republic, Ottoman Turkey, Egypt, Persia, and China were forced to accept varying degrees of Western control of their finances and foreign policy. Australia and New Zealand became European settler colonies. Canada, South Africa, the Philippines, and most of the West Indies remained parts of pre–nineteenth-century empires, although Canada in 1867 and South Africa in 1910 were granted extensive powers of self-government and the Philippines in 1898 changed masters from Spain to the United States. After gaining their independence from Spain and Portugal in the early 1800s, the new nations of Latin America retained full political sovereignty but saw many of their economic assets— banks, railroads, mines, and grazing lands—taken over by Western investors. Only Japan, by adopting the technology, military organization, and industrial economy of the West (a term now understood to include Europe and its offshoot, the United States), avoided an imperialist take-over and became an imperialist power itself. Never had world economic and political relationships been as one-sided as they were when World War I began in 1914.

The West's expansion resulted in part from the inner dynamics of capitalism, with its ceaseless drive for new markets, resources, and investment opportunities. It also resulted from nationalist rivalries among the Western powers themselves, most of whose leaders and citizens believed that prestige and prosperity depended on empire-building and overseas investment. The West's ascendancy was made possible by the huge economic and military disparity between Europe and the United States and that of the rest of the world. During the nineteenth century, once-powerful states such as the Ottoman Empire and China faced severe internal problems, and others, such as Mughal India, had already collapsed. Europe and the United States, however, continued to industrialize, develop new technologies, and build the most powerful armies and navies in history.

# Chapter 8

# The West in the Age of Industrialization and Imperialism

A S FAR-REACHING AS THE TRANSFORMATION of Western civilization since the Renaissance had been, no one in 1815 could have predicted the even greater changes about to occur in the nineteenth century. When Napoleon met defeat at Waterloo in 1815, Europe's population was 200 million, with as many as 25 million people of European descent living in the rest of the world. By 1914, these numbers were 450 million and 150 million, respectively. In 1815, most Europeans and Americans lived in villages and worked the land; by 1914, in highly industrialized nations such as Great Britain, a majority of the population lived in cities and worked in factories or offices. In 1815, despite two decades of revolution, most European governments were still aristocratic and monarchical; in 1914, representative government and universal manhood suffrage were the norms in much of Europe, the United States, and the British dominions of Canada, Australia, and New Zealand. In 1815, most governments limited their activities to defense, the preservation of law and order, and some economic regulation; in 1914, governments subsidized education, sponsored scientific research, oversaw public health, monitored industry, provided social welfare programs, and maintained huge military establishments, and, as a result, had grown enormously.

Europe's global role also changed dramatically. In 1815, European political authority around the world appeared to be declining. Great Britain no longer ruled its thirteen American colonies; Portugal and Spain were losing their American empires; and France recently had lost its prime Caribbean colony, Saint-Domingue, and had sold 800,000 square miles of North American territory to the United States through the Louisiana Purchase. Great Britain's decision to outlaw the slave trade in 1807 seemed to be a step toward a diminished European role in Africa, and there was nothing to suggest that Western nations had the means or inclination to extend their power in the Middle East or East Asia. Only the expansion of Great Britain

---

229

in India provided a hint of the future: the Western nations' takeover of Africa and Southeast Asia, their interference in the politics of China and the Middle East, and their dominance of the world's economy.

The most important cause of the West's expansion was the Industrial Revolution—a series of wide-ranging economic changes in which new technologies and energy sources transformed manufacturing, communication, and transportation. This revolution began in England in the late eighteenth century, when new machines and procedures were applied to the iron and textile industries. By 1914 industrialization had taken root in Europe, Japan, and the United States and was spreading to Canada, Russia, and parts of Latin America. Just as the discovery of agriculture had done many centuries earlier, industrialization profoundly altered the human condition.

# The Dynamics of Europe's Industrial Revolution

In 1750 the world's economy was dominated by three large regions, Europe, India, and China, all which were more or less equal in terms of economic development, technology, and standards of living. Each region produced approximately twenty-three percent of the world's gross domestic product, and together they produced just short of eighty percent of the world's manufactured goods. By 1900, however, a spectacular change had occurred. Europe by then produced sixty percent of the world's manufactured goods, and its offshoot, the United States, produced twenty percent. In contrast, China's share dropped to seven percent and India's to just under two percent. An immense gap between the West and the rest of the world had opened up.

What explains the West's meteoric economic rise? The simple answer is that Europe and the United States experienced what has come to be known as the Industrial Revolution, and except for Japan, no other part of the world did so. Although there is debate about the origins of the term "Industrial Revolution," its first use generally is credited to Arnold Toynbee, an English economic historian and social reformer who in 1882 delivered a series of lectures titled "The Industrial Revolution in England," which was published after his death in 1884. According to Toynbee, the "revolution" was a unique English phenomenon that occurred between 1760 and 1830, and its essential quality was the "substitution of competition for the medieval regulations which had previously controlled the production and distribution of wealth." Although historians no longer accept many of his ideas, few quibble with his choice of the word "revolution" in his title. Industrialization was a profound turning point in human affairs, certainly equal in importance to the political revolutions of the eighteenth and nineteenth centuries, and perhaps the equal of the discovery of agriculture, which had transformed human life thousands of years earlier.

The Industrial Revolution was characterized by a momentous increase in human productivity brought about by the use of new machines; new sources of energy, including coal, petroleum, and electricity; and the increased scale of manufacturing, with factories employing hundreds or thousands of workers. From its beginning in England, it continually changed and evolved as one innovation followed another in an outburst of inventiveness never seen in history. Whole new industries were created: Commercially viable railroads and electrical telegraph systems were introduced in the 1830s; the generation and utilization of electricity became widespread in the 1880s; and gasoline-powered internal combustion engines were introduced in the 1890s. New methods were developed for making steel, paper, and industrial chemicals. Refinements of gear shapers, lathes, drill presses, and other machine tools enabled manufacturers to make and maintain highly sophisticated and specialized devices for the production of everything from bicycles to cameras to eating utensils to automobiles. Industrialization was a dynamic, multifaceted process and a monument to human inventiveness, imagination, and perseverance. It brought about momentous changes in how humans led their lives.

# The Transformation of Textile Production in England

### 51 • RICHARD GUEST, A COMPENDIOUS HISTORY OF THE COTTON MANUFACTORY

The invention of efficient steam engines and the development of new methods for smelting iron, both of which occurred in England in the 1700s, were key events in the early Industrial Revolution, but innovations in the textile industry affected the greater number of human beings. Notable breakthroughs were John Kay's flying shuttle (1733), which speeded up weaving; Richard Arkwright's water frame (1769), which used water power to spin fine, strong yarns between rollers; James Hargreave's spinning jenny (1770), which enabled one person to spin eight, then sixteen, and finally over one hundred threads of yarn at once; a variety of carding and scribbling machines (1750s through the 1770s) to prepare raw wool for spinning; Samuel Compton's spinning mule (1779), which combined features of the water frame and jenny; and Edmund Cartwright's power loom (1785), which could be driven by water power or steam engines.

One of the first authors to appreciate the significance of these developments was Richard Guest, whose book, A *Compendious History of the Cotton Manufactory*, was published in 1823. A native of Lancashire, Guest witnessed the transformation of the cotton industry in northwest England from the 1780s onward. In his book he traces the gradual mechanization of spinning and weaving, describes new ways to organize the textile industry, presents statistics on cotton cloth production, and warns against sending new machinery to India, where, he feared, cheap labor would drive English manufacturers out of the world market. His book ends with his description of the development and early modifications of the power loom, which was invented by Edmund Cartwright in 1785 and was in general use by the 1820s.

## QUESTIONS FOR ANALYSIS

1. Why does Guest consider steam power one of the great inventions of the age?
2. Concerning Edmund Cartwright, what motivated him to design and build a power loom? What training did he have for such a task? Whom did he recruit to help him?
3. After a number of improvements in Cartwright's design, how quickly was the power loom adopted by cotton manufacturers in and around Manchester?
4. How was the weaving of cotton cloth affected by the introduction of the power loom?
5. How did the introduction of power looms affect worker productivity? How did it affect the quality of cotton textiles?

## National and General Importance of the Cotton Manufacture

The present age is distinguished beyond all others by the rapid progress of human discovery. . . .

One, however, which would seem to merit the attention of the Englishman from its having brought an immense increase of wealth and population to his territory, has obtained comparatively little attention. While admiration has been unboundedly lavished on other triumphs of the mind, the successive inventions and improvements of the Machinery employed in the Cotton Manufacture, have [not] obtained the notice . . . their national importance required. They have been the great means of increasing the population of the county of Lancaster, in the first ten years of the present century, from 672,731 to 810,539, and, in the subsequent ten years, to 1,052,859, . . . and of producing a corresponding increase of wealth and intelligence. Under the influence of the manufacture of which they have been the promoters, the town of Manchester has, from an unimportant provincial town, become the second in extent and population in England, and Liverpool has become in opulence, magnitude, elegance and commerce, the second Seaport in Europe. . . .

## Cartwright's Power Loom

In 1785, the Rev. E. Cartwright invented a Loom to be worked by water or steam. [Cartwright's] account of this invention is taken from the Supplement to the Encyclopaedia Britannica:[1]—

"Happening to be at Matlock, in the summer of 1784, I fell in company with some gentlemen of Manchester, when the conversation turned on Arkwright's spinning machinery. One of the company observed, that as soon as Arkwright's patent expired, so many mills would be erected, and so much cotton spun, that hands never could be found to weave it. To this observation I replied that Arkwright must then set his wits to work to invent a weaving mill. This brought on a conversation on the subject, in which the Manchester gentlemen unanimously agreed that the thing was impracticable; and in defence of their opinion, they adduced arguments which I certainly was incompetent . . . to comprehend. . . . I controverted [argued against], however, the impracticability of the thing, by remarking that there had lately been exhibited in London, an antomaton figure, which played at chess.[2] Now you will not assert, gentlemen, said I, that it is more difficult to construct a machine that shall weave, than

Source: Richard Guest, *A Compendious History of the Cotton Manufactory* (Manchester: Joseph Pratt, 1823), pp. 3, 4, 44–48.
[1]The first edition of the encyclopedia appeared in 1771. The supplement to the third edition was published in 1801.
[2]The Automaton Chess Player, also known as the Mechanical Turk, was a fake chess-playing machine constructed in 1770 in Austria. The "Turk's" moves were manipulated by a human chess master hidden inside the cabinet at which the Turk and its opponent were seated. In 1784 the mechanical chess player was exhibited in London as part of a European tour. It was not revealed as a hoax until the 1820s.

one which shall make all the variety of moves which are required in that complicated game.

"Some little time afterwards, . . . it struck me, that, as in plain weaving, there could only be three movements, which if they were to follow each other in succession, there would be little difficulty in producing and repeating them. Full of these ideas, I immediately employed a carpenter and smith to carry them into effect. As soon as the machine was finished, I got a weaver to put in the warp.[3] . . . To my great delight, a piece of cloth, such as it was, was the product.

As I had never before turned my thoughts to any thing mechanical, either in theory or practice, nor had ever seen a loom at work, or knew any thing of its construction, you will readily suppose that my first Loom must have been a most rude piece of machinery.

The warp was placed perpendicularly, the reed fell with a force of at least half an hundred weight, and the springs which threw the shuttle were strong enough to have thrown a Congreve rocket.[4] In short, it required the strength of two powerful men to work the machine at a slow rate, and only for a short time. Conceiving in my great simplicity, that I had accomplished all that was required, I then secured what I thought a most valuable property, by a patent, 4th April, 1785. This being done, I then condescended to see how other people wove; and you will guess my astonishment, when I compared their easy modes of operation with mine. Availing myself, however, of what I then saw, I made a Loom in its general principles, nearly as they are now made. But it was not till the year 1787, that I completed my invention, when I took out my last weaving patent. . . ."

Mr. Cartwright erected a weaving mill at Doncaster, which he filled with Looms. This concern was unsuccessful, and at last was abandoned, and some years afterwards, upon an application from a number of manufacturers at Manchester, Parliament granted Mr. Cartwright a sum of money [£10,000] as a remuneration for his ingenuity and trouble.

About 1790, Mr. Grimshaw, of Manchester, under a licence from Mr. Cartwright, erected a weaving factory turned by a Steam Engine. . . . [The] factory, however, was burnt down before it could be fully ascertained whether the experiment would succeed or not, and for many years no further attempts were made in Lancashire to weave by steam.

Mr. Austin, of Glasgow, invented a similar Loom, in 1789; which he still further improved in 1798, and a building to contain two hundred of these Looms was erected by Mr. Monteith, of Pollockshaws, in 1800. . . .

A factory for Steam Looms was built in Manchester, in 1806. Soon afterwards two others were erected at Stockport, and about 1809, a fourth was completed in Westhoughton. In these renewed attempts to weave by steam, considerable improvements were made in the structure of the Looms, in the mode of warping, and in preparing the weft for the shuttle. With these improvements, aided by others in the art of spinning. . . . cloth made by these Looms, when seen by those manufacturers who employ hand Weavers, at once excites admiration and a consciousness that their own workmen cannot equal it. The increasing number of Steam Looms is a certain proof of their superiority over the Hand Looms. In 1818, there were in Manchester, Stockport, Middleton, Hyde, Stayley Bridge, and their vicinities, fourteen factories, containing about two thousand Looms. In 1821, there were in the same neighbourhoods thirty-two factories, containing five thousand seven hundred

---

[3]The warp is the set of lengthwise yarns that are held in tension on a frame or loom. The weft is the thread or yarn drawn over and under the warp yarns to create cloth. Since warp yarn must be strong enough not to break while being held in tension during the weaving process, traditional warp yarns were made of wool, silk, or linen. Richard Arkwright's water frame made it possible to spin cotton thread strong enough for use in mechanical weaving.

[4]The reed is a comblike device used to push the weft yarn securely into place as it is woven. The Congreve Rocket was a British artillery rocket developed by Sir William Congreve in 1806.

and thirty-two Looms. Since 1821, their number has still farther increased, and there are at present not less than ten thousand Steam Looms at work in Great Britain.

It is a curious circumstance, that, when the Cotton Manufacture was in its infancy, all the operations, from the dressing of the raw material to its being finally turned out in the state of cloth, were completed under the roof of the weaver's cottage. . . . At the present time, when the manufacture has attained a mature growth, all the operations, with vastly increased means and more complex contrivances, are again performed in a single building. . . . Those vast brick edifices in the vicinity of all the great manufacturing towns . . . towering to the height of seventy or eighty feet, which strike the attention and excite the curiosity of the traveller, now perform labours which formerly employed whole villages. . . .

A very good Hand Weaver, a man twenty-five or thirty years of age, will weave two pieces of . . . shirting per week, each twenty-four yards long. . . . A Steam Loom Weaver, fifteen years of age, will in the same time weave seven similar pieces.

## The Beginning of the Railroad Age

### 52 • A GUIDE TO THE LIVERPOOL AND MANCHESTER RAILWAY

A new and important stage in the Industrial Revolution, one dominated by railroad construction and travel, began on September 15, 1830, when eight special trains pulled by steam locomotives and carrying over one thousand passengers made the seventy-two-mile roundtrip between the English port city of Liverpool and the industrial city of Manchester. This was the culmination of a series of technological breakthroughs that began in the early 1800s, when a number of English inventors designed and built wheel-mounted steam engines (locomotives) for rail transport. In the 1820s, steam locomotives designed by George Stephenson (1781–1834) were used to move goods on rails for the Hetton Coal Company and on a railway between Stockton and Darlington in the northeast.

The Liverpool and Manchester Railway, however, has the distinction of being the first modern railway. The brainchild of Liverpool and Manchester businessmen, it had a double track of iron rails, transported both freight and passengers, relied exclusively on locomotives, and provided regularly scheduled service between two major cities with all the accessories of stations, signals, bridges, tunnels, and trains of first-, second-, and third-class carriages. It also was wildly successful. Investors in the railroad anticipated four hundred to five hundred passengers a day, but within weeks it was carrying on average twelve hundred passengers a day; five years after the opening, it carried nearly half a million persons yearly. Attaining peak speeds of twenty-five miles per hour, it made the trip between Liverpool and Manchester in a little over an hour. With added income from moving freight, the railroad showed a healthy profit, making it possible to pay its several hundred investors a regular annual dividend of eight to ten percent.

Other eager investors soon created the world's first railway construction boom. Between 1830 and 1850 some six thousand miles of track were laid in England, creating a rail network that included all its major cities. By 1914 railroads crisscrossed

Europe and had spread around the world. The United States, with approximately 250,000 miles of track, knitted the country together with the transcontinental railroad in 1869, as did Canada in 1885 and Russia in 1903. Railroads were introduced to Asia, Africa, and South America, and by 1914 India had the fourth largest rail network after the United States, Germany, and Russia. In a matter of decades railroads transformed the world in countless ways.

The following selection is taken from a fifteen-page booklet produced by the Liverpool and Manchester Railway Company to help publicize the opening of the railroad in 1830. It draws heavily on writings of Henry Booth, a Liverpool merchant who served as secretary and treasurer of the railway from 1826 to 1846. It traces the company's brief history, describes the engineering problems the project encountered, provides information about the railway's costs, and presents a glowing picture of the railway's benefits.

## QUESTIONS FOR ANALYSIS

1. What motivated the Manchester businessmen to undertake the railway project?
2. What opposition to the project did its backers encounter? According to the author of the pamphlet, what were the opponents' motives?
3. What does the decision of the board of directors to settle the locomotive issue through a competition tell us about the board members' values and beliefs?
4. According to the pamphlet, how will railroad travel transform people's view of the world?
5. According to the pamphlet, how will the railroad affect the prices of goods and the practice of business?

### The Need for a Railway

During the last fifty years, the transit of goods between Liverpool and Manchester has taken place on the Mersey and Irwell Navigation or the Duke of Bridgewater's canal.[1] These, in their day, were great works, . . . but they have ceased to be adequate to the conveyance of goods between this town and Manchester. The quantity now exported daily exceeds *one thousands tons*! and the necessity of a new method of forwarding goods became apparent, when it is known that it sometimes takes as long to send cotton to Manchester from Liverpool as it did from America to the Mersey! Owing to the deficiency of water in summer, the barges cannot carry their usual freights; and from the operation of frost, in winter, the canals are frequently for weeks unnavigable. . . .

The delays and inconvenience of canal conveyance have been long felt by the merchants of Liverpool and Manchester; and as there are always abroad minds in search of new speculations, it was recommended in 1822 to diminish the distance between these two great towns by the means of a Rail-road. . . .

*Source: A Guide to the Liverpool and Manchester Railway with a History of the Work (Manchester: Rockcliff & Duckworth, 1830).*
[1]The Mersey and Irwell Navigation, begun in 1721, involved the construction of eight locks and a number of cuts in the two rivers; this made it possible for small boats to travel between Manchester and the Irish Sea. The longer and broader Bridgewater Canal, which opened in 1761, linked Leigh, a Manchester suburb, and Runcorn, a river port on the Mersey estuary.

## Opposition

To relieve individual proprietors from a dangerous responsibility, and to remove obstacles from the laying down of the road, an Act of Parliament was necessary. A part of the committee, therefore, hastened to London in the February of 1825, to superintend the progress of the proposed bills. . . . [The] measure encountered a decided and powerful opposition from those who have always been enemies to national improvement—monopolists and aristocrats. The proprietors of the Duke of Bridgewater's canal, the Mersey and Irwell Navigation, and the Leeds and Liverpool canal, were in the field, surrounded by all the influence which great wealth communicates. The channel of commerce was too unsightly to be permitted to deface the elegant uniformity of their domains, and they arrogantly thought that sanctity of their estates was to be preferred to the good of the country! . . .

Counsel was heard for and against the measure, and after some months spent in inquiry and arguing, the bill, on the 1st of June, was for the time withdrawn! An undertaking which now commands the wonder and approval of the world, failed to interest the legislature. The reasoning of monopolists was preferred to the evidence of scientific men.

[After a second prospectus was submitted in 1826 it was approved by a vote of 88 to 41.]

## Locomotives

Multifarious were the schemes proposed to the Directors of facilitating Locomotion. Communications were received from all classes of persons, each recommending an improved power, or an improved carriage: from professors of philosophy, down to the humblest mechanic, all were zealous in their proffers [offers] of assistance. . . . Every scheme, which the restless ingenuity or prolific imagination of man could devise, was liberally offered to the Company: the difficulty was to choose and to decide. . . .

Under these circumstances, a premium of £500 was offered for an improved locomotive Engine, which would accord with the provisions of the Act of Parliament one of which was, that it should not smoke. On the 6th of October the trial took place.

The Steam Engines which were entered on the lists to contend for the premium, were the "Novelty," a beautiful machine of a new construction, built by Messrs. Braithwaite and Ericsson, of London; the "Rocket," built by Messrs. Robt. Stephenson[2] and Co., of Newcastle, with a boiler of a new construction, . . . the "Sans Pareil," built by Mr. Timothy Hackworth, of Darlington; and the "Perseverance," by Mr. Burstall, of Leith.

The public are already familiar with the result. . . .

## Estimates of the Benefit of Railway

[The] Liverpool and Manchester Rail-way presents one great object for our admiration, almost unalloyed by any counteracting or painful consideration. We behold, at once, a new theatre of activity and employment presented to an industrious population, with all the indications of health and energy and cheerfulness which flow from such a scene. Or, if we take a wider range, and anticipate the extension of Rail-ways throughout the country, intersecting the island in every direction where the interchange of commodities, or the communication by travelling, will warrant the cost of their establishment; if we look to the construction of only one hundred Rail-ways, equal in extent to the Liverpool and Manchester, comprising a line of three thousand miles, and absorbing a capital of fifty or sixty millions of pounds sterling, what a source of occupation to the labouring community! What a change in the facility of giving employment to capital, and, consequently, in the value of money!

But perhaps the most striking result produced by the completion of this Rail-way, is the sudden and marvellous change which has been effected in our ideas of time and space. Notions which we have

---

[2]Robert, George Stephenson's son, was in charge of the shop that manufactured the locomotives. The Stephenson entry won a prize of £500 and the contract to build the locomotives.

received from our ancestors, and verified by our own experience, are overthrown in a day and a new standard erected, by which to form our ideas for the future. Speed—despatch—distance—are still relative terms, but their meaning has been totally changed within a few months; what was quick, is now slow— what was distant, is now near; and this change in our ideas will not be limited to the environs of Liverpool and Manchester—it will pervade society at large. . . . A transition in our accustomed rate of travelling, from eight or ten miles an hour, to fifteen or twenty . . . , gives a new character to the whole internal trade and commerce of the country. A saving of time is a saving of money. For the purposes of locomotion, about half the number of carriages will suffice, if you go twice the speed; or the aggregate travelling of the country may be doubled, or more than doubled, without any additional expense to the community. The same may be said of the number of waggons for the conveyance of merchandise. The saving of capital, therefore, in this department of business is considerable, from expedition alone. A great part of the inland trade of the country is conducted by travellers; and here, what a revolution in the whole system and detail of business, when the ordinary rate of travelling shall be twenty miles, instead of ten, per hour! The traveller will live double times; by accomplishing a given distance in *five* hours, which used to require *ten*, he will have the other five at his own disposal. The man of business, in Manchester, will breakfast at home—proceed to Liverpool by the Rail-way, transact his business, and return to Manchester before dinner. A hard day's journeying is thus converted into a morning's excursion. . . .

## Science and Industrialization

### 53 • EARL DEAN HOWARD, THE CAUSE AND EFFECT OF THE RECENT INDUSTRIAL PROGRESS IN GERMANY

The technological changes that drove the early Industrial Revolution had little to do with the discoveries of Europe's learned scientists. The inventors who revolutionized the textile industry included a wigmaker, carpenters, a clergyman, a clockmaker, a weaver, and many craftsmen, but only a few university graduates and not one person with formal training in science. George Stephenson, the "Father of Railways" and the foremost designer of locomotives in the early 1800s, was barely literate. Of the two most important contributors to the development of the steam engine, Thomas Newcomen was an ironmonger and lay preacher and James Watt was an instrument maker. The first scientific study of steam engines, Sadi Carnot's *Reflections on the Motive Power of Fire*, was published only in 1824, when thousands of steam engines were already in operation.

By the early 1900s, however, scientific research had become a powerful and essential source of technological innovation for a wide range of industries and a major factor in the West's continued economic expansion. During the nineteenth century, physicists abandoned their traditional focus on astronomy, mechanics, and optics and developed new subfields in electricity, acoustics, magnetism, thermodynamics, radiation, and the behavior of gases. Building on foundations laid in the late 1700s, chemists developed a new nomenclature, theoretical basis, and methodology and achieved literally thousands of important discoveries relating to the analysis and synthesis of compounds, organic chemistry, chemical reactions, and atomic theory. Important changes also took place in the teaching of science and engineering. Science gained a place in the curricula of European and American universities, where original research, not the transmission of inherited knowledge, became the focus. A key figure was Justus von Liebig (1803–1873), whose much-imitated program for training chemists at the University of Giessen included laboratory work, original research, seminars, and colloquia. Many countries underwrote the founding of schools specializing in engineering and other technical subjects.

Of the many ways science transformed technology and industry in the 1800s, several stand out. Research conducted on current electricity between the 1780s and the 1840s gave rise to the telegraph, telephone, electric lights, household appliances, and an industry dedicated to the generation of electricity. The emergence of chemistry resulted in new materials, dyes, fertilizers, and pharmaceuticals; it also led to new methods for producing steel and gunpowder, processing food, and refining petroleum.

As the following excerpt shows, Germany led the way in applying scientific discoveries to manufacturing. Its author is Earl Dean Howard (1876–1956), an American economist. As part of his graduate studies at the University of Chicago, in 1904–05 he attended the University of Berlin, where he completed the research for his thesis, "The Cause and Extent of the Recent Industrial Progress of Germany." It was published as a book in 1907.

## QUESTIONS FOR ANALYSIS

1. What are the concrete signs of Germany's "great progress" in the electrical industry?
2. What other sectors of the German economy would benefit from the growth of the country's electrical industry?
3. According to Howard, why have the Germans become dominant in the chemical industry?

It is in the electrical industry that Germany has made her greatest progress, one of the direct results, no doubt, of her excellent technical schools. In 1880 electricity was commercially employed only in telegraphy, and in 1882 the whole number of persons employed in the industry was too small to be separately enumerated. In 1895 there were 15,000 people engaged in the industry, and the number at the present time is estimated at 50,000. . . . This tremendous and rapid growth . . . was extraordinarily stimulating to other branches, and accounts for not a little of the boom from 1896 to 1900.

One of the principal uses of electricity is in street railways. In 1902 over 100 German cities had electric street railways, with a length of 2200 miles, and representing an investment of a billion dollars. Germany has over one third of all the electric street railways in Europe and over half of the total mileage. Ninety-one per cent of all the electric roads of Europe were built by German firms. The electric roads have not yet begun to compete with

Source: Earl Dean Howard, *The Cause and Effect of the Recent Industrial Progress in Germany* (Boston: Hughton, Mifflin and Company), 48–52.

the steam roads for long-distance traffic, as in the United States.

The six largest electrical companies have an invested capital in stocks and bonds of over $80,000,000, which has increased since 1894 from $16,000,000.

The General Electricity Company has three large factories employing 17,000 men. Their sales for the year 1899–1900 included 16,000 dynamos. . . . Their field includes all Europe, and extends to countries beyond the seas. They have established a branch company, with $2,500,000 capital, to handle their business in Argentina and Chile.

The export of electrical machinery in 1903 was $5,000,000. Great Britain is by far the best customer, taking in that year over twenty-five per cent of the whole export. . . .

In the chemical industry Germany is easily the first nation of the world. This industry affords the best illustration of the recent progress, and reveals more clearly than any others the causes which have made that country industrially great.

This splendid industry is the direct product of German technical education. The beginning was made when Professor Justus V. Liebig founded the first chemical laboratory in 1827, at the University of Giessen. The convincing success of this experiment led the several state governments to found and maintain advanced schools for scientific study. These technical schools and university laboratories may be regarded as the corner-stone of the nation's industrial greatness, and the whole foundation of its supremacy in the chemical industry. . . .

The most interesting branch of the chemical industry is the manufacture of dye-stuffs from coal-tar. It is in this field that the most recent and brilliant achievements of the German chemists have been won. In 1860 all the dyes used were organic, and Germany was almost entirely dependent on foreign countries for her supply. The annual import of dyes at that time cost the country 50,000,000 marks ($12,150,000). By 1900 the conditions had so changed that the import had sunk to almost nothing, and the export, on the other hand, had risen to 100,000,000 marks ($24,300,000). Almost without exception, the discovery and production of coal-tar dyes has remained in the hands of the Germans.

The raw material used is the bi-product of gas and coke manufacture, which was formerly a worse than useless waste. Now Germany not only utilizes all the coal-tar produced in that country, but imports large quantities . . . from Great Britain, Belgium, and Austria-Hungary. All this import and more is sold back to these countries again, multiplied many times in value, in the shape of dyes.

Four fifths of all the world's products of dyestuffs, as well as a large proportion of the medical preparations derived from coal-tar, are made in Germany. . . .

For centuries indigo [a blue colored dye derived from plants] had been one of the great items of import to the textile-producing countries. In 1892 the German Empire imported 3,556,740 pounds of natural or vegetable indigo, valued at $4,450,000. The discovery of a process for marking artificial indigo, made by a Munich chemist, Dr. Baeyer,[1] in 1897, has completely revolutionized this trade, for in 1902 the import of vegetable indigo had decreased to 833,000 pounds, while the export of artificial indigo amounted to 18,308,000 pounds in 1903.

Dr. Baeyer's discovery, which had such an important effect on a great industry, consisted of a process for the making of artificial indigo, called alizarene, from a coal-tar product, anthracene. As the result of this one discovery, Germany is not only relieved from the necessity of importing this dye-stuff at a great expense, but she is also able to realize from its export a very considerable national profit.

---

[1]Adolf von Baeyern (1835–1917) was a distinguished University of Munich chemist and winner of the Nobel Prize in 1905.

## GERMANY'S LARGEST CHEMICALS COMPANIES

| NAME OF COMPANY | NO. OF CHEMISTS / ENGINEERS | WORKMEN |
|---|---|---|
| CORPORATION FOR ANILINE PRODUCTION | 55 CHEMISTS 10 ENGINEERS 21 "EXPERTS" | 1550 |
| BADEN ANILINE AND SODA COMPANY | 148 CHEMISTS 75 ENGINEERS | 6300 |
| LEOPOLD CASSELLA AND COMPANY | 80 CHEMISTS | 1800 |
| BAYER & COMPANY DYE FACTORY | 145 CHEMISTS 27 ENGINEERS | 4200 |
| LUCIUS AND BRUNIG DYE WORKS | 129 CHEMISTS 36 ENGINEERS | 3500 |
| KALLE & COMPANY | 128 CHEMISITS | 500 |
| SIEGLE & COMPANY | 44 CHEMISTS | 106 |

**Multiple Voices V**

# Working Class and Middle Class in Nineteenth-Century Europe

## BACKGROUND

Poverty had always existed in Europe's preindustrial cities, where an unskilled, uneducated, and underemployed underclass was a permanent feature of urban life. It was even more pervasive in the countryside, where agricultural laborers and peasants, even the most industrious, were just one crop failure away from financial catastrophe and famine. Local governments, churches, and individual philanthropists provided support for the poor, but only a few thinkers seriously analyzed its causes or proposed ways to alleviate it. Most agreed that poverty was an unfortunate but inevitable aspect of the human condition—an inscrutable part of God's plan. Such attitudes began to change in the eighteenth century, when rural poverty worsened in many parts of Europe. One of the most famous analyses of poverty was provided at the very end of the century by the Englishman Thomas Malthus, whose *Essay on the Principle of Population* (1798) argued that poverty was the inevitable result of unbridled population growth, especially among the poor themselves.

During the nineteenth century, poverty increasingly became an urban problem. As a result of Europe's overall population growth, rural-to-urban migration, and the lure of jobs in factories and mines, old cities doubled or even tripled in population, and small villages were transformed into major urban centers. Within these cities, to the ranks of the traditional poor—invalids, widows, abandoned mothers, the un-employed, orphans, the sick, and the aged—were added a new "working class," made up of factory workers whose lives were marked by low wages, substandard housing, poor diet, harsh working conditions, and insecure employment.

The main beneficiaries of urbanization and industrialization were members of the middle class. Consisting of merchants, lawyers, bankers, doctors, skilled artisans, and shopkeepers in preindustrial Europe, the middle class expanded in the nineteenth century to include industrialists, managers, government officials, white-collar work-ers, and skilled professionals in fields such as engineering, architecture, account-ing, the sciences, and higher education. The values, interests, and ambitions of these groups increasingly set the tone for nineteenth-century Europe. Many members of the middle class provided leadership for movements on behalf of women's rights, public education, the abolition of slavery, prison reform, temperance, and other causes, but the class as a whole was divided on the issue of what, if anything, should be done to alleviate urban poverty and improve the lot of the workers. Insights into their views, along with those of workers and their sympathizers, are provided in the sources that follow.

## THE SOURCES

Our first source is taken from *The Manufacturing Population of Britain: Its Moral, So-cial, and Physical Condition* by Peter Gaskell (1806–1841), a physician who practiced in the industrial city of Manchester. Gaskell's book, published in 1833, appeared at a time when the English people were just beginning to appreciate how profoundly industrialization was changing their society. Drawing on his personal experiences as a physician and a wealth of statistical material, he presents a gloomy picture of working-class life.

Our second selection shows that alarm over conditions of the working poor was not limited to England. It is an excerpt from a pamphlet published in 1845 by Alexander Schneer, a minor government official, titled *Living Conditions of the Working Class in Breslau*. It is based on interviews with local physicians and overseers of the poor in Breslau, one of Germany's largest cities until it was incorporated into Poland after World War II.

Our third selection contains excerpts from two works by Samuel Smiles (1812–1904), a Scottish biographer, journalist, and businessman, who, more than any other writer, expressed the hopes, fears, and values of the middle class. He wrote biographies, his-tories, and travel books but gained worldwide fame through his inspirational books on character-building. With an upbeat message that hard work, discipline, and high moral standards guaranteed worldly success, his bestseller *Self Help* (1859) was followed by *Character* (1871), *Thrift* (1875), and *Duty* (1880). Our first excerpt, "Self-Help and Individualism," comes from *Self Help*; "Faults of the Poor" is from *Thrift*.

Our final selections were written later in the century. Both suggest that by then many workers had improved standards of living as a result of higher wages, better housing, sanitation improvements, public education, and government-subsidized systems of national health insurance. The fourth excerpt is from *An Essay on the Distribution of Wealth*, published in 1881 by a distinguished French economist, Pierre-Paul Leroy Beaulieu (1843–1916). Beaulieu, who had just been appointed to the chair of political economy at the prestigious Collège de France, sought to disprove the socialists' argument that industrialization impoverished the workers. The fifth selection is from *Letters from Berlin* (1891), a description of the lives of Berlin working-class families in the late 1880s based on interviews by the German journalist Otto von Leixner.

## QUESTIONS FOR ANALYSIS

1. Based on the descriptions of working-class life provided by the first two sources, what can be learned about working conditions in the mills and coal mines?
2. What may be learned or inferred about the domestic lives of working-class families?
3. Based on von Leixner's observations and Beaulieu's arguments, how does the situation of the late-nineteenth-century Berlin family and the average French laborer differ from that of the families described by Gaskell and Schneer? What may explain these differences?
4. Samuel Smiles directly addresses the issue of the causes of working-class poverty and suggests ways it might be alleviated. Gaskell, Schneer, and von Leixner also address the issue, although somewhat indirectly. In what ways do they agree and disagree?
5. Smiles opposes government initiatives to regulate working conditions in the mills and mines and to otherwise improve the lot of the poor. What are his reasons for opposing such measures?

---

## 1 • Peter Gaskell, *The Manufacturing Population of England: Its Moral, Social, and Physical Condition*

### Child Labor

The crowding together . . . of the young of both sexes in factories, is a prolific source of moral delinquency. The stimulus of a heated atmosphere, the contact of opposite sexes, the example of lasciviousness upon the animal passions—all have conspired to produce a very early development of sexual appetencies [longings]. Indeed, in this respect, the female population engaged in manufactures, approximates very closely to that found in tropical climates. . . . Unfortunately no regard, however slight, is paid to these matters by the majority of mill owners. A certain number of hands are required to superintend the labours of their untiring engine, with its complement of looms, for a certain number of hours, and for a certain amount of wages: so long as these are attained, he looks no farther. He considers the human beings who crowd his mill, from five o'clock in the morning to seven o'clock in the evening, but as so many accessories to his machinery, destined to produce a certain and well-known

*Source:* Peter Gaskell, *The Manufacturing Population of England: Its Moral, Social, and Physical Condition* (London: Baldwin and Cradock, 1833), pp. 18, 72, 109–110, 134–135, 162, and 163.

quantity of work, at the lowest possible outlay of capital. To him their passions, habits, or crimes, are as little interesting, as if they bore no relation to the errors of a system, of which he was a member and supporter. . . .

## Workers' Diet

The staple diet of the manufacturing population is potatoes and wheaten bread, washed down by tea or coffee. Milk is but little used. Meal is to some extent, either baked into cakes or boiled up with water, making a porridge at once nutritious, easy of digestion, and readily available. Animal food [meat] forms a very small part of their diet, and that which is eaten is often of an inferior quality. . . . Fish is bought to some extent, and even this not till it has undergone slight decomposition, having been first exposed in the markets, and, being unsalable, is then hawked about the back streets and alleys, where it is disposed of for a mere trifle. Eggs, too, form some portion of the operatives' diet. The staple, however, is tea and bread. . . . The plainness and want of solidity and proper stimulus in the food of the labourer, is attended by some other evils, bearing strongly upon his domestic habits. His labour is continued so uninterruptedly, that whether it is morning, or noon, or night, he leaves the mill or work-shop, and devours his watery meal with feelings of such mental depression and bodily exhaustion that he eagerly swallows a stimulus in the shape of spirits or beer, to supply by its temporary exciting influence the want of proper food on the one hand, and of due relaxation on the other. This habit of dram-drinking, so fatal in its consequences, is of the most extensive prevalence.

## Housing

In those divisions of the manufacturing towns occupied by the lower classes of inhabitants . . . the houses are of the most flimsy and imperfect structure. Tenanted by the week by an improvident and changeable set of beings, the owners seldom lay out any money upon them, and seem indeed only anxious that they should be tenantable at all, long enough to reimburse them for the first outlay. Hence, in a very few years they become ruinous to a degree. One of the circumstances in which they are especially defective, is that of drainage and waterclosets [a room with a toilet]; most of these houses are either totally undrained, or only very partially so. The whole of the washings and filth consequently are thrown into the front or back street, which being often unpaved and cut up into deep ruts, allows them to collect into stinking and stagnant pools, while fifty, or more even than that number, having only a single convenience common to them all, it is in a very short time completely choked up with excrement. Most of these houses have cellars beneath them, occupied if it is possible to find a lower class by a still lower class than those living above them. It would appear that upwards of 20,000 individuals live in cellars in Manchester alone.

## Physical Condition of the Workers

Any man who has stood at twelve o'clock at the single narrow door-way, which serves as the place of exit for the hands employed in the great cotton-mills, must acknowledge, that an uglier set of men and women, of boys and girls, . . . it would be impossible to congregate in smaller compass. Their complexion is sallow and pallid with a peculiar flatness of feature. . . . Their stature below the average height . . . being five feet six inches. Their limbs slender, and splaying badly and ungracefully. A very general bowing of the legs. Great numbers of girls and women walking lamely or awkwardly, with raised chests and spinal flexures. . . . Hair thin and straight; many of the men having but little beard, and that in patches of a few hairs. . . . A spiritless and dejected air . . . an appearance, taken as a whole, giving the world but "little assurance of man," or if so, "most sadly cheated of his fair proportions."

## 2 • Alexander Schneer, Living Conditions of the Working Class in Breslau

The following replies may provide answers about the nature of the living quarters, the cleanliness, the state of health as well as the state of morals of the classes under discussion.

**QUESTION:** What is the condition of the living quarters of the class of factory workers, day laborers and journeymen?

**REPLY OF THE CITY POOR DOCTOR, DR BLUEMNER:** It is in the highest degree miserable. . . . Many rooms are more like pigsties than quarters for human beings. The apartments in the city are, if possible, even worse than those in the suburbs. . . . The so-called staircase is generally completely in the dark. It is also so decrepit that the whole building shakes with every firm footstep; the rooms themselves are small and so low that it is hardly possible to stand upright, the floor is on a slope, since usually part of the house has to be supported by struts. The windows close badly, the stoves are so bad that they hardly give any heat but plenty of smoke in the room. Water runs down the doors and walls. The ground-floor dwellings are usually half underground. . . .

**QUESTION:** What is your usual experience regarding the cleanliness of these classes?

**DR BLUEMNER:** Bad! Mother has to go out to work, and can therefore pay little attention to the domestic economy [housekeeping], and even if she makes an effort, she lacks time and means. A typical woman of this kind has four children, of whom she is still suckling one, she has to look after the whole household, to take food to her husband at work, perhaps a quarter of a mile away . . . she therefore has no time for cleaning and then it is such a small hole inhabited by so many people. The children are left to themselves, crawl about the floor or in the streets, and are always dirty; they lack the necessary clothing to change more often, and there is no time or money to wash these frequently. . . .

**QUESTION:** What is the state of health among the lower classes?

**DR BLUEMNER:** Since these classes are much more exposed to diseases, they usually are the first to be attacked by epidemic and sporadic disorders. Chronic rheumatism is a common illness, since they are constantly subject to colds. In addition, we find hernia with men, diseases of the reproductive organs with women because they have to start work only a few days after childbirth. Children mostly suffer from scrofula, which is almost general.

**DR NEUMANN:** . . . The very frequent incidence of anemia among girls employed in factories deserves special mention. The hard work, the crowding of many individuals into closed rooms during their period of development, in which much exercise in the fresh air, plenty of sleep and only moderate exertion are most necessary, are sufficient explanation of this disease.

*Source:* From S. Pollard and C. Holmes, *Documents of European Economic History*, Vol. 1 (London: Edward Arnold, 1968), pp. 497–499.

## 3 • Samuel Smiles, Self Help and Thrift

### The Roots of Poverty (*Self Help*)

Whatever is done *for* men or classes, takes away the stimulus and necessity of doing for themselves; and where men are subjected to over-guidance and over-government, the inevitable tendency is to render them comparatively helpless.

Even the best institutions can give a man no active help. Perhaps the most they can do is to

*Source:* Samuel Smiles, *Self Help* (London: John Murray, 1859) and *Thrift* (London: John Murray, 1875).

leave him free to develop himself and improve his individual condition. But in all times men have been prone to believe that their happiness and well-being were to be secured by means of institutions rather than by their own conduct. . . . Laws, wisely administered, will secure men in the enjoyment of the fruits of their labor, whether of mind or body, at a comparatively small personal sacrifice; but no laws, however stringent, can make the idle industrious, the thriftless provident, or the drunken sober. Such reforms can only be effected by means of individual action, economy, and self-denial; by better habits, rather than by greater rights. . . .

What we are accustomed to decry as great social evils, will for the most part be found to be but the outgrowth of man's own perverted life; and though we may endeavor to cut them down and extirpate them by means of Law, they will only spring up again with fresh luxuriance in some other form unless the conditions of personal life and character are radically improved. If this view be correct, then it follows that the highest patriotism and philanthropy consist, not so much in altering laws and modifying institutions as in helping and stimulating men to elevate and improve themselves by their own free and independent individual action.

## Faults of the Poor *(Thrift)*

England is one of the richest countries in the world. Our merchants are enterprizing, our manufacturers are industrious, our labourers are hardworking. There is an accumulation of wealth in the country to which past times can offer no parallel. There never was more food in the empire; there never was more money. There is no end to our manufacturing productions, for the steam-engine never tires. And yet, notwithstanding all this wealth, there is an enormous mass of poverty.

Parliamentary reports have revealed to us the miseries endured by certain portions of our working population. They have described the people employed in factories, workshops, mines, and brickfields, as well as in the pursuits of country life. We have tried to grapple with the evils of their condition by legislation, but it seems to mock us. Those who sink into poverty are fed, but they remain paupers. Those who feed them, feel no compassion; and those who are fed, return no gratitude. . . .

With respect to the poorer classes,—what has become of them in the midst of our so-called civilization? . . . They work, eat, drink, and sleep: that constitutes their life. They think nothing of providing for tomorrow, or for next week, or for next year. They abandon themselves to their sensual appetites; and make no provision for the future. The thought of adversity, or of coming sorrow, or of the helplessness that comes with years and sickness, never crosses their minds. In these respects, they resemble the savage tribes, who know no better, and do no worse. Like the North American Indians, they debase themselves by the vices which accompany civilization, but make no use whatever of its benefits and advantages. . . .

This habitual improvidence—though of course there are many admirable exceptions—is the real cause of the social degradation of the artisan. This too is the prolific source of social misery. But the misery is entirely the result of human ignorance and self-indulgence. For though the Creator has ordained poverty, the poor are not necessarily, nor as a matter of fact, the miserable. Misery is the result of moral causes,—most commonly of individual vice and improvidence. . . .

All this may seem very hopeless; yet it is not entirely so. The large earnings of the working classes is an important point to start with. The gradual diffusion of education will help them to use, and not abuse, their means of comfortable living. The more extended knowledge of the uses of economy, frugality, and thrift, will help them to spend their lives more soberly, virtuously, and religiously. . . . Social improvement is always very slow. . . . It requires the lapse of generations before its effect can be so much as discerned; for a generation is but as a day in the history of civilization. . . .

### 4 • Pierre-Paul Leroy Beaulieu, *An Essay on the Distribution of Wealth*

Is the worker of today more weighed down by his work than before? His more substantial and varied diet, his cleaner and more spacious dwelling place; his more comfortable and admirable clothing and furnishings; his insurance against sickness and even old age; his greater savings . . . are these benefits all purchased by more time spent at work, by a sacrifice of his freedom and time spent relaxing, pursuing his hobbies, and in the company of his family? . . . The factual evidence enables us to give a definite answer. The work-day has been reduced to a level that makes it more humane. . . . Workers [formerly] were completely dominated by their work, from daybreak until they went home to bed, and were allowed only a few moments of rest in the course of the day. . . . Who would be so foolish to declare that the situation is still the same today? . . . Thirty or forty years ago a workday of 14 or 15 hours was not unusual both for domestic and factory industry. Nowadays the duration of work is not more than 12 effective hours, and even that is too much. French law has fixed it at this level; Swiss law has reduced it to eleven hours; in England it is down to nine and a half hours; in Paris and in all the major cities in innumerable occupations it does not exceed ten; in mines it is generally below this. . . . Thus out of 24 hours in the day the worker has thirteen for his own needs, and if we exclude time for sleep and meals, he has three or four hours to spend on his personal affairs, for family life, amusements, conversation, and reading, in addition to having the whole of Sunday free. This is certainly not what is sometimes called slavery.

The facts that we have assembled demonstrate with irrefutable evidence that all the social classes of the nation have shared in general progress, and that the working class has especially benefited in a three-fold sense of an improvement in their material well-being, greater security, and the growth of leisure. It may be true that the wealthy are becoming richer every day; but it can be stated now that it is false to say that the poor are becoming poorer. Nonetheless the partial and gradual improvements we describe do not touch the heart of those who have made themselves apostles of popular demands [a reference to socialists]. It is with arrogant disdain that these men speak of progress which they term as trivial and insignificant. They do not regard poverty as an absolute quality but rather as a relation between the standard of living of an individual and the standard of living of other members of society. Poverty is no longer the struggle to have the means to stave off hunger, cold, and illness; poverty is the condition of any man who cannot get for himself all the pleasures enjoyed by his fellows. Thus a laborer who is well fed, well clothed, with a good place to live, who has moreover, significant bank deposits and investments, who takes the train on Sundays or Mondays to spend a day in the country, returning to a balcony seat in a popular theater, declares himself to be poor because he does not have a town mansion, servants, a carriage, horses, or a loge in the best theater.

*Essai sur la repartition des richesse et sur le tendance â une moindre inégalité des conditions* (Paris: Guillaumin & Co., 1881), pp. 42–44. trans. by J. Overfield.

### 5 • Otto von Leixner, Letters from Berlin

As is the case with other social classes, there also exists among workers gradations in income from "master" and foreman to the young apprentice; and even among the former are differences according to various branches of industry. But the most fundamental difference is in moral character. If

*Source*: Otto von Leixner, *Soziale Briefe aus Berlin* (Berlin: F. Pfeilstucker, 1891), trans. by J. Overfield.

the husband is sober and decent, the wife frugal and hard-working, then a small salary suffices. If these characteristics are lacking, then even a larger salary is inadequate. . . . To prove this, I refer to my visits to families. . . .

The first household belongs to a relatively well-paid worker. He is employed as a molder in a bronze ware workshop, and is a hard-working, respectable man, and a worthy spouse and father. . . . He hardly attends political meetings, the tavern very rarely. His wife, who previously was a servant girl, is, despite her infirmities, very industrious and thrifty. Their apartment consists of a rather sizable room, with an attached kitchen. Although the husband, wife, and two children live and sleep here, everything is meticulously clean. Colorful calico curtains hang on the two windows, and plants are growing on the window sills. Two beds and a simple sleeping sofa for the children occupy one long wall; the others are taken up by a cupboard, wardrobe, and wash-stand. A table and chairs complete the furnishings.

The average income is 1700 marks.[1] 259 marks must be paid for rent. The small apartments are expensive, despite their deficiencies, because of high demand. . . . When the molder is paid on Saturday, he puts aside a part for the monthly rent. The wife receives 18 marks for household costs per week, in other words, 2.57 marks per day or 64 pfennig for each person; from this the bill for lighting must be paid. The husband pays for heating, specifically in the following manner: in winter, in other words for five months, 20 small coal briquettes are purchased (6 marks per 100) and a few pieces of kindling wood; they have to make do with this. When needed, they sit by the cookstove in the kitchen. . . .

Their daily food consumption is instructive. The following sketch is an average, and the menu is not always the same. The use of dried peas and lentils, potatoes, flour, bread, and milk is high. Meat products, except for some cheap sausage, is mostly chopped beef or lungs, in the form of meatballs or meatloaf. . . . To plan ahead for Sunday and holidays, the family cuts back on workdays. . . .

. . . Not even the smallest item is purchased on credit. This is a prime requirement if the small household is to remain on a sound footing. When larger expenses are necessary, then each week a partial amount is put aside, so that the expense can be paid for.

The husband takes coffee with him in the morning in a tin container, and in the evening and at midday he drinks at the most three glasses of beer, with each costing 10 pfennig (he hardly ever drinks anything stronger). On weekdays he smokes two cigars, on Sundays, three, at three pfennig each. He goes to the tavern perhaps once a week, but when he does, he is home by 10:30. . . .

. . . A glance at expenditures shows how much thriftiness is needed not to exceed the amount of income. . . . Amusements which cost money are rare. They consist of excursions to the zoo, where they take a lunch-basket, or to a country park. That is it. Very rarely, once every several years, they go to a cheap vaudeville theater. . . . The husband makes do; he borrows books from the public library and reads them in the evening if he is not too tired; the wife is satisfied with serialized novels and local news in the daily press, or she chats with neighbors after the children have gone to sleep.

So long as things remain on even keel, then a better paid worker, if he lives decently, can get by. . . . But if the husband and wife are frivolous, or irresponsible, then disaster begins. . . .

---

[1]The basic unit of the German currency. One mark equals 100 pfennig.

# New Perspectives on Humanity and Society

In 1873, the English naturalist Charles Darwin wrote a letter to the German philosopher and revolutionary Karl Marx in which he stated, "I believe we both earnestly desire the extension of human knowledge; and this in the long run is sure to add to the happiness of mankind." Whether Marx and Darwin added to human happiness is difficult to judge, but there is no doubting their enormous influence. Although nineteenth-century Europe produced more scientists, philosophers, artists, composers, novelists, poets, historians, and social theorists than ever before, and although these intellectuals produced an abundance of provocative new ideas, none matched the wide-ranging impact of Marx and Darwin.

Darwin (1809–1882) did not invent the theory of evolution. Several Europeans before him had theorized that species were mutable and that all plants and animals, including humans, evolved. Darwin's contributions were the wealth of data he marshaled to support the idea of evolution and his theory that evolution took place as a result of natural selection, not God's plan. Because Darwin cast doubt on the biblical creation story, in which God creates time, space, and the universe, including the first humans, in six days, his ideas rekindled debates about the relationship of science and religion. He also forced intellectuals to re-examine long-accepted notions about nature, morality, and, of course, humanity itself. In addition, Darwinism had important political ramifications: Imperialists, free traders, nationalists, and fascists all used (or misused) Darwinism to bolster their beliefs.

Just as Darwin was not the first proponent of evolution, Marx was not the first socialist. The first "utopian" socialists were early-nineteenth-century visionaries whose dreams of equality and justice lacked philosophical rigor and practical political sense. Marx, an academically trained philosopher knowledgeable in history, economics, and science, sought to establish an intellectual foundation for *scientific* socialism and to describe the mechanism by which communism would replace capitalism. Through class conflict, in a process Marx referred to as the *dialectic,* society developed through stages until it reached the age of industrial capitalism, when the oppressor class, the middle class or bourgeoisie, clashes with exploited factory workers, the proletariat. The proletariat will triumph, argues Marx, because capitalism, an intrinsically flawed system, will create the conditions for the proletarian revolution, the end of the dialectic, and a classless society.

Even dedicated disciples of Marx and Darwin concede that much of what they wrote was incomplete, incorrect, or hypothetical. Well before the collapse of most of the world's Marxist governments in the late twentieth century, critics could point to many ways in which Marx misjudged capitalism, workers' attitudes, and the causes of revolution. Opponents of Darwinism contend that its theories are unprovable and that natural selection cannot explain the miraculous complexity of living things.

Nonetheless, Darwin and Marx remain a part of that small group of nineteenth-century European thinkers whose work has left an indelible mark on history.

# The Marxist Critique of Industrial Capitalism

## 54 • KARL MARX AND FRIEDRICH ENGELS, THE COMMUNIST MANIFESTO

Karl Marx (1818–1883) was born in Trier, a city in western Germany that had been assigned to Prussia at the Congress of Vienna in 1815. Marx's parents were Jewish, but his father had become a Lutheran so he could continue his career as a lawyer. Young Marx studied law at the University of Bonn before enrolling at the University of Berlin, where he was influenced by the thought of the famous philosopher G. W. F. Hegel (1770–1831), especially his idea of the dialectic—the theory that history unfolds toward a specific goal in a process driven by the clash and resolution of antagonistic forces. After losing his job as a journalist for a Cologne newspaper because of his political views, in 1844 Marx moved to Paris, where he argued about capitalism and revolution with other radicals and continued his studies of economics and history. He also made the acquaintance of another German, Friedrich Engels (1820–1895), an ardent critic of capitalism despite the fortune he amassed from managing a textile mill in Manchester, England. In 1847, Marx and Engels joined the Communist League, a revolutionary society dominated by German political exiles in France and England. In 1848, a year of revolution in Europe, the two men wrote *The Communist Manifesto* to publicize the League's program. It became the most widely read socialist tract in history.

After 1848, Marx and Engels remained friends, with Engels giving Marx money so Marx could continue his writing and political activities while living in London. Both men continued to write on behalf of socialism, but Marx's works, especially his masterpiece, *Das Kapital* (*Capitalism*), assumed the far greater role in the history of socialism. Furthermore, his views of history, human behavior, and social conflict have influenced not only politics but also philosophy, religion, literature, and all the social sciences.

### QUESTIONS FOR ANALYSIS

1. How do Marx and Engels define class, and what do they mean by the "class struggle"?
2. According to Marx and Engels, how does the class struggle in nineteenth-century Europe differ from class struggles in previous eras?
3. According to Marx and Engels, what are the characteristics of the bourgeoisie?
4. Marx and Engels believe that bourgeois society is doomed and that the bourgeoisie will bring about their own destruction. Why?
5. The authors dismiss the importance of ideas as a force in human affairs. On what grounds? Ultimately, what is the cause of historical change in their view?
6. What may explain the popularity and influence of *The Communist Manifesto* among workers and those who sympathized with their plight?

## I. The Bourgeoisie and Proletariat

The history of all hitherto existing society is the history of class struggles.

Freeman and slave, patrician and plebeian, lord and serf, guild-master and journeyman, in a word, oppressor and oppressed, stood in constant opposition to one another, carried on an uninterrupted, now hidden, now open fight, a fight that each time ended, either in a revolutionary reconstitution of society at large, or in the common ruin of the contending classes. . . .

Our epoch, the epoch of the bourgeoisie, possesses, however, this distinctive feature: It has simplified the class antagonisms. Society as a whole is more and more splitting up into two great hostile camps, into two great classes directly facing each other—bourgeoisie and proletariat.

From the serfs of the Middle Ages sprang the chartered burghers of the earliest towns. From these burgesses the first elements of the bourgeoisie were developed.

The discovery of America, the rounding of the Cape, opened up fresh ground for the rising bourgeoisie. The East-Indian and Chinese markets, the colonization of America, trade with the colonies, the increase in the means of exchange and in commodities generally, gave to commerce, to navigation, to industry, an impulse never before known, and thereby, to the revolutionary element in the tottering feudal society, a rapid development.

The feudal system of industry, in which industrial production was monopolized by closed guilds, now no longer sufficed for the growing wants of the new markets. The manufacturing system took its place. The guild-masters were pushed aside by the manufacturing middle class; division of labor between the different corporate guilds vanished in the face of division of labor in each single workshop.

Meantime the markets kept ever growing, the demand ever rising. Even manufacture[1] no longer sufficed. Thereupon, steam and machinery revolutionized industrial production. The place of manufacture was taken by the giant, modern industry, the place of the industrial middle class by industrial millionaires, the leaders of whole industrial armies, the modern bourgeois. . . .

The bourgeoisie, wherever it has got the upper hand, has put an end to all feudal, patriarchal, idyllic relations. It has pitilessly torn asunder the motley feudal ties that bound man to his "natural superiors," and has left no other nexus between man and man than naked self-interest, than callous "cash payment." . . . In one word, for exploitation, veiled by religious and political illusions, it has substituted naked, shameless, direct, brutal exploitation. . . .

We see then: the means of production and of exchange, on whose foundation the bourgeoisie built itself up, were generated in feudal society. At a certain stage in the development of these means of production and of exchange, the conditions under which feudal society produced and exchanged, the feudal organization of agriculture and manufacturing industry . . . became no longer compatible with the already developed productive forces; they became so many fetters. They had to be burst asunder; they were burst asunder. . . .

A similar movement is going on before our own eyes. Modern bourgeois society with its relations of production, of exchange and of property, a society that has conjured up such gigantic means of production and of exchange, is like the sorcerer who is no longer able to control the powers of the nether world whom he has called up by his spells. . . . It is enough to mention the commercial crises that by their periodical return put the existence of the

*Source*: Karl Marx and Friedrich Engels, *The Manifesto of the Communist Party*, authorized English trans. by Samuel Moore (London: W. Reeves, 1888).

[1]"Manufacture" is used here in the sense of making goods by hand rather than machines.

entire bourgeois society on its trial, each time more threateningly. In these crises a great part not only of the existing products, but also of the previously created productive forces, are periodically destroyed. In these crises there breaks out an epidemic that, in all earlier epochs, would have seemed an absurdity—the epidemic of overproduction.

And how does the bourgeoisie get over these crises? On the one hand, by enforced destruction of a mass of productive forces; on the other, by the conquest of new markets, and by the more thorough exploitation of the old ones. That is to say, by paving the way for more extensive and more destructive crises, and by diminishing the means whereby crises are prevented.

The weapons with which the bourgeoisie felled feudalism to the ground are now turned against the bourgeoisie itself. But not only has the bourgeoisie forged the weapons that bring death to itself; it has also called into existence the men who are to wield those weapons—the modern working class—the proletarians. . . . Masses of laborers, crowded into the factory, are organized like soldiers. As privates of the industrial army they are placed under the command of a perfect hierarchy of officers and sergeants. Not only are they slaves of the bourgeois class, and of the bourgeois state; they are daily and hourly enslaved by the machine, by the overseer, and, above all, by the individual bourgeois manufacturer himself. . . .

The lower strata of the middle class—the small tradespeople, shopkeepers, and retired tradesmen generally, the handicraftsmen and peasants—all these sink gradually into the proletariat, partly because their diminutive capital does not suffice for the scale on which modern industry is carried on, . . . partly because their specialized skill is rendered worthless by new methods of production. Thus the proletariat is recruited from all classes of the population.

But with the development of industry the proletariat not only increases in number; it becomes concentrated in greater masses, its strength grows, and it feels that strength more. The various interests and conditions of life within the ranks of the proletariat are more and more equalized, in proportion as machinery obliterates all distinctions of labor, and nearly everywhere reduces wages to the same low level. The growing competition among the bourgeois, and the resulting commercial crises, make the wages of the workers ever more fluctuating. The unceasing improvement of machinery . . . makes their livelihood more and more precarious; the collisions between individual workmen and individual bourgeois take more and more the character of collisions between two classes. Thereupon the workers begin to form combinations (trade unions) against the bourgeois. . . . Here and there the contest breaks out into riots.

Now and then the workers are victorious, but only for a time. The real fruit of their battle lies, not in the immediate result, but in the ever expanding union of the workers. This union is helped on by the improved means of communication that are created by modern industry, and that place the workers of different localities in contact with one another. It was just this contact that was needed to centralize the numerous local struggles, all of the same character, into one national struggle between classes. . . .

Finally, in times when the class struggle nears the decisive hour, the process of dissolution going on within the ruling class, in fact within the whole range of old society, assumes such a violent, glaring character, that a small section of the ruling class cuts itself adrift, and joins the revolutionary class, the class that holds the future in its hands. Just as, therefore, at an earlier period, a section of the nobility went over to the bourgeoisie, so now a portion of the bourgeoisie goes over to the proletariat, and in particular, a portion of the bourgeois ideologists, who have raised themselves to the level of comprehending theoretically the historical movement as a whole.

## II. Proletarians and Communists

The distinguishing feature of communism is not the abolition of property generally, but the abolition of bourgeois property. But modern bourgeois private property is the final and most complete expression of the system of producing and appropriating products that is based on class antagonisms, on the exploitation of the many by the few.

In this sense, the theory of the Communists may be summed up in the single sentence: Abolition of private property. . . .

You are horrified at our intending to do away with private property. But in your existing society, private property is already done away with for nine-tenths of its population; its existence for the few is solely due to its nonexistence in the hands of those nine-tenths. . . .

The Communists are further reproached with desiring to abolish countries and nationality. The working men have no country. We cannot take from them what they have not got. . . .

National differences and antagonism between peoples are daily more and more vanishing, owing to the development of the bourgeoisie, to freedom of commerce, to the world market, to uniformity in the mode of production and in the conditions of life corresponding thereto.

The supremacy of the proletariat will cause them to vanish still faster. United action of the leading civilized countries at least, is one of the first conditions for the emancipation of the proletariat.

. . . In proportion as the antagonism between classes within the nation vanishes, the hostility of one nation to another will come to an end. . . .

We have seen above that the first step in the revolution by the working class is to raise the proletariat to the position of ruling class, to win the battle for democracy.

The proletariat will use its political supremacy to wrest, by degrees, all capital from the bourgeoisie, to centralize all instruments of production in the hands of the State, i.e., of the proletariat organized as the ruling class; and to increase the total of productive forces as rapidly as possible.

Of course, in the beginning, this cannot be effected except by means of despotic inroads on the rights of property, and on the conditions of bourgeois production; by means of measures which . . . are unavoidable as a means of entirely revolutionizing the mode of production.

These measures will of course be different in different countries.

Nevertheless, in the most advanced countries, the following will be pretty generally applicable.

1. Abolition of property in land and application of all rents of land to public purposes.
2. A heavy progressive or graduated income tax.
3. Abolition of all right of inheritance.
4. Confiscation of the property of all emigrants and rebels.[2]
5. Centralization of credit in the hands of the State, by means of a national bank with State capital and an exclusive monopoly.
6. Centralization of the means of communication and transport in the hands of the State.
7. Extension of the number of State factories and instruments of production: the bringing into cultivation of waste lands, and the improvement of the soil generally in accordance with a common plan.
8. Equal obligation of all to work. Establishment of industrial armies, especially for agriculture.
9. Combination of agriculture with manufacturing industries; gradual abolition of the

---

[2]Presumably individuals who resist the new regime or flee during the revolution.

distinction between town and country, by a more equable distribution of the population over the country.

10. Free education for all children in public schools. Abolition of children's factory labor in its present form. . . .

When, in the course of development, class distinctions have disappeared, and all production has been concentrated in the hands of a vast association of the whole nation, the public power will lose its political character. . . . If, by means of a revolution, [the proletariat] makes itself the ruling class, and as such sweeps away by force the old conditions of production, then it will, along with these conditions, have swept away the conditions for the existence of class antagonisms and of classes generally, and will thereby have abolished its own supremacy as a class. . . .

The Communists disdain to conceal their views and aims. They openly declare that their ends can be attained only by the forcible overthrow of all existing social conditions. Let the ruling classes tremble at a Communist revolution. In it the proletarians have nothing to lose but their chains. They have a world to win.

WORKING MEN OF ALL COUNTRIES, UNITE!

# The Principles of Darwinism

## 55 • CHARLES DARWIN, ON THE ORIGIN OF SPECIES AND THE DESCENT OF MAN

After pursuing his university education at Edinburgh and Cambridge, Charles Darwin (1809–1882) spent five years on the HMS *Beagle* as chief naturalist on a scientific expedition to the South Pacific and the west coast of South America. Darwin observed the bewildering variety of nature and began to speculate on how countless plant and animal species had come into existence. On his return to England, he developed his theory of evolution, basing his hypothesis on his own formidable biological knowledge, recent discoveries in geology, work on the selective breeding of plants and animals, and the theories of several authors that competition was the norm for all living things. In 1859, he published *On the Origin of Species*, followed in 1871 by *The Descent of Man*.

### QUESTIONS FOR ANALYSIS

1. What does Darwin mean by the terms *struggle for existence* and *natural selection*?
2. How does Darwin defend himself from religiously motivated attacks on his work?
3. What were some implications of Darwin's work for nineteenth-century views of progress? Of nature? Of human nature?
4. Defenders of laissez-faire capitalism sometimes drew upon Darwinian concepts in their arguments against socialism. Which concepts might they have used?
5. Similarly, Darwinian concepts were used to defend militarism and late-nineteenth-century Western imperialism. Which of Darwin's theories might have proved useful in such a defense?

## On the Origin of Species

### Struggle for Existence

It has been seen in the last chapter that amongst organic beings in a state of nature there is some individual variability. . . . But the mere existence of individual variability and of some few well-marked varieties . . . helps us but little in understanding how species arise in nature. How have all those exquisite adaptations of one part of the organization to another part, and to the conditions of life, and of one organic being to another being, been perfected? . . .

Again, . . . how is it that varieties, which I have called incipient species, become ultimately converted into good and distinct species, which in most cases obviously differ from each other far more than do the varieties of the same species? . . . All these results . . . follow from the struggle for life. Owing to this struggle, variations, however slight and from whatever cause proceeding, if they be in any degree profitable to the individuals of a species, in their infinitely complex relations to other organic beings and to their physical conditions of life, will tend to the preservation of such individuals, and will generally be inherited by the offspring. The offspring, also, will thus have a better chance of surviving, for, of the many individuals of any species which are periodically born, but a small number can survive. I have called this principle, by which each slight variation, if useful, is preserved, by the term Natural Selection, in order to mark its relation to man's power of selection. But the expression Survival of the Fittest is more accurate, and is sometimes equally convenient. . . .

I should premise that I use this term in a large and metaphorical sense including . . . not only the life of the individual, but success in leaving progeny. Two canine animals, in a time of dearth, may be truly said to struggle with each other which shall get food and live. But a plant on the edge of a desert is said to struggle for life against the drought. . . . A plant which annually produces a thousand seeds, of which only one of an average comes to maturity, may be more truly said to struggle with the plants of the same and other kinds which already clothe the ground. . . . In these several senses, which pass into each other, I use for convenience's sake the general term of Struggle for Existence.

A struggle for existence inevitably follows from the high rate at which all organic beings tend to increase. Every being, which during its natural lifetime produces several eggs or seeds, must suffer destruction during some period of its life, and during some season or occasional year, otherwise . . . its numbers would quickly become so inordinately great that no country could support the product. Hence, as more individuals are produced than can possibly survive, there must in every case be a struggle for existence, either one individual with another of the same species, or with the individuals of distinct species, or with the physical conditions of life. . . . Although some species may be now increasing, more or less rapidly, in numbers, all cannot do so, for the world would not hold them.

## The Descent of Man

### On the Manner of Development of Man from Some Lower Form

In this chapter we have seen that as man at the present day is liable, like every other animal, to multiform individual differences or slight variations, so no doubt were the early progenitors [ancestors] of man; the variations being formerly induced by the same general causes, and governed by the same general and complex laws as at

*Source:* Charles Darwin, "On the Origin of Species," in Charles Darwin, *The Origin of Species* (New York: Appleton and Company, 1896), pp. 75–78, and Charles Darwin, *The Descent of Man* (New York: Appleton and Company, 1896), pp. 62–63, 164–165, 613, 616–617.

present. As all animals tend to multiply beyond their means of subsistence, so it must have been with the progenitors of man; and this would inevitably lead to a struggle for existence and to natural selection. . . .

### On the Affinities and Genealogy of Man

Now as organisms have become slowly adapted to diversified lines of life by means of natural selection, their parts will have become more and more differentiated and specialized for various functions, from the advantage gained by the division of physiological labor. The same part appears often to have been modified first for one purpose, and then long afterwards for some other and quite distinct purpose; and thus all the parts are rendered more and more complex. But each organism still retains the general type of structure of the progenitor from which it was aboriginally derived. In accordance with this view it seems, if we turn to geological evidence, that organization on the whole has advanced throughout the world by slow and interrupted steps. In the great kingdom of the Vertebrata it has culminated in man. . . .

The most ancient progenitors in the kingdom of the Vertebrata . . . , apparently consisted of a group of marine animals, resembling the larvae of existing Ascidians.[1] These animals probably gave rise to a group of fishes, as lowly organized as the lancelet;[2] and from these the Ganoids,[3] and other fishes must have developed. From such fish a very small advance would carry us on to the Amphibians. We have seen that birds and reptiles were once intimately connected together; and the Monotremata[4] now connect mammals with reptiles in a slight degree. But no one can at present say by what line of descent the three higher and related classes, namely, mammals, birds, and reptiles, were derived

from the two lower vertebrate classes, namely, amphibians and fishes. In the class of mammals the steps are not difficult to conceive which led from the ancient Monotremata to the ancient Marsupials,[5] and from these to the early progenitors of the placental mammals. We may thus ascend to the Lemuridae,[6] and the interval is not very wide from these to the Simiadae.[7] The Simiadae then branched off into two great stems, the New World and Old World monkeys; and from the latter, at a remote period, Man, the wonder and glory of the Universe, proceeded.

### General Summary and Conclusion

I am aware that the conclusions arrived at in this work will be denounced by some as highly irreligious; but he who denounces them is bound to show why it is more irreligious to explain the origin of man as a distinct species by descent from some lower form, . . . than to explain the birth of the individual through the laws of ordinary reproduction. The birth both of the species and of the individual are equally parts of that grand sequence of events, which our minds refuse to accept as the result of blind chance. The understanding revolts at such a conclusion, whether or not we are able to believe that every slight variation of structure,—the union of each pair in marriage,—the dissemination of each seed,—and other such events have all been ordained for some special purpose. . . .

Man may be excused for feeling some pride at having risen, though not through his own exertions, to the very summit of the organic scale; and the fact of his having thus risen, instead of having been aboriginally placed there, may give him hope for a still higher destiny in the distant future. But we are not here concerned with hopes or fears, only

[1] Marine animals with a primitive backbone.
[2] Boney fish such as the sturgeon and gar, covered with large armorlike scales.
[3] Small translucent marine animals related to vertebrates.
[4] Egg-laying mammals such as the platypus.
[5] Mammals such as the kangaroo, whose females lack placentas and carry their young in an abdominal pouch.
[6] Largely nocturnal tree-dwelling mammals distinct from monkeys.
[7] Apes and monkeys.

with the truth as far as our reason permits us to discover it; and I have given the evidence to the best of my ability. We must, however, acknowledge, as it seems to me, that man with all his noble qualities, with sympathy which feels for the most debased, with benevolence which extends not only to other men but to the humblest living creature, with his god-like intellect which has penetrated into the movements and constitution of the solar system—with all these exalted powers—Man still bears in his bodily frame the indelible stamp of his lowly origin.

# The New Imperialism

Europe's overseas expansion continued in the late eighteenth and early nineteenth centuries despite the loss of American colonies by France, Great Britain, Portugal, and Spain. The British extended their authority in India; the French subdued Algeria between 1830 and 1847; and the European powers, led by England, forced China to open its ports to foreign trade after the Opium War (1839–1842). Then in the closing decades of the 1800s—the Era of Imperialism—the long history of Western expansion culminated in an unprecedented land grab. Between 1870 and 1914, Great Britain added 4.25 million square miles of territory and 66 million people to its empire; France, 3.5 million square miles of territory and 26 million people; Germany, 1 million square miles and 13 million people; and Belgium, 900,000 square miles and 13 million people. Italy, the United States, and the Netherlands also added colonial territories and subjects.

Anticipated economic gains, missionary fervor, racism, a faith in the West's civilizing mission, and confidence in the superiority of Western technology all contributed to the expansionist fever of the late 1800s. Another key factor was nationalism. Politicians, journalists, and millions of people from every walk of life were convinced that foreign conquests brought respect, prestige, and a sense of national accomplishment. To have colonies was the mark of a Great Power.

## A Defense of French Imperialism

### 56 • JULES FERRY, SPEECH BEFORE THE FRENCH CHAMBER OF DEPUTIES (MARCH 1884) AND PREFACE TO TONKIN AND THE MOTHER COUNTRY (1890)

Jules Ferry (1832–1893) was trained in the law but turned to journalism and politics in the 1860s. Having gained prominence as a harsh critic of the government of Napoleon III in the 1860s, after the establishment of the Third French Republic in 1870, he was elected to the Chamber of Deputies, where he became identified with the Opportunist Republicans, a center-left faction between the monarchists on the right and the Radicals and Socialists on the left. During his two terms as premier, or prime minister (1880–1881, 1883–1885), he led the fight to establish a system of free public education under the direction of the state rather than the Catholic Church. He also became an ardent proponent of French imperialism. During his premierships, France annexed Tunisia, Madagascar, and parts of Vietnam and took the first steps toward establishing colonies in Africa. In the following two excerpts, the first from a speech to the Chamber of Deputies in 1884, and the second from a book published in 1890, he states his reasons for supporting French expansionism, and in doing so also sheds light on the views of its critics.

## QUESTIONS FOR ANALYSIS

1. According to Ferry, what recent developments in world trade have made France's need for colonies more urgent?
2. What arguments against imperialism are proposed by Ferry's critics? How does Ferry counter them?
3. Aside from providing markets for French goods, what other economic advantages do colonies offer, according to Ferry?
4. How does Ferry's appeal for colonies reflect French nationalism?

## Speech to the Chamber of Deputies

M. JULES FERRY Gentlemen, it embarrasses me to make such a prolonged demand upon the gracious attention of the Chamber, but I believe that . . . there is some benefit in summarizing and condensing, in the form of the arguments, principles, motives, and various interests by which a policy of colonial expansion may be justified; it goes without saying that I will . . . never lose sight of the major continental interests which are the primary concern of this country.[1] . . .

In the area of economics, I will allow myself to place before you . . . the considerations which justify a policy of colonial expansion from the point of view of that need, felt more and more strongly by the industrial populations of Europe and particularly those of our own rich and hardworking country: the need for export markets. . . . I will formulate only in a general way what each of you, in the different parts of France, is in a position to confirm. Yes, what is lacking for our great industry, drawn irrevocably on to the path of exports by the treaties of 1860,[2] is more and more export markets. Why? Because next door to us Germany is surrounded by [tariff] barriers, because beyond the ocean, the United States has become protectionist, protectionist in the most extreme sense, because not only have these great markets . . . become more difficult to access for our industrial products, but also these great states are beginning to pour out products at a level not seen heretofore into our own markets. . . . It is not necessary to pursue this demonstration any further. . . .

Gentlemen, there is a second . . . order of ideas to which I have to give equal attention, but as

*Source:* Jules Ferry, *Discours et opinions,* Vol. 5 (Paris: Armand Cohn, 1897), pp. 557–564. Trans. James H. Overfield.
[1]A reference to the concerns of those who believed that French policy should concentrate on responding to the emergence of a strong united Germany and reversing the results of the Franco-Prussian War (1870–1871), which included the loss of the provinces of Alsace and northern Lorraine.
[2]Refers to the Cobden-Chevalier Treaty of 1860, which lowered tariffs between France and Great Britain.

quickly as possible, believe me; it is the humanitarian and civilizing side of the question. On this point the honorable M. Camille Pelletan[3] has jeered in his own refined and clever manner; he jeers, he condemns, and he says "What is this civilization which you impose with cannon-balls? What is it but another form of barbarism? Don't these populations, these 'inferior races,' have the same rights as you? Aren't they masters of their own houses? Have they called upon you? You come to them against their will; you offer them violence, but not civilization." . . . Gentlemen, I must speak from a higher and more truthful plane. It must be stated openly that, in effect, superior races have rights over inferior races.

**JULES MAIGNE** Oh! You dare to say this in the country which has proclaimed the rights of man!

**M. DE GUILLOUTET** This is a justification of slavery and the slave trade!

**JULES FERRY** If Monsieur Maigne is right, if the Declaration of the Rights of Man was written for the blacks of equatorial Africa, then by what right do you impose regular commerce upon them? They have not called upon you.

**RAOUL DUVAL** We do not want to impose anything upon them. It is you who wish to do so!

**JULES MAIGNE** To propose and to impose are two different things!

**GEORGES PERIN** In any case, you cannot bring about commerce by force.

**M. JULES FERRY** I repeat that superior races have a right, because they have a duty. They have the duty to civilize inferior races. . . .

Gentlemen, there are certain considerations which merit the attention of all patriots. The conditions of naval warfare have been profoundly altered. At this time, as you know, a warship cannot carry more than fourteen days' worth of coal, no matter how perfectly it is organized, and a ship which is out of coal is a derelict . . . abandoned to the first person who comes along. Thence the necessity of having on the oceans provision stations, shelters, ports for defense and reprovisioning. And for this reason we needed Tunisia, for this that we needed Saigon and the Mekong Delta, for this that we need Madagascar, that we are at Diego-Suarez and Vohemar[4] and will never leave them! Gentlemen, in Europe as it is today, in this competition of so many rivals which we see growing around us, some by perfecting their military or maritime forces, others by the prodigious development of an ever growing population; in a Europe of this sort, a policy of peaceful seclusion or abstention is simply the highway to decadence! Nations are great in our times only by means of the activities which they develop; it is not simply "by the peaceful shining forth of institutions" that they are great at this hour. . . .

[The Republican Party] has shown that it is quite aware that one cannot impose upon France a political ideal conforming to that of nations like independent Belgium and the Swiss Republic; that something else is needed for France: that she cannot be merely a free country, that she must also be a great country, exercising all of her rightful influence over the destiny of Europe, that she ought to propagate this influence throughout the world and carry everywhere that she can her language, her customs, her flag, her arms, and her genius.

---

[3]Pelletan (1846–1915) was a radical republican politician noted for his patriotism.

[4]Madagascar port cities.

**Preface to *Tonkin and the Mother Country***

Colonial policy is the child of the industrial revolution. For rich countries where there is much capital, where industry is steadily growing, and where even agriculture has been mechanized, . . . exports are necessary for general prosperity. But today every country seeks to do its own spinning and weaving, forging, and distilling. . . . With the arrival of the latest industrial giants, the United States and Germany; of Italy, newly revitalized; of Spain, enriched by the investment of French capital; of industrious little Switzerland, and moreover Russia waiting in the wings, Europe has embarked on a competitive course from which she will never be able to turn back. All over the world, . . . the raising of high tariffs has resulted in an increased volume of manufactured goods, the vanishing of traditional markets, and the emergence of fierce competition. . . . The European consumer-goods market is saturated; unless we declare modern society ruined, and prepare at the dawn of the twentieth century for its destruction through revolution . . . new consumer markets will have to be created in other parts of the world. . . . Colonialism is an international manifestation of the eternal laws of competition.

---

*Source:* Jules Ferry, *Tonkin et la Mère-Patrie* in Jules Ferry, *Discours et opinions*, Vol. 5 (Paris: Armand Cohn, 1897), pp. 557–564. Trans. James H. Overfield.

# The Imperialists' Delusions

## 57 • JOHN A. HOBSON, IMPERIALISM: A STUDY

As shown in Jules Ferry's speeches and writings, Western imperialism had its share of critics. Missionary groups, certain business interests, the military, conservatives, and nationalists tended to support colonialism. Left-leaning political groups and their supporters were skeptical of imperialism's benefits. Some believed that imperialism went against basic principles of social justice and freedom, while others argued that money spent on foreign ventures would better be spent on social programs. In France, many nationalists believed that imperialism was an unfortunate diversion from what should have been the focus of French policy—the need to contain the rising power of Germany.

In England, the leading critic of imperialism was the Oxford-educated economist J. A. Hobson (1858–1940), who wrote *Imperialism: A Study* in 1902 after serving as a correspondent covering the Second Boer War, or South African War, for the *Manchester Guardian*. The South African War was an imperialist war not against native Africans, but rather against the Boers, white descendants of mainly Dutch immigrants who lived in two independent south African republics, Transvaal and the Orange Free State. At issue were access to the republics' rich diamond and gold deposits and the political rights of the *uitlanders*, non-Dutch (mainly English) immigrants to the republics. The British won the war and incorporated the Boer republics into the Union of South Africa, but they paid a great price. The war dragged on from 1899 to 1902, cost the lives of 22,000 British soldiers and 35,000 Boers, and also cost the British dearly in terms of world opinion. To Hobson it epitomized the hypocrisy and failures of colonialism, which he spelled out in his widely read book.

## QUESTIONS FOR ANALYSIS

1. On what basis does Hobson reject the arguments about the economic benefits of overseas empire?
2. What arguments does Hobson develop to justify his skepticism about the "civilizing mission" of imperialism?
3. How, according to Hobson, does imperialism affect British and international politics?
4. What are Hobson's views of the recently colonized people of Asia and Africa? How do his views compare to those of Ferry?

No mere array of facts and figures . . . will suffice to dispel the popular delusion that the use of national force to secure new markets by annexing fresh tracts of territory is a sound and a necessary policy for an advanced industrial country like Great Britain. It has indeed been proved that recent annexations of tropical countries, procured at great expense, have furnished poor and precarious markets, that our aggregate trade with our colonial possessions is virtually stationary, and that our most profitable . . . trade is with rival industrial nations, whose territories we have no desire to annex, whose markets we cannot force, and whose active antagonism we are provoking by our expansive policy. . . .

The political effects . . . of the new Imperialism . . . may be thus summarised. It is a constant menace to peace, by furnishing continual temptations to further aggression upon lands occupied by lower races and by embroiling our nation with other nations of rival imperial ambitions; to the sharp peril of war it adds the chronic danger and degradation of militarism, which not merely wastes the current physical and moral resources of the nations, but checks the very course of civilization. It consumes to an illimitable and incalculable extent the financial resources of a nation by military preparation, stopping the expenditure of the current income of the State upon productive public projects and burdening posterity with heavy loads of debt. . . .

Seeing that the Imperialism . . . is clearly condemned . . . we may ask, "How is the British nation induced to embark upon such unsound business?" The only possible answer is that the business interests of the nation as a whole are subordinated to those of certain sectional interests that usurp control of the national resources and use them for their private gain. . . .

*Source:* John A. Hobson, *Imperialism: A Study.* (London: J. Nisbet & Company, 1902), pp. 51–56, 76, 160–161, 208–209, 266–267.

If the £60,000,000 which may now be taken as a minimum expenditure on armaments in time of peace were subjected to a close analysis, most of it would be traced directly to the tills of certain big firms engaged in building warships and transports, equipping and coaling them, manufacturing guns, rifles, ammunition, supplying horses, waggons, saddlery, food, clothing for the services, contracting for barracks, and for other large irregular needs. . . . Here we have an important nucleus of commercial Imperialism. . . .

With them stand the great manufacturers for export trade, who gain a living by supplying the real or artificial wants of the new countries we annex or open up. Manchester, Sheffield, Birmingham, to name three representative cases, are full of firms which compete in pushing textiles and hardware, engines, tools, machinery, spirits, guns, upon new markets. . . .

The making of railways, canals, and other public works, the establishment of factories, the development of mines, the improvement of agriculture in new countries, stimulate a definite interest in important manufacturing industries which feeds a very firm imperialist faith in their owners. . . .

The shipping trade has a very definite interest which makes for Imperialism. This is well illustrated by the policy of State subsidies now claimed by shipping firms as a retainer, and in order to encourage British shipping for purposes of imperial safety and defence.

The military services are . . . imperialist by conviction, and professional interest, and every increase enhances the political power they exert. . . .

To the military services we may add the Indian Civil Service and the numerous official and semi-official posts in our colonies and protectorates. Every expansion of the Empire is also regarded by these same classes as affording new openings for their sons as ranchers, planters, engineers, or missionaries. . . .

There exists in a considerable though not a large proportion of the British nation a genuine desire to spread Christianity among the heathen, to diminish the cruelty and other sufferings which they believe exist in countries less fortunate than their own, and to do good work about the world in the cause of humanity. Most of the churches contain a small body of men and women deeply, even passionately, interested in such work. Ill-trained for the most part in psychology and history, these people believe that religion and other arts of civilization are portable commodities which it is our duty to convey to the backward nations, and that a certain amount of compulsion is justified in pressing their benefits upon people too ignorant at once to recognize them. . . .

The actual history of Western relations with lower races occupying lands on which we have settled throws a curious light upon the theory of a "trust for civilization." When the settlement approaches the condition of genuine colonization, it has commonly implied the extermination of the lower races, either by war or by private slaughter, as in the case of Australian Bushmen, African Bushmen and Hottentots, [American] Red Indians, and [New Zealand] Maoris, or by forcing upon them the habits of a civilization equally destructive to them. This is what is meant by saying that "lower races" in contact with "superior races" naturally tend to disappear. How much of "nature" or necessity" belongs to the process is seen from the fact that only those "lower races" tend to disappear who are incapable of profitable exploitation either because they are too "savage" for effective industrialism or because the demand for labour does not require their presence. . . .

This is the root fact of Imperialism so far as it relates to the control of inferior races; when the latter are not killed out they are subjected by force to the ends of their white superiors.

# Images of Imperialism in Great Britain

## 58 • ADVERTISEMENTS AND ILLUSTRATIONS FROM BRITISH BOOKS AND PERIODICALS

Although late-nineteenth-century imperialism had its critics, in the major imperialist states it had broad support within the general population. This is especially true in Great Britain, the premier imperialist power, where novels, poetry, plays, children's books, advertisements, music hall entertainment, and publications of missionary societies were filled with positive imperialist images, themes, and motifs. Newly founded youth organizations such as the Boy Scouts and Girl Guides taught the value of service to Britain's imperial cause. The public's exposure to such material reinforced imperialism's appeal and strengthened support for the government's policies.

The following selections are examples of how British popular culture propagated imperial values. The first group of illustrations appeared in *An ABC for Baby Patriots* by Mrs. Earnest Ames. Designed to be read to young children, it was published in 1898 and went through several printings. The illustration that accompanies the letter "N" depicts a British naval officer showing off a flotilla of Royal Navy ships on maneuvers off Spithead in the English Channel. The foreigners are a German on the left and a Frenchman on the right. The others are self-explanatory.

The second illustration is taken from *The Kipling Reader,* a collection of stories written for young adults by Rudyard Kipling (1865–1936); the book was published in 1908 and illustrated by J. Macfarlane. Kipling, one of the most popular British writers of the era, is best remembered for his support of imperialism and his glorification of the heroism of the British soldier in India and Burma. This illustration depicts Scott, a character in the story "William the Conqueror." Set in India during a famine, the story centers on the romance that blooms between Scott and a young woman nicknamed "William" while they toil to save Indians from starvation. Scott has saved hundreds of babies by feeding them milk from a herd of goats he has managed to maintain. In this illustration, he approaches William, who sees "a young man, beautiful as Paris, a god in a halo of gold dust, walking slowly at the head of his flocks, while at his knee ran small naked Cupids."

The third illustration is an advertisement for Lipton Teas that appeared in 1897 in the *Illustrated London News.* The Lipton Company was founded by Thomas Lipton (1850–1931), who opened a small food shop in Glasgow in 1871 and by 1890 owned three hundred food stores throughout Great Britain. In 1890, the multimillionaire decided to cash in on the British taste for tea. Growing tea on plantations he owned in India and Ceylon and marketing it in inexpensive small packets that guaranteed freshness, the Lipton Company soon became synonymous with tea drinking throughout Europe and the United States. Lipton advertisements appeared regularly in the *Illustrated London News* in the 1890s and early 1900s.

The fourth and fifth illustrations are cartoons published in the weekly humor magazine *Punch.* "On the Swoop" appeared in 1894, when the European powers were consolidating their territorial claims in Africa. The German acquisition of Tanganyika had ruined the British imperialists' dream of establishing a string of contiguous colonies stretching from Cairo in Egypt to Cape Town in South Africa. "Britannia and Her Suitors" was published in 1901, when Great Britain was still avoiding entanglements in the diplomatic alliances then taking shape among the continental powers. It shows Britannia dancing with a figure representing its colonies, while in the background, the German emperor Wilhelm II, then allied only with weak Austria-Hungary, looks on unhappily. Farther in the background, Tsar Nicholas II of Russia dances with a figure representing France, with which Russia had been allied since 1894.

## QUESTIONS FOR ANALYSIS

1. What views of Africans and Asians are being communicated in each of the illustrations?
2. What message is being communicated about the benefits colonial subjects are accruing from their status?
3. What images are being communicated about the British in their role as imperialists?
4. What concrete examples of nationalism can you see in the various illustrations?
5. How many of the justifications for imperialism presented in Jules Ferry's speech (source 56) can you find represented in the illustrations?
6. Using evidence in the illustrations alone, what conclusions can you draw about the reasons for imperialism's popularity within the general British population?

N n    *N n*

N is the Navy
   We keep at Spithead.
It's a sight that makes foreigners
   Wish they were dead.

N,n.

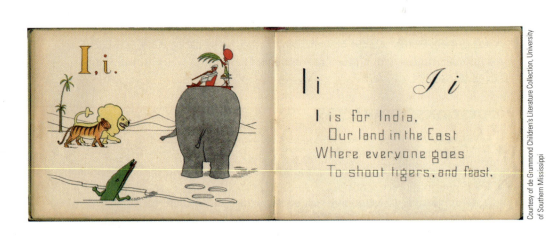

I, i.

I i    *I i*

I is for India,
   Our land in the East
Where everyone goes
   To shoot tigers, and feast.

W w    *W w*

W is the Word
   Of an Englishman True;
When given, it means
   What he says, he will do.

W,w.

From *An ABC for Baby Patriots*

From *The Kipling Reader*

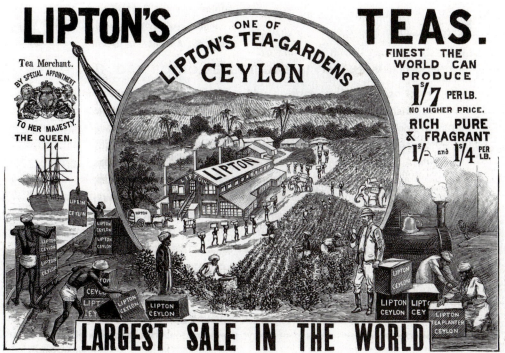

Advertisement for Lipton Teas, which appeared in the *Illustrated London News*, a weekly publication

*Punch Limited*

"Britannia and Her Suitors," from *Punch*, 1901

ON THE SWOOP!

From British Books and Periodicals, "On the Swoop," from *Punch*, 1894, Punch Cartoon Library & Archive

"On the Swoop," from *Punch*, 1894

# The Battle for Women's Suffrage in England

Women's political and legal rights became a subject of public debate during the French Revolution. In October 1789 thousands of women marched from Paris to the palace grounds at Versailles, where they forced the royal family and the National Assembly to relocate to Paris, the center of revolutionary agitation. Beginning in 1790, women formed political clubs to oppose laws and customs that were the foundation of France's patriarchal society. In response, legislators passed laws giving women the right to own property, marry without parental consent, initiate divorce, and take legal action against fathers of illegitimate children. In 1793, however, Jacobin revolutionaries outlawed women's political clubs and rejected women's demands for political equality. Having women vote, hold public office, and serve in the army would, they argued, undermine the family and divert women from their calling as wives and mothers. Women experienced more setbacks in the late 1790s, when moderate revolutionaries rescinded most of the laws that had improved women's legal status. Under Napoleon, the Civil Code of 1804 reaffirmed women's legal inferiority to men.

In the conservative atmosphere of the 1820s and 1830s, women's political activism declined, and prevailing opinion consigned middle- and upper-class women to a domestic role centered on childcare, housekeeping, supervising servants, and providing husbands with a tranquil home. By midcentury, however, women on both sides of the Atlantic once more began to speak out and organize on behalf of women's rights. A landmark in the history of feminism was the women's rights convention held in Seneca Falls, New York, in 1848; the delegates demanded the right to vote for women, divorce and property rights, and equal employment and educational opportunities. Such issues also became the focus of feminists in England in the 1850s and several continental European countries later in the century.

By the late 1800s women had made some gains, especially in the areas of family law and access to higher education. In addition, professions such as nursing and teaching provided new opportunities for many middle-class women, and a few women established careers as doctors and lawyers. Despite the efforts of women's suffrage organizations, however, granting women the vote met stiff resistance. Before World War I only Australia, New Zealand, Finland, Norway, and several western U.S. states had granted women full voting privileges.

## Women's Vote and How to Attain It

### 59 • EMMELINE PANKHURST, WHY WE ARE MILITANT

Organized efforts by Englishwomen to gain the vote began in 1847, when a group of women founded the Female Political Association and collected signatures on a prosuffrage petition they submitted to the House of Lords. In 1851,

Harriet Hardy Mill (1807–1858), the wife of philosopher John Stuart Mill, wrote a widely read pamphlet titled "Enfranchisement of Women." In 1867 John Stuart Mill, then a member of the House of Commons, proposed an amendment to a voting reform bill that would have given women the vote. It was rejected 194–73, a setback that led to the founding of the National Society for Women's Suffrage in 1868. In the following decades, women sought to advance their cause by making resolutions, publicizing their views, and performing symbolic acts such as appearing at polling places and requesting the vote, although they knew they would be turned away.

In the early 1900s, however, the feminist movement became more militant and confrontational. By 1900, Englishwomen could vote in local elections and stand for election to school boards and municipal offices. This was not enough for Emmeline Pankhurst (1858–1928), who, since the 1870s, had been a strong advocate for women's suffrage and better treatment of working-class and poor women. In 1903, she founded the Women's Social and Political Union (WSPU). Under the leadership of Pankhurst and her daughters, Christabel and Sylvia, the WSPU tried to advance the cause of women's suffrage by heckling politicians and then by smashing windows, slashing paintings in museums, burning letters in mailboxes, and finally martyrdom, when in May 1913 a young suffragist threw herself under the hooves of the king's racehorse at Epsom Downs and was killed before thousands of shocked spectators. When arrested, many "suffragettes," as they were called, went on hunger strikes. The government responded by approving the forced feeding of prisoners in 1909 and the Prisoners Act of 1913, by which fasting women were released from prison until they had eaten and then rearrested.

In October 1913, Emmeline Pankhurst traveled to New York City to defend the tactics of the WSPU in a speech delivered at Madison Square Garden. It was attended by a crowd of only three thousand, mainly owing to a last-minute change in scheduling—she had been held up by immigration authorities for two days after her arrival because of pending legal cases involving her in England.

## QUESTIONS FOR ANALYSIS

1. In Pankhurst's view, what was the condition of the women's suffrage movement in the first years of the 1900s?
2. According to Pankhurst, why had "nonmilitant" efforts on behalf of women's suffrage failed?
3. What event sparked the new militancy of the WSPU?
4. According to Pankhurst, why was it so important for women to gain the right to vote in parliamentary elections?
5. How does Pankhurst explain the difficulty women encountered in their efforts to win the vote?

I know that in your minds there are questions like these; you are saying, "Woman Suffrage is sure to come; the emancipation of humanity is an evolutionary process, and how is it that some women, instead of trusting to that evolution, instead of educating the masses of people of their country, instead of educating their own sex to prepare them for citizenship, how is it that these militant women are using violence and upsetting the business arrangements of the country in their undue impatience to attain their end?"

Let me try to explain to you the situation. . . .

The extensions of the franchise to the men of my country have been preceded by very great violence, by something like a revolution, by something like civil war. In 1832,[1] you know we were on the edge of a civil war and on the edge of revolution, and . . . it was after the practice of arson on so large a scale that half the city of Bristol[2] was burned down in a single night, it was because more and greater violence and arson were feared that the Reform Bill of 1832 was allowed to pass into law. In 1867[3] . . . rioting went on all over the country, and . . . as a result of the fear of more rioting and violence the Reform Act of 1867 was put upon the statute books.

In 1884 . . . rioting was threatened and feared, and so the agricultural laborers got the vote.[4]

Meanwhile, during the '80's, women . . . were asking for the franchise. Appeals, larger and more numerous than for any other reform, were presented in support of Woman's Suffrage. . . . More meetings were held, and larger, for Woman Suffrage than were held for votes for men, and yet the women did not get it. Men got the vote because they were and would be violent. The women did not get it because they were constitutional and law-abiding. . . .

Well . . . , on the eve of the General Election of 1905, a mere handful of us . . . set out on the wonderful adventure of forcing the strongest Government of modern times to give the women the vote. . . . The Suffrage movement was almost dead. The women had lost heart. You could not get a Suffrage meeting that was attended by members of the general public. . . .

Two women[5] changed that in a twinkling of an eye at a great Liberal demonstration in Manchester, where a Liberal leader, Sir Edward Grey, was explaining the program to be carried out during the Liberals' next turn of office. The two women put the fateful question, "When are you going to give votes to women?" and refused to sit down until they had been answered. These two women were sent to jail, and from that day to this the women's movement, both militant and constitutional, has never looked back. . . . Now we have nearly 50 societies for Woman Suffrage, and they are large in membership, they are rich in money, and their ranks, are swelling every day that passes. . . .

We are fighting to get the power to alter bad laws; but some people say to us, "Go to the representatives in the House of Commons, point out to them that these laws are bad, and you will find them quite

---

*Source:* Jane Marcus, ed., *Speech, Suffrage and the Pankhursts* (London: Routledge & Kegan Paul, 1987), pp. 153–157, 159–161.

[1] In 1831 and 1832, public excitement over voting reform peaked, as Parliament considered proposals to extend representation to new industrial cities and give voting rights to middle-class men.

[2] On Oct. 31, 1831, in response to the House of Lords' decision to turn down the Reform Act, a large crowd in Bristol burned down unpopular citizens' houses and released prisoners from the jails. Soldiers attacked the rioters, and hundreds were killed or severely wounded. Under pressure, Parliament passed the Reform Act of 1832.

[3] The Reform Bill of 1867 extended the right to vote to working-class men.

[4] This was the result of the Reform Bill of 1884, which gave the vote to male agricultural workers.

[5] One of these women was Emmeline Pankhurst's elder daughter, Christabel. The other was Annie Kenney (1879–1953) one of the few suffragists with a working class background.

ready to alter them." Ladies and gentlemen, there are women in my country who have spent long and useful lives trying to get reforms, and because of their voteless condition, they are unable even to get the ear of Members of Parliament, much less are they able to secure those reforms.

Our marriage and divorce laws are a disgrace to civilization. . . . I wonder that women have the courage to take upon themselves the responsibilities of marriage and motherhood when I see how little protection the law . . . affords them. I wonder that a woman will face the ordeal of childbirth with the knowledge that after she has risked her life to bring a child into the world she has absolutely no parental rights over the future of that child. Think what trust women have in men when a woman will marry a man, knowing, if she has knowledge of the law, that if that man is not all she in her love for him thinks him, he may even bring a strange woman into the house, bring his mistress into the house to live with her, and she cannot get legal relief from such a marriage as that. . . .

Take the industrial side of the question: have men's wages for a hard day's work ever been so low and inadequate as are women's wages today? Have men ever had to suffer from the laws, more injustice than women suffer? Is there a single reason which men have had for demanding liberty that does not also apply to women? . . . for women who are fighting for exactly the same thing?

All my life I have tried to understand why it is that men . . . think citizenship ridiculous when it is to be applied to the women of their race. . . . A thought came to me . . . : that to men women are not human beings like themselves. Some men think we are superhuman; they put us on pedestals; they revere us; they think we are too fine and too delicate to come down into the hurly-burly of life. Other men think us sub-human. . . . They think that we are fit for drudgery, but that in some strange way our minds are not like theirs, our love for great things is not like theirs, and so we are a sort of sub-human species. We are neither superhuman nor are we sub-human. We are just human beings like yourselves.

# Images of the Suffrage Campaign in England

## 60 • ENGLISH POSTERS AND POSTCARDS, 1908–1914

In the opening years of the twentieth century, English politicians debated the rights of striking workers, approved a host of social legislation, introduced inheritance taxes and a progressive income tax, curtailed the powers of the House of Lords, and agonized over the issue of home rule for Ireland. Of all the issues they faced, however, none brought forth as much passion and partisanship as the debate over women's suffrage. The militancy of the Women's Social and Political Union, a mass demonstration of three thousand prosuffrage women in London in 1907, and the arrest and hunger strike of Mary Wallace Dunlop in 1909 set the stage for the tumultuous events between 1910 and 1914. After Parliament on three occasions considered but failed to pass women's suffrage bills, prosuffrage militants responded with attacks on Parliament, window-breaking campaigns, arson, and the slashing of paintings in museums.

Against the backdrop of these events, all sides in the debate held rallies, wrote books, published magazines, and sent countless letters to newspaper editors. They also sought to win supporters though art. This was especially true for the suffragists, who founded the Artists' Suffrage League in 1907 and the Suffrage Atelier (workshop) in 1909. Both sought to advance the cause of women's suffrage by producing posters, postcards, banners, and illustrated leaflets. Opponents of women's suffrage could not equal their output in terms of quantity, but they certainly matched their zeal. The following selections provide an opportunity to analyze both sides' work.

The first examples were produced by opponents of suffrage, all in 1912. The first, "No Votes, Thank You," is a poster published under the auspices of the National League for Opposing Women's Suffrage (NLOWS), an organization founded in 1910. It shows a figure representing "true womanhood," and behind her a supporter of woman's suffrage brandishing a hammer for breaking windows. Three postcard illustrations follow: "A Perfect Woman," inspired by a quotation from "She Was a Phantom of Delight," a love poem written by William Wordsworth (1770–1850); "Votes for Women;" and "Hear Some Plain Things." These are followed by "A Suffragette's Home," the most famous of all the antisuffrage posters. A recruitment poster for NLOWS, it shows a husband returning home, where his prosuffrage wife has left a note, "Be back in an hour."

The first prosuffrage poster, "The Appeal of Womanhood" by Louise Jacobs was a direct response to "No Votes, Thank You." The female figure representing true womanhood stands up to defend the oppressed women behind her: a laundress, a mother, a prostitute, a widow, and a young girl holding chains in her hand. The words "white slavery" on the banner refer to the practice of kidnapping young girls and forcing them into prostitution; "sweated labour" refers to small industrial establishments where employees are forced to work long hours in poor conditions for low wages. "Convicts and Lunatics" appeared in 1908. It reflects the fact that women, who had been admitted to Oxford and Cambridge in the 1860s, still could not vote.

The next image, a publicity poster for the WSPU's magazine, *The Suffragette* features Joan of Arc as a symbol of the suffragists' struggle. Although the "Maid of Orleans" rallied French resistance against the English in the closing stages of the One Hundred Years' War, and indeed was put on trial and executed by the English, she came to represent to suffragists the courage of women standing up for a just cause. The final poster, produced by an anonymous artist in 1914, urges voters to vote against the Liberal party, whose Home Secretary, Reginald McKenna, was responsible for the so-called Cat and Mouse Act of 1913, which allowed for the temporary release of prosuffrage hunger strikers and their rearrest once they had recovered their health.

## QUESTIONS FOR ANALYSIS

1. How do the antisuffrage posters characterize women who favored the cause of votes for women?
2. What counter-images are presented in the suffragists' posters?
3. What, according to the posters of each side, will be the social implications of giving women the vote?

The Art Archive/Museum of London/Picture Desk

"No Votes, Thank You"

Mary Evans Picture Library/Alamy

"A Perfect Woman"

Bodleian Library, Oxford, John Johnson Collection: Postcards: Women's Suffrage

"Votes for Women"

"Hear Some Plain Things"

"A Suffragette's Home"

"The Appeal of Womanhood"

"Convicts and Lunatics"

"The Suffragette"

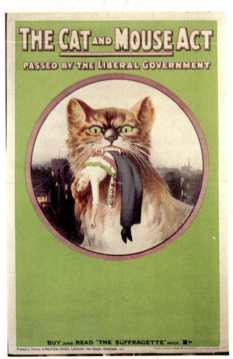

"The Cat and Mouse Act"

# Chapter 9

# Western Pressures, Nationalism, and Reform in Africa, Southwest Asia, and India in the 1800s

A FRICA, SOUTHWEST ASIA, and India shared a common experience in the nineteenth century: All three were caught up in a tidal wave of change set off by the political, economic, and cultural onslaught of Europe. In India, the British extended their empire until it encompassed most of the Indian subcontinent, while in Africa a half-dozen European states turned the continent into a giant colony. In Southwest Asia, Iran experienced growing British and Russian interference in its affairs, culminating in the Anglo-Russian Agreement of 1907, which divided the country into a Russian-dominated north, a British-dominated south, and a nominally independent center. The Ottoman Empire survived, but it lost thousands of square miles of territory to European powers in North Africa, a region that in 1800 was still part of the Ottoman Empire despite the de facto independence of its rulers. The Ottomans also lost territory in southeastern Europe after Greece, Serbia, Romania, Bulgaria, Montenegro, and Albania all won their independence. The sultan also was forced to hand over key government responsibilities to Europeans. Beginning in 1881, a committee of European businessmen and statesmen supervised the collection and disbursement of certain state revenues through the Ottoman Public Debt Administration, an agency created to guarantee payment of government debts to European creditors.

In all three regions, European penetration threatened ruling elites and traditional political institutions, making some irrelevant, destroying others, and inspiring reform in a few. It also brought about many economic changes. Europeans built railroads and installed telegraph lines, undertook huge engineering projects such as the Suez Canal, created new demands for raw materials and agricultural goods, and aggressively marketed their manufactured products. Europeans also introduced unsettling new ideas and values through missionary activity and the promotion of Western education and science. In a century of unparalleled change, the peoples of Africa, southwest Asia, and India were wrenched from their pasts and forced to face uncertain futures.

# Europe's Assault on Africa

The nineteenth century began with efforts by several European states to end their main business in Africa, the slave trade. Responding to religious, humanitarian, and economic arguments, Denmark outlawed the slave trade in 1792, and Great Britain and the United States did the same in 1807. Sweden in 1813, the Netherlands in 1814, and France in 1848 followed. Unexpectedly, however, African–European relations underwent a radical transformation in the closing decades of the nineteenth century, and virtually the entire continent was parceled out among European colonizers.

The European takeover of Africa began in earnest in the 1870s, a decade that saw intensified missionary activity, the discovery of gold and diamond deposits in southern Africa, heightened competition among European merchants in West Africa and the Niger delta region, and growing public interest in Africa as a result of missionaries' and explorers' writings. In 1878, the Welsh-American explorer Henry M. Stanley, working on behalf of King Leopold II of Belgium, was dispatched to the Congo River basin, where he convinced hundreds of chiefs to sign treaties that turned this vast region into the king's personal colony, the Congo Free State. In 1880, the Italian-born explorer Pierre Savorgnan de Brazza signed the first of dozens of treaties with African chieftains that were the basis for the French colonies in equatorial Africa. In 1881, the French established a protectorate over Tunisia, and in 1882, the British occupied Egypt. The Germans annexed Togo in 1883 and Cameroon in 1884. In 1884 and 1885, representatives of eleven European states, the Ottoman Empire, and the United States established guidelines for the further colonization of Africa at the Berlin West Africa Conference. By 1914, the scramble for Africa was over, and only Liberia and Ethiopia were still independent.

**Multiple Voices VI**

# A Sampling of African Colonial Treaties and Agreements

## BACKGROUND

During the 1800s, African kings and chiefs signed more than a thousand treaties and agreements with representatives of European states or trading companies, the cumulative effect of which was the near-total subjection of Africa to colonial rule. At first, such treaties mainly involved British efforts to suppress the slave trade. In midcentury, many agreements guaranteed Europeans access to exportable goods such as palm oil, peanuts, indigo, and ivory. By century's end, with the scramble for Africa in full swing, such treaties transferred territory, political authority, and exclusive access to minerals and other raw materials to European states or trading companies.

Most of these agreements were hardly treaties in the dictionary sense of an "arrangement or agreement made by negotiation." Vague and frequently misleading discussions of a proposed treaty's content, often accompanied by threats of force, were followed by the signing of a legalistic document in a European language that few African signees understood. Not surprisingly, months or years after an African leader affixed his "X" to a treaty, he and his people learned that the document had provisions he had never discussed and consequences he had never imagined. In the following selections, we present excerpts from three such treaties along with a letter written in response to one of them by an African king to Queen Victoria of Great Britain.

## THE SOURCES

The first document is a treaty signed in 1861 between Great Britain and King Docemo of Lagos, a city-state on the Niger Delta and a center of the slave trade since the fifteenth century. Great Britain had already signed several treaties with regional rulers to halt the slave trade, but the results had been deemed unsatisfactory. This treaty went further, in that Britain took control of actual territory. This step, it was hoped, would result in the suppression of slave smuggling out of Lagos, ensure access to the region's cotton, and serve as a warning to neighboring rulers to enforce the ban on slave trading.

The second treaty is one of the several hundred treaties signed in the early 1880s by chiefs in the Congo River Basin by which they transferred rights and powers to the International Association of the Congo, a consortium founded in 1879 by King Leopold II of Belgium and his associates. Supposedly a subgroup of the International African Association, a philanthropic organization founded by Leopold in 1876, the International Association of the Congo was meant to enrich the king by giving him personal control over a vast part of Africa. Leopold did his best to disguise the organization's true purpose by identifying it with the cause of bringing peace and enlightenment to Africa. The task of turning this huge region into a viable colony was given to the Welsh-American journalist/explorer Henry M. Stanley, whose agents used force and trickery to coerce chiefs into signing.

The last agreement, signed in 1888, was between King Lobengula of Matabeleland and business associates of Cecil Rhodes, the relentless British imperialist who already had enriched himself through his ownership of diamond mines around Kimberly, South Africa, and now was intent on extending his business interests and British authority farther north. Lobengula ruled a kingdom founded by the Ndebele people earlier in the century after they had migrated north to escape turmoil in southern Africa. After rejecting earlier requests of various Europeans to grant them concessions to mine gold in his territory, in 1888 he accepted the terms offered by Rhodes' group.

Lobengula realized he had been duped after learning he had given Rhodes and his associates rights to all the minerals in the kingdom, not, as he had thought, the right to dig "one big hole" in his territory with just ten men. In response, he ordered the execution of several of his counselors and sent the following note to Queen Victoria. Some months later, he received a response from one of the queen's advisors, who informed him that after looking into the matter, the queen had concluded that the men who had signed the treaty "may be trusted to carry out the working for gold in the chief's country without molesting his people." The king formally repudiated the treaty, but without effect.

## QUESTIONS FOR ANALYSIS

1. What specific powers will the rulers surrender by signing the treaties? What powers, if any, will they maintain?
2. What benefits do the rulers themselves receive as a result of signing the agreements?
3. What benefits will accrue to the European signatories of the treaties?
4. What benefits do the treaties promise for the subjects of the signatories of the treaties?
5. How, according to Lobengula, has he been misled in the agreement he signed?

---

## ▌ • Lagos Treaty of Cession, August 6, 1861

*Article 1.* In order that the Queen of England may be the better enabled to assist, defend, and protect the inhabitants of Lagos, and put an end to the slave trade in this and the neighbouring countries, and to prevent the destructive wars so frequently undertaken for the capture of slaves, I, Docemo, do . . . give, transfer, and grant and confirm unto the Queen of Great Britain, her heirs and successors forever, the port and Island of Lagos, with all rights, profits, territories, and appurtenances [incidental rights] whatsoever thereunto belonging . . . freely, fully, entirely, and absolutely, the

*Source:* From C. W. Newbury, ed., *British Policy towards West Africa, 1786–1874* (Oxford: Clarendon Press, 1965), pp. 429–430.

inhabitants of the said island and territories, as the Queen's subjects, and under her sovereignty, . . . being still suffered [allowed] to live there.

*Article 2.* Docemo will be allowed the use of the title of King in its usual African signification, and will be permitted to decide disputes between natives of Lagos with their consent, subject to appeal to British laws. . . .

In consideration of the cession as before-mentioned of the port and island and territories of Lagos, the representatives of the Queen of Great Britain do promise, subject to the approval of Her Majesty, that Docemo shall receive an annual pension from the Queen of Great Britain. . . .

*Additional Article to the Lagos Treaty of Concession, 18 February 1862.* King Docemo . . . perfectly agrees to all the conditions thereof; and with regard to the 3d Article consents to receive as a pension, to be continued during his lifetime, the sum of 1,200 (twelve hundred) bags of cowries[1] per annum, as equal to his net revenue; and I, the undersigned representative of Her Majesty, agree on the part of Her Majesty to guarantee to the said . . . annual pension . . . for his lifetime, unless he should break any of the Articles of the above Treaty, in which case his pension will be forfeited.

---

[1]Cowrie is a term for any number of marine snails that live in the coastal waters of the Indian and Pacific oceans. The snails produce thick polished shells that were widely used as currency in West Africa, especially during the era of the transatlantic slave trade. Although costs were involved in purchasing and transporting the shells to Europe from the Indian Ocean and then to Africa, they were otherwise worthless to Europeans.

---

## 2 • Treaty Between the International Association of the Congo and Tonki, Chief of Ngombi, and Mampuya, Senior Chief of Mafela, 1884

**Art. I.**—The chiefs of Ngombi and Mafela recognize that it is highly desirable that the [International Association of the Congo][1] should, for the advancement of civilization and trade, be firmly established in their country. They therefore now, . . . for themselves and their heirs and successors for ever, do give up to the said Association the sovereignty and all sovereign and governing rights to all their territories. They also promise to assist the said Association in its work of governing and civilizing this country, and to use their influence to secure obedience to all laws made by the said Association, and to assist by labour or otherwise, any works, improvements, or expeditions which the said Association shall cause at any time to be carried out in any part of these territories.

**Art. II.**—The chiefs . . . promise at all times to join their forces with those of the said Association, to resist the forcible intrusion or repulse the attacks of foreigners of any nationality or colour.

**Art. III.**—The country thus ceded has about the following boundaries, viz., the whole of the Ngombi and Mafela countries, and any others tributary to them. . . . All roads and waterways running through this country, the right of

---

*Source:* From Henry M. Stanley, *The Congo and the Founding of Its Free State. A Story of the Work of Exploration* (New York: Harper & Brothers, 1885), pp. 195–197.

[1]An altered version of this document was published in explorer Henry Stanley's *The Congo and the Founding of Its Free State* (1885). The original document showed the agreement as being between the chiefs and the International Association of the Congo (the political and business arm of Leopold's enterprise in the Congo). Before the book went to print, however, the manuscript was edited by King Leopold, who changed the contracting party to the International African Association (the philanthropic society of explorers and geographers founded by Leopold in 1876). This is one example of how Leopold attempted to fool the world about the aims of his project. We have used the language of the original contract.

collecting tolls on the same, and all game, fishing, mining, and forest rights, are to be the absolute property of the said Association, together with any unoccupied lands as may at any time hereafter be chosen.

**Art. IV.**—[The International Association of the Congo] agree to pay . . . one piece of cloth per month to each of the undersigned chiefs, besides present of cloth in hand; and the said chiefs hereby acknowledge to accept this bounty and monthly subsidy in full settlement of all their claims on the said Association.

**Art. V.**—[The International Association of the Congo] promises:—

1. To take from the natives of this ceded country no occupied or cultivated lands, except by mutual agreement.

2. To promote to its utmost the prosperity of the said country.

3. To protect its inhabitants from all oppression or foreign intrusion.

4. It authorizes the chiefs to hoist its flag, to settle all local disputes and to maintain its authority with the natives.

Agreed to, signed and witnessed, this 1st day of April, 1884.

HENRY M. STANLEY.
Tonki, his X mark,
Senior Chief of Ngombi.
Mampuya, his X mark,
Senior Chief of Mafela.

---

## 3 • Agreement Between Charles D. Rudd, et al., and Lobengula, King of Matabeleland, 1891

WHEREAS Charles Dunell Rudd of Kimberley, Rochfort Maguire of London, and Francis Robert Thompson of Kimberley hereinafter called the grantees . . . do hereby covenant and agree to pay to me, my heirs, and successors the sum of One hundred Pounds sterling British Currency on the first day of every lunar month and further to deliver at my Royal Kraal [homestead] one thousand Martini-Henry Breech-loading Rifles[1] together with one hundred thousand rounds of suitable ball cartridge; five hundred of the said Rifles and fifty thousand of the said cartridge to be ordered from England forthwith and delivered with reasonable dispatch . . . so soon as the said grantees shall have commenced to work mining machinery within my territory and further to deliver on the Zambesi river a Steamboat with guns suitable for defensive purposes upon the said river. . . . I Lobengula King of Matabeleland, Mashonaland and certain adjoining territories . . . do hereby grant and assign unto the said grantees . . . the complete and exclusive charge over all metals and minerals situated and contained in my Kingdoms, Principalities and dominions together with full power to do all things that they may deem necessary to win and procure the same and to hold collect and enjoy the profits and revenue if any derivable from the said metals and minerals . . . , and WHEREAS I have been much molested of late by diverse persons seeking and desiring to obtain grants and concessions of Land and Mining rights in my territories I do hereby authorize the said grantees, . . . to take all necessary and lawful

*Source:* Lewis Mitchell, *The Life of the Right Hon. Cecil John Rhodes, 1853–1902,* Vol. 2 (London: Edward Arnold, 1910), pp. 244–245.
[1]The Martini-Henry rifle, first produced in 1871, had been standard issue for British troops, but in 1888, the year in which this agreement was signed, it was replaced with the Lee-Metford rifle. Production of the Martini-Henry rifle ended in 1889. After he repudiated the agreement with Rudd, Lobengula refused to accept the first shipment of rifles the English had promised.

steps to exclude from my Kingdoms, principalities, and dominions all persons seeking land, metals, minerals, or mining rights therein and I do hereby undertake to render them such needful assistance as they may from time to time require for the exclusion of such persons.

This given under my hand this thirtieth day of October in the year of our Lord Eighteen hundred and Eighty-Eight at my Royal Kraal.

his

Lobengula X

Mark

---

### 4 • Letter of King Lobengula to Queen Victoria

Some time ago a party of men came to my country, the principal one appearing to be a man called Rudd. They asked me for a place to dig for gold, and said they would give me certain things for the right to do so. I told them to bring what they could give and I would show them what I would give. A document was written and presented to me for signature. I asked what it contained, and was told that in it were my words and the words of those men. I put my hand to it. About three months afterward I heard from other sources that I had given by that document the right to all the minerals of my country. I called a meeting of my *Indunas* [counselors], and also of the white men and demanded a copy of the document. It was proved to me that I had signed away the mineral rights of my whole country to Rudd and his friends. I have since had a meeting of my *Indunas* and they will not recognize the paper, as it contains neither my words nor the words of those who got it. . . . I write to you that you may know the truth about this thing.

*Source:* Quoted in E. D. Morel, *Black Man's Burden* (London: Arnold, 1920), pp. 34–35.

## Colonialism at Its Darkest

### 61 • A. E. SCRIVENER, *JOURNAL*

Among the claims made by supporters of nineteenth-century imperialism none had as much appeal as the assurance that Western expansion was a "civilizing mission" to bring law, order, literacy, modern medicine, Christianity, and a host of other benefits to the colonized. Tens of thousands of Europeans and Americans—mainly missionaries but also doctors and some administrators—took up residence in Africa or Asia and worked to fulfill this promise. On the whole, however, the results of their efforts fell short of expectations. Instead, one is struck by the immense gap between the professed altruism of imperialism's advocates and imperialism's actual record. Nowhere was the gap greater than in the Congo of King Leopold II of Belgium.

As noted in the introduction to Multiple Voices VI, shortly after the founding in 1876 of the International African Association, ostensibly for scientific and humanitarian purposes, King Leopold of Belgium dispatched the explorer Henry M. Stanley and other agents to the Congo River Basin, where they obtained treaties that gave the king and his business associates control in the region. In 1879 he founded and placed under his personal control the International Association of the Congo, an organization designed to enrich him and his associates. With control of what came to be known as the Congo Free State, the association sold monopolies to private businessmen and exploited the region's ivory, rubber, and minerals.

Beginning in the 1890s, as world demand for rubber tires, gaskets, hoses, and insulation materials soared, the collection of raw rubber became the focus of Leopold's money-making schemes. Agents of private companies and the Congo Free State forced villagers into the forest to collect the sap from rubber vines and maimed, whipped, or killed them if they failed to reach their quotas. Leopold tried to keep his horrific system of forced labor a secret, but missionaries and journalists gradually revealed its horrors. In 1908, after a full investigation, Belgium's parliament took away the Congo Free State from its king and placed it under state control.

A. E. Scrivener, an American Baptist missionary who had labored in the Congo since the late 1880s, recorded his observations of rubber-collecting operations after a guilt-ridden Belgian official allowed him to observe them firsthand in several villages. In 1904 Edmund Morel, a bitter opponent of African imperialism, published excerpts from Scrivener's journal in his book *King Leopold's Rule in Africa*. Our excerpt begins with Scrivener's first impressions of rubber collecting in a village.

## QUESTIONS FOR ANALYSIS

1. What incentives and what forms of coercion did the Belgians and their agents use to "encourage" rubber collection?
2. Aside from the collection of rubber sap, what other forms of forced labor does Scrivener describe?
3. Aside from their punishments for failing to reach their quotas, why did rubber sap collection create special hardships for the African villagers?
4. How do the Africans describe their first reactions to the Belgians?
5. What was the overall impact of the rubber-collecting operation on the region that Scrivener visited?

Everything was on a military basis, but so far as I could see, the one and only reason for it all was rubber. It was the theme of every conversation, and it was evident that the only way to please one's superiors was to increase the output somehow. I saw a few men come in, and the frightened look on their faces tells only too eloquently of the awful time they have passed through. As I saw it brought in, each man had a little basket, containing say, four or five pounds of rubber. This was emptied into a larger basket and weighed, and being found sufficient, each man was given a cupful of coarse salt, and to some of the headmen a fathom [two yards] of calico. . . .

I heard from the white men and some of the soldiers[1] some most gruesome stories. The former white man [overseer of the station] . . . would stand at the door of the store to receive the rubber from

Source: A. E. Scrivener, *Journal*, from Edmund Morel, *King Leopold's Rule in Africa* (London: Heinemann Ltd., 1904), pp. 183-186.

[1] The soldiers were African mercenaries.

the poor trembling wretches, who after . . . weeks of privation in the forests, had ventured in with what they had been able to collect. A man bringing rather under the proper amount, the white man flies into a rage, and seizing a rifle from one of the guards, shoots him dead on the spot. Very rarely did rubber come in, but one or more were shot in that way at the door of the store "to make the survivors bring more next time." . . . The people are regarded as the property of the State for any purpose for which they may be needed. That they have any desires of their own, or any plans worth carrying out in connection with their own lives, would create a smile among the officials. It is one continual grind, and the native intercourse [interaction] between one district and another in the old style is practically non-existent. Only the roads to and from the various posts are kept open, and large tracts of country are abandoned to the wild beasts. The white man himself told me that you could walk on for five days in one direction and not see a single village or a single human being. And this where formerly there was a big tribe!

---

> Scrivener continues his journey and joins a group of refugees who have fled from their village; his party has just arrived in the town of Ngongo.

---

Soon we began talking, and, without any encouragement on my part, they began the tales I had become so accustomed to. They were living in peace and quietness when the white men came in . . . with all sorts of requests to do this and to do that, and they thought it meant slavery. So they attempted to keep the white men out of their country, but without avail. The rifles were too much for them. So they submitted, and made up their minds to do the best they could. . . . First came the command to build houses for the soldiers and this was done without

a murmur. Then they had to feed the soldiers, and all the men and women—hangers-on who accompanied them. Then they were told to bring in rubber. . . . "What strange white men to give us cloth and beads for the sap of a wild vine." They rejoiced in what they thought was their good fortune. But soon the reward was reduced until they were told to bring in the rubber for nothing. To this they tried to demur [object to], but to their great surprise several were shot by the soldiers, and the rest were told, with many curses and blows, to go at once or more would be killed. Terrified, they began to prepare their food for the fortnight's absence from the village, which the collection of the rubber entailed. The soldiers discovered them sitting about. "What, not gone yet!" Bang! bang! bang! And down fell one and another dead, in the midst of wives and companions. There is a terrible wail, . . . and an attempt made to prepare the dead for burial, but this is not allowed. All must go at once to the forest. And off the poor wretches had to go without even their tinderboxes to make fires. Many died in the forests from exposure and hunger, and still more from the rifles of the ferocious soldiers in charge of the post. . . . I was shown round the place, and the sites of former big chiefs' settlements were pointed out. A careful estimate made the population of, say, seven years ago, to be 2000 people in and about the post, within the radius of, say, a quarter of a mile, All told they would not muster 200 now, and there is so much sadness and gloom that they are fast decreasing. . . . Lying about in the grass, within a few yards of the house I was occupying, were numbers of human bones, in some cases complete skeletons. I counted thirty-six skulls, and saw many sets of bones from which the skulls were missing. I called one of the men, and asked the meaning of it. "When the rubber palaver[2] began," said he, "the soldiers shot so many we grew tired of burying, and very often we were not allowed to bury, and so we just dragged the

---

[2]In this context, "commotion" or "trouble.

bodies out into the grass and left them. There are hundreds all round if you would like to see them." . . . In due course we reached Ibali. There was hardly a sound building in the place. . . . I saw long files of men come as at Mbongo with their little baskets under their arms, saw them paid their milktin-full of salt, and the two yards of calico flung to the head men; saw their trembling timidity, and in fact a great deal more, to prove the state of terrorism that exists, and the virtual slavery in which the people are held.

# Imperialist Economics and Rebellion in German East Africa

## 62 • RECORDS OF THE MAJI-MAJI REBELLION

The Germans were latecomers to imperialism, but after they gained control of territories in Africa and Oceania, they were quick to adopt the view that colonies existed to serve the economic interests of the colonial master. This was the principle that underlay their policies in German East Africa, a large and politically diverse region on Africa's east coast, surrounded by Kenya to the north, the Belgian Congo to the west, and Northern Rhodesia and Mozambique to the south. German economic policy lacked direction in the 1880s and 1890s as the Germans struggled to overcome African resistance and experimented with several strategies to force Africans to grow crops, especially cotton, needed for their home industries.

In 1902 the Germans implemented a plan to increase cotton cultivation in the coastal and southern sections of the colony. It required each village to provide a quota of laborers who were paid a paltry amount to work cultivating cotton a certain number of days a year on government estates, settler plantations, or village fields. To encourage Africans to accept these low-paying jobs, the Germans instituted a head tax payable in cash only. Opposition to the plan led to rebellion in 1905. Encouraged by religious leaders who supplied the rebels with *maji,* magic water that supposedly made warriors impervious to bullets, the rebellion spread throughout the colony's central and southern regions. The Germans fought back with Maxim guns, mass executions, and the burning of villages. The rebellion ended in 1907, at a cost of 75,000 African deaths, many the result of famine.

The following testimony was gathered by German officials in the wake of the rebellion. Most of the information deals with the experiences of the Matumbi, who lived in the southeastern part of the colony.

### QUESTIONS FOR ANALYSIS

1. What do these records and testimonies reveal about Germany's administration of its colony?
2. Why did the Africans object so strongly to German agricultural policy?
3. What other aspects of German rule did the Africans find objectionable?
4. What does the source reveal about German views of Africans and Germany's African colonies?
5. What information does the source provide about the role of women in the African village?

## Recollections of Ndundule Mangaya

The cultivation of cotton was done by turns. Every village was allotted days on which to cultivate at Samanga Ndumbo [a coastal town] and at the Jumbe's [chief's] plantation. One person came from each homestead, unless there were very many people. Thus you might be told to work for five or ten days at Samanga. So a person would go. Then after half the number of days another man came from home to relieve him. . . . It was also like this at the Jumbe's. If you returned from Samanga then your turn at the Jumbe's remained, or if you began at the Jumbe's you waited for the turn at Samanga after you had finished. No woman went unless her husband ran away; then they would say she had hidden him. Then the woman would go. When in a village a former clan head was seized to go to cultivate he would offer his slave in his stead. Then after arriving there you all suffered very greatly. Your back and your buttocks were whipped, and there was no rising up once you stooped to dig. The good thing about the Germans was that all people were the same before the whip. If a Jumbe or akida[1] made a mistake he received the whip as well. Thus there were people whose job was to clear the land of trees and undergrowth; others tilled the land; others would smooth the field and plant; another group would do the weeding and yet another the picking; and lastly others carried the bales of cotton to the coast. . . .

Now digging and planting were in the months of Ntandatu and Nchimbi, and this was the time of very many wild pigs[2] in this country. If you left the chasing of the pigs to the women she could not manage well at night. In addition, the pigs are very stubborn at that period and will not move even if you go within very close range. Only very few women can assist their husbands at night and these are the ones with very strong hearts. There were just as many birds, and if you did not have children it was necessary to help your wife drive away the birds, while at the same time you cleared a piece of land for the second maize crop, because your wife would not have time. And during this very period they still wanted you to leave your home and go to Samanga or to work on the jumbe's plantation. This was why people became furious and angry. The work was astonishingly hard and full of grave suffering, but its wages were the whip on one's back and buttocks. And yet he [the Germans] still wanted us to pay him the tax. Were we not human beings? And Maatumbi [members of the Matumbi tribe] since the days of old, did not want to be troubled or ruled by any person. . . . Given such grave suffering they thought it better for a man to die rather than live in such torment. . . . [When] he [the Germans] began to cause us to cultivate cotton for him and to dig roads and so on, then people said, "This has now become an absolute ruler. Destroy him."

## Recollection of Nduli Njimbwi Concerning Work on a Plantation Owned by a German Settler Named Steinhagen

During the cultivation there was much suffering. We, the labor conscripts, stayed in the front line cultivating. Then behind us was an overseer whose work it was to whip us. Behind the overseer there was a jumbe, and every jumbe stood behind his fifty men. Behind the line of jumbes stood Bwana Kinoo [Steinhagen] himself. . . . The overseer had a whip, and he was extremely cruel. His work was to whip the conscripts if they rose up or tried to rest, or if they left a trail of their footprints behind

---

*Source:* From C. G. K Gwassa and Joseph Iffile, "Records of the Maji-Maji Rising" (Nairobi: East African Publishing House, 1967), pp. 4-8.[Historical Association of Tanzania, Paper No. 4.

[1]Usually Muslims recruited from coastal towns who functioned as overseers or guards.
[2]A threat to cultivated crops.

them.[3] . . . And on the other side Bwana Kinoo had a bamboo stick. If the men of a certain jumbe left their footprints behind them, that jumbe would be boxed on the ears and Kinoo would beat him with the bamboo stick using both hands, while at the same time the overseer lashed out at us laborers.

### Excerpts from an Interview with a German Official Von Geibler Concerning the Communal Plots

Village plots were set up in each headman's area early in 1902 (September–October). . . . Each headman [village chief] made a plot for his area in the neighborhood of his headquarters. The principle was that every 30–50 men were to cultivate 2½ acres. . . . Where possible, the advice of the natives was obtained as to the crop to be grown. So far as possible, one crop was to be grown on each plot, according to the type of soil. Some 2,000 acres were cleared and cultivated. . . .

What was the labor situation and the supervision? . . . According to returns by the headmen, the number of able-bodied men amounted to:

1902–03 c. 25,000 men
1903–04 c. 26,000 men
1904–05 c. 25,000 men

During the last year, women and children had to be brought in to help, since the men frequently refused to work. . . .

The akidas were relied upon to report on the condition of the plots, and they were also responsible for punishing those whom the headmen reported as refractory workers. There was no European control of this. . . . Only once a year did a European visit the plots, to measure them out and select the land. . . . Work on most of the plots *was flatly* refused during 1904–05. The headmen complained that they no longer had the people in hand. The officials of the Commune believed at the time that they could detect a state of ferment.

Last year (1904–05), following reports from the akidas and from Sergeant Holzhausen, who was sent to inspect the headmen, numerous headmen were punished by the District Office with imprisonment in chains or solitary confinement for totally neglecting their village plots as a result of the natives' refusal to work. The last, in June, was headman Kibasila, who got one month in chains.

---

[3]Such a trail would have meant the person had walked away from his assigned work.

# The Ottoman Empire and Egypt

Ottoman Turkey, Iran, and Egypt, a virtually independent state within the Ottoman Empire, differed in many ways, but their rulers all faced a similar challenge in the nineteenth century. They all needed to devise and implement policies to withstand growing pressures from Europe, whose armies threatened their territories, whose businessmen threatened to take control of their economies, and whose ideas threatened many of their subjects' beliefs and values. Their states needed to be strengthened, and quickly, if they were to avoid the fate of India, where the efforts of India's princes failed to prevent a British takeover of the subcontinent.

For all three states the priority was military reform. Ottoman and Iranian defeats by Russia in the late eighteenth and early nineteenth centuries and Napoleon's invasion of Egypt between 1798 and 1801 revealed the gap between the well-armed and disciplined European armies and the poorly trained and frequently mutinous troops that opposed them. In response, the Ottoman sultans Selim III (see source 41) and Mahmud II (r. 1808–1839), as well as Crown Prince Abbas of Iran (1789–1833), sought to establish "new order" armies that were trained by European officers, outfitted in European-style uniforms, and armed with modern guns and artillery. Muhammad Ali, the Albanian general who ruled Egypt as an independent state within the Ottoman Empire from 1805 to 1848, went further. Beginning in the 1820s he set about creating a large conscript army trained according to European methods. Ottoman reformers in the 1830s followed his model by reorganizing the army, imposing conscription, and increasing the army's size from 24,000 to 120,000.

Meeting the costs of military modernization required new taxes, new methods of revenue collection, and above all, economic development. In the 1830s Muhammad Ali subsidized Egypt's first factories and took control of Egypt's agrarian economy by requisitioning approximately half of Egypt's arable land and planting indigo, sugar, flax, and especially cotton for export. He also required peasants to grow these same crops and sell them to the government at artificially low prices. Egypt's commercial importance attracted European investment in banks, railroads, and the building of the Suez Canal, which in turn gave rise to a large European community in Alexandria and Cairo. Economic development was slower in Ottoman-controlled lands, where European investors worried about the empire's political instability and poor credit rating. It was slower still in Persia, where foreign investment could be attracted only by granting concessions to European businessmen, who were given control of various industries (banking, tobacco, insurance, construction, food production, and oil, among others) in return for one-time payments and a small share of earnings.

Military modernization, political reorganization, and economic development—the essential components of "reform" in all three states—faced many obstacles. Large numbers of Ottoman subjects, Egyptians, and Iranians were indifferent or hostile to reform, and many government officials, military officers, and religious leaders who favored reform disagreed about what it should entail. Despite such difficulties, rulers in all three states accomplished a great deal. By the early 1900s, however, Egypt was a British protectorate, much of Iran was controlled by Russia and Great Britain, and the Ottoman Empire, shorn of its holdings in Europe and North Africa, was on the verge of collapse.

Meanwhile, immediate challenges in the form of wars, rebellions, religious dissent, indifferent rulers, and pressures from Western diplomats and businessmen had to be faced. In the end, however, it was the inability of Ottoman, Egyptian, and Iranian regimes to meet the costs of military modernization that doomed them to collapse or subservience to the West.

# Ottoman Reforms in the Tanzimat Era

## 63 • SULTAN ABDULMEJID, THE ISLAHAT FERMANI OF 1856

A new era of reform for the Ottoman Empire began on November 3, 1839, when before an assemblage of state officials, dignitaries, religious leaders, and foreign luminaries, Foreign Minister Mustafa Reshid Pasha read, on behalf of the sixteen-year-old Sultan Abdulmejid, a decree that spelled out a program to restore the empire to its lost glory after a one-hundred-fifty-year descent into "weakness and poverty." With language borrowed from the French Declaration of the Rights of Man and of the Citizen and the American Bill of Rights, the edict promised laws to prohibit bribery, regulate army recruitment and tax collection, and guarantee the security of life and property. Such laws would apply to all Ottoman subjects, with no distinction between Muslims, Christians, and Jews. This edict, known as the "Noble Edict" or the "Rose Chamber Edict," after the palace room in which it was read, launched a three-decade period of *Tanzimat, or* "restructuring."

Seventeen years later, in 1856, Sultan Abdulmejid issued the *Islahat Fermani* (Reform Edict), in which he renewed his government's commitment to reform and proposed a number of new policies. It represents the high point of efforts to reform the Ottoman Empire while maintaining the powers of the sultan and the traditional mix of Muslim, Christian, and Jewish subjects.

## QUESTIONS FOR ANALYSIS

1. What benefits were the sultan's non-Muslim subjects to receive as a result of this proclamation?
2. What efforts were made to improve the empire's system of justice?
3. What specific economic reforms are proposed? What do they reveal about the state of the empire's economy?
4. To what extent does this document extend meaningful political rights to the sultan's subjects?
5. In what respects does this document reflect European liberal ideas of individual freedom and religious toleration?

---

Let it be done as herein set forth. . . .

All the privileges and spiritual immunities granted by my ancestors from time immemorial, to all Christian communities or other non-Muslim faiths established in my empire shall be confirmed and maintained.

Every Christian or other non-Muslim community shall be bound within a fixed period, and with the concurrence of a commission composed of members of its own body, to proceed to examine its actual immunities and privileges, and to discuss and submit to my Sublime Porte[1] the reforms required

*Source:* E. A. van Dyck, *Report upon the Capitulations of the Ottoman Empire* (Washington D.C.: U.S. Government Printing Office, 1881, 1882), Part I, pp. 106–108.
[1]"Sublime Porte," or "High Gate," refers to the gate in Istanbul giving access to the buildings that house the offices of state officials. It came to refer to the sultan's government in much the same way that the term "the White House" refers to the U.S. presidency.

by the progress of civilization and of the age. The powers conceded to the Christian Patriarchs and Bishops[2] by the sultan Mehmed II[3] and his successors shall be made to harmonize with the new position which my generous and beneficent intentions ensure to these communities. . . . In the towns, small boroughs, and villages, where the whole population is of the same religion, no obstacle shall be offered to the repair, according to their original plan, of buildings set apart for religious worship, schools, hospitals, and cemeteries. . . .

Every distinction or designation tending to make any group inferior to another group, on account of their religion, language, or race, shall be forever eradicated from Administrative Protocol. The laws shall be put in force against the use of any injurious or offensive expression, either among private individuals or on the part of the authorities. . . .

As all forms of religion shall be freely professed in my dominions, no subject of my Empire shall be hindered in the exercise of the religion that he professes. No one shall be compelled to change their religion . . . and all the subjects of my Empire, without distinction of nationality, shall be admissible to public employments. . . . All the subjects of my Empire, without distinction, shall be received into the civil and military schools of the government. . . . Moreover, every community is authorized to establish public schools of science, art, and industry. . . .

All commercial and criminal suits between Muslims and Christian or other non-Muslim subjects, or between Christian or other non-Muslims of different sects, shall be referred to Mixed Tribunals [consisting of Muslim and non-Muslim judges]. The proceedings of these Tribunals shall be public; the parties shall be confronted, and shall produce their witnesses, whose testimony shall be received, without distinction, upon an oath taken according to the religious law of each sect. . . . Penal, correctional, and commercial laws, and rules of procedure for the Mixed Tribunals, shall be drawn up as soon as possible, and formed into a code. . . . Steps shall be taken for the reform of the penitentiary system. . . .

The organization of the police . . . shall be revised in such a manner as to give to all the peaceable subjects of my Empire the strongest guarantees for the safety both of their persons and property. . . . Christian subjects, and those of other non-Muslim sects, . . . shall, as well as Muslims, be subject to the obligations of the Law of Recruitment [for military service]. The principle of obtaining substitutes, or of purchasing exemption, shall be admitted. . . .

As the laws regulating the purchase, sale, and disposal of real property are common to all the subjects of my Empire, it shall be lawful for foreigners to possess landed property in my dominions. . . .

The taxes are to be levied from all the subjects of my Empire, without distinction of religion. The most prompt and energetic means for remedying the abuses in collecting the taxes shall be considered. The system of direct collection shall gradually, and as soon as possible, be substituted for the plan of farming,[4] in all the branches of the revenues of the state.

A special law having been already passed, which declares that the budget of the revenue and the expenditure of the state shall be drawn up and made known every year, the said law shall be most scrupulously observed. . . .

The heads of each community and a delegate, designated by my Sublime Porte, shall be

---

[2] A reference to the heads of the Greek and Armenian Christian churches in the empire.

[3] Mehmed the Great (r. 1451–1481O) authorized autonomous religious communities to give his non-Muslim subjects religious freedom and gain their support.

[4] Tax farming was a practice in which the government contracted with private financiers who collected taxes and kept a certain percentage for themselves.

summoned to take part in the deliberations of the Supreme Council of Justice on all occasions which might interest the generality of the subjects of my Empire. . . .

Steps shall be taken for the formation of banks and other similar institutions, so as to effect a reform in the monetary and financial system, as well as to create funds to be employed in augmenting the sources of the material wealth of my empire.

Everything that can impede commerce or agriculture shall be abolished. To accomplish these objects means shall be sought to profit by science, the art, and the funds of Europe, and thus gradually to execute them.

# The Costs of Modernization and Reform: The Case of Egypt

## 64 • KHEDIVE ISMAIL, SPEECH TO THE ASSEMBLY OF DELEGATES, 1869

As a result of massive deficits and the need to guarantee debt payments to outside investors, the Ottoman and Iranian governments were forced to relinquish control of tax collection and expenditures to foreign businessmen. In Egypt, government indebtedness, which spiraled out of control during the reign of Khedive Ismail (r. 1863–1879), had graver consequences.

Ismail's predecessor, Said Pasha, who entered into an agreement with the Frenchman Ferdinand de Lesseps to supply the labor, land, and almost half of the financing for the Suez Canal project, was the first Egyptian leader to borrow large amounts from European bankers, and at the time of his death in 1863, Egypt had a foreign debt of £6 million, an amount equal to £645 million in 2014 currency. Ismail, who had studied two years in Paris and was obsessed with all things European (in 1879 he proclaimed, "Our country is no longer in Africa; we are now part of Europe"), borrowed even more enormous sums to pay for the completion of the Suez Canal, new palaces, Egypt's sugar industry, an opera house and theater in Cairo, museums, schools, a new postal service, an expanded army and navy, the administration of newly conquered Sudan, gifts to the Ottoman sultan (in return for granting Ismail and his descendants the right to use the title "khedive," or prince), war with Ethiopia, and a host of personal expenses, including yachts, palaces, and Parisian gowns for his three wives. With the demand for Egyptian cotton exports plummeting after the end of the U.S. Civil War and his inability to say "no" to the next expensive project, by the mid-1870s the government's debt stood at £100 million. In 1875 he raised £4 million by selling the government's shares in the Suez Canal Company to the British government at one fourth of their value, but in 1876 he had no choice but to relinquish control of government finances to English and French officials, who cut expenditures to the bone and allocated sixty percent of all expenditures to debt service. This set in motion a train of events that led to the forced removal of Ismail from office in 1879, a nationalist rebellion led by Colonel Ahmad Urabi between 1879 and 1882, and the establishment of a British protectorate in 1882.

Ismail delivered the following speech in 1869 to the Assembly of Delegates, a body created by Ismail in 1866 mainly to make it seem that he was a constitutional monarch. Consisting of seventy-five members elected indirectly for three-year terms, the assembly had no legislative powers but could discuss matters relating to public works, taxes, education, and agriculture. As shown in the speech, in 1869 government debt also was on its agenda.

## QUESTIONS FOR ANALYSIS

1. Ismail makes the claim at the start of the speech that "the condition of our expenses is excellent." How strong is the evidence he presents to support such a claim?
2. What arguments does Ismail present to justify his government's expenditures?
3. From what Ismail tells us in his speech, which groups and which regions of the country most likely would benefit from his numerous projects?
4. Evaluate Ismail's efforts to improve Egyptian education. Keep in mind that in 1869 Egypt's population was approximately 6.3 million. Cairo's population was approximately 270,000, more than five percent of whom were foreigners.

---

The condition of our finances is excellent: they have been administered in such a way that we have been able to repay some large obligations without embarrassment to your government and without unusual sacrifices by the people.

Unfortunately, it is also true that this year the Nile did not attain its usual level and so . . . , the fields lacked the precious ingredient of water. Still, thanks to the measures taken by your government we have been able to arrange for the normal irrigation of the provinces of lower Egypt.[1] Although the same measures were undertaken in upper Egypt . . . our efforts were not crowned with equal success . . . and a rather large number of fields . . . were not irrigated. . . .

In this situation I was quick to come to the aid of the farmers struck by an unforeseen disaster by remitting taxes and tithes on non-irrigated fields. Also, I remitted their salt tax so that salt was delivered to them without charge, and I gave orders that they should be furnished with enough grain to sow their fields for planting. Finally, I exempted them

from labor on public works. These measures cost the government a sum in excess of 80,000 purses[2] . . . but contrary to what used to be done in such circumstances, we sustained the sacrifice without incurring debts that would have to be paid in the future.

Independently of these extraordinary measures, I also was able to come to the aid of each and every one of the people of upper Egypt thanks to the prosperous condition of our finances. I remitted the payment of the tax which was levied by the chamber last year and I granted new terms for the payment of the salt tax. . . .

We are confident that . . . these exceptional circumstances will not reappear for a long time and that this year the normal flood of the Nile will bring us its usual benefits. Nevertheless, . . . I wanted to prepare a proper program that would ensure the flooding of upper Egypt's fields under all circumstances. After conferring with our principal engineers . . . I named a commission that went to upper Egypt; after an on the spot study of the

---

*Source:* Robert G. Landen, *The Emergence of the Modern Middle East* (New York: Van Nostrand, 1970), pp. 65–72. Reprinted with the permission of the author.
[1]Upper Egypt refers to the Nile River Valley below Cairo; Lower Egypt refers to the Nile Delta Region.

[2]A purse was worth 25,000 paras, the standard silver coin of Ottoman Egypt. At the time 80,000 purses equaled £376,000.

scientific measures needed to assure the irrigation of the most elevated fields no matter what the level of the Nile flood might be, they proceeded immediately to put these measures into operation. . . .

The government has been able to bear some extraordinary expenses because of the resources that it has amassed through sage reductions in certain services as well as by the conclusion of the last loan. . . . A large part of this debt has been retired and our debt has been reduced today to approximately seventeen million pounds including the new loan. As for the sums borrowed by my government, they have been, as you have been informed, contracted in large part for public works and for expenses undertaken for the general well-being and progress of the country. Above these amounts, eight million pounds have been paid to the Suez Canal Company. . . . The government possesses almost half of the stock shares of the company and will have the right to 15% of the profits resulting from its operation; so soon we will have . . . a new source of revenue.

In order to justify the large size of our debt I need only enumerate the important projects which have been completed recently. I can cite in the first place the new 850 mile long railroad line. The results which this new means of communications has produced in the benefit of the country's prosperity are too apparent for me to have to dwell on them. . . . I can cite, moreover, 4 draw bridges built, 100 ordinary bridges of which 40 are in lower Egypt and 60 are in upper Egypt, 2 movable bridges . . . , the Suez dry-dock, the passenger dock and the enlargement of the port of Suez, and finally a great number of buildings and works of other types none-the-less useful—built in upper and lower Egypt, in the cities of Cairo and Alexandria and in other cities of Egypt.

From the financial point of view, . . . you will find in the establishment or in the reorganizing of many civil or military schools and in the organization of our land and sea military forces the justification for large expenses. . . . Since my accession our military establishment has been completely reformed and modernized; a large quantity of new model guns has been ordered. Factories for the manufacture of uniforms and military material have been established, warships and transports such as steam frigates, armored corvettes,[3] and 22 various sailing ships have been built or purchased and are at our disposition, some in the Mediterranean, some in the Red Sea. Today, thanks to God, our army and our navy are on a regular and respectable footing and we are completely able to provide for the country's security. . . .

I have to thank Providence that I have been able to realize in large part the ideas for increasing Egypt's prosperity which It inspired in me at the time of my accession to power. In my remarks addressed on that occasion to the consuls representing the several foreign powers, I emphasized five points. . . .

The first point relative to the suppression of the "corvée"[4] happily is no longer a question today. I have not avoided any sacrifice in order to gain its suppression and today, thanks to your helpful assistance, it is an accomplished fact. . . .

In the second point of my remarks, I called for the development of agriculture and commerce. Have I any need to remind you of what I have done to encourage this development? As for agriculture, it will suffice if I remind you that the works already listed have increased cultivated land by 327,485 feddans.[5] . . . As for commerce, it has profited greatly . . . thanks to the extension of the

---

[3]A small, lightly armed warship.

[4]Much of the early labor in the construction of the Suez Canal was carried out by poorly paid Egyptian peasants, twenty thousand of whom were conscripted annually for this purpose. Although from midcentury onward

conscripted soldiers performed some of the labor previously done by conscripted peasants, *corvée* labor was still being used at the end of the nineteenth century.

[5]A unit of area equal to slightly more than one acre.

railroads and the creation of facilities which have grown up because of them.

In the third point of my discourse I stated that public education was the foundation of the civilization of a country. You have been shown what I have done in this matter and you know the many schools which I have founded as well as the results I have obtained. . . .

*Schools of Cairo*

| | Students |
|---|---|
| Primary school | 388 |
| Preparatory school | 400 |
| Polytechnic and architecture school | 63 |
| School of administration and languages | 39 |
| School of surveying and accounting | 55 |
| School of arts and crafts | 82 |
| Design class | 11 |
| | TOTAL 1038 |

*Schools of Alexandria*

| | |
|---|---|
| Primary school | 108 |
| Preparatory school | 133 |
| School of seamanship | 31 |
| | TOTAL 272 |

*Provincial Schools*

| | |
|---|---|
| School of Tantah | 193 |
| School of Asyut | 95 |
| | TOTAL 288 |

*Schools Supported by the Ministry of War*

| | |
|---|---|
| Artillery school | 100 |
| Cavalry school | 70 |
| Infantry school | 217 |
| Staff school | 28 |
| Veterinary school | 21 |
| School of fencing | 24 |
| School of accounting | 32 |
| School of agriculture | 38 |
| School of ordnance | 26 |
| School of arts and crafts | 22 |
| | TOTAL 578 |

| Total: Schools, 22 | TOTAL: Students, 2176 |
|---|---|

In a fourth point I promised to draw up a civil list for my personal expenses. You know with what care I have carried out that engagement for several years. Finally, the fifth point of my remarks declared that a well-organized judicial structure was necessary to ease and strengthen relations between Europeans and locals[6]. . . . Knowing your ardent desire to see re-forms accomplished so that all this country's people can enjoy their advantages without distinction of nationality, I have the satisfaction of announcing to you that I have obtained the adherence of most of the great powers to the principle of judicial reform. . . . I hope that a special commission will be organized shortly to outline the organization of the new jurisdiction and to define its structure to the mutual advantage of the interested parties.

You see, gentlemen, that the prosperity of the county has been and is still my constant preoccupation. . . .

---

[6]With the influx of large numbers of foreigners into Egypt, adjudicating civil and criminal cases involving non-Egyptians became a problem. The solution was a system of Mixed Courts, staffed by Egyptian and foreign judges who would decide cases on the basis of French law. The Mixed Courts began functioning in 1875, four years before Ismail was removed from office and replaced by his son, Tewfik.

# India Under British Rule

As Great Britain took control of India during the nineteenth century, British administrators, policymakers, and the general public all agreed that this new colony should serve the economic interests of the mother country. It would be a source of raw materials, an area for investment, and a market for manufactured goods. Other issues, however, sparked debate. Most realized that at some point, the British would leave India and their colony would become a self-governing, independent state. They had no timetable for leaving, however, and they disagreed about how to prepare their Indian subjects for independence. They would bring some Indians into the colonial administration, but how many and at what levels? They would provide India with schools and colleges, but what kind of education would they offer? They would introduce European values and political principles to the Indians, but in doing so, how much Indian culture would be preserved?

The Indians were even more divided about the meaning and future of British rule. At first, many welcomed the British presence as a way to open the door to Western science, constitutional government, and economic development. Such views persisted into the twentieth century, but by the late 1800s, only a small minority embraced them unequivocally. Many Indians came to resent the British assumption that Western ways were superior to centuries-old Indian beliefs and practices. They also were offended by Britain's one-sided economic policies, which drained India's resources, stifled development, and damaged traditional industries. Finally, they were angered by Great Britain's reluctance to seriously consider Indian self-rule.

As the following documents reveal, an evaluation of the benefits and harm of British rule in India is no simple matter. Historians continue to debate the issue down to the present day.

# The Case for Western Schools

## 65 • RAMMOHUN ROY, LETTER TO LORD AMHERST

From the 1770s onward, directors of the East India Company, missionaries, and the London government all agreed that Britain had ethical and practical reasons to support schools for their Indian subjects. What they could not agree on was what these schools should teach. At first, the East India Company, in the interest of not disturbing traditional Indian culture and social relationships, sponsored studies in Persian, Arabic, and the ancient language of Sanskrit. Such an approach was favored by influential British scholars and intellectuals known as "Orientalists," who greatly admired Indian culture, and by most early missionaries, who accommodated their Indian audience by learning Indian dialects and translating the Bible into native languages. By the early 1800s, however, many Indians began to demand schools that taught English and Western curricula to prepare them for jobs made available to them by the East India Company. Their views were supported by a growing number of Englishmen, including some missionaries, who saw little or no value in Indian culture and sought to establish schools that would be agents of Anglicization. The debate between the two sides began in earnest in 1813, when Parliament voted funds "for the revival and promotion of literature and the encouragement of the learned natives of India" and appointed a Committee on Public Instruction to decide how the funds should be spent.

Rammohun Roy, "the father of modern India," was one of those who strongly supported Western-style schools. Born into a devout high-caste Hindu family in 1772, Roy showed an early genius for languages and a keen interest in religions. He learned Arabic, Persian, Greek, and Sanskrit and spent five years traveling across India seeking religious enlightenment. After mastering English, he entered the service of the East India Company, ultimately attaining the highest administrative rank possible for an Indian. In 1814, at age 42, he retired to Kolkata [Calcutta], where he founded several newspapers and schools and campaigned to abolish the practice of widow burning, or *sati*. He wrote the following letter in 1823 to the British governor-general of India, Lord Amherst, to oppose a British plan to sponsor a school in Kolkata to teach Sanskrit and Hindu literature.

In 1835, the debate over Indian education was settled when a committee appointed by the British government decided that the schools it sponsored should provide an English-style education. According to the committee's chair, Thomas Macaulay, the goal was to produce young men who were "Indian in blood and colour, but English in taste, in opinions, and in intellect."

### QUESTIONS FOR ANALYSIS

1. How would you characterize Roy's attitude toward the British? Does he seem comfortable offering the British advice?
2. What does he especially admire about Western learning and literature?

3. What does he view as the weaknesses of traditional Indian learning?
4. According to Roy, what implications would a Hindu-based educational system have for India's political future?

---

The establishment of a new Sanskrit School in Calcutta evinces the laudable desire of government to improve the natives of India by education—a blessing for which they must ever be grateful, and every well-wisher of the human race must be desirous that the efforts made to promote it should be guided by the most enlightened principles, so that the stream of intelligence may flow in the most useful channels.

When this seminary of learning was proposed, we understood that the government had ordered a considerable sum of money to be devoted to the instruction of its Indian subjects. We were filled with sanguine hopes that this sum would be laid out in employing European gentlemen of talent and education to instruct the natives of India in mathematics, natural philosophy, chemistry, anatomy, and other useful sciences, which the natives of Europe have carried to a degree of perfection that has raised them above the inhabitants of other parts of the world. . . .

We find that the government is establishing a Sanskrit school under Hindu pandits [learned men] to impart such knowledge as is already current in India. This seminary (similar in character to those which existed in Europe before the time of Lord Bacon[1]) can only be expected to load the minds of youth with grammatical niceties and metaphysical distinctions of little or no practical use to the possessors or to society. The pupils will there acquire what was known two thousand years ago with the addition of vain and empty subtleties since then produced by speculative men such as is already commonly taught in all parts of India.

The Sanskrit language, so difficult that almost a lifetime is necessary for its acquisition, is well known to have been for ages a lamentable check to the diffusion of knowledge, and the learning concealed under this almost impervious veil is far from sufficient to reward the labor of acquiring it. . . .

Neither can much improvement arise from such speculations as the following which are the themes suggested by the Vedanta.[2] In what manner is the soul absorbed in the Deity? What relation does it bear to the Divine Essence? Nor will youths be fitted to be better members of society by the Vedantic doctrines which teach them to believe that all visible things have no real existence, that as father, brother, etc., have no real entity, they consequently deserve no real affection, and therefore the sooner we escape from them and leave the world the better. . . .

If it had been intended to keep the British nation in ignorance of real knowledge, the Baconian philosophy would not have been allowed to displace the system of the schoolmen which was the best calculated to perpetuate ignorance. In the same manner the Sanskrit system of education would be the best calculated to keep this country in darkness, if such had been the policy of the British legislature. But as the improvement of the native population is the object of the government, it will consequently promote a more liberal and enlightened system of instruction, embracing mathematics, natural philosophy, chemistry, anatomy, with other useful sciences, which may be accomplished with the sums proposed by employing a few gentlemen of talent and learning educated in Europe and providing

---

*Source:* Rammohun Roy, *The English Works of Rammohun Roy* (Allahabad, India: Panini Office, 1906), pp. 471–474.
[1]The English philosopher and prophet of science, Francis Bacon (1561–1626).

[2]Vedanta refers to the philosophical portion of the ancient scriptures of India, the Vedas. Specifically, it refers to the Upanishads, but it also includes the Bhagavad Gita, the great epics of India, as well as other texts, hymns, and writings.

a college furnished with necessary books, instruments, and other apparatus.

In presenting this subject to your Lordship, I conceive myself discharging a solemn duty which I owe to my countrymen, and also to that enlightened sovereign and legislature which have extended their benevolent care to this distant land, actuated by a desire to improve the inhabitants, and therefore humbly trust you will excuse the liberty I have taken in thus expressing my sentiments to your Lordship.

# A Call to Expel the British

## 66 • THE AZAMGARH PROCLAMATION

On May 10, 1857, in Meerut in northern India, three Indian infantry regiments that were part of the army maintained by the British East India Company shot their British officers, released all prisoners from jail, and marched on the nearby city of Delhi, which fell to them on May 11. This sparked similar mutinies across northern India, and with scattered support from peasants, landowners, and a few native princes, the rebellion appeared to threaten the very basis of British authority in India. In the following months, however, British forces regrouped, and with the help of loyal Indian troops, crushed the rebels in 1858. Though brief, the Indian Rebellion (also called the Great Rebellion, the Indian Mutiny, the Revolt of 1857, the Uprising of 1857, and the Sepoy Mutiny) was bitterly fought, with atrocities committed by both sides. Two months after it ended, Parliament passed the India Act, which stripped the East India Company of its political authority and placed India directly under the Crown.

The meaning and significance of the Indian Rebellion continue to be debated. To some, it is considered to be the first expression of Indian nationalism; to others it was nothing more than a series of army mutinies that never garnered much support outside the north. There is more agreement about its causes. It was triggered by discontent among the Indian troops (sepoys) in the East India Company's Bengal army, discontent that boiled over into rebellion when the British introduced new cartridges greased with cow fat, which made them obnoxious to Hindu soldiers, and pig fat, which made them obnoxious to Muslims. This was only the spark, however. The rebellion gained support from many groups, some with specific grievances over British rule and others with vague fears about British intentions. Some of these grievances and concerns are revealed in the document that follows.

The document below, known as the Azamgarh Proclamation, was one of several such proclamations that were circulated to win support for the rebellion. This proclamation, supposedly issued in the city of Azamgarh, is thought to be the work of Mirza Mughal, the fifth son of the 82-year-old king of Delhi and Mughal emperor, Bahadur Shah. In some versions, the proclamation is ascribed to the king of Awadh (Oudh), whose territory had been annexed by the British in 1856. Whoever the author was, his goal was to bring Hindus and Muslims together to expel the British and restore Mughal authority. To forestall such a dream, the India Act of 1858, by which Parliament stripped the East India Company of its political authority, also abolished the Mughal Empire.

## QUESTIONS FOR ANALYSIS

1. What incentives does the author of the proclamation offer to those who would join the rebellion?
2. For each of the groups discussed (zamindars, merchants, artisans), what, according to the proclamation, have been the detrimental effects of British rule?
3. What role does religion play in the proclamation?
4. How do the views of the author of the proclamation differ from those of Rammohun Roy (source 65)?
5. What solutions for India's problems does the proclamation suggest?

It is well known to all that in this age the people of Hindustan [northern India], both Hindus and Muslims, are being ruined under the tyranny and oppression of the infidel and treacherous English. It is therefore the bound duty of those who have any sort of connection with any of the Muslim royal families to stake their lives and property for the well-being of the public . . . and I, who am the grandson of Bahadur Shah Ghazi, emperor of India, having . . . come here to get rid of the infidels and to liberate and protect the poor helpless people now groaning under their iron rule, have, by the aid of the Mujahidins [fighters for Islam against infidels] . . . raised the standard of Muhammad, and persuaded the orthodox Hindus who had been subject to my ancestors, and have been and are still partners in the destruction of the English, to raise the standard of Mahavir.[1]

Therefore, for the information of the public, the present proclamation is put in circulation, and it is the imperative duty of all to take it into their careful consideration, and abide by it. Parties anxious to participate in the common cause, but having no means to provide for themselves, shall receive their daily subsistence from me; and be it known to all, that the ancient works, both of the Hindus and Muslims, the writings of the miracle-workers, and the calculations of the astrologers, pundits, and

fortune-tellers, all agree in asserting that the English will no longer have any footing in India. . . .

Section I.—Regarding Zamindars [landholders].—It is evident that the British government, in making settlements with zamindars, have imposed exorbitant taxes, and have disgraced and ruined several zamindars by putting up their estates to public auction for arrears of rent. . . . In litigations regarding zamindars, the immense value of stamps [on official documents], and other unnecessary expenses of the civil courts, which are full of all sorts of crooked dealings, and the practice of allowing a case to hang on for years, are all calculated to impoverish the litigants. Besides this, the coffers of the zamindars are annually taxed with payments for schools, hospitals, roads, etc. Such extortions will have no manner of existence in the royal government; but, on the contrary, the taxes will be light, the dignity and honor of the zamindars safe, and every zamindar will have absolute rule in his own territory.

Section II.—Regarding Merchants.—It is plain that the infidel and treacherous British government has monopolized the trade of all the fine and valuable merchandise such as indigo, cloth, and other articles, leaving only the trade of trifles to the people, and even in this they are not without their share of the profits, which they secure by means of customs and stamp fees, etc., so that the people have

---

*Source:* In Charles Ball, *The History of the Indian Mutiny* (London: London Printing and Publishing, 1858–1859), Vol. 2, pp. 630–632.

[1]"Great Hero." In this context, a name for the Hindu god Vishnu.

merely a trade in name. . . . When the royal government is established, all these aforesaid fraudulent practices shall be abolished, and the trade of every article, without exception, both by land and water, shall be open to the native merchants of India, who will have the benefit of the government steam-vessels and steam carriages for the conveyance of the merchandise gratis; and merchants having no capital of their own shall be assisted from the public treasury. . . .

Section III.—Regarding Public Servants.—It is no secret that under the British government, natives employed in the civil and military services, have little respect, low pay, and no manner of influence; and all the posts of dignity and emolument [reward] in both departments, are exclusively bestowed on Englishmen. . . . But under the royal government, . . . the posts which the English enjoy at present will be given to the natives . . . together with landed estates, ceremonial dress, tax-free lands, and influence. Natives, whether Hindus or Muslims, who fall fighting against the English, are sure to go to heaven; and those killed fighting for the English, will, doubtless, go to hell. Therefore, all the natives in the British service ought to be alive to their religion and interest, and, abjuring their loyalty to the English, side with the royal government. . . .

Section IV.—Regarding Artisans.—It is evident that the Europeans, by the introduction of English articles into India, have thrown the weavers, cotton-dressers, carpenters, blacksmiths, and shoemakers, &c., out of employ, and have engrossed [taken over] their occupations, so that every description of native artisan has been reduced to beggary. But under the royal government the native artisans will exclusively be employed in the services of the kings, the rajahs, and the rich; and this will no doubt insure their prosperity. Therefore the artisans ought to renounce the English services, and assist the Mujahidin . . . engaged in the war, and thus be entitled both to secular and eternal happiness.

Section V.—Regarding Pundits, Fakirs,[2] and other learned persons.—The pundits and fakirs being the guardians of the Hindu and Muslim religions respectively, and the Europeans being the enemies of both religions, and as at present a war is raging against the English on account of religion, the pundits and fakirs are bound to present themselves to me, and take their share in this holy war, otherwise they will stand condemned. . . .

Lastly, be it known to all, that whoever, out of the above-named classes, shall, after the circulation of this [proclamation], still cling to the British government, all his estates shall be confiscated, and his property plundered, and he himself, with his whole family, shall be imprisoned, and ultimately put to death.

---

[2]The word *pundit* (or *pandit*) refers to learned Hindus who had committed holy texts to memory. *Fakir* refers to Islamic and occasionally Hindu mystics renowned for their acts of asceticism and supernatural powers.

## The Indian National Congress Debates British Rule

### 67 • DADABHAI NAOROJI, ADDRESS TO THE INDIAN NATIONAL CONGRESS, 1886; BAL GANGADHAR TILAK, TENETS OF THE NEW PARTY, 1907

A key event in India's political history occurred on December 28, 1885, when 72 delegates gathered in Mumbai to attend the first meeting of the Indian National Congress, an organization that provided much of the leadership for the Indian independence movement of the 1930s and 1940s and became India's most powerful political party after independence. The organization was the brainchild of Allan Octavian Hume (1829–1912), an Englishman who in 1882 had been dismissed from the Indian Civil Service after more than thirty years of service because of his advocacy for the Indians and tendency to criticize his superiors. He believed that an annual meeting of educated Indians to discuss and take stands on political issues would be a way to make their views known to the colonial administration.

In its early years, the Congress was dominated by middle- and upper-class Hindus who gathered to make speeches and pass resolutions on matters of interest to India's educated elite: access to higher positions in the Indian Civil Service and the army, a greater Indian voice in provincial legislative councils, the expansion of educational opportunities, and the lowering of certain taxes. They did not seek Indian independence. This is readily apparent in the speech delivered by the second president of the Congress, Dadabhai Naoroji (1825–1871), at the organization's second meeting in 1886 in Kolkata. Born into a prosperous Mumbai family, Naoroji abandoned a career as a mathematician at age thirty and moved to London, where he represented an Indian export business while seeking to educate the British public about Indian issues. During one of his many return visits to India, he was instrumental in founding the Indian National Congress, and served three terms as its president.

Just twenty years after Naoroji's speech, the Congress was rocked by a bitter conflict precipitated by a split between the Moderates, who favored cooperation with the British and gradual reform, and the Extremists, who sought immediate independence. Hostility to British rule, fueled by a revival of popular Hinduism and ongoing frustration with British policies, reached a flashpoint in 1905, when the British announced the partition of the province of Bengal, with one part predominantly Hindu and the other mainly Muslim. This was viewed as another example of British high-handedness and an effort to split the Hindu and Muslim communities. The leading spokesman for the Extremists was Bal Gangadhar Tilak (1856–1920), who, as editor of a widely read Marathi-language newspaper, thundered against British rule and defended Hindu traditions. His mottos—"Militancy Not Mendicancy" and "Freedom Is My Birthright and I Shall Have It"—spread throughout India. Viewing him as a dangerous rabble-rouser, the British imprisoned him in 1897 and 1908. In the following excerpt from an article written in early January 1907, Tilak states his ideas on Indian independence in the wake of the 1906 meeting of the Congress, at which a schism within the organization had been narrowly avoided.

## QUESTIONS FOR ANALYSIS

1. Naoroji begins his speech by claiming that an organization like the Indian National Congress could have come to existence only under British rule, not any previous Indian regime. What are his reasons for this view?

2. What, according to Naoroji, are the "numberless blessings" conferred on India by the British?
3. Overall, how would you characterize Naoroji's views of the British and their goals for India?
4. How do Tilak's views of the British differ from those of Naoroji?
5. According to Tilak, how and why have Indian views of British rule changed over time?
6. Why is Tilak convinced that a boycott will be such an effective weapon against the British?

## Dadabhai Naoroji, Speech to the Indian National Congress, 1886

The assemblage of such a Congress is an event of the utmost importance in Indian history. I ask whether in the most glorious days of Hindu rule, you could imagine the possibility of a meeting of this kind, where even Hindus of all different provinces of the kingdom could have collected and spoken as one nation. Coming down to the later empire of our [Muslim] friends, who probably ruled over a larger territory at one time than any Hindu monarch, would it have been possible for a meeting like this to assemble composed of all classes and communities, all speaking one language, and all having uniform and high aspirations of their own? . . .

It is under the civilizing rule of the Queen and people of England that we meet here together, hindered by none, and are freely allowed to speak our minds without the least fear and without the least hesitation. Such a thing is possible under British rule and British rule only. [Loud cheers] Then I put the *question* plainly: Is this Congress a nursery for sedition and rebellion against the British Government [cries of "no, no"]; or is it another stone in the foundation of the stability of that Government [cries of "yes, yes"]? There could be but one answer, and that you have already given, because we are thoroughly sensible of the numberless blessings conferred upon us, of which the very existence of this Congress is a proof in a nutshell. [Cheers] Were it not for these blessings of British rule I could not have come here, as I have done, without the least hesitation and without the least fear that my children might be robbed and killed in my absence; nor could you have come from every corner of the land, having performed, within a few days, journeys which in former days would have occupied as many months. [Cheers] . . . It is to British rule that we owe the education we possess; the people of England were sincere in the declarations made more than half a century ago that India was a sacred charge entrusted to their care by Providence, and that they were bound to administer it for the good of India, to the glory of their own name, and the satisfaction of God. [Prolonged cheering] When we have to acknowledge so many blessings as flowing from English rule . . . is it possible that an assembly like this . . . could meet for the purpose inimical to that rule to which we owe so much? [Cheers] . . . Let us speak out like men and proclaim that we are loyal to the backbone [Cheers]; that we understand the benefits English rule has conferred upon us; that we thoroughly appreciate the education that has been given to us, the new light which has been poured

*Source:* Naoroji speech: *Essays, Speeches, Addresses and Writings (on Indian Politics) of the Hon'ble Dadabhai Naoroji.* Edited by Chundal Lallubhai (Bombay: Caxton Printing Works, 1887), pp. 332–333. Tilak speech: *Bal Gangadhar Tilak, His Writings and Speeches,* 3rd edition (Madras: Ganesh, 1922), pp. 55–57, 61, 63–67.

upon us, turning us from darkness into light and teaching us the new lesson that kings are made for the people, not people for their kings; and this new lesson we have learned amidst the darkness of Asiatic despotism only by the light of free English civilization. [Loud cheers]

## Bal Gangadhar Tilak, Tenets of the New Party, 1907

. . . One thing is granted, namely, that this government does not suit us. As has been said by an eminent statesman—the government of one country by another can never be a successful, and therefore, a permanent government. . . . One fact is that this alien government has ruined the country. In the beginning all of us were taken by surprise. We were almost dazed. We thought that everything that the rulers did was for our good and that this English government had descended from the clouds to save us not only from foreign invasions but from internecine warfare, or the internal or external invasions, as they call it. We felt happy for a time, but it soon came to light that the peace which was established in this country did this . . . —that we were prevented from going at each other's throats, so that a foreigner might go at the throat of us all. *Pax Britannica* has been established in this country in order that a foreign government may exploit the country. . . . We believed in the benevolent intentions of the government, but in politics there is no benevolence. Benevolence is used to sugarcoat the declarations of self-interest and we were in those days deceived. . . . But soon a change came over us. English education, growing poverty, and better familiarity with our rulers, opened our eyes and our leaders'; especially, the venerable leader Naoroji, who was the first to tell us that the drain from the country was ruining it, and if the drain was to continue, there was some great disaster awaiting us. So terribly convinced was he of this that he went over from here to England and spent twenty-five years of his life in trying to convince the English people of the injustice that is being done to us. He worked very hard. He had conversations and interviews with secretaries of state, with members of Parliament—and with what result?

He has come here at the age of eighty-two to tell us that he is bitterly disappointed. . . .

You can now understand the difference between the old and the new parties. Appeals to the bureaucracy are hopeless. On this point both the new and old parties are agreed. The old party believes in appealing to the British nation and we do not. . . . Your industries are ruined utterly, ruined by foreign rule; your wealth is going out of the country and you are reduced to the lowest level which no human being can occupy. . . . The remedy is not petitioning but boycott. We say prepare your forces, organize your power, and then go to work so that they cannot refuse you what you demand. . . .

Self-government is our goal; we want a control over our administrative machinery. We don't want to become clerks and remain clerks. At present, we are clerks and willing instruments of our own oppression in the hands of an alien government, and that government is ruling over us not by its innate strength but by keeping us in ignorance and blindness to the perception of this fact. . . .

We shall not give them assistance to collect revenue and keep peace. We shall not assist them in fighting beyond the frontiers or outside India with Indian blood and money. We shall not assist them in carrying on the administration of justice. We shall have our own courts, and when time comes we shall not pay taxes. Can you do that by your united efforts? If you can, you are free from tomorrow. . . . This is a lesson of progress, a lesson of helping yourself as much as possible, and if you really perceive the force of it, if you are convinced by these arguments, then and then only is it possible for you to effect your salvation from the alien rule under which you labor at this moment.

# Chapter 10

# East and Southeast Asia Confront the West

D URING THE NINETEENTH CENTURY, ancient patterns of life in East and Southeast Asia were irrevocably altered by upheavals that felled governments, intensified social conflict, introduced new ideas and technologies, and transformed long-standing interstate relationships. These changes were caused in part by social and political forces generated within these societies themselves, and in part by new pressures from the West. Until the nineteenth century, Western involvement in the region had been limited to commerce and modest and generally ineffectual missionary activity. The only exceptions were a few coastal enclaves such as Melaka, which the Dutch took from the Portuguese in 1641; the Philippines, which Spain had ruled since the sixteenth century; and the island of Java, where the Dutch East India Company established indirect and informal control in the seventeenth century. Elsewhere, the region's rulers retained their power, and neither they nor their subjects were significantly attracted to or affected by Western culture.

This changed in the nineteenth century. Most of mainland Southeast Asia and many islands of the East Indies all joined the Philippines and Java as parts of Western empires. Thailand remained independent but lost territory to France and Great Britain. China faced severe internal problems and experienced relentless economic and military pressures from Western nations and Japan. Previous regimes had survived domestic turbulence and foreign threats, but this time, China's problems proved fatal, not just to the Qing Dynasty but also to China's two-thousand-year tradition of imperial rule. When the last Qing emperor was overthrown in the Revolution of 1911–1912, no new dynasty was established, and China faced a future without the authority of an emperor, the rule of scholar-officials, or the guidance of official Confucian ideology. Japan also faced internal conflict and foreign threats, but its experience sharply differed from that of China. Following an intense internal debate over Japan's future following the "opening" of Japan by American Commodore Matthew Perry in 1853, a group of patriotic aristocrats overthrew the Tokugawa shogunate in 1867, restored the emperor, and began laying plans for Japan's modernization. By the 1890s, Japan had escaped becoming a victim of imperialism and was on its way to becoming an imperialist power itself.

# Encounters with the West

Signs of changing Western aims and strategies in East and Southeast Asia were first noticeable in the late 1700s, when the British intensified their efforts to convince the Qing government to liberalize its commercial policies. They became more evident in the 1810s and 1820s, when the British founded a colony at Singapore on the southern tip of the Malay Peninsula, the Dutch imposed the harsh Culture System on Java, and the British took two provinces and demanded a huge indemnity from the king of Burma after their victory in the first Anglo-Burmese War (1824–1826). Three even more significant events soon followed: In 1842 Great Britain, in the wake of its victory in the First Opium War, imposed on China the first of the "unequal treaties"—the Treaty of Nanjing; in 1854, the Japanese government acquiesced to the demands of Commodore Matthew Perry by agreeing to open two ports for the provisioning of U.S. ships and a limited amount of trade; and in 1862 the Vietnamese emperor Tu Duc ceded control of three provinces to France after his army's defeat by a French invading force. Respectively, these latter three events smashed the myth of Chinese invincibility, ended Japan's centuries-old seclusion policy, and led to the near-complete colonization of Southeast Asia.

## Opium and Imperialism

### 68 • LIN ZEXU, LETTER TO QUEEN VICTORIA, 1839

In 1842, only a half-century after the Qianlong emperor sent King George III his condescending rejection of a British request for trade concessions (see source 47), the Daoguang emperor (r. 1820–1850) approved the Treaty of Nanjing, which required his government to open five ports to British merchants, cede Hong Kong to Great Britain, lower tariffs, pay Britain an indemnity of $21 million, and free all British prisoners. Acceptance of these humiliating terms was the result of China's defeat in the Opium War (1839–1842), the climax of Chinese efforts to halt the British sale of opium to China.

Although opium derivatives had been used in Chinese medicine for centuries, smoking opium as a narcotic dates only from the seventeenth century. Opium use increased in the late 1700s, when British merchants with access to the poppy-growing areas of India began to sell opium in China. By the early 1800s, millions of Chinese were addicts, and almost two million pounds of opium were being sold in China every year.

Chinese officials viewed the epidemic of opium smoking with alarm, but they disagreed on how to stop it. Some advocated the legalization of opium and the expansion of poppy growing in China to lessen imports. Those who favored more drastic measures won the support of the emperor, who banned opium use in 1838. One year later, he sent his official, Lin Zexu (1785–1850), to Guangzhou to confiscate the foreign merchants' stock of opium and stop the opium trade altogether.

Lin Zexu was a highly respected scholar-administrator who in previous provincial postings in Hubei and Hunan had tried to suppress opium smoking. In Guangzhou, he launched a campaign of moral persuasion and threats to enforce the emperor's ban. Insight into his thinking is provided by a letter he wrote to Great Britain's Queen Victoria in 1839, imploring her to halt her subjects' sale of opium.

Nothing came of his letter, and the noncooperation of British merchants in Guangzhou drove Lin to take more drastic steps. He arrested the leading English opium traders and blockaded the foreign quarter until its merchants handed over twenty thousand chests of opium. In response, the British government dispatched a fleet to Chinese waters and mobilized Indian troops to protect its interests. While the flotilla of almost fifty vessels was en route in late 1839, fighting had already started around Guangzhou. The Opium War had begun.

## QUESTIONS FOR ANALYSIS

1. What does Lin's letter reveal about Chinese views of foreign relations and the relationship between the Chinese emperor and other rulers?
2. What differences does Lin see in the motives of the Chinese and those of Europeans in regard to trade?
3. What moral arguments does Lin use to persuade the queen to order the end of opium trading? What other arguments does he use?
4. What seems to be Lin's understanding of the powers of the English monarchy?
5. How does Lin view the world outside of China? How do his views differ from and resemble those of the Qianlong emperor (source 47)?

His Majesty the Emperor. . . loves all the people in the world without discrimination. Whenever profit is found, he wishes to share it with all men; whenever harm appears, he likewise will eliminate it on behalf of all of mankind. His heart is the heart of the whole universe.

Generally, the rulers of your honorable country have been respectful and obedient. Time and again they have sent petitions to China, saying: "We are grateful to His Majesty for the impartial and favorable treatment he has granted to citizens of my country who have come to China to trade," I am pleased to learn that you are thoroughly familiar with the principle of righteousness and are grateful for the favor His Majesty has bestowed upon your subjects. Because of this fact, the Celestial Empire has been doubly considerate towards the people from England. You have traded in China for almost 200 years, and as a result, your country has become wealthy and prosperous.

*Source:* Dun J. Li, *China in Transition, 1517–1911* (New York: Van Nostrand Reinhold, 1969), 1st edition. © 1969, pp. 64–67.

As this trade has lasted a long time, there are bound to be unscrupulous as well as honest traders. Among the unscrupulous are those who bring opium to China...; they succeed so well that this poison has spread far and wide in all the provinces. You, I hope, will certainly agree that people who pursue material gain to the detriment of others can be neither tolerated by Heaven nor endured by men....

Your country is more than 60,000 *li*[1] from China. The purpose of your ships in coming to China is to realize a large profit. Since this profit is realized in China and is in fact taken away from the Chinese people, how can foreigners return injury for the benefit they have received by sending this poison. . . ? They. . . are so obsessed with material gain that they have no concern for the harm they cause. Have they no conscience? I have heard that you strictly prohibit opium in your country, indicating that you know how harmful opium is, but you choose to bring that harm to other countries such as China. Why?

Has China produced one item that is harmful to foreign countries? For instance, tea and rhubarb are so important to foreigners that they have to consume them every day.[2] Were China to concern herself only with her own advantage, how could foreigners continue to live? Where would the foreigners' profit come from? The products that foreign countries need and have to import from China are too numerous to enumerate: from food products. . . to useful necessities such as silk and porcelain. The imported goods from foreign countries, on the other hand, are merely playthings. . . Since we do not need these things, what harm would come if we should decide to stop foreign trade altogether? The reason why we unhesitantly allow foreigners to ship out such Chinese products as tea and silk is that we feel that wherever there is an advantage, it should be shared by all the people in the world. . .

I have heard that you are a kind, compassionate monarch... I have also heard that you have instructed every British ship that sails for Guangzhou not to bring any prohibited goods to China. . . . The fact that British ships have continued to bring opium to China results perhaps from the impossibility of making a thorough inspection of all of them owing to their large numbers. I am sending you this letter to reiterate the seriousness with which we enforce the law . . . and to make sure that merchants from your honorable country will not attempt to violate it again.

I have heard that the areas under your direct jurisdiction such as London, Scotland, and Ireland do not produce opium; it is produced instead in your Indian possessions . . . [where] the English people not only plant opium poppies that stretch from mountain to mountain but also open factories to manufacture this terrible drug. As months and years pass by, the poison they have produced increases in its wicked intensity, and its repugnant odor reaches as high as the sky. Heaven is furious with anger . . ., It is hereby suggested that you plow under all these opium plants and grow food crops instead, while issuing an order to punish severely anyone who dares to plant opium poppies again. If you adopt this policy . . . Heaven will protect you, and gods will bring you good fortune. Moreover, you will enjoy a long life and be rewarded with a multitude of children and grandchildren! In short, by taking this one measure, you can bring great happiness to others as well as yourself. Why do you not do it?. . .

Since a foreigner who goes to England to trade has to obey the English law, how can an Englishman not obey the Chinese law when he is physically within China? The present law calls for the imposition of the death sentence on any Chinese who has peddled or smoked opium. Since a Chinese could not peddle or smoke opium if foreigners had not brought it to China, it is clear that the true culprits

---

[1] One li equals approximately one third of mile.
[2] It was a widely held Chinese belief that Europeans would die of constipation if they did not consume rhubarb.

of a Chinese's death as a result of an opium conviction are the opium traders from foreign countries. Why should they be spared from capital punishment?... Just imagine how many people opium has killed! This is the rationale behind the new law which says that any foreigner who brings opium to China will be sentenced to death by hanging or beheading. Our purpose is to eliminate this poison once and for all and to the benefit of all mankind.

Our Celestial Empire towers over all other countries in virtue and possesses a power great and awesome enough to carry out its wishes. But we will not prosecute a person without warning him in advance; that is why we have made our law explicit and clear. If the merchants of your honorable country wish to enjoy trade with us on a permanent basis, they must fearfully observe our law by cutting off, once and for all, the supply of opium. Under no circumstance should they test our intention to enforce the law by deliberately violating it. You, as the ruler of your honorable country, should do your part to uncover the hidden and unmask the wicked. It is hoped that you will continue to enjoy your country and become more and more respectful and submissive. How wonderful it is that we can all enjoy the blessing of peace!

# Eastern Ethics and Western Science

### 69 • SAKUMA SHOZAN, REFLECTIONS ON MY ERRORS

After Commodore Perry left Tokyo in the summer of 1853, promising to return within a year to receive answers to his demands that Japan open its islands to U.S. trade, government officials, daimyo, samurai, intellectuals, merchants, and courtiers commenced an intense debate about the crisis at hand and their nation's future. Although the immediate reaction was to reject all things Western and "Expel the Barbarians," many soon realized that threats were no match for superior ships and firepower. Thus, as the debate went on, more Japanese were willing to consider the ideas of Sakuma Shozan, whose philosophy is summarized by the motto he made famous: "Eastern ethics and Western science."

Born of a samurai family in 1811, Sakuma had a Confucian education before entering the service of one of Japan's powerful aristocrats, Sanada Yukitsura. When the shogun put Sanada in charge of Japan's coastal fortifications in 1841, Sakuma was pushed into the world of artillery, naval strategy, and shipbuilding. He mastered Dutch, read all he could of Western science, learned how to make glass, and experimented with electricity. He also became an advocate of adopting Western weaponry. In the 1840s such views were unpopular within the shogun's government, and as a result both Sakuma and his lord were dismissed from the shogun's service. Sakuma experienced more problems in 1854, when at his urging a student of his attempted to stow away on one of Perry's ships as it left Japan. According to the Seclusion Laws, this was a capital offense, but through his aristocratic connections, Sakuma and his student received a jail sentence of only several months, followed by eight years of house arrest. Sakuma completed his deceptively titled "Reflections on My Errors" on his release from prison. Far from being an apology for his "errors," it was a self-defense made up of fifty-two brief commentaries on various issues. Although he claimed that the work was to be "locked up in a box" and shown only to his descendants, it was widely circulated among Japan's military and political leaders. After completing "Reflections" Sakuma became an advocate of the opening of Japan and cooperation between shogun and emperor. His ideas angered those who sought to abolish the shogunate completely, and they arranged his assassination in 1864.

## QUESTIONS FOR ANALYSIS

1. What is the meaning of the parable about the "man who is grieved by the illness of his lord or father"? What is the meaning of the story concerning Zao Wei?
2. What does Sakuma mean by "Eastern ethics"? Does he anticipate any difficulties reconciling ethics with Western science?
3. What does Sakuma see as the weakness of Japan's military leaders and Confucian scholars? How can these deficiencies be remedied?
4. Why does Sakuma view the study of science and mathematics as so important?
5. Aside from his admiration of Western science, how would you characterize Sakuma's attitude toward the West?

Take, for example, a man who is grieved by the illness of his lord or his father, and who is seeking medicine to cure it. If he is fortunate enough to secure the medicine, and is certain that it will be efficacious, then, certainly, without questioning either its cost or the quality of its name, he will beg his lord or father to take it. Should the latter refuse on the grounds that he dislikes the name, does the younger man make various schemes to give the medicine secretly, or does he simply sit by and wait for his master to die? There is no question about it: the feeling of genuine sincerity and heart-felt grief on the part of the subject or son makes it absolutely impossible for him to sit idly and watch his master's anguish; consequently, even if he knows that he will later have to face his master's anger, he cannot but give the medicine secretly. . . .

The gentleman has five pleasures, but wealth and rank are not among them. That his house understands decorum and righteousness and remains free from family rifts—this is one pleasure. That exercising care in giving to and taking from others, he provides for himself honestly, free, internally, from

shame before his wife and children, and externally, from disgrace before the public—this is the second pleasure. That he expounds and glorifies the learning of the sages, knows in his heart the great Way, and in all situations contents himself with his duty, in adversity as well as in prosperity—this is the third pleasure. That he is born after the opening of the vistas of science by the Westerners, and can therefore understand principles not known to the sages and wise men of old—this is the fourth pleasure. That he employs the ethics of the East and the scientific technique of the West, neglecting neither the spiritual nor material aspects of life, combining subjective and objective, and thus bringing benefit to the people and serving the nation—this is the fifth pleasure. . . .

The principal requisite of national defense is that it prevents the foreign barbarians from holding us in contempt. The existing coastal defense installations all lack method; the pieces of artillery that have been set up are improperly made; and the officials who negotiate with the foreigners are mediocrities who have no understanding of warfare. The

*Source:* From *Sources of Japanese Tradition*, by Tsumoda, de Bary, and Keene. Copyright © 1958 Columbia University Press. Reprinted with permission of the publisher.

situation being such, even though we wish to avoid incurring the scorn of the barbarians, how, in fact, can we do so? . . .

Of the men who now hold posts as commanders of the army, those who are not men of noble rank, are members of wealthy families. As such, they find their daily pleasure in drinking wine, singing, and dancing; and they are ignorant of military strategy and discipline. Should a national emergency arise, there is no one who could command the respect of the warriors and halt the enemy's attack. . . . For this reason, I have wished to follow in substance the Western principles of armament, and, by banding together loyal, valorous, strong men of old, established families not in the military class . . . to form a voluntary group which would be made to have as its sole aim that of guarding the nation and protecting the people. Anyone wishing to join the society would be tested and his merits examined; and, if he did not shirk hardship, he would then be permitted to join. Men of talent in military strategy, planning, and administration would be advanced to positions of leadership, and then, if the day should come when the country must be defended, this group could be gathered together and organized into an army to await official commands. It is to be hoped that they would drive the enemy away and perform greater service than those who now form the military class. . . .

Mathematics is the basis for all learning. In the Western world after this science was discovered military tactics advanced greatly, far outstripping that of former times. This development accords with the statement that "one advanced from basic studies to higher learning." In the *Art of War*[1] of Sunzi, the statement about "estimation, determination of quantity, calculation, judgment, and victory" has

reference to mathematics. However, since Sunzi's time neither we nor the Chinese have ceased to read, study, and memorize his teachings, and our art of war remains exactly as it was then. It consequently cannot be compared with that of the West. There is no reason for this other than that we have not devoted ourselves to basic studies. At the present time, if we wish really to complete our military preparations, we must develop this branch of study. . . .

What do the so-called scholars of today actually do? . . . Do they, after having learned the rites and music, punishment and administration, the classics and governmental system, go on to discuss and learn the elements of the art of war, of military discipline, of the principles of machinery? Do they make exhaustive studies of conditions in foreign countries? Of effective defense methods? Of strategy in setting up strongholds, defense barriers, and reinforcements? Of the knowledge of computation, gravitation, geometry, and mathematics? If they do, I have not heard of it! Therefore I ask what the so-called scholars of today actually do. . . .

In order to master the barbarians there is nothing so effective as to ascertain in the beginning conditions among them. To do this, there is no better first step than to be familiar with barbarian tongues. Thus, learning a barbarian language is not only a step toward knowing the barbarians, but also the groundwork for mastering them. . . .

Last summer the American barbarians arrived in the Bay of Uraga with four warships, bearing their president's message. Their deportment and manner of expression were exceedingly arrogant, and the resulting insult to our national dignity was not small. Those who heard could but gnash their teeth. A certain person on guard in Uraga suffered this insult in silence, and, having been ultimately unable to

---

[1]A classic work of military strategy written in the fourth century B.C.E.

do anything about it, after the barbarians had retired, he drew his knife and slashed to bits a portrait of their leader, which they had left as a gift. Thus he gave vent to his rage. In former times Zao Wei, having been demoted, was serving as an official in Shaanxi, and when he heard of the character of Chao Yuanhao, he had a person skillful in drawing paint Chao's image. Zao looked at this portrait and knew from its manly appearance that Chao would doubtless make trouble on the border in the future. Therefore Zao wished to take steps toward preparing the border in advance, and toward collecting together and examining men of ability. Afterwards, everything turned out as he had predicted. Thus, by looking at the portrait of his enemy, he could see his enemy's abilities and thereby aid himself with his own preparations. It can only be regretted that the Japanese guard did not think of this. Instead of using the portrait, he tore it up. In both cases there was a barbarian; in both cases there was a portrait. But one man, lacking the portrait, sought to obtain it, while the other, having it, destroyed it. Their depth of knowledge and farsightedness in planning were vastly different.

## The Fall of Vietnam

### 70 • PHAN THANH GIAN, LETTER TO EMPEROR TU DUC AND LAST MESSAGE TO HIS ADMINISTRATORS

In 1802, decades of civil war in Vietnam ended when Nguyen Anh unified the country under the Nguyen dynasty and as emperor took the name Gia Long. He and his successors sought to govern the country according to Confucian principles. Efforts to turn Vietnam into a model Confucian society led to the persecution of Vietnamese Catholics, who, as a result of mainly French missionary efforts, numbered 300,000 by the nineteenth century. When Catholics were implicated in a rebellion in 1833, Emperor Minh Mang (r. 1820–1841) ordered the imprisonment and execution of a number of converts and European missionaries. Three years later, he closed Vietnamese ports to European shipping. In response, the French sent naval vessels and troops to Vietnam, ostensibly to protect Christians but also to advance French imperialism. Fighting broke out in earnest in 1858, and although the Vietnamese staunchly resisted, Emperor Tu Duc (r. 1847–1883) accepted a settlement in 1862 by which he ceded three southern provinces around Saigon (currently Ho Chi Minh City) to the French.

Four years later, an anti-French rebellion broke out west of Saigon, then under the governorship of the prominent statesman Phan Thanh Gian (1796–1867). In response, the French sent in troops and demanded control of the provinces. In 1867, Phan Thanh Gian acquiesced and then committed suicide, but not before he wrote the following two letters, one to Emperor Tu Duc and the other to administrators in his district.

### QUESTIONS FOR ANALYSIS

1. What is the basis of Phan Thanh Gian's hope that the emperor can save Vietnam from further humiliation at the hands of the French?
2. What is Phan Thanh Gian's view of the French?

3. What evidence of Phan Thanh Gian's Confucian training do you see in the letter?
4. Why did Phan Thanh Gian decide to acquiesce to the French?

## Letter to Emperor Tu Duc

I, Phan Thanh Gian, make the following report, in expressing frankly, with my head bowed, my humble sentiments, and in soliciting, with my head raised, your discerning scrutiny. During the period of difficulties and misfortunes that we are presently undergoing, rebellion is rising around the capital, the pernicious [French] influence is expanding on our frontiers. . . .

My duty compels me to die. I would not dare to live thoughtlessly, leaving a heritage of shame to my Sovereign and my Father. Happily, I have confidence in my Emperor, who has extensive knowledge of ancient times and the present and who has studied profoundly the causes of peace and of dissension: . . . In respectfully observing the warnings of Heaven and in having pity on the misery of man . . . in changing the string of the guitar, in modifying the track of the governmental chariot, it is still possible for you to act in accordance with your authority and means.

At the last moment of life, the throat constricted, I do not know what to say, but, in wiping my tears and in raising my eyes toward you affectionately, I can only ardently hope that this wish will be realized. With respect, I make this report, Tu Duc, twentieth year, sixth moon, seventh day, Phan Thanh Gian.

## Last Message to His Administrators

It is written: He who lives in accordance with the will of Heaven lives in virtue; he who does not live according to the will of Heaven lives in evil. To work according to the will of Heaven is to listen to natural reason. . . . Man is an intelligent animal created by Heaven. Every animal lives according to his nature, as water flows to low ground, as fire goes out on dry ground. . . .

The empire of our king is ancient. Our gratitude toward our kings is complete and always ardent; we cannot forget them. Now, the French have come, with their powerful weapons of war to cause dissension among us. We are weak against them; our commanders and our soldiers have been vanquished. Each battle adds to our misery. . . . The French have immense warships, filled with soldiers and armed with huge cannons. No one can resist them. They go where they want, the strongest ramparts fall before them.

I have raised my spirit toward Heaven and I have listened to the voice of reason. And I have said: It would be as senseless for you to wish to defeat your enemies by force of arms as for a young fawn to attack a tiger. You attract uselessly great misfortunes upon the people whom Heaven has confided to you. I have thus written to all the mandarins and to all the war commanders to break their lances and surrender the forts without fighting.

But, if I have followed the Will of Heaven by averting great evils from the head of the people, I am a traitor to our king in delivering without resistance the provinces which belong to him. . . . I deserve death. Mandarins and people, you can live under the command of the French, who are only terrible during the battle, but their flag must never fly above a fortress where Phan Thanh Gian still lives.

*Source:* Letter to Emperor Tu Duc and Last Message to His Administrators, from *We the Vietnamese* by Francois Sully and Donald Kirk.

# The Emergence of Modern Japan

In the late nineteenth century, Japan accomplished what no other nation had been able to do. In only four decades, it set aside the bitter disputes of the 1850s and early 1860s and transformed itself from a secluded, preindustrial society, vulnerable to foreign exploitation, into a powerful, industrialized nation that shocked the world by winning wars against China in 1895 and Russia in 1905. What made this transformation even more remarkable was that it was accompanied by little social upheaval and that despite its magnitude the Japanese retained many of their hallowed ideals and beliefs.

Japan's transformation began in 1867, when a faction of aristocrats overthrew the Tokugawa shogunate and then orchestrated the move of the previously secluded and ceremonial emperor from Kyoto to Edo, where he assumed titular authority over a government they controlled. These events are known as the Meiji Restoration, based on the Japanese word *meiji* ("brilliant rule"), chosen by Emperor Mutsuhito as his reign name.

## Images of the West in Late Tokugawa and Meiji Japan

### 71 • PRINTS AND DRAWINGS, 1853–1891

Following the Europeans' arrival in Japan in 1542, their ideas, dress, weapons, and religion proved fascinating and attractive to many Japanese. Several hundred thousand Japanese converted to Catholicism, military leaders put European firearms to use, and some Japanese showed an interest in European fashion and cuisine. After the Tokugawa shoguns suppressed Christianity and implemented the seclusion policy in the 1600s, however, knowledge of the West was limited to merchants who traded with the Dutch in Nagasaki and a handful of intellectuals interested in European thought. For most Japanese, memory of the South Sea Barbarians disappeared.

Increased interactions with Westerners, culminating in the Perry expedition in 1853 and the opening of Japan to foreign trade in 1854, changed this dramatically. Inspired by a mixture of fear, awe, revulsion, and curiosity, the Japanese developed a deep interest in the West, and a flood of printed material about Europe and the United States appeared in the 1850s and 1860s. After the Meiji Restoration, imitation of the West for a time became a patriotic duty. Employing Western science, technology, military organization, and government practices would make Japan strong and prosperous; adopting Western fashion, etiquette, grooming habits, and architecture would make the Japanese respected and admired. In the late 1880s, however, a reaction against overzealous Westernization set in. Since then, the

Japanese have managed to strike a balance between borrowing from the West and preserving the essentials of their culture.

The following six illustrations provide insights into Japanese views of the West in the Meiji Era. The first two are tile prints that appeared soon after the arrival of Perry's ships. Forerunners of modern newspapers, such prints were produced quickly and anonymously after newsworthy events and sold for a few cents. The first print depicts one of Perry's "black ships," so called because of the dark smoke that belched from their smokestacks. The text provides information on the ship's dimensions and its voyage to Japan. The second print depicts Commander Henry Adams, Perry's second-in-command.

The next two illustrations appeared when the drive to emulate Europeans was under way. The first is part of a series of woodblock prints published in the 1880s entitled *Self-Made Men Worthy of Emulation*. The individual depicted is Fukuchi Genichiro (1841–1909), a journalist who served as editor-in-chief of Tokyo's first daily newspaper. He is shown covering the Satsuma Rebellion of 1877, a failed revolt by disgruntled samurai against the new Meiji order. The artist is Kobayashi Kiyochika (1847–1911), whose numerous woodblock prints show the influence of Western painting and perspective. The accompanying text reads:

> Fukuchi Genichiro was born in Nagasaki. . . . An exceptionally bright child, he could recognize characters at the age of five and had begun to read and write at about the age of seven. He resolved to enter the service of the shogunate and, upon coming of age, entered the government in the service of which he traveled three times to Europe. He then entered into a successful business career. In 1874 he became president of the Reporters' Association. He personally covered the Satsuma Rebellion in the south. Received by the emperor, he respectfully reported his observations to the throne. His style seemed almost supernatural in its logic, force, and lucidity. He is one of the truly great men of Meiji.

The next illustration (page 315) appeared in a popular book by Kanagaki Robun published in serial form in the 1870s. *Hiking through the West* tells the story of two Japanese travelers during a trip to London and back. The illustration depicts from right to left an "unenlightened man," dressed as a samurai; a "half-enlightened man"; and an "enlightened man."

Even as Japanese enthusiasm for things Western was peaking, some opposed Japan's rush to Westernize. Government censorship silenced most of these critics, but a few managed to get their ideas into print. Cartoonists Honda Kinichiro and Kobayashi Kiyochika were two such individuals. Honda's cartoons, usually with English captions and a Japanese text, appeared in the weekly humor magazine *Marumaru Chinbun*. His "Monkey Show Dressing Room" (page 316) was published in 1879, shortly after Dr. Edward S. Morse introduced Darwin's theory of evolution in a series of lectures at Tokyo University. The text reads, "Mr. Morse explains that all human beings were monkeys in the beginning. In the beginning—but even now aren't we still monkeys? When it comes to Western things we think the red beards [Westerners] are the most skillful at everything."

Kobayashi, the artist who made the print of Fukuchi Genichiro, published the second cartoon, on page 316, in the *Tokyo Daily News* in 1891. It depicts a New Year's dance held in the Rokumeikan, a pavilion built by the government in 1883 as a venue for formal balls and other entertainments involving Westerners and Japan's elite. Above the dance floor, filled with ill-matched Western and Japanese couples, is a sign that reads, "Hands Dance, Feet Stomp, Call Out Hurrah!"

### QUESTIONS FOR ANALYSIS

1. What impressions of the West are conveyed by the prints of Perry's ship and Commander Adams? What specific details help convey these impressions?
2. In the illustration from Hiking through the West, what are the significant differences between the three men? How does the artist convey a sense of the "enlightened man's" superiority?
3. What is there in the drawing of Fukuchi Genichiro and in the accompanying text that makes him "a man worthy of emulation"?
4. Why do you think the artist chose to depict Fukuchi while he was covering the Satsuma Rebellion?
5. What messages are Honda and Kobayashi attempting to convey about Japan's campaign to Westernize?
6. Compare and contrast the depiction of Westerners in "Hands Dance ..." with the earlier depiction of Commander Adams.

One of Commodore Perry's Black Ships

Commodore Perry's Second-in-Command, Commander Henry Adams

Kobayashi Kiyochika, Fukuchi Genichiro

From Kanagaki Robun, *Hiking through the West*

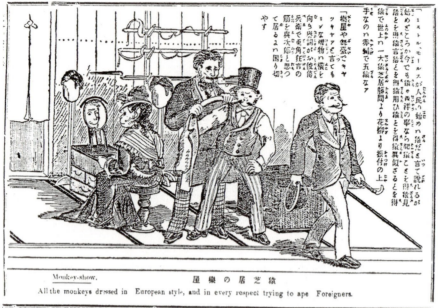

Monkey-show.

猿芝居の楽屋

All the monkeys dressed in European style, and in every respect trying to ape Foreigners.

Honda Kinichiro, "Monkey Show Dressing Room"

Kobayashi Kiyochika, "Hands Dance, Feet Stomp, Call Out Hurrah!"

# A Blueprint for Military Modernization

## 72 • YAMAGATA ARITOMO, OPINION ON MILITARY AFFAIRS AND CONSCRIPTION

Few individuals played a more important role in the history of Meiji Japan than Yamagata Aritomo (1838–1922), best known as the architect of the Japanese army, but also a statesman who influenced domestic policy, education, and the writing of Japan's constitution. Born into a low-ranking samurai family, he committed himself to the anti-foreign, antishogun movements of the 1860s and was a strong supporter of the imperial restoration. The new regime immediately assigned him its most pressing task, the modernization of Japan's military. After an eighteen-month trip to Europe to observe military practices, Yamagata submitted the following memorandum on the nation's military needs to his country's leaders in 1872. One year later, he framed the imperial decree that established a conscript army. This had revolutionary social implications for Japan, because it ended once and for all the samurai's monopoly on fighting and made military service the responsibility of every Japanese male, irrespective of his social standing.

### QUESTIONS FOR ANALYSIS

1. According to Yamagata, why is it necessary for Japan to strengthen its army and navy? In his view, what foreign enemy most threatens Japan?
2. What are some of the lessons Yamagata learned from his observations of Western military practices?
3. In his view, what lessons should Japan learn from the examples of Belgium and the Netherlands?
4. What can you infer from this document about the arguments being used against a military buildup?
5. What might be some of the ways in which the proposed military buildup would affect Japanese society as a whole?
6. What similarities can you see between Yamagata's memorandum and Sakuma's *Reflections on my Errors* (source 69)?

---

The status of our armed forces today is as follows: We have the so-called Imperial Guards whose functions are nothing more than to protect the sacred person of His Majesty and to guard the Imperial Palace. We have altogether more than twenty battalions manning the four military garrisons who are deployed to maintain domestic tranquility, and are not equipped to fight against any foreign threat. As to our navy, we have a few battleships yet to be completed. How can they be sufficient to counteract foreign threats? . . .

The first concern of the Ministry of Military Affairs is to set up a system to defend our homeland. For this purpose two categories of soldiers are required: a standing army and those on the reserve list. The number of troops differ from country to country. Of the major countries, Russia maintains the largest number of troops and the United States the smallest. . . . The Netherlands and Belgium are among the smallest countries, but they are located between large countries, and in order to avoid

*Source:* From *Japan: A Documentary History*, ed. David J. Lu (Armonk, NY: M.E. Sharpe, 1997), pp. 315-318. Translation

contempt and scorn from their neighbors, they diligently go about the business of defending their countries. Even though one of these countries has a total area not exceeding one-third of the area of our country, it maintains a standing army numbering not less than forty to fifty thousand. If we apply the existing standards prevailing in our country to judge these two countries, they may appear to be concerned only with military affairs to the neglect of other matters. However, they do attend to hundreds of other affairs of state and do not abandon them.

At a time like this it is very clear where the priority of the country must lie. We must have a well-trained standing army supplemented by a large number of reservists. We must build warships and construct batteries. We must train officers and soldiers. We must manufacture and store weapons and ammunition. The nation may consider that it cannot bear the expenses. However, even if we wish to ignore it, this important matter cannot disappear from us. . . .

Therefore the creation of a standing army for our country is a task which cannot be delayed. It is recommended that a certain number of strong and courageous young men be selected from each of the prefectures, and that such young men be trained in the Western-type military science and placed under rigorous drills, so that they may be deployed as occasion demands.

The so-called reservists do not normally remain within the military barracks. During peacetime they remain in their homes, and in an emergency they are called to service. All of the countries in Europe have reservists, and amongst them Prussia has most of them. There is not a single able-bodied man in Prussia who is not trained in military affairs. Recently Prussia and France fought each other and the former won handily.[1] This is due in large measure to the strength of its reservists.

It is recommended that our country adopt a system under which any able-bodied man twenty years of age be drafted into military service, unless his absence from home will create undue hardship for his family. There shall be no distinction made between the common man and those who are of the samurai class. They shall all be formed into ranks, and after completion of a period of service, they shall be returned to their homes. In this way every man will become a soldier, and not a single region in the country will be without defense. Thus our defense will become complete.

The second concern of the Ministry is coastal defense. This includes building of warships and constructing coastal batteries. Actually, battleships are movable batteries. Our country has thousands of miles of coastline, and any mobile corner of our country can become the advance post of our enemy. However, since it is not possible to construct batteries along the coastline everywhere, it is imperative to expand our navy and construct the largest warships. . . .

The third concern of the Military is to create resources for the navy and the army. There are three items under consideration, namely military academies, a bureau of military supplies, and a bureau of munitions depots. It is not difficult to have one million soldiers in a short time, but it is difficult to gain one good officer during the same span of time. Military academies are intended to train officers for these two services. If we pay little attention to this need today, we shall not be able to have the services of capable officers for another day. Therefore, without delay military academies must be created and be allowed to prosper. Students shall be adequately trained by the faculty consisting of experts from several countries. . . . The bureau of military supplies shall be in charge of procuring military provisions and manufacturing weapons of war for the two services. The bureau of munitions depots shall store such provisions and munitions. If we lack military provisions and weapons and our munitions depots are empty, what good will the million soldiers in the army or thousands of warships do? Therefore, well-qualified craftsmen from various countries must be hired to make necessary

---

[1] A reference is to the Franco-Prussian War (1870–1871).

machines and build strong storage houses. We must make our own weapons and store them, and must become self-sufficient without relying on foreign countries. The goal is to create a sufficient amount and if there is any surplus it may be sold to other countries.

Some people may argue that while they are aware of the urgency in the need for the Ministry of Military Affairs, they cannot permit all the national resources to be committed to the need of one ministry alone. They further aver that from the larger perspective of the imperial government, there are so many other projects covering a wide range of things which require governmental attention. . . . This argument fails to discern the fundamental issues. The recommendations herein presented . . . in no way asks for the stoppage of all governmental activities or for the monopolization of all government revenues. But in a national emergency, a new set of priorities must be established. Those of us who are given the task of governing must learn from the past, discern the present, and weigh all matters carefully.

In the past there was Emperor Peter[2] who was determined to make his country a great nation. He went overseas and studied naval sciences.

After his return he built many battleships and constructed St. Petersburg. He created a standing army numbering several million, and was able to engage in the art of international politics against five or six of the strongest nations. As to domestic politics, he was satisfied to leave them to a woman. There were one or two internal quarrels, but they were eradicated almost immediately. It is to him that the credit is due for making Russia a great nation.

Those of us who govern must first of all discern the conditions prevailing in the world, set up priorities and take appropriate measures. In our opinion Russia has been acting very arrogantly. Previously, contrary to the provisions of the Treaty of Sevastopol,[3] she placed her warships in the Black Sea. Southward, she has shown her aggressive intent toward Muslim countries and toward India. Westward, she has crossed the borders of Manchuria and has been navigating the Amur River. Her intents being thus, it is inevitable that she will move eastward sooner or later by sending troops to Hokkaido,[4] and then taking advantage of the seasonal wind move to the warmer areas.

---

[2]A reference to Tsar Peter the Great, who reigned from 1689 to 1725. Much of what Yamagata says about Peter in this paragraph is inaccurate, either because he received false information or because he distorted the facts to prove his point. His statements that Peter constructed "many battleships," recruited an army of "several million," fought "five or six" strong nations, and left domestic politics "to a woman" are all incorrect.

[3]There is no "Treaty of Sevastopol." Yamagata seems to have in mind the 1856 Treaty of Paris, which ended the Crimean War; it stipulated that the defeated Russians could send no warships into the Black Sea. Sevastopol is a city on the Black Sea.
[4]One of the islands of Japan north of Honshu.

# Patriotic Duty and Business Success

### 73 • IWASAKI YATARO, LETTER TO MITSUBISHI EMPLOYEES

From the moment the Meiji reformers seized power, they sought to modernize Japan's economy, especially in industries that produced goods for export or the military. After a rocky start in the 1870s, Japanese industrialization proceeded rapidly, and by 1900, the nation had become an important economic power through a combination of government subsidies and individual entrepreneurship.

The greatest success story in Japan's economic transformation was that of Iwasaki Yataro (1835–1885), the founder of one of the nation's most powerful business conglomerates, Mitsubishi. Born into a farming family, Iwasaki gained a rudimentary education and held several low-level business jobs before he found employment as an official in the service of the aristocratic Tosa clan in the mid-1860s. He was given the task of managing and reducing the Tosa domain's huge debt, which had resulted from purchases of firearms and artillery. His policies, which included paying some debtors with counterfeit money, quickly eliminated the domain's deficit. In 1871, when the domain abandoned its direct ownership of business enterprises, it gave Iwasaki eleven steamships and all the assets connected with its enterprises in the silk, coal, tea, and lumber industries. In return, Iwasaki was expected to pay off additional Tosa debts and provide employment for former samurai. With this to build on, he systematically wiped out foreign and domestic competition and through a series of shrewd business moves turned Mitsubishi (a name adopted in 1873) into Japan's second-largest conglomerate, with interests in shipbuilding, mining, banking, insurance, and manufacturing.

Iwasaki wrote the following letter to his employees in 1876 during Mitsubishi's battle with the British Peninsular and Oriental Steam Navigation Company over control of Japanese coastal trade. He had just cut fares in half but had also reduced wages by a third. His appeal to his workers' patriotism and his own sense of mission provide insights into the reasons for Japan's successful modernization.

## QUESTIONS FOR ANALYSIS

1. Why does Iwasaki believe that Japan must keep foreigners out of the coastal trade?
2. According to Iwasaki, what is at stake in the competition for control of Japan's coastal trade?
3. What advantages and disadvantages does Iwasaki's company have in its rivalry with its British rival?
4. How does Iwasaki attempt to inspire greater dedication and effort from his workers?

---

Many people have expressed differing opinions concerning the principles and advantages of engaging foreigners or Japanese in the task of coastal trade. Granted, we may permit a dissenting opinion which suggests that in principle both foreigners and Japanese must be permitted to engage in coastal trade, but once we look into the question of advantages, we know that coastal trade is too important a matter to be given over to the control of foreigners. If we allow the right of coastal navigation to fall into the hands of foreigners in peacetime it means loss of business opportunities and employment for our own people, and in wartime it means yielding the vital right of information to foreigners. In fact, this is not too different from abandoning the rights of our country as an independent nation.

Looking back into the past, . . . when we abandoned the policy of seclusion and entered into an era of friendly commerce with foreign nations,

---

*Source:* From *Japan: A Documentary History*, ed. David J. Lu (Armonk, NY: M.E. Sharpe, 1997), p. 191. Translation

we should have been prepared for this very task. However, due to the fact that our people lack knowledge and wealth, we have yet to assemble a fleet sufficient to engage in coastal navigation. Furthermore, we have neither the necessary skills for navigation nor a plan for developing maritime transportation industry. This condition is the cause of attracting foreign shipping companies to occupy our major maritime transport lines. . . .

I now propose to do my utmost, and along with my 35 million compatriots, perform my duty as a citizen of this country. That is to recover the right of coastal trade in our hands, and not to delegate that task to foreigners. Unless we propose to do so, it is useless for our government to revise the unequal treaties[1] or to change our entrenched customs. We need people who can respond, otherwise all the endeavors of the government will come to naught. This is the reason why the government protects our company, and I know that our responsibilities are even greater than the full weight of Mt. Fuji thrust upon our shoulders. There have been many who wish to hinder our progress in fulfilling our obligations. However, we have been able to eliminate one of our worst enemies, the Pacific Mail Company of the United States, from contention by application of appropriate means.[2] Now, another rival has emerged. It is the Peninsular & Oriental Steam Navigation Company of Great Britain which is setting up a new line between Yokohama and Shanghai, and is attempting to claim its right over the ports of Nagasaki, Kobe, and Yokohama. . . . How can we decline the challenge? Heretofore, our company has received protection from the government, support from the nation, and hard work from its employees through which it has done its duty. However, our company is young and not

every phase of its operation is well conducted. In contrast, the P & O Company is backed by its massive capital, its large fleet of ships, and by its experiences of operations in Oriental countries. In competing against this giant, what methods can we employ?

I have thought about this problem very carefully and have come to one conclusion. There is no other alternative but to eliminate unnecessary positions and unnecessary expenditures. This is a time-worn solution and no new wisdom is involved. Even though it is a familiar saying, it is much easier said than done, and this indeed has been the root cause of difficulties in the past and present times. Therefore, starting immediately I propose that we engage in this task. By eliminating unnecessary personnel from the payroll, eliminating unnecessary expenditures, and engaging in hard and arduous work, we shall be able to solidify the foundation of our company. If there is a will there is a way. Through our own effort, we shall be able to repay the government for its protection and answer our nation for its confidence shown in us. Let us work together in discharging our responsibilities and not be ashamed of ourselves. Whether we succeed or fail, whether we can gain profit or sustain loss, we cannot anticipate at this time. Hopefully, all of you will join me in a singleness of heart to attain this cherished goal, forbearing and undaunted by setbacks to restore to our own hands the right to our own coastal trade. If we succeed it will not only be an accomplishment for our company alone but also a glorious event for our Japanese Empire, which shall let its light shine to all four corners of earth. We can succeed or fail, and it depends on your effort or lack of effort. Do your utmost in this endeavor!

---

[1]The commercial treaties with Western powers agreed to by the shogunate after Perry's mission.

[2]The American firm withdrew from Japan when it was unable to compete with Mitsubishi's low prices, made possible largely by government subsidies.

# Reaction, Rebellion, and Reform in China

Although the Opium War revealed glaring deficiencies in the Chinese military and the relative backwardness of Chinese technology, it took the disastrous events of the 1850s to prod Chinese leaders into thinking seriously about reform. The 1850s saw the outbreak of three major rebellions, massive flooding of the Yellow River, and defeat by European armies in the Second Opium War (1858–1860). At the close of the war, which resulted in another humiliating treaty, a number of officials began to promote a program of Self Strengthening, which called for selective borrowing from the West in military and economic matters, but only as a means of propping up the country's traditional Confucian order, including imperial rule.

Despite its achievements, by the late 1890s the Self-Strengthening Movement had reached a dead end. For forty years, its supporters had worked to revive China by selectively and incrementally introducing aspects of Western science, technology, military organization, and jurisprudence. In the 1890s, however, China's shocking defeat in the Sino-Japanese War in 1895 and its inability to slow the partition of China by Western imperialists revealed the inadequacy of their approach. In response, in 1898 the Guangzhu emperor, at the urging of a small coterie of reform-minded advisors abandoned the moderate, slow-paced program of the self-strengtheners for a plan of rapid and comprehensive change. In one hundred days the emperor issued more than forty decrees on a wide range of subjects: modernization of the army, navy, police, and postal system; promotion of industry and agriculture; the founding of new schools and universities offering training in foreign languages, science, mathematics, and economics; the reform of the civil service examinations; and the overhaul of the administration at the imperial and provincial level.

The hopes of reformers were soon dashed. In September 1898, the Empress Dowager Cixi, who was Guangzhu's aunt and had served as his regent until he reached the age of nineteen, organized a coup d'état that placed the emperor under house arrest and reinstalled Cixi as regent. Her subsequent repeal of Guangzhu's edicts revealed the reformers' powerlessness in the face of conservative opposition.

Paradoxically, just two years later, a step taken by Cixi and supported by her most conservative advisors confirmed the need for immediate and far-reaching reforms. Her rash decision to lend military support to the ill-fated antiforeign revolt known as the Boxer Rebellion led to yet another military defeat, another humiliating treaty and general revulsion against the Manchus and their policies. In response, local elites, acting on their own, founded schools, published translations of Western books, and organized European-style police forces. Families sent their children to study in Europe, Japan, or the United States, and merchants joined boycotts of U.S. goods in response to U.S. anti-Chinese immigration policies. Even Cixi and her conservative entourage embraced reform. They announced the establishment of a national school system, founded new military academies, set a timetable for the achievement of constitutional government, changed the civil service examination system to include questions on more practical topics, and then abolished the examinations altogether. These ambitious policies, however, proved difficult to implement, and in any case failed to win the support of the Manchus' ethnic Chinese subjects, many of whom had come to believe that China was being victimized by two forms of foreign oppression, that of the West and that of the Manchus. Nor did the government's proposed reforms change the minds of those who believed China's salvation lay in a complete break from China's Confucian and imperial past. Long in coming, such a break occurred in October 1911, when an uprising and army mutiny in Wachung province sparked the revolution that led to the founding of the Republic of China on January 1, 1912 and the abdication the last Chinese emperor six weeks later.

# The Boxers and the Foreign Devils

## 74 • THREE DOCUMENTS ON THE BOXER REBELLION

The Righteous and Harmonious Fists (*Yihequan*), whose members were known to Westerners as Boxers because their martial exercises resembled boxing, was one of many secret societies that flourished in late Qing China. Centered in the northeastern provinces of Shandong, Hebei, and Shanxi, and drawing members mainly from the peasantry but also from the ranks of artisans, peddlers, ex-soldiers, and vagrants, the Boxers blamed foreigners, Christian missionaries, and their Chinese converts for the region's problems, which included flooding in 1898, a severe drought in 1900, and disruptions caused by railroad construction (which uprooted ancestors' graves) and the installation of telegraph lines (which appeared to bleed when rust-colored rainwater dripped off of them). Inspired by aspects of Daoism, Buddhism, folk beliefs, and even popular fiction, they were convinced of their supernatural powers, including invulnerability to bullets and swords. Beginning in 1898, Boxers spread over the countryside, burning Christian churches and chapels and slaughtering Chinese Christian converts. With their numbers swelling and their popular support increasing, in 1900 the Boxers began to drift into Beijing and Tianjin, two major cities, where they roamed the streets, harassed and killed Chinese converts, vandalized railroads, uprooted telegraph lines, and murdered six Europeans, including two English missionaries.

How to respond to the sudden rise of the Boxers was hotly debated by provincial governors, army officers, and Cixi and her advisors, all of whom were being pressured by foreign diplomats and Western missionary groups to disband or at least control the Boxers. At one extreme, officials who feared further conflict with the foreign powers and were wary of any and all popular movements recommended the annihilation of the Boxers through force. At the opposite extreme, those who saw Boxer violence as a way to discourage Western meddling in Chinese affairs believed the Boxers should be tolerated and even encouraged. In the end, however, only one person's opinion mattered, that of Cixi. On June 21, 1900, with Boxer violence increasing and reports of the first major clashes between Chinese and foreign troops reaching the court, she issued a "declaration of war," which committed the Chinese military to support the Boxers, who were now placed under the command of Manchu generals. With many generals holding back their troops rather than sacrificing them in a lost and ill-considered cause, within weeks a multinational force of six European states, Japan, and the United States easily defeated the Boxer/Manchu army, and Cixi and the Court fled to the distant city of Xi'an, where they remained for a year. The war officially ended in September 1901 with the signing of another humiliating treaty, one that included payment of a staggering indemnity of $333,900,000.

Three documents pertaining to the Boxer Rebellion follow. The first two are examples of the many proclamations the Boxers posted on walls or buildings to publicize their beliefs and powers. The third is the declaration of war issued by Cixi under the seal of the figurehead Guangzhu emperor on June 21, 1900.

## QUESTIONS FOR ANALYSIS

1. According to the two proclamations, how have Christians and foreigners harmed China?
2. How does the imperial declaration of war justify the government's decision to support the Boxers and fight the foreign powers?
3. What is there in the two proclamations that may explain why the Boxers rapidly attracted so much popular support?
4. The two proclamations and the declaration of war both express optimism that the Boxer/Chinese cause will triumph. What is the basis of their optimism?

## "The Gods Assist the Boxers"

The Gods assist the Boxers,
The Patriotic Harmonious corps,
It is because the Foreign Devils disturb the
    Middle Kingdom,
Urging the people to join their religion,
To turn their backs on Heaven,
To not venerate the Gods and forget their
    ancestors.

Men violate human obligations,
Women commit adultery,
Foreign Devils are not produced by
    mankind,
If you do not believe this,
Look at them carefully.

The eyes of all the Foreign Devils are bluish.

No rain falls,
The earth is getting dry,
This is because the churches block the
    skies.[1]
The Gods are angry;
The Genies[2] are vexed;
Both come down from the mountain to
    deliver the doctrine.

This is no false teaching,
The practices of boxing will not be in vain;
Reciting incantations and pronouncing
    magic words,
Burn up yellow written prayers,
Light incense sticks

---

*Source:* From *Peking and Tientsin Times* (May 5, 1900)
[1] After having experienced extensive flooding in 1898, Shandong province was in the midst of a severe drought in 1899-1900.

[2] Humans who are immortal and are endowed with special magical powers.

To invite the Gods and Genies of all the
    mountain grottoes.
The Gods come out from grottoes,
The Genies come down from mountains
To support the humans to practice the
    boxing.

When all the military feats and tactics are
    fully learned,
It will not be difficult to exterminate the
    "Foreign Devils" then.

Push aside the railway tracks,
Pull out the telegraph poles,
Immediately after this destroy the steamships.
Mighty France
Will grow cold and downhearted.
The English and Russians will certainly
    depart.
Let the various "Foreign Devils" all be killed.
May the whole Elegant Empire of the
    Great Qing Dynasty be ever prosperous!

## "Attention: All People in Markets and Villages"

Attention: all people in markets and villages of all provinces in China—now, owing to the fact that Catholics and Protestants have vilified our gods and sages, have deceived our emperors and ministers above, and oppressed the Chinese people below, both our gods and our people are angry at them, yet we have to keep silent. This forces us to practice the magic boxing so as to protect our country, expel the foreign bandits and kill Christian converts, in order to save our people from miserable suffering. After this notice is issued to instruct you villagers, no matter which village you are living in, if there are Christian converts, you ought to get rid of them quickly. The churches which belong to them should be all burned down. Everyone who intends to spare someone, or to disobey our order by concealing Christian converts, will be punished according to the regulation when we come to his place, and he will be burned to death to prevent his impeding our program. We especially do not want to punish anyone by death without warning him first. We cannot bear to see you suffer innocently. Don't disobey this special notice!

*Source:* From Ssu-yü Teng and John K. Fairbank, *China's Response to the West* Cambridge, Mass.: Harvard University Press, 1954), 190

## Imperial Edict to Declare War on Foreigners, June 21, 1900

Ever since the foundation of the dynasty . . . foreigners coming to China have been treated kindly. In the Daoguang [1821-1850] and Xian-feng [1851-1861] reigns they were allowed to trade. They also asked to propagate their religion, a request that the Throne reluctantly granted. At first they were amenable to Chinese control, but for the past thirty years they have taken advantage of China's forbearance to encroach on China's territory, trample on the Chinese people and demand China's wealth. Every concession made by the Chinese only heightened their reliance on violence. They oppressed peaceful citizens and insulted our gods and religious leaders. Their

*Source:* David G. Atwill and Yurong Y. Atwill, *Sources in Chinese History* (Upper Saddle River, New Jersey: Prentice Hall, 2010), p. 107.

actions provoked a burning fury within the people, hence the burning of chapels and the slaughter of converts by patriotic warriors. The Throne was anxious to avoid war . . . we were worried about protecting our people. Therefore time and again we issued edicts protecting legations and defending the converts. . . . Exceptional kindness was shown to the "people from afar." But these people knew no gratitude and increased their pressure. . . . These threats only serve to reveal their aggressive intentions. In all matters relating to international intercourse, we have never been lacking in civility. But while styling themselves as "civilized states," they continue to act with complete disregard to what is right, depending solely on military force.

I have now reigned for nearly thirty years and have treated the people as children, and the people in return have treated me as their divinity. In the midst of our reign we have been the recipient of the gracious favor of the Dowager Empress. Furthermore,

our ancestors have come to our aid, the gods have answered our call, and never has there been so universal a manifestation of loyalty and patriotism. With tears I have announced war in our ancestral shrines. Better to enter the struggle and do our utmost than seek some measures of self-preservation involving eternal disgrace. All our officials, high and low, are of one mind and therefore have assembled without official summons several hundred thousand patriotic soldiers. Even children are carrying spears in the service of the State. Those others rely on devious schemes, while our trust is in Heaven's justice. They depend on violence, we on humanity. Not to speak of the righteousness of our cause, our provinces number more than twenty, and our people over 400,000,000. It will not be difficult to vindicate the dignity of our country.

We conclude this decree by promising heavy rewards to those who distinguish themselves in battle or subscribe funds, and threatening punishment to those who show cowardice and act treacherously.

## The End of the Civil Service Examinations

### 75 • YUAN SHIKAI ET AL., MEMORIAL ON THE CIVIL SERVICE EXAMINATIONS AND IMPERIAL EDICT, SEPTEMBER 1905

For well over a thousand years, the imperial examination system, which at the local, provincial, and imperial levels tested candidates' knowledge of the Confucian classics, skill as calligraphers, and ability to write essays according to strict stylistic guidelines, was an integral part of Chinese culture. The system provided officials for the imperial bureaucracy and assured that a standardized Confucian curriculum dominated Chinese education. To its supporters, it ensured that the most qualified individuals, all sharing a set of core values, would advise the emperor and run the state. To its critics, whose numbers grew from the 1860s onward, the examinations encouraged rote memorization, fostered conservative thinking, and discouraged the study of foreign languages, mathematics, and science. In the 1890s reformers ordered that the examinations include more questions on practical government problems, with less emphasis on poetry and calligraphy, but went no further. As the pace of reform quickened in the early 1900s such tentative steps came to be viewed as inadequate, and in 1905, the figurehead Guangxu emperor issued the edict that abolished the civil service examinations.

The first excerpt that follows is the memorandum (memorial) addressed to the emperor in early 1905 by six provincial governors and generals, the most prominent of whom was Yuan Shikai, the governor of Zhili province and future dictator of China. It recommends the immediate abolition of the examination system rather than a gradual phase-out. The second excerpt is the edict abolishing the examinations issued by the Guangxu emperor in September 1905. Together they provide insights into the motives behind the decision to end the traditional examinations and the many challenges China faced in implementing its new educational program.

## QUESTIONS FOR ANALYSIS

1. According to the memorial and the rescript, what makes educational reform a matter of urgency?
2. According to the documents, what benefits to China will accrue from the new educational system being proposed?
3. What do the two documents tell us about the obstacles that will be faced in implementing the approach to education?

## Memorial on Education

In meditating upon the general conditions and considering carefully the trend of the times, your memoralists have become aware that the urgency of present circumstances is greater than ever before and that in the united exercise of our utmost strength an hour is worth thousands of gold pieces. Our strong neighbors are pressing in upon us and can we delay? During recent years all countries have been hoping that we should reform and have been urging us to change our system. They have all had misgivings that we are bound up to old systems, and have ridiculed us as being like a rat looking in both directions, undecided which one to take. While no change has been made . . . , in the twinkling of an eye peace will be restored between Japan and Russia[1] and the affairs of China will be in a still more dangerous condition. Then there will be a rude awakening. . . . As soon as conservative methods are boldly and rigorously abandoned and new methods adopted, those who see and hear what is being done will all . . . deal with us on a basis of mutual respect, and the students from China who are pursuing their studies in foreign countries will

also receive encouragement. Emphasizing the importance of schools will obviate the possibility of being carried away by gross superstition and idle rumors. . . . The establishment of schools is not solely for the training of learned men but for the general dissemination of knowledge among the people, so that all may receive the advantages and acquired powers of an elementary education. This will result in patriotic loyalty to the country and in increased ability to earn a livelihood. . . . Soldiers, farmers, artisans, and merchants will all follow their respective business with intelligent zeal. Women and children will not be left in idleness. . . . No place will be without a school and no person without an education. If this method be followed, why should our country not become wealthy and strong? Those who have carefully studied the situation know that the secret of Prussia's victory over France and of Japan's over Russia lay in their primary schools; in fact, the root of prosperity and strength is in the establishment of schools, and in this respect it is now only China that lags in the rear. If the examination system is not abolished and the schools are not established, how can general intelligence grow among students and people? . . .

---

*Source:* John C. Ferguson, "The Abolition of the Competitive Examinations in China," *Journal of the American Oriental Society* 27 (1906), pp. 79–86.

[1]The Russo-Japanese War began in February 1904 and would end officially on September 5, 1905, with the signing of the Treaty of Portsmouth. The Russians had sued for peace in May 1905.

[Another] important matter is the immediate establishment of normal schools [training schools for teachers]. The greatest cause of concern is not that there are no schools or no funds to establish them, but that there are no teachers. A special edict should also be issued commanding the provinces to send pupils who have finished their secondary studies to foreign countries to take courses in normal studies, some longer and some shorter. . . . If normal schools are established in all the provinces, teachers will be trained and the first step taken toward the advancement of schools. . . .

Another important matter is that a way of preferment should be left open to scholars of the old school. To this end during the next nine years students who have already taken their degree [by passing one of the traditional examinations] and also show proficiency in arithmetic, geography, science, politics, railroads, mining, police work, or western governmental science, may be sent from the various provinces to Beijing for examination. If they can pass successfully, they will be awarded with appointment.

## Imperial Rescript, September 2, 1905

Before the era of what is termed the Three Dynasties,[2] men for office were selected from the schools, and it must be confessed that the plan produced many talented men. It was indeed a most successful plan for the production of men of talents and for the molding of character. . . .

Just now we are passing through a crisis fraught with difficulties and the country is most urgently in want of men of talents and abilities (of the modern sort). Owing to the fact that, of late, modern methods of education have been daily on the increase amongst us, we repeatedly issued our commands to

all our viceroys and governors of provinces to lose no time in establishing modern schools of learning in such number that every member of this empire may have the means of going there to study and learn something substantial, in order to prepare himself to be of use to his country. We have indeed thought deeply on this subject.

---

> ### The Rescript Orders the Abolition of the Civil Service Examinations in 1906

---

We are certain that the official classes and gentry throughout the Empire, on learning of this will enthusiastically set about to start as many schools as possible, and thus give the blessings of modern education to every subject of the Throne. The Government being thus enabled to obtain men of talents and abilities, it follows that the cities and towns producing such bright lights of learning will also enjoy a reflected honor therefrom. We hereby further command our Ministers of Education . . . to lose no time in distributing at once to the various provinces the text-books for schools that have been prepared, so that we may have a uniform system of teaching in all our schools. We also command our viceroys and governors to insist that their subordinates, the prefects, sub-prefects, and district magistrates, shall make haste to establish primary schools in all the towns, hamlets, and villages within their respective jurisdictions, and that the utmost care be taken to select intelligent teachers for them, so that the minds of all our subjects be open for the reception of modern knowledge. Let all our officials be earnest and diligent in obeying these our commands and let there be no lagging and carelessness.

---

[2] The period from 220 to 289 C.E.—in other words, long before the beginning of the civil service examinations.

# PART FOUR

# The Global Community and Its Challenges in the Twentieth and Twenty-First Centuries

WHAT WILL FUTURE HISTORIANS say about the past one hundred years of human history? How will they interpret the era's wars, revolutions, economic transformations, new ideologies, technological breakthroughs, population trends, cultural changes, and countless other events and developments? How will they explain the contradictions between humankind's stupendous achievements and its abysmal failures? From the perspective of the early twenty-first century, no one can answer such questions. Future historians' views of the past century will be shaped by events that have not yet occurred and by values and concerns unique to their own era. What may seem to be matters of great consequence to us may be insignificant to them, while developments we barely notice may be important parts of their stories.

It would be surprising, however, if future historians did not note the importance of the dramatic shift in world political relationships following World War II. The world of the early 1900s was a Europe-dominated world. Europeans were among the best-educated and wealthiest people on earth. They ruled Africa and much of Asia, dominated the global economy, and played a preponderant role in world affairs. After World War II, however, Europe's primacy ended. The Europeans' colonial empires disintegrated, their dominance of international relations ended, and their economic importance declined in the face of global competition.

Future historians undoubtedly also will highlight the phenomenon of globalization, a word and concept that came into use at the end of the twentieth century to describe the unprecedented scale of integration and interaction that had come to dominate world relationships. Interactions among distant peoples, of course, were nothing new. Long-distance trade, migration, travel, wars of conquest, and the diffusion of ideas and technologies had been parts of history for thousands of years. Interaction on a global scale increased markedly in the fifteenth and sixteenth centuries, when Europeans opened sea routes to Africa, the Americas, and Asia and launched a new era in commerce, migration, and biological exchange. During the twentieth century, however, breakthroughs in communications and transportation virtually obliterated the limitations of time and space, and the exchange of goods and ideas among the world's peoples reached undreamed-of levels.

Future historians also will take note of other developments in the twentieth and early twentieth-first centuries: the ongoing rush of scientific, medical, and technological discoveries; the spectacular expansion of the world's population (from approximately 1.7 billion in 1900 to 7.2 billion in early 2014); the relative decline of the world's rural population and the growth of cities; and the emergence of a shared global culture, symbolized by the unlimited possibilities of the Internet and the ubiquity of McDonald's restaurants, Japanese and Korean automobiles, blue jeans, 24-hour cable news networks, and Chinese manufactured goods of every imaginable sort.

Future historians will undoubtedly take note of our recent history's inhumanities and cruelties: its appalling war casualties, its use of torture, and its genocides, not just against Jews in World War II but also against Armenians in World War I; Cambodians in the 1970s; Bosnians, Kosovars, and Tutsi in the 1990s; and the peoples of Darfur in the early 2000s. Will such developments be viewed as aberrations or the beginning of a new era of brutality and callousness in human relationships? Future historians surely will discuss the emergence of more than one hundred new independent states in Africa and Asia. Will their stories turn out to be celebrations of economic and political achievement or tales of ongoing failure and disillusionment? Historians will note that the twentieth and early twenty-first centuries were marked by both religious fervor and indifference, environmental disasters and growing environmental consciousness, and the globalization of culture and the continued appeal of national and ethnic identification.

In looking to the future, optimists affirm a faith in progress, holding fast to the dream that reasonable human beings can shape a future of peace, harmony, and a just sharing of the world's wealth. Pessimists, pondering the effects of continuing population growth, energy shortages, worsening pollution, global warming, and the persistence of intractable political conflicts, warn of a coming new "dark age." However things develop, events of the past hundred years have launched humankind on paths that will determine its future for years to come.

# Chapter 11

# The Western World in Crisis

N 1922, THE FRENCH INTELLECTUAL Paul Valéry spoke these words in a speech to a university audience in Switzerland:

> The storm has died away, and still we are restless, uneasy. . . . Almost all the affairs of men remain in terrible uncertainty. We think of what has disappeared, we are almost destroyed by what has been destroyed; we do not know what will be born, and we fear the future, not without reason. We hope vaguely, we dread precisely; . . . we confess that the charm of life is behind us, abundance is behind us, but doubt and disorder are in us and with us. There is no thinking man, . . . who can hope to overcome this anxiety, to escape this darkness, to measure the probable duration of this period when the vital relations of humanity are disturbed profoundly.[1]

How stark a contrast between Valéry's despondency and the optimism that preceded World War I. Before the war, the West's wealth and power reached unimagined heights, and most Americans and Europeans were self-satisfied, proud, and confident. They took for granted their moral and intellectual superiority and were convinced that their world dominance would last indefinitely. Only a few years later, assurance gave way to doubt, hope to despair, and moderation to fanaticism.

The turning point, especially for Europe, was World War I—the four-year exercise in death that resulted in thirty million casualties, billions of squandered dollars, and a disturbing realization that human inventiveness could have dark and devastating consequences. The war and the postwar treaties set the stage for three decades marked by economic depression, totalitarianism, diplomatic failure, contempt for human rights, and a second world war with a legacy of fifty to sixty million dead, the attempted annihilation of Europe's Jews, and the dropping of the first atomic bombs.

---

[1]Paul Valéry, *Variety*, translated from the French by T. Malcolm Crosby (New York: Harcourt Brace, 1927), p. 252.

Interwar intellectuals who shared Paul Valéry's anxiety and gloom prophesied the fall of European civilization and drew analogies between its decline and the fatal problems of fifth-century Rome. Post–World War II developments discredited much of their pessimism. European nations, even devastated Germany, recovered from the wars, affirmed a commitment to liberal democracy, rebuilt their economies, and embarked on a major project of economic and political cooperation. What changed was their role in the world. Their empires disappeared; dominance of international affairs shifted to the United States and the Soviet Union; and Asia provided fierce new economic competition. The era of European world dominance had come to an end.

# The Trauma of World War I

Why did Europeans find World War I so demoralizing, so unsettling, so devoid of any quality or result that might have justified its appalling costs and casualties? War, after all, was nothing new for Europeans. Dynastic wars, religious wars, commercial wars, colonial wars, civil wars, wars to preserve or destroy the balance of power, wars of every conceivable variety fill the pages of European history books. Yet none of these conflicts prepared Europeans for the war they fought between 1914 and 1918.

The sheer number of battlefield casualties goes far in explaining the war's devastating impact. Thirty-two belligerent nations mobilized approximately sixty-five million men, of whom just under ten million were killed and slightly more than twenty million were wounded. To present these statistics in another way, for approximately fifteen hundred consecutive days, on average six thousand men were killed every day. Losses on the Western Front were especially appalling. Here, after the Germans almost took Paris in the early fighting, the war became a stalemate until the armistice on November 11, 1918. Along a four-hundred-mile front stretching from the English Channel through Belgium and France to the Swiss border, defense—a combination of trenches, barbed wire, land mines, poison gas, and machine guns—proved superior to offense—massive artillery barrages followed by charges of troops sent "over the top" across no man's land to overrun enemy lines. Such attacks produced unbearably long casualty lists but minuscule gains of territory.

Such losses would have been easier to endure if the war had led to a secure and lasting peace, but the hardships and antagonisms of the postwar years rendered such sacrifice meaningless. After the war, winners and losers alike faced inflation, high unemployment, and, after a few years of prosperity in the 1920s, the economic catastrophe known as the Great Depression. Embittered by their defeat and harsh treatment in the Versailles Treaty, Germans abandoned democracy for Hitler's Nazi dictatorship in 1933. Japan and Italy, though on the winning side, were disappointed with their territorial gains, and this resentment played into the hands of ultranationalist politicians. Arabs, who had fought against Germany's ally, Ottoman Turkey, in the hope of achieving nationhood, were embittered when Great Britain and France denied their independence. The United States, disillusioned with war and Great Power wrangling, withdrew into diplomatic isolation, leaving Great Britain and France to enforce the postwar treaties. Britain and France expanded their colonial empires in Africa and the Middle East, but this was scant compensation for the sacrifices of the Great War, a war in which there were no true victors.

# The Romance of War

## 76 • POPULAR ART AND POSTER ART FROM GERMANY, ENGLAND, AND CANADA

When war came in 1914, crowds cheered, men rushed to enlist, and politicians promised that "the boys would be home by Christmas." Not having experienced a general war since the defeat of Napoleon in 1815, and with little thought to the carnage in the American Civil War or the Franco-Prussian War of 1870–1871, Europeans saw the war as a glorious adventure—an opportunity to fight for the flag or the Kaiser or the king, to wear splendid uniforms, and to win glory in battles decided by élan, spirit, and bravery. The war they fought was nothing like the war they imagined, and the disparity between expectations and reality was one of many reasons why World War I brought forth such despair and disillusionment.

The five illustrations shown here portray the eagerness and optimism of all belligerents at the war's start as well as their efforts to sustain this enthusiasm as the war dragged on. *The Departure* shows German troops departing for the battlefront in the late summer or fall of 1914. It is the work of the Swedish-born artist Bruno Wennerberg, who moved to Germany in 1898 and died there in 1950. This illustration appeared in the German periodical *Simplicissimus* in March 1915. Noted before the war for criticism of German militarism, *Simplicissimus* lent its full support to Germany's war effort once the war began.

The second poster, "Your King and Country Need You," is one of several recruitment posters inspired by a song of the same name recorded and popularized shortly after the war started. It is another departure scene, showing a young English officer and his father having a final handshake as a troop train prepares to depart. In the background another soldier bids farewell to his wife and child.

The third illustration, "Time for One More," is one of a series of war-related cards included by the Mitchell Tobacco Company in its packs of Golden Dawn Cigarettes in 1914 and early 1915. It shows a sergeant offering smokes to his soldiers before battle.

The fourth illustration, "To Build Anything, to Fight Anything," is a Canadian recruitment poster from 1916. Although Canada, like Australia, New Zealand, and

B. Wennerberg, The Departure

Your King and Country Need You

Advertisement card from Golden Dawn Cigarettes

"To Build Anything, to Fight Anything"

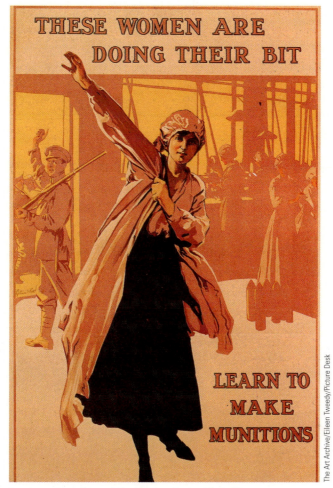

Septimus Scott, These Women Are Doing Their Bit

South Africa, controlled its internal affairs, its foreign policy was still directed by Great Britain. Hence, when Great Britain went to war, so did Canada. When war was declared, thousands of men, many of whom were English-born immigrants, volunteered for the Canadian Expeditionary Force, and in October 1914, 33,000 Canadian troops departed for Britain. Subsequently, recruitment became the responsibility of local militia units before conscription was decreed in 1917. This particular poster was used by the Fifth Canadian Pioneer Battalion in 1916, headquartered in Montreal. Pioneer battalions were frontline troops that performed a variety of engineering and construction tasks, including tunnelling, mining, wiring, railroad work, bridge construction, and building and repairing trenches.

The fifth illustration is a poster produced and distributed by the British Ministry of Munitions in early 1917 to encourage women to work in the munitions industry. It shows a young and attractive woman offering a jaunty salute to a passing soldier as she arrives for work. It gives no hint of the dangers of munitions work. During the war approximately three hundred "munitionettes" were killed in explosions or from chemical-related sicknesses. Women who worked with TNT came to be known as "canaries" because of their yellowish skin. Despite such hazards, almost a million women were working in munitions factories by war's end.

### QUESTIONS FOR ANALYSIS

1. What message about the war does each of the illustrations seek to convey?
2. In what ways does each illustration romanticize the life of a soldier or female munitions worker?
3. What impression of battle does the English tobacco card communicate?
4. What does a comparison of Wennerberg's illustration and the English poster of the munitions worker suggest about changing views of women's role during the war and in society at large?

# Twenty-Four Hours on the Western Front

## 77 • HENRY S. CLAPHAM, MUD AND KHAKI, MEMOIRS OF AN INCOMPLETE SOLDIER

Henry S. Clapham was born in 1875 in Hull, England, and graduated from Queen's College in Taunton, a boarding school for the sons of well-to-do families. After clerking in a law office, he married and began a legal career in London. In the fall of 1914 he enlisted in the army and by January 1915 was fighting in Belgium. Clapham fought there until October 1915, when a hand wound made him unfit for service. On his return to England, he resumed his career as a lawyer and, like many veterans, turned his diary notes into a book, *Mud and Khaki*, which appeared in 1917. It went through several printings and was republished in 1930.

Clapham's book describes his experiences fighting in and around Ypres, a Belgian city in the low, wet region that abuts the English Channel. It was the site of three major battles, one in the fall of 1914, another in 1915, and the last and bloodiest in 1917. Clapham fought in the Second Battle of Ypres, which began in April 1915, when the Germans launched an attack on entrenched enemy troops. The Germans abandoned the offensive in late May, but fighting continued in the general region through the summer.

The Second Battle of Ypres saw the introduction of poison gas on the Western Front. Chlorine gas, a product of the German dyestuff industry and developed by the German chemical company IG Farben, was released from cylinders or delivered by artillery shells. It made the lungs produce fluid, causing the victim to drown. Thousands of soldiers around Ypres died as a result of German gas attacks, but the effectiveness of the new weapon diminished when soldiers

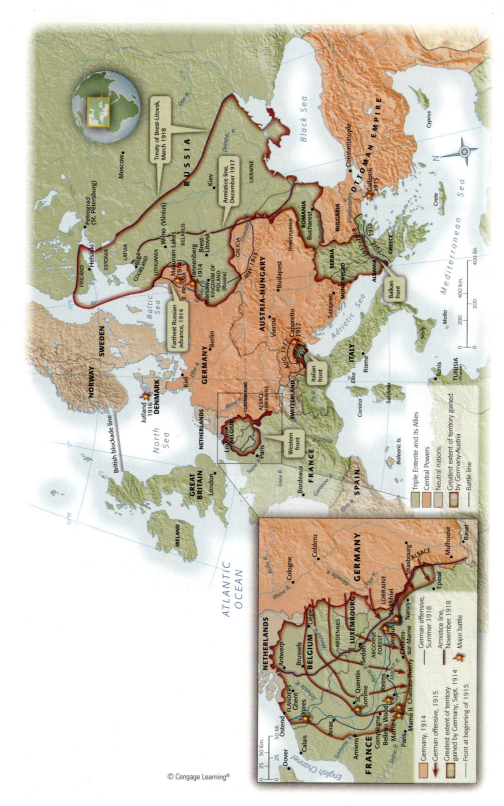

Treaty of Brest-Litovsk, March 1918

Armistice line, December 1917

Farthest Russian advance, 1914

British blockade line

Jutland 1916

Western front

Italian front

Balkan front

Treaty of Brest-Litovsk

Moscow

Petrograd (St. Petersburg)

Helsinki

FINLAND

NORWAY

SWEDEN

Baltic Sea

ESTONIA

LATVIA

Riga

COURLAND

LITHUANIA

Wilno (Vilnius)

Masurian Lakes 1914

E. PRUSSIA

Tannenberg 1914

Warsaw

KINGDOM OF POLAND (Russia)

BELARUS

Brest-Litovsk

R U S S I A

Kiev

UKRAINE

Dnieper R.

Dniester R.

Don R.

Black Sea

GALICIA

MAY 1915

Budapest

AUSTRIA-HUNGARY

Vienna

Caporetto 1917

AUG. 1917

TRANSYLVANIA

ROMANIA

Bucharest

SERBIA

Sarajevo

MONTENEGRO

BULGARIA

1917 1918

1915

ALBANIA

GREECE

Constantinople

Gallipoli 1915

Dardanelles

O T T O M A N   E M P I R E

Cyprus

Crete

Mediterranean Sea

Adriatic Sea

ITALY

Rome

Elba

Corsica

Sardinia

Sicily

Malta

TUNISIA (France)

Tunis

Balearic Is.

Kiel

GERMANY

Berlin

DENMARK

North Sea

NETHERLANDS

Rhine R.

LUXEMBOURG

ALSACE-LORRAINE

SWITZERLAND

Louvain

BELGIUM

Paris

FRANCE

Bordeaux

Seine R.

Loire R.

Garonne R.

Rhône R.

Po R.

Elbe R.

GREAT BRITAIN

London

IRELAND

ATLANTIC OCEAN

SPAIN

Ebro R.

0°

10°W

20°E

400 Mi.

400 Km.

200

200

0

N

Triple Entente and its Allies
Central Powers
Neutral nations
Greatest extent of territory gained by Germany-Austria
Battle line

**Inset map:**

NETHERLANDS

Antwerp

Brussels

BELGIUM

Ghent

FLANDERS

Ostend

Ypres

Calais

Dover

English Channel

Arras

Amiens

Somme R.

St. Quentin

Somme

Compiègne

FRANCE

Paris

Marne R.

Château-Thierry

Belleau Wood

Marne II

Reims

Châlons-sur-Marne

Sedan

ARGONNE FOREST

Verdun

St. Mihiel

LUXEMBOURG

Sedan

Liège

ARDENNES

Meuse R.

Scheldt R.

Aisne R.

Oise R.

Seine R.

Nancy

LORRAINE

Metz

Épinal

Strasbourg

ALSACE

Mulhouse

Basel

GERMANY

Cologne

Coblenz

Ruhr R.

Rhine R.

Moselle R.

Saar R.

MOSELLE R.

Germany, 1914
German offensive, 1915
Greatest extent of territory gained by Germany, Sept. 1914
Front at beginning of 1915
German offensive, Summer 1918
Armistice line, November 1918
Major battle

50 Mi.

50 Km.

25

25

0

© Cengage Learning®

World War I

were supplied with respirators, or gas masks, and learned that holding a wet handkerchief over one's nose and mouth provided some protection. Such countermeasures stimulated both sides to develop other types of poison gas, including phosgene, which causes asphyxiation, and mustard gas, which causes severe blistering.

## QUESTIONS FOR ANALYSIS

1. As far as can be determined by Clapham's account, how did the fighting he describes change the battle lines?
2. What aspects of the fighting did Clapham and the other men find most unnerving?
3. Wars inevitably cause immense human suffering, but the suffering in World War I for soldiers and civilians alike was especially traumatic and unbearable. What is there in Clapham's account that may explain this phenomenon?

### June 19, 1915

We started again at dusk and passed down the railway cutting, but, instead of turning off into the fields, we went on as far as the Menin Road, at what is known as "Hell Fire Corner." A few hundred yards down the road we found a resting place for the night in some shallow jumping-off trenches, a few yards back from the front line. It was very dark, and the trench was small, and sitting in a huddle I got a cramp and felt miserable.

The Huns[1] started by putting over big crumps[2] all around us. They seemed to aim for the relics of a building a hundred yards in the rear, and there the bricks were flying. . . . Then at 2:50 A.M. our own guns started and kept up a heavy bombardment of the trenches in front until 4:15, by which time it was quite light. . . .

At 4:15 a whistle blew. The men in the front line went over the top, and we scrambled out and took their places in the front trench. In front of us was a small field . . . split diagonally by an old footpath.

On the other side of the field was a belt of trees in which lay the Hun trench.

In a few moments flags went up there, to show that it had been captured and that the troops were going on. Another whistle, and we ourselves scrambled over the parapet[3] and sprinted across the field. Personally I was so over weighted that I could only amble. . . . I took the diagonal path, as the line of least resistance, and most of my section did the same.

When I dropped into the Hun trench I found it a great place, only three feet wide, and at least eight deep, and beautifully made of white sandbags . . . At that spot there was no sign of any damage by our shells, but a number of dead Huns lay in the bottom. There was a sniper's post just where I fell in, a comfortable little square hole, fitted with seats and shelves, bottles of beer, tinned meats, and a fine helmet hanging on a hook.

Our first duty was to change the [barbed] wire, so . . . I slipped off my pack, and, clambering out again, started to move the wire from what was now the rear, to the new front of the trench. It was rotten

Source: H. S. Clapham, *Mud and Khaki: Memoirs of an Incomplete Soldier* (Hutchinson & Co., 1930), pp. 141–153.
[1]A derogatory term for German soldiers. The Huns, legendary for their cruelty and ferocity, were a nomadic people of Central Asia whose invasions of the fourth and fifth centuries C.E. contributed to the fall of the Western Roman Empire.
[2]A heavy German shell that exploded with a cloud of black smoke.
[3]A mound built to protect the front of a trench.

stuff, most of it loose coils. . . . What there was movable of it, we got across without much difficulty, and we had just finished when we were ordered to move down the trench, as our diagonal advance had brought us too far to the right.

We moved down along the belt of woodland, which was only a few yards broad, to a spot where one of our companies was already hard at work digging a communication trench[4] back to our old front line. Here there was really no trench at all. One or more of our own big shells had burst in the middle, filling it up for a distance of ten yards and practically destroying both parapet and parados.[5] Some of us started building up the parapet with sandbags, and I saw the twins [two men in Clapham's unit] merrily at work hauling out dead Huns at least twice their own size.

There was a hedge along the back of the trench, so I scrambled through a hole in it, piled my pack, rifle, and other things . . . on the farther side, and started again on the wire. Hereabouts it was much better stuff, and it took us some time to get it across and pegged down. We had just got the last knife-rest across, when I saw a man who was placing sandbags on the parapet from the farther side swivel round, throw his legs into the trench, and collapse in a heap in the bottom. Several others were already lying there, and for the first time I realized that a regular hail of machine-gun bullets was sweeping over the trench.

. . . We all started work at a feverish pace, digging out the trench and building up some sort of shelter in front. One chap, a very nice kid, was bowled over almost at once with a bullet in the groin, and lay in the trench, kicking and screaming while we worked. . . .

The attacking battalions had carried several more trenches and we were told that two at least

had been held, but our own orders were to consolidate and hold on to the trench we were in at all costs. . . .

I had just filled a sandbag and placed it on the top of the parapet when I happened to glance down, and saw a slight movement in the earth between my feet. I stooped and scraped away the soil with my fingers and found what seemed like palpitating flesh. It proved to be a man's cheek, and a few minutes' work uncovered his head. I poured a little water down his throat, and two or three of us dug out the rest of him. He was undamaged except for his feet and ankles, which were a mass of pulp, and he recovered consciousness as we worked. The first thing he said was in English: "What Corps are you?" He was a big man, and told us he was forty-five and had only been a soldier for a fortnight.

We dragged him out and laid him under the hedge. There was nothing else we could do for him. He had another drink later, but he must have died in the course of the day. I am afraid we forgot all about him . . . The Captain was the next to go. He insisted on standing on the parados, directing operations, and got a bullet in the lungs. He could walk, and two men were detailed to take him down to the dressing-station. One came back, to be killed later in the day, but the other stopped a bullet *en route,* and followed the Captain.

When we had got our big Hun out, he left a big hole in the ground, and we found a dead arm and hand projecting from the bottom. We dug about, but did not seem to be able to find the body, and when I seized the sleeve and pulled, the arm came out of the ground by itself. We had to dig deeper for our own sake, but there was nothing else left, except messy earth, which seemed to have been driven into

---

[4]A shallow trench built from the front line to a relatively safe area in the rear. Used to supply front-line troops with food and ammunition and to transport killed and wounded soldiers away from the fighting.

[5]A mound built to protect the rear of a trench.

the side of the trench. The man helping me turned sick, for it wasn't pretty work. . . .

About 5:30 A.M. the Huns started shelling, and the new communication trench soon became a death-trap. A constant stream of wounded who had come down another trench from the north, passed along the rear. The Huns made a target of the two traverses (unluckily including our own), from which the communication trench opened, and numbers of the wounded were caught just behind us. The trench itself was soon choked with bodies. . . .

The shelling got worse as the day wore on and several more of our men went down. They plastered us with crumps, shrapnel, and whizz-bangs.[6] One of the latter took off a sandbag from the top of the parapet and landed it on my head. It nearly broke my neck. . . . Every minute several shells fell within a few yards and covered us with dust, and the smell of the explosives poisoned my mouth. All I could do was to crouch against the parapet and pant for breath, expecting every moment to be my last. And this went on for hours. I began to long for the shell which would put an end to everything, but in time my nerves became almost numbed, and I lay like a log until roused.

I think it must have been midday when something happened. An alarm was given and we manned the parapet, to see some scores of men retreating at a run from the trench in front. They ran right over us, men of half a dozen battalions, and many dropped on the way. As they passed, something was said of gas, but it appeared that nearly all the officers in the two front trenches had been killed or wounded, someone had raised an alarm of gas, and the men had panicked and run.

A lot of the runaways insisted on gathering by the hedge just behind us, in spite of our warnings not to do so, and I saw at least twenty hit by shrapnel within a few yards of us.

The Brigade-Major arrived, cursing, and called upon some of our own men to advance and re-occupy the trench in front. He led them himself, and they made a very fine dash across. I do not think more than twenty fell, and they reoccupied the trench and, I believe, the third also, before the Huns realized that they were empty. . . .

It was scorchingly hot and no one could eat, although I tried to do so. All day long we were constantly covered with debris from the shell-bursts. Great pieces fell all about us, and, packed like herrings, we crowded in the bottom of the trench. Hardly anything could be done for the wounded. If their wounds were slight, they generally risked a dash to the rear. Every now and then we stood to in expectation of a counterattack, but none developed.

About 6 P.M. the worst moment of the day came. The Huns started to bombard us with a shell which was quite new to us. It sounded like a gigantic firecracker, with two distinct explosions. These shells came over just above the parapet, in a flood, much more quickly than we could count them. After a quarter of an hour of this sort of thing, there was a sudden crash in the trench and ten feet of the parapet, just beyond me, was blown away and everyone around blinded by the dust. With my first glance I saw what looked like half a dozen bodies, mingled with sandbags, and then I smelt gas and realized that these were gas-shells. I had my respirator on in a hurry and most of our own men were as quick. The others were slower and suffered for it. One man was sick all over the sandbags and another was coughing his heart up. We pulled four men out of the debris unharmed. One man was unconscious, and died of gas later. Another was hopelessly smashed up and must have got it full in the chest.

We all thought that this was the end and almost hoped for it, but luckily the gas-shells stopped, and after a quarter of an hour we could take off our

---

[6]*Shrapnel* were hollow shells filled with bullets or pieces of metal that scattered on explosion. *Whizz-bangs* were shells fired by light German field guns.

respirators. I started in at once to build up the parapet again, for we had been laid open to the world in front, but the gas lingered about the hole for hours, and I had to give up delving in the bottom for a time. As it was it made me feel very sick.

A counter-attack actually commenced as soon as the bombardment ceased, and we had to stand to again. . . . As we leaned over the parapet, I saw the body of a Hun lying twenty yards out in front. It commenced to writhe and finally half-sat up. I suppose the gas had caught him. The man standing next me—a corporal in a county battalion—raised his rifle, and before I could stop him, sent a bullet into the body. It was a rotten thing to see, but I suppose it was really a merciful end for the poor chap, better than his own gas, at any rate.

The men in the front trenches had got it as badly as we had, and if the counter-attack was pressed, it did not seem humanly possible, in the condition we were in, to offer a successful defence. . . . Fortunately, our own guns started and apparently caught

the Huns massing. The counter-attack accordingly crumpled up.

In the midst of it all, someone realized that the big gap in the parapet could not be manned, and four of us, including myself, were ordered to lie down behind what was left of the parados and cover the gap with our rifles. It was uncomfortable work, as . . . the place was a jumble of dead bodies. We could not stand up to clear them away, and in order to get a place at all, I had to lie across the body of a gigantic Hun. . . .

We managed to get some sort of parapet erected in the end. It was more or less bulletproof, at any rate. At dusk some scores of men came back from the front line, wounded or gassed. They had to cross the open at a run or a shamble, but I did not see any hit. Then the Brigade-Major appeared, and cheered us by promising a relief that night. It still rained shells, although not so hard as before dusk, and we did not feel capable of standing much more of it.

# The Russian Revolution and the Founding of the Soviet Union

One of the most important results of World War I was the downfall of Russia's tsarist regime and its replacement by a Bolshevik dictatorship inspired by the doctrines of Karl Marx. Tsar Nicholas II, facing battlefield defeat, army defections, and rioting in St. Petersburg (Petrograd), abdicated in March 1917. He was replaced by a liberal provisional government charged with presiding over Russia until a constituent assembly could meet and write a new constitution. Seven months later, the Bolsheviks wrested power from the provisional government and set out to create the world's first communist state.

Nicholas II's Russia was full of discontent. Its millions of peasants no longer were serfs, but they still lived in abysmal poverty. Some moved to Moscow or St. Petersburg to work in factories, but without political power or labor unions, most exchanged the squalor of the rural village for the squalor of the urban slum. Meanwhile, many intellectuals, mostly from Russia's small middle class, became more deeply alienated from the tsar's regime and threw their support to political causes ranging from anarchism to constitutional monarchy. With the fervor of religious zealots, they argued, organized political parties, hatched plots, planned revolution, assassinated government officials, published pamphlets, and tried to stay one step ahead of the secret police.

Nicholas II raised his subjects' hopes in 1905, when after rioting in St. Petersburg he promised constitutional reforms and a parliament. Russians soon realized, however, that he had no intention of surrendering control of such crucial areas as finance, defense, and ministerial appointments. Meanwhile, workers and peasants cursed their government, and revolutionaries continued to plot. World War I provided the final push to a regime teetering on the brink of collapse.

The Marxist faction that orchestrated the downfall of the provisional government and took control of post-tsarist Russia was the Bolsheviks, which under the leadership of Vladimir Lenin (1870–1924) emerged in 1903 after a splintering of the Russian Social Democratic Labor Party. Lenin developed a distinctive political philosophy that affirmed Marx's idea that capitalism's demise and socialism's triumph could be achieved only through revolution. Lenin, however, broke with Marx in several respects. Whereas Marx believed that the revolution would result from an uprising of the industrial proletariat in mature industrialized societies, Lenin was confident that revolution was possible in countries like Russia with little industrialization and a small working class. The revolution would result from planning and organization by a small cadre of professional revolutionaries who would make all tactical and ideological decisions.

Living in exile in Zurich, Switzerland, when Tsar Nicholas abdicated, Lenin reentered Russia with the help of the German government, which hoped his presence would destabilize Russia and undermine its war effort. This is exactly what happened in October 1917 (in early November by the Gregorian calendar used in the West), when under Lenin's direction, a Bolshevik *coup d'état* resulted in the formation of the world's first Marxist state.

# Forging the Soviet State

## 78 • COMMUNIST DECREES, 1917–1918

On October 25, 1917, with the Bolsheviks in control of public buildings and other key points in Petrograd, Lenin confidently opened the Second Congress of Soviets with the words, "We shall now proceed to construct the Socialist order." As Lenin soon found out, building that new socialist order proved difficult. For one thing, although the Bolsheviks had a broad set of revolutionary aspirations for Russia, they had no blueprint for how to govern the country or how to restructure Russian society. Furthermore, the Bolsheviks were a minority party, as shown by the results of the elections for the Constituent Assembly in November 1917: The Bolsheviks received only twenty-nine percent of the vote, as opposed to fifty-eight percent for the Socialist-Revolutionaries, a party that garnered much of its support from the peasantry. Finally, they faced formidable problems—a ruined economy, continuing involvement in World War I until March 1918, and civil war from 1918 to 1921.

Despite these challenges, the Bolsheviks had no choice but to forge ahead. In their first year in power, they issued hundreds of decrees that touched on every aspect of Russian life and government. Some of these programs and policies lasted until the Soviet Union's demise in 1991.

What follows is a sample of the decrees issued by the Bolsheviks in 1917 and 1918. The Decree on Land, issued on October 26 by the Second Congress of Soviets only hours after the Bolsheviks seized power, recognized land seizures already carried out by the peasants.

The Decree on Suppression of Hostile Newspapers and the Decree Dissolving the Constituent Assembly both were steps toward one-party dictatorship. The Bolsheviks had supported convening a popularly elected Constituent Assembly, but the election of November 1917 resulted in only 168 Bolshevik deputies out of 703 and a clear Socialist-Revolutionary majority. The Assembly convened on January 5, 1918, only to be dissolved by the Bolsheviks on January 7. It was the Soviet Union's last democratically elected parliament until 1989.

The Edict on Child Welfare, issued in January 1918, was the brainchild of Alexandra Kollontai (1873–1952), who fled Russia in 1908 to escape arrest and, like Lenin, returned to Petrograd after the fall of the tsar's government. She became a member of the executive committee of the Petrograd Soviet and played a key role in the events leading up to the Bolshevik coup. As commissioner of social welfare under the Bolsheviks, she was responsible for laws that legalized abortion, liberalized marriage and divorce, and granted women equal standing with men.

The Decree on Nationalization of Large-Scale Industries was issued in June 1918 after the beginning of the civil war. Until then, industry had remained under private ownership, supposedly subject to "workers' control." Now it was nationalized without compensation to the owners.

## QUESTIONS FOR ANALYSIS

1. What rationale is provided for the "undemocratic" steps taken by the Bolsheviks to dissolve the Constituent Assembly and close down hostile newspapers?
2. What are the economic ramifications of the decrees on land use and the nationalization of industry? Who benefits, and who is hurt?
3. How will these decrees change essential features of Russian society and social relationships?
4. To what extent do the steps taken by the Bolsheviks as reflected in these decrees reflect Marx and Engels's views in *The Communist Manifesto* (source 54), especially in the section in which they discuss the first steps to be taken by the proletariat after its seizure of power?
5. In what specific ways do these decrees increase the role of the state? What implications might this have for the Soviet Union's future?

## Decree on Land, October 26, 1917

1. *Private ownership of land shall be abolished forever . . .*

   All land . . . *shall be alienated without compensation* and become the property of the whole people, and pass into the use of all those who cultivate it. . . .

2. All mineral wealth, e.g., ore, oil, coal, salt, etc., as well as all forests and waters of state importance, shall pass into the exclusive use of the state. All the small streams, lakes, woods, etc., shall pass into the use of the communities, to be administered by the local self-government bodies.

3. Lands on which *high-level scientific* farming is practiced, e.g., orchards, plantations, seed plots, nurseries, hot-houses, etc. *shall not be divided up, but shall be converted into model farms,* to be turned over for exclusive use *to the state or to the communities,* depending on the size and importance of such lands. . . .

4. The right to use the land shall be accorded to all citizens (without distinction of sex) desiring to cultivate it by their own labor, with the help of their families, or in partnership, but only as long as they are able to cultivate it. . . .

## Decree on Suppression of Hostile Newspapers, October 27, 1917

Everyone knows that the bourgeois press is one of the most powerful weapons of the bourgeoisie. Especially in this critical moment when the new authority, that of the workers and peasants, is in process of consolidation, it was impossible to leave this weapon in the hands of the enemy at a time when it is not less dangerous than bombs and machine guns. This is why temporary and extraordinary measures have been adopted for the purpose of cutting off the stream of mire and calumny in which the . . . press would be glad to drown the young victory of the people.

As soon as the new order will be consolidated, all administrative measures against the press will be suspended; full liberty will be given it within the limits of responsibility before the laws, in accordance with the broadest and most progressive regulations in this respect. . . .

## Decree Dissolving the Constituent Assembly, January 7, 1918

The October Revolution, by giving the power to the Soviets, and through the Soviets to the toiling and exploited classes, aroused the desperate resistance of the exploiters, and in the crushing of this resistance it fully revealed itself as the beginning of the socialist revolution. The toiling classes learnt by experience that the old bourgeois parliamentarism had outlived its purpose and was absolutely incompatible with the aim of achieving Socialism, and that not national institutions, but only class institutions (such as the Soviets), were capable of overcoming the resistance of the propertied classes and of laying the foundations of a socialist society. To relinquish the sovereign power of the Soviets, to relinquish the Soviet republic won by the people, for the sake of bourgeois parliamentarism and the Constituent Assembly, would now be a retrograde step and

*Source:* Decree on land: V. I. Lenin, *Selected Works* (Moscow: Foreign Languages Publishing House, 1950–1952), Vol. II, Book I, pp. 339–341. Suppression of Hostile Newspapers: English translation in *Bolshevik Propaganda:* Hearings before a Subcommittee of the Committee on the Judiciary, U.S. Senate, 56th Congress, 3rd Session, p. 1243. Dissolution of Constituent Assembly: V. I. Lenin, Draft Decree on the Dissolution of the Constituent Assembly: *Selected Work* (Moscow: Foreign Languages Publishing House, 1950–1952), Vol. II, Book I, 382–384. Edict on Child Welfare: From Alexandra Kollontai, *Selected Writings,* Alix Holt, ed. and trans. (Westport, CT: Lawrence Hill and Company, 1977), pp. 140–141. Decree of Nationalization of Large-Scale Industries: In James Bunyan, *Intervention, Civil War, and Communism in Russia, April–December 1918; Documents and Materials* (Baltimore: The Johns Hopkins Press, 1936), pp. 397–399.

cause the collapse of the October workers' and peasants' revolution. . . .

The Right Socialist Revolutionary and Menshevik[1] parties are in fact waging outside the walls of the Constituent Assembly a most desperate struggle against the Soviet power, calling openly in their press for its overthrow and characterizing as arbitrary and unlawful the crushing by force of the resistance of the exploiters by the toiling classes. . . . They are defending the saboteurs, the servitors of capital, and are going to the length of undisguised calls to terrorism, which certain "unidentified groups" have already begun to practice. It is obvious that under such circumstances the remaining part of the Constituent Assembly could only serve as a screen for the struggle of the counterrevolutionaries to overthrow the Soviet power.

Accordingly, the Central Executive Committee resolves: The Constituent Assembly is hereby dissolved.

### Edict on Child Welfare, January 1918

After a search that has lasted centuries, human thought has at last discovered the radiant epoch where the working class can freely construct that form of maternity protection which will preserve the child for the mother and the mother for the child. . . .

The new Soviet Russia calls all you working women, you working mothers with your sensitive hearts, you bold builders of a new social life, you teachers of the new attitudes, you children's doctors and midwives, to devote your minds and emotions to building the great edifice that will provide social protection for future generations. From the date of publication of this decree, all large and small institutions under the commissariat of social welfare that serve the child, from the children's home in the capital to the modest village creche [a day nursery], shall be merged into one government organization and placed under the department for the protection of maternity and childhood. As an integral part of the total number of institutions connected with pregnancy and maternity, they shall continue to fulfill the single common task of creating citizens who are strong both mentally and physically. . . . For the rapid elaboration and introduction of the reforms necessary for the protection of childhood in Russia, commissions are being organized under the auspices of the departments of maternity and childhood. . . . The commissions must base their work on the following main principles:

1. The preservation of the mother for the child: milk from the mother's breast is invaluable for the child.
2. The child must be brought up in the enlightened and understanding atmosphere provided by the socialist family.
3. Conditions must be created which permit the development of the child's physical and mental powers and the child's keen comprehension of life.

### Decree on Nationalization of Large-Scale Industries, June 28, 1918

For the purpose of combating decisively the economic disorganization and the breakdown of the food supply, and of establishing more firmly the dictatorship of the working class and the village poor, the Soviet of People's Commissars has resolved:

1. To declare all of the following industrial and commercial enterprises which are located in the Soviet Republic, with all their capital and property, whatever they may consist of, the property of the Russian Socialist Federated Soviet Republic. [A long list of mines, mills, and factories follows.]
2. The administration of the nationalized industries shall be organized . . . by the different departments of the Supreme Council of National Economy. . . .

---

[1]The Mensheviks split from the Bolsheviks at a meeting of the Social Democratic Labor Party in 1903, mainly over Lenin's insistence that the party should be directed by a small group of dedicated professional revolutionaries.

4. [The] members of the administration, the directors, and other responsible officers of the nationalized industries will be held responsible to the Soviet Republic both for the upkeep of the business and for its proper functioning. . . .

5. The entire personnel of every enterprise—technicians, workers, members of the board of directors, and foremen—shall be considered employees of the Russian Socialist Federated Soviet Republic; their wages shall be fixed in accordance with the scales existing at the time of nationalization and shall be paid out of the funds of the respective enterprises. . . .

6. All private capital belonging to members of the boards of directors, stockholders, and owners of the nationalized enterprises will be attached [taken by state authority] pending the determination of the relation of such capital to the turnover capital and resources of the enterprises in question. . . .

# The Soviet Path to Industrialization

### 79 • JOSEPH STALIN, THE TASKS OF BUSINESS EXECUTIVES

Joseph Stalin (1879–1953), the son of a shoemaker from the province of Georgia, was a candidate for the priesthood before he abandoned Christianity for Marxism and became a follower of Lenin in 1903. By 1917, he was secretary of the Bolshevik party, an office he retained after the revolution. Following Lenin's death in 1924, Stalin used his position in the party to defeat his rival, Leon Trotsky (1879–1940), the leader of the Red Army during the civil war and Lenin's heir apparent. Shortly after taking power in 1928, Stalin launched a bold restructuring of the Soviet economy.

In 1928, the New Economic Policy (NEP), begun under Lenin in 1921, guided Soviet economic life. Through the NEP Lenin had sought to restore agriculture and industry after seven years of war, revolution, and civil conflict. Although the state kept control of banks, foreign trade, and heavy industry, peasants could sell their goods on the open market, and owners of small businesses could hire labor, operate small factories, and keep their profits. The NEP saved the Soviet Union from economic collapse, but its concessions to capitalism troubled Marxist purists, and it did little to foster industrialization. Thus in 1928, Stalin replaced the NEP with the first Five-Year Plan, which established a centralized planned economy in which bureaucrats regulated agriculture, manufacturing, finance, and transportation. In agriculture, the plan abolished individual peasant holdings and combined them into large collective and state farms. In manufacturing, it emphasized heavy industry and the production of goods such as tractors, trucks, and machinery. Stalin launched second and third Five-Year Plans in 1933 and 1938.

In a speech delivered in 1931 to a conference of industrial managers, or "business executives," Stalin described his motives for instituting the Five-Year Plan.

### QUESTIONS FOR ANALYSIS

1. What factors convinced Stalin that the Soviet Union had the capacity to reach its industrial goals in 1931?
2. Why does Stalin believe that the Soviet system is superior to capitalism?

3. How does Stalin try to inspire the industrial managers to work for industrialization?
4. What does Stalin mean when he refers to the Soviet Union's responsibility to the "world proletariat"?
5. How do Stalin's views of the weaknesses of capitalism resemble those of Marx and Engels in the *Communist Manifesto*? (See source 54.)

Comrades! The deliberations of your conference are drawing to a close. You are now about to adopt resolutions. I have no doubt that they will be adopted unanimously. In these resolutions—I know something about them—you approve the control figures of industry for 1931 and pledge yourselves to fulfil them.

A Bolshevik's word is his bond. Bolsheviks are in the habit of fulfilling their pledges. But what does the pledge to fulfil the control figures for 1931 mean? It means ensuring a general increase of industrial output by 45 percent. And this is a very big task. More than that. Such a pledge means that you not only promise to fulfil our Five-Year Plan in four years—that is decided, and no more resolutions are needed on that score—*it means that you promise to fulfil it in three years in all the basic, decisive branches of industry.*

It is good that the conference gives a promise to fulfil the plan for 1931, to fulfil the Five-Year Plan in three years. But we have been taught by "bitter experience." We know that promises are not always kept. In the beginning of 1930, also, a promise was given to fulfil the plan for the year. At that time it was necessary to increase the output of our industries by 31 to 32 percent. But that promise was not kept to the full. Actually, the increase in industrial output in 1930 amounted to 25 percent. We must ask ourselves: will not the same thing occur again this year? The directors and managers of our industries now promise to increase the industrial output in 1931 by 45 percent. But what guarantee have we that this promise will be kept? . . .

In the history of states and countries, in the history of armies, there have been cases when every opportunity for success and for victory was on hand, but these opportunities were wasted because the leaders did not see them, did not know how to make use of them, and the armies suffered defeat.

Have we all the possibilities that are needed to fulfil the control figures for 1931?

Yes, we have these possibilities. What are these possibilities? What are the necessary factors that make these possibilities real?

First of all, adequate *natural resources* in the country: iron ore, coal, oil, grain, cotton. Have we these resources? Yes, we have. We have them in larger quantities than any other country. . . . What else is needed?

A *government* capable and willing to utilize these immense natural resources for the benefit of the people. Have we such a government? We have. . . . What else is needed?

That this government should enjoy the *support* of the vast masses of workers and peasants. Does our government enjoy such support? Yes, it does. You will find no other government in the world that enjoys such support from the workers and peasants as does the Soviet government. . . .

What else is needed to fulfil and over fulfil the control figures for 1931?

A *system* which is free of the incurable diseases of capitalism and which is greatly superior to capitalism. Crises, unemployment, waste, poverty among the masses—such are the incurable diseases of capitalism. Our system does not suffer from these diseases because power is in our hands, in the hands

*Source: Problems in Leninism* (Moscow: Foreign Languages Publishing House, 1947), pp. 359–360, 365–366.

of the working class; because we are conducting a planned economy, systematically accumulating resources and properly distributing them among the different branches of national economy. . . .

The capitalists are cutting the ground from under their own feet. And instead of emerging from the crisis they aggravate it; new conditions accumulate which lead to a new, and even more severe crisis: The superiority of our system lies in that we have no crises of over-production, we have not and never will have millions of unemployed, we have no anarchy in production; for we are conducting a planned economy. . . .

It is sometimes asked whether it is not possible to slow down the tempo a bit, to put a check on the movement. No, comrades, it is not possible! The tempo must not be reduced! On the contrary, we must increase it as much as is within our powers and possibilities. This is dictated to us by our obligations to the workers and peasants of the U.S.S.R. This is dictated to us by our obligations to the working class of the whole world.

To slacken the tempo would mean falling behind. And those who fall behind get beaten. But we do not want to be beaten. No, we refuse to be beaten! One feature of the history of old Russia was the continual beatings she suffered for falling behind, for her backwardness. She was beaten by the Mongol Khans. She was beaten by the Turkish beys. She was beaten by the Swedish feudal lords. She was beaten by the Polish and Lithuanian gentry. She was beaten by the British and French capitalists. She was beaten by the Japanese barons. All beat her—for her backwardness: for military backwardness, for cultural backwardness, for political backwardness, for industrial backwardness, for agricultural backwardness. She was beaten because to do so was profitable and could be done with impunity. . . . They beat her, saying: "You are abundant," so one can enrich oneself at your expense. They beat her, saying: "You are poor and impotent," so you can be beaten and plundered with impunity. Such is the law of the exploiters—to beat the backward and the weak. It is the jungle law of capitalism. You are backward, you are weak—therefore you are wrong; hence, you can be beaten and enslaved. You are mighty—therefore you are right; hence, we must be wary of you. That is why we must no longer lag behind.

# The German Catastrophe

On March 23, 1933, Germany's fourteen-year experiment with democratic government ended when its parliament, or Reichstag, voted 444–94 to grant dictatorial powers to Adolf Hitler, the leader of Nationalist Socialist German Workers' Party—the Nazis. Germany was not the only country where democratic, constitutional governments failed in the 1920s and 1930s. As late as 1921, except for Bolshevik Russia, all twenty-seven European states, including the six new states created by postwar treaties, had governments with parliaments, constitutions, and guarantees of basic freedoms. In 1922, however, when Benito Mussolini became dictator of Italy, this was the beginning of an authoritarian tide that swept across Europe, leaving only ten parliamentary democracies when World War II started in 1939. They included Finland, Sweden, Norway, Denmark, Czechoslovakia, Belgium, the Netherlands, Switzerland and only two major powers, Britain and France.

Most of the new authoritarian regimes were conservative in the sense that they represented the interests of large landowners, wealthy businessmen, the army, and certain elements within organized churches, all groups whose opposition to democracy predated World War I. Such governments shut down parliaments, abolished opposing political parties, ended free speech, and promised order, if necessary through force. But they offered no new ideologies, no blueprints for social change, and no grandiose plans for territorial expansion. In contrast stood the antidemocratic movement known as fascism, which took its name from the *Fasci italiani di Combattimento* (Italian League of Combat), the political party led by Benito Mussolini. Applied mainly to Mussolini's Italy and Hitler's Germany, but also to its sympathizers in other European states, fascism went beyond the rejection of liberalism, socialism, and democracy. It also glorified war, saw life in terms of struggle, promoted service to the nation as the supreme calling, and required absolute obedience to a single infallible ruler. Fascist regimes in Italy and Germany turned schools, theaters, newspapers, churches, museums, and radio broadcasts into instruments of propaganda. They also brought catastrophe to the people they ruled, the groups they hated, and the nations they attacked.

Nowhere did the collapse of democracy have more calamitous consequences than in Germany, which from 1933 to 1945 was ruled by Adolf Hitler, a man whose fanatical convictions about race, Germany's destiny, and his own infallibility resulted in a general European war that cost the lives of approximately fifteen million combatants. Hitler's Germany also was responsible for the deaths of an estimated seventeen million noncombatants who were deemed inferior, undesirable, or dangerous. They included Poles, Russians, Ukrainians, and other Slavic peoples; Gypsies; the mentally ill, the deaf, the intellectually challenged, and the physically disabled; communists and social democrats; homosexuals; religious dissidents; and above all Jews, of whom six million were killed.

# The Dreams of the Führer

## 80 • ADOLF HITLER, MEIN KAMPF

Born to an Austrian customs official and his German wife in 1889, Hitler moved to Vienna at the age of nineteen to seek a career as an artist or architect. His efforts failed, however, and he lived at the bottom of Viennese society, drifting from one low-paying job to another. In 1912, he moved to Munich, where his life fell into the same purposeless pattern. Enlistment in the German army in World War I rescued Hitler, giving him comradeship and a sense of direction he had lacked. After the war, a shattered Hitler returned to Munich, where in 1919, he joined the small German Workers' Party, which in 1920 changed its name to the National Socialist German Workers' Party, or Nazis.

After becoming leader of the National Socialists, Hitler staged an abortive *coup d'état* against the government of the German state of Bavaria in 1923. For this, he was sentenced to a five-year prison term (serving only nine months), during which he wrote the first volume of *Mein Kampf* (*My Struggle*). To a remarkable degree, this work, which he completed in 1925, provided the ideas that inspired his millions of followers and guided the National Socialists until their destruction in 1945.

## QUESTIONS FOR ANALYSIS

1. What broad purpose does Hitler see in human existence?
2. How, in Hitler's view, are the Aryans and Jews dissimilar?
3. What is Hitler's view of political leadership?
4. What role do parliaments play in a "folkish" state, according to Hitler?
5. How does Hitler plan to reorient German foreign policy? What goals does he set for Germany, and how are they to be achieved?
6. Based on these excerpts, what can you infer about his objections to the ideologies of democracy, liberalism, and socialism?

## Nation and Race

There are some truths that are so plain and obvious that for this very reason the everyday world does not see them or at least does not apprehend them. . . . So humans invariably wander about the garden of nature, convinced that they know and understand everything, yet with few exceptions are blind to one of the fundamental principles Nature uses in her work: the intrinsic segregation of the species of every living thing. . . . Each beast mates with only one of its own species: the titmouse with titmouse, finch with finch, stork with stork, field mouse with field mouse, house mouse with house mouse, wolf with wolf. . . . This is only natural.

Any cross-breeding between two not completely equal beings will result in a product that is in between the level of the two parents. That means that the offspring will be superior to the parent who is at a biologically lower level of being but inferior to the parent at a higher level. This means the offspring will be overcome in the struggle for existence against those at the higher level. Such matings go against the will of Nature for the higher breeding of life.

A precondition for this lies not in the blending of beings of a higher and lower order, but rather the absolute victory of the stronger. The stronger must dominate and must not blend with the weaker orders and sacrifice their powers. Only born weaklings can find this cruel, but after all, they are only weaker and more narrow-minded types of men; unless this law dominated, then any conceivable higher evolution of living organisms would be unthinkable. . . . The struggle for daily bread allows all those who are weak, sick, and indecisive to be defeated, while the struggle of the males for females gives to the strongest alone the right or at least the possibility to reproduce. Always this struggle is a means of advancing the health and power of resistance of the species, and thus a means to its higher evolution.

As little as nature approves the mating of higher and lower individuals, she approves even less the blending of higher races with lower ones; for indeed otherwise her previous work toward higher development perhaps over hundreds of thousands of years might be rendered useless with one blow. If this were not the case, progressive development would stop and even deterioration might set in. . . .

Whoever would live must fight. Whoever will not fight in this world of endless competition does

---

*Source:* Adolf Hitler, *Mein Kampf* (Munich: F. Eher Nachfolger, 1927), trans. by J. Overfield.

not deserve to live. . . . He interferes with the victory path of the best race and with it, the precondition for all human progress. . . .

It is an idle undertaking to argue about which race or races were the original standard-bearers of human culture and were therefore the true founders of everything we conceive by the word humanity. It is much simpler to deal with the question as it pertains to the present, and here the answer is simple and clear. What we see before us today as human culture, all the yields of art, science, and technology, are almost exclusively the creative product of the Aryans.[1] Indeed this fact alone leads to the not unfounded conclusion that the Aryan alone is the founder of the higher type of humanity, and further that he represents the prototype of what we understand by the word: MAN. He is the Prometheus[2] from whose brow the bright spark of genius has forever burst forth, time and again rekindling the fire, which as knowledge has . . . permitted humans to ascend the path of mastery over the other beings of the earth. Eliminate him—and deep darkness will again descend on the earth after a few thousand years; human civilization will die out and the earth will become a desert. . . .

The Jew provides the greatest contrast to the Aryan. With no other people of the world has the instinct for self-preservation been so developed as by the so-called chosen race. The best proof of this statement rests in the fact that this race still exists. Where can another people be found in the past 2,000 years that has undergone so few changes in its inner qualities, character, etc. as the Jews? What people has undergone upheavals as great as this one—and nonetheless has

emerged unchanged from the greatest catastrophes of humanity? What an infinitely tenacious will to live and to preserve one's kind is revealed in this fact. . . .

Since the Jew . . . never had a civilization of his own, others have always provided the foundations of his intellectual labors. His intellect has always developed by the use of those cultural achievements he has found ready at hand around him. Never has it happened the other way around.

For though their drive for self-preservation is not smaller, but larger than that of other people, and though their mental capabilities may easily give the impression that their intellectual powers are equal to those of other races, the Jews lack the most basic characteristic of a truly cultured people, namely an idealistic spirit.

It is a remarkable fact that the herd instinct brings people together for mutual protection only so long as there is a common danger that makes mutual assistance necessary or unavoidable. The same pack of wolves that an instant ago combined to overcome their prey will soon after satisfying their hunger again become individual beasts. . . . It goes the same way with the Jews. His sense of self-sacrifice is only apparent. . . . Jews act together only when a common danger threatens them or a common prey attracts them. When these two things are lacking, then their characteristic of the crassest egoism returns as a force, and out of this once unified people emerges in a flash a swarm of rats fighting bloodily against one another. . . .

That is why the Jewish state—which should be the living organism for the maintenance and improvement of the race—has absolutely no borders.

---

[1]Beginning in late eighteenth-century Europe *Aryan* came to be applied to speakers of any of the many languages, including all the major languages of Europe, that were part of the Indo-European family of languages. In the nineteenth century the term came to be used in a narrower racial sense as referring to light-skinned Caucasians who provided Europe's original racial stock. Their physical features included blond hair, blue eyes, light-colored skin, and elongated skulls; they were thought to be physically and intellectually superior to darker-skinned Caucasoid groups (Jews, Slavs, Mediterranean peoples, and others) and brown-, yellow-, and black-skinned peoples.

[2]In Greek mythology, Prometheus was the titan (offspring of Uranus and Gaia [Heaven and Earth]) who stole fire from the gods and gave it to humans, along with all other arts and civilization.

For the territorial definition of a state always demands a certain idealism of spirit on the part of the race which forms the state and especially an acceptance of the idea of work. . . . If this attitude is lacking then the prerequisite for civilization is lacking.

---

> Hitler describes the process by which Jews in concert with communists have come close to subverting and controlling the peoples and nations of Europe.

---

Here he stops at nothing, and his vileness becomes so monstrous that no one should be surprised if among our people the hateful figure of the Jew is taken as the personification of the devil and the symbol of evil. . . .

How close they see their approaching victory can be seen in the frightful way that their dealings with members of other races develop. The black-haired Jewish youth, with satanic joy on his face, lurks in wait for hours for the innocent girls he plans to defile with his blood, and steal the young girl from her people. With every means at hand he seeks to undermine the racial foundations of the people they would subjugate. . . .

Around those nations which have offered sturdy resistance to their internal attacks, they surround them with a web of enemies; thanks to their international influence, they incite them to war, and when necessary, will plant the flag of revolution, even on the battlefield.

In economics he shakes the foundations of the state long enough so that unprofitable business enterprises are shut down and come under his financial control. In politics he denies the state its means of self-preservation, destroys its means of self-maintenance and defense, annihilates faith in state leadership, insults its history and traditions, and drags everything that is truly great into the gutter. . . .

Religion is made an object of mockery, morality and ethics are described as old-fashioned, until finally the last props of a people for maintaining their existence in this world are destroyed.

## Personality and the Ideal of the Folkish[3] State

. . . The folkish state must care for the well-being of its citizens by recognizing in everything the worth of the person, and by doing so direct it to the highest level of its productive capability. . . . Accordingly, the folkish state must free the entire leadership, especially those in political leadership, from the parliamentary principle of majority rule by the multitude, so that the right of personality is guaranteed without any limitation. From this is derived the following realization. *The best state constitution and form is that which with unquestioned certainty raises the best minds from the national community to positions of leading authority and influence.* . . .

There are no majority decisions, rather only responsible individuals, and the word "advice" will once again have its original meaning. Each man will have advisers at his side, *but the decision will be made by one man.* The principle that made the Prussian army in its time the most splendid instrument of the German people will have to become someday the foundation for the construction of our completed state: *authority of every leader downward and responsibility upward.* . . .

This principle of binding absolute responsibility with absolute authority will gradually bring forth an elite group of leaders which today in an era of irresponsible parliamentarianism is hardly thinkable.

---

[3]The word Hitler uses, *völkisch,* is an adjective derived from *Volk,* meaning "people" or "nation," which Hitler defined in a racial sense; thus a "folkish" state is one that expresses the characteristics of and furthers the interests of a particular race, in this case the Aryans.

## The Direction and Politics of Eastern Europe

*The foreign policy of the folkish state has as its purpose to guarantee the existence on this planet of the race that it gathers within its borders. With this in mind it must create a natural and healthy ratio between the number and growth of the population and the extent and quality of the land and soil. . . . Only a sufficiently large space on the earth can assure the independent existence of a people. . . .*

*The National Socialist movement must seek to eliminate the disproportion between our people's population and our territory—viewing this as a source of food as well as a basis for national power—and between our historical past and our present hopeless impotence.* While doing so it must remain conscious of the fact that we as protectors of the highest humanity on earth are bound also by the highest duty that will be fulfilled only if we inspire the German people with the racial ideal, so that they will occupy themselves not just with the breeding of good dogs, horses, and cats but also show concern about the purity of *their own* blood. . . .

*State boundaries are made by man and can be changed by man. . . .* And only in force lies the right of possession. If today the German people are imprisoned within an impossible territorial area and for that reason are face to face with a miserable future, this is not the commandment of fate, any more than a revolt against such a situation would be a violation of the laws of fate; . . . the soil on which we now live was not bestowed upon our ancestors by Heaven; rather, they had to conquer it by risking their lives. So with us, in the future we will win soil and with it the means of existence of the people . . . only through the power of the triumphant sword.

But we National Socialists must go further: *The right to land and soil will become an obligation if without further territorial expansion a great people is threatened with its destruction.* And that is particularly true when the people in question is not some little nigger people, but the German mother of life, which has given cultural shape to the modern world. *Germany will either become a world power or will no longer exist. . . .*

*We take up where we broke off six hundred years ago. We put a stop to the eternal pull of the Germans toward the south and western Europe and turn our gaze to the lands of the east. We put an end to the colonial and commercial policy of the prewar period and shift to the land-oriented policy of the future.* When today we speak of new territory and soil in Europe, we think primarily of *Russia* and her subservient border states.

# The Nazi Message

## 81 • SIX POLITICAL POSTERS

The rise of the Nazis from an obscure regional right-wing party to the dominant political power in Germany owed much to their effective use of propaganda. Hitler was convinced that Germany had lost the propaganda battle to the Allies in World War I and vowed not to repeat its mistakes. Propaganda, he believed, was the best way to reach the masses, who lacked the interest, intellect, and attention span to grasp complex issues.

Hitler himself directed Nazi propaganda efforts until 1928, when Joseph Goebbels assumed greater responsibilities. After the Nazis took power, as Hitler's

Minister of Propaganda, Goebbels made use of radio and cinema, but in the heated days from 1930 to 1933, he relied on the Nazis' stock-in-trade—parades, mass rallies, speech-making, slogans, and posters. The political poster, widely used during the campaign for women's suffrage in the early 1900s and by all belligerents during World War I, was elevated to a high art by the Nazis. They specialized in large, brightly colored posters that were hung on walls or side panels of trucks. Their pictures, accompanied by brief slogans, communicated simple messages designed to appeal to different audiences—farmers, workers, veterans, women, and young people.

The six selections we have chosen are a sampling of the many dozens of posters produced in connection with the 1932 parliamentary and presidential elections. The first shows a down-and-out German family with the message, "Husbands! Wives! Millions of men without work! Millions of children without a future! Save the German family! Elect Adolf Hitler!" The second poster depicts a group of desperate people, with the words "Our Last Hope: HITLER." The third poster reads "Country People in Need. Who helps? Adolf Hitler." The fourth poster shows two figures, one of whom represents a middle-class "worker of the mind" (literally a worker of the forehead) and a lower-class "worker of the hand" (literally a worker of the fist), who are urged to vote for Hitler. The fifth poster, "The People Vote Slate 1, National Socialists," shows masses of Germans flocking into openings of a giant swastika, which was adopted as a Nazi symbol in 1920 and was associated with the party's belief in the superiority of the "Aryan race." The final poster features a worker under the motto "We build things up!" He is leaning on "our building stones": "Work, Freedom, Bread." He peers at two figures, one a caricature of Heinrich Brüning, Germany's chancellor from 1930 to May 31, 1932. Brüning's "Building Plan" includes "Promises, Government Cuts, Unemployment, and Emergency Decrees, Article 48." Article 48 refers to the provision of the German constitution that gave the president powers to pass laws and issue decrees without the consent of the Reichstag. Brüning had convinced Germany's president, Paul von Hindenburg, to invoke such powers on numerous occasions, most recently to ban activities of Nazi Storm Troopers, who had been largely responsible for the street violence in Germany's cities. The other figure represents a Social Democrat, whose sign reads, "Cuts in Social Services, Corruption, Terror, Agitation, Lies."

## QUESTIONS FOR ANALYSIS

1. On the basis of the content of the posters, what might one conclude about the problems confronting Germany in the early 1930s?
2. According to the message of the posters, what solutions to Germany's problems do the Nazis offer?
3. In the last three posters how are Hitler's supporters portrayed? What do these portrayals reveal about the appeal of Nazism?

Husbands! Wives!

Our Last Hope

Country People in Need

Workers of the Mind and Hand

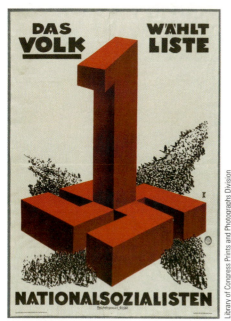

The People Vote Slate I

We Build Things Up

# The Legacy of World War II

In the two decades after World War I, weapons became more destructive, nationalism more fanatical, and leaders' ambitions more fantastic. As a result, the war that began in Asia in 1937 and in Europe in 1939—World War II—became the most devastating and destructive war in history. Modern communication and transportation systems enabled generals to plan and execute massive campaigns such as the German invasion of the Soviet Union in 1941 and the Allies' Normandy invasion in 1944. The airplane became an instrument of mass destruction, making possible the German assault on English cities in 1940, the Japanese attack on Pearl Harbor in 1941, the around-the-clock bombing of Germany by Britain and the United States from 1943 to 1945, and the American fire-bombing of Tokyo in 1945.

Only the closing months of the war, however, fully revealed the destructive possibilities of modern technology and large bureaucratic states. As Allied armies liberated Europe in the winter and spring of 1945, they found in the Third Reich's concentration and extermination camps the horrifying results of the Nazi assault on political enemies, religious dissidents, prisoners of war, Gypsies, Slavs, and especially Jews. Then on August 6, the United States dropped an atomic bomb on Hiroshima, Japan. It killed nearly eighty thousand people, seriously injured twice that number, and obliterated three-fifths of the city. On August 9, the United States dropped a second atomic bomb on Nagasaki, intending to demolish the Mitsubishi shipyards. It missed its target but destroyed half the city and killed seventy-five thousand people.

Decades later, the names Hiroshima and Nagasaki still evoke nightmares in a world where thousands of nuclear warheads exist and many nations have the capacity to manufacture nuclear weapons. Similarly, the Nazi campaign to exterminate Europe's Jews continues to haunt the imagination. Racism and ethnic hatreds are universally condemned, but they flourish in many parts of the world.

# "Führer, You Order. We Obey"

## 82 • RUDOLF HÖSS, MEMOIRS

On gaining power, the Nazis began to implement the anti-Jewish policies Hitler had outlined in *Mein Kampf* and the Nazis had promised in thousands of books, pamphlets, and speeches. Jewish shops were plundered while police looked the other way; Jewish physicians were excluded from hospitals; Jewish judges lost their posts; Jewish students were denied admission to universities; and Jewish veterans were stripped of their benefits. In 1935, the Nazis promulgated the Nuremberg Laws, which deprived Jews of citizenship and outlawed marriage between Jews and non-Jews. In November 1938, the regime organized nationwide violence against Jewish synagogues and shops in what came to be known as *Kristallnacht,* or "night of the broken glass."

After the war began in late 1939, conquests in eastern Europe gave the Nazis new opportunities to address the "Jewish problem." In early 1941, they began to deport Jews from Germany and conquered territories to Poland and Czechoslovakia, where their victims were employed as slave laborers or placed in concentration camps. In June 1941, special units known as *Einsatzgruppen* ("special action forces") were organized to exterminate Jews in territories conquered on the eastern front. In eighteen months, they killed more than one million Jews and smaller numbers of Gypsies and Slavs. Then in January 1942 Nazi leaders approved the Final Solution to the Jewish problem. Its goal was the extermination of European Jewry, to be accomplished in special camps where their murderous work could be done efficiently and quickly. When the war ended, the Nazis had not reached their goal of annihilating Europe's eleven million Jews. They did, however, slaughter close to six million, thus earning themselves a permanent place in the long history of man's inhumanity to man.

The following excerpt comes from the memoirs of Rudolf Höss (1900–1947), the commandant of the Auschwitz concentration camp in Poland from 1940 to 1943. After serving in World War I, Höss abandoned plans to become a priest and became involved in a number of right-wing political movements, including the Nazi Party, which he joined in the early 1920s. After serving a jail sentence for participating in the murder of a teacher suspected of "treason," Höss became a farmer and then, in 1934, a member of the Nazi SS, or *Schutzstaffel* (Guard Detachment). The SS, under its leader Heinrich Himmler, grew from a small security force to guard Hitler and other high-ranking Nazis into a powerful party organization involved in police work, state security, intelligence gathering, administration of conquered territories, and management of the concentration camps. After postings at the Dachau and Sachsenhausen camps, Höss was appointed commandant of Auschwitz, a huge, sprawling complex where more than a million Jews were gassed or shot and tens of thousands of prisoners served as slave laborers in nearby factories. In 1943, Höss became overseer of all the Third Reich's concentration camps, but he returned to Auschwitz in 1944 to administer the murder of four hundred thousand Hungarian Jews. After his capture in 1946, he was tried and convicted for crimes against humanity by the international military tribunal at Nuremberg. He was hanged on April 16, 1947. While awaiting trial, Höss was encouraged to compose a memoir to sharpen his recollection of his experiences. In the following passage, he discusses his views of the Jews and his reaction to the mass killings he planned and witnessed.

## QUESTIONS FOR ANALYSIS

1. What does Höss claim to be his attitude toward the Jews?
2. What distinctions, if any, does Höss make between the Russians and the Jews that he had exterminated?
3. What was Höss's attitude toward the Final Solution? How does Höss characterize his role in the mass extermination of the Jews?
4. How did his involvement in the Holocaust affect him personally? How, according to Höss, did it affect other German participants?
5. What would you describe as the key components of Höss's personality? To what extent was his personality shaped by Nazi philosophy?
6. What insight does this excerpt provide about the issue of how much the German people knew of and participated in the Holocaust?

As a fanatical National Socialist, I was thoroughly convinced that our ideas gradually would take hold and would come to be dominant in all countries. This would then break the dominance of the Jews. Anti-Semitism in the whole world really was nothing new. It always reappears when the Jews had forced themselves into positions of power and when their evil doings become visible to the general public. . . . I want to emphasize here that I myself have never hated the Jews. To me they were considered to be the enemy of our people. However, that was exactly the reason to treat them the same way as any other prisoners. I never made a distinction concerning this. Furthermore, the feeling of hatred is not characteristic of me. But I know what hate is, and how it manifests itself. I have seen it and I have recognized it . . .

When RFSS[1] modified his original order by which "All Jews without exception are to be destroyed," it was changed so that those able to work were to be separated from the rest and used in the arms factories. This made Auschwitz the assembly point for the Jews to a degree never known before. While the Jewish prisoners previously could still imagine that one day they might be released and as a result were less affected psychologically, for the Auschwitz Jews there was no such hope. They knew that without exception they would remain alive only so long as they could work. . . .

By the design of [Himmler] Auschwitz became the greatest human extermination center of all time. When he gave me the order personally in the summer of 1941 to prepare Auschwitz as a place

---

*Source:* Rudolf Höss, *Kommandant in Auschwitz: Autobiographische Aufzeichen von Rudolf Höss*, Martin Broszat, ed. (*Quellen und Darstellung zur Zeitgeschichte*, Vol. 5 (Stuttgart: Deutsche Verlags-Anstalt, 1958), pp. 120–125, 127, 129, 130. Trans. J. H. Overfield.

[1]The initials stand for *Reichsführer SS*, the title held by Heinrich Himmler. As such he was responsible for all internal security within the Third Reich and was the overseer of the concentration camps and extermination camps.

for mass killings and then carry them out, I did not have the slightest conception of what the scale or consequences would be. Of course, this order was something extraordinary, something monstrous. Nevertheless, the reasoning behind the extermination order seemed correct to me. I wasted no thoughts about it at the time. I had been given an order, and I had to carry it out. Whether this mass killing of the Jews was necessary or not was something about which I could not allow myself to form an opinion. . . . Since the Führer himself had ordered "The Final Solution of the Jewish Question," there was no second guessing for a veteran National Socialist, much less an SS officer. "Führer, you order. We obey" was not just a phrase or slogan. It was meant to be taken with bitter earnestness.[2]

Since my arrest it has been told to me repeatedly that I could have refused to obey this order, indeed that I might even have shot Himmler dead. I do not believe that among the thousands of SS officers, there was even one who would have allowed himself to have such a thought. . . . Of course, many SS officers grumbled and groaned about the many harsh orders. Even then, they carried out every one of them. . . . As leader of the SS, Himmler's person was sacrosanct. His fundamental orders in the name of the Führer were holy. There was no reflection, no interpretation, no analysis of these orders. They were carried out ruthlessly, regardless of the final consequences, even if it meant giving your life for them, as many SS officers did during the war. . . . Whatever the Führer and Himmler ordered was *always* right. Even democratic England has its saying, "My country, right or wrong," and every patriotic Englishman follows it.

Before the mass destruction of the Jews began, all the Russian politruks[3] and political commissars

in almost every camp were liquidated in 1941 and 1942. In accordance with the secret order issued by Hitler, special detachments of the Gestapo searched for and picked up the Russian politruks and commissars from all the prisoner-of-war camps. They transferred all they found to the nearest extermination camp for liquidation. . . . The first small transports of them were shot by firing squads of soldiers.

While I was away on duty, my deputy, Camp Commander Fritzsch, first tried gas for these killings. He used a gas called Cyclon B, prussic acid,[4] which was often used as an insecticide in the camp and was in good supply. When I returned, Fritzsch reported this to me, and we used it again for the next transport [of Russians]. The gassing was carried out in the detention cells of Block 11. Wearing a gas mask for protection, I observed the killing myself. Death occurred in the crammed cells immediately after the gas was thrown in. Only a short almost choking cry and it was all over. . . .

At the time I really didn't waste any thoughts about killing the Russian war prisoners. It was ordered; I had to carry it out. But I must admit openly that the gassings had a calming effect for me, since in the near future the mass annihilation of the Jews had to begin. Until now it had not been clear to me . . . how the mass killings were to be carried out. It would probably be by gas, but how, and what kind of gas? Now we had discovered the gas and the procedure. I had always shuddered at the prospect of exterminations carried out by firing squads, especially considering the huge numbers and the women and children who would have to be killed. . . . Now I was relieved that we were all saved from these bloodbaths, and the victims would be spared suffering until their last moment came. It is exactly this that concerned me

---

[2]All SS members swore the following oath: "I swear to you Adolf Hitler, as Führer and Chancellor of the Reich, loyalty and bravery. I vow to you and to the authorities appointed by you obedience unto death, so help me God."
[3]A Russian term for Communist Party members assigned to the army to ensure the military's loyalty to the government.

[4]Cyclon (or Zyklon) B is a blue crystalline substance; its active ingredient, hydrocyanic acid, sublimates into a gas upon contact with air. It causes death by combining with the red blood cells and preventing them from carrying oxygen.

the most when I heard of Eichmann's[5] accounts of the mowing down of the Jews with machine guns and pistols by the Einsatz-Kommmandos [mobile killing squads]. Gruesome scenes were supposed to have taken place: people running away after being shot, the killing of those who were wounded, especially the women and children. Another thing on my mind was the many suicides in the ranks of the Einsatz-Kommandos who could no longer endure wading in the bloodbath. A few of them had even gone insane. Most of the members of the Einsatz-Kommandos drank a great deal of alcohol to help get through this horrible work.

In the spring of 1942 the first transports of Jews arrived. . . . All of them were to be exterminated. They were led from the ramp across the meadow . . . to the farmhouse called Bunker I. Aumeier, Palitzsch, and a few other block leaders transported them and spoke to them as one might in a casual conversation, asking them about their occupations and their schooling in order to mislead them. After arriving at the farmhouse they were told to undress. At first they went very calmly into the rooms where they were supposed to be disinfected. But some of them at that point became suspicious and started talking about suffocation and extermination. Immediately panic set in. Those still standing outside were quickly pushed into the chambers, and the doors were bolted shut. In the subsequent transports those who were nervous or upset were picked out and watched closely at all times. As soon as any disturbance was noticed the troublemakers were inconspicuously led behind the farmhouse and killed with a small-caliber pistol, which could not be heard by the others. . . .

I also observed how some women who suspected or knew what was happening, even with mortal terror in their own eyes, still managed enough strength to play with their children and to talk to them lovingly. Once a woman with four children, all holding each other by the hand to help the smallest ones over rough ground, passed by me very slowly. She stepped very close to me and whispered while pointing to her four children, "How can you bring yourself to murder these beautiful, darling children? Don't you have any heart in your body?" . . .

On some occasions some women would suddenly start screaming terribly while undressing or pulled out their hair and acted as if they were crazy persons. Immediately they were led away behind the farmhouse and killed by a bullet in the back of the neck from a small-caliber pistol. . . . I remember too seeing a woman as the doors were being shut trying to shove her children out of the chamber, crying, "Why don't you at least let my precious children live?" There were many heartbreaking scenes like this which affected all who witnessed them. . . .

. . . With very few exceptions everyone assigned to do this monstrous "work," this "service," who gave serious thought to it like I did, have been deeply affected by these events. Many of the men involved approached me while I made my rounds through the killing areas and poured out their depression and anxieties to me, hoping that I could comfort them. During these conversations the question arose again and again, "Is it necessary that we do all this? Is it necessary that hundreds of thousands of women and children have to be destroyed?" And I, who countless times in my innermost being had asked the same question, could only put them off and attempt to console them by reminding them that it was Hitler's order. I had to tell them that it was necessary to exterminate all the Jews in order to forever free Germany and future generations from our most vicious enemy.

. . . However, secret doubts tormented all of us. Under no circumstances could I reveal my secret reservations to anyone. I had to convince myself to be like a rock when faced with the necessity of carrying out this horribly severe order, and I had to

---

[5]Adolf Eichmann (1906–1962) was a bureaucrat originally in charge of Jewish emigration. He later was given responsibility for organizing the deportation of Jews to the death camps. He fled to Argentina in 1946 but was captured by Israeli agents, who took him to Israel, where he was tried and executed in 1962.

show this in every way, to force all those under me to hang on mentally and emotionally. . . .

Day and night, hour upon hour I had to witness all that happened. I had to watch, whether it was the removal and burning of the bodies, the teeth being ripped out, the cutting of the hair[6]—the whole grisly business. I had to stand for hours in the horrible, haunting stench while the mass graves were dug open, and the bodies were dragged out and burned. I also had to watch the procession of death itself through the peephole of the gas chamber because the doctors wanted me to do it. I had to do all of this because I was the one to whom everyone looked, because I had to show everybody that I was not merely the one who gave the orders and issued the directives, but that I was also willing to be present at whatever task I assigned my men to perform. . . .

And yet, everyone in Auschwitz believed the Kommandant really had a wonderful life. Yes, my family was well taken care of in Auschwitz; every wish that my wife or my children had was fulfilled. The children could live free and easy. My wife's garden was a flower paradise. The prisoners tried to give my wife and children every consideration and thus attract their attention. . . . By the same token no former prisoner can say that he was treated poorly in any way or at any time in our house. My wife would have loved to give a gift to every prisoner who performed a service for us. The children constantly begged me for cigarettes for the prisoners. The children especially loved the ones who worked in the garden. In our entire family there was a deep love of farming and especially of animals of every kind. Every Sunday I had to walk with them across the fields and visit the stables, and we could never miss visiting the dog kennels. They especially loved our two horses and our colt. The prisoners who worked in the household were always dragging in some animal the children kept in the garden. Turtles, martens, cats, or lizards; there was always something new and interesting to be seen there. The children splashed around in the summertime in the wading pool in the garden or the Sola River. Their greatest pleasure was when daddy went into the water with them. But he had only a little time to share all these joys of childhood.

Today I deeply regret that I did not spend more time with my family. I always believed that I had to be constantly on duty. This exaggerated sense of duty always made my life more difficult than it actually was. My wife again and again admonished me, "Don't always think of your duty, think of your family too." But what did my wife know about the things that depressed me? She never found out.[7]

---

[6]Teeth extracted from the corpses were soaked in muriatic acid to remove muscle and bone before the gold fillings were extracted. Hair was used to make felt and thread.
[7]In an interview with a court-appointed psychiatrist during the Nuremberg trials in 1946, Höss stated that his wife actually did learn of his participation in the mass executions at the camp, and that afterward they became estranged and ceased having sexual relations.

# The Decision to Drop the Atomic Bomb

## BACKGROUND

The chain of events and decisions that led to the dropping of atomic bombs on Hiroshima and Nagasaki began with a letter sent to President Franklin D. Roosevelt in 1939 by Albert Einstein, the world-famous physicist who had fled Germany in 1933 to

364 • *The Global Community and Its Challenges*

escape the scourge of Nazi anti-Semitism. Although signed by Einstein, it was largely written by the less-well-known Hungarian physicist Leó Szilárd. The letter warned that German scientists were pursuing research on nuclear chain reactions with the goal of producing weapons of enormous power; it recommended that the U.S. government fund and coordinate similar research. In response, Roosevelt appointed a committee of scientists to investigate the possibility of uranium chain reactions. Only in 1941, however, after hearing the results of promising nuclear research in England, did he order an all-out effort to produce an atomic weapon. A year later, the project was placed under the control of the Army and code-named the Manhattan Project.

Led by Brigadier General Leslie Groves, the Manhattan Project became a huge, desperate enterprise, employing one hundred thirty thousand persons who worked under the direction of the country's leading nuclear physicists and engineers at thirty-seven installations and a dozen university laboratories. Success was achieved on July 16, 1945, when the first atomic bomb, twenty thousand times more powerful than the largest conventional bomb, was exploded in New Mexico. In less than a month, atomic bombs reduced Hiroshima and Nagasaki to ashes, and World War II was over.

President Truman only learned of the new weapon at his first cabinet meeting on April 13, a day after Roosevelt's death, and received a full briefing from Secretary of War Henry R. Stimson on April 25. In response, Truman appointed a small committee, chaired by Stimson and known as the Interim Committee, to advise him on the use of atomic weapons during and after the war. Throughout the late spring and summer, the committee met to discuss and make recommendations on a wide range of issues, including if and how atomic bombs should be used. In its deliberations, the committee was advised by high-ranking military officers, business leaders, and a small committee of scientists, known as the Scientific Panel.

The events and decisions that occurred in the late spring and summer of 1945 are described the sources that follow.

## THE SOURCES

The first source is an excerpt from a summary of comments made by General George Marshall during a meeting with Secretary of War Henry Stimson on May 29, 1945. Marshall was sworn in as army chief of staff by President Roosevelt on September 1, 1939, the day Germany invaded Poland, and still was serving in the closing weeks of the war. With Germany having surrendered on May 8, at the May 29 meeting, the two men discussed the final campaign against Japan.

The second source is an excerpt from a memoir written by Arthur Compton, a member of the Scientific Panel. A Nobel Prize winner for his work on x-rays, Compton was director of the Metallurgical Laboratory at the University of Chicago, where the world's first nuclear chain reaction was produced in December 1942. Here Compton describes a meeting of the Interim Committee on May 31, 1945.

The third and fourth sources were written by scientists who had participated in the Manhattan Project. The Franck Report, submitted to the Interim Committee on June 11, was prepared by the Committee on the Social and Political Implications of Atomic Energy, a group of scientists from the University of Chicago Metallurgical Laboratory who had reservations about the military use of atomic weapons. Its chairperson was James Franck, a German-born chemist and Nobel laureate for his work on the bombardment of atoms by electrons. A notable feature of the report is its consideration of the ramifications of using atomic energy in the postwar world. The next source is excerpted from a petition circulated by Leó Szilárd, the Hungarian-born physicist, and signed by sixty-nine other scientists. Szilárd, who, with Enrico Fermi, designed the first successful nuclear reactor, was deeply moved by the wartime destruction he had seen as a young man in Hungary during World War I. Although he had urged Einstein to write President Roosevelt about the need for research on the military uses of atomic energy in 1939, and had made major contributions to the Manhattan Project, he became increasingly dismayed as scientists lost control of the research to the military. In May and June of 1945, he sought to discourage the U.S. government from using the bomb. Szilárd was one of the signatories of the Franck Report and was the inspiration for the petition sent to President Truman on June 17.

The Interim Committee dismissed the recommendations of the Franck Report, and in all likelihood, President Truman never read Szilárd's petition. On July 16, while attending the Potsdam Conference in Germany, Truman learned of the successful test of an atomic bomb in New Mexico and received a full report on July 21. On July 25, he ordered the U.S. military to prepare for an atomic attack on Japan sometime after August 1. On July 26, the United States, China, and Great Britain issued the Potsdam Declaration, which urged Japan to surrender unconditionally or face "the prompt and complete destruction of the Japanese armed forces and . . . the utter devastation of the Japanese homeland." No mention was made of a new weapon. Although some Japanese civilian leaders continued to work for an agreement to end the war, Japan rejected the terms of the Potsdam Declaration, and the attacks on Hiroshima and Nagasaki followed.

The last sources were written by the two men who were most responsible for the decision to use atomic weapons. The first document is a brief letter dated August 11 from President Truman to Samuel Cavert, general secretary of the Federal Council of Churches, an ecumenical organization representing some thirty major Protestant and Orthodox denominations. On August 9, Cavert had sent a telegram to President Truman stating, "Many Christians are deeply disturbed over use of atomic bombs against Japanese cities because of their necessarily indiscriminate destructive effects and because their use sets extremely dangerous precedent for future of mankind." The last source is an excerpt from an article Secretary of War Henry Stimson wrote for *Harper's Magazine* in 1947 after his retirement from public service. In it, he describes the work of the Interim Committee and his reasons for advising the president to use the bomb.

## QUESTIONS FOR ANALYSIS

1. How many different ideas for using the atomic bomb as a means for ending the war can you find in the sources?
2. What were the arguments made by individuals who cautioned against the use of the atomic bomb or who thought it should be "demonstrated" rather than used against the enemy?
3. What points were made against such arguments?

4. What were the main arguments of those who believed that the bomb should be used against Japanese targets without prior warning?

5. Inevitably, the question must be asked: What would you have decided if you had been president?

---

### 1 • Memorandum of Conversation with General Marshall (May 29, 1945)

The Secretary [Stimson] referred to the burning of Tokyo and the possible ways and means of employing the larger bombs. . . .

General Marshall said he thought these weapons might first be used against straight military objectives such as a large naval installation and then if no complete result was derived from the effect of that, he thought we ought to designate a number of large manufacturing areas from which the people would be warned to leave—telling the Japanese that we intended to destroy such centers. There would be no individual designations so that the Japs would not know exactly where we were to hit—a number should be named and the hit should follow shortly after. Every effort should be made to keep our record of warning clear. We must offset by such warning methods the opprobrium which might follow from an ill-considered employment of such force.

The General then spoke of . . . the development of new weapons and tactics to cope with the . . . last-ditch defense tactics of the suicidal Japanese. He sought to avoid the attrition we were now suffering from such fanatical but hopeless defense methods—it requires new tactics. He also spoke of gas and the possibility of using it in a limited degree, say on the outlying islands where operations were now going on or were about to take place. . . . It did not need to be our newest and most potent—just drench them and sicken them so that the fight would be taken out of them—saturate an area, possibly with mustard [gas], and just stand off. . . . There would be the matter of public opinion which we had to consider, but that was something which might also be dealt with. The character of the weapon was no less humane than phosphorous and flame throwers and need not be used against dense populations or civilians—merely against these last pockets of resistance which had to be wiped out but had no other military significance. . . .

*Source:* Memorandum of Conversation with General Marshall, May 29, 1945, National Archives.

---

### 2 • Arthur Compton, Recollection of Interim Committee Meeting (May 31, 1945)

Throughout the morning's discussions it seemed to be a foregone conclusion that the bomb would be used. It was regarding only the details of strategy and tactics that differing views were expressed. At the luncheon following the morning meeting, I was seated at Mr. Stimson's left. In the course of the conversation I asked the Secretary whether it might not be possible to arrange a nonmilitary demonstration of the bomb in such a manner that the Japanese would be so impressed that they would see the uselessness of continuing the war. The Secretary opened this question for general discussion by those at the table. Various possibilities were brought forward. One after the other it seemed necessary that they should be discarded.

*Source:* From Arthur Compton, *Atomic Quest* (New York: Oxford University Press, 1956), pp. 238–241.

It was evident that everyone would suspect trickery. If a bomb were exploded in Japan with previous notice, the Japanese air power was still adequate to give serious interference. An atomic bomb was an intricate device, still in the developmental stage. Its operation would be far from routine. If during the final adjustments of the bomb the Japanese defenders should attack, a faulty move might easily result in some kind of failure. Such an end to an advertised demonstration of power would be much worse than if the attempt had not been made. It was now evident that when the time came for the bombs to be used we should have only one of them available, followed afterwards by others at all-too-long intervals. We could not afford the chance that one of them might be a dud. If the test were made on some neutral territory, it was hard to believe that Japan's determined and fanatical military men would be impressed. If such an open test were made first and failed to bring surrender, the chance would be gone to give the shock of surprise that proved so effective. On the contrary, it would make the Japanese ready to interfere with an atomic attack if they could. Though the possibility of a demonstration that would not destroy human lives was attractive, no one could suggest a way in which it . . . could be made so convincing that it would be likely to stop the war.

## 3 • The Franck Report (June 11, 1945)

Certain and perhaps important tactical results undoubtedly can be achieved, but we nevertheless think that the question of the use of the very first available atomic bombs in the Japanese war should be weighed very carefully, not only by military authority, but by the highest political leadership of this country. If we consider international agreement on total prevention of nuclear warfare as the paramount objective, and believe that it can be achieved, this kind of introduction of atomic weapons to the world may easily destroy all our chances of success. Russia, and even allied countries which bear less mistrust of our ways and intentions, as well as neutral countries, will be deeply shocked. It will be very difficult to persuade the world that a nation which was capable of secretly preparing and suddenly releasing a weapon, as indiscriminate as the rocket bomb and a thousand times more destructive, is to be trusted in its proclaimed desire of having such weapons abolished by international agreement. We have large accumulations of poison gas, but do not use them, and recent polls have shown that public opinion in this country would disapprove of such a use even if it would accelerate the winning of the Far Eastern war. It is true, that some irrational element in mass psychology makes gas poisoning more revolting than blasting by explosive, even though gas warfare is in no way more "inhuman" than the war of bombs and bullets. Nevertheless, it is not at all certain that the American public opinion, if it could be enlightened as to the effect of atomic explosives, would support the first introduction by our own country of such an indiscriminate method of wholesale destruction of civilian life.

Thus, from the "optimistic" point of view—looking forward to an international agreement on prevention of nuclear warfare—the military advantages and the saving of American lives, achieved by the sudden use of atomic bombs against Japan, may be outweighed by the ensuing loss of confidence and wave of horror and repulsion, sweeping over the rest of the world, and perhaps dividing even the public opinion at home.

From this point of view a demonstration of the new weapon may best be made before the eyes of representatives of all United Nations, on the desert or a barren island. The best possible atmosphere for the achievement of an international agreement could be achieved if America would be able to say to the world, "You see what weapon we had but

*Source:* The Franck Report (June 11, 1945), from U.S. National Archives, Washington, D.C.: Record Group 77, Manhattan Engineer District Records, Harrison-Bundy File, folder #76.

did not use. We are ready to renounce its use in the future and to join other nations in working out adequate supervision of the use of this nuclear weapon."

This may sound fantastic, but then in nuclear weapons we have something entirely new in the order of magnitude of destructive power, and if we want to capitalize fully on the advantage which its possession gives us, we must use new and imaginative methods. After such a demonstration the weapon could be used against Japan if a sanction of the United Nations (and of the public opinion at home) could be obtained, perhaps after a preliminary ultimatum to Japan to surrender or at least to evacuate a certain region as an alternative to the total destruction of this target. . . .

## 4 • The Szilárd Petition (June 17, 1945)

. . . We, the undersigned scientists, have been working in the field of atomic power. Until recently, we have had to fear that the United States might be attacked by atomic bombs during this war and that her only defense might lie in a counterattack by the same means. Today, with the defeat of Germany, this danger is averted and we feel impelled to say what follows:

The war has to be brought speedily to a successful conclusion and attacks by atomic bombs may very well be an effective method of warfare. We feel, however, that such attacks on Japan could not be justified, at least not unless the terms which will be imposed after the war on Japan were made public in detail and Japan were given an opportunity to surrender.

If such public announcement gave assurance to the Japanese that they could look forward to a life devoted to peaceful pursuits in their homeland and if Japan still refused to surrender, our nation might then, in certain circumstances, find itself forced to resort to the use of atomic bombs. Such a step, however, ought not to be made at any time without seriously considering the moral responsibilities which are involved.

The development of atomic power will provide the nations with new means of destruction. The atomic bombs at our disposal represent only the first step in this direction, and there is almost no limit to the destructive power which will become available in the course of their future development. Thus a nation which sets the precedent of using these newly liberated forces of nature for purposes of destruction may have to bear the responsibility of opening the door to an era of devastation on an unimaginable scale. . . .

*Source:* A Petition to the President of the United States, July 17, 1945, from U.S. National Archives, Record Group #77, Records of the Chief of Engineers, Manhattan Engineer District, Harrison-Bundy File, folder #76.

## 5 • President Harry Truman, Letter to Samuel Cavert (August 11, 1945)

My dear Mr. Cavert,

I appreciated very much your telegram of August 9. Nobody is more disturbed over the use of Atomic bombs than I am but I was greatly disturbed by the unwarranted attack by the Japanese on Pearl Harbor and their murder of our prisoners of war. The only language they seem to understand is the one we have been using to bombard them.

When you have to deal with a beast you have to treat him as a beast. It is regrettable but nevertheless true.

Sincerely yours,
Harry S. Truman

*Source:* President Harry Truman, Letter to Samuel Cavert, August 11, 1945, from Harry S. Truman Presidential Library and Museum.

## 6 • Henry Stimson, The Decision to Use the Atomic Bomb

In the middle of July 1945, the intelligence section of the War Department General Staff estimated Japanese military strength as follows: in the home islands, slightly under 2,000,000; in Korea, Manchuria, China proper, and Formosa, slightly over 2,000,000; in French Indo-China, Thailand, and Burma, over 200,000; in the East Indies area, including the Philippines, over 500,000; in the by-passed Pacific islands, over 100,000. The total strength of the Japanese Army was estimated at about 5,000,000 men. . . . As we understood it in July, there was a very strong possibility that the Japanese government might determine upon resistance to the end, in all the areas of the Far East under its control. In such an event the Allies would be faced with the enormous task of destroying an armed force of five million men and five thousand suicide aircraft, belonging to a race which had already amply demonstrated its ability to fight literally to the death.

The strategic plans of our armed forces for the defeat of Japan, as they stood in July, had been prepared without reliance upon the atomic bomb, which had not yet been tested in New Mexico. We were planning an intensified sea and air blockade, and greatly intensified strategic air bombing, through the summer and early fall, to be followed on November 1 by an invasion of the southern island of Kyushu. This would be followed in turn by an invasion of the main island of Honshu in the spring of 1946. The total U.S. military and naval force involved in this grand design was of the order of 5,000,000 men; if all those indirectly concerned are included, it was larger still.

We estimated that if we should be forced to carry this plan to its conclusion, the major fighting would not end until the latter part of 1946, at the earliest. I was informed that such operations might be expected to cost over a million casualties to American forces alone. Additional large losses might be expected among our allies, and, of course, if our campaign were successful and if we could judge by previous experience, enemy casualties would be much larger than our own.

It was already clear in July that even before the invasion we should be able to inflict enormously severe damage on the Japanese homeland by the combined application of "conventional" sea and air power. The critical question was whether this kind of action would induce surrender. It therefore became necessary to consider very carefully the probable state of mind of the enemy, and to assess with accuracy the line of conduct which might end his will to resist.

The face of war is the face of death; death is an inevitable part of every order that a wartime leader gives. The decision to use the atomic bomb was a decision that brought death to over a hundred thousand Japanese. . . . But this deliberate, premeditated destruction was our least abhorrent choice. The destruction of Hiroshima and Nagasaki put an end to the Japanese war. It stopped the fire raids and the strangling blockade; it ended the ghastly specter of a clash of great land armies. . . .

---

*Source:* From Harry L. Stimson, "The Decision to Use the Atomic Bomb," *Harper's Weekly*, February 1947, by Harper's Magazine.

# Chapter 12

# Anticolonialism, Nationalism, and Revolution in Africa, Asia, and Latin America

D URING THE NINETEENTH CENTURY, the industrialized nations of Europe and the
United States—"the West"—achieved unprecedented global dominance. For
India and most of Africa and Southeast Asia, this meant colonial status and out-
right political control by Western nations. For China, Iran, Turkey, and much of Latin
America, it meant the subordination of their economic interests to those of the
West and the reluctant acceptance of Western meddling in their political affairs.

In the first half of the twentieth century, however, Africans, Asians, and Latin
Americans challenged the West's ascendancy. In areas of formal empire, mounting
anticolonialism gave rise to organized parties and movements whose supporters
demanded more political power and, ultimately, independence. Such movements
were strongest in India, where opposition to British rule escalated from polite
requests by educated Indians for greater political responsibility to nationwide boycotts and mass demonstrations for independence. In Southeast Asia, despite French,
British, and Dutch repression, dozens of political parties and underground organizations worked for the peaceful end or violent overthrow of colonial regimes. In
Africa—although colonized only in the late 1800s and despite its ethnic and linguis-
tic diversity—articulate and forceful proponents of pan-Africanism, anticolonialism,
and nationalism also emerged. In the Arab Middle East, where nationalist aspirations
after World War I were dashed by the mandate system and the continuation of the

British protectorate in Egypt, opponents of Anglo-French political control sought independence for Egypt, Iraq, Lebanon, and Syria.

While nationalism in colonized areas was directed against foreign rule, in those parts of Asia and Latin America where independent states were subservient in some respects to U.S. and European interests, it focused on overcoming economic dependency and political weakness. In Turkey, this meant the implementation of a program of secularization and modernization under Mustafa Kemal Ataturk. In China, it resulted in a struggle to rebuild the country and end foreign interference in the face of warlordism, civil war, and Japanese aggression. In Latin America, nationalism inspired new plans for economic development after the demand for the region's minerals and agricultural products collapsed during the Great Depression of the 1930s. In several Latin American countries, such efforts intensified conflict between entrenched elites and populist leaders who promised social reforms.

When World War II ended in 1945, many Western leaders thought they could return to the world they had dominated before the war. In the immediate postwar years, the Dutch, French, and British used force to maintain their colonies and preserve their worldwide influence. They soon realized the futility of their efforts, due in part to the growth of nationalism and anticolonialism in the interwar years.

# African Society and Identity Under Colonial Rule

Colonialism in Africa involved more than authoritarian rule and economic exploitation. Despite its relative brevity, it profoundly affected African life. It fostered population growth, encouraged urbanization, undermined African religions, altered gender relationships, introduced new sports and pastimes, changed how people dressed and what languages they spoke, and created new African perspectives on their place in the world. Africans in the twenty-first century still debate whether such changes benefited or harmed Africa in the long run. Unquestionably, however, for most Africans who lived through them in the 1920s and 1930s, these changes were viewed as unsettling, dispiriting, and demeaning.

The Africans' experiences were dispiriting and demeaning because so much of what took place under colonialism was predicated on the assumption of black inferiority. Colonialism's message was that Africans were incapable of governing themselves, or at least incapable of governing themselves effectively; nor were they capable of managing a modern economy or of creating a viable culture and social order. For all these tasks they needed Europeans, who justified their authority by asserting their moral and intellectual superiority. Furthermore, Africans were told that to improve themselves as individuals—to become clerks or civil servants in the colonial administration or to become "assimilated" (for example, to become an évolué, or "evolved one" in French Africa)—they would have to shed their

Africanness and adopt the ideas, views, work habits, dress, and customs of Europeans. This was the price Africans needed to pay to overcome their backwardness.

Some Africans came to accept their supposed inferiority as a reality, causing them to discard their traditions in the pursuit of "civilization." Others, however, resisted colonialism's message and saw continuing value in Africa's cultures and beliefs.

# Eagles into Chickens

### 83 • JAMES AGGREY, PARABLE OF THE EAGLE

James Aggrey, an educator and clergyman who was among the most prominent Africans of his day, was born in 1875 in the Gold Coast, a British colony. He was educated in a Protestant mission school, became a convert to Christianity, and at age twenty-three traveled to the United States to study for the ministry. He remained in the United States for twenty years, studying economics and agriculture, speaking out against racial prejudice, and working among poor blacks of South Carolina. He returned to Africa in 1918 and died in 1927. "Parable of the Eagle" was written in the early 1920s.

### QUESTIONS FOR ANALYSIS

1. According to Aggrey's parable, what psychological and emotional damage results from colonialism?
2. If the lessons of Aggrey's parable had been translated into actual policy by colonial administrators, what aspects of colonial rule would have been affected?

A certain man went through a forest seeking any bird of interest he might find. He caught a young eagle, brought it home and put it among his fowls and ducks and turkeys, and gave it chickens' food to eat even though it was an eagle, the king of birds.

Five years later a naturalist came to see him and, after passing through his garden, said: "That bird is an eagle, not a chicken."

"Yes," said its owner, "but I have trained it to be a chicken. It is no longer an eagle, it is a chicken, even though it measures fifteen feet from tip to tip of its wings."

"No," said the naturalist, "it is an eagle still: it has the heart of an eagle, and I will make it soar high up to the heavens."

"No," said the owner, "it is a chicken, and it will never fly."

They agreed to test it. The naturalist picked up the eagle, held it up, and said with great intensity: "Eagle, thou art an eagle; thou dost belong to the sky and not to this earth; stretch forth thy wings and fly."

The eagle turned this way and that, and then, looking down, saw the chickens eating their food, and down he jumped.

The owner said: "I told you it was a chicken."

"No," said the naturalist, "it is an eagle. Give it another chance tomorrow."

So the next day he took it to the top of the house and said: "Eagle, thou art an eagle; stretch forth thy wings and fly." But again the eagle, seeing the chickens feeding, jumped down and fed with them.

*Source:* James Aggrey, "Parable of the Eagle," in Edwin Smith, *Aggrey of Africa* (London: Student Christian Movement, 1929).

Then the owner said: "I told you it was a chicken."

"No," asserted the naturalist, "it is an eagle, and it still has the heart of an eagle; only give it one more chance, and I will make it fly tomorrow."

The next morning he rose early and took the eagle outside the city, away from the houses, to the foot of a high mountain. The sun was just rising, gilding the top of the mountain with gold, and every crag was glistening in the joy of that beautiful morning.

He picked up the eagle and said to it: "Eagle, thou art an eagle; thou dost belong to the sky and not to this earth; stretch forth thy wings and fly!"

The eagle looked around and trembled as if new life were coming to it; but it did not fly. The naturalist then made it look straight at the sun. Suddenly it stretched out its wings and, with the screech of an eagle, it mounted higher and higher and never returned. It was an eagle, though it had been kept and tamed as a chicken! My people of Africa, we were created in the image of God, but men have made us think that we are chickens, and we still think we are; but we are eagles. Stretch forth your wings and fly! Don't be content with the food of chickens!

# "Westernism" and South African Blacks

## 84 • FLORENCE JABAVU, BANTU HOME LIFE

Few groups in Africa were affected by colonialism as much as women. In traditional African villages, a division of labor between men and women had existed in which women were responsible for planting, weeding, harvesting, food preparation, and child care, while men cleared the land, built houses, herded cattle, and helped with fieldwork. Such arrangements broke down in West Africa when cash-crop agriculture was introduced. Men took over the farming of cotton or cocoa, leaving the responsibility of growing food for domestic consumption exclusively to women. Disruption also took place in southern and eastern Africa, where men left their villages for wage-paying jobs in mines or cities. This meant long absences of husbands from their families, greater work and domestic responsibilities for women, and frequent breakdowns of family life.

All these issues were matters of concern for Florence Thandiswa Jabavu, who was born into the family of a prominent Presbyterian minister and school administrator in 1895 in the outskirts of Alice, a city in the Eastern Cape Province of South Africa. In 1911 she received a certificate in elementary education from a local mission school, where she remained for a time as a teacher. In 1915 and 1922 she made trips to England to study music at Kingsmead College, a missionary training school in Birmingham. In 1921, in what is thought to be an arranged marriage, she was wed to Davidson D. T. Jabavu, a well-known intellectual and political activist who taught African languages at the University of Fort Hare, an all-black university in Alice. In the 1920s Florence Jabavu became active in various movements on behalf of children and women in South Africa. In 1927 she founded the African Women's Self-Improvement Society, which taught women skills in household management, farming, child care, health, and hygiene. Her essay "Bantu Home Life" was written in 1928 and published in an anthology *Christianity and the Natives of South Africa*. It is a candid assessment of the impact of "Westernism" on the Bantu, a term used at the time to refer to all black South Africans.

## QUESTIONS FOR ANALYSIS

1. What, according to the author, have been the benefits of the introduction of "Christianity, education, and civilization"?
2. How have some of these "benefits" had harmful side effects?
3. According to Jabavu, during her lifetime what changes in South Africa have affected the position and status of men, women, and children?
4. What does Jabavu's essay reveal about the economic situation of black South Africans?
5. On the basis of the facts and arguments presented by Jabavu, how would you characterize her overall assessment of "Westernism's" impact on South African blacks?

### Effects of Westernism

The primitive life has to-day been considerably changed by Western modernism, by which we imply the introduction of Christianity, education and Western civilisation.

In outline these are the most apparent effects of the advent of these influences:

Windows have been introduced in the huts, making for some hygienic improvement; there is more furniture, in the shape of chairs, tables, bedsteads, saddles, crockery and linen; there is more bodily apparel in the form of trousers for men (compelled by government laws against nudity), overcoats, ornaments like brass bangles, making for vanity, stimulated by country trading shops. Employment amongst whites has produced new tastes for foods like coffee and sugar and the like, which in turn have resulted in greater living expense. Missions have established country day schools where the arts of reading and writing have been acquired, bringing the people in direct touch with civilisation, with the result that they have been attracted into towns whither they continuously drift to their supposed Eldorado.[1] This exodus is also explained by the fact that these new needs and tastes can no longer be provided by the meager earnings of rural life. Nevertheless this has given them a widened outlook and an enlarged world of hope and ambition. The mere act of travelling, bringing them into contact with new ideas, has proved to be a vast education inasmuch as they get to unlearn much of what they had been taught at the mission stations when they see the flagrant desecration of the Sabbath by whites in towns. Migration into towns also brings them into the ambit [scope] of pass laws with their resultant criminality.[2]

Government legislation on land questions together with the natural increase of population with its concomitant of congestion has resulted in much landlessness, which has in turn resulted in the homelessness of many people and the degradation of the ideals of home life. Westernism has, however, produced tranquility and order in place of the old unsettlement and tribal friction. The worst forms of superstition have been reduced. Death by smelling out[3] has been eliminated, and life is more

*Source:* "Bantu Home Life," from J. Dexter Taylor, *Christianity and the Natives of South Africa: A Yearbook of South African Missions* (Johannesburg: General Missionary Conference of South Africa, 1928).

[1]Originally applied to the legendary "Lost City of Gold" thought to exist in the region of present-day Guyana in South America. The term came to be used metaphorically for any place where wealth could be acquired rapidly.

[2]Pass laws as a means of controlling the movements of blacks in South Africa have a long history. As a result of legislation passed in 1923, when black males were outside their designated "homelands," they were required to carry a pass that showed how long and for what reason the bearer was permitted to be in a white area. Without a valid pass blacks could be fined, arrested, deported to a rural reserve, or forced to accept a low-paying job for a white employer.

[3]When witchcraft was thought to exist in a village, some chiefs would enlist the services of a "witch smeller," a uniquely gifted woman who at a gathering of all local women would identify those guilty of witchcraft after dancing herself into a frenzy. Those identified as witches were immediately killed.

secure. In mission stations life is now characterized by a new spiritual life due to the reading of the Bible and the conduct of family prayers, morning and evening—thus bringing about a new form of dignity, greater tenderness, more sympathy, absence of cruelty and new idealism.

The degrading customs of female puberty rites and circumcision ceremonies have been largely destroyed.

The position of man has been greatly altered. His authority is less absolute because under modern conditions he is unable to raise money to meet the increased needs of the family. The young men who are the most able-bodied males in the community are almost continually away working in the industrial centers for the support of their homes, and this has given them a new feeling of independence from the fathers who, being regularly at home awaiting the return of their sons, are placed in the humiliating position of being suppliant to their sons. This condition of things has undone the old fashioned form of discipline. Nowadays a man dare not, as in the kraal [rural settlement], chastise any delinquent boy, on pain of being brought before the magistrate and punished for assault in accordance with European law.

The old Bantu communalism is rapidly giving way to Western individualism.

It is encouraging, in face of all these disintegrating factors due to the transition stage, that we have constructive institutions that are destined to prove helpful to the development of the Bantu people in their upward progress in culture. Such are the innumerable elementary schools in the rural and urban areas; the secondary schools especially in the Cape and Natal Provinces, and the Fort Hare College which is the culminating achievement of missionary work. Bantu literature has developed by leaps and bounds under the encouragement of the mission press. . . .

## Weaknesses

The advent of Westernism has not . . . been an unmixed blessing. . . . The chief difficulty encountered by the Natives has been that they are striving after a civilisation of which they have very little inside knowledge, practical experience and guidance. Those who see the inside of a European's house are there only as servants and therefore never assimilate anything of the true home life except the externals. . . .

In following what they have seen they find life too costly for their circumstances and fail to make ends meet. Wages are always insufficient for the life they are anxious to lead, and the result is unsettledness and an unhappy home life and also lack of control over children. In one case a certain woman, whose husband was a teacher, finding the economic pinch severe, left her husband, to carry on her profession elsewhere, visiting her home only periodically. In another similar case the young married woman has gone to work at a place too far away for her even to make periodic visits to her husband. In two other cases both the young married women are engaged in work which makes it impossible for them to attend to their family at home during the day. Under the circumstances the children are left either with imperfect supervision or have to fend for themselves. In most cases the environment in which the civilised Native lives is squalid, there being no flowers nor trees to make the home attractive. The congestion of houses, themselves badly built, has made for bad health conditions resulting in appalling death-rate figures, particularly in infants and children. The figures of infantile mortality make sad reading. They range between 100 and 650 deaths per thousand, where under better conditions they would range between 30 and 200; e.g., in Virginia, U.S.A, they range between 32 and 156 according to a recent report.

The evil of drink has aggravated the situation because it has served to deplete the already insufficient income of the bread-winner. It has degraded the moral life of whole communities, so much so that it is quite common for one to find certain portions of

Native locations correctly but unfortunately called Sodom and Gomorah.[4] . . .

The women in their daily round of home duties have lost that variety of combined occupations which we have mentioned as being associated with kraal life.

On the one hand, men, owing to their migration to industrial centres, obtain a broadened view of life by coming in contact with a larger world; on the other hand, women, being tied down, tend to become narrow in vision and interest. The training of womanhood has much to do with the situation, because the tendency in training centres has been to lay the most emphasis upon the training of boys and men rather than girls and women. Notwithstanding the existence of such wide movements as the Women's Manyano,[5] which owe their origin to the initiative of Native women themselves, the missions have neglected to train their womenfolk with the same intensive method as they prepare the menfolk for being exhorters, lay preachers, evangelists, and other forms of leadership.

The woman as manager of the home has not been afforded a proportionate advance in the attitude with which she is viewed and should be respected. Consequently there is a sort of inferiority complex aided and abetted by Europeans to the disadvantage of the Native woman. This is gradually sapping the moral fibre of the race in its endeavours towards culture inasmuch as no race can advance without race pride. Such pride in the analysis depends upon the motherhood of the nation, and upon the self-confidence that can be engendered only by the mother in the home.

---

[4]Two cities mentioned in Genesis and other books of the Hebrew bible. Yahweh destroyed them with "fire and brimstone" because of their unrepentant sinfulness. Based on the theory that the cities' "sin" was male homosexuality, Sodom is the basis for the word *sodomite*.

[5]An organization of black Methodist women dedicated to prayer and women's spiritual and social advancement. Its present-day mission is the protection of women from domestic violence.

# Political Currents in the Middle East

The immediate aftermath of World War I brought political disaster to the Middle East. The Turks, who had fought on Germany's side, were forced in 1920 to accept the humiliating Treaty of Sèvres, which stripped Turkey of its Arab territories; limited the Turkish army to fifty thousand men; gave France, Britain, and Italy control of its finances; and proposed to cede parts of Turkey to Italy, Greece, and the new states of Kurdistan and Armenia. Sultan Mehmed VI, overwhelmed by problems of lawlessness, army desertions, and inflation, accepted the treaty and failed to offer resistance when the Greeks landed troops in western Anatolia in May 1919 to advance their territorial claims.

Arabs also experienced bitter disappointment. Promised self-rule for joining the Anglo-French alliance and fighting against their Ottoman overlords, they learned in 1919 that the British and French had agreed in 1916 to divide Arab lands between them and that this, rather than the promises of Arab independence, would determine the postwar settlement. In 1920, Iraq, Syria, Palestine, Lebanon, and Jordan all became British or French mandates, a status that resembled old-style colonialism in many respects. Arabs also were incensed by the continuation of the British protectorate in Egypt and British support for the establishment of a national homeland for Jews in Palestine. Farther east, another major Islamic state, Iran, under the decrepit rule of the Qajar Dynasty, seemed on the verge of becoming a British protectorate.

Efforts to reverse the postwar settlements succeeded in Turkey and Iran. Under Mustafa Kemal, the Turks rallied to drive out the Greeks and recover former Turkish territory claimed by the newly established Republic of Armenia. In 1922 the Turks abolished the sultanate, and in 1923 the European powers agreed to replace the Treaty of Sèvres with the Treaty of Lausanne, which recognized the integrity and independence of the new Turkish republic. Assuming near-dictatorial powers, Mustafa Kemal now had his opportunity to transform Turkey into a modern secular state. In Iran, which barely avoided becoming a British protectorate in 1919, Colonel Reza Khan (1878–1944) was named shah in 1925 and, like his hero Kemal, sought to build up his country through economic development, educational reform, and secularization.

Arab efforts to achieve independence and prevent Jewish migration to Palestine were less successful. Of the twenty Arab states that stretched from Morocco in the west to Iraq in the east, only Saudi Arabia and parts of Yemen were fully independent in the interwar years. Egypt and Iraq attained limited self-rule, but the presence of British troops and continuing British influence over foreign and military affairs were sources of resentment in both countries. The drive for independence was even more frustrating in French-controlled Lebanon and Syria. In the 1930s, the French reneged on promises to relinquish their authority, and Lebanon and Syria remained subject to the French mandate until 1943 and 1946, respectively. Arabs throughout the region also were angered by continuing Jewish migration to Palestine, which accelerated after the Nazi takeover of Germany.

While confronting these political problems, the people and leaders of the region faced other difficult issues. What could be done to end poverty and illiteracy? How might the teachings and expectations of Islam be reconciled with the realities and demands of modernization? Was modernization itself desirable, and, if so, how was it to be achieved? Was the goal of Arab nationalism the expulsion of the British and French and the stifling of Zionism, or was it the attainment of a single united Arab state? In the face of the changes that swept across the region in the first half of the twentieth century, finding answers to such questions became more urgent and more difficult.

# Secularism and Nationalism in Republican Turkey

## 85 • MUSTAFA KEMAL, SPEECH TO THE CONGRESS OF THE PEOPLE'S REPUBLICAN PARTY

The arch-symbol of secularism and nationalism in the Muslim world in the interwar years was Mustafa Kemal (1881–1938), a military hero during World War I who went on to serve as the first president of the Turkish republic. Disgusted by the Ottoman sultan's acquiescence to the Greek occupation of the Turkish port of Smyrna (Izmir) in 1919, Kemal assumed leadership of a resistance movement that by 1923 had overthrown the sultan, defeated the Greeks, and won the annulment of the punitive Treaty of Sèvres. Exercising broad powers as president until his death in 1938, Kemal sought to transform Turkey into a modern secular nation-state. To accomplish this, he broke the power of Islam over education and the legal system, encouraged industrialization, accorded women full legal rights, mandated the use of a new Turkish alphabet, and ordered Turks to adopt Western-style dress. Directing all Turks to adopt hereditary family names, he took the name Ataturk, or "Great Turk."

Having consolidated his authority, Kemal decided in 1927 to review his accomplishments and impress upon his subjects the need for continued support. He chose as the occasion the meeting of Turkey's only legal political party, the People's Republican Party, which he had founded. There he delivered an extraordinary speech that lasted six days.

In the following excerpts he discusses Turkey's past and future; explains his reasons for abolishing the caliphate, the ancient office by virtue of which Ottoman sultans had been the theoretical rulers of all Muslims; and justifies his suppression of the Progressive Republican Party, which despite its name had been a conservative party that opposed Turkey's modernization.

## QUESTIONS FOR ANALYSIS

1. According to Kemal, what "erroneous ideas" had guided the Ottoman state in the past?
2. Why does Kemal argue that nation-states, not empires, are the most desirable form of political organization?
3. What is Kemal's view of the West?
4. What are his views of Islam?
5. What arguments does Kemal offer against the continuation of the caliphate?
6. How does Kemal justify his suppression of the Progressive Republicans? What, in his view, were the positive results of this step?

### Nationalism and Empire

. . . Among the Ottoman rulers there were some who endeavored to form a gigantic empire by seizing Germany and Western Europe. One of these rulers hoped to unite the whole Islamic world in one body, to lead it and govern it. For this purpose he obtained control of Syria and Egypt and assumed the title of Caliph.[1] Another Sultan pursued the twofold aim, on the one hand of gaining the mastery over Europe, and on the other of subjecting the Islamic world to his authority and government. The continuous counterattacks from the West, the discontent and insurrections in the Muslim world, as well as the dissensions between the various elements which this policy had artificially brought together had the ultimate result of burying the Ottoman Empire, in the same way as many others, under the pall of history. . . .

To unite different nations under one common name, to give these different elements equal rights,

---

*Source:* Mustafa Kemal, *A Speech Delivered by Ghazi Mustapha Kemal* (Leipzig: F. F. Koehler, 1929), pp. 376–379, 589–594, 717, 721–722.

[1]A probable reference to Selim I, who conquered Egypt and Syria in 1515–1516; the "other sultan" referred to may be Suleiman I (r. 1520–1566).

subject them to the same conditions and thus to found a mighty State is a brilliant and attractive political ideal; but it is a misleading one. It is an unrealizable aim to attempt to unite in one tribe the various races existing on the earth, thereby abolishing all boundaries. Herein lies a truth which past centuries . . . have clearly shown in dark and sanguinary events.

In order that our nation should be able to live a happy, strenuous, and permanent life, it is necessary that the State should pursue an exclusively national policy and that this policy should be in perfect agreement with our internal organization and be based on it. When I speak of national policy, I mean it in this sense: To work within our national boundaries for the real happiness and welfare of the nation and the country by relying on our own strength in order to retain our existence. But not to lead the people to follow fictitious aims, of whatever nature, which could only bring them misfortune, and expect from the civilized world civilized human treatment, friendship based on mutuality. . . .

## The Issue of the Caliphate

I must call attention to the fact that Hodja Shukri, as well as the politicians who pushed forward his person and signature, had intended to substitute the sovereign bearing the title of Sultan or Padishah by a monarch with the title of Caliph.[2] The only difference was that, instead of speaking of a monarch of this or that country or nation, they now spoke of a monarch whose authority extended over a population of three hundred million souls belonging to manifold nations and dwelling in different continents of the world. Into the hands of this great monarch, whose authority was to extend over the whole of Islam, they placed as the only power that of the Turkish people, that is to say, only from 10 to 15 millions of these

three hundred million subjects. The monarch designated under the title of Caliph was to guide the affairs of these Muslim peoples and to secure the execution of the religious prescriptions which would best correspond to their worldly interests. He was to defend the rights of all Muslims and concentrate all the affairs of the Muslim world in his hands with effective authority. . . .

If the Caliph and Caliphate, as they maintained, were to be invested with a dignity embracing the whole of Islam, ought they not to have realized in all justice that a crushing burden would be imposed on Turkey, on her existence; her entire resources and all her forces would be placed at the disposal of the Caliph? . . .

I made statements everywhere that were necessary to dispel the uncertainty and anxiety of the people concerning this question of the Caliphate. . . . I gave the people to understand that neither Turkey nor the handful of men she possesses could be placed at the disposal of the Caliph so that he might fulfill the mission attributed to him, namely, to found a State comprising the whole of Islam. The Turkish nation is incapable of undertaking such an irrational mission.

For centuries our nation was guided under the influence of these erroneous ideas. But what has been the result of it? Everywhere they have lost millions of men. "Do you know," I asked, "how many sons of Anatolia have perished in the scorching deserts of the Yemen? Do you know the losses we have suffered in holding Syria and Iraq and Egypt and in maintaining our position in Africa? And do you see what has come out of it? Do you know? . . .

New Turkey, the people of New Turkey, have no reason to think of anything else but their own existence and their own welfare. She has nothing more to give away to others . . .

[2]These events took place in January 1923. After Sultan Mehmed V was deposed on November 1, 1922, his cousin was designated caliph. Shukri was a *hodja* (or *hojjd*), a Turkish religious leader; he hoped that the new Turkish state would continue to support the caliphate even after the sultanate was abolished. In 1924, however, Kemal abolished the caliphate.

## The Suppression of the Progressive Republicans

As you know, it was at the time that the members of the opposition had founded a party under the name of "Republican Progressive Party" and published its program. . . .

Under the mask of respect for religious ideas and dogmas the new Party addressed itself to the people in the following words:

"We want the re-establishment of the Caliphate; we do not want new laws; we are satisfied with the religious law; we shall protect the Medressas, the Tekkes, the pious institutions, the Softahs, the Sheikhs[3] and their disciples. Be on our side; the party of Mustafa Kemal, having abolished the Caliphate, is breaking Islam into ruins; they will make you into unbelievers. . . ."

Read these sentences, Gentlemen, from a letter written by one of the adherents of this program: . . . "They are attacking the very principles which perpetuate the existence of the Muslim world. . . . The assimilation with the Occident means the destruction of our history, our civilization. . . ." Gentlemen, facts and events have proved that the program of the Republican Progressive Party has been the work emanating from the brain of traitors. This Party became the refuge and the point of support for reactionary and rebellious elements. . . .

The Government and the Committee found themselves forced to take extraordinary measures. They caused the law regarding the restoration of order to be proclaimed, and the Independence Courts to take action. For a considerable time they kept eight or nine divisions of the army at war strength for the suppression of disorders, and put an end to the injurious organization which bore the name "Republican Progressive Party."

The result was, of course, the success of the Republic. . . .

## Civilization and Stability

Gentlemen, it was necessary to abolish the fez,[4] which sat on our heads as a sign of ignorance, of fanaticism, of hatred to progress and civilization, and to adopt in its place the hat, the customary headdress of the whole civilized world, thus showing, among other things, that no difference existed in the manner of thought between the Turkish nation and the whole family of civilized mankind. We did that while the law for the Restoration of Order[5] was still in force. If it had not been in force we should have done so all the same; but one can say with complete truth that the existence of this law made the thing much easier for us. As a matter of fact the application of the law for the Restoration of Order prevented the morale of the nation being poisoned to a great extent by reactionaries.

Gentlemen, while the law regarding the Restoration of Order was in force there took place also the closing of the Tekkes, of the convents, and of the mausoleums, as well as the abolition of all sects[6] and all kinds of titles such as Sheikh, Dervish, . . . Occultist, Magician, Mausoleum Guard, etc.[7]

---

[3]A *medressa* (also madrasah or madrassa) is an advanced school of Islamic learning; a *tekke* is a small teaching mosque usually built over the tomb of a saint; a *softah* is a student in an Islamic school; a *sheikh,* or *shaykh,* is a master of a religious order of Sufis, Muslims who adopted a mystical approach to their religion.

[4]The fez is a brimless hat popular among Turkish men during the nineteenth century; its lack of a brim allowed the wearer to touch his forehead to the ground while kneeling during prayer without removing the hat.

[5]The law, promulgated in March 1925, authorized the government to prohibit "all organizations, provocations, exhortations, initiatives and publications which disturb the social structures, law and order, and safety and incite to commit reactionary acts and subversion."

[6]Islamic religious orders.

[7]A *dervish,* or *darvish,* is a member of a Muslim, especially Sufi, religious order dedicated to leading lives of poverty and austerity. They are famous for their whirling dances that symbolize the movement of the heavenly spheres. An *occultist* was a Sufi who achieved a state of withdrawal from the world. A *mausoleum guard* guarded the tomb of a saint or holy person.

One will be able to imagine how necessary the carrying through of these measures was, in order to prove that our nation as a whole was no primitive nation, filled with superstitions and prejudices.

Could a civilized nation tolerate a mass of people who let themselves be led by the nose by a herd of Sheikhs, Dedes, Seids, . . . Babas and Emirs,[8] who entrusted their destiny and their lives to chiromancers [fortunetellers], magicians, dice-throwers and amulet sellers? Ought one to conserve in the Turkish State, in the Turkish Republic, elements and institutions such as those which had for centuries given the nation the appearance of being other than it really was? Would one not therewith have committed the greatest, most irreparable error to the cause of progress and reawakening?

Gentlemen, at the same time the new laws were worked out and decreed which promise the most fruitful results for the nation on the social and economic plane, and in general in all the forms of the expression of human activity . . . the Citizens' Legal Code, which ensures the liberty of women and stabilizes the existence of the family.

Accordingly we made use of all circumstances only from one point of view, which consisted therein: to raise the nation on to that step on which it is justified in standing in the civilized world, to stabilize the Turkish Republic more and more on steadfast foundations . . . and in addition to destroy the spirit of despotism forever.

---

[8]A *dede* was head of a Sufi order. *Seids*, or *sayyids*, were descendants of Muhammad through his daughter Fatima.

*Baba* was a popular surname among Sufi preachers. In this context *emir* is an honorary Turkish title.

## Impasse in Palestine

### 86 • REPORT OF THE PALESTINE ROYAL COMMISSION (THE PEEL COMMISSION), JULY 1937

Despite six wars, dozens of minor conflicts, frequent negotiations, and countless proposals and counterproposals, the Arab–Israel conflict over Palestine remains a source of ongoing tension in the Middle East. Its immediate cause was the founding of the state of Israel in 1948 and the displacement of approximately 750,000 Palestinian Arabs during and after the 1948 Arab–Israeli War. But its origins go back much further—all the way to 70 C.E., when the Jews were exiled from their Palestinian homeland by the Romans, forcing them to resettle in other parts of the Middle East, North Africa, Europe, and beginning in the 1500s, the Americas. Wherever they went, Jews were a small, frequently persecuted minority in predominantly Muslim or Christian societies. In their long exile they maintained a strong attachment to the "Land of Canaan," which, according to the Hebrew Scriptures, God had given them as their promised land after becoming His chosen people. Only in the nineteenth century, however, in response to growing anti-Semitism and fears of lost identity did some Jewish leaders conclude that Jews could escape persecution and preserve their traditions only if they had a homeland in Palestine. This movement came to be known as Zionism, derived from Mount Zion, one of the two major hills overlooking Jerusalem, the ancient Jewish capital.

The first advocates of Jewish resettlement in Palestine were eastern European Jews reacting to the anti-Jewish pogroms in Russian-controlled Poland and Ukraine in the 1880s and 1890s. Political Zionism, which advocates the foundation of a Jewish state, dates from the late 1890s, when the Vienna-based journalist Theodor Herzl published *Der Judenstaat* (The Jewish State) in 1896 and one year later convened the first international Zionist conference in Basel, Switzerland. Despite the indifference and outright opposition of many assimilated European Jews, and despite many disagreements among the Zionists themselves, on the eve of World War I, approximately 60,000 Jews, about half of whom were recent immigrants, lived in Palestine among 620,000 Muslims and 70,000 Christians.

The situation in Palestine became more volatile after World War I. The Palestinian Arabs, who identified themselves with Syria, were bitterly disappointed when Great Britain and France reneged on their wartime promises to support the creation of an independent Arab state and instead turned the former Arab provinces of the Ottoman Empire into mandates. Their disappointment deepened when the British, who held the Palestinian mandate, made good on the "Balfour Declaration," a wartime pledge to facilitate Jewish immigration to Palestine and make it a national home for Jews. Between 1919 and 1939, the number of Jews in Palestine grew from slightly under 10 percent to 30 percent. These Jews purchased land, established industries, founded schools and universities, and, with support from the Zionist Organization, laid the groundwork for the founding of an independent Jewish state. Meanwhile Arabs pressured British authorities to limit Jewish immigration and land transfers from Arabs to Jews. In 1936 Palestine erupted into sporadic violence, followed by Arab general strikes, tax boycotts, bombings, and property destruction directed against Jews and British officials.

In response, the British government sent the former secretary of state for India, Lord Robert Peel, to Palestine to head a commission to investigate the causes of the violence and recommend solutions. The commission published its report in mid-1937. Concluding that cooperation and compromise were impossible, it recommended partitioning Palestine into three parts: Jewish territory in the northwest; Arab territory in the east and south; and continued British control of Nazareth, Jerusalem, and a corridor between Jerusalem and the coast (see map on page 389). Although the proposals were endorsed by the British government, they bitterly divided the Jews, and were rejected totally by the Arabs. The political future of Palestine was not settled until 1948, when the independent state of Israel was born. But conflict and discord have continued.

## QUESTIONS FOR ANALYSIS

1. What do the Arab and Jewish lists of grievances reveal about the economic and social status of the two communities?
2. Given the two sides' lists of grievances, what reasonable chance did the British have of satisfying both sides?
3. Why, according to the report's authors, are the Arab and Jewish communities inherently and permanently incompatible?

4. Why do the the report's authors predict that the Arab–Jewish conflict will worsen?
5. Why, according to the report, does the use of force provide no long-term solution to the problems of the region?
6. How, according to the report, will continuation of the status quo damage Great Britain's standing in the world?
7. Overall, does the tone and content of the report seem more sympathetic to the Arabs or Jews?
8. Arabs resolutely rejected the commission's plan for partition. Among Jews the plan had supporters and opponents. What arguments might these groups have offered to defend their point of view?

## Conclusions and Recommendation

### *Arab Grievances*

(1) The failure to develop self-governing institutions.
(2) The acquisition of land by the Jews.
(3) Jewish immigration.
(4) The use of Hebrew and English as official languages.
(5) The employment of British and Jewish officers, and exclusion of Arabs from the higher posts.
(6) The creation of a large class of landless Arabs, and the refusal of Jews to employ Arab labourers.
(7) Inadequate funds for Arab education.

Whilst we [the commission] believe that these grievances are sincerely felt, we are of opinion that most of them cannot be regarded as legitimate under the terms of the Mandate and we are therefore not called upon to make recommendations on them. It is only in regard to the last that we are able to suggest any remedy. We would welcome increased expenditure on Arab education, especially in the direction of village agricultural schools.

### *Jewish Grievances*

(1) Obstruction in the establishment of the National Home owing to dilatory action in dealing with proposals demanding executive action.
(2) The display of "pro-Arab" proclivities by officials and their failure to carry out the Mandate. . . .
(3) Great delay in the decision of civil suits; inefficiency in criminal procedure, as instanced by the fact that 80 Jews were murdered during 1936, and no capital sentence was carried out.
(4) Toleration by the Government of subversive activities, more especially those of the Mufti of Jerusalem.[1]
(5) As regards the land, failure to introduce a land system appropriate to the needs of the country, the continuance of the system of *Masha'a*;[2] no arrangement for the consolidation of holdings, . . . difficulty in obtaining a satisfactory title to land when purchased; . . . insufficient encouragement of irrigation and drainage schemes.

---

*Source:* Report of the Palestine Royal Commission, June 22, 1937. Reprinted by Permission of Her Majesty's Copyright Office. Reproduced under the terms of the Click-Use license.
[1]A reference to Hajj Amin al-Husayni (1895 [?]-1974), who as Mufti of Jerusalem (the Sunni cleric who oversaw Islamic holy places in Jerusalem), helped organize attacks on Jews and British officials in 1937–1938. He also helped found the Arab Higher Committee, which called for nonpayment of taxes, organized an Arab general strike, and demanded an end to Jewish immigration. The committee was banned by the Mandate administration in September 1937. Amin al-Husayn fled to Lebanon and then Iraq to escape arrest. During World War II he lived in Rome and Berlin and made pro-Axis radio broadcasts for Arab audiences.
[2]The collective ownership of land by a village community.

(6) Reluctance really to facilitate [Jewish] immigration, . . . and uncontrolled illegal Arab immigration.

(7) Trans-Jordan should be opened to Jewish immigration.[3]

(8) The necessary steps have not been taken to secure the removal or alleviation of restrictions on the importation of Palestine citrus fruits into foreign countries.

(9) Progressive Jewish Municipalities are unduly restricted by Government rules and regulations.

(10) Failure to ensure public security.

---

> While the authors of the report rejected most Arab grievances as "illegitimate" under terms of the mandate, they proposed numerous administrative and policy changes in response to the grievances of the Jewish community. They concluded the section as follows:

---

These are the recommendations which we submit. . . . They are the best palliatives we can devise for the disease from which Palestine is suffering, but they are only palliatives. They might reduce the inflammation and bring down the temperature, but they cannot cure the trouble. The disease is so deep-rooted that, in our firm conviction, the only hope of a cure lies in a surgical operation.

### The Force of Circumstances

. . . An irrepressible conflict has arisen between two national communities within the narrow bounds of one small country. About 1,000,000 Arabs are in strife, open or latent, with some 400,000 Jews. There is no common ground between them. The Arab community is predominantly Asiatic in character, the Jewish community predominantly European. They differ in religion and in language. Their cultural and social life, their ways of thought and conduct, are as incompatible as their national aspirations. . . . The War [World War I] and its sequel have inspired all Arabs with the hope of reviving in a free and united Arab world the traditions of the Arab golden age. The Jews similarly are inspired by their historic past. They mean to show what the Jewish nation can achieve when restored to the land of its birth. National assimilation between Arabs and Jews is thus ruled out. . . . Neither Arab nor Jew has any sense of service to a single State.

The conflict has grown steadily more bitter. It has been marked by a series of five Arab outbreaks, culminating in the rebellion of last year. . . .

This intensification of the conflict will continue. . . . The educational systems, Arab and Jewish, are schools of nationalism, and they have only existed for a short time. Their full effect on the rising generation has yet to be felt. And patriotic "youth-movements", so familiar a feature of present-day politics in other countries of Europe or Asia, are afoot in Palestine. As each community grows, moreover, the rivalry between them deepens. The more numerous and prosperous and better-educated the Arabs become, the more insistent will be their demand for national independence and the more bitter their hatred of the obstacle that bars the way to it. As the Jewish National Home grows older and more firmly rooted, so will grow its self-confidence and political ambition. . . .

Meantime the "external factors" will continue to play the part they have played with steadily increasing force from the beginning. On the one hand, Saudi Arabia, the Yemen, Iraq and Egypt are already recognized as sovereign states, and Trans-Jordan as

---

[3]The emirate of Transjordan, to the east of the Jordan River, was created in 1921 to provide a kingdom for Abdullah I bin al-Hussein, who had led the Arab revolt against the Ottomans during World War I. The original mandate exempted Britain from the responsibility of encouraging Jewish immigration to Transjordan, so this grievance was rejected by the commission's report.

British Mandate of Palestine, 1920–1948

**Peel Commission Partition Plan, 1937**

- Proposed Jewish state
- Proposed Arab state
- Mandated territory

0  25  50 Km.
0  25  50 Mi.

LEBANON (French Mandate)

SYRIA (French Mandate)

Lake Huleh

Sea of Galilee

Haifa
Acre
Nazareth
NAZARETH ENCLAVE
Tulkarm
Nablus
Tel Aviv
Jaffa
Jericho
Jerusalem
Bethlehem
JERUSALEM ENCLAVE
Gaza
Hebron
Dead Sea
Beersheba

Jordan R.

*Mediterranean Sea*

32°N

EGYPT

*SINAI PENINSULA*

*NEGEV DESERT*

TRANSJORDAN (British Mandate)

30°N

34°E
36°E

© Cengage Learning®

an "independent government." In less than three years' time Syria and the Lebanon will attain their national sovereignty.[4] The claim of the Palestinian Arabs to share in the freedom of all Asiatic Arabia will thus be reinforced. . . . That they are as well qualified for self-government as the Arabs of neighboring countries has been admitted.

On the other hand, the hardships and anxieties of the Jews in Europe are not likely to grow less in the near future. . . . The appeal to the good faith and humanity of the British people will lose none of its force. The Mandatory [Great Britain] will be urged unceasingly to admit as many Jews into

Palestine as the National Home can provide with a livelihood and to protect them when admitted from Arab attacks. . . .

In these circumstances, we are convinced that peace, order and good government can only be maintained in Palestine for any length of time by a rigorous system of repression. . . . If "disturbances", moreover, should recur on a similar scale to that of last year's rebellion, the cost of military operations must soon exhaust the revenues of Palestine and ultimately involve the British Treasury to an incalculable extent. The moral objections to maintaining a system of government by constant repression

---

[4]Saudi Arabia was recognized as an independent state in 1927; Iraq became independent in 1932, although Britain maintained military bases and continued to exercise

influence over Iraqi foreign policy. The report exaggerates the progress toward independence in Egypt, Yemen, Syria, and Lebanon.

are self-evident. Nor is there any need to empha-size the undesirable reactions of such a course of policy on opinion outside Palestine.

And the worst of it is that such a policy leads nowhere. However vigorously and consistently maintained, it will not solve the problem. It will not allay, it will exacerbate the quarrel between the Arabs and the Jews. The establishment of a single self-governing Palestine will remain just as imprac-ticable as it is now. It is not easy to pursue the dark path of repression without seeing daylight at the end of it. . . .

In these last considerations lies a final argument for seeking a way out, at almost any cost, from the existing deadlock in Palestine. For a continuance or rather an aggravation—for that is what con-tinuance will be—of the present situation cannot be contemplated without the gravest misgivings. It will mean a steady decline in our prestige. It will mean the gradual alienation of two peoples who are traditionally our friends: for already the Arabs of Palestine have been antagonized and the patience of their kinsmen throughout the Arab world is being strained; and already the Jews, par-ticularly, we understand, in the United States, are

questioning the sincerity with which we are ful-filling the promises we made and suggesting that negligence or weakness on our part is the real cause of all the trouble. . . .

Manifestly the problem cannot be solved by giv-ing either the Arabs or the Jews all they want. . . . But, while neither race can justly rule all Palestine, we see no reason why, if it were practicable, each race should not rule part of it.

No doubt the idea of Partition as a solution of the problem has often occurred to students of it, only to be discarded. There are many who would have felt an instinctive dislike to cutting up the Holy Land. . . . Others may have felt that parti-tion would be a confession of failure. . . . Others, again, if they thought of Partition, dismissed it, no doubt, as impossible. The practical difficulties seemed too great: And great they unquestionably are. . . . Nevertheless . . . , those difficulties do not seem so insuperable as the difficulties inherent in the continuance of the Mandate or in any other alternative arrangement which has been proposed to us or which we ourselves could devise. Partition seems to offer at least a chance of ultimate peace. We can see none in any other plan.

# Anticolonialism in India and Southeast Asia

By the late nineteenth century, when Indians were in a full-scale debate about their relationship with Great Britain and some were demanding independence, many Southeast Asians were experiencing direct European political control for the first time. Nonetheless, in the first half of the twentieth century, developments in both areas showed some marked similarities. Nationalism swept through the Indian popu-lation, and despite their many differences in religion, education, and caste status, mil-lions of Indians came to agree that Great Britain should "quit India" and allow Indian self-rule. Nationalism also intensified in Southeast Asia, especially in Vietnam and the Dutch East Indies, where force was needed to suppress anticolonial movements in the 1920s and 1930s.

The reasons for this upsurge of anti-European sentiment included revivals of Hinduism in India, Buddhism in Myanmar, and Islam in Southeast Asia, all of which heightened people's awareness of their differences from the West; the emergence of Japan, which demonstrated that an Asian nation could become a major power; the carnage of World War I, which raised doubts about the Europeans' "superiority"; and the spread of Western political ideologies through education, travel, and growing literacy. Most telling, however, was anger over the disparity between the Europeans' stated good intentions and their actual record of economic exploitation, racial prejudice, and authoritarian rule. To these factors were added the influence of charismatic leaders such as Mohandas Gandhi, who drew the Indian masses into the nationalist movement; Jawaharlal Nehru, who guided the Indian Congress Party after 1941; Ho Chi Minh, who built a strong nationalist coalition in Vietnam; and Achmed Sukarno, who rallied Indonesian nationalists despite opposition from the Dutch.

World War II was the catalyst for the creation of independent nations throughout the region in the late 1940s and the 1950s, but events and leaders of the first half of the twentieth century set the stage for these developments.

# Gandhi's Vision for India

### 87 • MOHANDAS GANDHI, INDIAN HOME RULE

Mohandas Gandhi was born in 1869 in a village north of Mumbai on the Arabian Sea. His father was a government official who presided over an extended family with strict Hindu practices. Gandhi studied law in England, and after failing to establish a legal practice in Mumbai moved to South Africa in 1893 to serve the country's large Indian population.

In South Africa, he became incensed over discriminatory laws against Indians, many of whom were indentured servants employed by whites or petty merchants. During his struggle to improve the lot of South Africa's Indian population, Gandhi developed his philosophy of *satyagraha,* usually translated into English as "soul force." Satyagraha sought justice not through violence but through love, a willingness to suffer, and conversion of the oppressor. Central to Gandhi's strategy was nonviolent resistance: his followers disobeyed unjust laws and accepted the consequences—even beatings and imprisonment—to reach the hearts of the British and change their thinking.

Gandhi first wrote about his theories in 1909 after meeting with a group of Indians in England who favored force to oust the British. In response, he composed a one-hundred-page treatise, *Hind Swaraj* (Indian Home Rule). Although written well before he emerged as India's inspirational leader, it contains core principles that guided Gandhi throughout his life. In the preface to the 1938 edition of the work, he wrote, "I have seen nothing to make me alter the views expounded in it."

Composed as a dialogue between a "reader" and an "editor" (Gandhi), *Indian Home Rule* originally was written in Gujarati and published in installments in *Indian Opinion,* a newspaper he founded for South Africa's Indian community. The book was banned in India by the British, but English translations were published in South Africa in 1910 and the United States in 1924. The first Indian edition was published in 1938 after the British ban was lifted.

## QUESTIONS FOR ANALYSIS

1. What does Gandhi see as the major deficiency of modern civilization?
2. According to Gandhi, how has civilization specifically affected women?
3. Why does Gandhi have faith that Hindus and Muslims will be able to live in peace in India?
4. What, according to Gandhi, is true civilization, and what is India's role in preserving it?
5. What leads Gandhi to his conviction that love is stronger than force?
6. Why did Gandhi's attack on civilization gain him support among the Indian masses?

---

## Civilization

READER: Now you will have to explain what you mean by civilization. . . .

EDITOR: Let us first consider what state of things is described by the word "civilization." Its true test lies in the fact that people living in it make bodily welfare the object of life. We will take some examples: The people of Europe today live in better-built houses than they did a hundred years ago. This is considered an emblem of civilization, and this is also a matter to promote bodily happiness. Formerly, they wore skins, and used as their weapons spears. Now, they wear long trousers, and for embellishing their bodies they wear a variety of clothing, and, instead of spears, they carry with them revolvers containing five or more chambers. If people of a certain country, who have hitherto not been in the habit of wearing much clothing, boots, etc., adopt European clothing, they are supposed to have become civilized out of savagery. Formerly, in Europe, people plowed their lands mainly by manual labor. Now, one man can plow a vast tract by means of steam-engines, and can thus amass great wealth. This is called a sign of civilization. Formerly, the fewest

men wrote books that were highly valuable. Now, anybody writes and prints anything he likes and poisons people's minds. Formerly, men traveled in wagons; now they fly through the air, in trains at the rate of four hundred and more miles per day. This is considered the height of civilization. It has been stated that, as men progress, they shall be able to travel in airships and reach any part of the world in a few hours. Men will not need the use of their hands and feet. They will press a button, and they will have their clothing by their side. They will press another button, and they will have their newspaper. A third, and a motor-car will be in waiting for them. . . . Everything will be done by machinery. Formerly, when people wanted to fight with one another, they measured between them their bodily strength; now it is possible to take away thousands of lives by one man working behind a gun from a hill. This is civilization. Formerly, men worked in the open air only so much as they liked. Now, thousands of workmen meet together . . . for the sake of maintenance work in factories or mines. Their condition is worse than that of beasts. They are obliged to work, at the risk of their lives, at most dangerous occupations, for the sake of millionaires. Formerly, men were

---

*Source:* Mohandas Gandhi, *Indian Home Rule* (Madras, India: Ganesh & Co., 1922), pp. 30–35, 47–50, 63, 64, 85, 68, 90, 91.

made slaves under physical compulsion, now they are enslaved by temptation of money and of the luxuries that money can buy. . . . This is a test of civilization. Formerly, special messengers were required and much expense was incurred in order to send letters; today, anyone can abuse his fellow by means of a letter for one penny. True, at the same cost, one can send one's thanks also. Formerly, people had two or three meals consisting of homemade bread and vegetables; now, they require something to eat every two hours, so that they have hardly leisure for anything else. What more need I say? All this you can ascertain from several authoritative books. These are all true tests of civilization. . . .

This civilization is irreligion, and it has taken such a hold on the people in Europe that those who are in it appear to be half mad. They lack real physical strength or courage. They keep up their energy by intoxication. They can hardly be happy in solitude. Women, who should be the queens of households, wander in the streets, or they slave away in factories. For the sake of a pittance, half a million women in England alone are laboring under trying circumstances in factories or similar institutions. . . .

This civilization is such that one has only to be patient and it will be self-destroyed.

## The Hindus and the Muslims

**READER:** But I am impatient to hear your answer to my question. Has the introduction of Islam not unmade the nation?

**EDITOR:** India cannot cease to be one nation because people belonging to different religions live in it. The introduction of foreigners does not necessarily destroy the nation, they merge in it. A country is one nation only when such a condition obtains in it. That country must have a faculty for

assimilation. India has ever been such a country. In reality, there are as many religions as there are individuals, but those who are conscious of the spirit of nationality do not interfere with one another's religion. If they do, they are not fit to be considered a nation. If the Hindus believe that India should be peopled only by Hindus, they are living in dreamland. The Hindus, the Muslims, the Parsees[1] and the Christians who have made India their country are fellow-countrymen, and they will have to live in unity if only for their own interest. In no part of the world are one nationality and one religion synonymous terms; nor has it ever been so in India.

**READER:** But what about the inborn enmity between Hindus and Muslims?

**EDITOR:** That phrase has been invented by our mutual enemy [the British]. When the Hindus and Muslims fought against one another, they certainly spoke in that strain. They have long since ceased to fight. How, then, can there be any inborn enmity? Pray remember this too, that we did not cease to fight only after British occupation. The Hindus flourished under Muslim sovereigns and Muslims under the Hindu. Each party recognized that mutual fighting was suicidal, and that neither party would abandon its religion by force of arms. Both parties, therefore, decided to live in peace. With the English advent the quarrels recommenced. . . .

Hindus and Muslims own the same ancestors, and the same blood runs through their veins. Do people become enemies because they change their religion? Is the God of the Muslim different from the God of the Hindu? Religions are different roads converging to the same point. What does it matter that we take different roads, so long as we reach the same goal? Wherein is the cause for quarreling?

---

[1] Followers of the Zoroastrian religion who fled to India when Islamic armies conquered Persia in the seventh century C.E.

## What Is True Civilization?

READER: You have denounced railways, lawyers and doctors. I can see that you will discard all machinery. What, then, is civilization?

EDITOR: . . . I believe that the civilization India has evolved is not to be beaten in the world. Nothing can equal the seeds sown by our ancestors. Rome went, Greece shared the same fate, the might of the Pharaohs was broken, Japan has become westernized, of China nothing can be said, but India is still, somehow or other, sound at the foundation. The people of Europe learn their lessons from the writings of the men of Greece or Rome, which exist no longer in their former glory. In trying to learn from them, the Europeans imagine that they will avoid the mistakes of Greece and Rome. Such is their pitiable condition. In the midst of all this, India remains immovable, and that is her glory. It is a charge against India that her people are so uncivilized, ignorant, and stolid, that it is not possible to induce them to adopt any changes. It is a charge really against our merit. What we have tested and found true on the anvil of experience, we dare not change. Many thrust their advice upon India, and she remains steady. This is her beauty; it is the sheet-anchor of our hope.

Civilization is that mode of conduct which points out to man the path of duty. Performance of duty and observance of morality are convertible terms. To observe morality is to attain mastery over our mind and our passions. So doing, we know ourselves. The Gujarati[2] equivalent for civilization means "good conduct." If this definition be correct, then India, as so many writers have shown, has nothing to learn from anybody else, and this is as it should be.

## Passive Resistance

READER: Is there any historical evidence as to the success of what you have called soul-force or truth-force? No instance seems to have happened of any nation having risen through soul-force. I still think that the evil-doers will not cease doing evil without physical punishment.

EDITOR: . . . The force of love is the same as the force of the soul or truth. We have evidence of its working at every step. The universe would disappear without the existence of that force. But you ask for historical evidence. It is, therefore, necessary to know what history means. . . .

The fact that there are so many men still alive in the world shows that it is based not on the force of arms but on the force of truth or love. Therefore the greatest and most unimpeachable evidence of the success of this force is to be found in the fact that, in spite of the wars of the world, it still lives on.

Thousands, indeed, tens of thousands, depend for their existence on a very active working of this force. Little quarrels of millions of families in their daily lives disappear before the exercise of this force. Hundreds of nations live in peace. History does not and cannot take note of this fact. History is really a record of every interruption of the even working of the force of love or of the soul. . . . Soul-force, being natural, is not noted in history.

READER: According to what you say, it is plain that instances of the kind of passive resistance are not to be found in history. It is necessary to understand this passive resistance more fully. It will be better, therefore, if you enlarge upon it.

EDITOR: Passive resistance is a method of securing rights by personal suffering; it is the reverse of resistance by arms. When I refuse to do a thing that is repugnant to my conscience, I use soul-force. For instance, the government of the day has passed a law which is applicable to me: I do not like it; if, by using violence, I force the government to repeal the law, I am employing what may be termed body-force. If I do not obey the law and accept the penalty for its breach, I use soul-force. It involves sacrifice of self.

[2]An Indian dialect spoken in northwest India.

Everybody admits that sacrifice of self is infinitely superior to sacrifice of others. Moreover, if this kind of force is used in a cause that is unjust, only the person using it suffers. He does not make others suffer for his mistakes. Men have before now done many things which were subsequently found to have been wrong. No man can claim to be absolutely in the right, or that a particular thing is wrong, because he thinks so, but it is wrong for him so long as that is his deliberate judgment. It is, therefore, meet [proper] that he should not do that which he knows to be wrong, and suffer the consequence whatever it may be. This is the key to the use of soul-force. . . .

**READER:** From what you say, I deduce that passive resistance is a splendid weapon of the weak but that, when they are strong, they may take up arms.

**EDITOR:** This is gross ignorance. Passive resistance, that is, soul-force, is matchless. It is superior to the force of arms. How, then, can it be considered only a weapon of the weak? Physical-force men are strangers to the courage that is requisite in a passive resister. Do you believe that a coward can ever disobey a law that he dislikes? Extremists are considered to be advocates of brute-force. Why do they, then, talk about obeying laws? I do not blame them. They can say

nothing else. When they succeed in driving out the English, and they themselves become governors, they will want you and me to obey their laws. And that is a fitting thing for their constitution. But a passive resister will say he will not obey a law that is against his conscience, even though he may be blown to pieces at the mouth of a cannon.

What do you think? Wherein is courage required—in blowing others to pieces from behind a cannon or with a smiling face to approach a cannon and to be blown to pieces? Who is the true warrior—he who keeps death always as a bosom-friend or he who controls the death of others? Believe me that a man devoid of courage and manhood can never be a passive resister.

This, however, I will admit: that even a man, weak in body, is capable of offering this resistance. One man can offer it just as well as millions. Both men and women can indulge in it. It does not require the training of an army; it needs no Jiu-jitsu. Control over the mind is alone necessary, and, when that is attained, man is free like the king of the forest, and his very glance withers the enemy.

Passive resistance is an all-sided sword; it can be used anyhow; it blesses him who uses it and him against whom it is used. Without drawing a drop of blood, it produces far-reaching results.

# Nationalism and Revolution in Vietnam

## 88 • HO CHI MINH, APPEAL MADE ON THE OCCASION OF THE FOUNDING OF THE INDOCHINESE COMMUNIST PARTY (1930) AND LETTER FROM ABROAD (1941)

Born in 1890, Ho Chi Minh was tutored by his father and local teachers and briefly studied French, history, geography, and science at a prestigious academy in Hué. In 1911, however, at age twenty-one he took a low-level job on a French ocean liner sailing for Europe. This began a thirty-year period of continual movement and exile in which, however, he never lost his commitment to the cause of social revolution and independence for Vietnam. Toward the end of World War I he moved to Paris, where he gained a measure of fame when he petitioned the negotiators at the Paris

Peace Conference to accept a plan for Vietnamese independence. In 1920, he was one of the founders of the French Communist Party. In 1923, he made his first trip to the Soviet Union, where he was trained as an agent to advance the cause of communism in Indochina.

Using forged passports, disguises, and numerous aliases, from 1924 to 1941 Ho divided his time between the Soviet Union and China, with side trips to Italy, Switzerland, Germany, India, and Thailand. During these years, his main accomplishment was the founding of the two most important organizations in the Vietnamese independence movement: the Indochinese Communist Party (ICP) and the League for the Independence of Vietnam (Viet Minh). The ICP, founded in 1930 at a meeting of several Vietnamese Marxist groups in Hong Kong, organized strikes and peasant disturbances in the 1930s and managed to expand its organization in the face of French persecution. The Viet Minh, founded in 1941, brought together the ICP and other noncommunist nationalist organizations. During World War II it carried on an armed struggle against the Japanese, who occupied Vietnam with the acquiescence of the puppet French government installed by the Nazis in 1940. With the surrender of Japan, Ho Chi Minh, with his forces in control of northern Vietnam, proclaimed Vietnamese independence on September 2, 1945.

As president of the Democratic Republic of Vietnam, beginning in 1946 he led his country in a hard-fought war against the French, who sought to reclaim their colony. After eight years of fighting, in 1954 the country was divided into a communist north and a noncommunist south. Then as leader of North Vietnam, he oversaw the war against South Vietnam and its American allies until poor health forced him to the sidelines in 1965. Six years after his death in 1969, his dream of an independent, unified Vietnam was achieved when on April 30, 1975, the Vietnamese People's Army took Saigon, South Vietnam's capital, and in 1976 renamed it Ho Chi Minh City.

The following documents, the first composed in 1930 and the second in 1941, were published and distributed in Vietnam to encourage support for the ICP in one case and the Viet Minh in the other. Both documents show a visceral hatred of the French, but their rhetoric and rationale for resisting the foreign occupier are quite different.

## QUESTIONS FOR ANALYSIS

1. Both documents are addressed to specific groups of people. How does the composition of the two groups differ, and in what ways may these differences be significant?
2. How, according to the appeal of 1930, did World War I affect France and the world in general?
3. In 1930 Ho refers to the possibility of World War II. What does he think will be the issue in this war?
4. Why is Ho confident of victory for the Vietnamese revolutionaries despite French persecution?
5. Why according to Ho has the "moment come" for Vietnamese liberation in 1941?

## Appeal Made on the Occasion of the Founding of the Indochinese Communist Party (February 18, 1930)

*Workers, peasants, soldiers, youth and school students! Oppressed and exploited fellow-countrymen! Sisters and brothers! Comrades!*

Imperialist contradictions were the cause of the 1914-1918 World War. After this horrible slaughter, the world was divided into two camps: one is the revolutionary camp which includes the oppressed colonial peoples and the exploited working class throughout the world. Its vanguard is the Soviet Union. The other is the counter-revolutionary camp of international capitalism and imperialism, whose general staff is the League of Nations.[1]

That war resulted in untold loss of life and property for the peoples. French imperialism was the hardest hit. Therefore, in order to restore the forces of capitalism in France, the French imperialists have resorted to every perfidious scheme to intensify capitalist exploitation in Indochina. They have built new factories to exploit the workers by paying them starvation wages. They have plundered the peasants' land to establish plantations and drive them to destitution. They have levied new heavy taxes. They have forced our people to buy government bonds. In short, they have driven our people to utter misery. They have increased their military forces, firstly to strangle the Vietnamese revolution; secondly to prepare for a new imperialist war in the Pacific aimed at conquering new colonies: thirdly to suppress the Chinese revolution;[2] and fourthly to attack the Soviet Union because she helps the oppressed nations and the exploited working class to wage revolution. World War Two will break out. When it does the French imperialists will certainly drive our people to an even more horrible slaughter. . . .

However, the French imperialists' barbarous oppression and ruthless exploitation have awakened our compatriots, who have all realized that revolution is the only road to survival and that without it they will die a slow death. . . . Everywhere the masses have risen to oppose the French imperialists.

. . . If the French imperialists think that they can suppress the Vietnamese revolution by means of terror, they are grossly mistaken. For one thing, the Vietnamese revolution is not isolated but enjoys the assistance of the world proletariat in general and that of the French working class in particular. Secondly, it is precisely at the very time when the French imperialists are frantically carrying out terrorist acts that the Vietnamese Communists, formerly working separately, have united into a single party, the Indochinese Communist Party, to lead the revolutionary struggle of our entire people.

*Workers, peasants, soldiers, youth, school students! Oppressed and exploited fellow-countrymen!*

The Indochinese Communist Party has been founded. . . . It will help the proletariat lead the revolution waged for the sake of all oppressed and exploited people. From now on we must join the Party, help it and follow it in order to implement the following slogans:

1. To overthrow French imperialism and Vietnamese feudalism and reactionary bourgeoisie;

---

Source: (Appeal): Ho Chi Minh, *Down With Colonialism!*, ed. Walden Bello (London/New York: Verso, 2007), pp. 51–54. (Letter from Abroad): Ho Chi Minh, *Selected Articles and Speeches*, ed. Jack Woddis (New York: International Publishers, 1969), pp. 29–32.
[1]Founded at the Paris Peace Conference, the League of Nations was an international organization whose primary goals were the prevention of war through collective security, arms limitation, and the settling of international disputes through negotiation and arbitration. It also administered the mandate system, in which Germany's former colonies and Arab regions of the defunct Ottoman Empire were given over to France, Great Britain, South Africa, Belgium, New Zealand, and Australia until they were ready for self-rule.

[2]It is unclear what French "imperialist war in the Pacific" Ho is thinking of. By 1930, most Pacific islands had already been colonized. In China in 1930 local warlords, the Nationalist Party, and the Communist Party were involved in a three-way struggle for control of the country.

2. To make Indochina completely independent;

3. To establish a worker-peasant-soldier government;

4. To confiscate the banks and other enterprises belonging to the imperialists and put them under the control of the worker-peasant-soldier government;

5. To confiscate all the plantations and property belonging to the imperialists and the Vietnamese reactionary bourgeoisie and distribute them to the poor peasants.

6. To implement the 8-hour working day;

7. To abolish the forced buying of government bonds, the poll-tax and all unjust taxes hitting the poor;

8. To bring democratic freedoms to the masses;

9. To dispense education to all the people;

10. To realize equality between man and woman.

## Letter from Abroad (June 6, 1941)

*Venerable elders!*
*Patriotic personalities!*
*Intellectuals, peasants, workers, traders and soldiers!*
*Dear fellow-countrymen!*

Since France was defeated by Germany, its power has completely collapsed. Nevertheless, with regard to our people, the French rulers have become even more ruthless in carrying out their policy of exploitation, repression and massacre. . . . In the foreign field, bowing their heads and bending their knees, they resign themselves to ceding part of our land to Siam [Thailand] and shamelessly surrendering our country to Japan.[3] As a result our people are writhing under a double yoke of oppression. They serve not only as beasts of burden to the French bandits but also as slaves to the Japanese robbers. . . . Plunged into such tragic suffering, are we to await death with folded arms?

No! Certainly not! The twenty-odd million descendants of the Lac and the Hong[4] are resolved not to let themselves be kept in servitude. For nearly eighty years under the French pirates' iron heels we have unceasingly and selflessly struggled for national independence and freedom. The heroism of our predecessors, and the glorious feats of the insurgents of the provinces will live forever in our memory. The recent uprisings in the South . . . testify to the determination of our compatriots to follow the glorious example of their ancestors and to annihilate the enemy. . . .

Now, the opportunity has come for our liberation. France itself is unable to help the French colonialists rule over our country. As for the Japanese, on the one hand, bogged down in China, on the other, hampered by the British and American forces,[5] they certainly cannot use all their strength against us. If our entire people are solidly united we can certainly get the better of the best-trained armies of the French and the Japanese. . . .

A few hundred years ago, in the reign of the Tran, when our country faced the great danger of invasion by Yuan armies the elders ardently called on their sons and daughters throughout the country to stand up as one to kill the enemy.[6] Finally they saved their people and their glorious memory will live forever. Let our elders and patriotic personalities follow the illustrious example set by our forefathers.

---

[3]In October 1940, Thailand, sensing French weakness after their defeat by Germany, went to war with France to regain a number of disputed territories. After the Japanese invaded Indochina in September 1940, French officials permitted the Japanese to establish military bases in Vietnam.

[4]Lac is the name for the people of ancient Vietnam; Hung is the name of Vietnam's first dynasty, which ruled from c. 3000 to 258 B.C.E.

[5]In June 1941 Great Britain still controlled Malaya, Singapore, and Hong Kong; the United States had a military presence in the Philippines and maintained a formidable Pacific fleet. Britain and the United States did not declare war on Japan until December 1941.

[6]The Tran dynasty ruled Vietnam from 1225 to 1400. Prince Tran Hung Dao (1228–1300) commanded armies that repelled no less than three Chinese invasions during the era of Mongol Yuan Dynasty (1271–1368).

Notables, soldiers, workers, peasants, traders, civil servants, youth and women who warmly love your country! Let us unite and overthrow the Japanese, the French and their lackeys in order to save our people from their present dire straits.

*Dear fellow-countrymen!*

National salvation is the common cause of our entire people. Every Vietnamese must take part in it. He who has money will contribute his money, he who has strength will contribute his strength, he who has talent will contribute his talent. For my part I pledge to follow in your steps and devote all my modest abilities to the service of the country and am ready for the supreme sacrifice.

*Revolutionary fighters!*

The hour has struck! Raise aloft the banner of insurrection and lead the people throughout the country to overthrow the Japanese and the French! The sacred call of the Fatherland is resounding in our ears; the ardent blood of our heroic predecessors is seething in our hearts! The fighting spirit of the people is mounting before our eyes! . . .

The Vietnamese revolution will certainly triumph! The world revolution will certainly triumph!

# Latin America in an Era of Economic Challenge and Political Change

A popular slogan among Latin America's politicians, business leaders, and landowners in the late nineteenth century was "order and progress," and to an extent exceptional in the region's history, they achieved both. Around 1870, Latin America's economy entered a period of export-driven expansion that lasted until the 1920s. The region became a major supplier of wheat, beef, mutton, coffee, raw rubber, nitrates, copper, tin, bananas, and a host of other primary products to Europe and the United States and a major market for European and U.S. manufactured goods. Land prices soared, and English and U.S. capital flowed into Latin America as investments and loans.

Latin America's boom took place in a climate of relative political stability. In Argentina, Chile, and Brazil, this meant republican governments controlled by an oligarchy of landowning families, sometimes in alliance with wealthy businessmen; in Mexico, Peru, Ecuador, and Venezuela, it meant rule by a dictator (*caudillo*), who also usually represented the interests of landowners and businessmen. Oligarchs and dictators alike sought economic growth by maintaining law and order, approving land confiscations from the Church and peasantry, and keeping foreign business interests happy by maintaining low taxes and tariffs.

Latin America in these years is often viewed as an example of *neocolonialism*. Although nations in the region all had achieved political independence in the early 1800s, economic relationships reminiscent of the colonial era persisted. Latin America still depended on Europe and the United States as the markets for their exports of primary products, and depended on those same regions for manufactured goods and capital. The system's beneficiaries were the landowning elite, European and U.S. bondholders, and foreign businesses with investments in construction, railroads, shipping, and mining. Dependency on foreign markets, capital, and manufactured goods made Latin American governments vulnerable to diplomatic arm-twisting by their powerful economic "partners," and in some instances, military intervention.

By the 1930s, the neocolonial economy and the political order it supported both were in shambles as a result of the Great Depression. Demand for Latin America's exports plummeted, driving millions into unemployment and depriving the region of the foreign exchange needed to buy foreign manufactured goods. Foreign loans and investments dried up after the international banking system and stock markets collapsed. Governments faced insolvency, and capital shortages crippled plans to end the economic slump through industrialization. Latin Americans increasingly resented European and especially U.S. ownership of mines, oil fields, railroads, banks, processing plants, and prime agricultural land. Once welcomed as a means of attracting capital and encouraging growth, foreign ownership now was condemned as imperialist plunder.

# Economic Dependency and Its Dangers

## 89 • FRANCISCO GARCÍA CALDERÓN, LATIN AMERICA: ITS RISE AND PROGRESS

For most of the nineteenth century, the United States had relatively little involvement in Latin America. U.S. interests focused almost exclusively on Mexico, whose territories in present-day Texas, California, Nevada, Utah, New Mexico, most of Arizona and Colorado, and parts of Oklahoma, Kansas, and Wyoming became part of the United States after the Mexican War of 1846–1848. U.S. schemes to annex Cuba, Nicaragua, and the Mexican provinces of Yucatán and Lower California proved impractical or failed to generate support.

U.S.–Latin American relations changed beginning in the 1880s, however. As the United States industrialized, it gradually replaced Great Britain as the region's main purchaser of exports and supplier of manufactured goods. As U.S. businesses expanded their operations in Latin America, successive administrations in Washington pledged to protect their interests. In 1905, President Theodore Roosevelt announced that the United States reserved the right to intervene in the internal affairs of any state in the Western Hemisphere that was guilty of "chronic wrongdoing," a euphemism for failure to pay its debts or maintain law and order. Roosevelt's successor, William Howard Taft, was even more explicit. He stated that his foreign policy would include "active intervention to secure our merchandise and our capitalists' opportunity for profitable investment." These were not idle words. Between 1898 and 1934, the United States annexed Puerto Rico and intervened militarily in Cuba, Mexico, Guatemala, Honduras, Nicaragua, Panama, Colombia, and the Dominican Republic.

Denunciations of "Yankee imperialism" became commonplace during the Great Depression, but such criticisms had begun earlier. One of the first such critics was the Peruvian diplomat and author Francisco García Calderón. Born into a wealthy and politically prominent family in 1883, García Calderón entered the Peruvian foreign service soon after graduating from the University of San Marcos. A career diplomat with postings to London, Paris, Brussels, and Lisbon, he wrote numerous essays and books on Latin America. His most widely read publication was *Latin America: Its Rise and Progress,* which ranged over the region's history and discussed a number of contemporary social and political issues. First published in 1912, it attracted a wide readership only in the 1920s, when it went through numerous editions in several languages.

## QUESTIONS FOR ANALYSIS

1. According to García Calderón, how has U.S. foreign policy toward Latin America evolved since the time of the Monroe Doctrine?
2. How does he explain these changes?
3. According to García Calderón, what benefits have accrued to Latin America as a result of foreign investments? How has Latin America been hurt by such investments?
4. How does García Calderón characterize Latin Americans, and how do they differ from the "Anglo-Saxons" of the United States?
5. How have the Latin American states contributed to their own economic problems?
6. If one accepts the premises of García Calderón's arguments, what would the Latin American states have had to do to overcome the problems connected with foreign economic dependency?

The nation [the United States] which was peopled by nine millions of men in 1820 now numbers eighty millions—an immense demographic power; in the space of ten years, from 1890 to 1900, this population increased by one-fifth. By virtue of its iron, wheat, oil, and cotton, and its victorious industrialism, the democracy aspires to a world-wide significance. . . . Yankee pride increases with the endless multiplication of wealth and population, and the patriotic sentiment has reached such intensity that it has become transformed into imperialism. . . .

Interventions have become more frequent with the expansion of frontiers. The United States have recently intervened in the territory of Acre [in western Brazil], there to found a republic of rubber gatherers; at Panama, there to develop a province and construct a canal; in Cuba, to maintain order in the interior; in San Domingo, to support the civilizing revolution and overthrow the tyrants; in Venezuela, and in Central America, to enforce upon these nations the political and financial tutelage of imperial democracy. In Guatemala and Honduras the loans concluded with the monarchs of North American finance have reduced the people to a new slavery. Supervision of the customs and the dispatch of pacificatory [peace-keeping] squadrons to defend the interests of the Anglo-Saxon[1] have

*Source:* From Francisco García Calderón, *Latin America: Its Rise and Progress,* Bernard Miall, trans. (Charles Scribner's Sons and T. Fisher Unwin, Ltd., 1913), pp. 298, 301–303, 306, 311, 378–382.

[1]A loosely used term, "Anglo-Saxon" usually refers to people of English descent.

enforced peace and tranquility: such are the means employed. . . . Mr. Pierpont Morgan[2] proposes to encompass the finances of Latin America by a vast network of Yankee banks. Chicago merchants and Wall Street financiers created the Meat Trust in the Argentine. It has even been announced that a North American syndicate wished to buy enormous belts of land in Guatemala. . . . The fortification of the Panama Canal and the possible acquisition of the Galapagos Islands in the Pacific, are fresh manifestations of imperialistic progress.

• • •

Unexploited wealth abounds in [Latin] America. Forests of rubber . . . , mines of gold and diamonds, rivers which flow over beds of auriferous [gold-bearing] sand, . . . coffee, cocoa, and wheat, whose abundance is such that these products are enough to glut the markets of the world. But there is no national capital [for investment]. This contrast between the wealth of the soil and the poverty of the States gives rise to serious economic problems. . . .

Since the very beginnings of independence the Latin democracies, lacking financial reserves, have had need of European gold. . . . The necessities of the war [of independence] with Spain and the always difficult task of building up a new society demanded the assistance of foreign gold; loans accumulated. The lamentable history of these bankrupt democracies dates from this period.

For geographical reasons, and on account of its very inferiority, South America cannot dispense with the influence of the Anglo-Saxon North, with its exuberant wealth and its industries. South America has need of capital, of enterprising men, of bold explorers, and these the United States supply in abundance. The defense of the South should consist in avoiding the establishment of privileges or monopolies, whether in favor of North Americans or Europeans.

• • •

The descendants of the Spanish conquerors, who knew nothing of labor or thrift, have incessantly resorted to fresh loans in order to fill the gaps in their budgets. Politicians knew of only one solution of the economic disorder—to borrow, so that little by little the Latin-American countries became actually the financial colonies of Europe.

Economic dependence has a necessary corollary—political servitude. French intervention in Mexico[3] was originally caused by the mass of unsatisfied financial claims; foreigners, the creditors of the State, were in favor of intervention. England and France, who began by seeking to ensure the recovery of certain debts, finally forced a monarch upon the debtor nation. The United States entertained the ambition of becoming the sole creditor of the [Latin] American peoples: this remarkable privilege would have assured them of an incontestable hegemony over the whole continent.

The budgets of various States complicate still further an already difficult situation. They increase beyond all measure, without the slightest relation to the progress made by the nation. They are based upon taxes which are one of the causes of the national impoverishment, or upon a protectionist tariff which adds greatly to the cost of life. The politicians, thinking chiefly of appearances, neglect the development of the national resources for the immediate augmentation of the fiscal revenues;

---

[2]John Pierpont Morgan (1837–1913), founder of the investment bank J. P. Morgan and Company, was one of the wealthiest and most powerful financiers in the United States.

[3]In 1861, Spain, Great Britain, and France sent troops to Mexico to force the government to pay its debts. After gaining assurances of future payments, Spain and Great Britain withdrew their troops, but Emperor Napoleon III of France went forward with a plan to establish a new Mexican government under French protection. The French-sponsored candidate for emperor of Mexico was Archduke Ferdinand Maximilian of Hapsburg, brother of Austrian emperor Franz Josef. Maximilian served as emperor from 1863 to 1865, when the threat of U.S. intervention convinced Napoleon III to abandon his Mexican project.

thanks to fresh taxes, the budgets increase. These resources are not employed in furthering profitable undertakings, such as building railroads or highways, or increasing the navigability of the rivers. The bureaucracy is increased in a like proportion, and the budgets, swelled in order to dupe the outside world, serve only to support a nest of parasites. In the economic life of these countries the State is a kind of beneficent providence which . . . increases the common poverty by taxation, display, useless enterprises, the upkeep of military and civil officials, and the waste of money borrowed abroad. . . .

To sum up, the new continent, politically free, is economically a vassal. This dependence is inevitable; without European capital there would have been no railways, no ports, and no stable government in [Latin] America. But the disorder which prevails in the finances of the country changes into a real servitude what might otherwise have been a beneficial relation.

# Mexican Muralists and Their Vision

## 90 • JOSÉ CLEMENTE OROZCO, HISPANO-AMERICA—THE REBEL AND HIS INTERNATIONAL ENEMIES, AND DIEGO RIVERA, THE ARRIVAL OF CORTÉS AT VERACRUZ

In 1921 the Mexican government announced a program to promote Mexican national pride by encouraging Mexico's composers, choreographers, writers, and artists to explore Mexico's past, including its Indian past, in their works. In the 1920s many muralists took advantage of the offer to make available the walls of public buildings for their work. Among them the two most prominent were José Clemente Orozco and Diego Rivera, whose paintings of the historical experiences of Mexicans and other Latin American peoples brought them international fame.

José Clemente Orozco (1883–1949) hoped to become an architect, but at age twenty-six began training as a painter in the Mexican Academy of Fine Arts. As a Marxist and supporter of the Mexican Revolution, he introduced themes and topics dealing with the struggles of Mexico's Indian and mestizo (Spanish-Indian) populations. After achieving modest fame in Mexico, between 1927 and 1932 he lived in the United States, where he accepted commissions from Pomona College in California, the New School for Social Research in New York City, and Dartmouth College in New Hampshire. His work at Dartmouth, titled *The Epic of American Civilization*, in twenty-four scenes traces the history of the Americas from the arrival of the Aztecs in central Mexico to the modern industrial age. The section we show here, named *Hispano-America—The Rebel and His International Enemies,* shows an armed peasant standing amidst crumbling churches, an abandoned factory, politicians, soldiers, and capitalists. It is thought that the military figure on the right is General John J. Pershing, who in 1916–1917 led U.S. forces into Mexico against the paramilitary forces of Francisco "Pancho" Villa, who had attacked the town of Columbus, New Mexico, early in 1916. The masked figure behind him is thought to be President Woodrow Wilson, who ordered the attack.

Diego Rivera (1886–1957) came from a well-off family and spent ten years traveling and studying in Europe before returning to Mexico in 1920. Like Orozco, he joined the Communist party, became involved in the government-sponsored mural program of the 1920s, and accepted a number of commissions in the United States in the 1930s and 1940s. Among his best known works were the frescoes he painted for the interior walls of the National Palace of Mexico in Mexico City. The project was undertaken in 1929–1930, continued in 1935, and was not completed until after World War II, when Rivera agreed to paint a series of thirty-one frescoes for the second-floor lobby. They were to depict Mexican history from the pre-Hispanic period to 1917, the year in which seven years of revolutionary struggle culminated in the adoption of a new, progressive Mexican constitution. Ten of the eleven completed frescoes present an idealized vision pre-Hispanic culture that portrays the native people's achievements in agriculture, architecture, arts and crafts, and trade. The eleventh, *The Arrival of Hernán Cortés in Veracruz*, which is shown here, was anticipated to be the first of twenty panels dealing with post-conquest Mexican history.

The painting's title is somewhat misleading in that the painting's themes go well beyond the events of April 20, 1519, when Cortés and his men arrived at the site

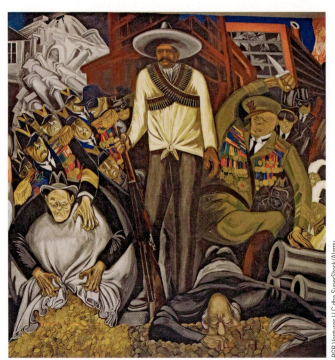

José Clemente Orozco, Hispano-America—The Rebel and His International Enemies

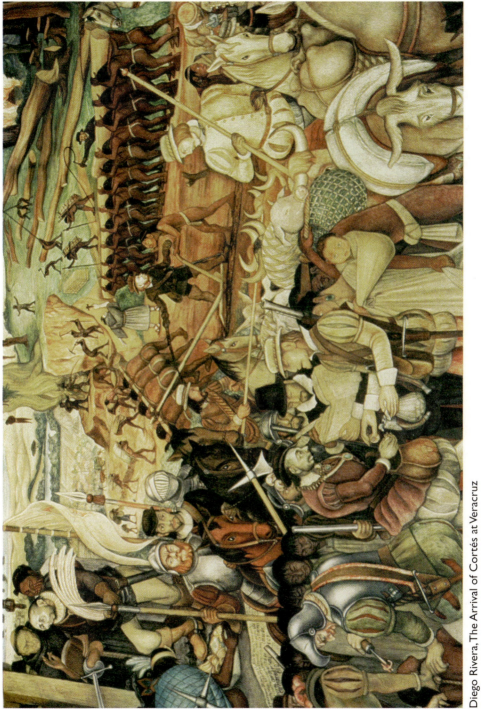

Diego Rivera, The Arrival of Cortés at Veracruz

Colonisation, 'The Great City of Tenochtitlan', detail from the mural, 'Pre-Hispanic and Colonial Mexico', north wall, 1945–52 (mural painting) (see also 136705 and 428081), Rivera, Diego (1886-1957)/Palacio Nacional, Mexico City, Mexico/Sean Sprague/Mexicolore/Bridgeman Images/© 2014 Banco de México Diego Rivera Frida Kahlo Museums Trust, Mexico, D.F./Artists Rights Society (ARS), New York

where they founded the first permanent Spanish settlement in Mexico, Rica Villa de la Vera Cruz ("Rich Town of the True Cross"). More broadly it is an indictment of the Spanish conquest and its dire consequences for the Mexican people. The two key figures in the painting are Cortés, who is depicted as an deformed, ashen-faced, almost goblin-like figure, and his second in command Pedro Alvarado, who is shown at the center of the painting exchanging gold coins with Cortés; he may also be the mounted figure herding animals in the right center and the figure in the lower left holding down the Indian slave as he is being branded. Notable details of the painting are the various forms of forced labor to which the Indians were subjected; a religious ceremony in the upper left corner, in which Cortés holds a sword over a kneeling Indian who is being converted the Christianity after laying down a plate filled with gold; the transaction at the center, where an official witnesses the document that founded the town of Veracruz, giving Cortés' lieutenants control of the town government, but simultaneously assigning to Cortés the title captain-general and the right to twenty percent of all spoils after the king's *quinto*—the "royal fifth"— had been deducted. The female to the right of Alvarado is sometimes identified as La Malinche, or Marina, the young slave girl who became Cortés' interpreter and mistress, but also may be Alvarado's native mistress. The baby she is carrying has stunning blue eyes, a noted feature of Alvarado.

## QUESTIONS FOR ANALYSIS

1. In Orozco's painting, what message is the painter communicating through the crumbling churches, the abandoned factories, the business owners, and the army officers?
2. What message does Orozco convey about the character and qualities of the central figure, the peasant?
3. What messages may Rivera be attempting to convey in the following details of his painting: the appearance of Cortés; the transaction at the painting's center; the branding scene in the lower left corner; the religious ceremony in the upper left corner?
4. In Rivera's painting what are the forms of labor exploitation to which the Indians are subjected? Why does Rivera depict a Catholic priest in the center of the slavery scenes?
5. To what degree do the paintings share common themes and messages?

# East Asia in an Era of Revolution and War

The histories of modern China and Japan began to radically diverge in the closing decades of the nineteenth century, when Japan transformed itself into a major economic and military power, while China, despite efforts of reformers, remained a feeble giant more than ever at the mercy of foreign powers. These foreign powers included Japan, which seized Taiwan and Korea, a Chinese client state, after the Sino-Japanese War of 1894–1895, was part of the coalition that suppressed the Boxer Rebellion in 1900–1901, and became the dominant power in the Chinese province of Manchuria after the Russo-Japanese War of 1905. These trends continued in the 1920s and 1930s.

Chinese revolutionaries who overthrew the Qing Dynasty in 1911 hoped that this break from the past, like Japan's Meiji Restoration, would be the first step toward their country's long-awaited revival. They were sorely disappointed. After General Yuan Shikai failed in his attempt to establish a new imperial dynasty in 1916, China was carved up by dozens of generally unscrupulous and irresponsible warlords—military strongmen whose local authority was based on their control of private armies. In the 1920s, warlord factions fought one another, and the energies of China's two major political parties—the Nationalist Party or Guomindang (GMD) and the Chinese Communist Party (CCP)—focused on reuniting the country by breaking the warlords' power. By 1931 most of the country had come under the nominal control of the Nationalists, whose leader Chiang Kai-shek (also known as Jiang Jieshi or Jiang Zhongzheng) ruled from Nanjing. By then, however, the alliance with the Communists had disintegrated, setting the stage for a GMD–CCP civil war that would continue until the Communists' victory in 1949.

In contrast to the turmoil and conflict in China, the 1910s and 1920s for Japan were decades of economic growth and democratic progress. During these years the political balance shifted away from the armed forces and bureaucracy to the political parties, whose power base was the elected Diet. This shift translated into gains for democracy, liberalism, and social reform; it also meant a foreign policy of international cooperation. In China, however, Japanese policy was shaped less by the Tokyo government than by two Japanese field armies: the China Garrison Army, established after the Boxer Rebellion to protect Japanese business interests in North China, and the larger Kwantung Army, established after the Russo-Japanese War to guard Japanese businesses in Manchuria. Convinced that Japan's economic future depended on gaining access to Chinese markets and raw materials and that extending Japanese military and political power in the region was needed to serve as a buffer against the Soviet Union, officers and agents of the two field armies used bribes, intimidation, subversion, and assassinations to keep China politically divided and pro-Japanese warlords in power.

In the 1930s, Japan's foreign policy became bolder and more reckless. With an economy already weakened by bank failures in 1927, disaster struck when the Great Depression hit the country in 1930. The economic crisis persuaded many Japanese, especially within the army, that the country's economic salvation lay in taking control of Manchuria and extending Japan's empire into Mongolia and northern China. They also believed that Japan needed to act quickly. Chinese nationalism, much of it directed against Japan, was growing; Chiang Kai-shek's reunification campaign was making progress; and the Manchurian warlord Zang Xueliang remained an implacable enemy of Japan. In 1931, taking matters into their own hands, officers in the Kwantung army arranged an explosion on the tracks of a Japanese-controlled railroad in Manchuria, and with the Tokyo government unable or unwilling to intervene, used this as an excuse to capture the region's important cities and establish the puppet state of Manchukuo in 1932. Six years after the Manchurian Incident, Japanese and Chinese troops clashed outside Beijing in early July 1937. It appeared at first to be no different from dozens of other Sino-Japanese flare-ups that had been quickly extinguished following negotiations and Chinese concessions. This time things turned out differently. Chiang Kai-shek, facing political pressure and public anger over his policy of nonresistance to Japanese aggression, refused to back down, and as a result, this minor skirmish escalated into a full-scale battle for Beijing and Tianjin. The Second Sino-Japanese War, the first act in World War II, had begun.

# The Maoist Version of Marxism

### 91 • MAO ZEDONG, REPORT ON AN INVESTIGATION OF THE PEASANT MOVEMENT IN HUNAN AND STRATEGIC PROBLEMS OF CHINA'S REVOLUTIONARY WAR

Mao Zedong, born into a well-to-do peasant family in Hunan province in 1893, as a university student participated in the anti-Qing revolution of 1911. During the next several years, while serving as a library assistant at Beijing University, he embraced Marxism and helped organize the CCP in 1921. During the 1920s he developed his unique Chinese variant of Marxism, one based on the premise that peasants, not the urban proletariat, would lead China to socialism.

After the break between the CCP and the GMD in 1927, Mao helped found the Red Army and played an important leadership role in the Chinese Soviet Republic, founded in 1931 in a remote and hilly region on the Hunan–Jiangxi border. In 1934, Chiang Kai-shek's troops surrounded the Communists' enclave, but as they moved in for the kill, more than one hundred thousand Communist troops and officials broke their encirclement and embarked on the Long March. This legendary trek lasted more than a year and covered six thousand miles before a remnant found safety in the mountains around Yan'an in northern Shaanxi province. Here Mao, now the party's leader, rebuilt his army and readied his followers for what would be fourteen more years of struggle against the Japanese and the GMD.

The following excerpts are drawn from two of Mao's most important writings. His "Report on an Investigation of the Peasant Movement in Hunan" was written in 1927 after he visited Hunan province to study peasant associations, groups of peasants who with the help of Communist organizers had seized land, humiliated or killed landlords, and taken control of their communities. In his report, Mao seeks to convince party members that the peasants can be the main source of revolution in China. His "Strategic Problems of China's Revolutionary War" is based on lectures he delivered at the Red Army College in late 1936. In it, Mao assesses China's military situation and outlines his strategy for victory over the GMD.

## QUESTIONS FOR ANALYSIS

1. What developments in Hunan reinforced Mao's convictions about the peasantry as a revolutionary force?
2. What criticisms have been made of the Hunan peasant movement, and how does Mao counter these criticisms?
3. What can be learned from these writings about Mao's views of the role of the Communist Party in China's revolutionary struggle?
4. According to Mao, what have been the sources of oppression of the Chinese people? Once these sources of oppression are removed, what will China be like?
5. According to Mao, what are the four unique characteristics of China's revolutionary war, and how do they affect his military strategy?
6. What are the characteristics of Mao's "active defense" as opposed to "passive defense"?
7. How do Mao's ideas about revolution resemble and differ from those of Marx?

## Report on an Investigation of the Peasant Movement in Hunan [1927]

. . . All the wrong measures taken by the revolutionary authorities concerning the peasant movement must be speedily changed. Only thus can the future of the revolution be benefited. For the present upsurge of the peasant movement is a colossal event. In a very short time, . . . several hundred million peasants will rise like a mighty storm, like a hurricane, a force so swift and violent that no power, however great, will be able to hold it back. They will smash all the trammels [shackles] that bind them and rush forward along the road to liberation. They will sweep all the imperialists, warlords, corrupt officials, local tyrants and evil gentry into their graves. Every revolutionary party and every revolutionary comrade will be put to the test, to be accepted or rejected as they decide. There are three alternatives. To march at their head and lead them? To trail behind them, gesticulating and criticizing? Or to stand in their way and oppose them? Every Chinese is free to choose, but events will force you to make the choice quickly. . . .

"Yes, peasant associations are necessary, but they are going rather too far." This is the opinion of the middle-of-the-roaders. But what is the actual situation? True, the peasants are in a sense "unruly." . . . Supreme in authority, the peasant association allows the landlord no say and sweeps away his prestige. This amounts to striking the landlord down to the dust and keeping him there. People swarm into the houses of local tyrants and evil gentry who are against the peasant association, slaughter their pigs and consume their grain. They even loll for a minute or two on the ivory-inlaid beds belonging to the young ladies in the households of the local tyrants and evil gentry. At the slightest provocation they make arrests, crown the arrested with tall paper-hats, and parade them through the villages, saying, "You dirty landlords, now you know who we are!" . . . This is what some people call "going too far." . . . Such talk may seem plausible, but in fact it is wrong. First, the local tyrants, evil gentry and lawless landlords have themselves driven the peasants to this. For ages they have used their power to tyrannize over the peasants and trample them underfoot; that is why the peasants have reacted so strongly. . . . Secondly, a revolution is not a dinner party, or writing an essay, or painting a picture, or doing embroidery; it cannot be so

*Source*: Mao Zedong, *Selected Works* (New York: International Publishers, 1954). Reprinted by permission.

refined, so leisurely and gentle, so temperate, kind, courteous, restrained and magnanimous. A revolution is an insurrection, an act of violence by which one class overthrows another. A rural revolution is a revolution by which the peasantry overthrows the power of the feudal landlord class. Without using the greatest force, the peasants cannot possibly overthrow the deep-rooted authority of the landlords which has lasted for thousands of years. . . . To put it bluntly, it is necessary to create terror for a while in every rural area. . . .

A man in China is usually subjected to the domination of three systems of authority: (1) the state system, . . . ranging from the national, provincial and county government down to that of the township; (2) the clan system, . . . ranging from the central ancestral temple and its branch temples down to the head of the household; and (3) the supernatural system [religion], ranging from the King of Hell down to the town and village gods belonging to the nether world, and from the Emperor of Heaven down to all the various gods and spirits belonging to the celestial world.[1] As for women, in addition to being dominated by these three systems of authority, they are also dominated by the men (the authority of the husband). These four authorities—political, clan, religious and masculine—are the embodiment of the whole feudal-patriarchal system and ideology, and are the four thick ropes binding the Chinese people, particularly the peasants. . . .

The political authority of the landlords is the backbone of all the other systems of authority. With that overturned, the clan authority, the religious authority and the authority of the husband all begin to totter. . . . In many places the peasant associations have taken over the temples of the gods as their offices. Everywhere they advocate the appropriation of temple property in order to start peasant schools and to defray the expenses of the

associations, calling it "public revenue from superstition." In Liling County, prohibiting superstitious practices and smashing idols have become quite the vogue. . . .

In places where the power of the peasants is predominant, only the older peasants and the women still believe in the gods, the younger peasants no longer doing so. Since the latter control the associations, the overthrow of religious authority and the eradication of superstition are going on everywhere. As to the authority of the husband, this has always been weaker among the poor peasants because, out of economic necessity, their womenfolk have to do more manual labor than the women of the richer classes and therefore have more say and greater power of decision in family matters. . . . With the rise of the peasant movement, the women in many places have now begun to organize rural women's associations; the opportunity has come for them to lift up their heads, and the authority of the husband is getting shakier every day. In a word, the whole feudal-patriarchal system and ideology is tottering with the growth of the peasants' power.

## Strategic Problems of China's Revolutionary War [1936]

What then are the characteristics of China's revolutionary war? I think there are four.

The first is that China is a vast semi-colonial country which is unevenly developed both politically and economically. . . . The unevenness of political and economic development in China—the coexistence of a frail capitalist economy and a preponderant semi-feudal economy; the coexistence of a few modern industrial and commercial cities and the boundless expanses of stagnant rural districts; the coexistence of several millions of industrial workers on the one hand and, on the other, hundreds of millions of peasants and handicraftsmen

---

[1]References to various deities rooted in Daoism and Buddhism that are part of Chinese folk religion.

under the old regime; the coexistence of big war-lords controlling the Central government and small warlords controlling the provinces; . . . and the co-existence of a few railway and steamship lines and motor roads on the one hand and, on the other, the vast number of wheel-barrow paths and trails for pedestrians only. . . .

The second characteristic is the great strength of the enemy. What is the situation of the Guomin-dang, the enemy of the Red Army? It is a party that has seized political power and has relatively stabilized it. It has gained the support of the prin-cipal counter-revolutionary countries in the world. It has remodeled its army, which has thus become different from any other army in Chinese history and on the whole similar to the armies of the mod-ern states in the world; its army is supplied much more abundantly with arms and other equipment than the Red Army, and is greater in numerical strength than any army in Chinese history. . . .

The third characteristic is that the Red Army is weak and small. . . . Our political power is dispersed and isolated in mountainous or remote regions, and is deprived of any outside help. In economic and cultural conditions the revolutionary base areas are more backward than the Guomindang areas. . . .

The fourth characteristic is the Communist Par-ty's leadership and the agrarian revolution.

This characteristic is the inevitable result of the first one. It gives rise to the following two fea-tures. On the one hand, China's revolutionary war, though taking place in a period of reaction in China and throughout the capitalist world, can yet be victorious because it is led by the Communist Party and supported by the peasantry. Because we have secured the support of the peasantry, our base areas, though small, possess great political power and stand firmly opposed to the political power of the Guomindang which encompasses a vast area; in a military sense this creates colossal difficulties for the attacking Guomindang troops. The Red Army, though small, has great fighting capacity, because its men . . . have sprung from the agrarian revolution

and are fighting for their own interests, and because officers and men are politically united.

On the other hand, our situation contrasts sharply with that of the Guomindang. Opposed to the agrarian revolution, the Guomindang is deprived of the support of the peasantry. Despite the great size of its army it cannot arouse the bulk of the soldiers or many of the lower-rank officers. . . .

Military experts of new and rapidly developing imperialist countries like Germany and Japan posi-tively boast of the advantages of strategic offensive and condemn strategic defensive. Such an idea is fundamentally unsuitable for China's revolutionary war. Such military experts point out that the great shortcoming of defense lies in the fact that, instead of gingering up [enlivening] the people, it demoral-izes them. . . . Our case is different. Under the slo-gan of safeguarding the revolutionary base areas and safeguarding China, we can rally the greatest major-ity of the people to fight single-mindedly, because we are the victims of oppression and aggression. . . .

In military terms, our warfare consists in the alternate adoption of the defensive and the offen-sive. . . . It remains a defensive until a campaign of "encirclement and annihilation" is smashed, and then it immediately begins as an offensive; they are but two phases of the same thing, as one campaign of "encirclement and annihilation" of the enemy is closely followed by another. Of the two phases, the defensive phase is more com-plicated and more important than the offensive phase. It involves numerous problems of how to smash the campaign of "encirclement and anni-hilation." . . .

In the civil war, when the Red Army surpasses the enemy in strength, there will no longer be any use for strategic defensive in general. Then our only directive will be strategic offensive. Such a change depends on an overall change in the rela-tive strength of the enemy and ourselves. The only defensive measures that remain will be of a partial character.

# Japan's Plan for a New Asia

## 92 • TOTAL WAR RESEARCH INSTITUTE, DRAFT OF BASIC PLAN FOR ESTABLISHMENT OF THE GREATER EAST ASIA CO-PROSPERITY SPHERE, JANUARY 1942

On December 7, 1941, in a ten-hour period Japanese forces not only destroyed the U.S. Pacific Fleet at Pearl Harbor, it also attacked independent Thailand; British-controlled Shanghai, Malaya, and Hong Kong; Guam, a U.S. territory in the Pacific; and the Philippines, which still was a U.S. dependency after achieving self-government in 1936. One day later Emperor Hirohito announced to the world that Japan was at war with the United States and the British Empire.

The decision for war grew out of a reorientation of Japanese strategic thinking that began to take shape in 1939, when it became clear there would be no quick victory in the war in China and no easy way to maintain Japanese control over Chinese territories the Japanese had conquered. With Japanese honor and reputation at stake, withdrawal from China was not an option, but how could the China War be brought to a successful conclusion in the face of British and American support for China and the reliance of Japan on imports, especially tin, rubber, and iron ore from British-controlled Malaya and oil from the United States and the Dutch-controlled East Indies? Increasingly the Japanese military and many politicians came to the conclusion that Japan's best option was to look southward and extend Japanese influence and power beyond Korea, North China, and Manchukuo (their puppet state in Manchuria) to Southeast Asia, even it meant war with the United States and Britain. They envisioned a new Asia, in which the peoples of East Asia, encompassing Korea, Taiwan, Manchukuo, large swaths of China, and the former European colonies in Southeast Asia and the South Pacific, would be freed of Western influence and brought under the benign guidance of Japan. In a radio address to the nation on June 29, 1940, Foreign Minister Hachirō Arita gave this new order a name, the Greater East Asia Co-Prosperity Sphere.

Subsequently, achieving the Greater East Asia Co-Prosperity Sphere formed the theoretical basis for Japan's Asian war. It was presented as such in an important speech by Premier Tōjō Hideki to the Japanese Diet on January 21, 1942, at a time when Japan already had occupied Hong Kong, Malaya, the Philippines, and key parts of the Dutch East Indies. It also was the subject of a report submitted to Japan's military and civilian leaders in January 1942 by the Total War Research Institute, an advisory body to the Cabinet founded in October 1940 and consisting of several dozen academics, business leaders, and military officers. The report provides a timetable for achieving the Greater East Asia Co-Prosperity Sphere and discusses how it will be administered and maintained. It reflects the optimism of Japanese planners before the setbacks of 1943 gradually revealed the folly of their ambitions.

## QUESTIONS FOR ANALYSIS:

1. What regions are to be included in the Greater East Asia Co-Prosperity Sphere?
2. According to the report what is the major purpose of the war against Britain and America? How will Japanese power be achieved in eastern Siberia, Australia, and Siberia?
3. Once the Greater East Asia Co-Prosperity Sphere is achieved how will it be administered and governed?
4. What limitations does the plan envision on the political independence of non-Japanese Asians once the co-prosperity sphere is established?
5. What changes in thought and culture are envisioned for non-Japanese peoples in the new Asian order.
6. The idea of the Greater East Asia Co-Prosperity Sphere is often seen as a cynical attempt to justify Japanese imperialism. Does the Research Institute's "basic plan" support such a view?

## Draft of Basic Plan for Establishment of Greater East Asia Co-Prosperity Sphere, January 1942

*The Plan.* The Japanese empire is a manifestation of morality and its special characteristic is the propagation of the Imperial Way. . . .

It is necessary to foster the increased power of the empire, to cause East Asia to return to its original form of independence and co-prosperity by shaking off the yoke of Europe and America, and to let its countries and peoples develop their respective abilities in peaceful cooperation and secure livelihood.

*The Form of East Asiatic Independence and Co-Prosperity.* The states, their citizens, and resources, comprised in those areas pertaining to the Pacific, Central Asia, and the Indian Oceans formed into one general union are to be established as an autonomous zone of peaceful living and common prosperity on behalf of the peoples of the nations of East Asia. The area including Japan, Manchuria, North China, the lower Yangtze River, and the Russian Maritime Province,[1] forms the nucleus of the East Asiatic Union. The Japanese empire possesses a duty as the leader of the East Asiatic Union. . . .

*Regional Division in the East Asiatic Union and the National Defense Sphere for the Japanese Empire.* . . . To enable the empire actually to become the central influence in East Asia, the first necessity is the consolidation of the inner belt of East Asia; and the East Asiatic Sphere shall be divided as follows for this purpose:

The Inner Sphere—the vital sphere for the empire—includes Japan, Manchuria, North China, the lower Yangtze Area and the Russian Maritime area.

The Smaller Co-Prosperity Sphere—the smaller self-supplying sphere of East Asia—includes the inner sphere plus Eastern Siberia, China, Indo-China and the South Seas.

The Greater Co-Prosperity Sphere—the larger self-supplying sphere of East Asia—includes the smaller co-prosperity sphere, plus Australia, India, and island groups in the Pacific. . . .

*Source:* Ryusaku Tsunoda, Wm. Theodore de Bary, Donald Keene, eds., *Sources of the Japanese Tradition* (New York: Columbia University Press, 1958), pp. 801-805, passim. Reprinted with the permission of the publisher.

[1]The northeast the part of Outer Manchuria in which Vladivostok was the major city.

For the present, the smaller co-prosperity sphere shall be the zone in which the construction of East Asia and the stabilization of national defense are to be aimed at. After their completion there shall be a gradual expansion toward the construction of the Greater Co-Prosperity Sphere.

*Outline of East Asiatic Administration.* It is intended that the unification of Japan, Manchukuo,[2] and China in neighborly friendship be realized by the settlement of the Sino-Japanese problems through the crushing of hostile influences in the Chinese interior, and through the construction of a new China in tune with the rapid construction of the Inner Sphere. Aggressive American and British influences in East Asia shall be driven out of the area of Indo-China and the South Seas, and this area shall be brought into our defense sphere. The war with Britain and America shall be prosecuted for that purpose.

The Russian aggressive influence in East Asia will be driven out. Eastern Siberia shall be cut off from the Soviet regime and included in our defense sphere. For this purpose, a war with the Soviets is expected. . . . Next the independence of Australia, India, etc. shall gradually be brought about. For this purpose, a recurrence of war with Britain and her allies is expected. . . . The construction of the Smaller Co-Prosperity Sphere is expected to require at least twenty years from the present time. . . .

*The Building of the National Strength.* . . .

In the economic construction of the country, Japanese and Manchurian national power shall first be consolidated, then the unification of Japan, Manchoukuo and China, shall be effected. . . . Thus a central industry will be constructed in East Asia, and the necessary relations established with the Southern Seas.

The standard for the construction of the national power and its military force, so as to meet the various situations that might affect the stages of East Asiatic administration and the national defense sphere, shall be so set as to be capable of driving off any British, American, Soviet or Chinese counter-influences in the future. . . .

## Political Construction

*Basic Plan.* The realization of the great ideal of constructing the Greater East Asia Co-Prosperity requires not only the complete prosecution of the current Greater East Asia War but also presupposes another great war in the future. . . .

The following are the basic principles for the political construction East Asia. . . .

(a) The politically dominant influence of European and American countries in the Smaller Co-Prosperity Sphere shall be gradually driven out and the area shall enjoy its liberation from the shackles hitherto forced upon it.

(b) The desires of the peoples in the sphere for their independence shall be respected and endeavors shall be made for their fulfillment, but proper and suitable forms of government shall be decided for them in consideration of military and economic requirements and of the historical, political and cultural elements peculiar to each area.

It must also be noted that the independence of various peoples of East Asia should be based upon the idea of constructing East Asia as "independent countries existing within the New Order of East Asia" and that this conception differs from an independence based on the idea of liberalism and national self-determination.

(c) During the course of construction, military unification is deemed particularly important, and the military zones and key points necessary for defense shall be directly or indirectly under the control of our country. . . .

## Thought and Cultural Construction

*General Aim in Thought.* The ultimate aim in thought construction in East Asia is to make East Asiatic peoples revere the imperial influence by

---

[2]The Japanese puppet state established in 1932 in Manchuria.

propagating the Imperial Way based on the spirit of construction, and to establish the belief that uniting solely under this influence is the one and only way to the eternal growth and development of East Asia.

And during the next twenty years . . . it is necessary to make the nations and peoples of East Asia realize the historical significance of the establishment of the New Order in East Asia, and in the common consciousness of East Asiatic unity, to liberate East Asia from the shackles of Europe and America and to establish the common conviction of constructing a New Order based on East Asiatic morality.

Occidental individualism and materialism shall be rejected and a moral world view, the basic principle of whose morality shall be the Imperial Way, shall be established. The ultimate object to be achieved is not exploitation but co-prosperity and mutual help, not competitive conflict but mutual assistance and peace, not a formal view of equality but a view of order based on moral classification, not an idea of rights but an idea of service, and not several world views but one unified world view.

*General Aim in Culture.* The essence of the traditional culture of the Orient shall be developed and manifested. And, casting off the negative and conservative cultural characteristics of the continents (India and China) on the one hand, and taking in the good points of Western culture on the other, an Oriental culture and morality, on a grand scale and subtly refined, shall be created.

# Chapter 13

# The Global Community from the 1940s through the 1980s

A FTER WORLD WAR I victors and vanquished alike failed to comprehend how many things the war had changed and dreamed that people and nations could return to patterns of life that had existed before the slaughter began. After World War II few people harbored such illusions. This war, it was realized, had irrevocably altered human affairs, setting the stage for a new era of change, not continuity. Such expectations proved to be accurate. The postwar era brought changes that were swift, wide-ranging, and profound.

Most notably, world political relationships were transformed. Before World War II seven or eight states could reasonably claim great power status; after the war only two, the United States and the Soviet Union, could do so. Divided by ideology and fearful of each other's intent, these two superpowers became intense rivals, whose efforts to extend their worldwide influence dominated international relations until the very end of the twentieth century. Against the backdrop of this Cold War, another remarkable political transformation took place: Empires for all intents and purposes disappeared. European empires in Asia, Africa, and Oceania were gradually dismantled in the 1950s and 1960s; the Soviet empire in Eastern Europe collapsed in the late 1980s; and the Soviet Union itself, basically a Russian-dominated imperial state, expired in 1991. As a result, approximately one hundred twenty new states came into existence in the postwar era.

Changes were not limited to international politics. Never before did human beings make so many revolutionary discoveries in science, medicine, and technology. They walked on the moon, made ground-breaking advances in molecular biology, designed, built, and programmed powerful computers, transformed agriculture through the Green Revolution, developed new vaccines and countless new surgical techniques, launched telecommunication satellites, and installed sophisticated telephone systems and computer networks that made possible instantaneous worldwide communication. Humans also learned to produce new weapons with destructive capacities so great that people routinely contemplated the obliteration of humanity if Soviet and U.S. nuclear arsenals were put to use. Such fears were well grounded. The atomic bomb dropped on Hiroshima in 1945 was equal in strength to 12,500 tons of TNT and destroyed an entire city. By the 1970s the United States and the Soviet Union had thousands of nuclear weapons, just one of which was equal in strength to *millions* of tons of TNT; such weapons could be delivered by missiles to targets across oceans or over the polar ice cap within minutes after launch.

Significant economic growth also took place in the postwar years, especially during the "twenty glorious years" of the 1950s and 1960s. Record levels of population growth, international trade, industrial productivity, and energy consumption all were attained, and despite the worldwide economic slump of the 1970s and 1980s, the economically advanced countries of Europe and North America, along with Australia and New Zealand, reached new heights of prosperity. Japan emerged from its defeat in World War II to become the world's second-greatest economic power after the United States. Regions such as the Middle East and states such as Nigeria and Venezuela assumed new economic importance because of their vast petroleum reserves. Not all the world prospered, however. During the postwar years the number of people living in poverty reached record levels, with most of them in Africa and South Asia and lesser numbers in Latin America and the Middle East.

These events and developments do not exhaust the list of significant changes that occurred between the mid-1940s and the mid-1980s. The attraction of religious fundamentalism; the demands of blacks, women, and homosexuals for equal rights; the emergence of a worldwide environmental movement; and the first stirrings of modern China as a major economic force all could be added to the list.

Then, beginning in the mid-1980s, changes of even greater consequence occurred. The Soviet Union entered a period of reform designed to reinvigorate an economic and political system whose flaws were openly admitted by its new leader, Mikhail Gorbachev. Reform, however, brought collapse rather than revival to the USSR. By the early 1990s the Soviet Union no longer existed, former East European satellites had rejected communism, and the Cold War was over. Few people doubted that another new era of change was about to begin.

# The End of a European-Dominated World

Despite the enormous costs and casualties of World War I, the European powers who had fought the war continued to dominate international relations in the 1920s and 1930s. Their colonial empires remained intact and even expanded. In the Middle East, France and Britain took over the Ottoman Empire's Arab provinces as League of Nations mandates, and in Africa, Italy conquered Ethiopia in 1935–1936. With the United States withdrawing into isolationism and the new communist regime in the Soviet Union shunned as a pariah, international affairs continued to be dominated by Great Britain, France, and to a lesser degree Germany and Japan.

The aftermath of World War II was far different. With ruined economies and exhausted populations, European states relinquished their dominance of world affairs to the United States and the Soviet Union, the two states that had been largely responsible for defeating the Axis powers. The unlikely alliance between the democratic, capitalist United States and the totalitarian, communist Soviet Union began to break down, however, in the closing stages of the war and disintegrated completely after the war ended. The establishment of Soviet-dominated regimes in postwar Eastern and Central Europe and the Soviet annexation of Latvia, Estonia, Lithuania, and parts of Poland confirmed the West's fears about communist designs for world domination. Simultaneously, staunch Western opposition to Soviet expansion reinforced Soviet convictions that capitalist nations were determined to destroy communism. Out of these mutual fears began the Cold War, the conflict that dominated world diplomacy until the late 1980s.

Another symptom of Europe's diminished international role after World War II was the loss of its colonies. Decolonization had many causes, including the military and financial exhaustion of postwar Britain and France, the expansion and subsequent collapse of Japan's Asian empire, Soviet and U.S. opposition to colonialism, and the upsurge of nationalism in the colonies themselves. By the mid-1960s, just short of ninety former European colonies, most of them in Asia and Africa, had become independent.

European states continued to play an important though secondary role in world affairs in the second half of the twentieth century. After their impressive postwar economic recovery, the people of Europe, especially Western Europe, enjoyed high incomes, excellent health care, and exceptional educational opportunities. But the age of European world dominance had ended.

# Soviet Perceptions of U.S. Ambitions

### 93 • NIKOLAS NOVIKOV, TELEGRAM, SEPTEMBER 27, 1946

In April 1945, the Allies, led by the United States and the Soviet Union, defeated Hitler and were planning for victory over Japan. In the months that followed, however, the antagonism and mutual distrust that had characterized U.S.–Soviet relations before the war resurfaced, as disagreements between the two emerging superpowers arose on a wide range of issues, including the treatment of defeated Germany, the occupation of Japan, Soviet troop deployments in Europe and Iran, the structure and purposes of the United Nations, the abrupt cessation of U.S. economic aid to the Soviet Union after the defeat of Hitler, and the control of nuclear weapons.

Against the backdrop of these disputes, hopes for cooperation and accommodation between the two states evaporated. In February 1946, in response to a confrontational and hostile speech by the Soviet leader Josef Stalin, the U.S. career diplomat

George Kennan at the request of the State Department wrote his famous "long telegram," in which he argued that the Soviet regime was inherently expansionist and that its influence had to be "contained" in areas of strategic importance to the United States. In March the British wartime leader Winston Churchill warned that an "iron curtain" was descending across Soviet-dominated Eastern Europe and called for an Anglo-American alliance to halt further Soviet expansion. And in September Clark Clifford, a close adviser of President Truman, in a memorandum to the president asserted that "Soviet leaders believe that a conflict is inevitable between the USSR and capitalistic states, and their duty is to prepare the Soviet Union for this conflict." Resisting the Soviet threat, he said, was the "gravest problem" facing the United States.

Western leaders were not alone in their pessimistic assessments of U.S.–Soviet relations in 1946. In the wake of the Foreign Ministers Conference in Paris in August, Nikolai Novikov, recently elevated to the position of ambassador to the United States, was ordered by Soviet foreign minister Viacheslav Molotov to prepare a memorandum on U.S. foreign policy goals. The result was the following dark assessment of U.S. intentions, sent as a cable to Molotov on September 27. We know that Molotov read the cable, but what happened next is unclear. Did Molotov show the telegram to Stalin and other high-ranking Soviet officials? Did Novikov's analysis contribute to the atmosphere of confrontation building in 1946? The answer to both questions is probably "yes," but until historians gain full access to Soviet archives, no one will know exactly what role Novikov's telegram played in the Cold War's murky beginnings.

## QUESTIONS FOR ANALYSIS

1. According to Novikov, what had been the preferred strategy of the United States in World War II? How and why had this strategy failed?
2. What specific evidence does Novikov cite to prove his assertion that the ultimate goal of U.S. foreign policy is world dominance?
3. In Novikov's view, how will the United States achieve its goal?
4. According to Novikov, what are the short-range goals of U.S. policy in these regions: Germany; Japan; the Near East; and Eastern Europe?
5. What is Novikov's evaluation of U.S. strengths and weaknesses?
6. If one were to accept the basic points of Novikov's arguments, what implications would they have for Soviet foreign policy and military planning?

The foreign policy of the United States, which reflects the imperialist tendencies of American monopolistic capital, is characterized in the postwar period by a striving for world supremacy. This is the real meaning of the many statements by President Truman and other representatives of American ruling circles: that the United States has the right to lead the world. All the forces of American diplomacy—the army, the air force, the navy, industry, and science—are enlisted in the service of this foreign policy. For this purpose broad plans for expansion have been developed and are being implemented through diplomacy and the establishment of a system of naval and air

*Source:* Nikolai Novikov, "Telegram, September 27, 1946," in Kenneth Jensen, ed., *Origins of the Cold War: The Novikov, Kennan, and Roberts Long Telegrams of 1946* (Washington, D.C.: United States Institute of Peace, 1993).

bases stretching far beyond the boundaries of the United States, through the arms race, and through the creation of ever newer types of weapons.

. . . This situation does not fully conform to the calculations of those reactionary circles which hoped that during the Second World War they would succeed in avoiding, at least for a long time, the main battles in Europe and Asia. They calculated that the United States of America, if it was unsuccessful in completely avoiding direct participation in the war, would enter it only at the last minute, when it could easily affect the outcome of the war, completely ensuring its interests. . . .

In this regard, it was thought that the main competitors of the United States would be crushed or greatly weakened in the war, and the United States by virtue of this circumstance would assume the role of the most powerful factor in resolving the fundamental question of the postwar world. These calculations were also based on the assumption . . . that the Soviet Union, which had been subjected to the attacks of German Fascism in June 1941, would also be exhausted or even completely destroyed as a result of the war.

Reality did not bear out the calculations of the American imperialists. . . . In actuality, despite all of the economic difficulties of the postwar period connected with the enormous losses inflicted by the war and the German fascist occupation, the Soviet Union continues to remain economically independent of the outside world and is rebuilding its national economy with its own forces. At the same time the USSR's international position is currently stronger than it was in the prewar period. . . . The enormous relative weight of the USSR in international affairs in general and in the European countries in particular, the independence of its foreign policy, and the economic and political assistance that it provides to neighboring countries, both allies and former enemies, has led to the growth of the political influence of the Soviet Union in these countries and to the further strengthening of democratic tendencies in them.

Such a situation . . . cannot help but be regarded by the American imperialists as an obstacle in the path of the expansionist policy of the United States. . . .

Obvious indications of the U.S. effort to establish world dominance are . . . to be found in the increase in military potential in peacetime and in the establishment of a large number of naval and air bases both in the United States and beyond its borders. In the summer of 1946, for the first time in the history of the country, Congress passed a law on the establishment of a peacetime army, not on a volunteer basis but on the basis of universal military service. The size of the army, which is supposed to amount to about one million persons as of July 1, 1947, was also increased significantly. The size of the navy at the conclusion of the war decreased quite insignificantly in comparison with war time. At the present time, the American navy occupies first place in the world, leaving England's navy far behind, to say nothing of those of other countries. Expenditures on the army and navy have risen colossally, amounting to 13 billion dollars according to the budget for 1946–47 (about 40 percent of the total budget of 36 billion dollars). This is more than ten times greater than corresponding expenditures in the budget for 1938, which did not amount to even one billion dollars.

Along with maintaining a large army, navy, and air force, the budget provides that these enormous amounts also will be spent on establishing a very extensive system of naval and air bases in the Atlantic and Pacific oceans. . . . A large number of these bases and points of support are located outside the boundaries of the United States. . . . The establishment of American bases on islands that are often 10,000 to 12,000 kilometers from the territory of the United States and are on the other side of the Atlantic and Pacific oceans clearly indicates the offensive nature of the strategic concepts of the commands of the U.S. army and navy. This interpretation is also confirmed by the fact that the American navy is intensively studying the naval approaches to the boundaries of Europe. For this purpose, American naval vessels in the course of 1946 visited the ports of Norway, Denmark, Sweden Turkey, and Greece. In addition, the American navy is constantly operating in the Mediterranean Sea.

All of these facts show clearly that a decisive role in the realization of plans for world dominance by the United States is played by its armed forces. . . .

One of the stages in the achievement of dominance over the world by the United States is its understanding with England concerning the partial division of the world on the basis of mutual concessions. The basic lines of the secret agreement between the United States and England regarding the division of the world consists . . . in their agreement on the inclusion of Japan and China in the sphere of influence of the United States in the Far East, while the United States, for its part, has agreed not to hinder England either in resolving the Indian problem or in strengthening its influence in Siam [Thailand] and Indonesia. . . .

The American policy in China is striving for the complete economic and political submission of China to the control of American monopolistic capital. . . . At the present time in China, there are more than 50,000 American soldiers. . . . The measures carried out in northern China by the American army show that it intends to stay there for a long time.

In Japan, despite the presence there of only a small contingent of American troops, control is in the hands of the Americans. Measures taken by the American occupational authorities in the area of domestic policy and intended to support reactionary classes and groups, which the United States plans to use in the struggle against the Soviet Union, also meet with a sympathetic attitude . . .

In recent years American capital has penetrated very intensively into the economy of the Near Eastern countries, in particular into the oil industry. At present there are American oil concessions in all of the Near Eastern countries that have oil deposits (Iraq, Bahrain, Kuwait, Egypt, and Saudi Arabia). American capital, which made its first appearance in the oil industry of the Near East only in 1928, now controls about 42 percent of all proven reserves in the Near East, excluding Iran. . . . The strengthening of U.S. military positions in the Near East and the establishment of conditions for basing the America navy at one or more points on the Mediterranean Sea . . . will therefore signify the emergence of a new threat to the security of the southern regions of the Soviet Union . . .

The present policy of the American government with regard to the USSR is also directed at limiting or dislodging the influence of the Soviet Union from neighboring countries. In implementing this policy in former enemy or Allied countries adjacent to the USSR, the United States attempts . . . to support reactionary forces with the purpose of creating obstacles to the process of democratization of these countries. In so doing, it also attempts to secure positions for the penetration of American capital into their economies. Such a policy is intended to weaken and overthrow the democratic governments in power there, which are friendly toward the USSR, and replace them in the future with new governments that would obediently carry out a policy dictated from the United States. . . .

One of the most important elements in the general policy of the United States, which is directed toward limiting the international role of the USSR in the post-war world, is the policy with regard to Germany. In Germany, the United States is taking measures to strengthen reactionary forces for the purpose of opposing democratic reconstruction. Furthermore, it displays special insistence on accompanying this policy with completely inadequate measures for the demilitarization of Germany.

The American occupation policy does not have the objective of eliminating the remnants of German Fascism and rebuilding German political life on a democratic basis, so that Germany might cease to exist as an aggressive force. . . . Instead, the United States is considering the possibility of terminating the Allied occupation of German territory before the main tasks of the occupation—the demilitarization and democratization of Germany—have been completed. This would provide the preconditions for the revival of an imperialist Germany, which the United States plans to use in a future war on its side. . . .

The numerous and extremely hostile statements by American government, political, and military figures with regard to the Soviet Union and its foreign policy are very characteristic of the current relationship between the ruling circles of the United States and the USSR. These statements are echoed in an even more unrestrained tone by the overwhelming majority of the American press organs. Talk about a "third war," meaning a war against the Soviet Union, even a direct call for this war—with the threat of using the atomic bomb—such is the content of the statements on relations with the

Soviet Union by reactionaries at public meetings and in the press. . . .

The basic goal of this anti-Soviet campaign of American "public opinion" is to exert political pressure on the Soviet Union and compel it to make concessions. Another, no less important goal of the campaign is the attempt to create an atmosphere of war psychosis among the masses, . . . thus making it easier for the U.S. government to carry out measures for the maintenance of high military potential. Of course, all of these measures for maintaining a highly military potential are not goals in themselves. They are only intended to prepare the conditions for winning world supremacy in a new war, the date for which, to be sure, cannot be determined now by anyone, but which is contemplated by the most bellicose circles of American imperialism.

# Dealing with the Communist Threat

## 94 • NATIONAL SECURITY COUNCIL, UNITED STATES OBJECTIVES AND PROGRAMS FOR NATIONAL SECURITY (NSC PAPER NUMBER 68)

By 1950, the Cold War was well under way. The Truman Doctrine (1947) pledged U.S. military aid to any country resisting a communist takeover, with Greece and Turkey being the first beneficiaries; the Marshall Plan (1947) sought to blunt the appeal of communism by allocating millions of dollars to rebuild the economies of Western Europe; in June 1948 Stalin ordered a blockade of all land routes from West Germany to Berlin in the hope of forcing out Berlin-based French, British, and U.S. troops, and in response the Western powers launched the year-long Berlin airlift to supply the city; and in 1949 the North Atlantic Treaty Organization was established to counter Soviet military strength in Eastern Europe.

Although no European countries became communist after Czechoslovakia did so in 1948, American fears of international communism deepened in 1949, when China became communist and the Soviets detonated their first atomic bomb. Against this background, President Truman directed the secretaries of state and defense to form a committee to prepare a position paper on a suitable U.S. response to the perceived communist threat. Under the chairmanship of Paul Nitze, the Director of Policy Planning for the State Department, the committee produced a blueprint for U.S. Cold War strategy in April 1950 that was approved by the National Security Council and passed on to the president in late April. Although the report had its share of critics, its assessments and recommendations were generally accepted. For the next twenty years it provided a blueprint for U.S. Cold War policy.

## QUESTIONS FOR ANALYSIS

1. According to this document, how did World War II fundamentally alter diplomatic relationships?
2. What view of the Soviet Union does this document present?
3. According to the report, what is the Soviet strategy for subverting the free world?
4. What does "containment" mean?
5. What must be done to ensure containment's effectiveness?
6. To what extent does NCS-68 confirm or refute Novikov's conclusions about U.S. foreign policy objectives as described in his September 1946 telegram to Molotov?

During the span of one generation, the international distribution of power has been fundamentally altered. For several centuries it had proved impossible for any one nation to gain such preponderant strength that a coalition of other nations could not in time face it with greater strength. The international scene was marked by recurring periods of violence and war, but a system of sovereign and independent states was maintained, over which no state was able to achieve hegemony.

Two complex sets of factors have now basically altered this historical distribution of power. First, the defeat of Germany and Japan and the decline of the British and French Empires have interacted with the development of the United States and the Soviet Union in such a way that power has increasingly gravitated to these two centers. Second, the Soviet Union, unlike previous aspirants to hegemony, is animated by a new fanatic faith, antithetical to our own, and seeks to impose its absolute authority over the rest of the world. Conflict has, therefore, become endemic and is waged, on the part of the Soviet Union, by violent or non-violent methods in accordance with the dictates of expediency. . . .

On the one hand, the people of the world yearn for relief from the anxiety arising from the risk of atomic war. On the other hand, any substantial further extension of the area under the domination of the Kremlin would raise the possibility that no coalition adequate to confront the Kremlin with greater strength could be assembled. It is in this context that this Republic and its citizens . . . stand in their deepest peril.

The issues that face us are momentous, involving the fulfillment or destruction not only of this Republic but of civilization itself. They are issues which will not await our deliberations. With conscience and resolution this Government and the people it represents must now take new and fateful decisions. . . .

Our overall policy at the present time may be described as one designed to foster a world environment in which the American system can survive and flourish. It therefore rejects the concept of isolation and affirms the necessity of our positive participation in the world community. This broad intention embraces two subsidiary policies. One is a policy which we would probably pursue even if there were no Soviet threat. It is a policy of attempting to develop a healthy international community. The other is the policy of "containing" the Soviet system. . . .

*Source:* NSC-68, U.S. Department of State, *Foreign Relations of the United States* 1950, Vol. 1.

As for the policy of "containment," it is one which seeks by all means short of war to (1) block further expansion of Soviet power, (2) expose the falsities of Soviet pretensions, (3) induce a retraction of the Kremlin's control and influence and (4) in general, so foster the seeds of destruction within the Soviet system that the Kremlin is brought at least to the point of modifying its behavior to conform to generally accepted international standards.

It was and continues to be cardinal in this policy that we possess superior overall power in ourselves or in dependable combination with other like-minded nations. One of the most important ingredients of power is military strength. In the concept of "containment," the maintenance of a strong military posture is deemed to be essential for two reasons: (1) as an ultimate guarantee of our national security and (2) as an indispensable backdrop to the conduct of the policy of "containment." . . . At the same time, it is essential to the successful conduct of a policy of "containment" that we always leave open the possibility of negotiation with the U.S.S.R. A diplomatic freeze—and we are in one now—tends to defeat the very purposes of "containment" because it raises tensions at the same time that it makes Soviet retractions and adjustments in the direction of moderated behavior more difficult. It also tends to inhibit our initiative and deprives us of opportunities for maintaining a moral ascendancy in our struggle with the Soviet system. . . .

It is quite clear from Soviet theory and practice that the Kremlin seeks to bring the free world under its dominion by the methods of the cold war. The preferred technique is to subvert by infiltration and intimidation. Every institution of our society is an instrument which it is sought to stultify and turn against our purposes. Those that touch most closely our material and moral strength are obviously the prime targets, labor unions, civil enterprises, schools, churches, and all media for influencing opinion. The effort is not so much to make them serve obvious Soviet ends as to prevent them from serving our ends, and thus to make them sources of confusion in our economy, our culture, and our body politic. The doubts and diversities that in terms of our values are part of the merit of a free system, the weaknesses and the problems that are peculiar to it, the rights and privileges that free men enjoy, and the disorganization and destruction left in the wake of the last attack on our freedoms, all are but opportunities for the Kremlin to do its evil work. Every advantage is taken of the fact that our means of prevention and retaliation are limited by those principles and scruples which are precisely the ones that give our freedom and democracy its meaning for us. None of our scruples deter those whose only code is, "morality is that which serves the revolution."

At the same time the Soviet Union is seeking to create overwhelming military force, in order to back up infiltration with intimidation. In the only terms in which it understands strength, it is seeking to demonstrate to the free world that force and the will to use it are on the side of the Kremlin, that those who lack it are decadent and doomed. In local incidents it threatens and encroaches both for the sake of local gains and to increase anxiety and defeatism in all the free world.

The possession of atomic weapons at each of the opposite poles of power, and the inability (for different reasons) of either side to place any trust in the other, puts a premium on a surprise attack against us. It equally puts a premium on a more violent and ruthless prosecution of its design by cold war, especially if the Kremlin is sufficiently objective to realize the improbability of our prosecuting a preventive war. It also puts a premium on piecemeal aggression against others, counting on our unwillingness to engage in atomic war unless we are directly attacked. . . .

Our position as the center of power in the free world places a heavy responsibility upon the United States for leadership. We must organize and enlist the energies and resources of the free world in a positive program for peace which will frustrate the Kremlin design for world domination by creating a situation in the free world to which the Kremlin will be compelled to adjust. Without such a cooperative effort . . . we will have to make gradual withdrawals under pressure until we discover one day that we have sacrificed positions of vital interest.

In summary, we must, by means of a rapid and sustained build-up of the political, economic, and military strength of the free world, and by means of an affirmative program intended to wrest the initiative from the Soviet Union, confront it with convincing evidence of the determination and ability of the free world to frustrate the Kremlin design of a world dominated by its will. Such evidence is the only means short of war which eventually may force the Kremlin to abandon its present course of action

and to negotiate acceptable agreements on issues of major importance.

The whole success of the proposed program hangs ultimately on recognition by this Government, the American people, and all free peoples, that the cold war is in fact a real war in which the survival of the free world is at stake. Essential prerequisites to success are consultations with Congressional leaders designed to make the program the object of nonpartisan legislative support, and a presentation to the public of a full explanation of the facts and implications of the present international situation. The prosecution of the program will require of us all the ingenuity, sacrifice, and unity demanded by the vital importance of the issue and the tenacity to persevere until our national objectives have been attained.

## Great Britain Lets Go of India

### 95 • DEBATE IN THE HOUSE OF COMMONS, MARCH 4 AND 5, 1947

A turning point in the dismantling of Europe's empires took place in August 1947 when the Indian people gained independence from Great Britain and the new states of India and Pakistan were created. After the greatest imperial power released its hold on the "jewel in the crown" of its empire, nationalist leaders throughout Asia and Africa demanded equal treatment, and European politicians found it more difficult to justify continued colonial rule.

British and Indian leaders had debated the timing and framework of Indian independence for years, but World War II brought the issue to a head. Many Indians, still embittered by the meager benefits they had received for their sacrifices in World War I, showed little enthusiasm for the British cause in World War II. In 1942, after Japan's conquest of Southeast Asia, the British government sent Sir Stafford Cripps to Delhi to offer India dominion status after the war if the leaders of the independence movement would support the war against Japan. Negotiations broke down, however, leading Gandhi to launch his last nationwide passive resistance campaign against British rule. Anti-British feeling intensified in 1943 when a disastrous famine took between one million and three Indian million lives and the pro-Japanese Indian National Army, organized by Subhas Bose, declared war on Great Britain with the goal of Indian independence.

A shift in British politics also affected India's future. The 1945 elections initiated six years of rule by the Labour Party, which had little enthusiasm for the idea of empire. Facing mounting restiveness in India, Prime Minister Clement Attlee dispatched a mission to India in early 1946 charged with preserving Indian unity in the face of growing Hindu–Muslim antagonism and arranging for India's independence as soon as possible. Although Hindus and Muslims could not reconcile their differences, on February 20, 1947, the Labour government announced its plan to end British rule in India. This led to an emotional two-day debate in Parliament in which Conservatives and some Liberals argued that independence should be delayed. Labour had a strong majority, however, and in March 1947, Parliament approved its plan for letting go of India. At midnight on August 14–15, 1947, predominantly Hindu India and predominantly Muslim Pakistan became independent.

The following excerpts are from the parliamentary debates of March 4 and 5, 1947. All the speakers oppose the proposal of Sir John Anderson, a Liberal representing the Scottish universities, that Great Britain should promise independence by June 1948 but withdraw the offer and require further negotiations if a suitable Hindu–Muslim agreement could not be achieved.

## QUESTIONS FOR ANALYSIS

1. What were the points of disagreement among members of Parliament about the benefits and harm of British colonial rule in India?
2. Some speakers who believed that British colonialism had benefited India still supported independence. Why?
3. The critics of British rule in India supported immediate independence. What was their line of argument?
4. According to the speakers, what military and economic realities make it impractical to continue British rule in India?
5. How do the speakers view developments in India as part of broader historical trends?
6. Most of the speakers were members of the Labour Party and thus sympathetic to socialism. What examples of socialist perspectives can you find in their speeches?

---

Mr. Clement Davies[1] (Montgomery) It is an old adage now, that "the old order changeth, yielding place to new," but there has been a more rapid change from the old to the new in our time than ever before. We have witnessed great changes in each one of the five Continents, and for many of those changes this country and its people have been directly or indirectly responsible. . . . In all the lands where the British flag flies, we have taught the peoples the rule of law and the value of justice impartially administered. We have extended knowledge, and tried to inculcate understanding and toleration.

Our declared objects were twofold—first, the betterment of the conditions of the people and the improvement of their standard of life; and, second, to teach them the ways of good administration and gradually train them to undertake responsibility so that one day we could hand over to them the full burden of their own self-government. Our teachings and our methods have had widespread effect, and we should rejoice that so many peoples in the world today are awake, and aware of their own individualities, and have a desire to express their own personalities and their traditions, and to live their own mode of life. . . . Our association

---

*Source: Parliamentary Debates, 5th ser., Vol. 434 (London: His Majesty's Printing Office, 1947).*

[1]A London lawyer and Liberal member of Parliament (MP) from 1929 until 1962.

with India during two centuries has been, on the whole—with mistakes, as we will admit—an honorable one. So far as we were able we brought peace to this great sub-continent; we have introduced not only a system of law and order, but also a system of administration of justice, fair and impartial, which has won their respect. . . . We have tried to inculcate into them the feeling that although they are composed of different races, with different languages, customs, and religions, they are really part of one great people of India.

The standard of life, pathetically low as it is, has improved so that during the last 30 years there has been an increase in the population of 100 million . . . We have brought to them schools, universities, and teachers, and we have not only introduced the Indians into the Civil Service but have gradually handed over to them, in the Provinces and even in the Central Government, the administration and government of their own land and their own people. . . . Then in 1946, there was the offer of complete independence, with the right again, if they so chose, of contracting in and coming back within the British Commonwealth of Nations.[2]

I agree that these offers were made subject to the condition that the Indian peoples themselves would co-operate to form a Central Government and draw up not only their own Constitution, but the method of framing it. Unfortunately, the leaders of the two main parties in India have failed to agree upon the formation of even a Constituent Assembly, and have failed, therefore, to agree upon a form of Constitution. . . .

What are the possible courses that could be pursued? . . . The first of the courses would be to restore power into our own hands so that we might not only have the responsibility but the full means of exercising that responsibility. I believe that that is not only impossible but unthinkable. . . . Secondly, can we continue, as we do at present, to wait until an agreement is reached for the formation of a Central Government with a full Constitution, capable of acting on behalf of the whole of India? The present state of affairs there and the deterioration which has already set in—and which has worsened—have shown us that we cannot long continue on that course.

The third course is the step taken by His Majesty's Government—the declaration made by the Government that we cannot and do not intend in the slightest degree to go back upon our word, that we do not intend to damp the hopes of the Indian peoples but rather to raise them, and that we cannot possibly go on indefinitely as we have been going on during these past months; that not only shall they have the power they now really possess but after June 1948, the full responsibility for government of their own peoples in India. . . .

Mr. Sorensen[3] (Leyton, West) I have considerable sympathy with the hon. and gallant Member for Ayr Burghs (Sir T. Moore),[4] because, politically, he has been dead for some time and does not know it. His ideas were extraordinarily reminiscent of 50 years ago, and I do not propose, therefore, to deal with so unpleasant and decadent a subject. When he drew attention to the service we have rendered to India—and we have undoubtedly rendered service—he overlooked the fact that India has had an existence extending for some thousands of years before the British occupation, and that during that period she managed to run schools, establish a chain of rest houses, preserve an economy, and reach a high level of civilization, when the inhabitants of these islands were in a condition of barbarism and

---

[2]The British Commonwealth of Nations was founded by Parliament in 1931 through the Statute of Westminster. It consisted of Great Britain and a number of its former colonies that chose to maintain ties of friendship and practical cooperation with Britain. In 1949 it was renamed the Commonwealth of Nations.

[3]A clergyman and Labour MP (1929–1931 and 1939–1954).
[4]A Conservative MP who had just spoken against Labour's plan for Indian independence.

savagery. One has only to discuss such matters with a few representative Indians to realize that they can draw up a fairly powerful indictment of the evil we have taken to India as well as the good. . . .

Whatever may have been the origin of the various problems in India, or the degree of culpability which may be attached to this or that party or person, a situation now confronts us which demands decision. . . . That is why, in my estimation, the Government are perfectly right to fix a date for the transference of power. . . . Responsibility is ultimately an Indian matter. Acute problems have existed in India for centuries, and they have not been solved under our domination. Untouchability, the appalling subjugation of women, the division of the castes, the incipient or actual conflict between Muslim and Hindu—all those and many others exist.

I do not forget what is to me the most terrible of all India's problems, the appalling poverty. It has not been solved by us, although we have had our opportunity. On the contrary, in some respects we have increased that problem, because, despite the contributions that we have made to India's welfare, we have taken a great deal of wealth from India in order that we ourselves might enjoy a relatively higher standard of life. Can it be denied that we have benefited in the past substantially by the ignorant, sweated labor of the Indian people? We have not solved those social problems. The Indians may not solve them either. There are many problems that the Western world cannot solve, but at least, those problems are India's responsibility. Indians are more likely, because they are intimate with their own problems, to know how to find their way through those labyrinths than we, who are, to the Indian but aliens and foreigners.

Here I submit a point which surely will receive the endorsement of most hon. Members of this House. It is that even a benevolent autocracy can be no substitute for democracy and liberty. . . .

I would therefore put two points to the House tonight. Are we really asked by hon. Members on the other side to engage in a gamble, first by continuing as we are and trying to control India indefinitely, with the probability that we should not succeed and that all over India there would be rebellion, chaos, and breakdown? Secondly, are we to try to reconquer India and in doing so, to impose upon ourselves an economic burden which we could not possibly afford? How many men would be required to keep India quiet if the great majority of the Indians were determined to defy our power? I guarantee that the number would not be fewer than a million men, with all the necessary resources and munitions of war.

Are we to do this at a time when we are crying out for manpower in this country, when in the mines, the textile industry, and elsewhere we want every man we can possibly secure? There are already 1,500,000 men under arms. To talk about facing the possibility of governing and policing India and keeping India under proper supervision out of our own resources is not only nonsense, but would provide the last straw that breaks the camel's back. . . .

FLIGHT-LIEUTENANT CRAWLEY[5] (BUCKINGHAM) Members opposite, who envisage our staying in India, must have some idea of what type of rule we should maintain. A fact about the Indian services which they seem to ignore is that they are largely Indianized. Can they really expect the Services, Indianized to the extent of 80 or 90 percent, to carry out their policy any longer? Is it not true that in any situation that is likely to arise in India now, if the British remain without a definite date for withdrawal, every single Indian member of the Services, will, in the mind of all politically conscious Indians become a political collaborator? . . . How could we get the Indianized part of the Services to carry out a policy which, in the view of all political Indians, is anti-Indian? The only conceivable way in which we

[5]An educator and journalist who was a Labour MP from 1945 to 1951.

could stay even for seven years in India would be by instituting a type of rule which we in this country abhor more than any other—a purely dictatorial rule based upon all the things we detest most.

Mr. Harold Davies[6] (Leek) . . . All the peoples of Asia are on the move. Can we in this House, by wishful thinking, sweep aside this natural desire for independence, freedom, and nationalism that has grown in Asia from Karachi to Peking,[7] from Karachi to Indonesia and Indo-China? That is all part of that movement, and we must recognize it. I am not a Utopian. I know that the changeover will

not be easy. But there is no hon. Member opposite who has given any concrete, practical alternative to the decision, which has been made by my right hon. friends. What alternative can we give?

This little old country is tottering and wounded as a result of the wars inherent in the capitalist system. Can we, today, carry out vast commitments from one end of the world to another? Is it not time that we said to those for whom we have spoken so long, "The time has come when you shall have your independence. That time has come; the moment is here"?

---

[6]An author and educator who was a Labour MP from 1959 to 1964.

[7]Karachi was soon to become Pakistan's first capital city.

# New Forces in the Global Economy

While the Cold War and decolonization transformed international politics in the 1950s and 1960s, two developments in the 1970s and 1980s brought about major changes in the world economy. The first was the emergence of the Organization of Petroleum Exporting Countries (OPEC) as an economic force. During the 1970s, OPEC's twelve Asian, African, and Latin American members shocked the world when they orchestrated a quadrupling of the price of oil in 1974 and then quadrupled it again in 1979. The second was the "economic miracle" that took place in Japan and somewhat later in South Korea, Taiwan, Hong Kong, and Singapore. These "Asian Tigers" emerged as centers of international finance and leading exporters of steel, automobiles, electronic goods, and consumer items. The Pacific Rim took its place alongside the United States and Western Europe as a major economic force.

The emergence of OPEC occurred against a background of soaring demand for oil during the two decades of worldwide economic expansion following World War II. World oil consumption grew from approximately 3.9 billion barrels in 1953 to 20.4 billion barrels in 1973. Nonetheless, prices stayed low, mainly because they were set by huge oil companies such as Texaco, Mobil, Standard Oil of California, British Petroleum, and the Royal Dutch/Shell Group, all of which were intent on keeping demand high and payments to oil producers low. In response, in 1960 five producers—Iran, Iraq, Saudi Arabia, Venezuela, and Kuwait—founded OPEC. Although membership in the 1960s and early 1970s expanded to include Qatar, Libya, Indonesia, Abu Dhabi, Ecuador, Gabon, and Nigeria, in 1973 the price of oil measured against inflation was only half of what it had been in the early 1950s.

This changed in late 1973 and 1974 when four Arab oil producers—Saudi Arabia, Iraq, Kuwait, and the United Arab Emirates—decided to use oil as a political weapon after the outbreak in October 1973 of the fourth Arab–Israeli war, known as the Yom Kippur War in Israel and the Ramadan War in Muslim countries. To support Egypt and Syria, which had launched an attack on Israel on October 6, these Arab states voted to stop oil deliveries to the United States, which was sending the Israelis weapons, and the Netherlands, which had made available its airfields to Israel-bound U.S. supply planes. This step, combined with across-the-board cuts in production, drove up the price of oil to $10 a barrel, a level that OPEC nations were able to maintain throughout the 1970s and push even higher after the outbreak of the Iran–Iraq war in 1979.

As gasoline prices soared in the United States during the 1970s, many Americans traded in their gas-guzzling Fords, Chevrolets, and Chryslers for fuel-efficient Japanese Toyotas, Datsuns, and Hondas. The fact that twenty years earlier the Japanese auto industry had scarcely existed underscores the rapid transformation of postwar Japan's economy. After their nation's defeat, Japanese leaders concluded that economic recovery depended on producing manufactured goods not just for domestic and regional markets, but for the entire world. With a supportive government, an industrious and well-educated workforce, high rates of savings, a talented entrepreneurial class, and an intense competitive spirit, the Japanese succeeded spectacularly. They moved from steel and shipbuilding in the 1950s to electronics, computers, consumer goods, and automobiles in the 1960s and 1970s. By the mid-1980s Japan had trade surpluses of more than $80 billion a year and one of the world's highest standards of living. By then South Korea, Taiwan, Singapore, and Hong Kong also had emerged as financial and industrial powers, and many commentators began to speak of the late twentieth century as the dawn of the Pacific Era in the world's economy.

# The Arab Oil Weapon

## 96 • ORGANIZATION OF ARAB PETROLEUM EXPORTING COUNTRIES, ADVERTISEMENT IN THE *GUARDIAN*, NOVEMBER 15, 1973

On October 8, 1973, representatives of the world's major oil companies and OPEC opened negotiations in Vienna over oil prices and profits. Just two days before the meetings began, Egypt and Syria, hoping to force Israel to relinquish the Arab territories it had won in the Six-Day War of 1967, attacked Israel, starting a war that would last three weeks. While the war raged on, negotiators in Vienna were unable to bridge the gap between the oil companies' offer and OPEC's demands. On October 14 the meeting broke up, and nine oil ministers, including those of Iran and the Arab oil states, convened two days later in Kuwait City to reconsider their position after the revelation that on October 13 the United States had begun a massive effort to supply Israel with weapons and ammunition. On October 16, they announced their decision to raise the price of oil seventy percent, to $5.11 a barrel. One day later Qatar, Abu Dhabi, Iraq, Libya, the United Arab Emirates, and Saudi Arabia announced a plan to cut production by five percent and to continue to cut it by another five percent per month until Israel withdrew from the territories it had occupied. Then on October 20, after it became known that the United States had proposed a $2.2 billion aid package for Israel, Saudi Arabia, followed by other Arab oil producers (but not Iraq), announced they would cut off all shipments of oil, every drop, to the United States. One week later the embargo was extended to the Netherlands.

The unleashing of the Arab oil weapon created panic among world statesmen and business leaders, a state of affairs the oil producers hoped to use to their political advantage even after fighting in the Middle East ended in late October. Countries supporting Israel—the United States, the Netherlands, and briefly Canada—would be embargoed; those deemed friendly to the Arab cause would be placed on a list of "exempt" countries and receive their prewar oil allocations; neutral countries would be subject to the monthly five percent cutbacks. Such incentives proved effective in the case of Japan, which after appearing on the list of "neutral states," was elevated to "exempt status" after the government endorsed various Arab positions.

The Arabs' diplomatic initiative was accompanied by a campaign to win over public opinion. In mid-November, the Organization of Arab Petroleum Exporting Countries took out full-page advertisements in major Western newspapers to explain its actions and spell out what governments must do to keep the oil flowing. The text of the following advertisement appeared in the November 15 edition of *The Guardian*, a London-based newspaper with distribution throughout the United Kingdom.

By early 1974 most Arab oil producers had concluded that the cutoffs were losing their effectiveness and that no further progress could be made on the diplomatic front until they ended. On March 18, with Syria and Libya dissenting, they voted to end the embargo and the monthly production reductions. But their use of the oil weapon had succeeded beyond their expectations. It was a true turning point in recent world history.

## QUESTIONS FOR ANALYSIS

1. The advertisement claims that the Arab oil-producing nations have made a "liberal and vital" contribution to the world economy. What is the basis of this claim?
2. According to the advertisement, why are Israel and its supporters to blame for the actions taken by the Arab oil producers?
3. According to the advertisement, why have the Netherlands and the United States been singled out for a total embargo? What alleged actions by the United States further justify the embargo?
4. What general and specific goals do the Arab oil-producing nations hope to achieve by using the oil weapon?

## Arab Oil Policy in the Middle East Conflict

It is an irrefutable fact that the Arab Petroleum Exporting Countries have made . . . and are continuing to make, a liberal and vital contribution to the enhancement of the World economy, and consequently to the well-being and prosperity of all nations, through exporting their gradually depleted, and irreplaceable, natural resources: OIL. Equally irrefutable is the fact that in many Arab countries production has long surpassed the limit required by their own local economy and the needs of future generations. . . . Nevertheless, they willingly decided to give first consideration to the mounting world-wide demand for their oil necessitated by the increasing requirements of energy as a key factor in maintaining the growth of production in all spheres. Thus, demonstrating their unequivocal desire to play their role in promoting . . . the well-being of mankind, they continued to increase their oil production and exports while being fully aware of the fact that by doing so they were indeed sacrificing their own interests.

On the other hand, for six years, the Arab Oil Exporting countries saw vast areas of the territories of three Arab countries[1] being perpetually occupied and ravished by the Israeli aggressors who acquired these Arab lands by force during the June War in 1967. During all these years, in spite of the innumerable peace offers and endeavours on the part of the Arab States and the peace-loving nations . . . , Israel remained intransigent and lent a deaf ear to all the efforts that have been made to induce her to respect and implement the U.N. resolution[2] calling upon her to withdraw from the Arab occupied territories. . . .

It is needless to say that the responsibility for the implementation of the U.N. resolutions, representing the consensus of the world community's will, lies squarely on the shoulders of all member-states, and particularly on the permanent members of the Security Council.[3] However, most of the major industrial powers failed to show any intention of taking meaningful and effective action indicating their willingness to discharge their responsibility as they should. On the contrary, some powers acted in such a manner as to encourage the Israeli aggressors to maintain their intransigence, and even consolidate their occupation of the Arab lands . . . , blatantly defying the World Organization [the U.N.] and breaking the principles of International law, as well as making mockery of the legitimate rights of the Arab people.

The 1967 Israeli aggression caused the closure of the Suez Canal,[4] thus disrupting world trade and inflicting immeasurable damage to the interests of the world community. During the present war, Israel did not hesitate in raiding, bombarding and destroying the oil export terminals in the East Mediterranean, thus aggravating the shortage of oil supplies to Europe.[5] Now, seeing for the third time that Israel, encouraged and abetted by the United

---

Source: *The Guardian*, 15 November 1973. Copyright Guardian News & Media Ltd.

[1] After the Six-Day War of 1967 Israel seized the Sinai Peninsula and the Gaza Strip from Egypt, the Palestinian West Bank and East Jerusalem from Jordan, and the Golan Heights from Syria.

[2] UN Security Council Resolution 242, adopted on November 22, 1967, in the aftermath of the Six-Day War, called for the withdrawal of Israeli armed forces from territories occupied in the recent conflict and the recognition by every state in the area of Israel's right to exist.

[3] Permanent members of the Security Council were at the time the Republic of China (Taiwan), the Soviet Union, the United States, the United Kingdom, and France.

[4] Israeli aggression "caused" the closing of the canal in the sense that its surprise attack on Syria and Egypt in June 1967 at the beginning of the Six-Day War led to Egypt's decision to close the canal to traffic. The blockade remained in effect until 1975.

[5] The "two previous wars" are the Six-Day War (1967) and the Suez War (1956). In the latter, Israel was allied with France and the United Kingdom in an effort to evict Egypt from the Suez Canal, which had been nationalized by Egypt in July 1956.

States, is persisting in its aggressive policy and defying Arab rights, the Arab Petroleum Exporting Countries have found themselves constrained to end their self-imposed economic sacrifices; namely producing quantities of their depleting oil resources far exceeding the requirements of their own economic needs. They will continue to pursue this course of action until such time as the international community decides to act and take decisive and effective measures to remedy the situation and induce Israel to withdraw from Arab lands and impress upon the United States how costly the latter's policy of unlimited and unequivocal support for Israel has proved to be to the major industrial countries.

Consequently, the Arab Petroleum Ministers, . . . , have resolved that all Arab Oil Exporting Countries shall forthwith cut their production respectively by no less than 5% of the September production, and maintain the same rate of reduction each month thereafter until the Israeli forces are fully withdrawn from all Arab territories occupied during the June 1967 War, and the legitimate rights of the Palestinian people are restored.

However, the Arab countries . . . wish to assure friendly countries . . . that they shall not be made to suffer from the Arab oil cut. Such countries will continue to receive the same quantities supplied to them from the Arab countries before the cut. On the other hand, countries which demonstrate moral and material support to the Israeli enemy will be subjected to severe and progressive reduction in Arab oil supplies, leading to a complete halt.

## The U.S.A. & Holland

Acting upon the above resolutions . . . the Arab Oil Exporting Countries found it necessary to impose a total embargo on oil exports to the U.S.A. and Holland in view of the active support given to the Israelis during this war. . . .

The Arabs wish to make it plainly and explicitly known, however, that this embargo is not intended in any way to castigate the peoples of the countries concerned, with whom the Arabs wish to maintain the closest and warmest friendly relations; but this embargo is indeed directed against the Governments, or those responsible in the Governments, for the anti-Arab policy which the Arabs could only reply to in kind.

Evidently, the Arabs' embargo on the export of strategic products to hostile and unfriendly countries—especially in time of war—is entirely in line with similar policies pursued by other countries at war, and even by the U.S.A., which went so far with this policy as to place an embargo on wheat and food supplies *to countries which have no special relations nor share common interests with the United States.*[6]

It is with deep regret that the Arab countries found it necessary to take this decision which is bound to bring suffering to the peoples of the countries concerned: but until such time as the Governments of the U.S.A. and Holland . . . reverse their positions and add their weight behind the World Community's consensus to end the Israeli occupation of Arab Lands and bring about the full restoration of the Legitimate rights of the Palestinian people, the Arab Oil Exporting Countries will not rescind their decision to impose a total embargo on oil exports to such countries.

---

[6]The United States used trade sanctions as part of its foreign policy throughout the twentieth century. In the postwar era the Export Control Act of 1949 gave the president the power to limit the export of weapons and military technology to the Soviet Union and its Eastern European satellites. In 1973 the only two countries subject to a total embargo, including food, were North Korea and Cuba.

# Japan's Economic Miracle

## 97 • AKIO MORITA, MADE IN JAPAN

After World War II, a former Japanese naval lieutenant, Akio Morita, and a defense contractor, Masaru Ibuka, borrowed $500 to form the Tokyo Telecommunications Engineering Corporation. With plans to produce consumer goods for the domestic market, they built a small factory in Tokyo and began to manufacture electric rice cookers. With an infusion of capital from Morita's father, the head of a family-owned sake brewery, the firm moved into consumer electronics with the marketing of a tape recorder in Japan in the early 1950s. Later in the decade the firm entered the international market with a miniaturized radio that used transistors, tiny new capacitors developed in the United States, rather than electronic tubes. Named "Sony" from the Latin word *sonus* for sound, the radios became so popular that Morita and Ibuka changed their company's name to the Sony Corporation in 1958. Beginning in the 1960s, the corporation branched out into chemicals, insurance, the recording industry, and real estate while introducing a stream of successful products, including transistorized tape recorders, videotape cameras and recorders, and color televisions. Although growth slowed in the 1970s, Sony rebounded in the 1980s and 1990s with new products such as the Walkman, digital audiotape, and compact disks and with acquisitions such as the purchase of Columbia Films in 1989.

During the 1980s Morita, having presided over a spectacular economic success story, entered semi-retirement. This gave him time to write his memoirs, which were published in English in 1986 with the title *Made in Japan*. In the book Morita discusses the unique features of Japanese business philosophy, underscoring the differences between Japanese and American practices. It became required reading in many U.S. business schools before the Japanese economy entered a prolonged slump in the 1990s.

### QUESTIONS FOR ANALYSIS

1. According to Morita, what were some of the obstacles Japan had to overcome to build its economy in the postwar years?
2. Why does Morita believe that good employee–employer relations are the key to business success?
3. What are some of the steps taken by the Sony Corporation to ensure good employee relations?
4. According to Morita, what are some of the differences between Japanese and U.S. business executives?
5. Why does Morita believe that Japanese business methods and philosophy are superior to those of Americans?

## Selling to the World

Although our company was still small and we saw Japan as quite a large and potentially active market, it was the consensus among Japanese industrialists that a Japanese company must export goods in order to survive. With no natural resources except our people's energy, Japan had no alternative. And so it was natural for us to look to foreign markets. Besides, as business prospered, it became obvious to me that if we did not set our sights on marketing abroad, we would not grow to be the kind of company Ibuka and I had envisioned. We wanted to change the image of Japanese goods as poor in quality, and, we reasoned, if you are going to sell a high-quality, expensive product, you need an affluent market, and that means a rich, sophisticated country. . . . But in 1958, the year after we produced our "pocketable" transistorized radio, only 1 percent of Japanese homes had a TV set, only 5 percent had a washing machine, and only two-tenths of 1 percent had an electric refrigerator. Fortunately, the Japanese economy began to grow vigorously from the mid-fifties onward. Double-digit increases in the gross national product and low inflation gave a great boost to consumer spending. Many people say Japan's true postwar era really began in 1955, the year we introduced the first transistorized radio in Japan. The country's GNP grew, amazingly, by 10.8 percent. Japanese households needed everything, and because of the high savings rate, which . . . was over 20 percent, the people could afford to buy. So with good and growing markets at home and potential markets abroad, the world was beginning to look bright. . . .

We were doing well, although we still had tough competition getting our name known in Japan, where brand consciousness and brand loyalty are very high. Overseas we were all on an even footing. And perhaps we were in a better position abroad than anybody. Quality Japanese consumer goods were virtually unknown before the war. The image of anything marked "Made in Japan" that had been shipped abroad before the war was very low. Most people in the United States and Europe, I learned, associated Japan with paper umbrellas, kimonos, toys, and cheap trinkets. In choosing our name we did not purposely try to hide our national identity . . . but we certainly did not want to emphasize it and run the risk of being rejected before we could demonstrate the quality of our products. But I must confess that in the early days we printed the line "Made in Japan" as small as possible. . . .

## On Management

There is no secret ingredient or hidden formula responsible for the success of the best Japanese companies. No theory or plan or government policy will make a business a success; that can only be done by people. The most important mission for a Japanese manager is to develop a healthy relationship with his employees, to create a family-like feeling within the corporation, a feeling that employees and managers share the same fate. Those companies that are most successful in Japan are those that have managed to create a shared sense of fate among all employees . . . and the shareholders.

I have not found this simple management system applied anywhere else in the world, and yet we have demonstrated convincingly, I believe, that it works. For others to adopt the Japanese system may not be possible because they may be too tradition-bound, or too timid. The emphasis on people must be genuine and sometimes very bold and daring, and it can even be quite risky. But in the long run—and I emphasize this—no matter how good or successful you are or how clever or crafty, your business and its future are in the hands of the people you hire. . . .

That is why I make it a point personally to address all of our incoming college graduates each year. The Japanese school year ends in March, and companies recruit employees in their last semester, so that before the end of the school year they know where they are going. They take up their new jobs in April. I always gather these new recruits together at headquarters in Tokyo, where we have an introductory or orientation ceremony. This year I looked out at more than seven hundred young, eager faces and gave them a lecture, as I have been doing for almost forty years. . . . The new employees are getting their first direct and sobering view of what it will be like in the business world. I tell them what I think is important for them to know about the company and about themselves. I put it this way to the last class of entering employees:

"We did not draft you. This is not the army, so that means you have voluntarily chosen Sony. This is your responsibility, and normally if you join this company we expect that you will stay for the next twenty or thirty years." . . .

"When you leave the company thirty years from now or when your life is finished, I do not want you to regret that you spent all those years here. That would be a tragedy. I cannot stress the point too much that this is your responsibility to yourself. So I say to you, the most important thing in the next few months is for you to decide whether you will be happy or unhappy here. So even though we recruited you, we cannot, as management, or a third party, make other people happy; happiness must be created yourself." . . .

The concept of lifetime employment arose when Japanese managers and employees both realized that they had much in common and that they had to make some long-range plans. The laws made it difficult legally, and expensive, to fire anybody, but that didn't seem like such a bad idea, since workers were badly in need of work, and struggling businesses needed employees who would remain loyal.

Without class disputes, despite the Communist and Socialist party propaganda, the Japanese, who are a homogeneous people, were able to cooperate to provide for their common welfare. I have often said that the Japanese company has become very much a social security organization.

In the postwar era, the tax laws make it useless for a company to pay an executive a lot of money, because the graduated tax rises sharply very quickly, and you are very soon in the highest bracket. Company-paid amenities such as worker dormitories and allowances for commuting, for example, help workers make up for the tax system. Tax shelters and tax avoidance are virtually unknown in Japan. Today, the salary for a top management official is rarely more than seven or eight times that of an entry-level junior executive trainee. This means Japan has no multimillion-dollar brass, and companies give no huge executive bonuses, no stock options, no deferred income, no golden parachutes, and therefore the psychological, as well as the real, gap between employees is narrower than in other countries. . . .

What we in industry learned in dealing with people is that people do not work just for money and that if you are trying to motivate, money is not the most effective tool. To motivate people, you must bring them into the family and treat them like respected members of it. Granted, in our one-race nation this might be easier to do than elsewhere, but it is still possible if you have an educated population. . . .

## American and Japanese Management Styles

If you ask a Japanese executive, "What is your most important responsibility?" he will invariably say that continued employment and improving the livelihood of the workers is at or near the top of the list. In order to do that, the company must make a profit. Making a profit will never be at the top of the list. Most of the American business executives I know put the highest priority on return to the investors or this year's profit. They have the responsibility because the investors gave it to them, and to stay in their jobs they have to continue to keep the investors happy. The board of directors represents the investors, and if top management fails to give the return the investors feel they need, he will be fired. For that reason he is entitled to use the factory and the machinery of the company, and also the workers, as tools to accomplish his aim. This can be detrimental.

Visiting an American television plant in the Midwest a few years ago, I commented to the manager that I thought he really needed to buy some more modern equipment in order to improve the company's productivity. He shocked me when he told me that his compensation was based on the company's financial performance and that he was not going to do anything, like making long-range investments, that might cut his compensation for the sake of the next manager who would be along in a year or so. . . .

Generally, in the United States, management's attitude toward the labor force and even the lower-level executives is very hierarchical, much more so than in Japan. . . . When I visited the Illinois television assembly plant of Motorola, one of the first things I noticed was that the offices were air-conditioned, but out on the shop floor it was stifling, people were dripping with sweat, and big noisy fans were blowing the hot air around. The workers were plainly uncomfortable, and I thought, "How can you get quality work from people laboring under such conditions? And what kind of loyalty can they be expected to show to the big bosses in their cool offices!" In Japan people often used to say that the shop floor where the goods were made was always more comfortable than the workers' homes. . . .

Amenities are not of great concern to management in Japan. . . . Just recently a U.S. company, the maker of highly complex computerized graphics equipment, formed a joint venture with a Japanese company and the Japanese partner said to his foreign associate: "We would like you to design the showroom, but please allow us to design the office space upstairs." . . . The showroom was beautifully appointed, with soft lighting and comfortable chairs for visitors and clients. The equipment was highlighted using modern display techniques, and there were video demonstrations and elegant four-color brochures on the company and its equipment. Upstairs, the entire office staff was housed in one big open room without partitions . . . in a simple, very Spartan arrangement. The U.S. partner raised his eyebrows, and his Japanese colleague explained, "If Japanese clients come into the office of a new and struggling company and see plush carpet and private offices and too much comfort, they become suspicious that this company is . . . devoting too much thought and company resources to management's comfort, and perhaps not enough to the product or to potential customers. If we are successful after one year, we might put up low partitions. After two or three years, we might give the top executive a closed office. But for now we have to all be reminded that we are struggling together to make this company a success."

# Problems and Prospects of Postcolonial Africa

As one African colony after another achieved independence in the 1950s and 1960s, euphoria swept across the continent. All the indignities of colonialism and all the ways it had branded Africans with the mark of inferiority could now be forgotten. Leaders and common people alike were ready to show the world they could govern themselves effectively. Their economic outlook was no less optimistic: With the heavy hand of the colonial master lifted from their economies, they anticipated growth and prosperity.

In the first three decades of independence, however, Africans experienced more difficulties and disappointments than anyone could have imagined. Many of the newly independent states were nations in name only, with boundaries drawn by colonial administrators without regard for cultural affinities, ethnic groupings, religious traditions, and economic viability. Throughout the continent, shallow national loyalties were undermined by regionalism and ethnic conflict, and soon civil wars and military coups took their toll on democratic governments. With few exceptions, the norm became one-party authoritarian regimes, dominated by short-sighted leaders who enriched themselves and their henchmen while their nations' economies crumbled. In some parts of Africa lawlessness, random violence, and warlordism overwhelmed even the dictators, and effective government essentially disappeared.

Blacks in South Africa faced a different challenge. Following South Africa's independence from Great Britain in 1910, blacks, along with Indians and colored (people of mixed blood), steadily lost ground politically and economically as a result of discriminatory laws imposed by the white minority. Beginning in the late 1940s a barrage of legislation sponsored by the Nationalist Party turned South Africa's discrimination policies into something harsher, the apartheid system. Nonwhites lost their remaining political rights; mixed marriages and interracial sex were outlawed; racial segregation was decreed for schools, universities, public transportation, restaurants, theaters, and sports facilities. Apartheid also demanded residential segregation, requiring blacks to live in urban townships or rural homelands known as Bantustans. Unlike European colonialism, which ended in Africa at the first signs of black nationalism, apartheid persisted despite black resistance and pressure from the international community. It ended only in 1994 when blacks received the right to vote for members of a parliament that would serve for five years and write a new constitution. The era of white rule in sub-Saharan Africa was finally over.

# Apartheid's Bitter Fruits

### 98 • NELSON MANDELA, THE RIVONIA TRIAL SPEECH

In 1912, two years after South Africa had been granted independence from Great Britain, blacks formed the African National Congress (ANC) to foster black unity and win political rights. At first the ANC sought to reach its goals through petitions and appeals to white politicians, but following the implementation of apartheid after World War II, it sponsored campaigns of passive resistance and supported strikes by black labor unions. The result was more government repression. Predictably, some blacks abandoned moderation for sabotage and terrorism. Among them was Nelson Mandela (1918–2013), the son of a tribal chieftain, who became a lawyer and an ANC activist in the 1940s. After the ANC was outlawed in 1960, and after he organized a three-day stay-at-home strike in 1961, Mandela went into hiding to avoid arrest. While eluding a nationwide manhunt, he helped found Umkhonto we Sizwe (Spear of the Nation), a branch of the ANC that carried out bombings in several cities. Arrested in 1962, he was tried and convicted of sabotage and plotting to overthrow the government and sent to the notorious prison on Robben Island, just off South Africa's southwestern coast. Here he spent eighteen of his twenty-seven years as a prisoner. He remained a prisoner until 1990, when he was released by President F. W. de Klerk as one of the first steps toward the abolition of the apartheid system. In 1994 he was elected as South Africa's first president in the post-apartheid era. He retired from politics in 1999, and after a long period of declining health died in early December 2013 at the age of 95.

The following excerpt comes from Mandela's most famous speech, sometimes given the title "I Am Prepared to Die" from its closing line. It was delivered on April 20, 1964, as he opened his defense against charges of sabotage and treason before Justice Quartus de Wet, the white judge who decided his case and imposed his sentence of life imprisonment on June 12, 1964.

## QUESTIONS FOR ANALYSIS

1. Why did Mandela decide that the ANC must resort to violence to achieve its goals?
2. What distinction does Mandela draw between sabotage and terrorism?
3. What attractions did Mandela and other ANC leaders see in communism?
4. What aspects of apartheid does Mandela find most degrading?
5. According to Mandela, how does apartheid affect the daily lives of the blacks?

I have already mentioned that I was one of the persons who helped to form Umkhonto. I, and the others who started the organization, did so for two reasons. Firstly, we believed that as a result of Government policy, violence by the African people had become inevitable, and that unless responsible leadership was given to . . . control the feelings of our people, there would be outbreaks of terrorism which would produce an intensity of bitterness and hostility between the various races of this country which is not produced even by war. Secondly, we felt that without violence there would be no way open to the African people to succeed in their struggle against the principle of White supremacy. All lawful modes of expressing opposition to this principle had been closed

by legislation, and we were placed in a position in which we had either to accept a permanent state of inferiority, or to defy the Government.

But the violence which we chose to adopt was not terrorism. We . . . were all members of the African National Congress, and had behind us the ANC tradition of non-violence and negotiation as a means of solving political disputes. We believed that South Africa belonged to all the people who lived in it, and not to one group, be it Black or White. We did not want an interracial war, and tried to avoid it to the last minute. . . .

The African National Congress was formed in 1912 to defend the rights of the African people. . . . For thirty-seven years—that is until 1949—it adhered strictly to a constitutional struggle. It put

*Source:* Nelson Mandela, *No Easy Walk to Freedom,* Ruth First, ed. (New York: Basic Books, 1965), pp. 163–168.

forward demands and resolutions; it sent delegations to the Government in the belief that African grievances could be settled through peaceful discussion and that Africans could advance gradually to full political rights. But White Governments remained unmoved, and the rights of Africans became less instead of becoming greater. . . .

Even after 1949, the ANC remained determined to avoid violence. At this time, however, there was a change from the strictly constitutional means of protest which had been employed in the past. The change was embodied in a decision which was taken to protest against apartheid legislation by peaceful, but unlawful, demonstrations against certain laws. Pursuant to this policy the ANC launched the Defiance Campaign. . . . This campaign was based on the principles of passive resistance. More than 8,500 people defied apartheid laws and went to jail. Yet there was not a single instance of violence in the course of this campaign. . . .

In 1960 there was the shooting at Sharpeville,[1] which resulted in the proclamation of a state of emergency and the declaration of the ANC as an unlawful organization. My colleagues and I, after careful consideration, decided that we would not obey this decree. The African people were not part of the Government and did not make the laws by which they were governed. We believed in the words of the Universal Declaration of Human Rights,[2] that "the will of the people shall be the basis of authority of the Government," and for us to accept the banning was equivalent to accepting the silencing of the Africans for all time. The ANC refused to dissolve, but instead went underground. . . .

The avoidance of civil war had dominated our thinking for many years, but when we decided to adopt violence as part of our policy, we realized that we might one day have to face the prospect of such a war. . . . We did not want to be committed to civil war, but we wanted to be ready if it became inevitable.

Four forms of violence were possible. There is sabotage, there is guerrilla warfare, there is terrorism, and there is open revolution. We chose to adopt the first method and to exhaust it before taking any other decision.

In the light of our political background the choice was a logical one. Sabotage did not involve loss of life, and it offered the best hope for future race relations. . . . Attacks on the economic life lines of the country were to be linked with sabotage on Government buildings and other symbols of apartheid. These attacks would serve as a source of inspiration to our people. In addition, they would provide an outlet for those people who were urging the adoption of violent methods and would enable us to give concrete proof to our followers that we had adopted a stronger line and were fighting back against Government violence. . . .

Another of the allegations made by the State is that the aims and objects of the ANC and the Communist Party are the same. . . . It is true that there has often been close cooperation between the ANC and the Communist Party. But cooperation is merely proof of a common goal—in this case the removal of White supremacy—and is not proof of a complete community of interests. . . . It is perhaps difficult for White South Africans, with an ingrained prejudice against communism, to understand why experienced African politicians so readily accept communists as their friends. But to us the reason is obvious. Theoretical differences amongst those fighting against oppression is a luxury we cannot afford at this stage. What is more, for many decades communists were the only political group in South Africa who were prepared

---

[1]The Sharpeville Massacre took place in 1960 when police killed 69 and wounded 178 in an anti-apartheid demonstration.

[2]Accepted by the United Nations on December 10, 1948.

to treat Africans as human beings and their equals; who were prepared to eat with us, talk with us, live with us, and work with us. They were the only political group which was prepared to work with the Africans for the attainment of political rights and a stake in society. Because of this, there are many Africans who, today, tend to equate freedom with communism.[3] . . .

Our fight is against real, and not imaginary, hardships or, to use the language of the State prosecutor, "so-called hardships." Basically, we fight against two features which are the hallmarks of African life in South Africa and which are entrenched by legislation which we seek to have repealed. These features are poverty and lack of human dignity. . . . South Africa is the richest country in Africa, and could be one of the richest countries in the world. But it is a land of extremes and remarkable contrasts. The Whites enjoy what may well be the highest standard of living in the world, whilst Africans live in poverty and misery. Forty percent of the Africans live in hopelessly overcrowded and, in some cases, drought-stricken Reserves, where soil erosion and the overworking of the soil make it impossible for them to live properly off the land. Thirty percent are laborers, labor tenants, and squatters on White farms and work and live under conditions similar to those of the serfs of the Middle Ages. The other 30 percent live in towns where they have developed economic and social habits which bring them closer in many respects to White standards. Yet most Africans, even in this group, are impoverished by low incomes and [the] high cost of living. . . .

The lack of human dignity experienced by Africans is the direct result of the policy of White supremacy. White supremacy implies Black inferiority. Legislation designed to preserve White supremacy entrenches this notion. Menial tasks in South Africa are invariably performed by Africans. When anything has to be carried or cleaned the White man will look around for an African to do it for him, whether the African is employed by him or not. Because of this sort of attitude, Whites tend to regard Africans as a separate breed. They do not look upon them as people with families of their own; they do not realize that they have emotions—that they fall in love like White people do; that they want to be with their wives and children like White people want to be with theirs; that they want to earn enough money to support their families properly, to feed and clothe them and send them to school. And what "house-boy" or "garden-boy" or laborer can ever hope to do this? . . .

. . . Children wander about the streets of the townships because they have no schools to go to, or no money to enable them to go to school, or no parents at home to see that they go to school, because both parents (if there be two) have to work to keep the family alive. This leads to a breakdown in moral standards, to an alarming rise in illegitimacy, and to growing violence which erupts, not only politically, but everywhere. . . . There is not a day that goes by without somebody being stabbed or assaulted. . . . And violence is carried out of the townships in the White living areas. People are afraid to walk alone in the streets after dark. House-breakings and robberies are increasing, despite the fact that the death sentence can now be imposed for such offenses. . . .

During my lifetime I have dedicated myself to this struggle of the African people. I have fought against White domination, and I have fought against Black domination. I have cherished the ideal of a democratic and free society in which all persons live together in harmony and with equal opportunities. It is an ideal which I hope to live for and to achieve. But if needs be, it is an ideal for which I am prepared to die.

---

[3]Elsewhere in his speech Mandela denied he was or had ever been a member of the South African Communist Party. This claim has been called into question by the English historian Stephen Ellis, who in 2012 presented evidence that Mandela had been a party member from 1960 until his arrest in 1962.

# The Challenge of Economic Development in Sub-Saharan Africa

## 99 • WORLD BANK, ACCELERATED DEVELOPMENT IN SUB-SAHARAN AFRICA: AN AGENDA FOR ACTION (THE "BERG REPORT")

Optimism about the economic future of postcolonial Africa did not last long. On achieving independence many African states launched ambitious economic plans to subsidize new industries, launch power projects, and build schools, universities, and hospitals. Such undertakings, financed by foreign aid, government borrowing, and exports of agricultural products and minerals, were accompanied by modest economic growth. During the 1970s, however, growth rates sunk, the region's trade imbalance grew from $1.5 billion to $8 billion, and government foreign debt increased from $6 billion to $32 billion. Idled factories, abandoned construction projects, hospitals without equipment or medicines, and ever-worsening shortages of consumer goods provided further evidence of economic failure. The human costs were enormous. By 1980 average annual per capita income in sub-Saharan Africa ranged from $59 to $115. Africans had shorter lifespans, lower literacy levels, and higher death rates among young children than the people of any other region in the world, including the poorest countries of Asia and Latin America.

By the end of the 1970s, African leaders and various international organizations responded to what was now perceived as a major economic crisis. In 1980, the economic ministers of fifty African states produced the Lagos Plan of Action for the Economic Development of Africa, which called for greater economic cooperation among African states, a continued commitment to education, and increased international aid, but no changes in government policies. One year later, another major report appeared, this one sponsored by the World Bank, an international organization that provided (and still provides) loans and other forms of assistance to alleviate poverty in developing countries. Prepared by the prominent American economist Eliot Berg, *Accelerated Development in Sub-Saharan Africa* (also known as the Berg Report) examined the roots of Africa's economic problems and called for changes in the policies and priorities of Africa's governments. It sharply criticized African states for favoring industry over agriculture, heavy government intervention in the economy, and trade policies aimed at protecting the domestic economy. It called for continued foreign aid to African governments, but only in return for commitment to what were called "structural adjustments." These typically involved austerity measures, privatization, the removal of price controls and subsidies, and the lifting of import and export restrictions.

Neither the Lagos Plan nor the Berg Report provided a quick cure for Africa's economic malaise. Africa's autocratic rulers, who benefited enormously from the status quo, resisted reforms, and if anything, Africa's economic problems worsened in the 1980s and 1990s. Many of these problems still exist in the early twenty-first century, but there are increasing numbers of success stories, at least some of which owe their accomplishments to recommendations in the Berg Report.

## QUESTIONS FOR ANALYSIS

1. How, according to the report, did the heritage of colonialism burden the African economy in the early years of independence?
2. What challenges to Africa's economic development resulted from African climate and geography?
3. According to the report, what were the causes of the continent's political instability in the postcolonial era? How did this political instability hurt economic growth?
4. According to the report, how have government trade policies impeded growth in the areas of agriculture and industry?
5. What benefits, in the view of the report's authors, will result from diminishing the state's role in the continent's economic affairs?
6. What benefits will accrue from emphasizing agriculture rather than industry as an engine of economic growth?

## Obstacles to Growth

One of the most critical problems of the past 20 years has been the scarcity of trained manpower. . . . Zaïre, which was left without a single African doctor, lawyer, engineer, or army officer at independence, was an extreme case, but foreigners occupied many positions of skill and responsibility even in the countries with the most advanced education systems; in Nigeria, Africans held fewer than 700 of the 3,000 senior posts in the civil service until the mid-1950s, and in Senegal, 1,500 French technical personnel occupied almost all of the top jobs in 1961. . . .

Throughout the region, trade and industry were almost entirely owned and managed by foreigners. As recently as 1975 there were only 80 African-owned shops in the Mozambican capital of Maputo, and after sixty years of colonial rule, African-owned and operated enterprises with more than ten employees were extremely rare, even in the relatively advanced economies of Kenya, Uganda, and Zimbabwe. . . .

This pattern of underdeveloped human resources is partially explained by the fact that even by the end of the 1950s, advanced education was still largely unavailable to most Africans: local facilities did not exist or, where they did, African enrollment was often restricted. Thus, in 1958, less than 10,000 African students were attending universities at home or abroad . . . , some 6,500 of whom were from Ghana and Nigeria. . . .

The number of people educated at the secondary level was also limited. In the late 1950s, the entire region produced only 8,000 secondary school graduates per year, 40 percent of whom were in Ghana and Nigeria. . . .

Just as educational and training needs were not being met, so too were health needs neglected. In 1960, for example, there was just one physician for every 50,000 people in Sub-Saharan Africa as compared to one per 12,000 in other low-income countries. . . .

The scarcity of managerial and technical cadres [trained personnel] at the time of independence

*Source:* World Bank, *Accelerated Development in Sub-Saharan Africa: An Agenda for Action* (Washington, D.C.: World Bank, 1981), pp. 9–14, 24–27, 40, 91, 95.

had strong adverse effects on public administration, industrial development, wage levels, and costs. Furthermore, the lack of education among the population reduced the stimuli for progressive change. . . .

Over the past two decades, a sizeable portion of the Sub-Saharan region was the scene of political and military conflict. . . . In the wake of independence, violent internal conflict burst forth in many of the new nations, stemming from the pluralism of African societies and the difficulties of postcolonial political consolidation. . . .

Civil and military strife and the political fragility which it reflected had several negative economic effects. First, it forced the post-independence leadership to give especially high priority to short-term political objectives. Second, it triggered large-scale displacement of people. In the 1970s, the number of refugees who had fled across national frontiers in Africa rose from 750,000 to over 5 million, accounting for about half of all refugees worldwide. . . . Third, civil strife induced a diversion of resources to military spending. . . .

[The] African economies at independence were unevenly developed. . . . Across the continent there were but few islands of modern economic development. For example, in West Africa, where peasant production of export crops was the primary motor of development, modern economic activity took place mainly in the forest and coastal zones extending 200 kilometers [c.125 miles] inland from the sea. In the vast interior, where most of the population was (and still is), evidence of economic change was barely visible. . . .

The dominance of subsistence production presented special obstacles to agricultural development. . . . Little was known about new crops, new methods of crop rotation, seed protection, or more productive farming techniques. Agricultural research and experimentation were lacking, but so too was most basic information about rainfall, river flow, soil quality, farming systems, and patterns of land use. Accordingly, the experimental and intellectual raw material necessary for progress in agriculture was very sparse. . . .

Moreover, basic infrastructure was, in some areas, almost nonexistent: roads, railroads, ports, buildings, and communications systems were scant and did not penetrate the hinterland. . . .

Africa is "preeminently tropical," . . . a fact which creates special obstacles to development. First, . . . most African soils are delicate, deficient in organic materials, and in general only moderately fertile. Well-watered areas are only about one quarter of the total; elsewhere, rains are inadequate in volume and highly variable in time. Moreover, the absence of frost . . . creates especially burdensome problems of weed and pest control. Second, the search for minerals is more difficult in the tropics than in temperate zones, where rock formations are well exposed. . . . Finally, because the tropical climate is especially hospitable to bacterial and parasitic diseases and to endemic diseases . . . , human energy and productivity are adversely affected. . . .

Geography has also had an impact. Africa's large physical size and dispersed population create special transport needs and problems. In addition, fourteen of the world's twenty landlocked developing countries are located on this continent. . . . These factors have obvious implications for road construction: long trunk routes generate relatively low volumes of traffic, and extensive feeder networks are required.

## A Flawed Trade Policy

There has been a common pattern of response to foreign exchange scarcity in most African countries. Government have relied increasingly on import restrictions rather than [currency] devaluation to conserve foreign exchange. More and more countries have imposed higher tarrifs, quotas, and bans on "nonessential" imports. . . . Quite separately from balance of payments policy, governments have tried to promote industrialization through tariff protection for local industry against competing imports. . . .

A trade and exchange-rate system that relies heavily on import restrictions biases the incentive system against agriculture in several ways. First, it forces farmers to purchase high-cost local implements. For example, in Upper Volta there is a 66 percent tariff on animal-drawn plows and a 58 percent tariff on engines used for irrigation pumps. Second, it raises the cost of consumer goods. Thus, in Kenya, imports of second-hand clothing have been banned and there is a 100 percent tariff on textiles. This measure has doubled the price of clothing and textiles and reduced real rural incomes by 10 percent. Third, and most importantly, this . . . policy serves to hold down the prices farmers receive for their export crops. Several African countries now find that producers of traditional export crops cannot be paid enough to cover the costs of production. . . .

A second consequence of the predominant trade and exchange-rate policy in Africa is that it is biased against exports. As with agriculture, export industries are sometimes burdened with high-cost domestically produced inputs that reduce their competitiveness in world markets. In Kenya, for example, a survey showed that the cost of locally produced cans alone was higher than the price of canned vegetables from Asian competitors located in the Arabian Gulf. . . .

There are two other ways in which the typical trade . . . system adversely affects the prospects for long-term industrial growth. First, protection typically favors packaging or assembly-type industries, which provide very few benefits to the economy either in foreign exchange, employment, or skill development. Second, the nearly complete protection given to industry gives no incentive for growth in productivity. Infant industries tend, therefore, never to grow up. As a result, they continue to impose high costs on consumers.

## Reducing Government's Role

During the past 20 years the public sector has greatly extended its economic role in Africa, as it has elsewhere. This growth has come not only from expansion of government per se, but also by extension of the state into commercial or productive activities—manufacturing, mining, transport, marketing—activities which were largely in private hands before independence. . . .

The parastatal[1] sector grew rapidly after independence. Before then, African participation in the modern private sector, especially industry, was very rare. Following independence, change took two main forms: nationalization of existing enterprises, which were almost invariably foreign owned, and investment of a very substantial share of government resources in parastatal enterprises in transport, public utilities, and manufacturing. The hope was that these public enterprises would be self-financing. . . . They would not only generate surplus for additional investment, but could also play an important role in modernization by developing skilled labor and enhancing managerial capacity.

These expectations have not been realized. With the exception of the mineral-exporting parastatals and some of those trading in export crops, public enterprises have thus far caused serious fiscal burdens. . . .

Unless there is a change in the operating effectiveness of parastatals, particularly in industry, they will not take their proper place as growth points. They will, instead, continue to be fiscal drains and major contributors to slow growth. . . .

## The Role of Industrialization

Industrialization has a crucial role in long term development; it is one of the best training grounds for skill development: it is an important source of structural change and diversification; and it can increase the flexibility of the economy and reduce dependence on external forces. Industrialization also provides employment, foreign exchange, and domestic savings. Although these developmental benefits justify incurring some additional cost to

---

[1]Parastatal refers to a company or agency owned and controlled by the government.

promote industry, they do not justify the promotion of industry at any cost. Manufacturing is only a small sector in Africa and can make only a modest, though growing, contribution to development during the next decade. Excessive investment in industry can starve other sectors of capital, foreign exchange, and high-level manpower, while expensive manufactured products can raise costs in other sectors and limit their growth.

Industrialization has failed to provide many of the benefits expected of it in Africa during the past decade. Respectable rates of growth of manufacturing production were achieved for several years after independence, but large savings of foreign exchange upon which much industrial investment was based have not materialized. . . .

No single industrial strategy will fit the diverse conditions, prospects, and goals of all African countries. There are, however, a few generally applicable principles. To begin with, a conscious effort should be made to seek out profitable industrial export opportunities. Even though the bulk of investment opportunities will be in production for the domestic market, sooner or later most countries will also have to increase manufactured exports to maintain industrial growth, expand employment opportunities, and diversify exports.

Moreover, the pace of industrialization should not be forced. In many cases the choice is not between having or not having an industry, but between having a small-scale, high-cost industry now or an optimum-scale, efficient industry a few years from now. Proper sequencing is vital.

# Religion and Politics in the Middle East and India

During much of the twentieth century, it would not have been unreasonable to conclude that religion was a dying force among the world's peoples. The Islamic Brotherhood's popularity in the Arab world and Hindu–Muslim strife accompanying Indian independence are examples of religion's continuing vigor, but in general organized religion was on the defensive. In the West, mainline Protestant churches experienced declining membership and attendance, and the Roman Catholic Church found it increasingly difficult to attract young men to the priesthood. In Turkey, Iran, Egypt, and Indonesia, governments embraced aggressively secularist policies as part of campaigns to modernize their economies, educational systems, and culture. Avowedly atheist regimes in the Soviet Union and communist China sought to obliterate religious belief and practice altogether.

Clearly, reports of religion's demise were premature. As the twentieth century unfolded, religiously inspired individuals and movements played a key role in world affairs. A Baptist minister, Martin Luther King, Jr., with broad support from the nation's religious leadership, led the civil rights movement in the United States. Religious people also played important roles in the struggle against apartheid in South Africa, movements on behalf of nuclear disarmament, and events that led to the downfall of communism in Eastern Europe in the 1980s. In Latin America Catholic clergy committed themselves to serving the poor, called for social justice and democracy, and denounced dictatorship. They did so at great risk. No fewer than eight hundred fifty priests, nuns, and bishops were murdered by right-wing death squads or individual assassins in the 1970s and 1980s.

The most striking sign of religion's vigor in recent history has been the phenomenon of religious fundamentalism. Fundamentalists, irrespective of their confessional allegiance, share two basic beliefs. First, they tend to reject modernism, secularism, and other intellectual and religious tendencies that challenge or belittle religious beliefs passed down by tradition or contained in sacred texts. Second, they tend to believe that these religious truths should regulate and inspire all aspects of public and private life.

In the late twentieth century, fundamentalist movements appeared in every major faith and in societies at every level of economic development. Fundamentalism was strongest, however, in the Middle East and parts of Africa, India, and Southeast Asia, where affirmation of traditional religious values provided a way to strengthen cultural identity and limit the influence of foreign, Western-inspired values. It also led to conflict and provided the impetus for earthshaking political changes.

# Islamic Law in the Modern World

## 100 • RUHOLLAH KHOMEINI, ISLAMIC GOVERNMENT

Ruhollah Mustafa Musavi Khomeini, whose name is synonymous with Islamic fundamentalism and Iran's Islamic Revolution of 1979, was born in 1902 in Khumayn, an Iranian village some sixty miles southwest of Tehran. Following the example of his father and grandfather, he became a religious scholar, and by the late 1930s he was director of the school of Islamic studies in Qum, a pilgrimage site and spiritual center for Iran's Shiite Muslims. In the late 1950s he became a vocal critic of Iran's reigning monarch, Shah Muhammad Reza Pahlavi, attacking him for his pro-U.S. policies, dictatorial rule, and efforts to weaken Islam's role in Iran. In 1963, his arrest and imprisonment led to nationwide demonstrations and rioting, which were suppressed by army troops at the cost of thousands of lives. Released from prison and exiled in 1964, Khomeini continued to denounce the shah, whose secularism, heavy-handed rule, and ill-conceived economic policies continued to cause widespread discontent. In January 1978 rioting again broke out in Qum, this time sparked by articles in the state-controlled press accusing Khomeini of treason. In the following months millions of Iranians, spurred on by Khomeini and other religious leaders, took to the streets chanting "death to the shah." In January 1979 the shah fled the country; in February Khomeini returned from exile; and in March a national referendum approved the establishment of the Islamic Republic of Iran.

Iran's new government was a republic in name only. Although it had an elected parliament and president, it was dominated by Khomeini and a small circle of likeminded Islamic clerics. They purged the shah's supporters from the government, suppressed political and religious dissent, instituted religious courts to enforce Islamic law, and used the army and schools as instruments of religious indoctrination. Although Khomeini had promised to address the problems of poverty and social inequality in Iran, his efforts foundered in the face of war with Iraq in the 1980s, inflation, and rapid population growth. Nonetheless, by the time of his death in 1989 millions of Muslims in Iran and elsewhere venerated Khomeini as a heroic defender of Islam against the forces of secularism and imperialism, and his austere, uncompromising version of Islam had become a major force in world politics.

The following selection is an excerpt from *Islamic Government*, Khomeini's best-known work. The book is based on a series of lectures he delivered while in exile in 1970 to students at a religious school in the Iraqi city of Najaf. Khomeini's goal was to inspire his student listeners to work for the establishment of an Islamic state and to assume executive and judicial positions within it.

## QUESTIONS FOR ANALYSIS

1. According to Khomeini, who are the enemies of Islam and what are their goals?
2. How, according to Khomeini, do the enemies of Islam distort Islamic doctrine and practice? How does he counter their arguments?
3. How does Khomeini characterize the relationship between Islam and modern science and technology?
4. What are the shortcomings of existing governments in the Islamic world according to Khomeini?
5. What benefits will accrue to society if Islamic laws are rigorously enforced?
6. What is the meaning of the term *jihad* as used by Khomeini?

### Misconceptions About Islamic Law

At a time when darkness prevailed over the West, when America was populated by half-savage Indians, when tyrannical regimes in Byzantium and Persia[1] exercised discrimination and excessive use of force with total disregard for public opinion and existing laws—at that time God, exalted and mighty, made laws that were revealed to the greatest prophet, Muhammad, may God's peace and prayers be with him, that are astounding in their magnitude. Laws and principles were laid down for all human affairs. Before man's birth until he is lowered into his grave, laws have been drawn up to govern him. . . . Provisions of Islamic law contain rules for all aspects of society. Under this system all of mankind's needs are met, beginning with the relationship between neighbors, of children and tribe, and with fellow citizens, and with all aspects of married life and even with regulations concerning war and peace, international relations, punishments, commerce, industry and agriculture. The law also regulates . . . what a couple eats when married and in the period when a child is nursing. Islam regulates the duties of the parents, . . . the relationship between husband and wife, and the relationship of each of them with their children. In all these spheres, Islam has laws to produce perfect and virtuous human beings.

The agents of imperialism write at times in their books and papers: The penalties of Islam are cruel and harsh. . . . I wonder how these people think.

*Source:* Ruhollah Khomeini, *Islamic Government*. U.S. Government Publication, *Translations on the Near East and Northern Africa*, no. 1897, Joint Publications Research Service, no. 72663 (Arlington, VA, 1979), pp. 3–5, 15, 18, 52, 53, 55–57, 61.

[1]During Muhammad's lifetime (570–632 C.E.) the region north of Arabia was dominated by two large empires, the Byzantine Empire in Asia Minor and the Sassanid Empire in Persia (Iran).

. . . I have learned that they executed some time ago ten persons, one after the other, for smuggling ten grams of heroin. . . .

Punishing an alcohol drinker with eighty whip lashes is harsh, but executing people for smuggling ten grams of heroin is not harsh when most forms of social corruption are caused by alcohol! Traffic accidents on the highways, incidents of suicide and even heroin addiction—according to some people—are the consequences of drunkenness and alcohol drinking. Yet, they do not ban alcohol because the West has permitted it. . . .

If an alcohol drinker is to be given eighty lashes or an [unmarried] adulterer is to be punished with one hundred lashes and if a married adulterer or adulteress are to be stoned, you hear them scream: These are cruel and harsh sentences derived from the harshness of the Arabs. On the other hand, no objection must be made against the bloody massacres that have been taking place in Vietnam[2] for fifteen years on the lands of the masters of these rules despite the exorbitant costs that are extorted from the pockets of people. . . .

### Science, Materialism, and Islam

So far we have sketched the destructive plans of the imperialists. We must add to them certain internal factors as well, notably the powerful effect the material progress of the enemy has had on weakening the people, causing them to despise themselves.

. . . When some states advance industrially and scientifically, some of us feel inferiority and begin to think that our failure to do the same is due to our religion and that the only means to achieve such progress is to abandon religion and its laws and to violate the Islamic teachings and beliefs. When the enemies went to the moon, these people imagined that religion was the obstacle preventing them from doing the same! I would like to

tell these people: The laws of the Eastern or the Western camps are not what led them to this magnificent advance in invading outer space. . . . Let them go to Mars or anywhere they wish; they are still backward in the sphere of securing happiness to man, backward in spreading moral virtues and backward in creating psychological and spiritual progress on par to the material progress. They are still unable to solve their social problems because solving these problems and eliminating hardship requires . . . moral spirit. The material gains in the sphere of overcoming nature and invading space cannot accomplish this task. Wealth, capabilities and resources require the Islamic faith, creed and ethics to become complete and balanced, to serve man and to turn him away from injustice and poverty. We alone possess such morals and laws. Therefore, we should not cast aside our religion and our laws, which are directly connected with man's life and which harbor the nucleus of reforming people and securing their happiness in this world and in the hereafter. . . .

### The Timelessness of Islamic Law

It is obvious that the need for implementing laws was not exclusive to the prophet's age and that this need continues because Islam is not limited by time or place. Because Islam is immortal, it must be implemented and observed forever. If what was permissible by Muhammad is permissible until the day of resurrection [the end of time] and what was forbidden by Muhammad is forbidden to the day of resurrection, then Muhammad's restrictions must not be suspended, his teachings must not be neglected, punishment must not be abandoned, tax collection must not be stopped and defense of the nation of the Muslims and of their lands must not be abandoned. The beliefs that Islam came for a limited period and for a certain place violates the essentials of the Islamic

---

[2]When Khomeini delivered his speech in 1970, the Vietnam war, also known as the Second Indochinese War, had been going on since 1956 and would last another five years

beliefs. Considering that the implementation forever of laws after the renerable prophet, . . . one of the essentials of life, then it is necessary for government to assist and for this government to have the qualities of an executive and administrative authority. Without this, social chaos, corruption and ideological and moral deviation would prevail. This can be prevented only through the formation of a just government that runs all aspects of life.

## The Faults of Existing Governments

The only means that we possess to unite the Muslim nation, to liberate its lands from the grip of the imperialists and topple the governments of imperalism, is to seek to establish our Islamic government. The efforts of this government will be crowned with success when we become able destroy the heads of treason, the idols, the human images and the false gods who disseminate injustice and corruption on earth. . . .

To achieve their unjust economic goals, the imperialists employed the help of their political agents in our countries. As a result of this, there are hundreds of millions of starving people who lack the simplest health and educational means. On the other side, there are individuals with excessive wealth and corruption is widespread. The starving people are in a constant struggle to improve their conditions and to free themselves from the tyranny of the aggressive rulers. But the ruling minorities and their government agencies are also seeking to extinguish this struggle. . . .

Do you think that all that the information the radio says is true? Go to the villages and the rural areas and you will hardly find a single clinic in every one hundred or two hundred villages! They have not thought of the starved and of the naked, they have not allowed them to think and they have not permitted Islam to solve their problem. Islam, as you know

well, solved the problem of poverty and decided at the very outset that "the alms are for the poor."[3] Islam arranged and organized this but they are not allowing Islam to get to the Muslims in any way.

The nation is living in a state of hardship while the authorities go on with their extravagant spending and with increasing taxes. They purchase the Phantom jets[4] so that the Israelis may be trained on them. Considering that Israel is in a state of war with the Muslims, then whoever helps and supports it is in turn in a state of war with the Muslims. . . .

## A Final Charge to His Listeners

If you speak about Islam with utter sincerity and if you stress to the people its fundaments, laws, rules and systems, people will welcome and follow this religion. . . . I have witnessed this myself. When I make a speech I feel a change in the people and I feel the impact on them because they are displeased with the condition under which they live. Fear of the tyrants is filling their hearts and they are in direct need of people who speak courageously and firmly. Sons of Islam, be strong and firm in explaining your cause to the people so that you may defeat your enemy with all his weapons, troops and guards. Highlight the facts to the people and urge them on. Inject the spirit of jihad in the market and street people, in the worker, the peasant and the university man. All will rise for the jihad. All demand freedom, independence, happiness and dignity. Make the teachings of Islam available to all, because Islam is for all, and you will find that it will lead them to the path, light their way, correct their thoughts and beliefs and will make them offer and sacrifice so that the agencies of the policy of tyranny and imperialism may be destroyed and so that the Islamic government may rise on firm foundations.

---

[3]The third pillar of Islam is charity.
[4]Under the shah Iran purchased more than 200 Phantom jets, making it the second largest purchaser after Israel of these planes.

# The Place of Hinduism in Modern India

## 101 • GIRILAL JAIN, EDITORIALS

Religious tension between India's majority Hindu and smaller communities of Muslims and Sikhs divided India's political leaders in the 1930s and early 1940s; set off communal rioting that caused the deaths of tens of thousands in 1946; and ultimately led to the founding of two separate states, predominantly Muslim Pakistan and predominantly Hindu India, after the end of British rule in August 1947. In the year following independence as many as fourteen million Muslims, Hindus, and Sikhs crossed borders to escape entrapment in a state that was hostile to their faith. Newly formed governments were unable to deal with migrations of such staggering magnitude, and violence and slaughter occurred on both sides of the border. As many as five hundred thousand deaths resulted.

Despite partition and the mass migrations of 1947 and 1948, independent India remained religiously divided among Hindus (approximately eighty-two percent of the population), Muslims (approximately thirteen percent), and smaller communities of Christians, Sikhs, Parsis, Jains, and Buddhists. In 1949, under the leadership of the Congress Party, a constituent assembly that also served as India's first parliament approved a constitution that declared India to be a secular state committed to religious freedom and partiality to no single religious group.

None of India's religious groups has been completely satisfied with the results of India's commitment to secularism. Many Hindus remain convinced that the government has bent over backward to protect Muslims and Sikhs; Muslims and Sikhs, conversely, continue to believe that the government has pandered to Hindus. Religious tensions intensified in the 1980s as Muslims began to make converts among low-caste Hindus in the south, Sikhs agitated for an independent Punjab, and Hindus in 1982 organized their own political party, the Bharatiya Janata (Indian People's Party), or BJP, whose goal was the "Hinduization" of India.

A leading spokesman for Hindu nationalism was Girilal Jain, a journalist who served as editor-in-chief of the New Delhi *Times of India* between 1978 and 1988. Born into a poor rural family in 1922 and educated at Delhi University, Jain was drawn to Hindu nationalism and the BJP in the 1980s. He wrote the following editorials at a time when Hindu–Muslim tensions were peaking over the Babri mosque, built in the city of Ayodhya in the sixteenth century on a site believed by Hindus to be the birthplace of one of the most revered Hindu gods, Lord Rama. Hindus demanded the destruction of the mosque, which was no longer used, so that a temple in honor of Rama could be built. In 1989 Hindu nationalists began laying the foundations for a Hindu temple near the mosque, and in 1990, the year in which Jain wrote his editorials "The Harbinger of a New Order" and "Limits of the Hindu Rashra [Polity]" for the *Sunday Mail,* they attacked and damaged the mosque. In December 1992, one hundred fifty thousand Hindus stormed the mosque and destroyed it, precipitating a government crisis and causing violence that took two thousand lives. In September 2010, judges from the High Court of Allahabad (the supreme court for the state of

Uttar Pradesh) gave control of the main disputed section of the property to Hindus, with the remaining property to Muslims and a Hindu sect. In August 2011 India's supreme court agreed to consider an appeal of the verdict.

## QUESTIONS FOR ANALYSIS

1. What does Jain mean when he says that the issues that concern the BJP have to do with "civilization," not religion?
2. How does Jain define the West? How does he view the West's role in Indian history?
3. Why, according to Jain, is the controversy over the Ayodhya mosque so significant for India's future?
4. In Jain's view, why have the Muslims been satisfied to go along with the secularist policies of the Indian state?
5. What is Jain's vision of India's future?

### The Harbinger of a New Order

A specter haunts dominant sections of India's political and intellectual elites—the specter of a growing Hindu self-awareness and self-assertion. Till recently these elites had used the bogey of Hindu "communalism" and revivalism as a convenient device to keep themselves in power and to "legitimize" their slavish imitation of the West. Unfortunately for them, the ghost has now materialized.

Millions of Hindus have stood up. It will not be easy to trick them back into acquiescing in an order which has been characterized not so much by its "appeasement of Muslims" as by its alienness, rootlessness and contempt for the land's unique cultural past. Secularism, a euphemism for irreligion and repudiation of the Hindu ethos, and socialism, a euphemism for denigration and humiliation of the business community to the benefit of ever expanding rapacious bureaucracy, . . . have been major planks of this order. Both have lost much of their old glitter and, therefore, capacity to dazzle and mislead. . . .

The Hindu fight is not at all with Muslims; the fight is between Hindus . . . and the state, Indian in name and not in spirit and the political and intellectual class trapped in the debris the British managed to bury us under before they left. The proponents of the Western ideology are using Muslims as auxiliaries and it is a pity Muslim "leaders" are allowing themselves to be so used. . . .

### Limits of The Hindu Rashtra

India . . . has been a battleground between two civilizations (Hindu and Islamic) for well over a thousand years, and three (Hindu, Muslim and Western) for over two hundred years. None of them has ever won a decisive enough and durable enough victory to oblige the other two to assimilate themselves fully into it. So the battle continues. This stalemate lies at the root of the crisis of identity the intelligentsia has faced since the beginning of the freedom movement in the last quarter of the nineteenth century. . . .

The more resilient and upwardly mobile section of the intelligentsia must, by definition, seek to come to terms with the ruling power and its mores, and the less successful part of it to look for its roots and seek comfort in its cultural past. . . . Thus in the medieval period of our history there grew up a

*Source:* Girilal Jain, "On Hindu Rashtra" and "The Harbinger of a New Order." From Konrad Elst, *Ayodya and After* (New Delhi: Crescent Printing Works, 1991).

class of Hindus in and around centers of Muslim power who took to the Persian-Arabic culture and ways of the rulers; similarly under the more securely founded and far better organized and managed [British] Raj[1] there arose a vast number of Hindus who took to the English language, Western ideas, ideal, dress and eating habits; . . . they, their progeny and other recruits to their class have continued to dominate independent India.

They are the self-proclaimed secularists who have sought, and continue to seek, to remake India in the Western image. . . . Behind them has stood, and continues to stand, the awesome intellectual might of the West, which may or may not be anti-India, depending on the exigencies of its interests, but which has to be an antipathetic to Hinduism. . . .

Some secularists may be genuinely pro-Muslim. . . . But, by and large, that is not the motivating force in their lives. They are driven, above all, by the fear of what they call regression into their own past which they hate and dread. Most of the exponents of this viewpoint have come and continue to come understandably from the Left, understandably because no other group of Indians can possibly be so alienated from the country's cultural past as the followers of Lenin, Stalin and Mao, who have spared little effort to turn their own countries into cultural wastelands.

The state in independent India has, it is true, sought, broadly speaking, to be neutral in the matter of religion. But this is a surface view of the reality. The Indian state has been far from neutral in civilizational terms. It has been an agency, and a powerful agency, for the spread of Western values and mores. It has willfully sought to replicate Western institutions, the Soviet Union too being essentially part of Western civilization. It could

not be otherwise in view of the orientation and aspirations of the dominant elite of which Nehru[2] remains the guiding spirit. . . . Muslims have found such a state acceptable principally on three counts. First, it has agreed to leave them alone in respect of their personal law. . . . Secondly, it has allowed them to expand their traditional . . . educational system in madrasahs[3] attached to mosques. Above all, it has helped them avoid the necessity to come to terms with Hindu civilization in a predominantly Hindu India. This last count is the crux of the matter. . . .

In the past up to the sixteenth century, great temples have been built in our country by rulers to mark the rise of a new dynasty or to mark a triumph. . . . In the present case, the proposal to build the Rama temple has also helped produce an "army" which can in the first instance achieve the victory the construction can proclaim.

The raising of such an "army" in our democracy, however flawed, involves not only a body of disciplined cadres, which is available in the shape of the RSS,[4] a political organization, which too is available in the Bharatiya Janata Party, but also an aroused citizenry. . . . The Vishwa Hindu Parishad[5] and its allies have fulfilled this need in a manner which is truly spectacular.

The BJP-VHP-RSS leaders have rendered the country another great service. They have brought Hindu interests, if not the Hindu ethos, into the public domain where they legitimately belong. But it would appear that they have not fully grasped the implications of their action. Their talk of pseudosecularism gives me that feeling. The fight is not against what they call pseudosecularism; it is against secularism in its proper definition whereby man as animal usurps the place of man as spirit. . . .

---

[1]*Raj* is Hindi for reign, or rule; often used to refer to the British colonial administration.
[2]Jawaharlal Nehru (1899–1964), India's first prime minister, was an ardent secularist.
[3]Schools devoted to Islamic studies.

[4]RSS stands for the Rashtriya Swayamsevak Sangh, a militant Hindu organization founded in 1925, dedicated to the strengthening of Hindu culture.
[5]The Vishwa Hindu Parishad (VHP), or World Hindu Society, was founded in 1964. It is dedicated to demolishing mosques built on Hindu holy sites.

# Women Between Tradition and Change, 1960s–1970s

During the twentieth century, political leaders of industrialized nations, revolutionaries such as Lenin and Mao, and nationalist heroes as different as Ataturk and Gandhi all supported the idea of women's equality with men. The United Nations Charter of 1945 committed the organization to the same idea, and in 1948 the UN Universal Declaration of Human Rights reaffirmed the goal of ending all forms of gender-based discrimination. Beginning in the 1960s, powerful feminist movements with agendas ranging from equal educational access to legalized abortion took root in Western nations and to a lesser degree in Asia, Latin America, and Africa.

Despite these commitments to gender equality, progress for women worldwide was uneven. In developed industrial societies, women undoubtedly made great strides. Large numbers of women entered professions such as law, medicine, and university teaching; contraception and abortions were legalized in many nations; and laws forbidding gender-based discrimination were passed. Nonetheless, even in countries with strong feminist movements women still earned less than men did for doing the same jobs, were underrepresented in managerial positions, and played less significant roles in politics than did men. Furthermore, movements for gender equality met strong opposition from individuals and groups that were convinced that such movements threatened the family, undermined morality, and left women unhappy and unfulfilled.

In less economically developed parts of the world, efforts to improve the status of women faced much greater obstacles. Movements to improve women's legal status were hindered by the small pool of educated women and by the gap between middle-class, urban women and the millions of women in urban slums or rural villages who struggled against poverty. Religious fundamentalists in the Islamic world and elsewhere also sought to keep women in traditional roles. Even in China and India, both of which adopted strong antidiscrimination laws, it proved difficult to modify, let alone eradicate, centuries-old educational patterns, work stereotypes, marriage customs, and attitudes. More so than in any other area of modern life, tradition held its own against movements and ideologies seeking to liberate African, Asian, and Latin American women from the burdens of patriarchy and inequality.

## Feminism's Rebirth in the United States

### 102 • NATIONAL ORGANIZATION FOR WOMEN, 1966 STATEMENT OF PURPOSE

After having won the right to vote in most Western democracies by the 1920s, the feminist movements of the late nineteenth and early twentieth centuries lost momentum. In the 1930s and 1940s, women diverted their energies to surviving the

Great Depression and contributing to their nations' efforts in World War II. After 1945, as prosperity returned to the United States and Europe, women were generally content to accept the domestic roles prescribed for them by the family-oriented ethos of the postwar era.

Beginning in the 1960s, feminism reemerged as a powerful force, with much of its impetus and energy derived from movements originating in the United States. The revival of feminism gathered strength in the early 1960s with the appointment by President John F. Kennedy of the Presidential Commission on the Status of Women in 1961, the publication of Betty Friedan's *The Feminine Mystique* in 1963, and the inclusion of gender as one of the categories protected by the Civil Rights Act of 1964. The National Organization for Women (NOW), which was founded in 1966 and concentrated on redressing gender-based vocational and educational inequalities, assumed leadership of the women's movement.

The following excerpt is from the Statement of Purpose adopted by NOW in 1966. It was written by Betty Friedan, the author of *The Feminine Mystique* and the organization's first president.

## QUESTIONS FOR ANALYSIS

1. According to the NOW Statement of Principles, why are the mid-1960s the right time to advance the "unfinished revolution" of women's equality?
2. According to the NOW statement, what factors have kept women from full equality with men?
3. What evidence does the NOW statement provide to show that women's status and prospects declined in the 1950 and 1960s?

Enormous changes taking place in our society make it both possible and urgently necessary to advance the unfinished revolution of women toward true equality, now. With a life span lengthened to nearly 75 years it is no longer either necessary or possible for women to devote the greater part of their lives to child-rearing; yet childbearing and rearing—which continues to be a most important part of most women's lives—still is used to justify barring women from equal professional and economic participation and advance.

Today's technology has reduced most of the productive chores which women once performed in the home and in mass-production industries based upon routine unskilled labor. This same technology has virtually eliminated the quality of muscular strength as a criterion for filling most jobs, while intensifying American industry's need for creative intelligence. In view of this new industrial revolution created by automation in the mid-twentieth century, women can and must participate in old and new fields of society in full equality—or become permanent outsiders.

Despite all the talk about the status of American women in recent years, the actual position of women in the United States has declined, and is declining, to an alarming degree throughout the 1950's and 60's. Although 46.4% of all American women between the ages of 18 and 65 now work outside the home, the overwhelming majority—75%—are

*Source:* National Organization for Women Statement of Purpose (1966), reprinted with permission. This is a historical document (1966) and may not reflect the current language or priorities of the organization.

in routine clerical, sales, or factory jobs, or they are household workers, cleaning women, hospital attendants. About two-thirds of Negro women workers are in the lowest-paid service occupations. Working women are becoming increasingly—not less—concentrated on the bottom of the job ladder. . . . In 1964, of all women with a yearly income, 89% earned under $5,000 a year; half of all full-time year-round women workers earned less than $3,690; only 1.4% of full-time year-round women workers had an annual income of $10,000 or more.

Further, . . . too few women are entering and finishing college or going on to graduate or professional school. Today, women earn only one in three of the B.A.'s and M.A.'s granted, and one in ten of the Ph.D.'s.

In all the professions considered of importance to society, and in the executive ranks of industry and government, women are losing ground. Where they are present it is only a token handful. Women comprise less than 1% of federal judges; less than 4% of all lawyers; 7% of doctors. . . . And, increasingly, men are replacing women in the top positions in secondary and elementary schools, in social work, and in libraries—once thought to be women's fields.

Official pronouncements of the advance in the status of women hide not only the reality of this dangerous decline, but the fact that nothing is being done to stop it. . . . Until now, too few women's organizations and official spokesmen have been willing to speak out against these dangers facing women. Too many women have been restrained by the fear of being called "feminist." There is no civil rights movement to speak for women, as there has been for Negroes and other victims of discrimination. The National Organization for Women must therefore begin to speak. . . .

WE DO NOT ACCEPT the token appointment of a few women to high-level positions in government and industry as a substitute for serious continuing effort to recruit and advance women according to their individual abilities. To this end, we urge American government and industry to mobilize the same resources of ingenuity and command with which they have solved problems of far greater difficulty than those now impeding the progress of women.

WE BELIEVE that this nation has a capacity at least as great as other nations, to innovate new social institutions which will enable women to enjoy the true equality of opportunity and responsibility in society, without conflict with their responsibilities as mothers and homemakers. . . . We question the present expectation that all normal women will retire from job or profession for 10 or 15 years, to devote their full time to raising children, only to reenter the job market at a relatively minor level. . . . Above all, we reject the assumption that these problems are the unique responsibility of each individual woman, rather than a basic social dilemma which society must solve. True equality of opportunity and freedom of choice for women requires such practical, and possible innovations as a nationwide network of child-care centers, which will make it unnecessary for women to retire completely from society until their children are grown, and national programs to provide retraining for women who have chosen to care for their children full-time.

WE BELIEVE that it is as essential for every girl to be educated to her full potential of human ability as it is for every boy—with the knowledge that such education is the key to effective participation in today's economy and that, for a girl as for a boy, education can only be serious where there is expectation that it will be used in society. . . . Moreover, we consider the decline in the proportion of women receiving higher and professional education to be evidence of discrimination. This discrimination may take the form of quotas against the admission of women to colleges and professional schools; lack of encouragement by parents, counselors and educators; denial of loans or fellowships; or the traditional or arbitrary procedures in graduate and professional training geared in terms of men, which inadvertently discriminate against women. . . .

WE REJECT the current assumptions that a man must carry the sole burden of supporting himself, his wife, and family, and that a woman is automatically entitled to lifelong support by a man upon her marriage, or that marriage, home and family are primarily woman's world and responsibility. . . . We believe that a true partnership between the sexes demands a different concept of marriage, an equitable sharing of the responsibilities of home and children and of the economic burdens of their support. We believe that proper recognition should be given to the economic and social value of homemaking and child-care. To these ends, we will seek to open a re-examination of laws and mores governing marriage and divorce, for we believe that the current state of "half-equity" between the sexes discriminates against both men and women, and is the cause of much unnecessary hostility between the sexes.

WE BELIEVE that women must now exercise their political rights and responsibilities as American citizens. They must refuse to be segregated on the basis of sex into separate-and-not-equal ladies' auxiliaries in the political parties, and they must demand representation according to their numbers in the regularly constituted party committees . . . participating fully in the selection of candidates and political decision-making, and running for office themselves.

IN THE INTERESTS OF THE HUMAN DIGNITY OF WOMEN, we will protest, and endeavor to change, the false image of women now prevalent in the mass media, and in the texts, ceremonies, laws, and practices of our major social institutions. Such images perpetuate contempt for women by society and by women for themselves. We are similarly opposed to all policies and practices—in church, state, college, factory, or office—which, in the guise of protectiveness, not only deny opportunities but also foster in women self-denigration, dependence, and evasion of responsibility, undermine their confidence in their own abilities and foster contempt for women. . . .

WE BELIEVE THAT women will do most to create a new image of women by acting now, and by speaking out in behalf of their own equality, freedom, and human dignity—not in pleas for special privilege, nor in enmity toward men, who are also victims of the current, half-equality between the sexes—but in an active, self-respecting partnership with men. By so doing, women will develop confidence in their own ability to determine actively, in partnership with men, the conditions of their life, their choices, their future and their society.

# Women and Religious Fundamentalism: The Example of Iran

## 103 • ZAND DOKHT, THE REVOLUTION THAT FAILED WOMEN

Although the Pahlavi rulers of Iran, Reza Shah (1925–1941) and Muhammad Reza Shah (1941–1979), gave women political rights, allowed them to abandon the veil for Western-style dress, and encouraged female literacy and higher education, in the 1970s, millions of Iranian women shared the widespread disgust with the Pahlavi government's autocracy, corruption, and secularism. Women played a prominent role in the massive demonstrations that preceded Reza Shah's downfall in 1979 and led to his replacement by an Islamic fundamentalist regime under Ayatollah Ruholla Khomeini (1902–1989) (source 100). True to its Islamic principles, Khomeini's government revoked Pahlavi-era legislation on women and the family and enforced strict Islamic practices.

Many Iranian women who had taken advantage of educational opportunities and had benefited professionally during the Pahlavi years opposed the Islamic republic's effort to turn back the clock. In 1979, representatives from various women's organizations founded the Women's Solidarity Committee, dedicated to the protection of Iranian women's rights. Although later banned in Iran itself, a branch of the organization was maintained in London by Iranian women living in England. In the 1980s it published pamphlets and newsletters on issues pertaining to women's status in Iran. The following selection, written by Zand Dokht, appeared in one of their publications in 1981.

## QUESTIONS FOR ANALYSIS

1. According to Zand Dokht, in what specific ways did the Islamic Revolution in Iran affect women?
2. According to the author, how do Iran's new leaders envision a woman's role in society?
3. How does the author explain the fact that so many Iranian women supported the revolution that toppled the shah?
4. Why in the author's view did Pahlavi-era reforms fail to satisfy large numbers of Iranian women?

---

When Khomeini created his Islamic Republic in 1979, he relied on the institution of the family, on support from the women, the merchants, and the private system of landownership. The new Islamic constitution declared women's primary position as mothers. The black veil, symbol of the position of women under Islam, was made compulsory. Guards were posted outside government offices to enforce it, and women were sacked from their jobs without compensation for refusing to wear the veil. . . .

Schools were segregated, which meant that women were barred from some technical schools, even from some religious schools, and young girls' education in the villages was halted. Lowering the marriage age for girls to 13, reinstating polygamy and *Sigben* [temporary wives] . . . meant that women did not need education and jobs, they only needed to find husbands.

The Ayatollahs[1] in their numerous public prayers, which grew to be the only possible national activity, continuously gave sermons on the advantages of marriage, family, and children being brought up on their mother's lap. They preached that society would be pure, trouble free, criminalless (look at the youth problem in the West) if everybody married young, and if men married as many times as possible (to save the unprotected women who might otherwise become prostitutes). . . . Another *masterpiece* of the revolutionary Islamic government was to create a system of arranged marriages in prisons, between men and women prisoners, to "protect" women after they leave prison.

Because abortion and contraception are now unobtainable, marriage means frequent pregnancy. If you are 13 when you get married, it is likely that you will have six children by the time you are 20.

---

*Source:* From Miranda Davies, ed., *Third World, Second Sex* (London: Zed Press, 1983), pp. 152–155. Reprinted by permission of Zed Books.

[1]Ayatollah is a title of respect for high Shiite Muslim religious leaders.

This, in a country where half the total population are already under 16, is a tragedy for future generations.

Religious morality demands that all pleasures and entertainments be banned. Wine, music, dancing, chess, women's parts in theater, cinema, and television—you name it. Khomeini banned it. He even segregated the mountains and the seas, for male and female climbers and swimmers. . . .

Perhaps nowhere else in the world have women been murdered for walking in the street open-faced. The question of the veil is the most important issue of women's liberation in Muslim countries. The veil, a long engulfing black robe, is the extension of the four walls of the home, where women belong. The veil is the historical symbol of woman's oppression, seclusion, denial of her social participation and equal rights with men. It is a cover which defaces and objectifies women. To wear or not to wear the veil, for Muslim women is "the right to choose." . . .

Why do women, workers, and unemployed, support this regime which has done everything in its power to attack their rights and interests? The power of Islam in our culture and tradition has been seriously underestimated . . . and it was through this ideology that Khomeini directed his revolutionary government. The clergy dealt with everyday problems and spoke out on human relationships, sexuality, security, and protection of the family and the spiritual needs of human beings. It was easy for people to identify with these issues and support the clergy, although nobody knew what they were later to do.

Women's attraction to Khomeini's ideas was not based simply on his Islamic politics, but also on the way he criticized the treatment of women—as secretaries and media sex objects—under the Shah's regime. Women were genuinely unsatisfied and looking for change. Some educated Iranian women went back to Iran from America and Europe to aid the clergy with the same messages, and became the government's spokeswomen. They put on the veil willingly, defended Islamic virtues and spiritual values while drawing from their own experiences in the West. They said it was cold and lonely. Western women were only in pursuit of careers and self-sufficiency, and that their polygamous sexual relationships had not brought them liberation, but confusion and exploitation. These women joined ranks with an already growing force of Muslim women, to retrieve the tradition of true/happy Muslim women—in defense of patriarchy.

The mosque is not just a place of prayer, it is also a social club for women. It provides a warm, safe room for women to meet, chat, or listen to a sermon, and there are traditional women-only parties and picnics in gardens or holy places. Take away these traditional and religious customs from women as the Shah—with his capitalist and imperialist reforms, irrelevant to women's needs—tried to do and a huge vacuum is left. Khomeini stepped in to fill that vacuum. The reason why Khomeini won was that the Shah's social-economic program for women was dictatorial, bureaucratic, inadequate (especially in terms of health education) and therefore irrelevant to women's needs. . . .

# A Chinese Woman's Life Story

### 104 • "MING," RECOLLECTIONS

The following memoir is one of several interviews of Chinese women conducted by the Dutch scholar Denise Verschuur-Basse and published in her 1991 book, *Chinese Women Speak*. At the time of her interview, Ming (not her real name) was in her mid-twenties and a teacher.

Ming lived in a China that under Communist rule was officially committed to the liberation of women from the bonds of patriarchy and Confucianism. The constitution of 1950, adopted one year after the Communists took power, guaranteed equality between men and women, and the Marriage Law, also adopted in 1950, gave women the right to choose their own husbands and divorce. Girls were given access to education, could no longer have their feet bound, and were brought into the workforce in unprecedented numbers.

At the time of Ming's birth in 1965, China was experiencing a quiet interval between two periods of upheaval. The Great Leap Forward, Mao Zedong's disastrous effort to increase agricultural and industrial output through the mass mobilization of ideologically committed workers, had ended in 1960. The Great Cultural Revolution, Mao's effort to revitalize the revolution by purging the country of "reactionaries" and "bourgeois elements," would begin in 1966. Ming was eleven years old in 1976 when Mao died and thirteen in 1978 when China abandoned ideological purity for economic development. From then on she lived in a China increasingly open to foreign investment and private enterprise. As Ming's memoir reveals, however, it remained a China where many old attitudes and practices survived despite major political and economic changes.

## QUESTIONS FOR ANALYSIS

1. How did Ming's mother respond to her husband's abuse? What was her explanation for not seeking a divorce? What factors other than those stated might have played a role in her decision?
2. What do Ming's recollections reveal about the changes that took place concerning women and families in her lifetime and that of her parents?
3. Ming emphasizes that traditional attitudes about family relationships and women have persisted more in rural areas than they have in cities. What may explain this phenomenon?
4. Ming concludes that the "spirit of Confucius" still persists in China in the 1980s. To what extent do her own experiences confirm this observation?

---

My parents' marriage was arranged by their parents. My father is, in my opinion, the standard type of man you find in the countryside. He thinks that women should listen to men, and he does not respect them in the least. My mother was often beaten by my father. She didn't defend herself. For us children, our mother's submission was very painful. . . .

Often, my father's mother and my aunts would comfort my mother, because she would go see them to tell them about her situation. But then she was brought back home to us, and it always happened again; there was no other means of pressure. . . .

My mother had been educated until the beginning of high school. But in spite of her level, she never thought of divorcing. In the countryside it was very difficult. Even today, women do not think of divorcing, nor does the family. . . . One day I asked my mother why she did not divorce. I said to her, "you can get a divorce, the law permits it,"

*Source:* Denyse Verschuur-Basse, *Chinese Women Speak* (Westport, Conn., London: Praeger, 1991), pp. 59–65.

but my mother answered: "It is because of you, I do not want my children to be separated. . . ." Indeed, in case of divorce, the children are often separated. In our case, there might have been two children in my mother's care and one in my father's. Even when my mother would go to see the director of my father's work unit and explained the case to him, the whole committee would say, "It will get better, don't worry, it will most certainly get better!" But no one would have ever proposed the possibility of getting a divorce. . . .

Men like my father are still abundant in the countryside. My father behaved quite well toward my brother, but very differently toward my sister and myself. He does not like girls, and from a very early age we had a difficult relationship with him.

I was admitted to high school because of my teachers. Once, my father came to get me there. It was the first time he had done it. He wanted to introduce me to a boy, to arrange my marriage. It was the son of a friend. He had already discussed it with the father. . . . I absolutely wanted to finish high school. My father did not want me to. As I was among the top three students in my class, a teacher tried to persuade my father to let me finish my studies. Up to that time, my father was paying for part of my studying, and from then on, he refused to continue paying. . . . I absolutely hated my father, and I was forced to go back to the countryside.

So then I helped my mother. . . . She encouraged me to try for the entrance exam to university the next year, and I succeeded thanks to her. . . . My father, on the other hand, was trying to blackmail me. He would say, "If you agree to get married, you can go to university. . . . If you don't, you can't." I knew very well that if I got married, I would never go to university. . . . It was at that moment that I decided that I would definitely enter university, and I would be doing it partly for

my mother who was working so hard in the fields, planting and harvesting fruits and vegetables. . . .

My sister and my brother still live at home. My mother has already proposed a fiancé to my sister. She wanted someone who did not live too far away, so that they could take care of her later. My sister was in despair. After a long hesitation, I decided to discuss it with my mother. I felt very awkward to be opposing my mother. . . . My mother understood, and she accepted the refusal of her daughter. But generally, in the countryside, it is still the parents who look for partners for their children, and it is still rare for young people to go against the choice of their parents. . . .

Nowadays in the countryside, in most families it is the women who handle the money. The man listens to what the woman has to say; the women have a lot of influence. In earlier times, they would let their husband beat them and didn't react. Now they react, and they defend themselves. The fathers take more care of their children now than they used to, but the women are still left with the household tasks. . . .

Contraception before marriage is not accepted in the countryside; it is looked upon badly before marriage. But a great number of couples live together and even have children before being married. . . . But they must marry. Nowadays in the countryside, when people get married, it is the state that dictates when they can have a child.[1] There are production quotas. You might have the right to have a child in two or four years' time; it is up to the state to decide. If the state, the family planning agent, has decided that there can be five children for this village this year, it will look up when people got married and allow five couples to have a child. If a child is conceived outside of the family plan, in theory abortion is obligatory. But some parents have a child outside of the plan and do not declare it. Then the child has no identity card, and the parents have to pay a fine.

----

[1]China's family planning policy, often referred to as the "one-child" policy, was adopted in 1979 in response to perceived social, economic, and environmental problems. The policy allowed many exceptions. For example, rural families could have a second child if their firstborn was a girl or disabled. In November 2013 the law was modified so that couples in which one partner was an only child could have two children.

If people want a second child, for example, a son after a girl (sons are still preferred to daughters), here again, there will be a fine. The parents must pay up to 700 yuan per year. . . . This system is changing because it leads to all sorts of problems. For example, in the region where I come from, if one has a child out of plan, and if the parents are managers, they can lose their position as managers, and the premiums and salaries are diminished. It is still very carefully monitored and the fines depend on the salaries. . . .

Infanticide of little girls is still quite common in the countryside. . . . It happens mainly in the poorer areas, which are also the most backward. The people have no choice. And I agree with them. If the government gave cash premiums to all those who did not have any children, then there would be many less children, because in the countryside children represent help, a workforce. Also, when the children get married, there is a larger income in the family, and when the parents get old, it is better to be dependent on several children than on just one.

A new reform, which is still somewhat unknown, makes it possible, in certain cases, to have a second child if the first one is a girl. . . .

The latest changes have brought certain advantages to women. They can study and have a job. But in the countryside, there are only very few women who are lucky enough to study as I did; they rarely get more than a few years of primary school. From a job opportunity point of view, very often only the youngest are given jobs in local industries. I think that changes have come about since 1911. Already in 1912, and also in 1919, there were women's movements, women's demonstrations and claims. Around 1900, the director of the University of Beida in Beijing decided that women would have access to university equal to that of men.[2]

But as for the rest, the spirit of Confucius is still present. The three constraints borne by women, according to Confucius, still exist: to look for a husband, to stay a widow, and to be faithful. The greatest crime was, and still is, to remarry. The greatest honor, or rather the greatest constraint, was thus to have only one man, to devote oneself to one man. And the woman was to respect the parents of her husband, while the man was permitted to look for several women.

---

[2]The Revolution of 1911 overthrew the Qing dynasty; the Republic of China was founded in 1912; the May 4th Movement of 1919 began as a student protest against post–World War I treaty arrangements and broadened into a movement for China's revival through science and democracy. Beida is the colloquial name for Peking University, a major research university in Beijing founded in 1898.

# Communism's Retreat

The Cold War era was a time of moral and ideological absolutes. On one side was the communist world, characterized by authoritarian, one-party governments, centralized economic planning, and a commitment to the worldwide victory of Marxism over capitalism. On the other side was the "free world," a bloc of nations led by the United States, with the goal of defending capitalism and spreading liberal democracy. For more than forty years, these two blocs formed formidable military alliances, built up huge nuclear arsenals, supported giant intelligence establishments, and competed for support among nonaligned nations. For both sides, the dualisms of the Cold War—communism versus capitalism, the United States versus the Soviet Union, NATO versus the Warsaw Pact—gave direction and meaning to international politics.

There were times when the Cold War seemed about to end, but on each occasion, old tensions returned. Peaceful coexistence in the late 1950s gave way to renewed acrimony after the downing of a U.S. spy plane over Soviet territory in 1960, the building of the Berlin Wall in 1961, and the Cuban missile crisis of 1962. U.S.–Soviet relations improved in the 1970s, but again deteriorated after the Soviet invasion of Afghanistan in 1979. In the early 1980s, President Ronald Reagan branded the Soviet Union an "evil empire," and Soviet suspicions of the United States deepened. No one expected anything other than continuing U.S.–Soviet conflict.

By 1991, however, the Cold War was over. In one state after another, communist regimes in Eastern Europe either collapsed or were voted out of power and replaced by democracies. Within the Soviet Union, Premier Mikhail Gorbachev in 1985 initiated policies of *glasnost* (openness) and *perestroika* (restructuring) to rejuvenate Soviet society. But his efforts to save the Soviet Union by democratization and economic liberalization failed. By the end of 1991, the Soviet Union itself had ceased to exist.

Profound changes also took place in China. After the death of Mao Zedong in 1976, China's new leader, Deng Xiaoping, deemphasized ideology and egalitarianism in favor of pragmatism and economic development. He ordered the opening of small private businesses, fostered a market economy in agriculture, sought foreign investment, supported scientific and technological education, and encouraged Chinese exports of manufactured goods. The result was economic growth rates of twelve percent annually in the early 1990s. China remained officially communist, but with its commitment to "market socialism," it was far different from the isolated, ideology-driven China of previous decades.

# China's New Course

## 105 • DENG XIAOPING, SPEECHES AND WRITINGS

Born into the family of a well-off landowner in 1904, Deng Xiaoping studied in China and in post–World War I France, where he supported himself as a kitchen helper and laborer. He also embraced Marxism, which he studied more deeply in Moscow in 1925–1926. On his return to China in 1927, he joined the Communist Party and became one of Mao's most loyal followers.

After the communists took control of China in 1949, Deng became a Politburo member, with responsibility for overseeing economic development in southwest China. He supported the strategy of developing China's economy by following the Stalinist model of agricultural collectivization, centralized planning, and investment in heavy industry. This was scrapped in 1958 when Mao instituted the Great Leap Forward. Mao's experiment was a spectacular failure, and in its wake, Deng and other moderates dismantled the communes and reintroduced centralized planning.

This made Deng a prime candidate for vilification after Mao launched the Great Cultural Revolution in 1966. Designed to revive revolutionary fervor and rescue

China from materialism and Soviet-style bureaucratization, the revolution unleashed the energies of millions of young people who were urged to rise up and smash "bourgeois" elements throughout society. Deng fell from power, was paraded through the streets in a dunce cap, and was put to work in a mess hall and tractor repair shop. As the Cultural Revolution faded, Deng was reinstated as a party official, and after Mao's death in 1976, he led the moderates in their struggle with the radical faction led by Mao's widow, Jiang Qing. Deng's faction won, and in December 1978, the Central Committee of the Chinese Communist Party officially abandoned Mao's emphasis on ideology and class struggle in favor of a moderate, pragmatic policy designed to achieve the Four Modernizations in agriculture, industry, science and technology, and the military.

To encourage economic growth, the government fostered free markets, competition, and private incentives. Although Deng claimed that China had entered its "second revolution," it was an economic revolution only. When millions of Chinese demonstrated for democracy in the spring of 1989, the government crushed the demonstration in Beijing with soldiers and tanks, thus ensuring the continuation of the party dictatorship. After 1989, Deng withdrew from public life, and he died in early 1997. The following excerpts are from speeches and interviews given by Deng between 1983 and 1986.

## QUESTIONS FOR ANALYSIS

1. According to Deng, what had been the shortcomings of China's economic development planning under Mao Zedong?
2. According to Deng, how is China's new economic policy truly Marxist and truly socialist?
3. How does Deng view China's role in the world? What implications will China's new economic priorities have for its foreign policy?
4. What is Deng's rationale for opposing democracy in China?

### Maoism's Flaws

Comrade Mao Zedong was a great leader. . . . But he made the grave mistake of neglecting the development of the productive forces. I do not mean he didn't want to develop them. The point is, not all of the methods he used were correct. For instance, the people's communes were established in defiance of the laws governing socio-economic development. The most important lesson we have learned, among a great many others, is that we must be clear about what socialism is and how to build it. . . .

The goal for Marxists is to realize communism, which must be built on the basis of highly developed productive forces. What is a communist society? It is a society in which there is vast material wealth and in which the principle of from each according to his ability, to each according to his needs is applied. . . .

Our experience in the 20 years from 1958 to 1978 teaches us that poverty is not socialism, that

*Source:* Deng Xiaoping, *Fundamental Issues in Present-Day China* (Beijing: Foreign Languages Press, 1987), pp. 42–44, 69–72, 101–102, 105–109, 162–163. Reprinted by permission.

socialism means eliminating poverty. Unless you are developing the productive forces and raising people's living standards, you cannot say that you are building socialism.

After the Third Plenary Session[1] we proceeded to explore ways of building socialism in China. . . . The first goal we set was to achieve comparative prosperity by the end of the century. . . . So taking population increase into consideration, we planned to quadruple our GNP [Gross National Product], which meant that per capita GNP would grow from $250 to $800 or $1,000. We shall lead a much better life when we reach this level, although it is still much lower than that of the developed countries. That is why we call it comparative prosperity. When we attain that level, China's GNP will have reached $1,000 billion, representing increased national strength. And the most populous nation in the world will have shaken off poverty and be able to make a greater contribution to mankind. With a GNP of $1,000 billion as a springboard, within 30 or 50 more years—50, to be more accurate—China may reach its second goal, to approach the level of the developed countries. How are we to go about achieving these goals? . . . We began our reform in the countryside. The main point of the rural reform has been to bring the peasants' initiative into full play by introducing the responsibility system and discarding the system whereby everybody ate from the same big pot. Why did we start in the countryside? Because that is where 80 per cent of China's population lives. If we didn't raise living standards in the countryside, the society would be unstable. Industry, commerce and other sectors of the economy cannot develop on the basis of the poverty of 80 per cent of the population. After three years of practice the rural reform has proved successful. . . . The countryside has assumed a new look. The living standards of 90 per cent of the rural population have been raised. . . .

Urban reform is more complicated and risky. This is especially true in China, because we have no experience in this regard. Also, China has traditionally been a very closed society, so that people lack information about what's going on elsewhere. . . .

It is our hope that businessmen and economists in other countries will appreciate that to help China develop will benefit the world. China's foreign trade volume makes up a very small portion of the world's total. If we succeed in quadrupling the GNP, the volume of our foreign trade will increase considerably, promoting China's economic relations with other countries and expanding its market. Therefore, judged from the perspective of world politics and economics, China's development will benefit world peace and the world economy. . . .

## True Socialism

Our modernization programme is a socialist programme, not anything else. All our policies for carrying out reform, opening to the outside world and invigorating the domestic economy are designed to develop the socialist economy. We allow the development of individual economy, of joint ventures with both Chinese and foreign investment and of enterprises wholly owned by foreign businessmen, but socialist public ownership will always remain predominant. The aim of socialism is to make all our people prosperous, not to create polarization. If our policies led to polarization, it would mean that we had failed; if a new bourgeoisie emerged, it would mean that we had strayed from the right path. In encouraging some regions to become prosperous first, we intend that they should help the economically backward ones to develop. Similarly, in encouraging some people to become prosperous first, we intend that they should help others who are still in poverty to become better off, so that there will be common prosperity rather than polarization. A limit

---

[1] The Third Plenary Session of Eleventh Central Committee of the Chinese Communist Party, held in December 1978, approved the Four Modernizations Program favored by Deng.

should be placed on the wealth of people who become prosperous first, through the income tax, for example. In addition, we should encourage them to contribute money to run schools and build roads. . . . We should encourage these people to make donations, but it's better not to give such donations too much publicity.

In short, predominance of public ownership and common prosperity are the two fundamental socialist principles that we must adhere to. We shall firmly put them into practice. And ultimately we shall move on to communism.

## Special Economic Zones

In establishing special economic zones[2] and implementing an open policy, we must make it clear that our guideline is just that—to open and not to close.

I was impressed by the prosperity of the Shenzhen[3] Special Economic Zone during my stay there. The pace of construction in Shenzhen is rapid. It is particularly fast in Shekou, because the authorities there are permitted to make their own spending decisions up to a limit of U.S. $5 million. Their slogan is "time is money, efficiency is life." In Shenzhen, it doesn't take long to erect a tall building; the workers complete a storey in a couple of days. . . . Their high efficiency is due to the "contracted responsibility system," under which they are paid according to their performance, and to a fair system of rewards and penalties.

A special economic zone is a medium for introducing technology, management and knowledge. It is also a window for our foreign policy. Through the special economic zone we can import foreign technology, obtain knowledge and learn management, which is also a kind of knowledge. . . . Public order in Shenzhen is reportedly better than before, and people who slipped off to Hong Kong have begun to return. One reason is that there are more job opportunities and people's incomes and living standards are rising, all of which proves that cultural and ideological progress is based on material progress.

## China's Foreign Relations

Reviewing our history, we have concluded that one of the most important reasons for China's long years of stagnation and backwardness was its policy of closing the country to outside contact. Our experience shows that China cannot rebuild itself with its doors closed to the outside and that it cannot develop in isolation from the rest of the world. It goes without saying that a large country like China cannot depend on others for its development; it must depend mainly on itself, on its own efforts. Nevertheless, while holding to self-reliance, we should open our country to the outside world to obtain such aid as foreign investment capital and technology. . . .

## China's Political Future

The recent student unrest[4] is not going to lead to any major disturbances. But because of its nature it must be taken very seriously. Firm measures must be taken against any student who creates trouble at Tiananmen Square. . . . In the beginning, we mainly used persuasion, which is as it should be in dealing with student demonstrators. But if any of them disturb public order or violate the law, they must be dealt with unhesitatingly. Persuasion includes application of the law. When a disturbance breaks out in a place, it's because the leaders there didn't take a firm, clear-cut stand. This is not a problem that has arisen in just one or two places or in just the last couple of years; it is the result of failure over the past several years to take a firm, clear-cut stand against bourgeois liberalization. It

---

[2]Special Economic Zones were restricted areas where foreign firms could set up businesses and house their personnel.
[3]A district in southern China's Guangdong province, situated just north of Hong Kong. One of the first Special Economic Zones.

[4]Deng made these remarks in December 1986, when student demonstrations and speechmaking on behalf of the pro-democracy movement had been going on in Beijing's Tiananmen Square for several years.

is essential to adhere firmly to the Four Cardinal Principles;[5] otherwise bourgeois liberalization will spread unchecked—and that has been the root cause of the problem. . . .

In developing our democracy, we cannot simply copy bourgeois democracy, or introduce the system of a balance of three powers. I have often criticized people in power in the United States, saying that actually they have three governments. Of course, the American bourgeoisie uses this system in dealing with other countries, but when it comes to internal affairs, the three branches often pull in different directions, and that makes trouble. We cannot adopt such a system. . . .

Without leadership by the Communist Party and without socialism, there is no future for China. This truth has been demonstrated in the past, and it will be demonstrated again in future. When we succeed in raising China's per capita GNP to $4,000 and everyone is prosperous, that will better demonstrate the superiority of socialism over capitalism, it will point the way for three quarters of the world's population and it will provide further proof of the correctness of Marxism. Therefore, we must confidently keep to the socialist road and uphold the Four Cardinal Principles.

We cannot do without dictatorship. We must not only affirm the need for it but exercise it when necessary. Of course, we must be cautious about resorting to dictatorial means and make as few arrests as possible. But if some people attempt to provoke bloodshed, what are we going to do about it? We should first expose their plot and then do our best to avoid shedding blood, even if that means some of our own people get hurt. However, ringleaders who have violated the law must be sentenced according to law. Unless we are prepared to do that, it will be impossible to put an end to disturbances. If we take no action and back down, we shall only have more trouble down the road.

The struggle against bourgeois liberalization is also indispensable. We should not be afraid that it will damage our reputation abroad. China must take its own road and build socialism with Chinese characteristics—that is the only way China can have a future. We must show foreigners that China's political situation is stable. If our country were plunged into disorder and our nation reduced to a heap of loose sand, how could we ever prosper? The reason the imperialists were able to bully us in the past was precisely that we were a heap of loose sand.

---

[5]Issued by Deng in 1979, the Four Cardinal Principles were (1) the socialist path, (2) the dictatorship of the proletariat, (3) party leadership, and (4) Marxism/Leninism/Mao Zedong thought.

## A Plan to Save Communism in the Soviet Union

### 106 • MIKHAIL GORBACHEV, ON RESTRUCTURING AND THE PARTY'S PERSONNEL POLICY, JANUARY 27, 1987

In the 1970s and early 1980s, the Soviet Union was viewed as one of the world's two superpowers, with an enormous army, a huge industrial establishment, a record of impressive technological achievement, and a seemingly unshakable authoritarian government. In reality, industrial output and agricultural production were stagnating, the people's morale was plummeting, and the fossilized bureaucracy was mired in policies and theories that no longer worked. Against this background Mikhail Gorbachev became general secretary of the Communist Party in March 1985.

Gorbachev, who was fifty-four years old when he took power, was born of peasant parents and had studied law and agricultural economics at Moscow State University. After filling a variety of positions in the Communist Party, he became a member of the Politburo in 1979. On becoming general secretary he spoke in general terms of the need for new policies based on *glasnost*, or openness, and *perestroika*, or restructuring. He launched a campaign to curb drunkenness, permitted wider and more accurate reporting of information and events, pointed out some of the failings of the Soviet regime, and gradually weeded out long-serving officials and replaced them with younger, reform-minded men. Beginning in March 1986 he began to spell out his vision of the Soviet Union's future. Among his most important speeches was his address in January 1987 to a meeting of several hundred delegates attending the meeting of the Central Committee of the Communist Party of the Soviet Union, a body that met twice a year and directed all party and government activities between general party congresses. The new general secretary called for fundamental changes in every dimension of Soviet life.

## QUESTIONS FOR ANALYSIS

1. What developments in the Soviet Union led Gorbachev to the conclusion that Soviet society and government were in need of reform?
2. In Gorbachev's analysis, what or who was to blame for Soviet society's loss of momentum?
3. According to Gorbachev, what are the salient features of the new policy of *perestroika* (restructuring)?
4. How, according to Gorbachev, will the lives of everyday Soviet citizens be changed as a result of restructuring?
5. What proposals does Gorbachev offer to rejuvenate the Soviet economy?
6. What kinds of changes does Gorbachev recommend to make the Soviet Union more democratic?
7. How do Gorbachev's and Deng Xiaoping's ideas of reform for their two countries (see source 105) resemble one another? How are they different?
8. Gorbachev characterizes his proposed reforms as "revolutionary." Do you agree with this characterization?

## The Need for Restructuring

Almost 7 decades ago the Leninist party raised over the country the victorious banner of socialist revolution, of struggle for socialism, freedom, equality, social justice and societal progress and against oppression and exploitation, poverty, and oppression of nationalities. . . . The Soviet Union achieved truly epoch-making success as it built socialism, won the victory in the Great Patriotic War [World War II], strengthened the national economy and made their homeland a mighty Power.

Our achievements are enormous and undeniable. . . . But the Party is obliged to see life in its entirety

Source: J. L. Black, ed., *USSR Documents, 1987: The Gorbachev Reforms* (Gulf Breeze, Florida Academic International Press, 1988).

and complexity. No achievements, even the mightiest ones, should obscure . . . our mistakes and deficiencies. We have talked about this, and today we must repeat once more: At a certain stage the country began to lose momentum, difficulties and unsolved problems began to pile up, and stagnation and other phenomena alien to socialism appeared.

Of course the country's development did not stop. Tens of millions of Soviet people worked honestly, and many Party organizations and cadres [party leaders] acted vigorously in the interests of the people. All of this restrained the negative processes, but it could not prevent them. . . .

The principal cause was that the country's leaders were unable to promptly or fully appreciate the need for changes and the danger of the mounting crisis . . . to work out a clear-cut line aimed at overcoming them and making fuller use of the possibilities inherent in the socialist system. Conservative inclinations, inertia, a desire to brush aside everything that didn't fit into habitual patterns and unwillingness to tackle urgent social and economic questions prevailed. . . .

Comrades, all this had a negative effect on the development of many spheres of society. . . . Over the past three Five-Years Plans, growth rates declined by more than 50%. For most indices, plans had not been fulfilled since the early 1970s. . . . During the past few Five-Year Plans . . . a sort of deafness to social questions appeared. . . . While successfully resolving questions of the population's employment and providing fundamental social guarantees, we have been unable to fully realize the possibilities of socialism in improving living conditions and the food supply, organizing transportation, medical service and education and in solving a number of other urgent problems. Violations of the most important principle of socialism—distribution according to work—disappeared and the struggle against unearned income was waged indecisively. . . . Large sums of money were paid out in unwarranted bonuses and various kinds of additional incentives, and reports were padded for the sake of personal gain. A dependent mind-set grew, and a "wage-leveling"

mentality began to take root in people's minds. This hit at those toilers who were able and wanted to work better, while it made life easier for those whose idea of working involves little effort.

The stratum of people, including young people, whose goal in life came down to material well-being and personal gain by any means increased. Their cynical position poisoned the minds of those around them. . . . The growth of drunkenness, the spread of drug addiction, and the increase in crime became indices of the falloff in social mores. Instances of a scornful attitude toward laws, hoodwinking [swindling], bribetaking and the encouragement of servility . . . had a pernicious effect. Genuine concern for the people was supplanted by the mass handing out of awards, titles, and bonuses. . . . Soviet society was increasingly penetrated by stereotypes from bourgeois mass culture, imposing banality, primitive tastes, and spiritual emptiness. . . .

## The Meaning of "Restructuring"

In essence what is involved here is a change of direction and measures of a revolutionary nature. Restructuring means resolutely overcoming the processes of stagnation. . . . and creating a reliable and effective mechanism of accelerating the social and economic development of Soviet society. The main idea of our strategy is to combine the achievements of the scientific and technological revolution with a planned economy and set the entire potential of socialism in motion.

Restructuring means reliance on the vital creativity of the masses, the all-around development of democracy and socialist self-government, the encouragement of initiative and independent activity, the strengthening of discipline and order, and the expansion of openness [glasnost] and self-criticism in all spheres of life; it means respect for the value and worth of the individual. . . .

Restructuring means a decisive turn toward science, a businesslike partnership between science and practice . . . , the ability to put any undertaking on a solid scientific footing, and a readiness on the part of scientists to actively support the Party's course at aimed at the renewal of society.

Restructuring means . . . the fuller satisfaction of the Soviet people's requirements for good working, living, recreational, educational, and medical-service conditions; it means constant concern for the spiritual health and culture of every person and society as a whole.

Restructuring means the consistent implementation of the principles of social justice; it means the unity of rights and obligations; and it means ennoblement of honest, high-quality labor and the overcoming of pay-leveling behavior. . . .

The ultimate aim of restructuring is the thoroughgoing renewal of all aspects of the county's life.

## Economic Reforms

The branches of the economy that are directly involved in satisfying the needs of the population— such as the agro-industrial complex, light industry, trade and the service sphere—have begun to operate on principles that ensure broad independence and increase responsibility. . . . With the aim of stepping up the struggle for high quality in manufactured articles, a system of state product acceptance has been introduced at 1,500 leading enterprises.

The system of foreign economic activity is being restructured. The rights of enterprises and branches with respect to foreign economic ties have been expanded. New forms of cooperation— . . . , specialization and production on a cooperative basis with foreign partners—are receiving further development. . . .

New principles for raising pay in the production branches have been worked out and are being implemented. We have firmly embarked on a course that rejects "wage-leveling" and consistently observes the socialist principle of distribution according to the quantity and quality of work. At the same time, unwarranted restrictions on individual enterprise have been lifted. Favorable conditions for its development are now being created. . . .

On the basis of an analysis of the situation in housing construction, and taking into account the programmatic goal of providing every family with a separate apartment by the year 2000, additional reserves for stepping up the pace of housing construction and improving its quality have been found.

A program has been outlined for the erection and reconstruction of medical institutions, capacities for the production of Soviet-made medicines and medical equipment are being increased, and work is being accelerated to introduce and develop new forms of medical services and to organize medical science. In connection with this program, measures are being carried out to improve the population's working and living conditions, to expand preventive health care, to eradicate drunkenness and alcoholism, and to reduce the sickness rate. The wages of medical personnel are being raised.

Thus, comrades, even a brief survey of what has been planned and begun shows how extensive the restructuring work now under way in the county is.

## Social Democracy and Self-Government

The further democratization of Soviet society has become an urgent task for the Party. . . . This does not mean any breakup of our political system. We should use all its possibilities with maximum effectiveness, fill the work of the Party, the Soviets,[1] state agencies, public organizations and labor collectives[2] with profound democratic content, and breathe new life into all the cells of the Soviet organism. . . . The process is already underway. The life of the Party organization is becoming

---

[1] A local council, originally elected only by manual workers, with certain administrative powers and the right to choose representatives to serve in a hierarchy of soviets culminating in the Supreme Soviet, the highest legislative body in the USSR.

[2] The body of workers at a factory.

more vigorous. Criticism and self-criticism are expanding. The mass news media have begun to work more effectively. Soviet people have a very good feeling for the favorable influence of openness, which is becoming the norm.

What paths for the deepening of democracy in Soviet society does the Politburo see? We will be able to boost effectively people's initiative and creativity if our democratic institutions vigorously influence the state of things in every work collective, whether it concerns planning, organization of labor, distribution of material and other benefits, or selection and promotion of the most competent people to leading positions. . . . Endowing general meetings and councils of labor collectives with the power to resolve questions connected with production, social matters and personnel will be a major political measure in shifting, to use the words of V.I. Lenin, to real people's self-government.

The question of the election of the managers of enterprises and production facilities . . . should be singled out. . . . We have begun the wide-ranging changeover of enterprises to full economic accountability, self-financing and paying their own way. . . . This means that the income of an enterprise and all forms of incentives for the member of the labor collectives will depend wholly on the final results of work. . . . In these conditions workers and collective farmers are far from indifferent as to who heads their enterprise. . . . Since the collective's well-being depends on the abilities of its leaders, the working people should have real opportunities to influence their selection. . . .

The Politburo considers the improvement of the Soviet electoral system to be a fundamental area in the democratization of our life. . . .

The existing mechanism of the electoral system ensures representation for all strata of the populations in the elective bodies of power. The working class, the collective farm peasantry, the intelligentsia, women and men, veterans and young people, and all the country's nations and nationalities are represented in the present Soviet at all levels. The elective bodies reflect the social, occupational and national structure of Soviet society and the diversity of interest of the entire population. In itself, this is an enormous achievement of socialist democracy. But, like all political, economic and social institutions, the electoral system cannot remain set in concrete, sitting on the sidelines of restructuring and the new processes developing in society.

On a concrete level, most proposals come to suggesting that meeting of voters in labor collectives . . . discuss several candidates, as a rule, that elections be held in larger elections districts, and that several deputies be elected from each district. Comrades think that this will enable every citizen to express his attitude toward a broader range of candidates and will enable Party and Soviet agencies to get a better knowledge of the population's mood and will. . . .

In improving the social atmosphere, it is also necessary to continue to develop openness. It is a powerful lever for improving work in all sectors . . . and an effective form of control by all the people. . . .

# Chapter 14

# The World Since 1990

THE WORLD SINCE 1990 has had its share of promising, even inspiring, events and developments. In South Africa the dismantling of the apartheid system and the election of Nelson Mandela as the country's first black president in 1994 ended one of the world's most vicious racist regimes. "Intractable" political conflicts in Northern Ireland, Bosnia, and Sri Lanka were resolved or contained. The number of nuclear weapons in the world dropped from a high of just under 60,000 in 1985 to just over 17,000 in 2013, and nuclear tests, except for those carried out recently by North Korea, have ceased altogether. Even though world military expenditures since the mid-1990s steadily increased, the number of interstate wars reached its lowest level since the early twentieth century, and the number of battlefield and civilian deaths from wars declined.

Extraordinary scientific and technological advances continued. Progress was made in the fight against HIV/AIDS, cancer, and dozens of other diseases; scientists sequenced and mapped the multiple variations of all 20,500 genes in the human genome; observations made with the Hubble telescope revolutionized astronomy; researchers using the Large Hadron Collider, a mammoth particle accelerator, deepened our understanding of the minuscule elementary particles that are the building blocks of the universe. A stream of innovations in computer technology revolutionized how people communicated, shopped, banked, worked, gained information, and entertained themselves.

The world in the past twenty-five years also became wealthier. Despite the global economic slump following the collapse of the U.S. housing market in 2007, the market value of all final goods and services produced in the world's economy (gross world product) increased from an estimated $27.5 trillion in 1990 to $74.2 trillion in 2013 ($53.7 trillion in 1990 dollars); the value of international trade doubled in the 1990s and tripled in the 2000s until it reached $19.4 trillion in 2013; annual production of motor vehicles grew from approximately 48.6 million units in 1990 to almost 88 million units in 2013. As a result of this economic growth hundreds of millions of people have been lifted out of poverty.

Balanced against such achievements were any number of discouraging events and developments. Despite the near-universal belief that the end of the Cold War and the collapse of communism would initiate a new liberal democratic era, the progress of democracy has been tenuous and limited. It failed to take root in Russia and the former states of the Soviet Union; struggled to survive in much of Africa; made no progress in China and only scant progress in the Middle East, despite U.S. efforts to export it to Iraq and the widespread prodemocracy demonstrations during the Arab Spring of 2011.

Although major interstate wars were avoided, long-standing conflicts between India and Pakistan and between Israel and the Palestinians persisted, and civil wars continued or began in Syria, Nepal, Myanmar, the former Yugoslavia, and dozens of states in sub-Saharan Africa. Genocides took place in Bosnia, Rwanda, and the Darfur region of Sudan. North Korea and Iran continued their nuclear weapons programs despite threats and pressures from the international community. Religious extremism and religious divisions led to ethnic conflicts, destabilized governments, and inspired acts of terrorism, including al-Qaida's attack on the World Trade Center and the Pentagon in 2001.

Despite overall economic growth, at present more than 3 billion people still live on less than $2.50 a day, and of these, approximately 1.2 billion live in *extreme* poverty (less than $1.25 a day). Much of this poverty is concentrated in the Indian subcontinent and sub-Saharan Africa, where recent economic growth has caused modest reductions in poverty but mainly has benefited economic and political elites. These two regions' experience highlights another worldwide trend: the almost universal growth in income inequality over the past quarter-century. Prime examples are the two countries with the world's largest economies, China and the United States.

Humanity had a similar mixed record in its response to myriad issues pertaining to sustainability and the environment. Green political parties and environmental organizations continued to grow; recycling of industrial and household waste increased; cars, appliances, televisions, furnaces, and light bulbs became more efficient; and many dozens of international conferences discussed and proposed programs to deal with water quality, deforestation, climate change, overpopulation, agricultural sustainability, species extinction, and the protection of the world's oceans. Conversely, major corporations continued to bankroll campaigns to oppose profit-threatening environmental initiatives; politicians defended harmful environmental practices to protect local interests; many governments pursued policies to protect jobs and maintain low prices rather than the environment; individuals found it difficult to abandon potentially harmful habits and practices whose consequences will not be felt for many decades.

The end of the Cold War, followed closely by the beginning of a new millennium, inspired an extraordinary outpouring of books, speeches, and scholarly articles in which experts—some real and some self-proclaimed—speculated about humanity's future. Their visions ranged from unremitting optimism to abject hopelessness, with many shades of opinion in between. Such predictions make interesting reading, but the fact is that human beings over time have proved to be poor forecasters of future events. Only one thing is certain. History is the story of the thoughts and deeds of the billions of human beings who have lived and died over the past 200,000 years. This will not change. For good or ill, humanity's fate is in our hands.

# From Cold War to Cold Peace

Between 1989 and 1991, in a sequence of events no one had anticipated, worldwide communism collapsed, the Soviet Union disintegrated, and the Cold War ended. Universally viewed as a historic turning point, these changes were followed by an outburst of optimism about the future. U.S. president George H. W. Bush envisioned a new era in international relations—an "American peace"—in which the world's nations would work together to advance peace and freedom under the guidance of the one remaining superpower, the United States. Others went further. The American political scientist Francis Fukayama argued in *The End of History and the Last Man*, published in 1991, that the collapse of Soviet totalitarianism, following on the heels of fascism's defeat in World War II, "ended history" in the sense that it confirmed for all time that liberal democracy had triumphed over every other form of government in the battle of ideas. The world, he asserted, had entered an era that would see "the universalization of Western liberal democracy."

The anticipated new era has had a rocky start. The United States remains the world's sole superpower, but it has struggled to fulfill its role as the world's moral guide, overseer, and promoter of freedom. This was partly the result of self-inflicted wounds, especially the decision of President George W. Bush to invade Iraq in 2003 despite worldwide protests and thin support from world leaders. After the quick U.S. "victory," however, no weapons of mass destruction were uncovered, and Iraq descended into a state of ongoing sectarian violence. U.S. standing in the world fell further after revelations of its abuse of prisoners at Iraq's Abu Ghraib prison, its use of "harsh interrogation techniques" in the War on Terror, and the revelation in 2013 that the National Security Agency was monitoring the email of thirty-five world leaders. Angela Merkel, Germany's chancellor, likened the NSA's policies to those of the Stasi, East Germany's notorious secret service during the Cold War era.

Other events did not follow the hopeful script written in the heady days following the Cold War's end. In fairness, no one at the time could have predicted how much the world would be changed by events such as the emergence of transnational terrorist organizations such as al-Qaida and China's astounding economic growth. In 2010 China overtook Japan to become the world's second largest economy, and with annual double-digit increases in military spending since 1989, it now has the world's second largest military budget. This, along with alleged cyber-attacks by the Chinese military on U.S. government computer systems, raised Sino–U.S. tensions and increased support in Japan for the nationalist policies of Prime Minister Shinzo Abe.

In addition to Japan, nationalism experienced a revival in many countries in the post–Cold War era, but none more so than in Vladimir Putin's Russia. Appointed acting president of Russia on December 31, 1999, and subsequently serving three terms as president and one term as prime minister, Putin, a dictator in all but name, has strived to revive Russia's great-power status after the humiliations of the 1990s. In combination with a number of U.S. policy decisions that have displeased the Russians, the result was a deterioration of U.S.–Russian relations over issues such as NATO expansion, human rights, Syria, Russia's use of gas and oil sales as an instrument of policy, the internal politics of former Soviet states, and the Russian occupation of Georgian province of South Ossetia in 2008.

President Obama set out to repair the U.S.–Russian relationship after taking office in 2009, and the countries have been able to cooperate to a degree in efforts to curb Iran's nuclear weapons program. In 2013, however, the United States canceled an Obama–Putin summit after Russia granted asylum to Edward Snowden, who had stolen and publicized 1.7 million classified National Security Agency documents. In 2014 U.S.–Russian relations reached a low point when Russia occupied and annexed the Ukrainian province of Crimea and aided Russian separatists in eastern Ukraine. In response the United States and other industrialized nations expelled Russia from the Organization for Economic Co-Operation and Development and imposed a range of economic sanctions on Russia. As a result, the United States and Russia are no longer locked in a struggle for world dominance, as they were during the Cold War, but in this new era of "cold peace," mutual mistrust and antagonism continue.

# "The Dawn of a New Era"

## 107 • GEORGE H. W. BUSH, STATE OF THE UNION MESSAGES, JANUARY 29, 1991, AND JANUARY 28, 1992

George H. W. Bush was born in 1924 into a wealthy family in Milton, Massachusetts, and received his college degree at Yale after serving as a Navy aviator during World War II. On graduating he moved to western Texas, founded an oil company, and entered politics, winning a seat in the House of Representatives in 1966. After failing in his bid for the Senate in 1970, Bush was appointed ambassador to the United Nations and over the next decade held posts as Republican Party chair, special envoy to the People's Republic of China, and director of the Central Intelligence Agency. Between 1980 and 1988 he served as vice president under Ronald Reagan, and in 1988 he was elected president.

During his presidency the two most important events were the end of the Cold War, in which he played a relatively small role, and the First Persian Gulf War, in which a U.S.-led coalition invaded Iraq and liberated Kuwait, which Iraq's ruler, Saddam Hussein, had invaded in 1990. Bush commented on the significance of these two events in his last two State of the Union messages. The first, delivered on January 29, 1991, took place over a year after the Soviet Union's Eastern European satellites had achieved independence and just days after the coalition's invasion of Iraq had begun. The second speech, delivered on January 28, 1992, took place only a few weeks after the dissolution of the Soviet Union.

## QUESTIONS FOR ANALYSIS

1. According to Bush, what are the characteristics of the "new world order" he envisions?
2. Why, in his view, is the United States uniquely qualified to assume leadership in this new era?
3. In this leadership role, how should the United States use its power?
4. According to Bush, what changes can Americans expect to see in their lives now that the Cold War is over?
5. Bush is optimistic about future Russian–U.S. relations. In his view, what recent events encourage such optimism?

### State of the Union, January 29, 1991

I come to this House of the people to speak to you and all Americans, certain that we stand at a defining hour. Halfway around the world, we are engaged in a great struggle in the skies and on the seas and sands.[1] We know why we're there: We are Americans, part of something larger than ourselves. For two centuries, we've done the hard work of freedom. And tonight, we lead the world in facing down a threat to decency and humanity. What is at stake is more than one small country; it is a big idea: a new world order, where diverse nations are drawn together in common cause to achieve the universal aspirations of mankind—peace and security, freedom, and the rule of law. Such is a world worthy of our struggle and worthy of our children's future.

The community of nations has resolutely gathered to condemn and repel lawless aggression . . . The world has said this aggression would not stand, and it will not stand. Together, we have resisted the trap of appeasement, cynicism, and isolation that gives temptation to tyrants. The world has answered Saddam's invasion with 12 United Nations resolutions, starting with a demand for Iraq's immediate and unconditional withdrawal, and backed up by forces from 28 countries of 6 continents. With few exceptions, the world now stands as one. . . .

The end of the cold war has been a victory for all humanity. A year and a half ago, in Germany, I said that our goal was a Europe whole and free. Tonight, Germany is united.[2] Europe has become whole and free, and America's leadership was instrumental in making it possible. . . . For two centuries, America has served the world as an inspiring example of freedom and democracy. For generations, America has led the struggle to preserve and extend the blessings of liberty. And today, in a rapidly changing world, American leadership is indispensable. Americans know that leadership brings burdens and sacrifices. But we also know why the hopes of humanity turn to us. We are Americans; we have a unique responsibility to do the hard work of freedom. And when we do, freedom works. . . .

The world can, therefore, seize this opportunity to fulfill the long-held promise of a new world order, where brutality will go unrewarded and aggression

---

*Source:* American Presidency Project: http://www.presidency.ucsb.edu/ws/index.php?pid=19253.

[1] A reference to the Persian Gulf War, which began on January 17 with a massive air attack that destroyed the Iraqi air force, antiaircraft facilities, and command and control facilities.

[2] The unification of the Federal Republic of Germany (West Germany) and the German Democratic Republic (East Germany) took place on October 3, 1990.

will meet collective resistance. Yes, the United States bears a major share of leadership in this effort. Among the nations of the world, only the United States of America has both the moral standing and the means to back it up. We're the only nation on this Earth that could assemble the forces of peace. This is the burden of leadership and the strength that has made America the beacon of freedom in a searching world. The winds of change are with us now. The forces of freedom are together, united. . . .

## State of the Union, January 28, 1992

We gather tonight at a dramatic and deeply promising time in our history and in the history of man on Earth. For in the past 12 months, the world has known changes of almost Biblical proportions. And even now, months after the failed coup that doomed a failed system,[1] I'm not sure we've absorbed the full impact, the full import of what happened. But communism died this year.

Even as President, with the most fascinating possible vantage point, there were times when I was so busy managing progress and helping to lead change that I didn't always show the joy that was in my heart. But the biggest thing that has happened in the world in my life, in our lives, is this: By the grace of God, America won the cold war.

I mean to speak this evening of the changes that can take place in our country, now that we can stop making the sacrifices we had to make when we had an avowed enemy that was a superpower. Now we can look homeward even more and move to set right what needs to be set right. I will speak of those things. But let me tell you something I've been thinking these past few months. It's a kind of roll call of honor. For the cold war didn't end; it was won. And I think of those who won it, in places like Korea and Vietnam. . . . The long roll call, all the G.I. Joes and Janes, all the ones who fought faithfully for freedom, who hit the ground and sucked the dust and knew their share of horror. . . . The world saw not only their special valor but their special style: their rambunctious, optimistic bravery, their do-or-die unity unhampered by class or race or region. . . . What a group of kids we've sent out into the world.

And there's another to be singled out . . . , I mean . . . the American taxpayer. No one ever thinks to thank the people who pay a country's bill or an alliance's bill. But for half a century now, the American people have shouldered the burden and paid taxes that were higher than they would have been to support a defense that was bigger than it would have been if imperial communism had never existed. . . .

So now, for the first time in 35 years, our strategic bombers stand down. No longer are they on' round-the-clock alert. Tomorrow our children will go to school and study history and how plants grow. And they won't have, as my children did, air raid drills in which they crawl under their desks and cover their heads in case of nuclear war. My grandchildren don't have to do that and won't have the bad dreams children had once, in decades past. There are still threats. But the long, drawn-out dread is over. . . .

Much good can come from the prudent use of power. And much good can come of this: A world once divided into two armed camps now recognizes one sole and preeminent power, the United States of America. And they regard this with no dread. For the world trusts us with power, and the world is right. They trust us to be fair and restrained. They trust us to be on the side of decency. They trust us to do what's right . . .

Two years ago, I began planning cuts in military spending that reflected the changes of the new era.

---

*Source:* American Presidency Project: http://www.presidency.ucsb.edu/ws/index.php?pid=20544.

[1] A coup organized by hardline communist elements in the Soviet government and military to depose Premier Gorbachev and seize power began on August 18, 1991. It failed to generate support and collapsed on August 21. Gorbachev, who had been seized and imprisoned, returned to power, but he was politically crippled. His resignation and the dissolution of the Soviet Union took place in December 1991.

But now, this year, with imperial communism gone, that process can be accelerated. Tonight I can tell you of dramatic changes in our strategic nuclear force . . . After completing 20 planes for which we have begun procurement, we will shut down further production of the B-2 bombers. We will cancel the small ICBM program. We will cease production of new warheads for our sea-based ballistic missiles. We will stop all new production of the Peacekeeper missile. And we will not purchase any more advanced cruise missiles.

This weekend I will meet at Camp David with Boris Yeltsin[2] of the Russian Federation. I've informed President Yeltsin that if the Commonwealth, the former Soviet Union, will eliminate all land-based multiple-warhead ballistic missiles, I will do the following: We will eliminate all Peacekeeper missiles. We will reduce the number of warheads on Minuteman missiles to one and reduce the number of warheads on our sea-based missiles by about one-third. And we will convert a substantial portion of our strategic bombers to primarily conventional use. President Yeltsin's early response has been very positive, and I expect our talks at Camp David to be fruitful. . . . The reductions I have approved will save us an additional $50 billion over the next 5 years. By 1997, we will have cut defense by 30 percent since I took office. These cuts are deep, and you must know my resolve: This deep, and no deeper. To do less would be insensible to progress, but to do more would be ignorant of history. . . .

There are those who say that now we can turn away from the world, that we have no special role, no special place. But we are the United States of America, the leader of the West that has become the leader of the world. And as long as I am President, I will continue to lead in support of freedom everywhere, not out of arrogance, not out of altruism, but for the safety and security of our children. This is a fact: Strength in the pursuit of peace is no vice; isolationism in the pursuit of security is no virtue.

---

[2]Boris Yeltsin (1931–2007) was a Soviet politician who broke with Gorbachev in 1987 over the slow progress of reform. In June 1991 he was elected president of the Soviet Russian republic, which became an independent state after the dissolution of the Soviet Union. He was reelected in 1996 but resigned in 1999 for health and political reasons.

## The Dangers of Unilateralism

### 108 • VLADIMIR PUTIN, ADDRESS TO THE 2007 MUNICH SECURITY CONFERENCE

After the resignation of Russia's elected president, Boris Yeltsin, in 1999, political authority passed into the hands of the Vladimir Putin, and there it has remained. A former KGB officer and an ardent nationalist who was deeply humiliated by Russia's political and economic decline before and after the Cold War, Putin had one overriding goal—to rebuild Russia to the point where it again would be recognized as a great power. To achieve it he pursued an assertive but flexible foreign policy based on his assessment of national self-interest rather than ideology. At first relations between Russia and the United States were reasonably cordial. President George W. Bush and Putin had two meetings in 2001, with each leader coming away convinced he could work with the other. The United States encouraged Russia's entry into the World Trade Organization, and the two countries explored ways Russia might be able to contribute to the U.S. oil supply. Most importantly, Putin, who had his own problem with Islamic terrorism, was quick to offer his sympathy and assistance to the United States after the 9/11 attacks in New York and Washington.

In 2003, however, three developments worsened U.S.–Russian relations. The first was the unilateral American decision to attack Iraq, which Putin viewed as unnecessary and dangerous. The second was Putin's crackdown on political opponents, resulting in arrests of prominent rivals, tighter control over the press and political parties, and alleged abuses in the 2004 presidential election. Western denunciations of such steps were deeply resented by Putin. The third factor was the U.S. role in encouraging democratic movements in the former Soviet states of Georgia, Ukraine, and Kyrgyzstan. These actions were viewed as a plot to encircle Russia with pro-Western governments.

By 2007 U.S.–Russian relations had deteriorated, but nonetheless, the world was stunned by the speech Putin delivered at the Munich Security Conference in February of that year. Before an audience that included Robert Gates, U.S. Secretary of Defense, and a number of U.S. legislators, he denounced U.S. policies in unusually harsh terms. Headlines around the world declared the end of the "new world order" and the possibility of a new cold war.

## QUESTIONS FOR ANALYSIS

1. At the beginning of his speech Putin offers several reasons why a unipolar world is dangerous and unsustainable. What are they?
2. What observations does Putin make about the effects of using force to settle international disputes?
3. What better alternative does he suggest for settling such disputes?
4. What position does Putin take on the following issues: disarmament; NATO expansion; the installation of antiballistic missiles in Poland; economic aid to alleviate poverty?
5. How would you describe the overall tone of Putin's speech?

---

This conference's structure allows me to avoid excessive politeness and the need to speak in roundabout, pleasant but empty diplomatic terms. This conference's format will allow me to say what I really think about international security problems. And if my comments seem unduly polemical, pointed or inexact to our colleagues, then I would ask you not to get angry with me. . . .

### The Realities of a Unipolar World

The history of humanity certainly has gone through unipolar periods and seen aspirations to world supremacy. And what hasn't happened in world history? However, what is a unipolar world? However one might embellish this term, at the end of the day it refers to one type of situation, namely one center of authority, one center of force, one center of decision-making. It is a world in which there is one master, one sovereign. And at the end of the day this is pernicious not only for all those within this system, but also for the sovereign itself because it destroys itself from within. And this [unipolar world] certainly has nothing in common with democracy. Because, as you know, democracy is the power of the majority in light of the interests and opinions of the minority. Incidentally,

*Source:* President of Russia Website: http://archive.kremlin.ru/eng/speeches/2007/02/10/0138_type82912type82914type82917type84779_118123.shtml.

Russia—we—are constantly being lectured about democracy. But for some reason those who lecture us do not want to learn themselves.

I consider that the unipolar model is not only unacceptable but also impossible. . . . And this is not only because if there was individual [one-country] leadership in today's world, the military, political and economic resources would not suffice [to sustain it]. What is even more important is that the model itself is flawed because at its root it can provide no moral foundations for modern civilization. Even so what is happening in today's world . . . is an attempt to introduce precisely this concept into international affairs. . . . And with what results? Unilateral and frequently illegitimate actions have not resolved any problems. Moreover, they have caused new human tragedies and created new centers of tension. Judge for yourselves: wars as well as local and regional conflicts have not diminished. . . . And no fewer people perish in these conflicts—even more are dying than before. Significantly more, significantly more! Today we are witnessing an almost uncontained hyper-use of military force in international relations, force that is plunging the world into an abyss of permanent conflicts. As a result we do not have sufficient strength to find a comprehensive solution to any one of these conflicts. Finding a political settlement also becomes impossible.

We are seeing a greater and greater disdain for the basic principles of international law. And independent legal norms are, as a matter of fact, coming increasingly closer to one legal system. One state and, of course, first and foremost the United States, has overstepped its national borders in every way. This is visible in the economic, political, cultural and educational policies it imposes on other nations. Well, who likes this? Who is happy about this?

In international relations we increasingly see the desire to resolve a given question according to so-called criteria of political expediency, based on the current political climate. And of course this is extremely dangerous. It results in the reality of no one feeling safe. I want to emphasize this—no one feels safe! Because no one can feel that international law is like a stone wall that will protect them. Of course such a policy stimulates an arms race. Force's dominance inevitably encourages . . . countries to acquire weapons of mass destruction. . . .

I am convinced that we have reached that decisive moment when we must seriously think about the architecture of global security. And we must proceed by searching for a reasonable balance between the interests of all participants in the international dialogue. Especially since the international landscape is so varied and changes so quickly. . . . The combined GDP [gross domestic product] . . . of countries such as India and China is already greater than that of the United States. And a similar calculation with the GDP of the BRIC countries—Brazil, Russia, India and China—surpasses the cumulative GDP of the EU [European Union]. . . . There is no reason to doubt that the economic potential of the new centers of global economic growth will inevitably be converted into political influence and will strengthen multipolarity.

In connection with this, the role of multilateral diplomacy is significantly increasing. The need for principles such as openness, transparency and predictability in politics is beyond debate and the use of force should be a really exceptional measure, comparable to using the death penalty in the judicial systems of certain states. However, today we are witnessing the opposite tendency, namely a situation in which countries that forbid the death penalty,[1] even for murderers and other dangerous criminals, are cheerfully participating in military operations that are difficult to consider legitimate. And as a matter of fact, these conflicts are killing people—hundreds and thousands of civilians!

---

[1]Capital punishment was and still is banned in the European Union.

But at the same time the question arises whether we [the international community] should be indifferent and aloof to various internal conflicts inside countries, to authoritarian regimes, to tyrants, and to the proliferation of weapons of mass destruction. . . . Can we be indifferent observers in view of what is happening? . . . Of course not. But do we have the means to counter these threats? Certainly we do. It is to look at recent history. . . . The use of force can only be considered legitimate if the decision is sanctioned by the UN. And we do not need to substitute NATO or the EU for the UN. When the UN will truly unite the forces of the international community and can really react to events in various countries, when we will leave behind this disdain for international law, then the situation will be able to change. Otherwise the situation will simply result in a dead end, and the number of serious mistakes will be multiplied.

## Nuclear Weapons and Disarmament

It is important to conserve the international legal framework relating to weapons destruction and therefore ensure continuity in the process of reducing nuclear weapons. Together with the United States we agreed to reduce our nuclear strategic missile capabilities to up to 1700–2000 nuclear warheads by 31 December 2012.[2] Russia intends to strictly fulfil the obligations it has taken on. We hope that our partners will also act in a transparent way and will refrain from laying aside a couple of hundred superfluous nuclear warheads for a rainy day. And if today the new American Defense Minister[3] declares that the United States will not hide these superfluous weapons in a warehouse or, as one might say, under a pillow or under the blanket, then I suggest that we all rise and greet this declaration by standing up. It would be a very important declaration. Russia strictly adheres to and intends to further adhere to the Treaty on the Non-Proliferation of Nuclear Weapons[4] as well as the multilateral supervision regime for missile technologies. The principles incorporated in these documents are universal ones.

At the same time, it is impossible to sanction the appearance of new, destabilizing high-tech weapons. Needless to say it refers to measures to prevent a new area of confrontation, especially in outer space. Star wars[5] is no longer a fantasy—it is a reality. . . . In Russia's opinion, the militarization of outer space could have unpredictable consequences for the international community, and provoke nothing less than the beginning of a [new] nuclear era. And we have come forward more than once with initiatives designed to prevent the use of weapons in outer space.

## NATO Expansion

I think it is obvious that NATO expansion[6] does not have any relation with the modernization of

---

[2]Putin is referring to SORT (Strategic Offensive Reduction Treaty) signed by presidents Bush and Putin in 2002 and subsequently approved by the U.S. Senate and Russian Duma. The treaty was criticized for having weak verification provisions and its failure to require the destruction of nuclear weapons, only their removal from operational deployment. In 2011 it was replaced by the New START (Strategic Arms Reduction Treaty).

[3]Secretary William Gates was in Putin's audience.

[4]An international treaty that first went into effect in 1970. It is designed to prevent the spread of nuclear weapons and weapons technology, to promote cooperation in the peaceful uses of nuclear energy, and to advance the cause of general disarmament. One hundred ninety nations have signed the treaty, although North Korea withdrew in 2003. India,

Pakistan, Israel, and South Sudan are the only UN members not to have signed the treaty.

[5]A reference to the Strategic Defense Initiative announced by President Reagan in 1983. It launched a research program involving the use of ground-based and space-based weapons to intercept intercontinental ballistic missiles before they could reach the United States.

[6]By 2007 ten former Soviet satellites and republics had joined NATO: the Czech Republic, Hungary, Poland, Bulgaria, Estonia, Latvia, Lithuania, Romania, Slovakia, and Slovenia. Member nations commit themselves to the advancement of democratic values and recourse to consultation to prevent conflict. They are also obligated to come to the aid of any member when attacked.

the Alliance itself or with ensuring security in Europe. On the contrary, it represents a serious provocation that reduces the level of mutual trust.... And what happened to the assurances our western partners made after the dissolution of the Warsaw Pact? Where are those declarations today? No one even remembers them. . . . The stones and concrete blocks of the Berlin Wall have long been distributed as souvenirs. And now they are trying to impose new dividing lines and walls on us—these walls may be virtual but they are nevertheless dividing, ones that cut through our continent. And is it possible that we will once again require many years and decades, as well as several generations of politicians, to disassemble and dismantle these new walls? . . .

## The Issue of Poverty

Today many talk about the struggle against poverty. What is actually happening in this sphere? On the one hand, financial resources are allocated for programs to help the world's poorest countries—and at times substantial financial resources. But to be honest [such efforts] are linked with the development of that same donor country's companies. And on the other hand, developed countries simultaneously keep their agricultural subsidies and limit some countries' access to high-tech products. And let's tell things as they are—one hand distributes charitable help and the other hand not only preserves economic backwardness but also reaps the profits from it. The increasing social tension in depressed regions inevitably results in the growth of radicalism and extremism, feeds terrorism and local conflicts. . . . It is obvious that the world's leading countries should see this threat. And that they should therefore build a more democratic, fairer system of global economic relations, a system that would give everyone the chance and the possibility to develop. . . .

## Russia's Role in the World

We very often . . . hear appeals by our partners, including our European partners, to the effect that Russia should play an increasingly active role in world affairs. . . . Russia is a country with a history that spans more than a thousand years and has practically always used the privilege to carry out an independent foreign policy. We are not going to change this tradition today. . . . And of course we would like to interact with responsible and independent partners with whom we could work together in constructing a fair and democratic world order that would ensure security and prosperity not only for a select few, but for all.

# Globalization and Its Critics

Although the term *globalization* is new, the phenomenon it describes—cultural, political, ecological, and economic contacts and interactions among the world's regions and peoples—is centuries old. Since 1500, such global interactions have multiplied, with increases taking place in three stages: the first from 1500 to 1800, the second from the mid-1800s to 1914, and the third from the 1980s to the present. In all three periods world trade, migration, and transnational investment increased. In all three technology played a role—in the first, advances in ship construction, cartography, and navigation techniques; in the second, railroads, steamships, the telegraph, and countless machines and inventions that were part of the Industrial Revolution; and in the third, supertankers, jumbo jets, and, above all, computers and the Internet. In all three periods new forms of business organization emerged, financial structures changed, and new economic theories evolved. All three periods had winners and losers, and all three were marked by controversy.

In the most recent stage of globalization, controversy has centered on a set of economic policies and principles known as *neoliberalism*, a word and concept that entered the American vocabulary in the 1980s, when it came to be understood as an ideology that broadly favored individualism, free markets, limited government, and policies such as privatization of state-owned businesses, tax cuts, deregulation, and the removal of controls on global financial flows. It is an updated version of classical nineteenth-century European liberalism and has little in common with twentieth- and twenty-first century American liberalism, which favors government activism as a means of achieving social, economic, and environmental goals.

The emergence of neoliberalism as the ideological handmaiden of globalization came after a long period in which classical liberalism was in retreat. During the Great Depression tariffs were raised to protect struggling domestic industries. In the newly formed Soviet Union the state took over banks and major industries, collectivized agriculture, and instituted a planned economy run by bureaucrats. During both world wars other national governments took steps to regulate their economies by controlling wages, establishing production quotas, setting prices, rationing food, and mobilizing strategic resources. The leading economic thinker of the era was the Englishman John Maynard Keynes, who argued that state intervention was necessary to moderate "boom and bust" cycles and limit the potential damage of economic depressions.

During the 1950s and 1960s tariffs remained high, Keynesianism was viewed as economic gospel, and nationalization and state planning were embraced by many European governments and most of the newly independent states of Asia and Africa. These also were years, however, in which the seeds of neoliberalism were planted. The General Agreement on Tariffs and Trade (which was established in 1947 under U.S. auspices and morphed into the World Trade Organization in 1994) worked successfully to reduce tariffs and other impediments to free trade. Regional organizations such as the European Economic Community, founded in 1957, effectively limited or eliminated trade restrictions. Advocates of free trade and limited government drew inspiration from the works of Friedrich Hayek, an Austrian economist who touted the benefits of individual freedom, and Milton Friedman, a University of Chicago economist who criticized Keynesianism. Their ideas gained traction in the 1970s, when the postwar boom gave way to a decade and a half in which government deficits mushroomed, growth slackened, prices soared, and unemployment rates reached their highest level since the Great Depression. Their ideas were transformed into policy in the 1980s when British Prime Minister Margaret Thatcher embarked on a decade-long campaign to privatize national industries, cut taxes, and curb the power of unions, and U.S. President Ronald Reagan followed a similar course, cutting taxes and deregulating the airline, trucking, railroad, and telecommunications industries.

In the 1990s, as the pace of globalization quickened, market-based reforms were extended or undertaken in the United States, the United Kingdom, and much of Europe; were implemented in India, China, Russia, and former Soviet satellites such as Poland; and were adopted by many African states, often under pressure from the World Bank as a condition for receiving technological and economic aid. With the collapse of communism, the decline of labor unions, and dwindling faith in socialism, global capitalism was once more ascendant, and its supporters were confident that a new wave of capitalist expansion would make the world wealthier, more democratic, and more peaceful. Such optimistic forecasts did not go unchallenged, however, and from the perspective of 2014, it is still unclear what the final results of this latest quantum leap in economic globalization will be.

# "Globaphobia" Is No Answer

## 109 • GARY BURTLESS, ROBERT Z. LAWRENCE, ROBERT E. LITAN, AND ROBERT SHAPIRO, GLOBAPHOBIA: CONFRONTING FEARS ABOUT OPEN TRADE

The following defense of free trade, a key element in the neoliberal agenda, was published in 1998 by four economists connected with the Brookings Institution in Washington, D.C. Founded in 1916 and named after St. Louis businessman Robert Brookings, an early benefactor of the organization, the Brookings Institution maintains a program of research and publication on public policy issues in the areas of foreign relations, economics, and governance. It supports the work of approximately one hundred scholars. Centrist and nonpartisan, its goal is to improve the performance of U.S. institutions and the quality of public policy by linking scholarship and decision making.

### QUESTIONS FOR ANALYSIS

1. What do the authors mean when they use the term "globalization"?
2. According to the authors, what factors have contributed to the recent acceleration of globalization?
3. According to the authors, in what ways is free trade good for the American economy?
4. In the views of the authors, why do so many people have reservations about free trade and globalized markets?
5. The authors concede that some individuals will experience pain as a result of free trade. How and in what ways will this occur, and what should policymakers do about it?

The fate of the U.S. economy has become increasingly linked with the economies of other nations for two reasons. One is . . . the result of deliberate policy. Since the end of the World War II, nations around the world, led by the United States, have been steadily lowering trade barriers—in recent cases, unilaterally. Average tariffs imposed by high-income countries like the United States have dropped from over 40 percent to just 6 percent, while barriers to services trade have come down. Many countries have negotiated free trade agreements with their neighbors.

*Source:* Gary Burtless, Robert Z. Lawrence, Robert E. Lipton, and Robert J. Shapiro, *Globaphobia: Confronting Fears about Open Trade* (Washington, D.C.: The Brookings Institution, 1998), pp. 6–11.

The other force behind globalization is one over which politicians have little or no control: the continuing progress of technology. Faster and bigger airplanes move people and goods more quickly and cheaply. The cost of communication . . . continues to plummet. Although most investment stays at home, large pools of liquid capital nonetheless flow around the world at a quickening pace in search of the best returns. . . .

Whatever the reasons behind it, globalization has aroused concern and outright hostility among some in the United States. Both were much in evidence in the fall of 1997, during the tense debate in Congress over the extension of "fast-track" trade negotiating authority for the president and in the ultimate decision to postpone a vote on the issue until some time in 1998.[1] . . . Opinion surveys show that at least half of the American population believes that "globalization"—whatever people assume the term means—does more harm than good and that expanded trade will lead to lower wages for American workers. . . . A similar, if not greater, degree of hostility to world economic integration is common to Europe.

We have written this book to demonstrate that the fear of globalization—or "globaphobia"—rests on very weak foundations. . . .

First, the United States globalized rapidly during the golden years before 1923, when productivity and wages were growing briskly and inequality was shrinking, demonstrating that living standards can advance at a healthy rate while the United States increases its links with the rest of the world. . . .

Second, even though globalization harms some American workers, the protectionist remedies suggested by some trade critics are, at best, short-term palliatives and, at worst, harmful to the interests of the broad class of workers that they are designed to help. Sheltering U.S. firms from imports may grant some workers a short reprieve from wage cuts or downsizing. But protection dulls the incentives of workers and firms to innovate and stay abreast of market developments. As a result, its benefits for individual workers and firms are often temporary. . . .

Third, erecting new barriers to imports also has an unseen boomerang effect in depressing exports. . . . While higher barriers to imports can temporarily improve the trade balance, this improvement would cause the value of the dollar on world exchange markets to rise, undercutting the competitive position of U.S. exports and curtailing job opportunities for Americans in export industries. Moreover, by increasing the costs of inputs (whether imported or domestic) that producers use to generate goods and services, protection further damages the competitive position of U.S. exporters. This is especially true in high-tech industries, where many American firms rely on foreign-made parts or capital equipment. The dangers of protection are further compounded to the extent it provokes retaliation by other countries. In that event, some Americans who work in exporting industries would lose their jobs, both directly and because higher barriers abroad would induce some of our exporting firms to move their plants (and jobs) overseas. In short, protection is not a zero-sum policy for the United States: it is a *negative sum* policy.

Fourth, globaphobia distracts policymakers and voters from implementing policies that would directly address the major causes of the stagnation or deterioration in the wages of less-skilled Americans. *The most significant problem faced by underpaid workers in the United States is not foreign competition. It is the mismatch between the skills that employers increasingly demand and the skills that many young adults bring to the labor market.* For the next generation of workers, the problem can be addressed by improvements in schooling and public and private training. The more difficult challenge is faced by today's unskilled adults, who find themselves unable to respond to the help wanted ads in

---

[1]Fast-track negotiating authority is the authority of the president to negotiate international trade agreements that Congress can approve or reject but cannot amend or filibuster.

daily newspapers, which often call for highly technical skills. It is easy to blame foreign imports for low wages, but doing so will not equip these workers with the new skills that employers need. . . .

Fifth, Americans in fact have a vested interest in negotiating additional reductions of overseas barriers that limit the market for U.S. goods and services. These barriers typically harm the very industries in which America leads the world, including agriculture, financial services, pharmaceuticals, aircraft, and telecommunications. . . .

Sixth, it cannot be stressed too heavily that open trade benefits consumers. Each barrier to trade raises prices not only on the affected imports but also on the domestically produced goods or services with which they compete. Those who would nonetheless have the United States erect barriers to foreign goods—whether in the name of "fair trade," "national security," or some other claimed objective—must face the fact that they are asking the government to tax consumers in order to achieve these goals. And Americans must decide how willing they are to pay that tax. By contrast, lowering barriers to foreign goods delivers the equivalent of a tax cut to American consumers, while encouraging U.S. firms to innovate. The net result is higher living standards for Americans at home.

Finally, to ensure support for free trade, political leaders must abandon the argument traditionally used to advance the cause of trade liberalization: that it will generate *more* jobs. . . . Total employment depends on the overall macroeconomic environment (the willingness and capacity of Americans to buy goods and services) not on the trade balance. . . . Lower trade barriers in other countries mean *better* jobs for Americans. Firms in industries that are major exporters pay anywhere from 5 to 15 percent more than the average national wage. The "price" for gaining those trade opportunities—reducing our own trade barriers—is one that Americans should be glad to pay.

In spite of the enormous benefits of openness to trade and capital flows from the rest of the world and notwithstanding the additional benefits that Americans would derive from further liberalization, it is important to recognize that open borders create losers as well as winners. Openness exposes workers and company owners to the risk of major losses when new foreign competitors enter the U.S. market. Workers can lose their jobs. This has certainly occurred in a wide range of industries exposed to intense foreign competition—autos, steel, textiles, apparel, and footwear. Indeed, the whole point of engaging in trade is to shift resources—capital and labor—toward their most productive uses, a process that inevitably causes pain to those required to shift. In some cases, workers are forced to accept permanent reductions in pay, either in the jobs they continue to hold . . . or in new jobs they must take after suffering displacement. . . . Indeed, the job losses of thousands of similar workers in traded goods industries may tend to push down the wages of *all* workers—even those in the service sector—in a particular skill category. . . .

The losses suffered by displaced workers . . . are vividly portrayed on the nightly news, but few Americans realize that cars, clothes, and shoes are cheaper, better made, or more varied as a result of their country's openness to the rest of the world. Workers who make products sold outside the United States often fail to recognize how much their jobs and wages depend on America's willingness to import as well as its capacity to export. People contributing to a pension fund seldom realize that their returns (and future pensions) are boosted by the fund's ability to invest overseas, and almost no borrower understands that the cost of a mortgage or car loan is lower because of America's attractiveness to foreigners as a place to invest their money. All of these benefits help improve the standard of living of typical Americans, and they can be directly or indirectly traced to our openness. They are nearly invisible to most citizens, however; certainly far less visible than the painful losses suffered by workers when a factory is shut down.

# The False Promises of Global Capitalism

## 110 • INTERNATIONAL FORUM ON GLOBALIZATION, THE SIENA DECLARATION

Opposition to the neoliberal project of extending free market capitalism across the globe has come from groups and individuals with a wide range of ideological orientations, including trade unionists, environmentalists, anarchists, socialists, Keynesian economists, feminists, proponents of human and animal rights, and individuals concerned with the growing gap between the rich and poor. The ire of these groups has been directed against multiple targets, but none more so than two organizations that originated in the immediate post–World War II era, the World Trade Organization (WTO) and the World Bank. The WTO, founded in 1995, grew out of the General Agreement on Tariffs and Trade, which, under United Nations auspices and heavy U.S. influence, in 1947 created a set of trade-related rules through which member nations sought to lower tariffs and remove other restrictions on world trade. The World Bank, founded at the Bretton Woods Conference in 1944, provides technological and economic aid to less developed countries, in most cases only after the recipient country has agreed to open its economy to foreign trade and investment, shrink government spending, and reduce deficits. Since the early 1990s annual meetings of these organizations have attracted protests, the most famous of which accompanied the annual meeting of the WTO in Seattle in 1999. It attracted forty to fifty thousand activists, resulted in hundreds of arrests, and made headlines around the world.

The International Forum on Globalization is one of the many organizations formed to oppose certain aspects of the new global economy. Founded in 1994 by a group of activists, economists, and researchers, the San Francisco-based organization promotes equitable, democratic, and ecologically sustainable economies through publications and meetings. In 1998 at a forum it sponsored in Siena, Italy, it issued the following statement of its concerns and principles. Known as the Siena Declaration, it was written at a time when the economies of Southeast Asia and Japan were recovering from a financial crisis that had begun in early 1997 in Thailand when a decade-long building boom collapsed, several major financial institutions failed, and the Thai currency lost half its value. Thailand's problems plunged the region into a severe recession and raised fears of a global economic meltdown.

### QUESTIONS FOR ANALYSIS

1. According to the authors of the document, what groups and organizations have been mainly responsible for causing the recent financial crisis and the broader problems of the global economy?
2. What powers does the document ascribe to organizations such as the World Bank, the World Trade Organization, and the International Monetary Fund and trade agreements such as the North American Free Trade Agreement?

3. According to the declaration, how have recent economic developments affected the economies of developing countries, especially their food supplies?

4. How, according to the declaration, have recent economic developments weakened democracy?

5. The declaration states that the goal of the institutions it is criticizing is to create a "corporate utopia." Why will they ultimately fail to achieve such a goal?

---

1. The undersigned have long predicted that corporate-led economic globalization, as expressed and encouraged by the rules of global trade and investment, would lead to an extreme volatility in global financial markets and great vulnerability for all nations and people. These rules have been created and are enforced by the World Trade Organization (WTO), the International Monetary Fund (IMF),[1] the General Agreement on Tariffs and Trade (GATT), the North American Free Trade Agreement (NAFTA),[2] the Maastricht Agreement,[3] the World Bank and other global bureaucracies that currently discipline governments in the area of trade and financial investment. This volatility is bringing massive economic breakdown in some nations, insecurity in all nations, unprecedented hardships for millions of people, growing unemployment and dislocation in all regions, direct assaults on environmental and labor conditions, loss of wilderness and biodiversity, massive population shifts, increased ethnic and racial tensions, and other disastrous results. Such dire outcomes are now becoming manifest throughout the world, and are increasing daily.

2. The solutions to the crises that are currently being offered by the leadership of the above-named trade bureaucracies, and the leaders of most western industrialized states, as well as bankers, security analysts, corporate CEO's and economists—the main theoreticians, designers and promoters of the activities that have led us to this point—are little more than repetitions, even expansions, of the very formulas that have already proven socially, economically and environmentally disastrous. The experts who now propose solutions to the financial meltdown are the very ones who, only months ago, were celebrating Indonesia, Thailand, South Korea and other "Asian Tigers" as poster-children for the success of their designs. They later stated that the Asian crisis was fully contained. Notably, these experts have been wrong in nearly every predicted outcome of their policies.

Now these "leaders" advocate that we solve the problem by further opening markets, further opening and liberalizing the rules of investment (as they promote such draconian formulas as the Multilateral Agreement on

---

*Source:* http://www.twnside.org.sg/title/siena-cn.htm

[1] The International Monetary Fund, a specialized agency of the United Nations, was created at the Bretton Woods Conference of 1944. Its goal is to secure the stability of world financial markets by making loans to countries in financial difficulty. In 1997–1998 it provided countries in the Asian debt crisis with $110 billion in short-term loans with a requirement that they cut public spending, raise interest rates, and deregulate sectors of their economies.

[2] The North American Free Trade Agreement, implemented on January 1, 1994, eliminated most barriers to trade and investment involving the United States, Canada, and Mexico.

[3] The Maastricht Treaty, which went into force in late 1993, created the European Union; along with much else it provided for the introduction of a central banking system and a common currency, the euro.

Investment,[4] and expanded IMF powers), further suppressing the options of nation-states and communities to regulate commerce for the good of their own publics and environments, further discouragement of such models as "import substitution"[5] that have the chance to enable nations to feed and care for themselves, and further centralization of control within the same governing bodies as at present. In other words, more of the same.

According to these architects of globalization, it is only a matter of "fine tuning" or "first aid" while on the way to continued expansion of the same failed dream of theirs. They cite "cronyism" among the Third World's nations as contributing to the problem, but say nothing of the cronyism exhibited by the U.S. Treasury–Wall Street–IMF collaborations by which western bankers bail out other western bankers for their disastrous policies.

Clearly, the architects of the present crisis have not understood what they have wrought, or, if they have understood it, cannot afford to admit it.

3. As for the tens of millions of people who now suffer from this experiment, the expert solutions include no bailouts. Many of these people, formerly self-sufficient in food, are now dependent on the absentee-ownership system of the global economy. Now abandoned, they are left to seek solutions outside the system, from foraging in the (fast disappearing) forests, to barter systems, to social upheaval as means of expression. Many are finding that their attempts to return to prior means of livelihood—such as small-scale local farming—are impossible, as their former lands have been converted to industrial corporate agricultural models for export production. Land on which people formerly grew food to eat has been converted to corporate production of luxury commodities—e.g. coffee, beef, flowers, prawns—to be exported to the wealthy nations. Poverty, hunger, landlessness, homelessness, and migration are the immediate outcome of this. Insecure food supplies, lower food quality, and often dangerous contaminated foods are a secondary outcome. The situation is unsustainable.

4. Its creators like to describe the global economic system as the inevitable outgrowth of economic, social and technological evolution. They make the case that centralized global economies that feature an export-oriented free trade model, fed by massive deregulation, privatization, and corporate-led free market activity in both commodity trade and finance—free of inhibiting environmental, labor and social standards—will eventually bring a kind of utopia to all people of the planet. Now it is clear that it is a corporate utopia they have in mind. But even this will fail to achieve its goals, as the entire process is riven with structural flaws. No system that depends for its success on a never-ending expansion of markets, resources and consumers,

---

[4] Drafting a Multilateral Agreement on Investment (MAI) was begun in 1995 at the annual meeting of the Organization for Economic Cooperation and Development, a group of economically developed countries committed to promoting democracy and world trade. At the time twenty-seven countries were involved. The MAI's objective was to provide a multilateral framework for international investment with effective dispute-settlement procedures, open to OECD and non-OECD countries. When a draft of the proposal was released in 1997, critics objected to the secrecy of the negotiations and the limitations it would impose on the ability of nations to enforce labor and environmental laws when dealing with foreign corporate investors. In response to the uproar, France withdrew its support for the agreement in 1998, effectively killing the proposal.

[5] Import substitution industrialization (ISI) is a trade and economic policy favored by many developing countries based on the premise that a country should attempt to reduce its foreign dependency through the local production of industrialized products.

or that fails to achieve social equity and meaningful livelihood for all people on the planet, can hope to survive for very long. Social unrest, economic and ecological breakdown are the true inevitabilities of such a system.

5. It is appropriate to recall that the present structures of globalization did not grow in nature as if they were part of a natural selection, evolutionary process. Economic globalization in its present form was deliberately designed by economists, bankers, and corporate leaders to institute a form of economic activity and control that they said would be beneficial. It is an invented, experimental system; there is nothing inevitable about it. Globalization in its recent form even had a birthplace and birthdate: Bretton Woods, New Hampshire, 1944. It was there that a design was agreed to by the leading industrial nations. The WTO, the IMF, the World Bank, et al. were instruments that grew out of the design plan, to facilitate and further the process.

Great expectations have led to despair. After 50 years of this experiment, it is breaking down. Rather than leading to economic benefits for all people, it has brought the planet to the brink of environmental catastrophe, social unrest that is unprecedented, economies of most countries in shambles, an increase in poverty, hunger, landlessness, migration and social dislocation. The experiment may now be called a failure.

6. With the crisis now obvious in Asia, Russia, Brazil, Mexico and soon, predictably, in other places including western industrial nations, many peoples of the world, and many nation-states, have begun to recognize that the globalization experiment is doomed to fail. They have begun to specifically ask if globalization—especially free trade in financial flows—is in the best interest of their own nation, or any nation. We have seen serious corrective actions recently taken by China, India, Hong Kong, Malaysia, Russia and Chile which, by various means, have tried to counter the destabilizing force of unregulated private investment that has proved to benefit no one but the crony capitalists who advocate it. . . . Importantly, the nations that have put, or maintained, controls on capital have demonstrated a higher degree of stability, and are better able to act successfully in the interests of their own resource and economic bases and in the interests of their own populations.

We applaud such actions and urge more nations to investigate and adopt currency and investment controls, as appropriate to their unique situations, rather than continuing to take dictates from distant bureaucracies who have proved they do not know what they are doing.

7. Though the current crisis tends to be reported as strictly "financial" in nature, it is worth noting that the problems are deeper and more endemic to the inherent flaws in the design of the global economy itself. All peoples of the world have been made tragically dependent upon the arbitrary, experimental acts of giant self-interested corporations, bankers and speculators. This is the result of the global rules that remove real economic power from nations, communities and citizen democracies, while giving new powers to corporate and financial speculators that act only in their own interests; and that suppress the abilities of local economies, regions and nations to protect resources, public health and human rights, This has left the peoples of the world in a uniquely isolated, vulnerable condition; dependent upon the whims of great, distant powers. This too is an unsustainable condition.

8. Any truly effective solution to the current financial crisis, and the larger crises of economic globalization, must include the following ingredients, among others:

a) Recognition and acknowledgment that the current model, as designed and implemented by present-day, corporate led global trade bureaucracies is fundamentally flawed, and that the current crises are the inevitable, predictable result of these flaws.

b) Convening of a new Bretton Woods-type international conference which would bring to the table not only representatives of nation-states, bankers and industry, but an equal number of citizen organizations from every country to design economic models that turn away from globalization and move toward localization, re-empower communities and nation-states, place human, social and ecological values above economic values (and corporate profit), encourage national self-sufficiency (wherever possible) including "import substitution," and operate in a fully democratic and transparent manner.

c) Efforts to build on the experiences of Chile, Malaysia, India and the other countries that have placed controls on capital investment and currency speculation. Encourage all activity that reverses present policies that expand the freedoms of finance capital and transnational corporations, while suppressing the freedoms of individuals, communities, and nation-states to act in their own behalf.

d) Immediately cancel all efforts toward completion of the Multilateral Agreement on Investment (MAI), or the expansion of the International Monetary Fund to include ingredients of the MAI that give added freedom to finance capital to operate free of national control.

Finally, the undersigned wish to state that we are not opposed to international trade and investment, or to international rules that regulate this trade and investment, so long as it complements economic activity that nation-states can achieve for themselves, and so long as the environment, human rights, labor rights, democracy, national sovereignty and social equity are given primacy.

Signed By:
The Board of Directors,
International Forum on
Globalization

# Terrorism and the War Against It

Terrorism—the use of violence by an individual or group to instill fear in a target audience and gain recognition for a cause—has a long history. Many of its histories begin with the first century C.E., when Roman authorities financed dissidents and malcontents to murder enemies in subject territories or neighboring states, and members of a small Jewish sect assassinated officials and prominent individuals to bring about the end of Roman rule in Palestine. Terrorism's history includes the Persian religious sect, the Assassins, who used murder to undermine Turkish rule in Southwest Asia; Catholics who sought to overthrow England's Protestant government by plotting to blow up the houses of Parliament in 1605; and European and American anarchists and radical socialists who assassinated some fifty prominent politicians and heads of state from the late 1800s through the early 1900s.

After subsiding during and after World War I, terrorism revived after World War II. Since the late 1940s, terrorist acts have taken place in every part of the world and have been carried out by groups espousing many different causes: militant Zionists in post–World War II Palestine; anticolonialists in Africa and Asia; left-wing radicals in Europe; Ku Klux Klan members in the United States; Arabs bent on the destruction of Israel; religious extremists in India, Northern Ireland, Indonesia, and Africa;

enemies of apartheid in South Africa; and Chechen separatists in Russia, to name but a few. They also include obscure religious sects such as Aum Shinrikyo, whose members killed twelve and injured thousands by releasing sarin gas in the Tokyo subway system in 1995; alienated individuals such as Theodore Kaczynski, the American opponent of technology whose letter bombs killed three and injured twenty-three before his arrest in 1997; and self-proclaimed patriots like Timothy McVeigh, who sought to strike a blow against the "tyranny" of the U.S. government in 1995, when his truck bomb destroyed the federal building in Oklahoma City and killed 168.

In recent decades, terrorism has been identified with the Middle East, whose people are both victims of terrorism and a major source of recruitment, organizational effort, and financing for terrorist activities. Bombings, hijackings, kidnappings, and assassinations planned or occurring in the region took many thousands of lives from the 1970s through the 1990s, but it was the attacks on the World Trade Center and the Pentagon on September 11, 2001, that caused a seismic shift in world politics and made the prevention of terrorism the twenty-first century's first great challenge.

# The Worldview of Osama bin Laden

### 111 • OSAMA BIN LADEN, DECLARATION OF JIHAD AGAINST AMERICANS OCCUPYING THE LAND OF THE TWO HOLY MOSQUES

Osama bin Laden, the founder of al-Qaida, was born in 1957 in Saudi Arabia, the son of a billionaire owner of a construction company and a cultured Syrian woman who was his tenth or eleventh wife. As a young man bin Laden led a privileged existence of private schooling, Scandinavian vacations, and English lessons in Oxford. At age seventeen, he enrolled as a civil engineering student at King Abdulaziz University in Jeddah, Saudi Arabia, where he became interested in Islamic theology and forged friendships with Islamic radicals. In 1980, he went to the Pakistani–Afghan border to aid Afghan holy warriors, or mujahedeen, who were fighting Soviet troops who had invaded Afghanistan in late 1979 to prop up the pro-Soviet regime. Using his inheritance (perhaps as much as $300 million), he organized an office to provide support and weapons for the thousands of Muslim volunteers; from the mid-1980s onward, he joined the fighting. Out of these contacts and activities, al-Qaida (meaning "the base" in Arabic) took shape under bin Laden's guidance.

On his return to Saudi Arabia, bin Laden became an outspoken critic of the Saudi regime for its corruption, secularism, and acceptance of the U.S. military presence during and after the first Persian Gulf War. In 1991, he fled to Sudan, where he extended and expanded al-Qaida to include as many as several thousand agents who worked in cells ranging from the Philippines to the United States. Between 1992 and 1995, al-Qaida was linked to attacks on U.S. troops in Yemen and Somalia, the bombing of an American-operated Saudi National Guard training center in Riyadh, and unsuccessful plots to assassinate Pope John Paul II, U.S. president Clinton, and Egyptian president Hosni Mubarak. Under U.S. pressure, Sudan expelled bin Laden in 1996, forcing al-Qaida to relocate to Afghanistan, which was coming under the control of the radical Islamic group known as the Taliban. Between 1996 and 2000, al-Qaida was responsible for more acts of terrorism, including the car bombing of an apartment building in Dhahran, Saudi Arabia, that killed 19 U.S. soldiers; the simultaneous bombings of U.S. embassies in Tanzania and Kenya that killed 234 and injured several thousand; and the attack on the USS *Cole* in Aden, Yemen, that killed 17 U.S. sailors and wounded 39. After the attacks of September 11, 2001, the United States invaded Afghanistan, ended Taliban rule, and smashed al-Qaida headquarters and training camps. Bin Laden eluded capture until May 2, 2011, when a team of U.S. Navy SEALs invaded his compound in Abbottabad, Pakistan, and killed him.

Bin Laden published little and as leader of a secret terrorist organization gave few interviews or public speeches. One exception is the speech he delivered to his followers in Afghanistan in August 1996 in which he "declared war" on the United States. Printed in Arabic-language newspapers and audiotaped for worldwide distribution, bin Laden's speech describes his motives and priorities.

## QUESTIONS FOR ANALYSIS

1. How does bin Laden perceive the Muslims' place in the world? Who are their main enemies?
2. Why does bin Laden oppose the existing government of Saudi Arabia?
3. What are the goals of the "Zionist-Crusaders alliance," according to bin Laden?
4. What lessons can be learned, according to bin Laden, by the U.S. response to terrorist attacks and military setbacks in Beirut, Aden, and Somalia?
5. Why is bin Laden convinced that Muslims will triumph in their struggle with the United States?
6. What do you perceive as bin Laden's ultimate political and religious goals?

---

It should not be hidden from you that the community of Islam has suffered from aggression, iniquity and injustice imposed on them by the Zionist-Crusaders alliance and their collaborators. . . . Their blood was spilled in Palestine and Iraq. The horrifying pictures of the massacre of Qana[1] in Lebanon are still fresh in our memory. Massacres in Tajikistan, Burma, Kashmir, Assam, the Philippines, Fatani, Ogaden, Somalia, Eritrea, Chechnya and in Bosnia-Herzegovina[2] took place, massacres that send shivers in the body and shake the conscience. All of this and the world watched and listened, and not only didn't respond to these atrocities, but also with a conspiracy between the USA and its allies and under the cover of the iniquitous United Nations the dispossessed

*Source:* "Declaration of Jihad Against Americans Occupying the Land of the Two Holy Mosques," from http://azzam.com/html/articlesdeclaration htm.

[1]In April 1996, the Israelis launched a two-week bombardment of territory in southern Lebanon against the terrorist group Hezbollah. On April 18, one hundred civilians were killed when the Israelis shelled the battalion headquarters of a UN peacekeeping force where some eight hundred Lebanese had taken refuge. The Israelis blamed "technical

and procedural errors," an explanation questioned by an official UN report.

[2]This is a rather wide-ranging list. The massacres in Assam, a province of northeastern India, were carried out by an Assam separatist group in 1990 and claimed several dozen victims, not all of whom were Muslims. Attacks on Burmese (Myanmar) Muslims in the early 1990s were carried out by Buddhists.

people were even prevented from obtaining arms to defend themselves.

The people of Islam awakened and realized that they are the main target for the aggression of the Zionist-Crusaders alliance. All false claims and propaganda about "Human Rights" were hammered down and exposed by the massacres that took place against the Muslims in every part of the world. . . .

Today we work to lift the iniquity that had been imposed on the Umma [the Muslim community] by the Zionist-Crusaders alliance, particularly after they have occupied the blessed land of Jerusalem . . . and the land of the two Holy Places.[3] . . . We wish to study the means by which we could return the situation [in Saudi Arabia] to its normal path and to return to the people their own rights, particularly after the great damage and the great aggression on the life and the religion of the people. . . .

Injustice [in Saudi Arabia] had affected the people in industry and agriculture. It affected the people of the rural and urban areas. And almost everybody complains about something. The situation at the land of the two Holy Places became like a huge volcano at the verge of eruption that would destroy the Kuffar [non-believers] and the corruption and its sources. . . . People are fully concerned about their everyday living; everybody talks about the deterioration of the economy, inflation, ever increasing debts and jails full of prisoners.

Through its course of actions the regime has torn off its legitimacy:

1. Suspension of the Islamic Sharia law and exchanging it with man-made civil law. . . .
2. The inability of the regime to protect the country and allowing the enemy of the Umma, the American crusader forces, to occupy the land for the longest of years. . . . As a result of the policy imposed on the country, especially in the oil industry where production is restricted

or expanded and prices are fixed to suit the American economy, ignoring the economy of the country. Expensive deals were imposed on the country to purchase arms. People are asking what then is the justification for the very existence of the regime?

But to our deepest regret the regime refused to listen to the people. . . .

The regime is fully responsible for what has been incurred by the country and the nation; however, the occupying American enemy is the principal and the main cause of the situation. Therefore efforts should be concentrated on destroying, fighting and killing the enemy until, by the Grace of Allah, it is completely defeated. . . .

• • •

It is incredible that our country is the world's largest buyer of arms from the USA and the area's biggest commercial partner of the Americans who are assisting their Zionist brothers in occupying Palestine and in evicting and killing the Muslims there, by providing arms, men and financial support. To deny these occupiers . . . the enormous revenues from their trade with our country is a very important help for our Jihad against them. . . .

We expect the women of the land of the two Holy Places and other countries to carry out their role in boycotting the American goods. If economic boycott is intertwined with the military operations of the Mujahedeen [holy warriors], then defeating the enemy will be even nearer, by the Permission of Allah. . . .

• • •

A few days ago the news agencies had reported that the Defense Secretary[4] of the Crusading Americans had said that "the explosions at Riyadh and

---

[3]Mecca, the birthplace of Muhammad and the site of the Kaaba, Islam's holiest shrine, and Medina, the city to which Muhammad and his followers fled in 622 C.E. Both are in Saudi Arabia.

[4]William Perry, secretary of defense between 1994 and 1997.

Al Khobar[5] had taught him one lesson: that is, not to withdraw when attacked by coward terrorists."

We say to the Defense Secretary that his talk can induce a grieving mother to laughter! . . . Where was this false courage of yours when the explosion in Beirut took place in 1983? You were turned into scattered bits and pieces at that time; 241 marine soldiers were killed.[6] And where was this courage of yours when two explosions made you leave Aden in less than twenty-four hours![7] But your most disgraceful case was in Somalia;[8] where you moved an international force, including twenty-eight thousand American soldiers. . . . However, when tens of your soldiers were killed in minor battles and one American pilot was dragged in the streets of Mogadishu you left the area carrying disappointment, humiliation, defeat and your dead with you. Clinton appeared in front of the whole world threatening and promising revenge, but these threats were merely a preparation for withdrawal. You have been disgraced by Allah and you withdrew; the extent of your impotence and weaknesses became very clear. . . .

Since the sons of the land of the two Holy Places feel and strongly believe that fighting against the nonbelievers in every part of the world is absolutely essential; then they would be even more enthusiastic, more powerful and larger in number upon fighting on their own land, the place of their births. . . . They know that the Muslims of the world will assist and help them to victory. I say to you William [Perry] that these youths love death as you love life. They inherit dignity, pride, courage, generosity, truthfulness and sacrifice from father to father.

They are most . . . steadfast at war. They inherit these values from their ancestors. . . .

These youths believe in what has been told by Allah and His messenger about the greatness of the reward for the Mujahedeen martyrs. . . .

Those youths know that their reward in fighting you, the USA, is double their reward in fighting someone else. They have no intention except to enter paradise by killing you. . . .

In the heat of battle they do not care, and cure the insanity of the enemy by their "insane" courage. Terrorizing you, while you are carrying arms on our land, is a legitimate and morally required duty. It is a legitimate right well known to all humans and other creatures. Your example and our example is like a snake which entered into a house of a man and got killed by him. The coward is the man who lets you walk, while carrying arms, freely on his land and provides you with peace and security.

Those youths are different from your soldiers. Your problem will be how to convince your troops to fight, while our problem will be how to restrain our youths to wait for their turn in fighting. . . . The youths hold you responsible for all of the killings and evictions of the Muslims and the violation of the sanctities, carried out by your Zionist brothers in Lebanon; you openly supplied them with arms and finance. More than 600,000 Iraqi children have died due to lack of food and medicine and as a result of the unjustifiable aggression imposed on Iraq and its nation.[9]

The children of Iraq are our children. You, the USA, together with the Saudi regime are responsible for the shedding of the blood of these innocent children. . . .

---

[5]In November 1995, a car bomb at a Saudi National Guard training center in Riyadh killed five Americans; the bombing of Khobar Towers, a U.S. Air Force housing complex in Dhahran, Saudi Arabia, killed nineteen Americans.

[6]President Reagan ordered the withdrawal of Marine peacekeepers after a bomb killed 241 Marines and Navy personnel in October 1983 in Beirut.

[7]The Pentagon withdrew one hundred Army personnel after the U.S. embassy in Aden was bombed in 1993.

[8]President Clinton ordered the withdrawal of U.S. peacekeepers from Somalia by March 1994 after a clash with Somali warlords in Mogadishu in October 1993 resulted in the deaths of eighteen Army Rangers.

[9]The alleged victims of economic sanctions imposed on Iraq after the first Persian Gulf War (1991).

It is a duty now on every tribe on the Arab Peninsula to fight in the cause of Allah and to cleanse the land from those occupiers. Allah knows that their blood is permitted to be spilled and their wealth is a booty to those who kill them. . . . Our youths know that the humiliation suffered by the Muslims as a result of the occupation of their Holy Places cannot be removed except by explosions and Jihad.

# The War on Terror

## 112 • ALBERTO GONZALES, MEMORANDUM OF JANUARY 25, 2002 AND JAY BYBEE, MEMORANDUM OF AUGUST 2, 2002

On September 20, 2001, nine days after the attacks on the World Trade Center and the Pentagon, President George W. Bush announced in a speech to Congress that the United States was at war, a "war on terror," that would continue until al-Qaida and "every terrorist of global reach has been found, stopped, and defeated." The first stage of the war could not have gone better. In early October, with support from its traditional allies and world powers such as Russia and China, the United States launched a massive bombing campaign against Taliban-controlled Afghanistan, which had provided a haven for al-Qaida after its expulsion from Sudan. Taliban forces soon crumbled, abandoning the capital Kabul in early November and withdrawing from their last major bastion, Kandahar, in December. The United States and its allies could now go forward to create a new government that would bring stability and human rights to Afghanistan and cooperation in the struggle against al-Qaida.

As President Bush had warned in his September 20 speech, the war on terror would involve more than "instant retaliation and isolated strikes" and would not be won by a single battle. The war on terror would also be a war of covert missions and secret attacks to gradually shut down the enemy's cells, take out its leaders, and cripple its finances. As Vice President Dick Cheney had stated just a few days earlier, this phase of the war would require spending "time in the shadows," where "the work will have to be done quietly, without any discussion, using sources and methods that are available to our intelligence agencies." It would mean working "in the dark side."

It would take several years before it was gradually revealed what working in the dark side meant. It meant redefining or simply ignoring a body of international law, U.S. law, and U.S. military regulations concerning the humane treatment in wartime of unlawful combatants, prisoners, civilian detainees, and those suspected of committing or planning crimes. It included the practices of "extraordinary rendition," in which a prisoner or kidnapped person was transported for interrogation to countries where torture was practiced, and "forced disappearances," in which individuals were sent for interrogation to secret CIA prisons known as "dark sites." At these and other locations, including Guantanamo Naval Base in Cuba, Abu Ghraib Prison in Baghdad, and Bagram Airfield in Afghanistan, detainees were subjected to various "harsh interrogation techniques" that included beatings, forced nudity, sleep deprivation, solitary confinement, confinement in small dark boxes, mock burials, food deprivation, exposure to temperature extremes, stress positions, sexual humiliation, and waterboarding.

Such policies were opposed at the start of the war on terror by Secretary of State Colin Powell and subsequently by individuals from the FBI and the armed forces. Their arguments were countered by a small group within President Bush's administration led by Secretary of Defense Donald Rumsfeld and Vice President Dick Cheney. In their efforts to win over the president and others in the administration, Rumsfeld and Cheney enlisted the help of a number of administration lawyers who between 2001 and 2003 provided interpretations of international treaties and U.S. laws that legitimized hardline policies. Excerpts from two of these opinions follow.

The first memorandum, issued on January 25, 2002, under the signature of Attorney General Alberto Gonzales, but probably written by David Addington, Vice President Cheney's chief legal counsel, came at the end of a debate within the administration over the applicability of the Geneva Conventions to the war on terror. A body of international law dating back to 1882 and updated in 1929 and 1949, the Geveva treaties, to which the United States and Afghanistan were signatories, set standards for the treatment of prisoners and specifically protected them from humiliating and degrading treatment, mutilation, and torture. President Bush had already decided to ignore the Geneva Conventions on this matter, but his decision was challenged in a memorandum written by William Taft IV, a legal counsel for Colin Powell. The Gonzales memorandum urged the president to adhere to his earlier decision, and it succeeded.

The second memorandum was submitted to Attorney General Gonzales on August 1, 2002, under the signature of Jay Bybee, head of the Office of Legal Counsel (OLC), an office that advises the president on legal matters. Mainly the work of another OLC lawyer, John Yoo, it was written in response to queries from the Central Intelligence Agency about legal limits on the interrogation of prisoners. The United Nations Convention on Torture, to which the United States became a signatory in 1994, obligated nations to prevent torture and cruel and inhuman treatment of prisoners within their borders and barred them from extraditing anyone to a state where there was reason to think they will be tortured. In compliance with the UN Convention, in 1994 the Congress passed and the president signed legislation that made also it illegal to use torture outside the United States.

## QUESTIONS FOR ANALYSIS

1. What legal arguments does the Gonzales memorandum make to justify his position that the Geneva Convention does not apply to Taliban and al-Qaida fighters?
2. What arguments does he make based on the unique features of the war against terrorist organizations?
3. How does the Gonzales memorandum respond to the arguments presented in the Taft memorandum?

4. Concerning the Bybee memorandum, what would you consider to be its overriding purpose or goal?

5. What level of physical and mental pain must be reached before an act can be considered torture?

6. How do the Bybee memorandum's views of presidential powers protect interrogators from criminal prosecution?

## Alberto Gonzales, Memorandum to President Bush, January 26, 2002

. . . The Office of Legal Counsel [OLC] of the Department of Justice has opined that, as a matter of international and domestic law, GPW [the Geneva Convention on Prisoners of War] does not apply to the conflict with al Qaeda. OLC has further opined that you have the authority to determine that GPW does not apply to the Taliban. As I discussed with you, the grounds for such a determination may include:

• . . . that Afghanistan was a failed state because the Taliban did not exercise full control over the territory and people, was not recognized by the international community, and was not capable of fulfilling its international obligations . . .

• . . . that the Taliban and its forces were, in fact, not a government, but a militant, terrorist-like group. . . .

The consequences of a decision to adhere to what I understood to be your earlier determination that the GPW does not apply to the Taliban include the following:

Positive:

• Preserves flexibility: As you have said,[1] the war against terrorism is a new kind of war. It is not the traditional clash between nations adhering to the laws of war that formed the backdrop for GPW. The nature of the new war places a high premium on other factors, such as the ability to quickly obtain information from captured terrorists and their sponsors in order to avoid further atrocities against American civilians, and the need to try terrorists for war crimes such as wantonly killing civilians. In my judgment, this new paradigm renders obsolete Geneva's strict limitations on questioning of enemy prisoners and renders quaint some of its provisions requiring that a captured enemy be afforded such things as commissary privileges, scrip [currency in place of legal tender], athletic uniforms, and scientific instruments.

By concluding that GPW does not apply to al Qaeda and the Taliban eliminates any argument regarding the need for case-by-case determination of POW [prisoner of war] status.[2] It also holds open options for future conflicts in which it may be more difficult to determine whether an enemy force as a whole meets the standard for POW status.

• Substantially reduces the threat of domestic criminal prosecution under the War Crimes Act (18 U.S.C. 2441). That statute, enacted in 1996, prohibits the commission of a "war crime" by or against a U.S. person, including U.S. officials. "War crime" for these purposes is defined to include any grave breach of GPW or any violation of common Article 3 thereof (such as "outrages against personal dignity"). . . . Punishments for violations of Section 2441 include the death penalty. A determination that the GPW is not applicable to the Taliban would mean that Section 2441 would not apply to actions taken with respect to the Taliban. . . .

*Source:* http://www2.gwu.edu/~nsarchiv/NSAEBB /NSAEBB127/02.01.25.pdf.

[1] A reference to President Bush's September 20 speech.

[2] The Geneva Convention requires that all captured enemies, including saboteurs, spies, and civilians, were to be treated as prisoners of war "until their status has been determined by a competent tribunal."

On balance, I believe that the arguments for reconsideration and reversal [of Bush's early decision on the Geneva Conventions] are unpersuasive.

• The argument that the U.S. has never determined that GPW did not apply is incorrect. In at least one case (Panama in 1989) the U.S. determined that GPW did not apply even though it determined for policy reasons to adhere to the convention. More importantly, as noted above, this is a new type of warfare—one not contemplated in 1949 when the GPW was framed—and requires a new approach in our actions towards captured terrorists. . . .

• The statement that other nations would criticize the U.S. because we have determined that GPW does not apply is undoubtedly true. It is even possible that some nations would point to that determination as a basis for failing to cooperate with us on specific matters in the war against terrorism. On the other hand, some international and domestic criticism is already likely to flow from your previous decision not to treat the detainees as POWs. And we can facilitate cooperation with other nations by reassuring them that we fully support GPW where it is applicable and by acknowledging that in this conflict the U.S. continues to respect other recognized standards.

• In the treatment of detainees, the U.S. will continue to be constrained by its commitment to treat the detainees humanely and, to the extent appropriate and consistent with military necessity, in a manner consistent with the principles of GPW. . . .

## Memorandum from Jay Bybee to Alberto Gonzales, August 2, 2002

You have asked for our Office's views regarding the standards of conduct under the Convention Against Torture and Other Cruel, Inhuman and Degrading Treatment or Punishment as implemented by Sections 2340-2340A of title 18 of the United States Code. As we understand it, this question has arisen in the context of the conduct of interrogations outside of the United States. . . .

"Specifically Intended": To violate Section 2340A, the statute requires that severe pain and suffering must be inflicted with specific intent. . . . In order for a defendant to have acted with specific intent, he must expressly intend to achieve the forbidden act. . . . As a result, the defendant had to act with the express "purpose to disobey the law" in order for the *mens rea*[1] element to be satisfied. Here, because Section 2340 requires that a defendant act with the specific intent to inflict severe pain, the infliction of such pain must be the defendant's precise objective. . . . Thus, even if the defendant knows that severe pain will result from his actions, if causing such harm is not his objective, he lacks the requisite specific intent. . . . Instead, a defendant is guilty of torture only if he acts with the express purpose of inflicting severe pain or suffering on a person within his custody or physical control. . . .

"Severe Pain or Suffering": . . . Section 2340 makes plain that the infliction of pain or suffering per se [in itself], whether it is physical or mental, is insufficient to amount to torture. Instead, the text provides that pain or suffering must be "severe." The statute does not, however, define the term "severe." The dictionary defines "severe" as "unsparing in exaction, punishment, or censure" or "Inflicting discomfort or pain hard to endure; sharp; afflictive; distressing;

---

*Source:* http://www.torturingdemocracy.org/documents/20020801-1.pdf.

[1]Literally means "guilty mind." It refers to the intent of the defendant in a criminal case at the time the criminal act (*actus reus*) was committed. The argument here is that since the intent of interrogators is not specifically to cause pain, but rather to gain information, they cannot be held guilty for alleged acts of torture.

violent; extreme; as severe pain, anguish, torture." . . . Thus, the adjective "severe" conveys that the pain or suffering must be of such a high level of intensity that the pain is difficult for the subject to endure.

Congress's use of the phrase "severe pain" elsewhere in the United States Code can shed more light on its meaning. . . . Significantly, the phrase "severe pain" appears in statutes defining an emergency medical condition for the purpose of providing health benefits. . . . These statutes define an emergency condition as one "manifesting itself by acute symptoms . . . such that a prudent layperson, . . . could reasonably expect the absence of immediate medical attention to result in placing the health of the individual . . . (i) in serious jeopardy, (ii) serious impairment to bodily functions, or (iii) serious dysfunction of any bodily organ or part." . . . Although these statutes address a substantially different subject from Section 2340, they are nonetheless helpful for understanding what constitutes severe physical pain. . . . These statutes suggest that "severe pain," as used in Section 2340, must rise to a similarly high level—the level that would ordinarily be associated with a sufficiently serious physical condition or injury such as death, organ failure, or serious impairment of body functions—in order to constitute torture.

"Severe Mental Pain or Suffering": . . . As an initial matter, Section 2340(2) requires that the severe mental pain must be evidenced by "prolonged mental harm." To prolong is to "lengthen in time" or to "extend the duration of, to draw out." . . . Accordingly, "prolong" adds a temporal dimension to the harm to the individual, namely, that the harm must be one that is endured over some period of time. Put another way, the acts giving rise to the harm must cause some lasting, though not necessarily permanent, damage. For example, the mental strain experienced by an individual during a lengthy and intense interrogation—such as one that state or local police might conduct upon a criminal suspect—would not violate Section 2340(2). On the other hand, the development of a mental disorder such as posttraumatic stress disorder, which can last months or even years, or even chronic depression, which also can last for a considerable period of time if untreated, might satisfy the prolonged harm requirement. . . .

"The President's Commander-in-Chief Power": Even if an interrogation method arguably were to violate Section 2340A, the statute would be unconstitutional if it impermissibly encroached on the President's constitutional power to conduct a military campaign. As Commander-in-Chief, the President has the constitutional authority to order interrogations of enemy combatants to gain intelligence information concerning the military plans of the enemy. The demands of the Commander-in-Chief power are especially pronounced in the middle of a war in which the nation has already suffered a direct attack. In such a case, the information gained from interrogations may prevent future attacks by foreign enemies. Any effort to apply Section 2340A in a manner that interferes with the President's direction of such core war matters as the detention and interrogation of enemy combatants thus would be unconstitutional. . . .

There can be little doubt that intelligence operations, such as the detention and interrogation of enemy combatants and leaders, are both necessary and proper for the effective conduct of a military campaign. Indeed, such operations may be of more importance in a war with an international terrorist organization than one with the conventional armed forces of a nation-state, due to the former's emphasis on secret operations and surprise attacks against civilians. It may be the case that only successful interrogations can provide the information necessary to prevent the success of covert terrorist attacks upon the United States and its citizens. Congress can no more interfere with the President's conduct of the interrogation of enemy combatants than it can dictate strategic or tactical decisions on the battlefield.

# New Patterns of Immigration

Migration has always been a part of human history, but never did it play as prominent a role as it did in the last half-century, when more human beings chose or were forced to migrate than ever before. According to the United Nations *International Migration Report 2013*, the number of international migrants, legal and illegal, stood at 54.2 million in 1990, 117.45 million in 2000, 220.7 million in 2010, and 231.5 million in 2013. In 2013 slightly more than three in every one hundred human beings were international migrants.

The geography of migration also changed. Europe, for example, was transformed from a land of emigrants to a land of immigrants. Between 1500 and the mid-twentieth century Europe provided most of the millions of immigrants who added to the populations of the Americas, Australia, New Zealand, and parts of Africa. In the late twentieth century, however, this outflow virtually stopped, and Europe became a destination for migrants from the Middle East, the Caribbean, Africa, and Asia. Migration also changed in the United States, Australia, and Canada, when in the late 1900s all three nations abandoned quota systems that discriminated against non-Europeans. As a result, Asians in Australia, Asians and West Indians in Canada, and Asians, West Indians, and Latinos in the United States became the dominant immigrant groups.

Many factors contributed to these changes: growing economic disparities between rich and poor nations; demographic patterns resulting slow-growing, aging populations in industrialized states, and younger, fast-growing populations in Africa, Latin America, and South Asia; ethnic strife and political conflict in many parts of the world; cheaper and faster means of transportation; new technologies that make possible instant communication between immigrants and family and friends at home; the creation of free trade areas that encourage movements of labor; the liberalization of immigration laws in Canada, Australia, and the United States; and in developing nations, fewer restraints on women's freedom of movement. In other words, changing migration patterns were one part of the transnational revolution that has reshaped societies around the globe.

Migration can be disruptive, even traumatic, for the migrants themselves, the countries they are leaving, and the countries of their destination. This especially has been the case since the 1980s, when the number of migrants swelled and many of them practiced religions, spoke languages, and came from racial stock different from those of most of their new country's citizens. Thus as the number of immigrants rose, so too did the number of individuals and organizations demanding immigration restrictions. Opponents of immigration worried and continue to worry about immigration's economic effects, the difficulty of assimilating newcomers, pressures on government services, and on a deeper level the erosion of distinct national cultures in an era of globalization.

# Too Many Immigrants

## 113 • ROY H. BECK, THE CASE AGAINST IMMIGRATION

The number of immigrants to the United States diminished dramatically from the 1920s through the 1960s, largely due to restrictive legislation passed in the 1920s. This downward trend was reversed with the passage of the Immigration and Nationality Act in 1965. This law abolished a quota system adopted in 1924 that had favored immigrants from western Europe, limited those from southern and eastern Europe, and totally excluded Asians. The new law made family reunification and the nation's need for skills the key determinants of who would be admitted rather than nationality. The act's provision for family reunification meant that when a single family member gained legal immigrant status, it opened the door to his or her spouse, children, parents, brothers, and sisters. Thus a single immigrant could begin a chain reaction that enabled a large extended family to immigrate. After the new legislation, legal immigration, mainly from Asia, Latin America, and the Caribbean, rose from an average of 450,000 immigrants per year in the 1970s, to 730,000 in the 1980s, and to over a million in the 1990s and early 2000s. These figures do not include illegal immigrants, whose numbers rose from approximately 3.5 million in 1990 to approximately eleven to twelve million in 2010. Just over half of the illegal immigrants are Mexicans.

It is not surprising, therefore, that against a backdrop of economic recession, a movement to curb legal and illegal immigration to the United States gathered strength in the early 1990s. A leading spokesperson for immigration reform was the journalist Roy H. Beck, whose 1994 *Atlantic Monthly* article on the impact of Asian immigration on the Wisconsin town of Wausau gained him national attention. Deeply concerned about environmental issues and poverty, he was convinced that population growth and high immigration were at the root of many social and economic problems in the United States. In 1996 he wrote the widely read book *The Case Against Immigration*, from which the following excerpt is drawn. Since 1997 he has been the director of NumbersUSA, an anti-immigration organization whose lobbying efforts contributed to the defeats of the comprehensive immigration bill proposed by President George W. Bush in 2007 and the so-called DREAM Act (Development, Relief, and Education for Alien Minors Act) in 2011. The latter would have provided a path to citizenship through military service or educational achievement for illegal immigrants who had arrived in the United States as minors.

## QUESTIONS FOR ANALYSIS

1. According to Beck, what have been the most damaging effects of high immigration on U.S. society?
2. In Beck's view, which groups have been most adversely affected by high immigration? Which groups have benefited?
3. Why, according to Beck, has Congress been slow to react to the "immigration crisis," despite widespread support among the general populace for immigration reform?

Although we often hear that the United States is a nation of immigrants, we seldom ask just what that means. It can be difficult to ask tough questions about immigration when we see nostalgic images of Ellis Island, recall our own families' coming to America, or encounter a new immigrant who is striving admirably to achieve the American dream.

But tough questions about immigration can no longer be avoided as we enter a fourth decade of unprecedentedly high immigration and struggle with its impact on job markets, on the quality of life and social fabric of our communities, and on the state of the environment. . . .

Until recently, policymakers and politicians of every stripe had ignored what public opinion polls found to be the public's growing dissatisfaction with the abnormally high level of immigration. Majority public opinion can be shallow, fleeting, and wrong, but an honest look at major trends during the recent mass immigration shows that ordinary Americans' concerns can hardly be dismissed as narrow and unenlightened:

• Whole industries in the 1970s and 1980s reorganized to exploit compliant foreign labor, with the result that conditions have deteriorated for all workers in those industries.

• Long trends of rising U.S. wages have been reversed.

• Poverty has increased.

• The middle-class way of life has come under siege; income disparities have widened disturbingly.

• Aggressive civil rights programs to benefit the descendants of slavery have been watered down, co-opted, and undermined because of the unanticipated volume of new immigration. A nearly half-century march of economic progress for black Americans has been halted and turned back.

• The culture—and even language—of many local communities has been transformed against the wishes of their native inhabitants. Instead of spawning healthy diversity, immigration has turned many cities into caldrons of increased ethnic tension and divisiveness.

• A stabilizing U.S. population with low birth rates (like other advanced nations) has become the most rapidly congesting industrialized nation in the world (resembling trends in Third World countries). Vast tracts of remaining farmland, natural habitat, and ecosystems have been destroyed to accommodate the growing population. . . .

• Numerous organized crime syndicates headquartered in the new immigrants' home countries have gained solid beachheads of operations. Law enforcement agencies have been confounded just as they thought they were near victory over the crime organizations that other ethnic groups had brought with them. . . .

. . . Some observers fear that the volume of non-European immigration threatens to swamp America's cultural heritage; others welcome an ever more multicultural society. Nonetheless, the chief difficulties that America faces because of current immigration are not triggered by *who* the immigrants are but by *how many* they are. . . . It is time to confront the true costs and benefits of immigration numbers, which have skyrocketed beyond our society's ability to handle them successfully. . . .

Who wins and who loses? A glance through the roster of immigration winners quickly finds business owners who have followed a low-wage labor strategy. Land developers, real estate agents, home mortgage officials, and others who tend to profit from population growth are winners. Owners of high-tech industries have lowered their costs by importing skilled immigrants who will work at lower wages than college-educated Americans. People who can afford nannies, gardeners, and housekeepers have benefitted from lower costs. . . . Others have won by having the security, prestige, or pay of their jobs enhanced by the high immigrant flow. That would include immigration lawyers, refugee resettlement agency personnel, officials of immigrant-advocacy groups, and educators and other social services employees who work the immigrants.

Unfortunately, the roster of immigration losers is much larger and includes some of America's most vulnerable citizens: poor children, lower-skilled workers, residents of declining urban communities, large numbers of African Americans, the unskilled immigrants who already are here and face the most severe competition from new immigrants, and even some of America's brightest young people, who lose opportunities to pursue science-based careers because of some corporations' and universities' preferences for foreign scientists and engineers. . . .

. . . Finally, it is the local community as a whole that is forced to assume the costs of immigration. . . . Some of the subsidy is monetary: social services to foreign workers who do not earn enough money to rise above poverty; issuance of new school bonds to educate the foreign workers' children; additional infrastructure to handle an expanding population that cannot pay enough taxes to cover the costs; social services to American workers who lose jobs or drop into poverty wages because of the foreign job competition.

. . . We cannot deny that cutting immigration will hurt some citizens. Most immigration lawyers might lose their livelihood and have to enter other specialties. Not surprisingly, they and their organization, the American Immigration Lawyers Association, have been the most aggressive in fighting any reductions whatsoever. . . . Also suffering from the change—at least temporarily—would be the businesses which the lawyers represent and which have decided to rely heavily on

foreign labor. . . . A number of national church bureaucracies and other private refugee organizations might have to cut their staffs. On the other hand, the charitable organizations should be able to find plenty of humanitarian work to do overseas—where nearly all refugees are, anyway—as well as among the black underclass and other impoverished citizens here in America. . . . Then there are the ethnic immigrant organizations that had counted on a continuing flow of their countrymen to boost the power of their budding political machines. . . .

Those few groups that stand to lose money, power, or prestige with a cut in immigration wield tremendous power on Capitol Hill. People representing the broad public interest will have to speak very loudly to be heard. The majority of members of Congress previously earned their living in self-employed occupations or as executives; they think like employers who love a labor surplus instead of like most Americans who depend on paychecks and benefit from tight-labor markets. . . .

Immigration is so high now that the cuts proposed in Congress reduce the numbers only back to the level of the Great Wave.[1] In fighting that slight reduction, the National Association of Manufacturers[2] proclaimed the great myth about immigration: "Legal immigration strengthens and energizes America. Throughout America's history, legally admitted immigrants have been a source of strength and vitality to our nation. Our current legal immigration policies are specifically designed to reflect American values and serve national interests."

Nothing could be further from the truth, if "national interest" is defined by what is good for the majority of the public. High immigration almost always has reflected the values and served the interest of a small elite at the *expense* of the national interest.

---

[1]The "Great Wave" of immigration to the United States from the 1890s to the 1910s.

[2]The National Association of Manufacturers, founded in 1895, is an organization of U.S. industrial and business firms

joined together to further their trade, business, and financial interests, and to publicize the advantages of free enterprise. It is located in Washington, D.C., where it carries on extensive lobbying activity.

# France Struggles with Multiculturalism

## 114 • THE STASI REPORT: THE REPORT OF THE COMMISSION OF REFLECTION ON THE APPLICATION OF THE PRINCIPLE OF SECULARITY IN THE REPUBLIC

How best to integrate millions of new arrivals into European society gained the attention of policymakers, intellectuals, and the general public in the 1970s, when it became apparent that immigration and the existence of large non-Western ethnic minorities were becoming permanent features of European life. During the 1950s and 1960s, it had been expected that most immigrants at some point would return to their birth country and that those who stayed would be would be integrated into European society in a process of gradual assimilation. The model was the American "melting pot," in which millions of immigrants through education, intermarriage, and their daily experiences gradually cast off their identity as Germans, Poles, and Italians and became "Americans" in their values and loyalties.

By the 1980s, however, it was apparent that the assimilation model was not working in Europe. Members of different ethnic and religious groups, especially Muslims, tended to cluster in well-defined neighborhoods or districts, which limited their contacts with other groups in public schools and daily life. Marriage outside one's group was rare. Many individuals returned to their (or their family's) country of origin to find spouses. Furthermore, legal requirements were such that relatively few immigrants sought and received citizenship.

As a result, in the 1980s two other approaches to the "immigrant problem" emerged. One approach found expression in the platforms of of right-wing nationalist political parties that made opposition to immigration and immigrants' rights a top priority. These parties and their supporters favored a halt to all immigration, the abandonment of efforts to accommodate the unique needs and demands of the ethnic populations, and even incentives to recent immigrants to return to their countries of origin.

Another approach came to be known as multiculturalism. Rejecting what they considered to be the underlying racist premise of assimilationism, which took for granted the superiority of Western values and culture over those of newly arrived ethnic groups, multiculturalists celebrated difference, and claimed that the diversity provided by immigrants enriched and strengthened society. Governments, therefore, should take steps to accommodate Muslims, for example, by subsidizing the building of mosques, providing imams to serve as prison and army chaplains, and even taking into account Islamic law when adjudicating legal cases pertaining to marriage, divorce, and inheritance. Schools should encourage Islamic studies, and businesses should increase minority hiring.

Debates about immigration policy and multiculturalism consumed politicians, the press, and the general public across Europe, but nowhere were these debates as tense and divisive as they were in France, which by the late 1990s and early 2000s had a substantial immigrant population, most of them Muslims from the Maghreb (Mediterranean Africa), sub-Saharan Africa, and Turkey. The controversy began in the mid-1990s, when a series of disputes developed over how to deal with the relatively small number of Muslim girls who insisted on wearing to school the traditional Muslim headscarf, which covered their hair and neck. This was in keeping with the Muslim dress code, which required women to dress modestly while in public. At several schools, officials responded by expelling the girls, claiming that wearing this symbol of their religious affiliation disrupted instruction and violated the cherished French principle of *laicité* (secularity), which required absolute religious neutrality in public institutions such as schools. There followed several years of uncertainty in which the Minister of Education upheld the expulsions, but the Council of State, a body of the national government that acts as an administrative court, offered the opinion that according to another dimension of secularity—religious freedom—wearing the headscarf was permitted.

In 2003, in the midst of ever-increasing public controversy over the wearing of the headscarf, growing concern over Islamic fundamentalism, and pressures from anti-immigrant political parties, President Jacques Chirac appointed Bernard Stasi (1930–2011), a career politician and civil servant, to head a commission to report on the "applicability of the principle of secularity" in the Republic. The twenty-person committee, which included only one Muslim, took input from the public and interviewed over one hundred individuals from varying backgrounds. In December 2003 the committee submitted its report to President Chirac. It retraced the history of the principle of secularity back to the French Revolution, and, as the following excerpt shows, provided examples of how the need to accommodate the religious concerns of Muslims and other groups was disturbing the country. It made a number of recommendations, one of which became a topic of national and worldwide discussion and debate. This was the recommendation that the "wearing or displaying of conspicuous signs and symbols of religious belief, such as large Christian crosses, the Jewish skullcap, or Yarmulke, and Islamic headscarves" should be banned from public schools. This was also the commission's only recommendation that in the short term was acted upon. In March 2004 the "headscarf ban" was approved by the Chamber of Deputies by a vote of 494 to 36, setting off another protracted and heated discussion of secularity, republican values, what it meant to be French, and what it meant to be a French Muslim.

Subsequently, the government continued to make laws pertaining to the dress of Muslim women. In 2011 it made it a crime for a woman to appear in public wearing a face veil or a burka (a full body cloak), and in early 2012 the Senate approved a law to ban the wearing of headscarves by teachers in nursery schools and nannies, even if they were working in a private home. The Chamber of Deputies, however, decided to table it, a step that optimists considered a positive sign that tensions over the religious practices of Europe's seventeen million Muslims were beginning to subside.

## QUESTIONS FOR ANALYSIS

1. Aside from the alleged "disturbances" caused by the wearing of headscarves, in what other ways has the principle of secularity been threatened by Muslim demands and actions?
2. According to the report, in what ways have French institutions other than schools been threatened by Muslim demands and actions?

3. What explanation does the report offer for the isolation and anger of ethnic minorities?
4. French feminists were divided over the issue of the "headscarf ban." What arguments, for and against the ban, might they have made?
5. According to the report, what is the potential of sports in bringing ethnic and religious groups together in France? Why at the time of the report were sports failing to achieve this potential?
6. In what ways does the Stasi Report confirm the arguments of those who oppose multiculturalism?

## Public Services and the World of Work: Some Disturbing Abuses

New and increasing difficulties have loomed up. They provide evidence that the requirement of secularity in public services, notably in the schools and workplace, is being weakened by demands that tend to make the convictions of one's own community prevail over general rules. The principle of secularity is today being undermined in more sectors than it may appear. The commission is aware that the difficulties we discovered are still in the minority. But they are real, painful, and harbingers of dysfunctions, all the more disturbing due to the recent and rapid spread of these phenomena. . . .

### At School

In school, the wearing of a conspicuous religious symbol—a large cross, yarmulke,[1] or headscarf — is already enough to disturb the tranquility of daily school life. But the difficulties go far beyond this excessively publicized question.

In fact, the normal course of study is also impaired by the persistent demands for absences one day a week, or by the interruption of instruction or of examinations for reasons of prayer or fasting. Behaviors that challenge the whole curriculum of

teaching history or the earth and life sciences disrupt the study of these disciplines. Some young women resort to unjustifiable medical certificates in order to be exempted from physical education and sports. Tests that are part of examinations are disturbed by the refusal of young women to be heard by a male examiner. Teachers and administrators, simply because they are female, see their authority challenged by students or their parents.

Universal access to school is weakened by school withdrawals for religious reasons. . . . Recourse to teaching by correspondence courses has been observed. Moreover, certain private schools under contract[2] only accept students who can provide proof of their allegiance to the institution's own religion; these schools do not offer instruction in those parts of the required curriculum that in their opinion do not agree with certain aspects of their worldview.

All these positions are illegal. Even if they are only the actions of an activist minority, they cause serious harm to the principles that govern public service. It is damaged in its very foundations.

### At the Hospital

The hospital is no longer spared these types of uncertainties. . . . It already has had to come to terms

---

*Source: Rapport de la Commission de réflexion sur l'application du principe de laïcité dans la République remis au Président de République le 11 décembre 2003. Paris: La Documentation française 2003. Translation by J. Overfield.*

[1]A skullcap worn by Jewish males and occasionally females. When and where the yarmulke is worn depends on personal choice and the branch of Judaism to which a person belongs.
[2]Private schools that are chartered by and receive funding by the state.

with certain religious prohibitions such as the opposition of Jehovah's Witnesses to blood transfusions.[3] More recently, religiously-inspired refusals have multiplied from husbands or fathers to have their wives or daughters treated or deliver a baby under the care of a male physician. Some women for these reasons have been denied epidurals.[4] Some caregivers have been rejected because of their alleged religious beliefs. More generally, certain religious concerns of the patients can upset the hospital routine: corridors are transformed into private places for prayer; cafeterias similar to those of the hospital are set up to provide traditional food in defiance of sanitary regulations.

Here again, the foundations of public service are directly affected: principles of equality, continuity, and respect for sanitary rules and health requirements.

## In the Justice System

In the prisons numerous difficulties have appeared. The Law of December 9, 1905[5] and the code of penal procedure make provisions for the expression of spiritual and religious life among the prisoners. But in an environment where collective pressures are very strong, influences can be brought to bear so that prisoners assent to certain religious practices. At the time of visits from family and friends, prisoners are strongly urged to adopt "religiously correct" behavior. In this tense situation prison administrators are perhaps tempted in the interest of maintaining order in the prison to regroup the prisoners according to their religious background. Such a solution begins a vicious cycle by reinforcing group control over the most vulnerable prisoners.

The courts are not spared these issues. A judge was asked to recuse himself because of his alleged religious beliefs. After having been chosen, jurors have expressed the wish to be seated while wearing ostentatious religious symbols. The minister of justice (keeper of the seals) has refused to allow a lawyer to be sworn in while wearing a headscarf. . . .

## Behaviors That Are on the Increase

During Days of Introduction to Defense and the French Military,[6] difficulties have been confirmed. Certain girls have not wanted to take part in the course of co-educational first aid and have refused on principle to carry out first aid on males. More generally, the managers of public facilities . . . are petitioned to offer time slots to users for non-co-ed use. This way of thinking is dangerous and discriminatory. It opens the door to other forms of discrimination, for example, those pertaining to nationality or ethnic background. Such actions gravely weaken public services, especially for the poorest citizens, who should be their main beneficiaries. Public officials have given in to various religious demands. Civil servants have demanded to wear in the workplace a yarmulke or headscarf to show their religious affiliation. Recently medical interns have demanded the same thing.

## Pressured Public Servants Facing Change

Confronted with the situations that have been described, public servants find themselves in a confusing situation. There is a state of uneasiness and discomfort that is stirred up in those who are in this position, preventing them from doing their

---

[3]Jehovah's Witnesses is a Christian denomination founded in the 1870s by the American Charles Taves Russell. Among its beliefs is the conviction that the world is in its "last days" before it will be destroyed by God and replaced by an earthly paradise ruled by God and 144,000 true believers. Members of the church refuse military service and blood transfusions. Jehovah's Witnesses established a presence in France in the early 1900s, but it was not recognized as a true religion by the government until 2000.

[4]Epidural analgesia is a method of relieving pain in labor by introducing drugs through a catheter placed in the lower back.
[5]The law that established separation of church and state in France.
[6]Days on which teenage boys and girls visit military installations. where they are introduced to the French armed forces and learn certain basic skills related to civil defense.

jobs. . . . Hospital personnel exhaust themselves in negotiations with patrons, to the detriment of the care they are to provide on urgent matters. . . .

## A World of Work Which Is Not Spared

In the 1960s large-scale businesses knew how to decide the religious issues they encountered because of the national origins of their employees. They rearranged the menus in their cafeterias; the work schedule was adapted in regard to specific breaks to take into account the time of Ramadan.[7] Lastly, some businesses set aside rooms for prayer on their premises. These steps involved encouraging the integration of the foreign workforce . . . to the extent they did not hinder the success of the business. The situation now is different. Businesses are no longer confronted with the expression of needs, but with demands, mainly as a result of the arrival of in the workplace of a new generation of activists. Business managers must deal with employees who wear the headscarf and refuse to shake hands with male colleagues. Some do not recognize the authority of the higher staff when it is a matter pertaining to women.

• • •

These demands present a triple menace. They weaken the harmony that must exist among employees, no matter what their sex and philosophical convictions might be. They affect relations with clients. . . . Finally, they cause security risks.

Such behavior sometimes turns against those who embrace it. Business executives have observed that because of the headscarf and the demands that go with it, young women deprive themselves of any chance of being hired, or if they are already employed, any chance of advancement. Some female employees refuse to apply for managerial positions to avoid having to oversee the work of male co-workers; thus they imprison themselves in

subordinate positions. Such behavior is a form of "self-discrimination."

## Community Narrowing More Imposed Than Sought After

Field workers interviewed by the commission all drew attention to a social and urban environment favorable to the development community-based thinking that makes primary allegiance to a particular group more important than a sense of belonging to the Republic. Until the past few years this phenomenon was barely noticeable in France.

A few figures illustrate the gravity of the situation. It was pointed out to the commission that in seven hundred districts, made up of several nationalities, difficulties are growing: unemployment rates of forty percent and acute school attendance problems are social indicators three times more prevalent than in other parts of the country. The inhabitants of these neglected areas have the feeling that that they are the victims of social banishment that condemns them to rely on themselves. This is especially the case with young people. Thirty two percent of the population is under twenty years of age: which is to say this is a predicament for themselves and for the Republic.

In certain instances schooling and sport are unable to combat this social narrowing, for they no longer serve the function of being a melting pot. Children withdraw to attend private schools or obtain exemptions from parts of the school curriculum: schools become socially and ethnically homogenous. The growth of sports facilities in the heart of these districts no longer provides opportunities for interactions among persons of different nationalities and cultures on the playing field. The number of community teams is increased, and no longer participate in competitions organized by sports confederations, which were occasions for intermingling. Sporting activities for women in these districts

---

[7]The month is which Muslims refrain from eating, drinking, smoking, and sex during daylight hours; its purpose is to teach Muslims patience, spirituality, humility, and submissiveness to God. The month is believed to be the time in which the first verses of the Quran were revealed to Muhammad.

have notably declined. Females are in fact excluded from the playing fields and swimming pools. Female and co-ed sports clubs are disappearing. . . . On the whole these phenomena undermine confidence in the Republic and identification with the nation.

Activist community groups exploit this real social malaise to make militant converts. They develop an aggressive strategy against individuals to bend them to their preconceived community-based standard. These groups thus act in neglected districts, submitting the weakest part of the population to permanent stress.

## A Serious Decline in the Situation of Young Women

"The situation of girls in the city is approaching the level of a true tragedy," so testified an associate director [official] who brought out that the first victims of the decline in the social situation are young women. Another young woman, who testified behind closed doors because she feared recriminations from her community, put it thusly, "The Republic is not protecting its children."

Young women once more are finding themselves victims of a resurgence of sexism, which is reflected in various pressures and forms of verbal, psychological, and physical violence. Young men force them to wear unrevealing and asexual clothing and to lower their gaze when in view of a man; with failure to conform, they are stigmatized as "whores." Several organizations are alarmed by the increasing resignations of many of their foreign-born female members, who consider themselves forbidden from any social life.

In such a situation some girls and women agree to wear the headscarf, but others wear it under constraint or pressure. This also applies to preadolescent girls, on whom wearing the headscarf is imposed, sometimes by force. Once veiled, girls can traverse the stairwells of public buildings and walk on the streets without fear of being insulted, indeed of being abused, as had been the case when their head was uncovered. Paradoxically, the headscarf thus offers them protection that should be provided for by the state. Those who do not wear the veil and consider it a sign of their perceived inferiority because it enfeebles and isolates women are singled out as shameless and even as "infidels."

Young women are victims of other forms of violence: genital mutilation, polygamy, and repudiation by their families. The personal status of women does not always allow women to oppose this; on the basis of bilateral agreements,[8] the laws of the country of origin can be applied to them, including provisions directly contrary to sexual equality and basic rights. Arranged marriages are imposed on them in certain communities, especially Turkish, North African, African, and Pakistani. In bringing in foreigners as future spouses, families try to side-step the autonomy and emancipation chosen by their daughters, and occasionally by their sons. Sometimes a girl is "married" during a visit to the country of origin, which means the end of schooling. . . .

## Racist and Xenophobic Displays

A number of persons heard by the commission made a point about open hostility directed against Muslims. These acts, which sometimes rise to the level of the profanation of tombs and physical violence, indicate the shape of anti-Muslim hatred. In the view of many, all foreigners, especially if they are North Africans or Turks, are dismissed and reduced to a single religious identity, ignoring all the other aspects of their culture. This stereotyping is accompanied by a perception that identifies Islam with social-political radicalism, thus ignoring the fact that a great majority of Muslims confess to a faith and a credo perfectly compatible with the laws of the Republic.

---

[8]Agreements between France and an immigrant's country of origin.

# Internet Freedom: U.S. and Chinese Views

China's astonishing economic growth over the past two decades has been accompanied by an equally amazing explosion of the Chinese people's Internet use. In 1995, just one year after the Internet became available to China's general population, the country had 16 million users, consisting of only 0.4% of the population. The number rose to 103 million in 2005 and reached 618 million in 2013. This made China the world leader in terms of Internet usage and created a formidable challenge for China's rulers, who understood the importance of the Internet for the country's economic and technological development but feared the political dangers of the Internet's ease of use and openness.

As a result, beginning in the 1990s, the Chinese government has instituted regulations that make China a world leader in Internet repression and control. In December 1997, the State Council made it illegal to use the Internet for inciting law-breaking, terrorism, and the overthrow of the socialist system; promoting falsehoods that threatened the social order; and damaging the reputation of state organizations. It also banned vaguely defined "other activities" against China's constitution, laws, and administrative regulations. In 1998 the government introduced the Golden Shield Project (the "Great Firewall of China"), a content-filtering system that blocks blacklisted sites and sites that contain certain words or names. Although Internet controls were loosened in the summer of 2008, when China hosted the Olympics, they were reinstituted and tightened after the athletes left. It is estimated that the government employs 2 million individuals to monitor and control Internet content and that more than 1.3 million websites are closed to Chinese users.

Foreign corporations doing business in China were expected to accept and adhere to the government's regulations. Yahoo!, which entered the mainland Chinese market in 2004, and Microsoft MSN, which entered a year later, also agreed to "self-censorship," which meant that they would not respond to or supply complete information in response to certain search requests. Both companies have been accused of providing the Chinese government with information leading to the arrest of Chinese dissidents. When the Internet giant Google entered the Chinese market in 2006, it too accepted government controls and agreed to practice self-censorship despite its stated goal to "organize the world's information and make it universally accessible and useful."

The efforts of China (and other authoritarian states) to censor the Internet have been criticized by organizations such as Reporters Without Borders and Amnesty International. They also have been a source of tension between China and the United States and other Western democracies, which have persistently criticized China's human rights record, especially after the crackdown against student demonstrators in Beijing in June 1989. Since then, the United States has pressured China to end its repressive policies by issuing reports on human rights abuses, threatening trade sanctions, and having China criticized in public forums, such as meetings of the

United Nations Human Rights Commission. China has rejected such criticism, claiming that its human rights record has been distorted by foreign governments that have no business interfering in its internal affairs.

# Internet Freedom and Human Rights

## 115 • HILLARY RODHAM CLINTON, REMARKS ON INTERNET FREEDOM, JANUARY 21, 2010

On January 12, 2010, David Drummond, the chief legal officer for Google, announced in a blog entitled "A New Approach to China" that Google had been the target of "a highly sophisticated and targeted attack on our corporate infrastructure originating from China that resulted in the theft of intellectual property from Google." Drummond also asserted that the main purpose of the cyber-attacks had been to access the Gmail accounts of prominent Chinese dissidents. He further claimed that in the course of Google's investigations of these attacks, it was discovered that "dozens of U.S.-, China- and Europe-based Gmail users who are advocates of human rights in China appear to have been routinely accessed by third parties." Drummond claimed such attacks "go the heart of a much bigger global debate on freedom of speech" and suggested that Google might be forced to leave China unless the restrictions on Internet use were lifted.

A week later, Secretary of State Hillary Rodham Clinton delivered a sweeping "Internet freedom" speech in which she called for nations to band together to punish cyber-attacks meant to quiet citizens and disrupt businesses abroad. Although China was one of many nations Clinton criticized, those who heard or read the speech (including the Chinese) knew that her speech was a reaction to Drummond's blog and a direct condemnation of Chinese Internet policies.

### QUESTIONS FOR ANALYSIS

1. According to the secretary, what motivates the United States to defend Internet freedom?
2. How, specifically, will increased Internet freedom contribute to the spread of democracy and better government?
3. How in particular will economically backward societies benefit from unrestricted Internet usage?
4. According to Clinton, how specifically have authoritarian governments attempted to restrict Internet access and usage?

The spread of information networks is forming a new nervous system for our planet. When something happens in Haiti or Hunan, the rest of us learn about it in real time—from real people. . . . And we can respond in real time as well. As we sit here, any of you—or maybe more likely, any of

Source: From the U.S. State Department website.

our children—can take out the tools that many carry every day and transmit this discussion to billions across the world.

Now, in many respects, information has never been so free. There are more ways to spread more ideas to more people than at any moment in history. And even in authoritarian countries, information networks are helping people discover new facts and making governments more accountable.

During his visit to China in November [2009], for example, President Obama held a town hall meeting with an online component to highlight the importance of the internet. In response to a question that was sent in over the internet, he defended the right of people to freely access information, and said that the more freely information flows, the stronger societies become. He spoke about how access to information helps citizens hold their own governments accountable, generates new ideas, encourages creativity and entrepreneurship. The United States belief in that ground truth is what brings me here today.

Because amid this unprecedented surge in connectivity, we must also recognize that these technologies are not an unmitigated blessing. . . . The same networks that help organize movements for freedom also enable al-Qaida to spew hatred and incite violence against the innocent. And technologies with the potential to open up access to government and promote transparency can also be hijacked by governments to crush dissent and deny human rights.

In the last year, we've seen a spike in threats to the free flow of information. China, Tunisia, and Uzbekistan have stepped up their censorship of the internet. In Vietnam, access to popular social networking sites has suddenly disappeared. And

last Friday in Egypt, 30 bloggers and activists were detained.[1] . . . So while it is clear that the spread of these technologies is transforming our word, it is still unclear how that transformation will affect the human rights and the human welfare of the world's population.

On their own, new technologies do not take sides in the struggle for freedom and progress, but the United States does. We stand for a single internet where all of humanity has equal access to knowledge and ideas. And we recognize that the world's information infrastructure will become what we and others make of it. Now, this challenge may be new, but our responsibility to help ensure the free exchange of ideas goes back to the birth of our republic. . . .

So as technology hurtles forward, we must think back to that legacy. We need to synchronize our technological progress with our principles. . . .

. . . As I speak to you today, government censors somewhere are working furiously to erase my words from the records of history. But history itself has already condemned these tactics. Two months ago, I was in Germany to celebrate the 20th anniversary of the fall of the Berlin Wall. The leaders gathered at that ceremony paid tribute to the courageous men and women on the far side of that barrier who made the case against oppression by circulating small pamphlets called samizdat. Now, these leaflets questioned the claims and intentions of dictatorships in the Eastern Bloc and many people paid dearly for distributing them. But their words helped pierce the concrete and concertina wire [a type of barbed wire] of the Iron Curtain.

The Berlin Wall symbolized a world divided and it defined an entire era. Today, remnants of that wall sit inside this museum[2] where they belong,

---

[1] In other words, approximately a year before the beginning of the Arab Spring of late 2010 and 2011, when a wave of demonstrations across the Middle East and North Africa challenged the established political order. Participants in the demonstrations used social media to organize demonstrations and communicate with one another.

[2] The speech was delivered at the Newseum, an interactive museum of news and journalism in Washington, D.C.

and the new iconic infrastructure of our age is the internet. Instead of division, it stands for connection. But even as networks spread to nations around the globe, virtual walls are cropping up in place of visible walls. . . .

There are, of course, hundreds of millions of people living without the benefits of these technologies. In our world, as I've said many times, talent may be distributed universally, but opportunity is not. And we know from long experience that promoting social and economic development in countries where people lack access to knowledge, markets, capital, and opportunity can be frustrating and sometimes futile work. In this context, the internet can serve as a great equalizer. By providing people with access to knowledge and potential markets, networks can create opportunities where none exist.

Over the last year, I've seen this firsthand in Kenya, where farmers have seen their income grow by as much as 30 percent since they started using mobile banking technology; in Bangladesh, where more than 300,000 people have signed up to learn English on their mobile phones; and in Sub-Saharan Africa, where women entrepreneurs use the internet to get access to microcredit loans and connect themselves to global markets.

Now, these examples of progress can be replicated in the lives of the billion people at the bottom of the world's economic ladder. In many cases, the internet, mobile phones, and other connection technologies can do for economic growth what the Green Revolution[3] did for agriculture. You can now generate significant yields from very modest inputs. And one World Bank study found that in a typical developing country, a 10 percent increase in the penetration rate for mobile phones led to an almost 1 percent increase in per capita GDP [Gross Domestic Product]. . . .

A connection to global information networks is like an on-ramp to modernity. In the early years of these technologies, many believed that they would divide the world between haves and have-nots. But that hasn't happened. There are 4 billion cell phones in use today. Many of them are in the hands of market vendors, rickshaw drivers, and others who've historically lacked access to education and opportunity. Information networks have become a great leveler, and we should use them together to help lift people out of poverty and give them a freedom from want.

• • •

The freedom to connect is like the freedom of assembly, only in cyberspace. It allows individuals to get online, come together, and hopefully cooperate. Once you're on the internet, you don't need to be tycoon or a rock star to have a huge impact on society.

The largest public response to the terrorist attacks in Mumbai [2008] was launched by a 13-year-old boy. He used social networks to organize blood drives and a massive interfaith book of condolence. In Colombia, an unemployed engineer brought together more than 12 million people in 190 cities around the world to demonstrate against the FARC[4] terrorist movement. The protests were the largest antiterrorist demonstrations in history. And in the weeks that followed, the FARC saw more demobilizations and desertions than it had during a decade of military action. And in Mexico, a single email from a private citizen who was fed up with drug-related violence snowballed into huge demonstrations in all of the country's 32 states. In Mexico City alone, 150,000 people took to the streets in protest. . . .

---

[3]"Green Revolution" refers to a number of innovations, including irrigation projects, new plant varieties, and the use of chemical fertilizers and pesticides, that increased worldwide agricultural production from the 1940s through the late 1970s.

[4]FARC refers to the Revolutionary Armed Forces of Colombia, the military wing of the Colombian communist party.

Now, the principles I've outlined today will guide our approach in addressing the issue of internet freedom and the use of these technologies. And I want to speak about how we apply them in practice. . . .

. . . And I'm proud that the State Department is already working in more than 40 countries to help individuals silenced by oppressive governments. We are making this issue a priority at the United Nations as well, and we're including internet freedom as a component in the first resolution we introduced after returning to the United Nations Human Rights Council.

We are also supporting the development of new tools that enable citizens to exercise their rights of free expression by circumventing politically motivated censorship. We are providing funds to groups around the world to make sure that those tools get to the people who need them in local languages, and with the training they need to access the internet safely. . . .

Increasingly, U.S. companies are making the issue of internet and information freedom a greater consideration in their business decisions. I hope that their competitors and foreign governments will pay close attention to this trend. The most recent situation involving Google has attracted a great deal of interest. And we look to the Chinese authorities to conduct a thorough review of the cyber instrusions that led Google to make its announcement. And we also look for that investigation and its results to be transparent.

The internet has already been a source of tremendous progress in China, and it is fabulous. There are so many people in China now online. But countries that restrict free access to information or violate the basic rights of internet users risk walling themselves off from the progress of the next century. Now, the United States and China have different views on this issue, and we intend to address those differences candidly and consistently in the context of our positive, cooperative, and comprehensive relationship.

## China Responds

### 116 • EDITORIALS FROM THE PEOPLE'S DAILY

It did not take long for the Chinese government to respond to the fallout from Drummond's blog and Secretary of State Clinton's speech on internet freedom. A number of Chinese officials publicly criticized the speech, and *The People's Daily,* an official organ of the Chinese Communist Party, did the same in a series of editorials. Excerpts from three of these editorials follow.

After their appearance the Google controversy continued. On March 23, 2010, Google began to redirect all search queries from Google China to Google Hong Kong, which enabled them to bypass Chinese regulators and provide uncensored search results. On March 30, 2010, the Chinese government banned searching via all Google search sites in mainland China, but the ban was lifted the following day. On June 30, 2010, Google ended the automatic redirect of Google China to Google Hong Kong and instead placed a link to Google Hong Kong to avoid getting its Internet content provider license revoked. Less than a year later, Google announced in June 2011 that suspected Chinese hackers had tried to steal passwords of hundreds of Google email account holders, including senior U.S. government officials, Chinese activists, and journalists. The claim sparked an angry response from Beijing, which said blaming China was "unacceptable."

## QUESTIONS FOR ANALYSIS

1. According to the Chinese editorial writers, how is the United States hoping to benefit from the Google controversy?
2. How do the writers justify the Internet restrictions imposed by the Chinese government?
3. In the view of the editorial writers, what lesson is to be drawn from the breakup of the Soviet Union in the early 1990s?
4. According to the editorial writers, why is the U.S. attack on Chinese Internet policy hypocritical?
5. According to the author of "To Defend 'Freedom' . . . ," what may be the true reasons Google is threatening to leave China?

## Google, Do Not Take Chinese Netizens Hostage, January 19, 2010

. . . It is a lie to claim that the Internet is an absolutely free space without regulations. The truth is that it is the extension of the real world. Therefore, implementing monitoring according to a country's national context is what any government has to do. World countries including the U.S. do not permit the existence of a laissez-faire Internet world either. To combat terrorism after the "9/11" terrorist attack, the U.S. has permitted police to search civilian emails and even monitor their communications without permission. Western countries such as Canada, Australia, New Zealand, the U.K., Germany and Sweden have also passed similar bills.

In recent years, China has sincerely opened up to the outside world. However, China follows its own course while learning from the west and its reluctance to copy the Internet control and supervision mode of the U.S. does not contradict its adherence to the "4 Cardinal Principles"[1] released in the early stage of the opening up and reform. At that time, even in China, some people raised doubts about the Chinese government's choice. However, when looking back, we now can find that the government's

choice is correct. . . . Therefore, China must not follow the western world's practice on crucial issues such as Internet control and supervision. Of course, China is progressing and its Internet industry should advance accordingly. However, China must have its own plan on how to regulate and deregulate the Internet and should not and will not follow orders from Google's CEO and the U.S. Department of State.

Google's CEO Eric Schmidt stated that he "loves China and the Chinese people." . . . Google should show its sincerity by taking practical actions and should first abide by China's laws and not seek any privilege in China, [and] stop launching surprise attacks against China if it really "loves China." At the same time, Google should take the Chinese people's feelings into consideration and stop using Chinese customers as hostage to confront the Chinese government. . . .

We do not hope that giant multinational enterprises such as Google will become pure political tools for the U.S. to export its own concepts of values. A lot of Chinese people like Google, but they do not want to become tools being used by Google.

Source: http://English.peoplesdaily.com.cn/90001/90780/91344/6873383.html.

[1]Announced by Deng Xiaoping in 1979, the four cardinal principles could not be questioned or debated. They were (1) upholding the socialist path; (2) the people's democratic dictatorship; (3) the leadership of the Communist Party of China; and (4) Marxist-Leninist-Mao Zedong thought. The implication was that political issues other than these four could be debated.

## "Internet Freedom" and "Smart Power" Diplomacy, January 25, 2010

The United States has lambasted "China's policies to administer the Internet." . . .

In her speech in Washington D.C., Hillary Clinton mentioned China four times and referred to it as among a number of countries where there has been a "spike in threats to the free flow of information." . . .

If the moral high ground is short of real, practical support, however, it can hardly walk on and stand. Take for [example] the attack on Google; the United States urged China to make a thorough-going probe . . . but the U.S. should first look into attack problems itself. Not long ago, the largest Chinese search engine Baidu[1] was attacked and the domain name registration service provider was right in the U.S. territory.

Then, let us look at "network freedom" in the U.S.: In order to resist Internet pornography, the U.S. "Children's Internet Protection Act" . . . requires all public network resources to curb Internet child porn, a serious crime in the country; in order to respond to threats, the Pentagon has developed a new type of troops—cyber troops, and also adopted several measures to beef up the military's cyber warfare capacity; shortly after the September 11, 2001 terrorist attacks, the U.S. Congress approved the Patriot Act to grant its security agencies the right to search telephone and e-mail communications in the name of anti-terrorism. . . .

It is thus evident that with any freedom, people are not meant to do whatever they want, but they still need the norms of law and order, which constitute the basic premise of "network freedom."

*Source:* http://english.peopledaily.com.cn/90001/90780 /91343/6878072.html.

[1]Founded in 2000, Baidu is a Chinese web services company. It is publicly traded on the NASDAQ stock market.

## To Defend "Freedom" or to Defend "Hegemony," January 26, 2010

The "Google case" is a politicized business issue in the final analysis. Google senior vice president, David Drummond, said on January 13 in the official blog that "Google might have to pull all of its operations out of China." As for the reason, Google said it suffered a "highly sophisticated and targeted attack on our operation." . . .

On the Google retreat, is it really attributed to the so-called "cyber-attack" and "Internet censorship"? . . .

At present, [the] Google search engine in China accounts merely for 35 percent market share, far behind Baidu China's largest search engine; Google's annual income from the country constitutes only less than 2 percent of its total global income.

Some of China's Internet industry insiders maintain that Google has been looking for an excuse for its failure due to its "inability to adapt" and loss to Chinese domestic firms.

It is not difficult, however, to see the shadow of the US government behind the highly politicized "Google" case. . . .

As a matter of fact, the U.S.'s international conduct is determined by its "imperial mindset"; as the "United Morning News," Singapore's leading newspaper and a major Chinese morning daily, said in a recent commentary that one of its [the United States'] salient features is to direct other nations' policies so as to maximize its own interests.

*Source:* http://english.peopledaily.com.cn/90001/90780 /91343/6879251.html.

Around the "Google" incident, the United States has not only focused on the commercial interest of domestic companies and safeguard its own national security . . . but also is trying hard to limit China's cyberspace. This is something totally unacceptable.

To date, Google executives have expressed the hope to go on negotiating with the Chinese government and continue to stay in China, and Google has perhaps come to realize that China could do without it, whereas Google will definitely have no future without China.